STALIN AND THE BOMB

The Soviet Union and Atomic Energy
1939–1956

DAVID HOLLOWAY

YALE UNIVERSITY PRESS
New Haven & London
1994

Set in Linotron Bembo by Best-set Typesetter Ltd., Hong Kong
Printed and bound in Great Britain by St Edmundsbury Press

Library of Congress Cataloging-in-Publication Data

Holloway, David, 1943–
    Stalin and the bomb: the Soviet Union and atomic energy, 1939–56
    /David Holloway.
        p.   cm.
    Includes bibliographical references and index.
    ISBN 0–300–06056–4
        1. Atomic weapons—Government policy—Soviet Union—History.
2. Nuclear energy—Research—Soviet Union—History.   3. Science and
state—Soviet Union—History.   4. Soviet Union—Foreign relations.
I. Title.
UA770.H632   1994   94–8216
355.8′25119—dc20   CIP

A catalogue record for this book is available from the British Library.

For Arlene, James, and Ivor

Contents

Illustration Sources

The author and publisher would like to make acknowledgment to the following sources for photographs:

V.I. Vernadskii, Moscow: Planeta, 1988 **1**; V. Ia. Frenkel', *Iakov Ilich Frenkel'*, Moscow: Nauka 1966 **2**; Vospominaniia ob A.F. Ioffe, Leningrad: Nauka, 1973 **3**, **32**; Dr. Viktor Frenkel' **4**, **6**, **7**; G.E. Gorelik, V.I. Frenkel' *Matvei Petrovich Bronshtein*, Moscow: Nauka, 1990 **5**, **9**, **10**; J.G. Crowther, *Soviet Science*, London: Kegan Paul, 1936 **8**; A.I. Leipunskii, *Izbrannye trudy. Vospominaniia*, Kiev: Naukova Dumka, 1990 **11**; Dr. Raisa Kuznetsova **12**, **13**, **14**, **19** (photo of Igor Kurchatov), **22**, **23**, **26**, **28**, **38**; Georgii Flerov **15**; *Aleksandr Evgenievich Fersman, Zhizn' i deiatel'nostn*, Moscow: Nauka, 1961 **16**; F. Kedrov, Kapitsa: *Zhizn' otkrytiia*, Moscow: Moskovskii rabochii, 1984 **17**; Lev Gumilevskii, *Vernadskii*, Moscow: Molodaia Gvardiia, 1967 **18**; *Atom Sluzhit sotsializmu*, Moscow: Atomisdat, 1977 **19** (photo of Isaak Kikoin) **31**, **33**; Dr. A. Iu. Semenov **19** (photo of Iakov Zel'dovich), **24**, **25**, **42**; *Akademik A. I. Alikhanov Vospominaniia, pis'ma, dokumenty*, Leningrad: Nauka, 1989 **19** (photo of Abram Alikhanov), **35**; *Atomnaia Nauka i Tekhnika v SSSR*, Moscow: Atomizdat, 1977 **19** (photos of Avraamii Zaveniagin, Mikhail Pervukhin, Viacheslav Malyshev and Igor Tamm); U.S. Army, Harry S. Truman Library **20**, **21**; *Ogonek*, September 1989 **27**; *Marshal Zhukov*, Moscow: Planeta, 1987 **29**; Postcard, Moscow: Planeta, 1983 **30**, **33**; *Akademiik S.P. Korolev: uchenyi, inzhener, chelovek*, Moscow: Nauka, 1986 **34**; Sovetskaia atomnai nauka: tekhnika, Moscow: Atomizadt, 1967 **36**; Dr. Iurii Smirnov **37**, **43**; V. Chalmaev, Malyshev, Moscow: Molodaia Gvardiia, 1978 **39**; L.A. Artsimovich, *Izbrannye trudy: Atomnaia fizika i fizika plazmy*, Moscow: Nauka, 1978 **40**; AEA Technology Photographic Services, Harwell, England **41**; Jamie Doran **44**, **45**, **46**, **47** and **48**

Acknowledgments

WHEN I BEGAN the research that led to this book, I did not think that I would be able to meet any of the participants in the Soviet nuclear project. The opportunity to do so has made the book much more interesting to write and, I hope, to read. The late Georgii Flerov kindly encouraged me to write about the Soviet project, and gave me helpful interviews and documents. Peter Kapitsa and Andrei Sakharov, both now dead, agreed to speak to me at a time when neither was free to discuss his role in this history in detail. Igor' Golovin, who worked closely with Igor' Kurchatov in the 1950s and later wrote Kurchatov's biography, gave me several very helpful interviews. I am especially grateful to Iulii Khariton, a key figure in the Soviet nuclear weapons project, for his willingness to give me interviews, for inviting me to visit Arzamas-16, and for reading and commenting on parts of the manuscript.

Several of the Western scientists who figure in these pages also gave me help. Sir Rudolf Peierls spoke to me of his impressions of Soviet physics and physicists, and the late Lady Peierls kindly shared with me her vivid memories of the Leningrad physics community in the 1920s. Hans Bethe and Victor Weisskopf gave me several very helpful interviews, and commented on the manuscript.

I am grateful to colleagues in Russia, Britain, and the United States for their help. Viktor Frenkel' gave me the benefit of his encyclopedic knowledge of Soviet physics. Gennadii Gorelik was similarly generous, and let me use the transcripts of interviews he conducted for his own work on Andrei Sakharov. Major-General Anatolii Boliatko's comments on my manuscript helped to sharpen the analysis. I had many useful discussions with Iurii Smirnov and Vladislav Zubok. Margaret Gowing encouraged me when I began this research, and commented on drafts of the manuscript; her own work on the British nuclear project provides a model of what nuclear history should be. Barton Bernstein was unstinting in his help with sources and in his comments on the manuscript; I have learned a great deal from his work on American nuclear weapons policy. I thank Alexander Dallin and

Jonathan Haslam for many discussions and for their comments on the manuscript, and John Lewis, Xue Litai, Sergei Goncharov, and Norman Naimark for stimulating conversations and help with sources. Sidney Drell, from whom I have learned much over the years, gave me his comments on the draft manuscript.

I owe a special debt of gratitude to Aleksei and Agnessa Semenov who not only helped with the book, but provided friendship and hospitality in Moscow too.

My thanks are due also to Herb Abrams, Lorna Arnold, Arsenii Berezin, George Bunn, Robert Conquest, John Dunlop, Lynn Eden, Matthew Evangelista, John Harvey, Paul Josephson, Arnold Kramish, Scott Sagan, David Shoenberg, Kathryn Wethersby and Victor Zaslavsky, who have helped me in various ways with this project.

I received considerable help in Russia while I was working on this book. I am particularly grateful to the following people and institutions: Andrei Kokoshin, formerly deputy director of the Institute for the Study of the USA and Canada; Zhores Alferov, director of the Leningrad Physicotechnical Institute; Galina Sinitsyna of the Radium Institute in Leningrad; Raisa Kuznetsova, curator of the Kurchatov museum at the Kurchatov Institute of Atomic Energy; Pavel Rubinin of the Institute of Physical Problems; Vladimir Vizgin of the Institute of the History of Science and Technology. The Russian Minister of Atomic Energy, Viktor Mikhailov, gave me permission to visit Arzamas-16. At the Institute of Military History Major-General Iurii Kirshin kindly arranged interviews for me.

I am grateful to those students who assisted me with my research over the years: Stacy Williams, Marina Landau, Kimberly Zisk, Anne Garvey, Ifan Go Arthur Knachikian. Sasha Pursley provided invaluable assistance in the final stages. My thanks to Helen Morales and Betty Bowman for their work with the manuscript.

The Woodrow Wilson International Center for Scholars awarded me a fellowship which allowed me to begin research on this project. The Nuclear History Project and the Cold War International History Project provided the opportunity to try out my ideas before colleagues. I owe a great intellectual debt to the Center for International Security and Arms Control at Stanford. It has been my good fortune to have many good colleagues there, among them Coit Blacker, Michael May, William Perry and Condoleezza Rice. The collegial interdisciplinary community of the Center has provided the ideal conditions for writing a book of this kind. It will be clear that, having received so much help, I alone am responsible for the errors and deficiencies in this book.

Work on this book has been supported at various times by the Nuffield Foundation, the Ford Foundation, the Weingart Foundation, the William and Flora Hewlett Foundation, the Carnegie Corporation of New York, the John D. and Catherine T. MacArthur Foundation, and by the Institute for the Study of World Politics. None of these centers or foundations takes responsibility for the statements or views expressed in this book.

John Nicoll and Candida Brazil of Yale University Press have shown a combination of patience and efficiency for which I am most grateful.

My greatest debt is to my wife, Arlene, and our sons, James and Ivor, for their support and encouragement. I dedicate this book to them, with love.

Note on Transliteration

I have used a modified version of the Library of Congress system. I have not used it, however, for well-known names, e.g. Beria, not Beriia. I have used it, however, for scientists even though some of those used different versions of their names in English. For example, I have used Kapitsa, Khariton, and Fok, instead of Kapitza, Chariton, and Fock.

Abbreviations

ABM	anti-ballistic missile
AEC	United States Atomic Energy Commission
CERN	Conseil Européen pour la Recherche Nucleaire
Cheka	Extraordinary Commission for Combating Counter-Revolution and Sabotage, forerunner of the OGPU and NKVD
CPSU	Communist Party of the Soviet Union
FIAN	Physics Institute, Academy of Sciences
GAC	General Advisory Committee of the AEC
GDL-OKB	Valentin Glushko's design bureau
GKO	State Defense Committee
GRU	Chief Intelligence Directorate of the General Staff
GSFG	Group of Soviet Forces in Germany
ICBM	intercontinental ballistic missile
JCAE	Joint Committee on Atomic Energy, U.S. Congress
JCS	United States Joint Chiefs of Staff
KB-11	Design Bureau 11
KEPS	Commission for the Study of Natural Productive Forces
KPA	Korean People's Army
LFTI	Leningrad Physicotechnical Institute
LIPAN	Laboratory of Measuring Instruments of the Academy of Sciences
MGB	Ministry of State Security
MTR	magnetic thermonuclear reactor
MVD	Ministry of Internal Affairs
NII	Research Institute
NKGB	People's Commissariat of State Security
NKVD	People's Commissariat of Internal Affairs
NSC	United States National Security Council
OGPU	Joint State Political Administration, predecessor of the NKVD
PLA	Chinese People's Liberation Army

PUWP	Polish United Workers' Party, i.e. Communist Party
RNII	Reactive Research Institute
SAC	United States Strategic Air Command
SAMs	surface-to-air missiles
UFTI	Ukrainian Physicotechnical Institute
WSEG	Weapons Systems Evaluation Group, United States Department of Defense
ZhETF	*Journal of Experimental and Theoretical Physics*

Introduction

THE HISTORY OF nuclear weapons, it has been said, is at once fascinating and repulsive. It is an exciting tale of discovery and invention, but it tells of weapons that could destroy all life on earth. The history of nuclear weapons in the Soviet Union is doubly fascinating and doubly repellent. Its fascination is enhanced by the mystery in which it has been shrouded for so long. Its repulsiveness is magnified by the brutality of the Stalin regime for which Soviet nuclear weapons were first created.

Soviet nuclear weapons policy excited great, though fearful, interest in the West during the Cold War. Those on whom the weapons were targeted naturally wanted to know more about them, and about the plans and intentions that lay behind them. Soviet nuclear weapons policy was the subject of numerous books and reports. Some of these still have considerable value, but the range of issues they could explore was limited.[1] They were largely devoted to military strategy and doctrine, and could say little about the way in which nuclear weapons policy was made.

It was not possible to analyse Soviet policy – as one could study American or British policy – in terms of the interplay of individuals, institutions, and circumstances. Soviet nuclear weapons policy was often presented therefore as the product of the Soviet system, or of Marxist-Leninist ideology, or of an individual leader's policy goals. Only now, with the end of the Cold War and the collapse of the Soviet Union, is it becoming possible to write differently about Soviet nuclear weapons policy, to place it more securely in the context of Soviet history and the history of the Cold War.

This book examines Soviet policy in relation to atomic energy from the discovery of nuclear fission at the very end of 1938 to the mid-1950s, when the Soviet Union tested thermonuclear weapons. It asks why the Soviet Union built nuclear weapons, and how it did so; what the implications of the nuclear project were for Soviet society and politics; and what effect nuclear weapons had on Soviet foreign and military policy. It tries to set the Soviet nuclear project in its comparative context, and also to show how it

I

was affected by, and in turn influenced, other nuclear projects. In this connection I have been fortunate in being able to draw on the fine studies that have been done of nuclear weapons policy in the United States, Britain, France, and China.[2]

This book, however, also treats the Soviet nuclear project as a subject that raises its own questions, not merely as a matter of solving puzzles that arise in writing about the nuclear policies of other states. The period it covers was a terrible one for the people of the Soviet Union: the purges of the 1930s, the bloody war with Germany, the repressive rule of Stalin's last years. The post-Stalin thaw provided only partial alleviation. Soviet scientists, engineers, workers, managers, and political leaders lived and worked in conditions that were very different from those that existed in the West, and their actions can be understood only if that context is taken into account.

Although the later chapters treat different aspects of Soviet policy separately, the book is organized chronologically. It starts with the development of physics in the Soviet Union in the 1920s and 1930s, before the discovery of nuclear fission. It ends with three closely related events in a crucial six-month period in 1955–6: the Soviet Union's first test of a superbomb in November 1955; Khrushchev's renunciation, in February 1956, of Lenin's thesis that war was inevitable between capitalist states; and the visit of Igor' Kurchatov, scientific director of the Soviet nuclear project, to Britain in April 1956. The reason for going beyond Stalin's death in March 1953 is that the Stalin years become more comprehensible when one examines the way in which his successors dealt with his nuclear legacy. Moreover, the changes in 1955–6 marked the end of one phase in nuclear relations between the Soviet Union and the Western powers.

The first two chapters of the book examine Soviet science in the 1920s and 1930s: the physics community in the political and social context of the Stalinist system; and the state and development of nuclear science before the discovery of fission. Chapter 3 analyzes the Soviet response to the discovery of nuclear fission in the period up to the German attack on June 22, 1941. The fourth chapter examines the decision to start a small-scale nuclear project during the war, while the fifth traces the progress of that project before August 1945. Chapters 6 and 7 examine the effect of Hiroshima on Soviet policy, and the organization of the Soviet crash program. Chapter 8 examines the effect of the bomb on the wartime alliance in the eighteen months after Hiroshima. Chapter 9 analyzes the creation of the atomic industry, and Chapter 10 the design and testing of the first Soviet atomic bomb. Chapter 11 analyzes Stalin's military policies: the steps taken to counter the atomic threat from the United States, and the development of systems to deliver Soviet nuclear weapons. The impact of the atomic bomb on Soviet foreign policy during Stalin's last years is discussed in Chapters 12 and 13. Chapter 14 examines how the Soviet

Union developed and tested thermonuclear weapons. Chapter 15 discusses Soviet thinking about nuclear weapons in the three years after Stalin's death, and Chapter 16 looks at Soviet policy on the peaceful uses of atomic energy.

Because little has been written about the history of the Soviet nuclear project, there is a certain set of questions that anyone writing on the topic has to address. When, for example, did the Soviet Union decide to build the atomic bomb? What role did espionage play in the Soviet nuclear project? How did Stalin understand the political significance of the bomb before and after Hiroshima? Did he fear an American attack in the postwar years, or was he confident that there would be no war? Did he believe that the Soviet Union could win a nuclear war? None of these questions has been given a definitive answer in the existing literature. But if they are not answered, there will be important gaps in our understanding of Soviet history and of international relations during the most intense period of the Cold War.

The scope of the book is defined, however, not merely by the desire to fill gaps in our knowledge of nuclear history, but by three broad themes. The first is the development of nuclear weapons and their delivery vehicles. The second is the relationship between science and politics. The third is the impact of nuclear weapons on international relations. These themes are often treated separately in studies of the policies of Western states. I have chosen to weave them together, for two reasons. The first is practical. The sources for the history of the Soviet project are still, in spite of greater openness, very much more fragmentary than those for the American or British projects. It makes sense, therefore, to look at the project from a number of different angles, in the hope that the view from one will fill out the view from the others.

The second reason is substantive. The different themes are interrelated, as I hope the book will show. The relationship between scientists and political leaders affected the way in which decisions were taken about nuclear weapons, and the nuclear project in turn affected the relationship between scientists and political leaders. Decisions about nuclear weapons were triggered by international rivalry, and in turn affected international relations. Scientists understood better than others the destructive effects of nuclear weapons, and helped to shape the political leaders' understanding of those weapons; this new understanding in turn affected foreign policy. This is the nexus of relationships that the book examines.[3]

The first theme – the development of nuclear weapons – provided the initial impetus for the book. During the Cold War political scientists argued about the dynamics of the Soviet–American nuclear arms race. Was it an action–reaction phenomenon, in which actions (or potential actions) by one side provoked a reaction by the other side? Or was it driven by an internal dynamic in one or both of the countries? The "internal dynamic" model came in various guises – the military-industrial complex or bureau-cratic politics, for example – but the basic premise was that the explanation for Soviet and/or American weapons decisions had to be sought within those countries, and not in the rivalry between them.[4]

American policy was analysed extensively in terms of these different approaches, but it was difficult to apply the action–reaction and internal dynamic models to the Soviet Union. The action–reaction model assumed that the Soviet Union was a state like any other, but that assumption begged the interesting question: to what degree did the particular character of the Soviet state affect its policy-making process, and its policies? The internal dynamic model, on the other hand, was too often used to generate assumptions about Soviet policy – that the Soviet leaders, as Leninists, for example, must believe that the Soviet Union would win a nuclear war. But these assumptions remained assumptions in the absence of evidence. The basic question remained: to what extent should Soviet nuclear policy be explained in terms of the international balance of power, and to what extent in terms of the particular character of the Soviet state?

One way to approach this question is to look at the process of techno-logical innovation in the Soviet Union. Soviet technological performance was generally poor compared to that of other countries, because the command-administrative system placed obstacles in the way of innovation. Some branches of industry performed better than others, however. The defense sector was the most successful, because the political leadership gave it the highest priority. Intervention by the political leadership gave the military sector its dynamism, and this intervention was frequently triggered by technological developments abroad. This in itself invalidates the notion that Soviet weapons decisions were the product of an internal dynamic alone.[5] On the other hand, the patterns of weapons innovation were different in the Soviet Union and the United States, as Matthew Evangelista has shown.[6] Consequently it does not make sense to treat the arms race as a competition between two identical states. Soviet nuclear weapons policy has to be studied in both its international and domestic contexts. This is not a very startling conclusion, but it does suggest that a history of Soviet nuclear weapons policy that ignores either the domestic or the international context will be seriously deficient. I have tried therefore to set the nuclear project squarely in both contexts, and to point to the interplay of internal and external factors at different junctures.

This book is not merely about the development of nuclear weapons. Its second theme is the relationship between science and politics. This re-lationship was a very complex one in the Soviet Union.[7] The communists regarded science and technology as progressive, but also claimed, in the Stalin years, to have the right to define what constituted valid science. The regime supported science, but also destroyed scientific disciplines. The destruction of genetics in the Soviet Union has been the subject of several studies.[8] But the case of physics is no less interesting.[9] Why and how did it survive and prosper? Did the Soviet leaders trust the advice they received from nuclear scientists? What mechanisms existed for providing the leadership with scientific advice? Did their special knowledge give the nuclear scientists political power? These questions have a direct bearing on the decisions to develop and procure weapons, and it is difficult to understand nuclear policy without taking them into account.

The relationship between science and politics has broader implications too. The development of science and technology in the Soviet Union was strongly influenced by the ideological, institutional, and political character of the regime. But science and technology, in their turn, can exert an influence on ideology, institutions, and politics. Russian intellectuals before and after the October Revolution regarded science as a force for rationality and democracy. They believed that it had a cultural value in and of itself, above and beyond the knowledge that was accumulated. Was this belief a delusion? Did the association of science with the Stalin regime – especially in the nuclear project – corrupt and discredit science? Or did science in fact constitute a civilizing force in Soviet society?

The same question may be asked of the relationship between science and international politics. No field better exemplified the international character of science than nuclear physics in the 1920s and 1930s. Yet the Soviet nuclear project – like other nuclear projects – was a prime example of science in the service of the state. What, in the Soviet scientists' minds, was the relationship between the national and international aspects of science? Did the international connections of physicists have any importance for Soviet policy, or for the course of international politics?

The third major theme of the book is the effect of nuclear weapons on international relations. Historians have argued about the role of the atomic bomb in the breakdown of the Grand Alliance and the origins of the Cold War. Would it have made a difference if Roosevelt and Churchill had accepted the advice of the Danish physicist Niels Bohr to tell Stalin about the atomic bomb before it was used? What was the effect of US atomic diplomacy on the Soviet Union, and on US–Soviet relations? Was there a missed opportunity to halt the arms race by arranging a ban on testing thermonuclear weapons? These questions have been much discussed in the West, but they involve the Soviet Union, and the lack of Soviet sources has been a serious obstacle to answering them.[10] My aim in writing this book has been to throw light on these questions by piecing together a careful and systematic analysis of Soviet nuclear policy.

This history raises more general questions about nuclear weapons: are they a stabilizing or destabilizing force in international relations, as some political scientists and historians have variously argued? Or have they had little effect on international relations, as others have claimed? These questions have not lost their importance with the end of the Cold War. Much of our thinking about the impact of nuclear weapons on international relations naturally derives from our understanding of the Cold War.[11] As we come to learn more about the Cold War through the opening up of Soviet and Chinese archives, our understanding of the role of nuclear weapons may change.

These are the questions that have shaped this book. In seeking to answer them I have drawn on sources of different kinds: archives, interviews, memoirs, diaries, journal articles, official documents, as well as secondary sources on science, technology, politics, and international relations. A great deal of new material became available while I was writing the book. The Soviet and Russian press published interviews with participants in the nuclear project, and new documents became available for the study of foreign and military policy. Some very helpful articles were published by Russian historians, especially on the history of Soviet science. I was able to work in archives I thought I would never visit, and to interview people I thought I could never meet.

All of these sources have been extremely helpful. They remain, nevertheless, unsatisfactory by comparison with those which historians of American and British nuclear policy can use. I have been able to work in Russian archives, but some of the most important archives remain closed. The records of the main nuclear policy-making bodies are not yet accessible. The Presidential Archive, where the papers of the top policy-making bodies are kept, is not open to foreign researchers. I have made considerable use of interviews and memoirs. These are important sources, but they have their drawbacks. Memories can be faulty and selective; memoirists may exaggerate their own role. Interviews and memoirs are most useful when they can be checked against contemporary documents, but that was not always possible in the research for this book. I tried to be careful in assessing the available material, for the history of the Soviet project has become encrusted with many stories of doubtful reliability. I have tried to strip those legends away, and to point to them only when they themselves are evidence about something else.

The need for care in handling evidence is strikingly illustrated by a recent book by Pavel Sudoplatov, who headed the department responsible for processing atomic intelligence at the end of World War II. In his memoirs, *Special Tasks: The Memoirs of an Unwanted Witness – A Soviet Spymaster*,[1] Sudoplatov claims that Niels Bohr, Enrico Fermi, J. Robert Oppenheimer, and Leo Szilard knowingly passed atomic secrets to the Soviet Union during and after World War II. Claims of this kind receive a great deal of publicity in the press, but the specific evidence produced by

---

[1] Pavel Sudoplatov and Anatoli Sudoplatov with Jerrold L. and Leona P. Schecter, *Special Tasks: The Memoirs of an Unwanted Witness – A Soviet Spymaster*, Boston: Little, Brown and Company, 1994. For a detailed discussion of the inaccuracy of these particular allegations, see my review in *Science*, May 27 1994.

Sudoplatov in support of this claim was soon shown to be untrue or misleading.

I started work on this book when there was an intense nuclear arms race and the Soviet Union still existed. The end of the Cold War and the collapse of the Soviet Union not only made it possible to gain access to new sources, but also put the story into quite a different context. This is a book about a system that failed, and about a conflict that is over. There is a temptation to treat the history of the Soviet Union merely as the history of a system that was bound to fail, and to indict all those who were associated with the Soviet side of the Cold War. But the collapse of the system did not seem inevitable after World War II, and the history of the Cold War is far too complex to be captured by an indictment of one side. I have tried to explore, as far as I could, what people did – and what they thought they were doing – in the context of their own time. That time and that context are quickly becoming remote, and increasingly difficult to comprehend. Yet it is important to do so, for we still live – and will live for a long time – with the consequences of decisions taken and implemented in the period covered by this book.

CHAPTER ONE

Ioffe's Institute

I

ON FEBRUARY 3, 1923 the Physicotechnical Institute held a reception to celebrate its move into a new building in Lesnoe, on the northern outskirts of Petrograd.[1] The institute's new home had been built as an almshouse just before World War I, but had been used as a psychiatric hospital during the war. In 1922 the Soviet authorities gave it to the Physicotechnical Institute, and now, after much effort, it had been made ready. Gas and electricity had been installed, and a well-equipped workshop built. Instruments and apparatus imported from Germany had been moved into the new laboratories. The People's Commissariat of Education had allowed the institute to take furniture from the storerooms of the Winter Palace.

At five o'clock the celebration began. Besides the staff of the institute, who numbered about sixty, there were party and government officials present, and representatives from the Academy of Sciences – about 150 people in all. Abram Ioffe, the director of the Institute, welcomed the guests with an address on "Science and Technology", in which he stressed that Soviet physics must grow strong and develop quickly. To do this, he said, it would have to find its own new ideas, and not trail along behind foreign science. Physics had a historic role to play in the development of industry, and would exert an active influence on technology. This was the basis on which the State Physicotechnical X-Ray Institute (to give it its full name) was organized. Soviet physics was not to be an abstract science. Though profoundly theoretical, it would make an effective contribution to technology, and to the economic development of the country.

After Ioffe's speech, the guests were taken to inspect the new laboratories. In a letter to his wife, Ioffe expressed satisfaction at the impression that the new building had created: "everyone was struck by the sight of a perfectly equipped European scientific institute, clean and elegant."[2] Then followed supper, for which the city authorities had made a special food allowance. After that came a piano recital, and humorous sketches and verses. The celebration ended at five o'clock in the morning.

Almost forty years later, Nikolai Semenov, deputy director of the institute and largely responsible for making the new building ready, recalled that there had been an exciting, youthful atmosphere at the opening ceremony. He and his colleagues, he wrote, could not know that from their number would come many of the physicists who would master atomic energy, but they did feel that a bright future awaited them. [3]

II

Ioffe's speech touched on two important themes in the history of Russian science – its relationship to Western science, and its ties with industry. Natural science had been imported into Russia from Europe by Peter the Great at the beginning of the eighteenth century. It was only in the mid-nineteenth century, however, that Russian scientists began to win international reputations, and Russian scientific institutions to rely predominantly on native rather than on foreign scholars. A more or less cohesive scientific community now began to emerge in Russia, with its social and intellectual ties maintained by a network of learned societies, scientific circles, and congresses.[4]

Even when it was assimilated into Russian culture, science was regarded by many Russians as an activity that embodied Western values. Political reformers and revolutionaries saw it as a rationalizing force that would help to dispel superstition and undermine the ideological basis of the Tsarist autocracy. The Tsarist authorities, for their part, distrusted the scientific spirit because they regarded it as critical of authority. Science was seen by its friends and enemies alike as progressive and democratic.

The Bolsheviks' view of science was very much in the revolutionary tradition of the nineteenth century. Science was especially important for them because they claimed that Marxism was a *scientific* theory. This claim rested upon the assertion that Marxism, like the natural sciences, was based on a materialist rather than an idealist conception of reality (i.e. it regarded the world as real, not merely as the creation of our minds or senses), and that Marxists used the same dialectical method as natural scientists in their analysis of the capitalist mode of production. Marxists asserted that their theory enabled them to make a scientific analysis of capitalism and of the revolutionary process which would lead to its replacement by socialism. The claim to scientific status is less stark in German or Russian because the term "scientific" has a broader meaning in those languages than it has today in English. Nevertheless Marxism's assertion of philosophical and methodological continuity with the natural sciences was a significant element in its claim to authority.[5]

The Bolsheviks believed, moreover, that science and technology would flourish in a society based upon the principles of scientific socialism. They did not reject the science and technology of capitalism. On the contrary,

Lenin argued that it was "necessary to take all the culture that capitalism has left and to build socialism out of it . . . to take all the science, the technology, all the knowledge and art. Without this we cannot build the life of communist society."[6] He understood that science and technology were necessary for defense and for economic development. In March 1918, when the Soviet government had to sign the punitive Treaty of Brest-Litovsk with Germany, he drew the lesson that "it is necessary to master the highest technology or be crushed."[7] When he coined the slogan "Communism = Soviet power + the electrification of the whole country" in 1920 he was doing more than popularizing the plan for electrification. He was also conveying the message that socialism was to be created by technological progress as well as social revolution.[8]

The Bolsheviks found, however, that their own enthusiasm for science was not matched by political support from Russian scientists. Most scientists had welcomed the revolution of February 1917 because they regarded the Tsarist autocracy as a brake on education and science, but they were suspicious of the Bolsheviks, who, they feared, might destroy Russian science and culture.[9] The Bolsheviks recognized this antipathy. Their Second Party Program, adopted in March 1919, declared that the greatest possible use should be made of scientific and technical specialists, "in spite of the fact that in most cases they have inevitably been nourished upon capitalist ideology and have been trained in bourgeois habits."[10]

The Bolsheviks took steps to enlist the support of the scientific community. They tried to protect leading scientists from the famine, disease, and war that swept Soviet Russia in the first years of its existence. In December 1919 they decreed that outstanding scientists should receive better food allowances and working conditions. Their purpose was, as the decree said, to preserve the scientific skills needed in constructing and defending a socialist society. In January 1920 the writer Maksim Gorkii established a special commission in Petrograd to improve the living conditions of scientists. The commission was given the power to ensure the normal functioning of research institutes and higher educational establishments. In the following year a central commission was set up in Moscow with the same purpose. These measures did not save the scientific community from all the vicissitudes of life in a war-torn country, but they did indicate that the Bolsheviks believed that science and technology were important for the revolution.[11]

Before World War I Russian science had been largely an academic pursuit, poorly supported by government. Scientists, moreover, did not have close ties with industry, much of which was controlled by foreign companies that relied on research done abroad, while Russian capitalists showed little interest in financing science. But the war brought major changes in the relationship between science and industry, because dependence on industrial imports, including many chemicals essential for the manufacture of weapons, was recognized to be a factor in Russia's military weakness. The war encouraged closer ties between science and industry and stimulated scientific research. Science was now seen as an important area of government policy.[12]

The Bolsheviks, in spite of their general commitment to science, had given little thought to how it should be organized and supported; they had, after all, to attend to the more urgent business of seizing power. Since they had no plans of their own, they were willing to look with favor on projects that had been frustrated under Tsarist rule. They supported the establishment of new research institutes in the first years of their rule, and one of these was the State Physicotechnical X-ray Institute, under the direction of Abram Ioffe.

III

Ioffe was born into a moderately well-off Jewish family in the small Ukrainian town of Romny in 1880. After graduating from the St Petersburg Technological Institute in 1902, he went to Munich to work in the laboratory of Wilhelm Röntgen, the discoverer of X-rays, and received his doctorate in 1905 for a study of the electrical conductivity of dielectric crystals.[13] In the following year he returned to Russia, even though Röntgen put him forward for a position at Munich University.[14] Ioffe explained to Röntgen why he had decided to remain in Russia:

I consider it my duty given the present sad and critical position in [Russia] to do all in my power (even if it is very little) in this bitter struggle [against political reaction], or at least not to turn aside from the dangers connected with it. I certainly do not want to become a "politician" – I have no predisposition for that, I can find satisfaction only in science.[15]

Ioffe's patriotism entailed a commitment to foster science and learning in Russia, but it did not imply support of the existing political system. He received other offers from foreign universities and institutes later in his career – Berkeley offered him a professorship in 1926, for example – but he turned them down.[16]

In St Petersburg Ioffe's career was hampered by the fact that he was a Jew (though he became a Lutheran to marry his first wife), and by the education system, which did not recognize his German doctorate. He had to accept a position as laboratory assistant at the Polytechnical Institute. He was, however, able to pursue his research and to give lectures, and he soon began to make his mark on Russian physics and to attract able students. He became a close friend of the Viennese physicist Paul Ehrenfest, who lived in St Petersburg from 1907 to 1912 and was largely responsible for bringing modern theoretical physics to Russia. Ioffe's work soon won him recognition. In 1913 he was appointed professor in the Polytechnical Institute, and in 1915 the Academy of Sciences awarded him a prize for a study of the magnetic field of cathode rays.[17]

When he was a student at the Technological Institute Ioffe, along with several hundred other students, was expelled for taking part in protests. He was reinstated only after he had signed two declarations promising not to break the rules again.[18] Apart from this, he seems not to have engaged in any kind of political activity before 1917. He was opposed to the Tsarist autocracy, but, like most Russian scientists, he viewed the Bolsheviks with caution, and in 1918 he left St Petersburg for the Crimea. Soon, however, he decided "to tie his fate with the land of the Soviets," as he later wrote, and returned to Petrograd in September 1918, one of the first Russian scientists to give his support to the Bolsheviks.[19] He continued to enjoy authority in the scientific community, and in November he was elected corresponding member of the Academy of Sciences, which remained largely antipathetic to the Bolsheviks until the late 1920s; in 1920 he became a full Academician.[20]

Ioffe's early career showed some of the features that later characterized his work for Soviet physics. He greatly valued his ties with Germany, and nearly every year until World War I he spent some time in Munich working with Röntgen.[21] He was a gifted teacher, and able to communicate his own intellectual enthusiasm to his students. In 1916 he organized a seminar on the new physics in his laboratory at the Polytechnic Institute. Among the eleven regular members were two future Nobel laureates, Peter Kapitsa and Nikolai Semenov, as well as others such as Iakov Frenkel' and P.I. Lukirskii, who would later win major reputations.[22]

This seminar formed the nucleus of Ioffe's new institute. Ioffe was asked by M.I. Nemenov, a professor at the Women's Medical Institute in Petrograd, to help organize a special center to study X-rays. Nemenov had been pressing for some years for this center, but his efforts were unsuccessful until 1919 when he received support from Anatolii Lunacharskii, the People's Commissar of Education. Ioffe became head of the physicotechnical department in the new institute. Disagreements soon arose, however, between Ioffe and Nemenov about the way in which the institute should be organized, and these resulted in its being split in 1921 into three parts, with the physicotechnical department becoming the State Physicotechnical X-Ray Institute.[23]

It was one thing to establish an institute; it was another to provide the conditions for serious research. In June 1920 Ioffe wrote to Ehrenfest, who was now at the University of Leiden:

We have lived through difficult years and have lost many people, but now we are starting to live again. . . . We are doing a lot of work, but little has been completed yet, since a year has been spent in organizing work in the new conditions, setting up workshops and struggling with famine. Now our chief misfortune is the complete lack of foreign literature, of which we have been deprived since early 1917. And my first and main request to you is to send us journals and the main books on physics.[24]

In February 1921 Ioffe set off on a six-month visit to Western Europe to buy scientific journals, books, and instruments, and to establish relations with foreign colleagues. The trip proved difficult to arrange: Western governments were reluctant to grant visas, and Lenin's intervention was required to secure hard currency from the limited Soviet reserves. But eventually the money was forthcoming, and several other scientists were sent abroad in the same year for the same purpose.

Ioffe spent most of his time in Germany and Britain, buying equipment and literature and reestablishing contact with Western scientists. In Germany he attended a colloquium at which his work with Röntgen was discussed. In London he was joined by Kapitsa, whose wife and two children had recently died in the epidemics sweeping Russia. Ioffe took Kapitsa with him to Cambridge where Ernest Rutherford agreed to take Kapitsa into the Cavendish Laboratory.[25]

There was still much to do in organizing the institute and training physicists. "Physics is in a particularly bad state," Semenov wrote to Kapitsa in March 1922, "because in general it has only begun to wake up in Russia . . . for its development we must have favorable external conditions, instruments, equipment, workshops, a supply of co-workers. . . . Perhaps I exaggerate, but I think that the economic collapse of our institute would set back for decades the development of physics in Russia."[26] Semenov appealed to Kapitsa to return to Petrograd to help in the education of physicists, "not of chatterboxes and idlers, but of real scientists – systematic and tenacious, who know the instruments and methods, who look on science not only as pleasure, but also as a cause."[27] But Kapitsa did not heed Semenov's plea. He felt that he was at the center of the leading school of physics in the world. "To return to Petrograd," he wrote to his mother, "and torment myself with the absence of gas, electricity, water and apparatus is simply impossible. It is only now that I have felt my strength. Success gives me wings and I am carried along by my work."[28] Kapitsa remained in Cambridge for another twelve years.

In 1919 Ioffe organized a new faculty at the Polytechnical Institute to give students an education combining physics and engineering.[29] The Physicomechanical Faculty became an important source of recruits to Ioffe's institute. Many of the institute's staff taught at the Polytechnic, which was located across the road from the new institute building, and Ioffe encouraged the best students to do research at his institute even before they graduated. Isaak Kikoin, for example, entered the Physicomechanical Faculty in 1925. He and his fellow students dreamed of doing research in Ioffe's institute, and in his second year he was invited to work there.

"Already within the walls [of the Polytechnical Institute] we learned to think of science as the basic affair of our life and worked in the laboratory practically without break," he wrote many years later. "... It is not surprising that we grew fairly rapidly in a scientific sense."[30] After graduating in 1930 and spending a short time studying in Munich with Walter Gerlach, Kikoin was appointed head of the electromagnetic laboratory at Ioffe's institute. After World War II he was to take charge of the gaseous diffusion and centrifuge methods of separating the isotopes of uranium.

The creation of the Physicomechanical Faculty is a good example of Ioffe's ability to create the conditions in which his school of physics could flourish. His institute, according to its 1921 statute, was supposed to conduct research into X-rays, electronic and magnetic phenomena, and the structure of matter, and to implement the technical applications of this research.[31] One of Ioffe's major problems was to secure financial and material support for this work. The People's Commissariat of Education, to which the institute was subordinate, did what it could to provide it with funds. Lunacharskii was eager to foster the development of science in Russia, and to secure the cooperation of scientists with the young Soviet state. But the commissariat's resources were limited, and financial problems remained severe. The institute earned some money by producing and selling X-ray tubes and other equipment, but this was too little to provide it with adequate support.[32] In 1924 Ioffe approached the Scientific-Technical Department of the Supreme Council of the National Economy, which was responsible for the country's industrial research, with a proposal to set up a new laboratory that would concentrate on applied research for industry. His proposal was accepted, and the new laboratory, which Ioffe directed, overlapped considerably with the institute.[33] This arrangement was a clever device for gaining increased support for research, and further evidence of Ioffe's ingenuity as an organizer.

During the 1920s the institute concentrated on the mechanical properties of crystals, the physics of dielectrics and dielectrical breakdown, the physics of metals, thermodynamic engineering, and theoretical physics. Much of this work had potential applications in the electric power and metallurgical industries, with which the institute maintained close relations. By the end of the decade the institute and the laboratory had grown into a large and complex research establishment, employing more than one hundred full-time physicists, many of whom had studied or done research in the West.[34] The institute had become a leading center of European physics at a time when quantum mechanics had revolutionized physics. Some of its members had international reputations: Iakov Frenkel' headed the theoretical department, while some younger theorists – Dmitrii Ivanenko, Vladimir Fok, Lev Landau – were making names for themselves; Semenov had begun the research that led to the publication in 1934 of a study of chain reactions for which he received the Nobel Prize for chemistry in 1956.[35]

In the early 1930s Ioffe's institute was reorganized. The laboratory
and the institute were combined formally, and in 1931 the whole organization was divided into three separate institutes: the Leningrad Institute
of Chemical Physics, with Semenov as director; the Leningrad Physicotechnical Institute (LFTI), headed by Ioffe himself; and the Leningrad
Institute of Electrical Physics, under the direction of A.A. Chernyshev.
Ioffe also took the initiative in setting up physicotechnical institutes in the
provinces to extend the research network out from Leningrad and Moscow
to the new industrial centers that were expanding rapidly under the first
Five-Year Plan. Four such institutes were created, in Khar'kov, Sverdlovsk,
Dnepropetrovsk, and Tomsk. Most of the staff for these institutes came
from the Leningrad *Fiztekh* (as Ioffe's institute was known). These off-
shoots became, in time, important research centers in their own right.[36]

IV

The reorganization of Ioffe's institute was designed to encourage technological progress in industry. It came at a time when the Soviet authorities
were putting increasing pressure on scientists to contribute to the industrialization drive. Stalin had proclaimed the goal of "catching up and overtaking the technology of the developed advanced capitalist countries."[37] The
urgency with which the Bolsheviks wanted to pursue industrial growth
made it impossible to rely on indigenous research alone. The Fifteenth
Party Congress had called in 1927 for the "widest use of West European
and American scientific and scientific-industrial experience."[38] During the
First Five-Year Plan, from 1928 to 1932, the Soviet Union imported large
quantities of foreign machinery and plant.[39] But the Second Five-Year Plan
(1932–7) gave greater attention to the development of indigenous technology. The Seventeenth Party Congress in 1934 declared that by the end of
the plan period the Soviet Union would be transformed "into a technologically and economically independent country, and into the most technologically advanced state in Europe."[40]

This goal showed how ambitious Soviet industrial policy was. In 1929
Stalin, who had now defeated his political opponents on both the left and
the right of the Party, set his own brutal stamp on the Soviet economy. He
launched the forced collectivization of agriculture, thereby destroying the
economic power of the peasantry. At the same time he imposed drastic
increases in the targets for industrial production. The justification he
offered for this policy was the need to overcome Russia's traditional
backwardness and its suffering at the hands of its enemies: "We are fifty or
a hundred years behind the advanced countries. We must make good this
distance in ten years. Either we do it, or they crush us."[41]

Ioffe had been indefatigable in propounding to party and government
leaders the view that physics would provide the basis for future technol-

ogy.[42] But in 1931 he suffered a serious setback. Experiments done in his laboratory had suggested that it would be possible to make thin insulating film with high resistance to electric breakdown, and thus to produce cheaper and better insulators which would reduce the cost of transmitting high-voltage electric current over long distances. The idea was of great interest to the government, which decided in October 1929 to allocate 300,000 roubles, as well as 60,000 roubles in foreign currency, to support further research; special funds were also made available to buy instruments abroad. Agreements were concluded with American firms and with the Siemens company in Berlin for development work.[43]

Ioffe's initial experiments were confirmed at the Siemens laboratory in Berlin. These encouraging results prompted Valerian Kuibyshev, head of the Supreme Council of the National Economy, to tell the Sixteenth Party Congress in July 1930 that

this work is not yet completed, but Academician Ioffe thinks that after a year's work it will be brought to a successful conclusion. The results of this work will lead to a serious transformation in the matter of insulation and in electrical engineering in general.[44]

But further experiments in Leningrad failed to reproduce the results obtained in Berlin. In 1931 Landau, who was in the theoretical department of Ioffe's institute and had just returned from two years in Western Europe, pointed out that the theoretical assumptions underlying Ioffe's experiments were incorrect. New experiments confirmed that the initial results had been wrong. The research done by Siemens led to some improvement in insulators, but Ioffe's initial hopes had not been realized, and in January 1932 he had to confess to the Seventeenth Party Conference that the work on thin-layer insulation had not met with the expected success.[45] He was intensely disappointed, and deeply offended by the behavior of Landau, who called him an illiterate.[46] It was one thing to say that physics should provide the basis for future technology; it was quite another to translate that slogan into reality.

The relationship between physics and industry was the focus of a session of the Academy of Sciences in March 1936. The Soviet leadership was concerned that, in spite of the large resources being devoted to science, Soviet physicists were failing to contribute enough to the industrialization drive. The aim of the meeting was to make it clear to Soviet physicists that their main task was to provide the scientific basis for socialist production. This message was to be conveyed by subjecting Ioffe and his Institute – the dominant school of Soviet physics – to "criticism and self-criticism' for failing to do enough to help industry. The meeting was carefully orchestrated on the basis of instructions from the party leadership.[47] On the day the session opened the government newspaper *Izvestiia* carried an article deploring the failure of Ioffe's institute to do more to help industry.[48] This set the tone of the meeting, which was attended by several hundred scientists and officials. It was held in Moscow, to which the Academy had moved two years before.

Ioffe began his report by saying that his institute had been founded with the aim of making physics the scientific basis of socialist technology. As a result of its work, the Soviet Union had become one of the leading centers of physics in the world:

I consider the growth of Soviet physics and of its specific gravity in world science a fundamental result of our activity. I think it would not be an exaggeration to say that, instead of one of the last places [in the world], our physics has taken fourth place, and technical physics perhaps even third place.[49]

The Physicotechnical Institute of 1918 had become a network of fourteen institutes and three higher technical schools, with 1,000 scientific workers, of whom about one hundred could be considered major independent scientists.[50]

Ioffe claimed that his institute had made a significant contribution to the Soviet economy. Its most important achievements were an acoustic method for measuring stresses; new methods for studying the structure of steel and alloys; the invention of new insulating materials; the protection of electric lines and high-voltage transformers; work on polymers and artificial rubber; and new methods of biological measurement.[51] But industrial engineers, he said, were reluctant to present their needs to the physicists, and showed little interest in the proposals put forward by Soviet science:

Some people expect physics to direct technology, to create new manufactures, others consider it to be of no practical value. Often it is required that physics introduce its own methods almost by force, without taking account of engineering and economic factors. And only a few understand that the main duty of physics is to answer the enquiries of technology, when they have their origin in the state of production, and to prepare new methods. The physicist is basically a consultant on technology, not its director.[52]

Physics, said Ioffe, had played a rather small part in the first two five-year plans, because the transfer of American technology did not require significant participation by physicists. But physicists would play an increasingly important role in coming years, because they would have to take part in developing new technology.[53]

In the debate that followed none of Ioffe's claims went unchallenged. He was complimented for his part in fostering the growth of physics, but the general tone of the discussion was highly critical. His claims for the standing of Soviet physics were disputed by several speakers, most notably by Aleksandr Leipunskii, a former student who was now director of the Ukrainian Physicotechnical Institute in Khar'kov. Leipunskii argued that it was quite misleading to say that the Soviet Union occupied fourth place in the world in physics. If first place was ascribed to Britain, second to America, and third to France, said Leipunskii, then it was important to remember that there was a large gap between third and fourth places. Moreover, given the extensive contact that existed between scientists of the different West European countries, West European science had to be viewed as a whole, and "there exists a pretty fair qualitative leap between West European science and ours." The Soviet Union did not occupy a leading position in any area of physics, and had no school comparable to those of Niels Bohr in Denmark or Ernest Rutherford in England.

Leipunskii also took issue with Ioffe's judgment that the Soviet Union held third place in technical physics, behind the United States and Germany. Technical physics was to be judged not by the number or quality of papers written, but by the things that were produced. Ioffe's classification placed the Soviet Union ahead of Britain, but Leipunskii, who had recently returned from a year in Cambridge, argued that this assessment was mistaken. Ioffe was wrong to give the impression that everything was in order with Soviet physics, especially since he was right to say that the Soviet Union now faced the task of developing its own technology independently of the West. This could be done only if the Soviet Union had an advanced science, and a superior ability to apply science to practice.[54]

Leipunskii's criticism of Ioffe's complacency about the state of Soviet physics was supported by other speakers. But the issue that received most attention was the one that worried the authorities most: the gap between science and industry, the failure to translate new scientific ideas into production. Academician Dmitrii Rozhdestvenskii, who had founded the State Optical Institute in Leningrad, took particular exception to Ioffe's view that the physicist should merely act as a consultant to industry. Ioffe's institute, Rozhdestvenskii said, was too remote from industry, unlike the State Optical Institute. Science needed closer contact with industry if it was to provide the initiative for technological progress, and itself grow on the basis of advancing technology.[55]

Many of the speakers remarked that physicists were unwilling to engage in industrial work. One spoke of *Fiztekh's* "academism" and "aristocratism."[56] A.A. Armand, head of the research sector of the People's Commissariat of Heavy Industry, complained that

among our physicists there is cultivated, unfortunately, the opinion that there is nothing for physicists to do in industry, that a man who is able to transform physical data into practical things is not a physicist and is not worth a penny, that he is an artisan, and that only the person who opens a new path to physics, who works on the atomic nucleus, on quantum mechanics, is a physicist, and that a physicist need not go into engineering work.[57]

Ioffe's institute came in for criticism on other grounds too. Leipunskii spoke of the unsystematic character of its work, and claimed that the stress laid upon the prospects for future technology interfered with the institute's efforts to meet industry's current needs.[58] Others, recalling Ioffe's misfortune with thin-layer insulation, spoke of the low level of theoretical work and of careless experiments. The sharpest attack on this score came from Landau, who also complained that Ioffe had introduced a boastful and bragging style into Soviet physics.[59]

Ioffe acknowledged the justice of some of these criticisms but defended himself against most of the charges. He had been wrong, he said, to assess the standing of Soviet physics in the way he had, and his remarks had been too optimistic, but he had wanted to show that "in the totality of our scientific work we have [something of] significant value – both cultural and economic."[60] Physicists were indeed to blame for not pushing harder for innovation, but there was considerable resistance from industry too, which was more interested in what was being done in the West than in the proposals of Soviet scientists. Ioffe quoted an example that he said was typical. In its work on insulation his institute had developed and tested acetyl-cellulose as an insulating material. But in spite of every kind of pressure, Soviet industry would not produce it. Only after some representatives from the Khar'kov Electromechanical Factory had seen that kind of insulation at Metro-Vickers in England did the Khar'kov factory organize production of the material.[61]

Ioffe also rejected Rozhdestvenskii's suggestion that different fields of physics be linked with the appropriate branch of industry. Rozhdestvenskii had said that nuclear research could be combined with work on high-voltage technology. Ioffe dismissed this, saying that "if you try to divide up physics according to [Rozhdestvenskii's] scheme in these technical institutes, then I don't know what such physics will be worth. And it must be said that high-voltage technology will not thrive from being put under the leadership of specialists in atomic affairs."[62]

Yet Rozhdestvenskii had raised the fundamental question: why was science still being used more successfully in capitalist industry than in the Soviet Union? His own answer was that

in the end, the capitalist looks after his own pocket very well, and knows perfectly well how to buy scientists and make them work for him. . . . Here, in a socialist country, what collective will takes the place of the capitalist's ability to use science? We have not organized such an apparatus, or else it works badly. Meanwhile, it should be insisted that socialism needs such an apparatus.[63]

In the mid-1930s the Soviet government, according to one study, spent a larger proportion of its national income than the United States on research and development.[64] The Soviet authorities expected science to produce tangible results, and became impatient when it did not do so. But the chief obstacle to technological innovation came not from the scientists but from the system of economic planning and management that was created in the

1930s to carry out the policy of rapid industrialization. This highly central-ized, hierarchical system interposed departmental barriers between research and production, and made innovation a difficult bureaucratic exercise. The practice of setting ambitious production targets for industrial enterprises also created a disincentive for industry to introduce new products or processes, since these might interfere with production and result in failure to meet plan targets. Besides, the willingness of engineers and managers (who were generally engineers) to show initiative had been dampened by the Shakhty trial of 1928 and the Industrial Party trial of 1930, in which engineers had been accused of sabotaging coal mines near the town of Shakhty and of conspiring to overthrow the Soviet regime. These trials had been followed by widespread arrests of engineers.[65]

The chronic defects of the Stalinist economy – the "command-admin-istrative system," as it is now called – have been extensively analyzed by various authors.[66] Since the obstacles to innovation were systemic, Ioffe can hardly be assigned all the blame for the failure to introduce research into production. The State Optical Institute was held up as a model for physics institutes at the March session of the Academy. But that institute was soon working almost exclusively on applied physics, and Rozhdestvenskii and other leading physicists were driven to conduct their research elsewhere; it could not serve, therefore, as a useful model for a general physics institute.[67] Ioffe, with his slogan that physics was the basis of future technology, had not understood that innovation would be problematic, that it would not happen automatically as a result of scientific discovery.

G.M. Krzhizhanovskii, vice-president of the Academy and an old Bol-shevik who had been responsible for the plan to electrify the country, and N.P. Gorbunov, the Academy's permanent secretary, sent a report to Viacheslav Molotov, the head of the government, about the Academy Session. Their report was deeply critical of Ioffe, who had tried, they said, to avoid serious discussion of his institute's work, and had been unrespon-sive to criticism. His institute had done very little for industry, they wrote. They described at length the scientific and organizational mistakes for which Ioffe had been criticized, and did so in a way that laid him open to the charge of sabotage.[68]

After the Academy Session, the Soviet authorities kept up pressure on scientists to play their part in the industrialization drive. In August 1936 the Heavy Industry Commissariat organized a conference at which the head of the science department of the Party Central Committee, Karl Bauman, declared that

in the USSR, as nowhere else in the world, all the conditions have been created for the flourishing of science, for the development of research work. We are surging forward, the cultural-technical level of the workers is growing constantly, the Stakhanovite movement is expanding – all this creates limitless scope for the practical realization of the institutes' achievements. There are precise directions from the Party about scientific work. The institutes face a basic task: to contribute in every way possible to the realization of the Party's slogan – to catch up and overtake the economically and technologically advanced capitalist countries. However, scientific work still lags behind practice.[69]

At the same conference A.A. Armand, head of the Heavy Industry Commissariat's research section, commented on the slow progress of research. Although the institutes had done some good work, he said, "a significant part [of that work] was done only after it became known that analogous work had been done abroad."[70]

The tendency to look to the West, and to neglect Soviet research unless the same work had been done abroad, had been commented on by Ioffe at the March session. The psychology of "catch up and overtake" militated against technological innovation on the basis of original Soviet research. This slogan implied that the Soviet Union was following the path that the more advanced countries had already traveled. It was less risky to do something that had already been done abroad than to try out an untested Soviet idea. Proposals from Soviet scientists were likely to be ignored unless they had been validated by foreign experience.

The difficulties of innovation modified Ioffe's view of the role his institute should play. Soon after the débâcle of thin-layer insulation in 1931 he began to press for the institute's transfer from the industrial sector to the Academy of Sciences. He was eager to develop fundamental research, and this was made difficult by the demands placed on the institute by the People's Commissariat of Heavy Industry and then by the People's Commissariat of Medium Machine-Building, to which it was subordinate in the 1930s. Ioffe wanted to concentrate on creating the foundation for future technologies, rather than on responding to industry's day-to-day concerns. The Academy approved of the move in 1932, but the industrial commissariats were reluctant to lose the institute.[71]

At its March 1936 session the Academy of Sciences adopted a resolution, which had been prepared before the meeting, criticizing Ioffe's institute and calling for much greater efforts on its part to ensure that scientific results were translated rapidly into production.[72] Ioffe took some steps to improve the institute's ties with industry, and encouraged defense work at the institute – on the demagnetizing of ships and on radar.[73] At the same time he continued to lobby for the transfer of the institute from the industrial sector to the Academy of Sciences, where it would be less directly tied to practical tasks.

V

Physicists came under increasing pressure in the 1930s to show their loyalty to the Party and the state. The intellectual climate of the country changed drastically for the worse at the end of the 1920s. The Academy of Sciences lost the relative intellectual autonomy it had enjoyed in the 1920s and was brought under increasing party and government control.[74] Collaboration with the regime was no longer enough; the Party now demanded political and ideological commitment. Scientific disciplines came under scrutiny from militant party philosophers who wanted to root out any political or philosophical deviations that scientific theories might betray.[75] These philosophers claimed the right to judge whether theories in the natural sciences were really scientific or not. What was at issue in these discussions was the question of authority in science: who had the right to say what constituted a valid scientific theory – the scientists or the Communist Party?[76]

The dangers of this situation were illustrated most clearly by the destruction of Soviet genetics at the hands of Trofim Lysenko, who made far-reaching claims for his own ideas about agriculture and attacked his opponents as anti-Marxist and anti-Soviet. "Lysenko and . . . his supporters," Semenov said many years later, "by using the conditions of the personality cult, transferred the struggle against those with different ideas from the level of scientific discussion to the level of demagogy and political accusations."[77] Among the techniques of argument Lysenko used were: "quotation-mongering" – appealing to the writings of Marx, Engels, Lenin, or Stalin in support of an argument; and "label-sticking" – attacking an opponent by associating him with an anti-Soviet political or philosophical position. By shifting the terms of the debate, Lysenko appealed to political authority, rather than to the scientific community, to assess the validity of his ideas.

Not all sciences suffered as biology had done. Physics fared much better, though it did not escape ideological policing entirely.[78] Militant philosophers, in alliance with a small number of older physicists who could not adjust to relativity theory or quantum mechanics, assailed the physicists for their unwillingness to be guided by dialectical materialism, and for the "idealism" inherent in quantum mechanics.[79] The intellectual level of these attacks was not high, and the party philosophers were divided among themselves. Some rejected recent advances in theoretical physics, on the grounds that they contravened the materialism espoused by Lenin in his *Materialism and Empirio-Criticism*. Others believed that these advances, and the epistemological issues they raised, were not only compatible with dialectical materialism, but confirmed its usefulness as a methodological guide.[80]

The 1930s saw a number of skirmishes between physicists and philosphers. One of the first of these took place at a conference in November 1931 where Iakov Frenkel' made it clear that he did not believe that dialectical materialism should have a guiding role in science. Frenkel' was summoned to explain his position before the party fraction (group) at the conference, and he did so in uncompromising terms:

What I have read in Engels and Lenin does not delight me at all. Neither Lenin nor Engels is an authority for physicists. Lenin's book [*Materialism and Empirio-Criticism*] is a model of acute analysis, but amounts to little more than the assertion of elementary truths that it's not worth breaking a lance over. . . . As a Soviet person I personally cannot sympathize with an opinion that is harmful to science. There cannot be proletarian mathematics, proletarian physics etc.[81]

No other physicist was so outspoken or so courageous in criticizing dialectical materialism, and for the next two decades party philosophers regarded Frenkel' as their chief target among the physicists. That was a dangerous and exposed position to be in, and Frenkel' was fortunate to escape arrest.[82]

Physicists employed various tactics against the efforts to force dialectical materialism on scientists: some argued that quantum mechanics offered a brilliant confirmation of dialectical materialism; others that dialectical materialism could indeed provide guidance for physicists, but that the philosophers knew too little physics to be able to say anything useful; still others that philosophers and physicists had different areas of expertise and should confine themselves to those areas.[83] Whatever the arguments used, the physicists were largely united in resisting the claims of party philosophers to be able to adjudicate on scientific theories in light of their conformity with dialectical materialism.

The solidarity of the physicists on this point can be seen in the preparations for the March 1936 session of the Academy of Sciences. At a preparatory meeting in January 1936 the chairman of the organizing committee, G.M. Krzhizhanovskii, asked whether it would make sense to include a philosophical discussion at the session. "We ought to understand," he said, "whether everything is in order in the sense of philosophical attitudes [of the physicists]."[84] Ioffe rejected the idea, arguing that while such discussions were important and useful, they needed special preparation. Only confusion would result from such a discussion at the March meeting, he said, because the theoretical physicists had not analyzed all their theories from the point of view of dialectical materialism, and not one of the philosophers (with the exception of B.M. Gessen, who was a member of the organizing committee) knew modern physics.

The case for putting philosophy on the agenda was made by A.M. Deborin, a member of the Academy, and secretary of its social sciences department. Deborin declared that there was no doubt that many Soviet physicists stood on the "ground of idealism." Soviet physics, he suggested, lagged behind Soviet reality and the Soviet worldview. Moreover, some of the physicists' concepts – notably indeterminacy – drew them close, at a philosophical level, to Fascism. He proposed that the March session be used to make a sharp turn from idealism to the materialist dialectic. This was an ominous argument, and could have had very unpleasant consequences if it had been endorsed by the party leadership. Deborin received some support from B.M. Vul, a physicist who was close to party circles, but Ioffe, Frenkel', Igor' Tamm, and Fok firmly rejected his arguments, and Krzhizhanovskii decided not to include a philosophical discussion on the agenda of the March session.

There was relatively little political rhetoric at the session, and the tone of the discussion was matter-of-fact and businesslike.[85] Although the philosophical attacks on physics continued, and grew more intense during the Great Terror of 1937–8, the party leadership did not give them definitive backing until after World War II. In spite of the philosophical pressure, with its political accusations and threats, Soviet physics escaped the fate of genetics. The ideological policing nevertheless reflected the regime's distrust of scientists.

Biologists and physicists alike were criticized for not doing enough to help the Soviet regime achieve its economic goals, but physics prospered while genetics was largely destroyed and biology more generally badly damaged.[86] There was no doubt an element of luck in this, and personalities too played a role. Besides, theoretical physics was more esoteric and less accessible than genetics, and it was therefore easier to repel the philosophers by arguing that they did not know what they were talking about. With the exception of some marginal figures, the physicists were united in their defense of physics against the criticisms of the philosophers.

There was another difference too. David Joravsky has argued convincingly that the Lysenko affair should be seen not merely as a clash between natural science and dialectical materialism, but also as a product of the terrible condition of Soviet agriculture after collectivization. Soviet plant breeders were unable to come forward with proposals for dramatic increases in grain yields, even though they were winning an international reputation for the scientific breeding of improved crop varieties. Their cautious realism was irrelevant to the momentous problems which faced Soviet agriculture.[87] By offering increased crop yields, Lysenko's theories reinforced the claim that the Soviet Union was creating the most advanced agricultural system in the world. Soviet officials may have complained that Soviet physics was not doing enough to help industry, but industry was growing rapidly nonetheless. Soviet leaders did not need a "Lysenkoist" physics to bridge the gap between political goals and reality. Much of the work done by physicists was helpful to industry, and those parts of physics that came under the strongest ideological attack – most notably, quantum mechanics – did not become caught up in the dangerous nexus that existed between science and practical utility in the Stalin years.

VI

Physics was one of the weaker sciences in prerevolutionary Russia, and lacked the strong national tradition that existed, for example, in chemistry and mathematics. Most research was done in universities, where it was poorly supported.[88] By the mid-1930s Soviet physics had progressed considerably: new generations of physicists had been trained, and new institutes set up. There were now two important schools of physics besides Ioffe's. These were headed by Dmitrii Rozhdestvenskii and Leonid Mandel'shtam, both of whom had, like Ioffe, spent several years in the West before 1917. Rozhdestvenskii studied in Leipzig and Paris, while Mandel'shtam was at Strasbourg University from 1899 to 1914, first as a student, then as a professor.[89]

Rozhdestvenskii helped to create the State Optical Institute, which was set up in 1918. Like Ioffe he held the belief, which was shared by many Russian scientists at the time, that scientists and engineers ought to work closely together. The Optical Institute, he wrote in 1919, was an establishment "of a new type, in which scientific and technical tasks were inseparably linked," and such institutes would lead very quickly to an unprecedented flowering of science and technology.[90] The State Optical Glass Factory was put under the direction of his institute, and Rozhdestvenskii played an active part in developing the optical industry.

Mandel'shtam, who had returned to Russia from Strasbourg on the eve of World War I, was "not a scientist of the organizing type."[91] He did not seek to play a public role, and eschewed the kind of propaganda for physics in which Ioffe engaged. He devoted himself to research and teaching, and was widely regarded as the most brilliant of the older generation of Soviet physicists.[92] After he became head of the Department of Theoretical Physics at Moscow University in 1925, he drew a number of able physicists to him and established the leading school of physics in Moscow. In the mid-1930s, after the Academy of Sciences had moved from Leningrad to Moscow, he worked closely with Sergei Vavilov, the director of the Academy's Physics Institute (FIAN), to turn that institute into a powerful center of research.[93]

It is Ioffe, however, who deserves most of the credit for the growth of Soviet physics. His institute has been called the "maternal nest," the "cradle," the "forge," the "alma mater" of Soviet physics.[94] Although he was never more than a very superficial Marxist in his philosophical views, his vision of physics as the basis for technology matched the Bolshevik aim of making the Soviet Union a great industrial state, and he was able to win support for his work by conveying this to the party leaders.

Ioffe was a considerable scientist in his own right, and is widely regarded as one of the founders of the physics of semiconductors. But from the 1920s on his outstanding qualities were those of an impresario of physics: publicizing its value, recruiting talented young scientists, choosing directions of research, getting resources from the government, and building up research institutes. In pursuing these goals he engaged in the boasting and bragging that Landau complained of, and in the fantasizing and dreaming that others criticized. Moreover, he annoyed some of his colleagues in the Academy by the way in which he praised the Bolsheviks for what they had done for science. These failings were traits not only of his personality, but also of the times he lived in – times that encouraged grandiose claims and extravagant promises about the future.

Ioffe wanted his institute to be a great center of European science. He placed particular weight on contacts with foreign scientists, believing that exchange visits, international congresses, conferences and seminars were essential for the normal development of science. Personal contacts, in Ioffe's view, were the best form of communication, and the main stimulus to creative work. He did his utmost to foster such contacts, and from 1924 to 1933 spent some time each year traveling in Europe or the United States.[95] He claimed that it was because of his contacts with foreign scientists that Soviet physics had lost its provincial character. In the 1920s and early 1930s he sent more than thirty of his institute's researchers abroad to do research, and more than once paid for these trips with honoraria and consultancy fees he received in the West (the rest of this money was used to buy literature and equipment for the institute).[96] He also invited foreign scientists to come to the Soviet Union to do research and to take part in conferences.

In 1930 Iakov Frenkel' wrote to his wife from New York that "physicists are a narrow caste, the members of which are well known to one another in all parts of the globe, but at the same time completely unknown even to their closest compatriots."[97] In the mid-1930s, however, communication with foreign scientists became much more difficult. After 1933 Ioffe was not allowed to travel abroad again until 1956. In 1936 he complained that the restrictions on foreign travel were hampering the intellectual development of young physicists, but his complaints had no effect. The restrictions on Ioffe were evidently intended as punishment for the defection of Georgii Gamov (George Gamow) in 1933. Gamov was one of the leading younger theoretical physicists, and attended the Solvay conference in Belgium in 1933 with Ioffe. He decided to defect with his wife.[98]

Kapitsa too was affected by the shift in policy. He had stayed in Cambridge, becoming a Fellow of Trinity in 1925, and a Fellow of the Royal Society and corresponding member of the Soviet Academy of Sciences in 1929. In the summer of 1931 Nikolai Bukharin, who had lost to Stalin in the political struggles within the party leadership and was now head of the research sector of the Supreme Council of the National Economy, visited Cambridge where Rutherford showed him around the Cavendish Laboratory. Kapitsa invited him to dinner at his house; after dinner Bukharin asked Kapitsa to come back to the Soviet Union, and promised that he would have the most favorable conditions for his work if he did. Kapitsa avoided giving a direct answer, but stayed in Cambridge.[99]

In the autumn of 1934, when he made one of his regular trips to the
Soviet Union, Kapitsa was prevented by the Soviet government from
returning to Cambridge. He was extremely depressed by this. For two
years he could do no research; he was engaged in the organization of a new
institute, the Institute of Physical Problems, which was created for him in
Moscow, and his laboratory in Cambridge was eventually bought by the
Soviet government. He again took up the work he had been doing in
Cambridge in low-temperature physics and magnetism.[100]

In letters he wrote at the time to his wife in Cambridge (he had
remarried in 1927) and to the Soviet authorities Kapitsa painted an un-
flattering picture of the scientific community in Moscow. He was bitter
because he felt that his former friends and colleagues, including Ioffe, were
shunning him, fearing that he was a dangerous person to be associated with.
He was dismayed by the contrast between Moscow and Cambridge. There
was no real scientific community in Moscow, he wrote, and no place
where the physicists of the city would gather to discuss their work; this was
one of the reasons why Soviet physicists sought recognition abroad rather
than at home. "If we are the strongest state in relation to politics and
economics," he wrote, "then in relation to progress in science and technology we are a complete colony of the West."[101] Science was undervalued in
the Soviet Union, and the authorities did not treat scientists with respect.[102]

The curtailing of contacts with foreign scientists in the mid-1930s was a
consequence of the worsening of the political situation inside the country.
The assassination of Sergei Kirov, the Leningrad party secretary, on
December 1, 1934 ushered in a period of intense repression, culminating in
the savage purge of 1937–8, during which 7–8 million people were
arrested.[103] Western physicists who traveled to the Soviet Union in these
years were aware of the terror that pervaded Soviet society, and of the fear
among their Soviet colleagues.[104] David Shoenberg, a Cambridge physicist
who worked at Kapitsa's new institute in 1937–8, wrote later that the
purge was "rather like a plague and you could never tell who would catch
it next."[105] Numerous scientists were caught up in the infernal machine
of the People's Commissariat of Internal Affairs (NKVD) in those years.
The Ukrainian Physicotechnical Institute in Khar'kov was especially badly
affected, as will be seen in the next chapter. It has been estimated that as
many as one hundred physicists were arrested in Leningrad in 1937–8.[106]
Whatever the precise figure, it is clear that the physics community was
badly hit by the purge.

Several of the leading figures at Ioffe's institute were arrested, including
P.I. Lukirskii, head of the Department of X-rays and Electronics, V.
Frederiks, head of the Laboratory of Liquid Crystals, and M.P. Bronshtein,
a brilliant young theoretician. Lukirskii was released in 1942, but
Bronshtein was shot in 1938, and Frederiks died in the camps.[107] No one

was safe in those terrible years, but the purge worked in an arbitrary way
and Ioffe and Frenkel' were spared.

In the early years of the revolution an implicit compact had been
concluded between the Bolsheviks and scientists like Ioffe: If the scientists
contributed their knowledge to the building of socialist society, the Bolsheviks would help them to realize their projects for investigating and transforming nature. This was never an easy relationship, and it became more
difficult as time passed. In retrospect the 1920s seemed like a Golden Age,
in spite of the great hardships. Semenov wrote of it as a "wonderful and
truly romantic period." Others have painted the same picture of Ioffe's
institute in those years. It was an exciting time in physics, especially for
young physicists in an expanding institute.[108]

The 1930s were a much more difficult decade. The Soviet authorities
made increasing demands on scientists to contribute to industrialization,
but the economic system created obstacles to the introduction of new
technology. Stalinist repression weighed heavily on the scientific community, and international contacts were cut back. Ioffe received support
from the state for his efforts to foster the growth of Soviet physics and,
thanks in large measure to his work, Soviet physics did flourish in the
prewar years. But he and his colleagues had to endure restrictions and
repressions of a kind that he cannot have envisaged when he made his
optimistic speech about science and technology at the opening of his
institute's new building in February 1923.

CHAPTER TWO

Nuclear Prehistory

I

THE DISCOVERY OF RADIOACTIVITY in Paris in 1896 was the first step on a circuitous path that led to the development of nuclear weapons. Henri Becquerel found that uranium salts emitted radiation which (like X-rays, discovered the year before) could penetrate cardboard and blacken a photographic plate, and also ionize the atmosphere. The nature and source of this radiation provided a fruitful area of research. Marie and Pierre Curie found two new elements, polonium and radium, the latter many millions of times more radioactive than uranium. They also established that radioactivity is a property of the atoms of particular elements. In the early years of this century Ernest Rutherford and Frederick Soddy discovered that radioactive elements decay because their atoms emit particles, with the result that at any given moment some part of the atoms of radioactive elements are changing into atoms of another element.

In spite of its esoteric character, research into radioactivity quickly captured the public imagination. Radioactive elements had practical uses in research and medicine, but it was as a potential source of energy on a large scale that they excited most interest. Soddy was among the most eloquent and influential prophets of the energy that was stored in the atoms of radioactive elements. "Radium had taught us," he wrote, "that there is no limit to the amount of energy in the world available to support life, save only the limit imposed by the boundaries of knowledge."[1]

Vladimir Vernadskii, a Russian mineralogist with broad scientific and philosophical interests, was equally excited by the discovery of radioactivity. In a lecture to the General Assembly of the Academy of Sciences in December 1910 he argued that steam and electricity had changed the structure of human societies. "And now in the phenomena of radioactivity new sources of atomic energy are opening up before us," he declared, "exceeding by millions of times all the sources of energy that the human imagination has envisaged."[2] He urged that Russian deposits of radioactive minerals be charted, "for possession of large supplies of radium will give the possessors of it might and power" incomparably greater than the might of those who own gold, land, or capital.[3]

Vernadskii was one of the most remarkable figures in Russian science. He was born in St Petersburg in 1863 into a well-to-do family: his father was a professor of political economy, and an active member of the liberal intelligentsia. Vernadskii helped to found the liberal Constitutional Democratic Party (the Kadets) during the Revolution of 1905. He was elected to the Academy of Sciences in the following year for his mineralogical research. He believed in science as a force for civilization and democracy, and wanted the Russian scientific community to make its voice heard on important matters of the day. He tried several times to organize a Russian equivalent of the British Association for the Advancement of Science, but without success.[4]

Thanks to Vernadskii, the study of Russian radioactive minerals began in 1911, with support from the government and public donations. The Academy of Sciences sent expeditions to look for uranium deposits in the Urals, the Caucasus, and Central Asia.[5] In the summer of 1914 the Academy expedition found "weakly radioactive vanadites of copper and nickel" in the Fergana Valley in Central Asia, and concluded that some of these deposits could be exploited on an industrial scale.[6] This deposit was not mined, however, and the only uranium mine in Russia before 1917 was owned by a private company, the Fergana Society for the Extraction of Rare Metals, which had been set up in 1908. During the building of the Central Asian Railway at the end of the nineteenth century, prospectors had discovered copper ores at Tiuia-Muiun in the Fergana Valley. When these ores were found to contain pitchblende, the Fergana Company was formed and worked the mine until 1914. The ore was taken to St Petersburg where it was refined into uranium and vanadium preparations for export to Germany. The residues contained radium, but the company did not know how to extract it, and would not give Russian scientists access to its supplies.[7] Vernadskii was very unhappy about this, and in his lecture to the Academy in December 1910 insisted that the radium ores "ought to be investigated by us, by Russian scientists. Our scientific institutions ought to take charge of this work."[8]

World War I restricted the search for radioactive minerals. In March 1918, however, the head of the Chemical Industry Department of the Supreme Council of the National Economy, L.Ia. Karpov, learned that the Fergana Company still had a supply of mining residues and uranium ore in Petrograd. This, it was estimated, would yield 2.4 grams of radium, which would be useful to the medical service and the Artillery Directorate of the Red Army. Karpov ordered the seizure of this supply and asked the Academy of Sciences to set up a factory to extract radium from it. The Academy agreed and formed a new department with responsibility for all questions connected with rare and radioactive minerals.[9] Vernadskii was named chairman of this department, even though he was not in Petrograd at the time, and one of his protégés, the geologist Aleksandr Fersman, was chosen as deputy chairman, while another, the radiochemist Vitalii Khlopin, was made secretary.[10] In May 1918 the radioactive material was evacuated from Petrograd, which was under threat by German forces, and was moved about the country until May 1920 when it reached a chemical plant in Bondiuga (now Mendeleevsk) in Viatka province. It was there that in December 1921 the first Russian radium was extracted from Russian uranium ore by an original process devised by Khlopin.[11]

Vernadskii took no part in this effort, for he had fled from the territory controlled by the Bolsheviks and did not return to Petrograd until March 1921. In September 1917 he had become assistant to the Minister of Education in the Provisional Government, and shortly after the Bolshevik seizure of power he left Petrograd for the Ukraine, where the Reds had not yet gained control. He was opposed to the Bolsheviks, but felt, as he later said, "morally incapable of participating in the civil war."[12] He wrote to Fersman from Kiev that he wanted to do all he could to ensure "that scientific (and all cultural) work in Russia is not interrupted but strengthened."[13] In the summer of 1918 he took part in establishing the Ukrainian Academy of Sciences in Kiev, and was elected its first president.

On a trip to Rostov, where General Denikin's government was based, Vernadskii found himself unable to return to Kiev. He went instead to the Crimea where his son George was a professor at the newly established Tauridian University in Simferopol. There he was elected rector of the university. He intended to leave for Constantinople on a British ship before the Red Army took the Crimea, but the professors and students asked him not to abandon them, and he remained behind as others were evacuated. His son left for Constantinople and, after spending some years in Czechoslovakia, moved to the United States where he became a professor of history at Yale University. But Vernadskii himself was arrested, and taken by train to Moscow, along with his wife and daughter. Lunacharskii, fearing that the local *Cheka* would deal with its prisoners in its own way, had persuaded Lenin to send a telegram to the Crimea ordering that Vernadskii and some of the other professors be brought to Moscow. When they arrived there they were released, and in April 1921 Vernadskii returned to Petrograd where, after being detained for three days, he resumed his multifarious activities.[14]

Vernadskii soon turned his attention to the creation of an institute that would bring together all the Russian work on radium. This was a project he had long had in mind, and now that the radium factory had started production the time seemed ripe. With the help of Khlopin and Fersman the Radium Institute was established in January 1922, on the basis of the radium department of Nemenov's institute. The Radium Institute had three departments: chemistry, which was headed by Khlopin; mineralogy and geochemistry, under Vernadskii's direction; and physics, under L.V. Mysovskii. [15]

Vernadskii defined the institute's purpose very broadly. "The Radium Institute," he wrote, "ought now to be so organized that it can direct its work towards the mastering of atomic energy."[16] With characteristic vision, he was already concerned about the dangers such mastery might bring. In February 1922 he wrote that

We are approaching a great revolution in the life of humankind, with which none of those it has experienced before can be compared. The time is not far off when man will get atomic energy in his hands, a source of power that will give him the possibility of building his life as he wishes. This could happen in the coming years, it could happen in a hundred years' time. But it is clear that it must be.

Will man be able to use this power, direct it towards good, and not towards self-destruction?

Is he mature enough to be able to use the power that science must inevitably give him?

Scientists ought not to close their eyes to the possible consequences of their scientific work, of scientific progress. They ought to feel responsible for all the consequences of their discoveries. They ought to connect their work with the best organization of all mankind.

Thought and attention ought to be directed to these questions. And there is nothing in the world more powerful than free scientific thought.[17]

This passage reflects not only Vernadskii's interest in atomic energy, but also his belief in the importance of "free scientific thought," which was a recurrent theme in his writings.

Vernadskii played little part in directing the Radium Institute in its early years for in May 1922 he left Petrograd to deliver a course of lectures on geochemistry at the Sorbonne, and did not return until 1926. In Paris he wrote a number of monographs, including one on the biosphere, which was published in Russian and in French. In this he tried to give a precise analysis of the extent of the biosphere – defined as that part of the atmosphere and the earth where living matter exists – and of the geochemical and biochemical processes taking place in it. He made some effort to stay in the West to continue his research, but in March 1926 finally returned to Leningrad. He was now impressed by the commitment to science that he saw in Russia, and believed that communist ideas were losing their force. Towards the end of 1925 he wrote to a friend that the "utopia of communism, which is perishing ideologically, is not dangerous."[18]

After his return to Leningrad, Vernadskii made no secret of his view that Marxism was an outmoded theory of social and political organization. He took a leading part in trying to prevent the "Bolshevization" of the Academy of Sciences in the late 1920s. He was not opposed to the aim of linking science and industry, but he did resist the imposition of tight party control, for he feared that this would stifle intellectual freedom. He objected to the activities of Marxist philosophers of science, and warned that "scientists must be saved from the tutelage of representatives of philosophy."[19] Vernadskii was attacked in the press for his philosophical and political views; one of his attackers was A.M. Deborin, whose election to the Academy he had opposed. Some of his closest associates were sent to the camps; B.L. Lichkov, one of his assistants, was arrested in 1930. Vernadskii did his best to help the victims of repression by writing letters to the authorities and providing financial help to the families of the victims.[20]

Vernadskii continued with his research during this terrible period. He was becoming increasingly interested in the concept of the "noosphere." This was a term he had heard in Paris from the Jesuit scientist Teilhard de Chardin. For Vernadskii the noosphere was the stage when scientific thought begins to exercise an ever more powerful and profound influence on the biosphere.[21] "The noosphere is a new geological phenomenon on our planet," he wrote. "In it for the first time man becomes a powerful geological force. He can and should restructure by his labor and thought the sphere of his life, restructure [it] radically by comparison with what went before."[22] The transition to the noosphere is the central theme of a book he wrote in 1938 entitled *Scientific Thought as a Planetary Phenomenon*. In this book, which could not be published during his life, Vernadskii criticized very sharply the way in which the state-supported philosophical dogma of dialectical materialism was hindering free scientific thought in the Soviet Union.[23] He remained optimistic, nevertheless, that a new era was beginning in which science would become a more powerful force; and this new era, he believed, would be more democratic, because science would strengthen the democratic basis of the state.[24]

Most of the responsibility for running the Radium Institute fell on Khlopin, especially after 1930 when Vernadskii set up a new biogeo-chemical laboratory in Moscow. Vitalii Khlopin was almost thirty years younger than Vernadskii, and his father, a well-known doctor, had been a friend of Vernadskii's and active in the Kadet Party. Khlopin took a degree in chemistry at St Petersburg University in 1912, and in 1915 went to work in Vernadskii's mineralogical laboratory. He was elected a corresponding member of the Academy of Sciences in 1933, and a full member in 1939. In the same year he took over from Vernadskii as director of the Radium Institute. Khlopin lacked Vernadskii's broad vision of science, and focused in his own work on the chemistry of radioactive elements, which became the strongest field in the institute.[25]

Once the institute had been established, a State Radium Fund was set up: all radium produced in Soviet Russia was declared to be state property, to be held in custody by the institute. The government placed the factory in Bondiuga under the institute's control, but the factory was closed down in 1925, and radium production was moved to a rare metals plant in Moscow. Mining was started again in Tiuia–Muiun in 1924, after a break of ten years, but the ore was very low-grade, and the mine was closed down in the late 1930s. Some other deposits of uranium were discovered in the Fergana Valley, and in the Krivoi Rog area in the Ukraine, but these were not mined until much later.[26] Radium was discovered in the 1920s in the borehole water of the Ukhta oilfield in the Komi province in the north of Russia, and this became the main source of radium in the interwar period; little was done to discover exactly what uranium deposits the Soviet Union possessed.[27] Radium extraction was the responsibility of OGPU, the predecessor of the NKVD. "A surprising anachronism, which I would earlier have considered impossible," Vernadskii wrote in his diary. "An interest in practical science and the gendarmerie. Can that be for the future?"[28]

II

Radioactivity opened new opportunites for investigating the structure of the atom. The discovery of radioactive decay by Rutherford and Soddy had shown that atoms are not indestructible. In 1911 Rutherford advanced the idea that the atom has a nucleus, in which most of the mass of the atom is concentrated. Eight years later he succeeded in changing nuclei of nitrogen into nuclei of oxygen by bombarding them with alpha particles. This was the first time that nuclei had been altered artificially, and it opened up a period in which atomic structure was investigated by bombarding nuclei with particles.

Russian physicists did no serious work on radioactivity before 1917.[29] In December 1919 D.S. Rozhdestvenskii, director of the newly established State Optical Institute, gave a talk in which he reported on work he had done on the structure of complex atoms by means of spectral analysis. This was the first notable Russian work on atomic structure, and in the terrible conditions of wartime Petrograd it stirred some excitement.[30] Rozhdestvenskii asked Lunacharskii to send a radiogram to Ehrenfest and Hendrik Lorentz in Leiden, telling them of his work. Much to his chagrin, he later discovered that his research had been anticipated by Western physicists.[31] Rozhdestvenskii's paper led to the setting up of a commission to study the theory of atomic structure, but this did not produce anything of significance.[32]

Soviet interest in nuclear physics was transformed by the *annus mirabilis* of 1932. Several important discoveries were made in that year. James Chadwick at the Cavendish Laboratory discovered the neutron. John Cockcroft and E.T.S. Walton, also at the Cavendish Laboratory, split the lithium nucleus into two alpha particles.[33] Georgii Gamov, who was on the staff of the Radium Institute, played a role in this experiment. He had developed in 1928 a theory of alpha-decay on the basis of the new quantum mechanics. This suggested that relatively low-energy particles could tunnel their way through the protective barrier surrounding the nucleus, and that it was therefore worthwhile to build machines capable of accelerating particles through a few hundred thousand electron volts (keV) without waiting until energies of tens of millions of electron volts (MeV) could be achieved. Cockcroft and Walton had taken up this suggestion and built a machine capable of accelerating protons to 500 keV, which they used to split the lithium nucleus. In the same year Ernest O. Lawrence in Berkeley used a new machine which he had developed – the cyclotron – to accelerate protons to an energy of 1.2 MeV. At the California Institute of Technology Carl Anderson identified the positive electron, or positron. Harold Urey at Columbia University discovered the hydrogen isotope of mass 2, deuterium.

Soviet scientists learned of the discoveries of 1932 with great excitement. They were keenly aware of what was being done in the West, and they responded quickly to the new developments. Dmitrii Ivanenko, a theoretician at Ioffe's institute, proposed a new model of the atomic nucleus, which incorporated the neutron.[34] At the Ukrainian Physicotechnical Institute in Khar'kov a group of physicists repeated Cockcroft and Walton's experiment before the end of 1932. In the same year the Radium Institute decided to build a cyclotron, and Vernadskii, though without success, tried to get support for a major expansion of the institute.[35] In December 1932 Ioffe set up a nuclear physics group in his institute, and in the following year he obtained 100,000 roubles from the People's Commissar of Heavy Industry, Sergo Ordzhonokidze, for new equipment for nuclear research.[36]

Ioffe decided to organize an All-Union conference on the atomic nucleus in order to create closer ties among the various Soviet centers working in nuclear physics.[37] He also invited a number of physicists from abroad to the conference, which eventually took place in September 1933. Among those who spoke were Frédéric Joliot, Paul Dirac, Franco Rasetti, a colleague of Enrico Fermi's, and Victor Weisskopf, then Wolfgang Pauli's assistant in Zurich. This conference did a great deal to stimulate Soviet nuclear research, and among the young physicists who took part were a number who later played leading roles in the atomic project: Igor' Kurchatov, Iulii Khariton, Lev Artsimovich, and Aleksandr Leipunskii.[38]

Ioffe did not direct his young colleagues to move into nuclear physics, but he encouraged and supported them when they decided to do so. Before 1932 the only work in the institute that could be counted as nuclear physics was Dmitrii Skobel'tsyn's research on cosmic rays. By the beginning of 1934 there were four laboratories in the institute's nuclear department with about thirty research scientists in all. Nuclear physics had become the second most important area of research at the institute, after semiconductors.[39] According to Khariton, who had been a student of Ioffe's and was now working with Semenov in the Institute of Chemical Physics, it took courage on Ioffe's part to encourage nuclear physics,

because at the beginning of the '30s everyone considered nuclear physics to be a subject having absolutely no relationship to practice or technology. . . . The study of a topic that seemed to be so remote from technology and practice was far from easy and could threaten various unpleasantnesses.[40]

Everyone knew that vast amounts of energy were locked up inside the nucleus, but nobody knew how, or even whether, this energy could be released and harnessed. In 1930 Ioffe had written that nuclear energy might provide the solution to the energy crisis that would overtake humankind in two or three hundred years' time, but he could not promise practical results in the short, or even the medium, term.[41] "In those years there could be no thought of nuclear weapons or nuclear energy," Anatolii Aleksandrov, who was then at Ioffe's institute, has written, "but in the physics of the nucleus great new problems and interesting tasks for researchers had been discovered."[42]

At the March 1936 session of the Academy of Sciences Mysovskii argued that although radioactive elements did have practical applications in medicine, biology, and industry, earlier ideas about nuclear reactions as powerful sources of energy had proved to be mistaken.[43] Igor' Tamm disagreed. It was clear, he said, that "inside nuclei there is hidden an absolutely inexhaustible supply of energy," which would sooner or later be mastered. "I do not see," he added, "any basis for doubting that sooner or later the problem of using nuclear energy will be solved," but no sensible questions could yet be asked about how or when this energy would be harnessed, because nuclear phenomena were not properly understood. Optimistic though he was about atomic energy, Tamm did assert – only nine years before Hiroshima – that "the idea that the use of nuclear energy is a question for [the next] five or ten years is really naive."[44]

III

Ioffe's institute was the main Soviet center for nuclear physics in the 1930s, and the first head of the nuclear department there was Igor' Kurchatov, who became scientific director of the Soviet nuclear program in 1943 and held that position until his death in 1960. Kurchatov was born in January 1903 at Simskii Zavod in the southern Urals, where his father was a surveyor, and his mother a teacher. In 1912 the family moved to Simferopol in the Crimea, for the sake of their daughter's health – but to no avail, for she soon died of tuberculosis. Kurchatov went to school at the gymnasium in Simferopol, and in 1920 entered the Tauridian University, of which Vernadskii had just been elected rector, to study physics. Teaching seems to have been haphazard at best, even though Frenkel' was lecturing there during Kurchatov's first year and Professor S.N. Usatyi, a relative of Ioffe's, came from Sevastopol' to teach physics. Kurchatov graduated a year early, in 1923.[45]

Kurchatov next went to Petrograd to study shipbuilding at the Polytechnical Institute. To support himself he found a job at the Pavlovsk Observatory outside the city, where he published his first scientific paper, on the radioactivity of snow. In the summer of 1924 he quit the Polytechnical Institute and returned to the south to support his family, because his father had been exiled to Ufa for three years, for reasons that remain obscure.[46] Later that year Kurchatov moved to the Baku Polytechnical Institute, where he worked for a year as an assistant to Usatyi, who had moved from Simferopol. As a student Kurchatov had become friendly with his classmate Kirill Sinel'nikov, who was now at Ioffe's institute. Sinel'nikov told Ioffe about Kurchatov, and in the spring of 1925 the twenty-two-year-old Kurchatov received an invitation from Ioffe to join his institute.[47]

The institute was very much Ioffe's "kindergarten." Ioffe did his best to provide his young scientists with a good training in physics. He organized regular seminars to keep them abreast of current research, and in the incoming journals he marked the papers that they should read, demanding an explanation if they did not do so. He visited each laboratory once a week to find out what was being done.[48]

The atmosphere in the institute combined dedication to science with liveliness and enthusiasm. Isaak Kikoin has written that

we worked around the clock, and other interests, apart from science, did not exist for us. Even girls did not often manage to separate us from our studies, and when we married we were already so "spoiled" by the habit of working a lot, that our wives had to resign themselves to that.[49]

Naum Reinov, who worked in one of the institute workshops, paints a less earnest picture. He was surprised at first by the fact that the scientists did not work regular hours, and wandered about the corridors smoking or exchanging jokes. Soon, however, he came to the conclusion that "these people were possessed by their science."[50] Living conditions were hard. When Anatolii Aleksandrov went to the institute in 1930, he had to sleep with eight others in a freezing cold room, and to cover his head with a blanket to stop the rats from gnawing his ears.[51]

Kurchatov worked at first in Ioffe's laboratory on the physics of dielectrics. This was a central part of the institute's work since the insulating properties of dielectrics under extremely high voltages had potentially important applications in the electric power industry. Under Ioffe's supervision, Kurchatov, working with Sinel'nikov and another physicist, conducted experiments which seemed to suggest that the breakdown voltage would increase as the thickness of the material decreased. This work formed part of the basis for Ioffe's ill-fated claim about thin-layer insulating material.[52]

In the course of this research Kurchatov turned to the study of anomalies in the dielectric properties of Rochelle salts, and his research led to the discovery of a special class of crystals which behaved in an electrical field exactly like ferromagnets in a magnetic field. This phenomenon is now called ferroelectricity (Kurchatov gave it its Russian name "segneto-electricity" after the French chemist Segnier). Kurchatov investigated it with colleagues in Leningrad, including his brother Boris who had joined him there, and with Sinel'nikov in Khar'kov.[53] This research established Kurchatov's reputation as a physicist. Khariton later called this work "elegant and beautiful."[54]

In spite of the success of this research, Kurchatov decided at the end of 1932 to shift to nuclear physics. This was an abrupt and unexpected change, and meant a break with Ioffe's own research on semiconductors. It was also a move away from research that had some prospect of immediate application to an area that was judged at the time to be very remote from practical use. But Kurchatov appears to have felt that he had done all he wanted to in the study of ferroelectricity, and that nuclear physics was an exciting and promising field. He may have been influenced by his friend Sinel'nikov, who had spent 1928 to 1930 in Cambridge, and was now head of the high-voltage laboratory in Khar'kov. Whatever the reasons, Kurchatov made his move "decisively, quickly, without looking back as, incidentally, he always acted in such cases."[55]

Kurchatov was not the only physicist to switch to nuclear physics in 1932. Abram Alikhanov, who like Kurchatov was about thirty years old, moved from X-ray physics to nuclear physics in the same year, and was put in charge of the positron laboratory, where he did research with his brother Artem Alikhan'ian on the materialization of electron-positron pairs, and later on beta-spectra.[56] Another young physicist, Lev Artsimovich, who had joined the institute two years before at the age of twenty-one, also moved into nuclear physics and was put in charge of the high-voltage laboratory. Artsimovich worked closely with the Alikhanov brothers.[57] The fourth laboratory head in the nuclear department was Dmitrii Skobel'tsyn, who was somewhat older than the three other men, having been born in St Petersburg in 1892. He had studied cosmic rays since the early 1920s, and had spent two years in Paris, at Marie Curie's institute.[58] Skobel'tsyn was cold and reserved in manner, whereas Alikhanov was hot-tempered, and Artsimovich a sharp-witted, and sometimes sharp-tongued, man with an interest in everything.[59]

Kurchatov was known as the "general," because he liked to take the initiative and issue commands. One of his favorite phrases, according to a close colleague, was "to task."[60] He had an energetic manner and liked to argue. He could swear expressively but, if the memoirs of those who worked with him are to be believed, he did not give offense. He had a good sense of humor.[61] In 1927 he married Marina, the sister of his friend Sinel'nikov. She was at first upset by her husband's practice of spending his evenings in the laboratory, but became reconciled to it.[62] We have one or two glimpses of Kurchatov in these years from Sinel'nikov's wife, an Englishwoman he had met in Cambridge. In letters to her sister she portrays Kurchatov as single-minded about his work and in general a rather determined and purposeful individual. But she writes also that he "is such a nice soul, like a teddy-bear, no one could ever be cross with him."[63]

In the descriptions of Kurchatov's character there is always a sense of distance, as though behind the energetic manner there was another person who was not being disclosed so readily. He could put a shield between himself and the people around him by "hamming it up" or by adopting an ironic tone towards himself as well as towards others. All the memoirs convey, alongside the hearty and extrovert manner, an impression of seriousness and reserve. One of those who worked closely with him in the 1950s describes Kurchatov as a man with many layers to his personality, and therefore ideally suited to secret work.[64]

Kurchatov devoted most of 1933 to studying the literature on nuclear physics and preparing apparatus for research. He organized the construction of a small cyclotron, but this achieved only a very low beam current and was not used for experiments. He also constructed a high-voltage proton accelerator of the Cockcroft–Walton type and used it to study nuclear reactions in boron and lithium. In the spring of 1934 he altered the direction on his work when he read the first notes by Enrico Fermi and his group about nuclear reactions caused by neutron bombardment. Kurchatov dropped his proton-beam experiments and began to study the artificial radioactivity created in some isotopes by irradiation with neutrons.[65] Between July 1934 and February 1936 he and his collaborators published seventeen papers on artificial radioactivity. His most original contribution during this period was the hypothesis that the multiple half-lives of some radioisotopes could be explained by nuclear isomerism – the existence of isotopes with the same mass number and atomic number but with different energies.[66] The other phenomena investigated by Kurchatov were neutron–proton interactions and the selective absorption of neutrons by nuclei of different elements.

These questions were very much at the center of nuclear physics in the mid-1930s. Maurice Goldhaber, who was working on the same problems at the Cavendish Laboratory at the time, has said that there were a number of important centers in nuclear physics.

There was the Cavendish, which I think was foremost, and then the Rome school when Fermi was there was top-notch; and the Joliot-Curie crowd in Paris. Then there was Kurchatov and his people. They did good work. I always guessed it was Kurchatov who was the most important man in atomic energy in Russia because I had read his papers. He was not far behind us considering the time difference in receiving journals. There were always interesting papers coming out of Kurchatov's school.[67]

Kurchatov and his colleagues were very much part of the international community of nuclear physicists, even though personal contacts had now become more difficult.

Kurchatov was dissatisfied, however, because he felt that he was following in Fermi's tracks, and not blazing his own trail.[68] In 1935 he thought that he had discovered the resonance absorption of neutrons, but he and Artsimovich, with whom he was collaborating, disagreed about the interpretation of the results, and before a decisive experiment could be done Fermi and his colleagues published a paper on the existence of this phenomenon. Kurchatov was disappointed, for the Leningrad physicists were eager to make their mark too, and to prove that they were as good as any other research group.[69]

Kurchatov was hampered by the lack of neutron sources for his research. The only place in Leningrad that had them was the Radium Institute, and Kurchatov therefore arranged to work together with Mysovskii, the head of the Radium Institute's physics department.[70] There was a certain tension between the physics community and the Radium Institute. Vernadskii had no respect for Ioffe, whom he regarded as an ambitious and dishonest man.[71] Igor' Tamm had angered Vernadskii by suggesting in 1936 that the Radium Institute's cyclotron be handed over to Ioffe's institute. The physicists, Vernadskii responded, had been slow to recognize the importance of radioactivity and still had an inadequate understanding of the field. The Radium Institute, he insisted, had to work in nuclear physics, which had developed from the study of radioactivity. The cyclotron, which was now about to go into operation, was needed for the Radium Institute's work, and should not be taken away from it; and in the event it was not.[72]

Progress on the cyclotron was slow, however, and it was only in February 1937 that a proton beam of ~500 keV was obtained; energies of ~3.2 MeV were achieved in July 1937, but the operation of the cyclotron was extremely unstable.[73] Kurchatov was frustrated by this poor performance because he wanted to use the cyclotron for his own research. In the spring of 1937 he started working in the Radium Institute's cyclotron laboratory one day a week and gradually took charge of it. The cyclotron began to be used for research in 1939, but it was not until the end of 1940 that it went into normal operation.[74]

The nuclear physicists at Ioffe's institute pressed for a cyclotron of their own.[75] Kurchatov and Alikhanov had talked in 1932 about building a large cyclotron, but this idea was put aside because the Radium Institute had decided to go ahead with its own machine. In January 1937, however, Ioffe wrote to Sergo Ordzhonikidze, People's Commissar of Heavy Industry, asking for the resources to build a cyclotron at his institute, and requesting that two of his physicists be sent to Berkeley to study the cyclotron (this was the month before Ordzhonikidze's suicide).[76] The People's Commissariat supported this proposal, and in June 1939 – nearly two and a half years after Ioffe's letter – a government decree was adopted allocating the resources for the cyclotron.[77] No one went to Berkeley.

In the late 1930s Kurchatov ran a neutron seminar at which work being done in the institute was discussed, along with papers that had appeared in the physics journals. One of the participants in that seminar, Isai Gurevich, said later that

if it hadn't existed, the immense tasks which had to be performed during the war and after it would have needed even more years, in addition to those spent on it [sic]. Because that seminar was a school of neutron physics without which nothing would have resulted.[78]

The seminar had about fifteen members, many of whom were later to play important roles in the atomic project.[79]

Ioffe sent many of his young physicists abroad to do research, and he recommended Kurchatov for such trips. A visit to the United States was planned for Kurchatov in the winter of 1934–5, and in September 1934 Frenkel' wrote to Ernest Lawrence to request an invitation to Berkeley for Kurchatov. Lawrence wrote to Kurchatov on 1 October, inviting him to his laboratory "for a period of time."[80] But Kurchatov did not go abroad, perhaps because his father's exile made him appear politically unreliable to the NKVD. After the mid-1930s Soviet physicists were, in any event, increasingly cut off from personal contacts with their Western colleagues: at the 1933 nuclear conference half the papers had been given by foreign scientists, but at the 1937 conference physicists from abroad gave only five of the twenty-eight papers, and there were no foreign participants at the 1938 nuclear conference.[81] Soviet physicists nevertheless continued to think of themselves as part of an international community, and to follow the foreign journals closely.

IV

Leningrad was not the only place where nuclear research was done in the 1930s. The other major center was the Ukrainian Physicotechnical Institute (UFTI) in Khar'kov, which Ioffe had set up in 1928 with the encouragement of the Ukrainian authorities. Ioffe wanted to create a first-class physics institute that would maintain strong ties with industry in the

Ukraine, and he sent some of his own people from Leningrad to form the nucleus of the new institute.[82] Kurchatov spent periods of two or three months working at UFTI in the 1930s.[83]

Ioffe tried to get his old friend Ehrenfest to go to Khar'kov, and wrote to him that the institute needed a "broadly educated physicist," but although Ehrenfest spent several months there he did not stay.[84] A number of foreign scientists did work in Khar'kov, however: Alexander Weissberg, a Viennese communist who headed the low-temperature experimental station; Martin Ruhemann, who was in charge of one of the low-temperature laboratories; Friedrich Houtermans, a lively and original physicist from Germany; and Fritz Lange, a German physicist who later worked on the centrifuge method of isotope separation.[85]

UFTI's first director was Ivan Obreimov, a specialist in optics, who had been one of Ioffe's earliest students. He was an excellent physicist, but not a very forceful director.[86] He was succeeded in 1932 by Aleksandr Leipunskii, who was regarded as one of the ablest of the younger physicists. Leipunskii's interests were primarily in atomic and nuclear physics. In 1932 he and Sinel'nikov, along with two colleagues, repeated Cockcroft and Walton's experiment. He spent more than a year at the Cavendish Laboratory in the mid-1930s. He was a party member, which was unusual among serious physicists in the 1930s. He was highly respected in the physics community and seemed destined to play an important role in Soviet science.[87]

UFTI began to thrive in the early 1930s. It was well funded and equipped, and by the middle of the decade it had a bigger staff and a bigger budget than Ioffe's institute.[88] Its leading scientists were able and well trained: Shubnikov, who headed the low-temperature research, had spent 1926 to 1930 in the low-temperature laboratory in Leiden, one of the leading European centers in this field, and was regarded as a very talented experimentalist; Landau, perhaps the most brilliant Soviet physicist of his generation, headed the theoretical department in the mid-1930s. Many foreign physicists came to visit, among them Niels Bohr, John Cockcroft, and Paul Dirac.[89] Victor Weisskopf spent eight months there in 1932.[90] The institute published a journal of Soviet physics in German.

Alexander Weissberg wrote in *The Accused*, his classic book on the Great Purge, that until early 1935 the institute was an "oasis of freedom in the desert of Stalinist despotism," and that "left in peace the scientists of the institute would have produced valuable results in due course."[91] But the atmosphere in the institute became soured by personal feuds and political intrigues after a new director was appointed in 1934. Sinel'nikov's wife, in a letter to her sister in England in June 1935, wrote that "the institute is full of intrigues, firstly it was the Scientists against the Administrative department, but now it seems to me wheels within wheels and some of the scientists are using dirty methods to obtain their own ends."[92] In September she wrote that "I guess the whole Institute just wants dynamiting and then a fresh start making."[93] When Victor Weisskopf visited Khar'kov at the end of 1936 some of the émigrés he spoke to advised him not to accept the professorship he had been offered in Kiev; he went to the University of Rochester in New York instead.[94]

Bad though things may have been in 1935 and 1936, they were to get worse. Many of UFTI's leading members were arrested in the Great Purge and accused of fantastic plots against the state.[95] The effect on the institute was devastating. Weissberg recalls that in arguments with his cell-mates he assessed the damage in this way:

"Listen," I said. "Our Institute is one of the most important of its kind in Europe. In fact, there is probably no other institute with so many different and well-equipped laboratories. The Soviet Government has spared no expense. Our leading scientists were partly trained abroad. They were constantly being sent to leading physicists all over the world at Government expense to supplement their knowledge and experience. Our Institute had eight departments, each headed by a capable man. And what's the situation now? The head of the laboratory for crystallology, Obremov, is under arrest, and so is the head of the low-temperatures laboratory, Shubnikov. The head of the second low-temperatures laboratory, Ruhemann, has been deported. The head of the laboratory for atom-splitting, Leipunsky, is under arrest, and so is the head of the X-ray department, Gorsky, the head of the department for theoretical physics, Landau, and the head of the experimental low-temperatures station, myself. As far as I know, Slutski, the head of the ultra-short-wave department, is the only one still at work."[96]

Sinel'nikov, who was in charge of the high-voltage laboratory, escaped arrest too.

Before his arrest Landau had moved to Moscow to head the theoretical group at Kapitsa's new institute. On the day he was arrested, April 28, 1938, Kapitsa wrote to Stalin to seek his release. He pointed out that Landau was, with Fok, one of the two strongest theoretical physicists in the Soviet Union and that his loss to the institute, as well as to Soviet and world science, would be a serious one. "Of course, learning and talent, no matter how great they may be, do not give a man the right to break the laws of his own country," Kapitsa continued, "and if Landau is guilty, he ought to answer for it. But I beg you, in view of his exceptional talents, to give the appropriate orders that his case be treated very attentively." Kapitsa's letter was both courageous and clever. He explained how Landau might have made enemies. "His personality, which is – to put it simply – bad, should be taken into account," he wrote. "He is a tease and a bully, and enjoys looking for mistakes in others, and when he finds them, especially if they are made by important old men like our Academicians, he begins to tease them irreverently."[97] Kapitsa kept up his efforts on behalf of Landau, who was released exactly a year after he had been arrested. Kapitsa had to write a short letter to L.P. Beria, the new head of the NKVD, saying that he would be responsible for Landau's good conduct.[98]

Shubnikov, Rozenkevich, and Gorskii were shot in alphabetical order on November 8, 9, and 10, 1937.[99] Leipunskii was arrested in July 1938 and released a month later. Obreimov, who was arrested in 1938 was released in May 1941, thanks to Kapitsa's efforts. Weissberg and Houtermans were handed over to the Gestapo shortly after the Soviet–German Pact of August 1939.[100] The effect of the purge on the institute was profound: UFTI was greatly weakened, and very far from being the kind of research center its leading members had hoped, some years earlier, that it would become. On the eve of the discovery of nuclear fission the Soviet authorities had wrecked one of the country's most important physics institutes.

V

In the early and mid-1930s the main physics institutes were part of the research and development network of the industrial commissariats. The Academy of Sciences had no major physics institute of its own. In the early 1930s Georgii Gamov tried to organize an institute of theoretical physics on the basis of the physics department of the Academy's Physical and Mathematical Institute in Leningrad, but Ioffe and Rozhdestvenskii squashed this proposal. As a result of these discussions, however, the Academy in 1932 asked Sergei Vavilov to organize a physics institute.[101] (Vavilov was the brother of Nikolai Vavilov, the world-famous geneticist and plant breeder, who was one of Lysenko's chief targets; Nikolai was arrested in August 1940 and died in January 1943.) Vavilov, who was mainly interested in luminescence and the nature of light, was a capable organizer and determined to turn the small physics department with its handful of researchers into a large institute covering all the main areas of physics. When the Academy moved to Moscow in 1934, Vavilov's physics department moved with it and became a separate institute, the Physics Institute of the Academy of Sciences (FIAN). Many of the leading Moscow physicists – including Mandel'shtam and Tamm – joined its staff.[102]

Because Vavilov wanted his institute to do research in the most important fields he persuaded some of his younger colleagues, including Pavel Cherenkov and Il'ia Frank, to work in nuclear physics. At Vavilov's suggestion, Cherenkov investigated the luminescence of solutions of uranium salts under the action of gamma rays. He discovered "Cherenkov radiation," the bluish light emitted by a beam of high-energy charged particles passing through a transparent medium, like the bow wave created by a boat passing through water. Tamm and Frank soon developed a theory to explain this effect. For this work they and Cherenkov received the Nobel Prize for physics in 1958.[103]

Vavilov, like Ioffe, had to defend nuclear physics against its critics. Commissions periodically came to inspect the institute, Il'ia Frank later recalled, and offered two different kinds of criticism:

If it was a commission from some government department then it noted that since nuclear physics was a useless science, there was no reason to develop it. In the discussions in the Academy of Sciences the grounds of criticism were different: none of the recognized authorities here is doing nuclear physics, and the young people will produce nothing.[104]

Vavilov tried to strengthen his nuclear physics group by recruiting people from other institutes. Before the Academy moved to Moscow, Mysovskii took part in the nuclear research in Vavilov's laboratory, but he did not want to leave Leningrad. After 1934 Skobel'tsyn acted as consultant, and in January 1939 he moved to Moscow to join the institute's permanent staff.[105]

Vavilov wanted more than this, however, for he was trying to make FIAN the main center of nuclear physics. He raised with Ioffe the possibility of transferring some of the Leningrad nuclear physicists to Moscow, arguing that it was in the Academy, and not in the industrial sector, that the most favorable conditions for nuclear physics could be created.[106] Vavilov was thought by some people to be trying to gather everything into his own hands, and to destroy the Leningrad school of nuclear physics.[107] That is certainly how it seemed to Ioffe, who was very depressed at the prospect that his nuclear physicists, whom he had encouraged and protected, might move to Moscow.[108] Vavilov, said Ioffe, "thinks that it is necessary to close down completely the nuclear laboratory in Leningrad, while I think that to have only a nuclear laboratory in Moscow will be too little for the whole [Soviet] Union."[109] Apart from Skobel'tsyn, however, none of the nuclear physicists at Ioffe's institute yielded to Vavilov's blandishments.

Vavilov, however, did not abandon his efforts to build up his institute as a center of nuclear physics. At the end of 1938 he made a report on nuclear physics to the Presidium of the Academy of Sciences, which adopted a resolution noting the

unsatisfactory organizational state of this work, as expressed in the splintering of nuclear laboratories among different departments, in the irrational distribution of powerful modern technical means of investigating the atomic nucleus among institutes, in the incorrect distribution of leading scientific workers in this field, and so on.[110]

The Presidium thought that all work on the atomic nucleus and cosmic rays should be brought into the Academy of Sciences, as well as into the Ukrainian and Belorussian Academies. It asked the government to allow FIAN to start work on a new building in 1939 so that nuclear research could be concentrated as soon as possible in Moscow. It also decided to set up a Commission on the Atomic Nucleus to make decisions about the planning and organization of nuclear research, with Vavilov as chairman and Ioffe, Alikhanov, and Kurchatov among its members.[111]

The Presidium's decisions were a blow to Ioffe. His institute was not yet part of the Academy and was therefore likely to lose its nuclear group if the Presidium's plans were realized, especially since the industrial commissariats were not interested in nuclear physics. Moreover, the new commission gave Vavilov considerable say in the organization of the field. This was bad for Ioffe because Vavilov had apparently tried to hold up the *Fiztekh* cyclotron.[112] But before the commission could get down to serious work, the significance of nuclear physics was transformed by the discovery of fission at the end of 1938.

VI

This chapter has looked at the response of Russian scientists to the discovery of radioactivity, and to the discoveries of the *annus mirabilis* of 1932. Vernadskii was the leading figure in pressing for research on radioactivity and for exploration for uranium deposits. He was inspired in part by the belief that this research would lead to the harnessing of atomic energy for practical purposes. By the 1930s, however, that prospect seemed more distant than it had done in the early years of the century. What drew Soviet physicists to nuclear research in 1932 was not the promise of practical results, but the prospect of interesting physics. They may have hoped that their work would prove useful, but they thought that practical applications, if they ever resulted, were far in the future.

It was the scientists themselves, not the managers of science policy, who took the initiative in expanding nuclear research, and who persisted with it in the face of skepticism on the part of practical-minded administrators. In making this choice Soviet physicists saw themselves as part of an international community: they paid close attention to what was being done abroad, they wanted to contribute to the flood of new discoveries, and to gain recognition from their Western colleagues for their research. Rudolf Peierls, who knew the Soviet physics community well in the 1930s, has said that when it came to the choice of research problems "he did not have the impression in those days that in the way science operated there was any real difference" between the Soviet Union and other countries.[113]

Physics, as was seen in the last chapter, represented a sphere of relative intellectual autonomy in a society dominated by a regime with totalitarian pretensions. This intellectual autonomy was sustained by a set of social relationships – of authority, status, and reward – that were different from those in the society at large. The authority of the Party did not hold sway here, in spite of the efforts of party philosophers; as Frenkel' had said, "neither Lenin nor Engels is an authority for physicists." This was a statement not about the attitude of physicists to the regime – those attitudes varied – but about their attitude to the integrity of physics as an intellectual enterprise. The defense of physics implied that there were limits to the Party's authority, that physicists had the right to decide which physical theories were valid and which problems were interesting, and also to look to the international physics community for recognition. The decision to expand nuclear research after 1932 shows the Soviet physics community acting in this way.

It is true, of course, that scientists had to justify their choices to the authorities. One way of doing so was to point to the potential practical uses of atomic energy, thereby showing commitment to the goals and values of the regime. In his opening address to the second All-Union conference on the atomic nucleus in September 1937, Ioffe said that "for us, Soviet physicists, it is a basic truth that any science, including physics, can develop and can raise the most important problems only if it is indeed linked in the closest way with those practical applications that flow from it." He went on to say that only mastery of the atomic nucleus could lead to the ancient goal of obtaining cheap energy, or the alchemist's dream of obtaining precious elements from cheap ones.[114] In October of the following year the physics group of the Academy of Sciences adopted a resolution that nuclear physics should in the near future concentrate on work connected with practical technical problems, but it did not specify what these might be.[115] Such statements were little more than pious utterances, designed to placate the authorities and to support requests for funds.

A more realistic picture of physicists' attitudes is provided by a description of a meeting of the academic council of FIAN in 1938. The laboratories' plans for applied research were being discussed, with reports about the practical uses of research – the spectral analysis of metals, radiogeodesy, and fluorescent lamps, for example.

When it came to the turn of the atomic nucleus laboratory, its representative began to mumble uncertainly something about the possibility of measuring the thickness of reservoir walls according to the dispersion of gamma-rays from a radioactive source that the institute had. One of the members of the council, now a well-known physicist, could not contain himself and said: "Using physics for the needs of the economy is a serious business, and we are doing much that is really important. But it should not be turned into a game. The physics of the atomic nucleus is a very important sphere of fundamental scientific research and it needs to be developed, but it does not have and we do not know when it will have any practical significance at all."[116]

Everyone agreed with the speaker and the meeting continued.

In spite of the difficulties it faced, Soviet nuclear physics reached a high standard in the 1930s. Victor Weisskopf, who had a high regard for Soviet physicists, found that they did not lag behind in their understanding of nuclear structure when he visited the Soviet Union at the end of 1936.[117] Ioffe, in his closing remarks to the 1937 conference on the atomic nucleus, said that there were now more than one hundred Soviet scientists doing research in nuclear physics – about four times more than at the time of the first nuclear conference in 1933. Of the thirty papers given, he said, a significant number had "fundamental importance" and showed the "broad development of our science."[118] In the following month the Presidium of the Academy noted with particular satisfaction the growth of "young scientific cadres" in nuclear physics.[119]

CHAPTER THREE

Reacting to Fission

I

WHEN ENRICO FERMI and his colleagues began to study artificial radioactivity in 1934 by bombarding different elements with neutrons, they found indications that transuranic elements (i.e. elements higher in the periodic table than uranium) were created. Chemists in other countries, including Vitalii Khlopin in Leningrad, attempted to identify these elements by radiochemical analysis, and believed that they had indeed established the existence of transuranic elements. The German chemist Ida Noddack suggested that Fermi's conclusion was wrong, and that the uranium might be splitting into elements in the middle of the periodic table, but no one heeded her argument.[1] In December 1938, however, Otto Hahn and Fritz Strassmann at the Kaiser Wilhelm Institute for Chemistry in Berlin discovered that when they bombarded uranium with neutrons it split into elements in the middle of the periodic table, and was not transformed into elements higher than uranium. This was a completely unexpected discovery. As chemists Hahn and Strassmann were sure of the results of their analysis, but they wrote in their paper that "as 'nuclear chemists' working very close to the field of physics" they were reluctant to come to a conclusion that "goes against all previous experience in nuclear physics."[2]

Hahn and Strassmann's paper appeared in *Die Naturwissenschaften* on January 6, 1939, but before it was published Hahn wrote to his close colleague Lise Meitner to tell her about the experiment. Meitner had fled Germany because of the racial laws, and was now living in Sweden. She showed the letter to her nephew, the physicist Otto Frisch, who was spending Christmas with her; Frisch too was a refugee from Nazism, and was working at Niels Bohr's institute in Copenhagen. In trying to explain the result of Hahn and Strassmann's experiment, Meitner and Frisch decided that "the uranium nucleus might indeed resemble a very wobbly, unstable drop, ready to divide itself at the slightest provocation, such as the impact of a single neutron."[3] After separation the two drops would be driven apart by their mutual electrical repulsion, with a mass (or energy) loss equivalent to 200 million electron volts (MeV). The most energetic chemical reactions release only a few electron volts, and even ordinary radioactive processes release only several MeV. Consequently, this new reaction, for which Frisch and Meitner used the term "fission," was very much more powerful. Their paper was published in *Nature* on February 18.

News of the discovery of fission spread quickly. On January 16, 1939 Enrico Fermi, who had just fled from Rome because his Jewish wife was threatened by the Fascist laws on race, learned of it in New York from Niels Bohr, who had arrived that day from Europe. About the same time Frédéric Joliot in Paris read Hahn and Strassmann's paper, and on January 26 Bohr informed a wider audience at a conference in Washington, DC. The discovery opened a period of great excitement in scientific research; by December 1939 over a hundred papers on fission had been published.[4] This excitement was tinged, however, by foreboding about the use to which nuclear fission might be put, for the threat of war was hanging over Europe.

Soviet physicists learned of the discovery of fission when the journals arrived.[5] The news evoked the same reactions as in the West: great excitement, and new lines of research. Khlopin and his colleagues at the Radium Institute proceeded to investigate the chemical character of the fission products. The discovery of fission cast doubt on the existence of transuranic elements. Khlopin, however, was still very much interested in the possibility of transuranics, and conducted experiments to see whether they were created by fission.[6] In the course of this research Khlopin discovered some hitherto unknown patterns of disintegration by fissioned uranium nuclei, and although he did not succeed in identifying transuranic elements, he concluded that the disintegration chains did indeed indicate the existence of transuranics.[7] He wrote to Vernadskii on April 1, 1939 that the "experiments which we have so far managed to conduct using the cyclotron make it very probable that transuranics nevertheless exist, i.e. that the disintegration of uranium under the action of neutrons proceeds along a variety of different paths." He hoped, he wrote, that he would have a final answer to this question in the next few weeks, but the answer eluded him, and transuranic elements were first identified in Berkeley in 1940.[8]

In Ioffe's institute too the discovery of fission caused excitement. The first Soviet theoretical work on fission was done by Iakov Frenkel', who used the liquid-drop model of the nucleus to provide a theoretical explanation of fission in terms of the stability of heavy nuclei. He reported on this work to Kurchatov's nuclear seminar on April 10, and his paper was soon published in one of the Soviet journals.[9]

The first question tackled by Kurchatov's laboratory was whether or not secondary neutrons were released during the fission, and if so how many. This was a key question, for only if more than one neutron were released would a self-sustaining chain reaction be possible. Several groups in Europe and the United States investigated this problem simultaneously. Georgii Flerov and Lev Rusinov concluded that 3 ± 1 neutrons were emitted per fission. They made a first report on their experiments to Kurchatov's nuclear seminar on April 10, the same day on which Frenkel' spoke. By that time, however, Joliot and two of his collaborators, Hans von Halban and Lew Kowarski, had already published a paper showing that secondary neutrons were emitted, and on April 22 they reported that the average number of neutrons emitted per fission was 3.5.[10]

Once these experiments had been completed, Kurchatov wanted to test the hypothesis that it was the rare isotope, uranium-235, that fissioned with slow neutrons.[11] The probability of causing fission was much greater for slow than for fast neutrons, and Bohr had come to the conclusion early in February that fission with slow neutrons occurred in uranium-235, and not in the dominant isotope, uranium-238. He had published a note to this effect in *Physical Review* on March 15.[12] This was a point of great importance, because uranium-235 constitutes only 0.7 per cent of natural uranium. Bohr believed – as did everyone else – that it would be enormously difficult to separate uranium-235, and he was therefore extremely skeptical about the possibility of making practical use of atomic energy. "It would take the entire efforts of a country to make a bomb," he said to colleagues in March.[13] Many physicists disagreed with Bohr's hypothesis that it was only uranium-235 that fissioned, but no definitive test would be possible until samples of uranium enriched with 235 became available. Kurchatov nevertheless directed Rusinov and Flerov to investigate this question. They concluded that Bohr was right, and reported this result to the nuclear seminar on June 16, 1939.[14]

Soviet scientists were asking the same questions as their Western colleagues, and were closely attuned to what was being done in the West. But their research made little impact outside the Soviet Union. The work done in Kurchatov's laboratory in 1939 was not published until 1940, by which time it had lost whatever interest it might have had. It was difficult to be the first with significant results when scientists in other centers were pushing ahead so rapidly; and the problem was complicated by the fact that it took the journals weeks to reach Soviet scientists.[15]

The most important Soviet theoretical work in this period was done by Iulii Khariton and Iakov Zel'dovich on the conditions under which a nuclear chain reaction would take place. The papers these two men published in 1939–41 foreshadowed the key role they were to play in the development of Soviet nuclear weapons. Khariton was born in 1904 in St Petersburg, where his father was a journalist and, after the revolution, director of the House of Writers, an important center of literary life. In 1921, when he was still a second-year student at the Polytechnical Institute, he was invited by Semenov to come and work with him at Ioffe's institute. In 1925 Khariton and Zinaida Val'ta conducted experiments on the oxidation of phosphorous vapors at low pressures. They discovered that oxidation did not take place below a critical pressure of the oxygen. When they published their results the German chemist, Max Bodenstein wrote that what they had found was impossible and must be the result of experimental error. Further experiments by Semenov confirmed the results obtained by Khariton and Val'ta, and led to the work on chain reactions for which Semenov received the Nobel Prize for chemistry in 1956.[16]

In 1926 Khariton went to Cambridge, where he had been accepted at the Cavendish Laboratory on Kapitsa's recommendation. Here he worked under Ernest Rutherford and James Chadwick, doing research on the sensitivity of the eye to weak impulses of light, and on alpha-radiation.[17] When Khariton returned to Leningrad in 1928 with his Cambridge PhD, he took charge of a new laboratory to study explosives. On his way back to the Soviet Union he visited Germany, where his mother was now living. Many years later he said that this visit had convinced him that the political situation in Germany was dangerous and that he should engage in work that would be useful for his country's defense.[18] Khariton's laboratory became part of the new Institute of Chemical Physics in 1931, when it was split off from Ioffe's institute.[19]

Zel'dovich, who was ten years younger than Khariton, was also from a highly educated Jewish family: his father was a lawyer and his mother had studied languages at the Sorbonne. On a visit to Ioffe's institute at the age of seventeen he had asked questions which produced a very favorable impression on one of the laboratory heads. As a result he was invited to come and work there.[20] By the time this was finally arranged, the laboratory had become part of the Institute of Chemical Physics.

In the summer of 1939, on the bus to Lesnoe, Zel'dovich learned from another physicist about a paper in which the French physicist Francis Perrin had tried to estimate the critical mass needed for a chain reaction in uranium.[21] Zel'dovich's interest was aroused, and he talked to Khariton about Perrin's calculation. They studied Perrin's paper but were not convinced by his analysis, and decided to investigate the problem themselves.[22] It was a natural topic for them to pursue, since chain reactions were a major focus of research at Semenov's institute.

Zel'dovich and Khariton at first did their nuclear research in the evening, but they soon realized that it was such an important problem that they should devote all their time to it. They began to take part in Kurchatov's seminar, where they became familiar with the latest research in nuclear physics. In October 1939 they sent two papers to the Soviet physics journal ZhETF (Zhurnal eksperimental'noi i teoreticheskoi fiziki). The first of these considered the possibility of a fast-neutron chain reaction in uranium-238.[23] Bohr had argued that uranium-238 would not fission with slow neutrons; if a fast-neutron chain reaction were to take place, the neutrons emitted during fission would have to cause the next fission before they were slowed down. Zel'dovich and Khariton defined the theoretical conditions under which a chain reaction could take place and concluded, on the basis of existing experimental data, that they could not be met in uranium-238, either in uranium oxide or in pure metallic uranium.[24]

In their second paper Zel'dovich and Khariton studied the possibility of a slow-neutron chain reaction in natural uranium.[25] Experiments done by Fermi with Leo Szilard and Herbert Anderson at Columbia University in New York, and by Joliot and his collaborators in Paris, had shown that resonance absorption, in which uranium-238 captures neutrons before they slow down sufficiently to cause fission in uranium-235, would have a serious effect on the possibility of a chain reaction in natural uranium. Fermi and his colleagues had done their experiment with uranium in a tank of water, and concluded that "even at the optimum concentration of hydrogen it is at present quite uncertain whether neutron production will exceed the total neutron absorption."[26] In other words it was not clear whether hydrogen would slow down (or moderate) the neutrons sufficiently to prevent resonance absorption and make a chain reaction possible.

Zel'dovich and Khariton reinterpreted the results obtained by Joliot and Fermi in light of their own theory of the conditions for a chain reaction, and concluded that a chain reaction would not be possible in a uranium-water system. For a chain reaction "it is necessary to use heavy hydrogen [deuterium]," they wrote, "or, perhaps, heavy water, or some other substance which will ensure a small enough capture cross-section [i.e. probability of capture], in order to slow down the neutrons. . . . The other possibility consists in enriching uranium with the isotope 235." If the proportion of uranium-235 in natural uranium were increased from 0.7 per cent to 1.3 per cent, they calculated, water or hydrogen could be used as a moderator.[27]

At the fourth All-Union nuclear conference, which was held in Khar'kov in November 1939, Khariton spoke about the work that he and Zel'dovich were doing. A report on the conference concluded that

from these calculations, which at first glance lead to pessimistic conclusions, it is apparent, however, what path can be taken to realize a chain reaction. It is enough to raise the concentration of the isotope uranium-235 in uranium for a reaction to become possible. If, on the other hand, deuterium [i.e. heavy hydrogen] is used as a moderator instead of hydrogen, then there will be practically no absorption in the moderator, and a reaction will apparently also be possible. Both paths seem now to be fairly fantastic if one remembers that tons of uranium are needed for a reaction. However, in principle the possibility of using nuclear energy has been discovered."[28]

There was some discussion at the conference about the use of atomic energy for power generation and for explosives, but no one thought that these were a matter for the near future.[29]

Niels Bohr and John Wheeler had published a major paper on the theory of fission in *Physical Review* on September 1, two days before the outbreak of war in Europe. Among other things, this paper provided a theoretical basis for Bohr's hypothesis that it was uranium-235 that fissioned with slow neutrons. Aleksandr Leipunskii, who gave an overview of the state of research at the Khar'kov conference and devoted much of his paper to the Bohr–Wheeler theory, said that uranium separation would be impossible for a long time to come, and described the possibility of a slow-neutron chain reaction as "very doubtful." Moreover, he added, nothing could be said about the prospects for a fast-neutron chain reaction, because there were no data about such things as the probability that fast neutrons would be slowed down.[30]

Most Soviet scientists were skeptical about the possibility of utilizing atomic energy. Igor' Tamm is reported to have said in August 1939, upon hearing of the work of Zel'dovich and Khariton, "Do you know what this new discovery means? It means a bomb can be built that will destroy a city out to a radius of maybe ten kilometers."[31] But this was an exception. Ioffe commented in a report to the Academy of Sciences in December 1939 that it was unlikely that there would be a technological payoff "this time" from nuclear physics.[32] Kapitsa remarked at some point in 1939 that nuclear reactions would absorb more energy than they yielded. The isotopes of uranium would have to be separated, and to do this it would be necessary "to expend more energy than one could count on obtaining from nuclear reactions." It would be very surprising, he said, if the possibility of using atomic energy were to become reality.[33]

Research into the conditions for a fission chain reaction continued after the Khar'kov conference. Kurchatov had proposed several experiments to see whether uranium-238 would fission with fast neutrons. He assigned one of these experiments to Flerov and Konstantin Petrzhak, a young researcher at the Radium Institute. The aim of the experiment was to observe how the flow of neutrons from a sphere of uranium changed when neutron sources with different energy spectra were placed inside it. Petrzhak and Flerov devised a highly sensitive ionization chamber to register the fission events. When they began their experiment early in 1940 they found, much to their surprise, that the ionization chamber continued to click – and thus to register fission – even after they had removed the neutron source. They soon decided that they had discovered spontaneous fission – fission without bombardment by neutrons. This had been predicted theoretically by Frenkel', and by Bohr and Wheeler, but Petrzhak and Flerov provided the first experimental demonstration of this phenomenon.[34]

In order to eliminate the possibility of error Kurchatov instructed Petrzhak and Flerov to do various control experiments. One of these was conducted under ground in the Dinamo metro station in Moscow to check that fission was not being caused by cosmic rays. Eventually Kurchatov was satisfied that they had indeed discovered spontaneous fission. Khlopin and Kurchatov reported on the discovery to the Academy of Sciences in May 1940, and papers soon appeared in Soviet journals.[35] Kurchatov, ever attentive to the opinion of foreign physicists, sent a short cable to the American journal *Physical Review*, which published it on July 1, 1940. Flerov and Petrzhak wanted to name Kurchatov as one of the authors since he had designed the experiments and helped to analyze the results, but he refused, apparently fearing that his younger colleagues would get no credit for their work if his name appeared on the paper.[36] This discovery received a good deal of attention in the Soviet Union where it was taken to show that Kurchatov and his colleagues were now working on the same level as the leading research centers in the West. Flerov said later that "before the war our desire for priority was very strong. Everyone fought to be first."[37] The American Willard Libby had tried, but failed, to discover spontaneous fission by experiment. This made the Soviet success all the sweeter.

On March 7, 1940 Zel'dovich and Khariton submitted their third paper to *ZhETF*, which published it in May.[38] Their first two papers had investigated the conditions for a chain reaction in a system of infinite size; now they examined the kinetics of a chain reaction close to the critical condition. A chain reaction would develop only in a lump of critical size. A nuclear chain reaction would produce an enormous amount of energy, they wrote, and make it possible to realize "several applications of uranium."[39] An attempt to achieve a chain reaction could therefore be expected soon, in spite of the great practical difficulties that stood in the way. But no judgment could be made about the use of nuclear fission for the generation of power or for explosives, unless the kinetics of the chain reaction were understood. It was particularly important to understand the transition from the subcritical to the supercritical state, because this transition would take place very quickly. The period between neutron generations, they wrote, was calculated in thousandths of a second for slow neutrons, and in ten-millionths of a second for fast neutrons.[40]

Zel'dovich and Khariton calculated that once a system was close to the critical condition, the thermal expansion of the uranium (which would allow neutrons to escape from the uranium) and the release of delayed neutrons would exercise a decisive influence on the transition to the critical state, making that transition much easier to regulate:

these characteristics of the system (above all, regulation through thermal expansion) make it safe to conduct experimental research and to use the uranium chain decay [chain reaction] for energy. The explosive use of the chain decay requires special devices for a very rapid and profound transition into the supercritical region and for a reduction of natural thermal regulation.[41]

This paper pointed to physical processes which were to prove crucial in reactor design. It also showed that Zel'dovich and Khariton were thinking about slow-neutron and fast-neutron chain reactions, and that they had in mind the use of atomic energy for bombs as well as power generation. Although the paper did not explicitly define the conditions for initiating a powerful nuclear explosion – significant supercriticality in the initial state and fast-neutron multiplication – it did, as a later Soviet commentary asserted, point directly to them.[42]

II

In the 1930s nuclear physicists were the very model of an international scientific community, and the dramatic progress of the decade was built on discoveries by scientists in several different countries. Theoretical and experimental results were communicated quickly through the international community, and a discovery in one laboratory spurred further work in others. This is very evident in the physicists' reaction to the discovery of fission. Soon, however, the situation began to change as nuclear physics was transformed from an area of research remote from practical application into a key factor in international relations.

The first person to see that nuclear physicists would have to take account of the military implications of their work was Leo Szilard, a Hungarian physicist who had moved to Britain in 1933 to escape the Nazi persecution of the Jews. Szilard understood at once what fission might mean, for in 1933 he had hit upon the idea of a chain reaction as the way to release the energy bound up in the atomic nucleus. It had not occurred to him that a chain reaction might be possible in uranium, nor did he anticipate the discovery of fission, but he was sufficiently worried by the prospect of a nuclear chain reaction to take out a British patent in order to restrict the use that might be made of his idea.[43]

In January 1939 Szilard, who was now living in New York, suggested to Enrico Fermi that research on fission should be kept secret. Fermi thought the prospect of a chain reaction remote, and his response to Szilard was "Nuts!"[44] Szilard then wrote to Frédéric Joliot to sound him out about imposing secrecy on research. Joliot ignored this approach, and he and his collaborators, Halban and Kowarski, published the paper in which they showed that neutrons were liberated when a uranium nucleus fissioned.[45]

Szilard persisted in his efforts, and in March he prevailed upon Fermi to ask *Physical Review* to delay the publication of a paper the Columbia physicists had written on the number of secondary neutrons emitted per fission. At Szilard's instigation, Victor Weisskopf sent a cable to Halban saying that publication was being delayed and asking whether Joliot and his collaborators were willing to do the same. Joliot declined, and on April 7, the day on which he cabled his final answer to Szilard, the French group sent to *Nature* the paper in which they calculated that between three and four neutrons were emitted per fission.[46]

When this paper appeared on April 22 it had a major impact on research elsewhere, because it showed that a chain reaction might indeed be a possibility. It impelled Professor G.P. Thompson of Imperial College to draw the British government's attention to the possibility of an atomic bomb, and to the importance of denying to Germany the uranium held by the Union Minière Company in Belgium. Responsibility for the uranium problem was assigned to the Air Ministry's Committee on the Scientific Survey of Air Defence. Research was started on the possibility of achieving a chain reaction, but there was little sense of urgency because the prospect of an atomic bomb seemed remote. The outbreak of war in September 1939 limited research still further because most physicists now became engaged in other kinds of war work.[47]

It was in April 1939 too that German scientists alerted their government to the implications of nuclear fission. Nikolaus Riehl, a former student of Hahn and Meitner's who headed scientific research at the Auer Company, drew the attention of Army Ordnance to potential applications of nuclear fission. Other scientists wrote to the Ministry of Culture and the Ministry of War. By September 1939 the Army Ordnance Department had set up a project to study nuclear fission. The Ministry of War took over the Kaiser Wilhelm Institute for Physics in Berlin and replaced the director, Peter Debye. From now on all reference to the possibility of atomic bombs or uranium reactors was excluded from the German press.[48]

In France Joliot and his colleagues were much more interested in the use of nuclear chain reactions for the production of nuclear power, and believed this to be a more immediate prospect than an atomic bomb. After the outbreak of war, however, Joliot explained to Raoul Dautry, the Minister of Armament, that research on uranium could lead either to a powerful new weapon or to an abundant source of energy. Dautry promised Joliot all the help he needed, and in March 1940 he sent Jacques Allier, an engineer who was now working in military intelligence, to Norway to obtain the stock of heavy water owned by the Norsk Hydro Electric Company, the only producer of heavy water in significant quantities. Allier managed to obtain the whole stock of 185.5 kilograms and move it to Paris. French nuclear research was brought to an end by the German invasion in May 1940. Halban and Kowarski escaped to England with the precious heavy water. Joliot stayed in Paris to sustain French science under the Nazi occupation.[49]

In the United States, which was still at peace, Szilard pressed for an expansion of research, out of fear that Germany had already embarked on an atomic bomb project. He contrived to bring the issue to President Roosevelt's attention by having Albert Einstein write to the president, on August 2, 1939, to warn him that recent research had made it conceivable

that "powerful bombs of a new type" could be constructed. At the end of
the letter Einstein noted that Germany had banned the sale of uranium
from the mines in Czechoslovakia, which it had occupied in March. In
response to this letter, Roosevelt established a government Committee on
Uranium in October 1939.[50]

Szilard also continued his campaign for a ban on publication of fission
research, but made little headway in the early months of 1940. He withheld
one of his own papers, and prevailed upon one or two of his colleagues to
do the same. But in June 1940 the Berkeley physicists Edwin McMillan
and Philip Abelson published a letter in *Physical Review* on the production
by nuclear fission of element 93, which was later named neptunium.
This evoked protests in Europe as well as in America from physicists who
believed that it was dangerous to publish an article which implied that
fission might lead to the production of fissionable transuranic elements;
if that were so, it would be possible to build a bomb without tackling
the very complex problem of separating uranium-235. Shortly thereafter,
voluntary restrictions on the publication of papers on fission were accepted
by the editors of the main American scientific journals and by leading
scientists.[51]

The behavior of Soviet scientists was quite different. There is no evidence that they tried to alert their government to the possible implications
of nuclear fission before the summer of 1940, and no special organization
was created before then to coordinate research on fission.[52] Soviet scientists
continued to publish freely on fission in 1940; no effort was made, by the
government or by the scientists themselves, to restrict publication. The
contrast with the response of scientists in other countries is striking and
reflects the strategic and political position of the Soviet Union. Unlike
Britain, France, and Germany, the Soviet Union had not been drawn into
the European war (though it had invaded Poland in September 1939 and
was at war with Finland from November 1939 to March 1940). Unlike the
United States, it did not have a significant group of refugee physicists to
sound the alarm about a Nazi atomic bomb. Besides, expressions of alarm
at the prospect of a German bomb would not have been compatible with
the Nazi–Soviet Pact of August 1939 or the Friendship Pact which followed it in September. The Soviet pacts with Nazi Germany also discouraged Western physicists from contacting their Soviet colleagues about
stopping the publication of papers on fission.

In spite of the alarm that scientists had raised, at the beginning of 1940
there was no full-scale project under way anywhere to develop the atomic
bomb. Although it appeared that a chain reaction was possible, this was still
not firmly established; nor had anyone formulated precisely the conditions
for an explosive chain reaction. Besides, it was not clear whether uranium-
235 could be separated on a large enough scale for a bomb. Most physicists

thought that tons of enriched uranium would be needed, and it was widely believed that this would be prohibitively expensive.[53]

The breakthrough came in March 1940, when Rudolf Peierls and Otto Frisch, who were then at the University of Birmingham, wrote a memorandum "On the Construction of a 'Superbomb'; based on a Nuclear Chain Reaction in Uranium."[54] Frisch and Peierls asked a set of basic questions. If you had a lump of pure uranium-235, would a fast-neutron chain reaction be possible? If so, how much uranium-235 would you need? What would be the consequences of such a chain reaction? How could the uranium-235 be separated? They provided answers which showed that a nuclear bomb was much more feasible than people had thought. They concluded that a fast-neutron chain reaction would be possible in 1 kilogram of metallic uranium-235, and that the destructive effect of a 5-kilogram bomb would be equivalent to that of several thousand tons of dynamite. They pointed out that a slow-neutron chain reaction could not produce an effective bomb, because the uranium would heat up and expand to let the neutrons escape, thus stopping the reaction. They proposed that the uranium-235 could be separated by a thermal diffusion method, which they described briefly. This memorandum prompted the British government to set up a committee to explore the possibility of an atomic bomb. The Maud Committee, as it was known, coordinated research in Britain on this problem, and completed its report in July 1941.

Margaret Gowing has written of the Frisch–Peierls memorandum that "the questions may seem obvious enough today but they were not at the time. In America they were not asked for many months, until after the British work was available. The German physicists, including the brilliant Heisenberg, apparently did not ask them at all."[55] It was to be some months before these questions were formulated by Soviet physicists.

III

The *New York Times* science correspondent, William Laurence, was following nuclear research closely in 1940, with particular attention to what was going on in Germany. At the end of April he learned from Peter Debye, who was visiting the United States, that a large part of the Kaiser Wilhelm Institute for Physics was being turned over to research on uranium. He took this as confirmation of his suspicions that Nazi Germany was working to develop an atomic bomb. At the same time he learned that two minute samples of uranium-235 had been separated by Alfred Nier at the University of Minnesota and that these had been used by John Dunning at Columbia University to confirm experimentally that it was this isotope that fissioned with slow neutrons. He decided that the time had come to write the "big story."[56]

On Sunday May 5, 1940, the *New York Times* carried Laurence's story on its front page, under the headline "Vast Power Source In Atomic Energy Opened by Science." Laurence wrote of Dunning's experiments and claimed that "improvement in the methods of extraction of this substance [i.e. uranium-235] was the only step that remained to be solved for its introduction as a new source of power." He noted the enormous explosive power of uranium-235, and the "tremendous implications this discovery bears on the possible outcome of the European war." He also reported – with some exaggeration – that "every German scientist in this field, physicists, chemists and engineers . . . have [*sic*] been ordered to drop all other researches and devote themselves to this work alone."[57]

Laurence hoped that his story would alert policy-makers to the danger that Nazi Germany might be building an atomic bomb. When no summons to Washington followed, he felt discouraged.[58] But his article produced an effect he had not anticipated, and probably never learned of. George Vernadsky, who was now teaching history at Yale University and knew, of course, of his father's interest in uranium and atomic energy, sent him Laurence's article. Vernadskii was staying at a sanatorium in Uzkoe, near Moscow, when his son's letter arrived, and he was greatly excited by Laurence's story.[59] He was particularly struck by Laurence's report of the experiments with uranium-235. The first question to spring to his mind was whether the Soviet Union had enough uranium ore to enable it to exploit atomic energy. He and Khlopin, who was also staying at Uzkoe, wrote to the Department of Geological and Geographical Sciences of the Academy of Sciences proposing that a plan be drawn up for uranium exploration. "Uranium metal," they wrote, "which has found only limited application and has always been regarded as a by-product of the extraction of radium, is now acquiring absolutely exceptional significance. The surveys of known deposits and the search for new ones are proceeding at a completely inadequate pace and are not united by a general idea."[60]

In response to this memorandum the Academy, as *Izvestiia* reported on June 26, set up a "troika" consisting of Vernadskii, Vitalii Khlopin, and Aleksandr Fersman to work out "a plan of measures which it would be necessary to realize in connection with the possibility of using intraatomic energy."[61] Several days later Vernadskii wrote to the vice-president of the Academy, explaining why he thought the matter so urgent:

According to the available information (received by me almost by accident and in incomplete form due unfortunately to the artificial obstacles placed in the way of our reading the foreign press), it has become clear that in the USA and Germany energetic and organized work is now proceeding in this direction, in spite of world military events. Our country can in no case stand aside and ought to provide the opportunity and the financial means for broad, organized and rapid work in this area of first-class significance.[62]

Vernadskii was playing the same role he had played before World War I when he had pressed for expeditions to look for uranium.

Once again Vernadskii relied on Khlopin and Fersman to help him. On July 5, 1940 Vernadskii wrote to his son in New Haven:

Thank you for the clipping you sent from Washington from the *New York Times* about uranium. This was the first news about this discovery to reach me, and to reach Moscow in general. I quickly set things moving. On 25.VI a "troika" was formed in the Academy under my chairmanship (Fersman and Khlopin) with the right of cooptation. Fersman is in Murmansk – but I started work quickly. We have to make use of the summer and autumn. I did not expect when Soddy first explained clearly the possibility of using intraatomic energy (more than 35 years ago) that I would live to see not only practical discussion of this phenomenon, which has a great future, but also work in this area. I think now that the possibilities that are being opened up for the future here are greater than the application of steam in the XVIIIth century and of electricity in the XIXth.[63]

In other letters he repeated the parallel between atomic energy and electricity. It was this prospect, rather than the more immediate danger from Germany that Laurence had described, that impelled him to action. His comment that work was proceeding rapidly in the United States and Germany, "in spite of world military events," not because of them, bears this out.

Vernadskii and Khlopin sent a letter on July 12 to Nikolai Bulganin, deputy premier and chairman of the government's Council on the Chemical and Metallurgical Industries, drawing attention to the discovery of fission, and to the huge quantities of energy it released.[64] This appears to have been the first attempt by Soviet scientists to alert a senior government official to the importance of nuclear fission. Vernadskii and Khlopin wrote that the discovery that uranium-235 fissions with slow neutrons would make it possible to regulate nuclear fission. Several very great difficulties stood in the way of the practical utilization of atomic energy, "but it seems to us that these are not difficulties of principle." They asked the government to take steps "that would enable the Soviet Union not to lag behind foreign countries in resolving this question." The Academy should be instructed to design an apparatus for isotope separation, and speed up the planning of the new "superpowerful" cyclotron at FIAN.[65]

When the Presidium of the Academy met on July 16 to consider Vernadskii's report, it asked him, along with Fersman and S.I. Vol'fkovich, a chemist, to write a further memorandum about the Academy's work in this area, and about the development of methods of isotope separation. It also asked them to draft a memorandum for the government on the significance of atomic energy, on the creation of a state uranium fund, and on exploration for uranium deposits.[66] Vernadskii was pleased with the outcome of the meeting, but he felt that not everyone shared his vision.

"The huge majority do not understand the historical significance of the moment," he wrote in his diary on the following day; "I wonder am I mistaken or not?"[67] In a letter to Lichkov some days later he wrote that

uranium has acquired significance as a source of atomic energy. With us uranium is a scarce metal; we extract radium from deep brine, and any quantity can be obtained. There is no uranium in these waters.[68]

A new commission was to be set up, he wrote, but he had "made an announcement" that Khlopin ought to be chairman. Having taken the initiative, Vernadskii, who was seventy-seven and busy with other scientific projects, now passed over the leading role to Khlopin.

The government decided, on the basis of Vernadskii's memoranda, to approve the creation of a Commission on the Uranium Problem, which was to be attached to the Presidium of the Academy of Sciences.[69] The commission was established on July 30, 1940. Khlopin was named chairman, with Vernadskii and Ioffe as his deputies. Besides Khlopin, three other members were former students of Vernadskii's: Aleksander Fersman, A.P. Vinogradov, a geochemist who was now Vernadskii's deputy at the Biogeochemical Laboratory, and D.I. Shcherbakov, a geologist at the Academy's Institute of Geological Sciences. Besides Ioffe, the physicists on the commission were Kurchatov, Khariton, Vavilov, Kapitsa, Mandel'shtam, and P.P. Lazarev, whose main interests were in biophysics and geophysics rather than in the nucleus. The membership was completed by A.N. Frumkin, director of the Academy's Institute of Physical Chemistry, and G.M. Krzhizhanovskii, now head of the Academy's Institute of Energetics.[70]

The Presidium of the Academy asked the commission to determine what research the Academy should do, to organize the development of methods for separating the isotopes of uranium, to initiate research into the control of nuclear fission, and to coordinate and direct the Academy's research in this area. A team headed by Fersman was to go to Central Asia before the end of the year to study the uranium deposits there, to organize a conference in Tashkent on uranium exploration, and to draw up a plan for the creation of a state uranium fund. The Academy proposed to hold a conference on radioactivity at the Radium Institute, and to speed up work on the cyclotrons at the Radium Institute, Ioffe's Institute, and FIAN. In defining the commission's responsibilities the Academy had followed Vernadskii's advice very closely.

The commission set to work quickly. At one of its first sessions, which was attended by industrial officials and geologists, Khlopin explained that recent research " 'made probable' the realization of a so-called chain reaction," with the release of an exceptionally great amount of energy. He warned that "very many difficulties stand in the way," and that the "mechanism of this reaction is insufficiently elucidated."[71] He explained that such a reaction could be realized with uranium-235. It was necessary, however, to try to achieve a chain reaction in uranium-238 as well, which "is not completely impossible theoretically; it is possible that this question will be solved and work is going on in this direction. On the other hand, if it is not possible to do that, then calculations show that by means of the enrichment of isotope-235, not separated in a pure form but in a mixture with isotope-238, such a chain reaction could be reproduced. These are the two directions in which physicists ought to work."[72]

A chain reaction would require "quantities measured in tens of kilograms of this mixture," Khlopin said, stressing that the supply of uranium was now the fundamental problem. The Soviet Union was "for the time being not very rich in it. . . . We must above all find out what reserves we can dispose of, that is – can we provide the necessary quantity? Then, having learned what state our raw material base is in today – to find out whether the geological search for uranium deposits is being conducted properly."[73]

The Uranium Commission faced great difficulties in providing Soviet physicists with the uranium compounds and metallic uranium they wanted for their experiments. In other countries uranium compounds were a by-product of radium production, but the Soviet radium industry was able to supply the country's needs by extracting radium from the borehole water in the oilfields at Ukhta. As a result, there was little uranium in the country in 1940, though some institutes had small quantities of uranium salts.[74] There was no serious demand for uranium, and little had been done to look for deposits. The Tiuia-Muiun mine had been closed down, and although some new deposits had been discovered, they had not been explored in a systematic way.[75] Soviet geologists did not know what uranium reserves the country had.[76]

IV

The Presidium of the Academy asked the Uranium Commission to prepare a plan of research by September 20, 1940. On August 29, before the commission responded to this directive, Kurchatov, Khariton, Flerov, and Rusinov submitted to the Academy a plan of their own entitled "On the utilization of the energy of uranium fission in a chain reaction."[77] The possibility of utilizing atomic energy had been established in principle, they wrote, but further research was needed.

The first task was to determine the conditions for a chain reaction in metallic uranium. Flerov would undertake this investigation, but would need one kilogram of pure metallic uranium. The second task followed from the first: if it seemed that a chain reaction was possible in metallic uranium, the neutrons emitted by the fission of uranium-238 nuclei would have to be studied; 300 kilograms of metallic uranium would be needed for these experiments. These two questions indicate that Kurchatov and his colleagues – apparently at the instigation of Flerov – had not given up all hope of a chain reaction in a mixture of natural uranium and water. The next three research topics in the plan reflected their interest in a system consisting of natural uranium and a moderator: the capture cross-sections of heavy hydrogen (deuterium), helium, carbon, oxygen, and other light elements were to be measured; the conditions for a chain reaction in a mixture of uranium and heavy water were to be calculated; and the feasibility of obtaining tons of heavy water assessed. Finally, they proposed research into the methods of separating the isotopes of uranium.

Kurchatov and his colleagues urged the Academy to create a special fund of several tons of uranium for chain reaction experiments. The lack of uranium was a major constraint on research. For one of the early experiments in his laboratory Kurchatov had sent his younger colleagues to buy up all the uranium nitrate in the photographic shops in Leningrad.[78] Such improvisations were no longer enough. The experimental physicists needed larger quantities of uranium in order to obtain the data they needed to reach a definite conclusion about the feasibility of a chain reaction. Kurchatov wrote to Khlopin on September 9 to say that he needed 500–1,000 grams of pure metallic uranium to investigate the possibility of a chain reaction in uranium-238. A little while later he wrote again to ask when uranium metal might become available, and what measures could be taken to speed things up.[79]

There is no hint of research on the atomic bomb in the Leningrad physicists' plan.[80] They were aware that nuclear fission might have military applications, but their primary interest at this time was to establish whether a fission chain reaction was indeed possible, rather than to achieve a specific practical goal. In an article written in the early summer of 1940 Zel'dovich and Khariton surveyed the research on fission, and calculated that about 2.5 metric tons of uranium oxide and 15 metric tons of heavy water would be needed for a slow-neutron chain reaction.[81] They made no reference to fast-neutron chain reactions.

At a meeting on September 28, almost a month after Kurchatov and his colleagues had sent their plan to the Academy, the Uranium Commission decided to prepare its own plan of research.[82] Khlopin and Leipunskii, who was now working at the Radium Institute, drew up this plan. They identified five main areas of research: the mechanism of fission of uranium and thorium; the possibility of a chain reaction in natural uranium; the development of methods for separating the isotopes of uranium; the development of methods for obtaining and studying volatile compounds of uranium metal; exploration for rich sources of uranium ore and the methods of processing it.[83] Whether Khlopin and Leipunskii knew of the plan prepared by Kurchatov and his colleagues is not clear. Ioffe's relations with Vernadskii and Khlopin were very poor, and although Kurchatov headed the physics department at the Radium Institute from April 1939 to October

1940, his relations with Khlopin appear to have been complicated.[84] This may explain why Kurchatov sent his plan to the Academy Presidium, and not directly to Khlopin.

On October 15 the Presidium of the Academy approved the plan prepared by Khlopin and Leipunskii. The Academy allocated additional funds to the Radium Institute and to the Biogeochemical Laboratory for work on the uranium problem in 1941. It promised to ask the government to supply 1.5 metric tons of uranium compounds a year, to create a state uranium fund, and to buy up industry's supply of uranium salts, 300 kilograns. It also announced steps to improve the supply of uranium: it set up a permanent raw materials subcommission of the Uranium Commission under Fersman; it resolved to draw the importance of uranium to the attention of the various government geological agencies, and to try to have the Central Asian Rare Metals Trust put in charge of uranium exploration in Central Asia. Finally the Academy allocated just under a million roubles for completion of the Radium Institute's cyclotron building.[85]

The future of nuclear research was the subject of a "very lively" discussion at the fifth All-Union conference on nuclear physics, which was held in Moscow from 20 to 26 November 1940.[86] About 200 scientists attended. Kurchatov delivered the main paper on fission, reviewing the progress of the previous year and discussing the possibility of a chain reaction.[87] He argued that a chain reaction could be achieved in a mixture of water and uranium enriched with the isotope uranium-235, or in a mixture of natural uranium and heavy water. (He expressed doubts about the effectiveness of helium, carbon, or oxygen as moderators, because he thought their cross-sections were too high.) In both cases great difficulties would have to be overcome: uranium isotopes would have to be separated for the first approach, and hydrogen isotopes for the second. Kurchatov provided a table in which he compared the amounts of uranium and heavy water required with the amounts then available: half a metric ton of enriched uranium would be needed, but only minute quantities then existed in the world; similarly, 15 metric tons of heavy water would be required, but there was only half a metric ton in the laboratories of the world. Kurchatov also considered the possibility of using protactinium for a chain reaction but the ratio of what was available to what was needed was even worse.[88] "Although the possibility of a nuclear chain reaction has now been established in principle," he concluded, "tremendous practical difficulties will arise in any attempt to realize it in any of the systems that have so far been investigated. . . . Perhaps the next few years will reveal other ways of solving this problem, but if this should not be the case, only new and very effective methods for separating the isotopes of uranium and hydrogen will make possible the practical realization of a nuclear chain reaction."[89]

Kurchatov's paper was restrained and sober in tone, but it did point to the need for extraordinary measures if a chain reaction was to be achieved. According to Igor' Golovin, who took part in the conference, the paper

sparked off a lively discussion during the break about the desirability of
approaching the government for more funds for nuclear research. The basic
issue was whether enough was known about nuclear chain reactions to
justify the expense of making a serious effort to separate uranium-235 and
produce heavy water in the necessary quantities. After the break, "Khlopin
returned to the rostrum," Golovin has written, "and declared that he had
come to the conclusion that it was too early to ask the government for large
grants since the war was going on in Europe and the money was needed for
other purposes. He said that it was necessary to work a year more and then
make the decision whether there would be some grounds to involve the
government and to ask for a few million for construction of a uranium pile
to excite the chain reaction there."[90] Kurchatov had apparently prepared a
memorandum asking the government for more resources, but Khlopin's
statement ruled out such an approach.[91] Khlopin was not the only person
to take a cautious line. Ioffe too, in a public lecture given during the
conference, made it clear that he did not think that atomic energy would
be harnessed until the distant future.[92]

Four days after the Moscow conference, on November 30, 1940, the
Uranium Commission met to hear reports from Fersman and Khlopin
about the expedition that they had headed, earlier in the autumn, to study
uranium deposits in Central Asia.[93] Fersman painted a gloomy picture.
Ten metric tons of uranium a year could be exracted by 1942–3, he said,
if a mine were organized. But the creation of a raw material base would
require a substantial capital investment, and the need for uranium for
atomic energy could be assessed only approximately; consequently he
proposed that other ways of using uranium – in the metallurgical, paint,
and pharmaceutical industries – be looked into. Khlopin declared that
the tentative reserves of uranium would need to be confirmed, and the
scale of exploitation work determined. He proposed that back-up funds be
identified to ensure that uranium-235 or uranium enriched to 3–4 per cent
with uranium-235 could be made available. He argued also for a special
fund to procure 2 metric tons of uranium. The commission approved these
proposals.[94]

While Khlopin focused on the problem of uranium supply, Khariton and
Zel'dovich continued to work on the conditions for a nuclear chain
reaction. In the course of this research they asked the same question that
Frisch and Peierls had asked earlier in the year: supposing you had a lump
of pure uranium-235, what would the critical mass be? Just as Frisch and
Peierls had done, they concluded from the Bohr–Wheeler theory that in
uranium-235 almost every neutron collision produces fission.[95] Working
with Isai Gurevich of the Radium Institute, they calculated the critical mass
for a fast-neutron chain reaction in a lump of pure uranium-235 surrounded by a heavy neutron reflector.[96] In a paper submitted to *Uspekhi
fizicheskikh nauk* in 1941 they referred briefly to these calculations: "in order

to realize a chain reaction in uranium with the liberation of tremendous quantities of energy approximately ten kilograms of the pure uranium-235 isotope would be sufficient."[97] (The war began before this paper could be published, and it did not appear until forty years later.[98]) The 10-kilogram estimate by Khariton and Zel'dovich was an order of magnitude greater than the Frisch–Peierls estimate of 1 kilogram, but that difference was small compared with the earlier estimates that tons of uranium-235 would be needed.[99] Like Frisch and Peierls, Khariton and Zel'dovich also gave some thought to the initiation of an explosive chain reaction, and calculated that if the lump of uranium-235 were compressed by means of conventional explosives, a chain reaction would take place.[100] The one point of difference is that Frisch and Peierls proposed a method of isotope separation, while Zel'dovich and Khariton did not. In 1937 Khariton had published a paper on isotope separation by the centrifuge method in which he had argued that this method was rational only for small quantities. Zel'dovich and he did not propose a particular method of separation in 1940.[101]

The parallel with the Frisch–Peierls memorandum is striking. That memorandum had of course not been published and there is no reason to suppose, and no evidence to suggest, that Zel'dovich and Khariton knew of it through espionage. The critical mass calculations by Khariton and Zel'dovich were a logical continuation of their earlier work. Semenov, as director of their institute, was naturally aware of their research, and understood that it pointed to the feasibility of an atomic bomb. He wrote to the Scientific-Technical Administration of the People's Commissariat of the Petroleum Industry, to which the Institute of Chemical Physics was then subordinate, claiming that a bomb could now be built with destructive power incomparably greater than that of any existing explosive, and arguing for an expansion of research; he asked that the letter be passed on to the People's Commissar.[102] Since no copy of this letter has been found, it is impossible to say precisely what its contents were, or exactly when it was written. It may have been written in the second half of 1940, or perhaps in the early months of 1941; but it may also have been written before Khariton and Zel'dovich did their calculations on the critical mass of uranium-235. In any event, it elicited no response. Here the parallel with the Frisch–Peierls memorandum breaks down, for the work done by Khariton and Zel'dovich did not lead to the establishment of anything like the crucially important Maud Committee. Semenov should perhaps have written to someone higher up in the government.[103]

In the second half of 1940 there was growing awareness among Soviet scientists of the possible military significance of nuclear fission. The situation in Europe had worsened. Germany dominated the continent after its stunning defeat of France in June. The Red Army had fought poorly in the war with Finland. There was a perceptible increase in the sense of danger in the Soviet Union, and this helped to draw attention to the military uses of atomic energy. Moreover, by the late summer of 1940 the effect of the war on nuclear research was becoming evident to Soviet scientists, who began to notice that foreign publications on nuclear fission were appearing less frequently. Vernadskii became aware of this in August 1940, and there was some discussion of it among the Leningrad physicists.[104] Ioffe hinted at it in a letter to Niels Bohr on December 5, 1940, just after the Moscow conference on nuclear physics. "Unfortunately," he wrote, "we have almost no news about scientific results outside our country." Bohr soon replied from Copenhagen, which was now occupied by Nazi Germany, but he offered little information about recent research.[105]

V

The Uranium Commission continued with its work, and research proceeded on a broad front, but without any great urgency. In a lecture in March 1941 Khlopin said that "we are, of course, still very far from solving this task [harnessing atomic energy]; however, there is some hope of its being solved positively and work is going on in that direction."[106] The cyclotron at the Radium Institute began normal operation at the end of 1940. Kurchatov turned his attention to construction of the cyclotron at Ioffe's institute. He and Alikhanov shared the responsibility for this, with Kurchatov supervising the design and construction, and Alikhanov responsible for obtaining the necessary funds and materials. By the summer of 1941 the cyclotron building was nearly ready, and the machine was planned to start operation on January 1, 1942.[107] Once it had been clearly established that uranium-235 was the fissionable isotope, interest in the methods of separation began to grow. The two most popular methods among Soviet physicists were thermal diffusion and centrifugal separation. The Radium Institute, the Biogeological Laboratory, and the Dnepropetrovsk Physicochemical Institute were all working on thermal diffusion.[108] Many physicists, however, believed that this was not a promising approach to separation on an industrial scale, because the separation process would consume as much energy as would be yielded by the uranium-235 obtained.[109] V.S. Shpinel' of UFTI thought diffusion methods too slow for separating the isotopes of heavy elements, and considered the centrifuge, which was being investigated by Fritz Lange at UFTI, to be the most promising approach.[110] Other methods were also explored. Kurchatov persuaded Artsimovich to begin experiments on electromagnetic isotope separation at Ioffe's institute, and at the Radium Institute some research was done on separation by means of a linear accelerator.[111] In January 1941 the Biogeochemical Laboratory undertook to prepare uranium hexafluoride (a gaseous form of uranium) for use in separation, and Vernadskii began to look for suitable premises for this work.

The scope of Soviet nuclear research can be judged from the list of topics discussed at the meeting of the Uranium Commission on May 17, 1941: chain reaction calculations, methods of isotope separation, the use of fluorescent tests for detecting uranium, and the work of the Leningrad and Ukrainian Physicotechnical Institutes.[112] The commission's work was hampered by two things, however. The first was what Vernadskii referred to in his diary as the "routine and ignorance of Soviet bureaucrats." In the spring of 1941 the government proposed to stop exploration of the uranium deposit at Tabashar, even though it had still not been established what kind of deposit it was, or how deep the ore ran. Only a protest from Khlopin, Vernadskii, and Fersman persuaded the government to reverse this decision.[113]

The second impediment was the tension between Vernadskii's group and the physicists. This was partly rooted in old rivalries, but it also reflected disagreement over the relative priority to be given to nuclear theory and to uranium exploration. In his diary for May 16, 1941 Vernadskii recorded a conversation he had had with one of the Academy vice-presidents:

I pointed out to him that now obstruction was caused by the physicists (Ioffe, Vavilov – I did not name names). They are directing their efforts to the study of the atomic nucleus and its theory and here . . . much of importance is being done – but life requires the mining-chemical direction.[114]

Two weeks later he wrote that "The physicist directs his attention to the theory of the nucleus, and not to the real task which faces the physical chemist and the geochemist – the separation of isotope 235 from uranium."[115]

Although there was rivalry between Vernadskii's group and the physicists, it did not assume ideological or political overtones. The disagreements were sharp, but neither side resorted to the Stalinist techniques of argument; there were no accusations of sabotage or anti-Marxism. These men were too committed to science – or rather to the dominant theories in physics – to resort to those techniques; they did not cross the line into the dangerous language of Stalinist politics.

The bad feelings between Khlopin and Ioffe are clear from an exchange of letters in December 1940. On December 2 Ioffe resigned from the Uranium Commission. The uranium problem was undergoing rapid change, he wrote:

It is absolutely essential that the commission's decisions should take account of all possible facts. Nevertheless the physicists (Kurchatov et al.) are not taking part in the most important meetings, and the other members of the commission, including you, are, as past experience has shown, inadequately informed about the new possibilities that are opening up, and about the elimination of others which can no longer be depended upon.[116]

The immediate pretext for this letter was an invitation for Ioffe to the November 30 meeting of the Uranium Commission, which had arrived three days late. Khlopin replied that physicists had been present at all the "responsible meetings": "You yourself, Acad. S.I. Vavilov, Acad. P.P. Lazarev, Acad. A.I. Leipunskii, Iu.B. Khariton and others. As for I.V. Kurchatov, for reasons that I do not understand he has not been to one meeting of the commission, although he has always received an invitation, except to the last one."[117]

The reference to Kurchatov's not attending the meetings of the Uranium Commission is intriguing. Memoirs about Kurchatov often portray him as destined all along for greatness, but in this period there were few signs of the power and authority he was later to acquire. He was a respected scientist, and he inspired the loyalty of his colleagues. But he was not regarded as a really outstanding physicist; when Ioffe's institute nominated him for the Academy of Sciences in 1938, he was not elected.[118] He wanted to press ahead with work on nuclear chain reactions, but his research plan was not accepted by the Academy. It was an exciting time for Kurchatov because his field was developing so rapidly – Gurevich describes him as being in a "holiday mood" after the discovery of fission – but it was a frustrating period for him as well.[119]

Although they no longer had close personal contacts with Western colleagues, Soviet scientists followed foreign research very closely. The experiments done by Joliot's group in Paris, for example, and by Fermi in New York, were studied carefully. So too was Bohr and Wheeler's theory of fission. Soviet nuclear scientists were especially interested in the paper published in *Physical Review* in June 1940 by the Berkeley scientists Edwin McMillan and Philip Abelson announcing the production of neptunium and positing the existence of element 94.[120] This was the paper that had elicited protests from physicists in Britain and the United States, and had led to the cessation of publications on fission.

Western physicists took less note of Soviet work. Although some Soviet research – on the number of secondary neutrons emitted per fission, for example – was preempted by publications by other research groups, there were two important Soviet contributions in this period – the discovery of spontaneous fission, and the theory of chain reactions. These did not receive much attention in the West, however. At the Moscow nuclear conference in November 1940 a resolution was passed nominating Flerov and Petrzhak for one of the newly established Stalin prizes. But the referee who reviewed their nomination apparently turned them down on the grounds that Western physicists had not said anything about their discovery.[121] Similarly, the papers by Khariton and Zel'dovich, which provided the most extensive discussion of chain reactions to be published in this period, elicited no response outside the Soviet Union.

There were various reasons for this apparent lack of interest. Research on fission had been made secret in the main countries by the summer of 1940, so it is not surprising that the Soviet work was not cited in Western journals. Scientists in the United States and Britain were especially concerned about what was going on in Germany, and did not pay particular attention to Soviet research. Lack of personal contact made it less likely that the work of Soviet physicists would be known abroad. The lack of communication was not complete, however. Niels Bohr took note of Soviet research. In his letter of December 23, 1940 to Ioffe, he wrote that "it is exceedingly interesting that the experiments of Petrzhak and Flerov actually seem to confirm our [Bohr and Wheeler's] expectation. . . . It is most desirable that these important experiments will soon be further extended."[122] Bohr's knowledge of the Soviet discovery of spontaneous fission may have helped, along with his high regard for Soviet physics in general, to inspire his efforts in 1944 and 1945 to head off a nuclear arms race.

CHAPTER FOUR

Making a Decision

I

THERE WAS GREAT APPREHENSION in Moscow after the German defeat of France in June 1940. Most of Europe now lay under the Nazi yoke, and although Britain was still fighting, it had no forces on the European continent: might not Hitler now turn eastward? In an effort to strengthen the Soviet position, Stalin annexed the three Baltic states, as well as Bessarabia and northern Bukovina, in the summer of 1940. In the latter half of the year Germany began to build up its forces along the Soviet border. Stalin did not believe, however, that Hitler would attack the Soviet Union before Britain had been defeated or had concluded a peace treaty with Germany. He was impressed by Bismarck's view that Germany could never win a war on two fronts, and he thought that Hitler had drawn the same conclusion from German history.[1] In February 1941 he remarked to General K.A. Meretskov, who had just been replaced as Chief of the General Staff by General Georgii Zhukov, that the Soviet Union might manage to stay out of the war until 1942.[2] In May he told a reception for new graduates from the military academies that Germany might attack, but he hoped, he said, that war could be postponed until 1942, when the Red Army would be better trained and better equipped.[3]

Stalin was anxious to put off Soviet involvement in the war as long as possible. The Red Army, still in disarray from the terrible purge of 1937–8, had fought badly in the winter war with Finland in 1939–40. The contrast with the brilliant campaign of the *Wehrmacht* against France in May and June 1940 did not go unnoticed in Berlin or Moscow. Stalin needed time to make the Red Army ready by reforming its structure and building up its stocks of arms and equipment.[4] He was afraid, however, to mobilize the Red Army fully or to bring it up to full combat readiness along the border, for fear that this might provoke the war he was so anxious to avoid. He received numerous warnings, from the British and American governments as well as from his own intelligence services, about Hitler's intention to attack the Soviet Union, but he dismissed these warnings as provocations designed to draw the Soviet Union into war with Germany. He had in mind the experience of 1914 when mobilization had helped to precipitate war; and he suspected that the British and American governments, as well as the German High Command, wanted to provoke war between the Soviet Union and Germany.[5]

Stalin apparently believed that if Germany decided to attack it would first issue an ultimatum, and that this would provide him with time either to grant political and economic concessions, or to bring the Red Army up to full readiness. The Red Army's High Command compounded this misconception by assuming, in spite of the German *Blitzkrieg* strategy in the West, that the war would start with frontier battles before the main forces were engaged. This assumption proved unfounded, and the German High Command completed the deployment of its forces along the Soviet border before the Soviet Union did. Germany launched its attack on the morning of June 22, 1941 without any prior ultimatum, thereby seizing the strategic initiative.[6]

In the opening days of the war the Red Army suffered terrible losses in men and material as it was thrown back in confusion. Soviet troops put up stiff resistance at a few points, but they could not stop the onward sweep of the *Wehrmacht*. The fate of the Soviet Union now hung in the balance. As Stalin realized the scale of the disaster, he fell into a state of shock.[7] "All that which Lenin created we have lost forever," he said.[8] (Or, in alternative versions: "Lenin left us a state and we have turned it to shit"; "Lenin left us a great inheritance and we, his heirs, have fucked it all up.")[9] Stalin's own fate hung in the balance too. His policies over the previous fifteen years had killed millions of people and inflicted enormous suffering upon the Soviet Union. He had justified such brutal policies by arguing that the Soviet Union had to defend itself against its enemies and make itself ready for war. Now the war had come, and he had been taken by surprise. Stalin apparently feared that the other members of the Politburo would remove him from power, but they were too much his creatures even to try to do so. They asked him to head a new committee that would exercise supreme power during the war.[10]

On June 30 the State Defense Committee was created. Stalin, who was not only general secretary of the Communist Party but had taken over from Molotov as chairman of the Council of People's Commissars in May 1941, was named chairman of the new committee. Viacheslav Molotov, who had been chairman of the People's Commissars from 1930 to 1941 and People's Commissar of Foreign Affairs since 1939, was appointed deputy chairman of the State Defense Committee. Molotov was widely regarded as the second figure in the Party and the state. Marshal Kliment Voroshilov, who had been People's Commissar of Defense from 1925 to 1940, was also a member. Voroshilov was a weak-willed and incompetent figure, and not a serious force in the leadership. The other two members were Lavrentii

Beria, who had become head of the NKVD in 1938, and Georgii Malenkov, Central Committee secretary and head of the Cadres Director- ate of the Central Committee.

Twelve days after the invasion, Stalin finally broadcast to the Soviet people. He addressed them in unprecedented fashion: "Brothers and Sis- ters! I turn to you, my friends . . ." He defended the pact with Germany by saying that "no peace-loving state could have rejected such a pact with another country, even if scoundrels like Hitler and Ribbentrop stood at its head," and claimed that the pact had given the Soviet Union time to prepare for war. He called for the full mobilization of the economy, and for partisan warfare in the occupied territories. He urged the people to rally round the "Party of Lenin and Stalin" in the struggle against the invader.[11]

The advance of the German armies continued. By the end of November Germany had gained control of the territory on which 45 per cent of the Soviet population lived and 60 per cent of Soviet coal, iron, steel, and aluminum were produced.[12] The first major check to the German advance came only at the beginning of December, when the Red Army mounted a counteroffensive at the gates of Moscow.

II

On the day after the German attack the Presidium of the Academy of Sciences held an extraordinary meeting at which scientists and scholars spoke of their wish to devote all their energies and abilities to the war effort.[13] Several leading chemists wrote to Stalin shortly afterwards, propos- ing that a new organization be created to direct science to the needs of defense. The chemists were quickly summoned to a meeting with Molo- tov, who decided to create a new mechanism to draw scientists into the war effort. Sergei Kaftanov, head of the government's Committee on Higher Education, was appointed the State Defense Committee's "plenipoten- tiary" for science, and on July 10 a Scientific-Technical Council, compris- ing leading members of the Academy – among them Ioffe, Kapitsa, and Semenov – was set up under Kaftanov's chairmanship. This council was responsible for organizing war work in research establishments and for evaluating research and engineering proposals. At first it dealt primarily with chemistry and physics, but later it extended its activities to geology and other fields. Kaftanov was given a small staff to help him run the council and to maintain contact with industry and the military. He himself reported directly to the State Defense Committee.[14]

Even before the creation of this council, research institutes had begun to move to a war footing. Within five days of the German attack 30 of the staff of Ioffe's institute had either been drafted or had volunteered for military service; a month later that number had risen to 130. The institute was reorganized, with priority now given to the areas of military research in which it had already been engaged: radar, armor, and the demagnetizing of ships.[15] This pattern was repeated elsewhere, and ultimately 90 to 95 per cent of research at the physics institutes was devoted to war purposes.[16]

Kurchatov decided to drop his research on fission, and his laboratory was disbanded. Some of its equipment was moved to Kazan' when Ioffe's institute was evacuated there in July and August; the rest, including the unfinished cyclotron, remained in Leningrad. Kurchatov joined a group headed by Anatolii Aleksandrov to work on the protection of ships against magnetic mines.[17] He threw himself into this work with customary energy. He spent three months in Sevastopol', the headquarters of the Black Sea Fleet, and left early in November when the city was under siege by German forces. After a dangerous voyage he landed in Poti on the eastern shore of the Black Sea and spent several weeks setting up the demagnetizing service there. Early in 1942 he traveled to Kazan', which was bitterly cold, short of food, and crowded with evacuees. On the day after his arrival, he fell ill with pneumonia. He had a hereditary weakness of the lungs, and this bout of illness lasted for two months. In April 1942 he and other members of the demagnetizing team were awarded a Stalin prize for their work, but poor health made it impossible for him to return to the Navy, and he took over the armor laboratory at the Physicotechnical Institute.[18]

Most nuclear scientists abandoned their research to work for the war effort. The Academy's Physics Institute was evacuated from Moscow to Kazan', where its nuclear group adapted its knowledge and techniques to the development of acoustic apparatus for the detection of aircraft, and to quality control of arms production.[19] The Institute of Chemical Physics also moved to Kazan', and Khariton and Zel'dovich dropped their research on fission chain reactions. They both worked on the powder fuel for the "Katiusha" rocket artillery, and Khariton later helped to develop anti-tank grenades and cheap, surrogate explosive substances.[20] The Ukrainian Physicotechnical Institute was evacuated thousands of kilometers from Khar'kov to Alma-Ata and to Ufa, where it concentrated on developing new weapons and helping local industry.[21] Only the Radium Institute, which also moved to Kazan', continued to work on the synthesis of uranium compounds for use in isotope separation, but this research was on a very small scale.[22]

With the outbreak of war the Uranium Commission ceased to function. Vernadskii was evacuated to the resort of Borovoe in Kazakhstan, along with a group of elderly Academicians. In his diary on July 13 and 14 he expressed the fear that Germany might use gas or "uranium energy" on the battlefield, but his belief in Soviet victory did not waver.[23] On July 15, the day before he left Moscow, he wrote to his son that "I am profoundly glad that we are now indissolubly linked with the Anglo-Saxon democracies. It is precisely here that our historic place is."[24] He hoped that victory would lead to radical changes in the Soviet Union in the direction of democracy and freedom of thought. The defeat of Nazism would move the world closer to the noosphere.[25]

A more specific concern about the effect of science on human life was voiced by Peter Kapitsa at an anti-Fascist rally of scientists in Moscow on October 12. Kapitsa had not forgotten the atomic bomb. "My personal opinion is that the technical difficulties which stand in the way of utilizing intra-atomic energy are still very great," he said. "This matter is still very doubtful, but it is very probable that there are great possibilities here. We are posing the question of using atomic bombs which possess huge destructive force."[26] A future war would be even more terrible than this one, said Kapitsa, and "therefore scientists should now warn people about this danger, so that all the public figures of the world will strain every nerve to eliminate the possibility of another war, a war of the future."[27] Kapitsa was speaking of the possible effect of science on war, not urging that an effort be made to develop the atomic bomb for use in the war against Germany.

There was, however, one physicist who had a sense of urgency about nuclear research. This was Kurchatov's twenty-eight-year-old colleague, Georgii Flerov, who had joined up at the outbreak of war and been sent to the Leningrad Air Force Academy to train as an engineer for work on Pe-2 dive bombers. He could not put nuclear research out of his mind. He wrote to Ioffe in Kazan', asking to be allowed to address a seminar there. He obtained permission to travel from Ioshkar-Ola, to which the Air Force Academy had been evacuated, to Kazan', 120 kilometers away. There he spoke to a group that included Ioffe and Kapitsa in mid-December 1941.[28]

Flerov spoke in his customary enthusiastic and lively manner, according to Isai Gurevich, who attended the seminar. His arguments made an impression on his audience, who were also worried by the fact that publication on nuclear fission had stopped in the West. "The impression was left that this was very serious and well-grounded," Gurevich recalls, "that work on the uranium project should be renewed. But there was a war going on. And I am not absolutely sure what the result of, say, a secret vote would have been, if the seminar had had to decide whether to begin work immediately or begin after a year or two."[29] Flerov returned to the Air Force Academy on December 22, without having persuaded Ioffe, who was now a vice-president of the Academy and a member of its Presidium, to seek a renewal of nuclear research. No matter how convincing Flerov's case, this was not a propitious time to be making such a request. The Red Army was fighting to halt the German advance outside Moscow, and war production had not yet recovered from the catastrophic disruption caused by the German invasion.

The irrepressible Flerov did not let the matter drop, however. He wrote at once to Kurchatov, setting out the argument he had made in Kazan'.[30] His letter covered thirteen pages of a school notebook.[31] He began by arguing that a slow-neutron chain reaction in natural uranium was imposs-ible, and that a chain reaction in enriched uranium, or in natural uranium with a moderator, would be so expensive as to make nuclear power uneconomical.[32] But a fast-neutron chain reaction, he wrote, could pro-duce an explosion equivalent to 100,000 metric tons of TNT, and was therefore worth the time and effort. "The basic direction of research, in our opinion," he wrote, "ought to be investigation of the conditions for the development of just these 'dynamite' chain nuclear reactions – fast-neutron reactions."

The first condition for a fast-neutron chain reaction, Flerov noted, was that, given a sufficiently large amount of active material, each fission would lead to at least one other fission. He discussed the number of neutrons released per fission, as well as the capture and fission cross-sections of uranium-235 and protactinium-231.[33] Both of these materials, he wrote, could be used as the active material, and the critical mass for either had been estimated to be between half a kilogram and 10 kilograms.[34] The second condition for an explosive chain reaction was a rapid "jump-like" transition to the supercritical state. If the transition were too slow, only a small proportion of the uranium nuclei would fission. The transition to the supercritical state had to be made quickly enough to preclude premature detonation by stray neutrons. Flerov's research on spontaneous fission was relevant here, because he feared that neutrons emitted in spontaneous fission could initiate a chain reaction prematurely.[35] The third condition was that significant supercriticality had to be obtained immediately, to prevent the chain reaction from dying out quickly.

Flerov provided calculations for all these conditions. He also provided a sketch of an experimental bomb. He proposed that a rapid transition into the supercritical state be ensured by compressing the active material. In Flerov's sketch the uranium-235 or protactinium-231 is divided into two hemispheres, and conventional high explosives are used to propel one hemisphere very rapidly into the other in order to form a critical mass. This mechanism is similar to that suggested by Frisch and Peierls; it later came to be known as a "gun-assembly device."[36]

At the end of his letter Flerov added a PS: "I have read the whole article through from beginning to end, and feel that I have been thinking too much about these questions, it is hard to judge how valuable everything I have written is – see for yourself." But Flerov was more convinced of the force of his own arguments than this PS suggests; and indeed, the con-ditions that he discussed proved to be important for the design of an atomic bomb. Flerov hoped that his letter would persuade Kurchatov to take up nuclear research again. "Perhaps my letter will help this process of the return of the 'prodigal son'," he wrote to a friend in Leningrad.[37] Kurchatov did not receive the letter until after he had recovered from his bout of pneumonia; he did not reply to it.[38]

Early in 1942 Lieutenant Flerov's unit was stationed in Voronezh, close
to the front line. The university in Voronezh had been evacuated, but the
library was still there. "The American physics journals, in spite of the war,
were in the library, and they above all interested me," Flerov wrote later.
"In them I hoped to look through the latest papers on the fission of
uranium, to find references to our work on spontaneous fission."[39] When
Flerov looked through the journals he found that not only had there been
no response to the discovery that he and Petrzhak had made, but that there
were no articles on nuclear fission. Nor did it seem that the leading nuclear
physicists had switched to other lines of research, for they too were missing
from the journals.[40]

From "the dogs that did not bark" Flerov deduced that research on
fission had now gone secret in the United States. That meant, he concluded, that the Americans were working to build a nuclear weapon. More
worrying was the fact that Nazi Germany had "first-class scientists . . . ,
significant supplies of uranium ore, a heavy water plant, the technology for
obtaining metallic uranium, methods for separating isotopes."[41] Flerov
decided to sound the alarm. It was at this point, apparently, that he wrote
to Kaftanov, the State Defense Committee's "plenipotentiary" for science.
He pointed to the absence of publications on fission in foreign journals:
"this silence is not the result of an absence of research. . . . In a word, the
seal of silence has been imposed, and this is the best proof of the vigorous
work that is going on now abroad." He also suggested that "it would be
very good to ask the British and the Americans about the results they have
obtained recently."[42]

When he received no reply from Kaftanov, Flerov decided to make use
of the Soviet citizen's last resort: he wrote to Stalin in April 1942. He felt
like a man who was trying to break through a stone wall with his head, he
explained. He did not think that he was overestimating the importance of
the uranium problem. It would not produce a revolution in civilian
technology, but "in military technology a real revolution will take place. It
will take place without our participation, and all that is only because in the
scientific world now, as before, inertia flourishes." Perhaps he had lost
perspective, he wrote, but he did not think that programmatic goals like
the uranium problem should all be deferred until after the war.[43]

In case anyone should think that he was merely trying to escape from the
front, and to return to research for selfish reasons, Flerov proposed that a
meeting be organized to discuss nuclear research. Ioffe, Fersman, Vavilov,
Khlopin, Kapitsa, Leipunskii, Landau, Alikhanov, Artsimovich, Frenkel',
Kurchatov, Khariton, and Zel'dovich should be invited, as well as Migdal,
Gurevich, and Petrzhak.[44] Flerov asked for the right to speak for an hour
and a half. "Your presence, Iosif Vissarionovich, is very desirable," he
added, "whether in person or not." He was aware that this was not the time
for scientific tournaments, he wrote, but he saw no other way of proving

that he was right, since his letter and five telegrams to Kaftanov had been ignored and his talks with Ioffe had led nowhere; the Presidium of the Academy of Sciences would talk about anything but nuclear research.

"This is the wall of silence which I hope you will help me to break through," he wrote,

since this letter is the last, and after it I will lay down my arms and wait until the problem is solved in Germany, Britain, or the USA. The results will be so huge that there will be no time to decide who was guilty of the fact that we abandoned this work here in the Union.

In addition, all this is being done so skillfully that we will not have formal grounds against anyone. Nobody has ever said, anywhere, that a nuclear bomb is not feasible, yet the opinion has been created that this goal belongs in the realm of fantasy.[45]

Flerov urged that all those invited to the meeting be asked to write down their view of the "uranium problem," and to attach a figure to the probability that it could be solved. Those who felt that they could not do this should still be required to attend the meeting.

The urgency of Flerov's desire to persuade the Soviet government to set up a nuclear project is very evident from this letter, and is in sharp contrast to the caution exhibited by Khlopin and Ioffe. Yet Flerov's impetuousness was potentially dangerous for those whom he criticized. With his reference to a possible trial of those who were "guilty" of abandoning nuclear research, he put the issue into the sinister language of Stalinist politics. Whether Stalin saw the letter is not clear, and the meeting for which Flerov called did not take place. But the letter was given to Kaftanov, who was doubtless unhappy to see himself accused of negligence in a matter affecting the interests of the Soviet state.[46]

III

As Soviet nuclear physicists dispersed to various kinds of war work, Britain and the United States were expanding their nuclear projects. The Maud Committee completed its secret report in July 1941. It concluded that "it will be possible to make an effective uranium bomb which, containing some 25 lb of active material, would be equivalent as regards destructive effect to 1,800 tons of T.N.T. and would also release large quantities of radioactive substances, which would make places near to where the bomb exploded dangerous to human life for a long period."[47] The committee had studied the problem of isotope separation very carefully and recommended gaseous diffusion as the most effective method, rather than the thermal diffusion method that Peierls and Frisch had suggested. Studies by Professor Francis Simon at Oxford had shown that separation on an industrial scale by gaseous diffusion was feasible. The committee calculated that the uranium-235 for the first bomb could be available by the end of 1943, and referred in passing to "a new element of mass 239 [i.e. plutonium] which will very probably have similar fission properties to uranium-235."[48]

The Maud Committee presented its case with great cogency, and put the possibility of the atomic bomb in a new light. In September 1941 the Defence Services Panel of the Cabinet Scientific Advisory Committee reviewed its work, and concluded that "the development of the uranium bomb should be regarded as a project of the very highest importance."[49] It would take between two and five years to make the bomb, the panel estimated, and probably more than two. It recommended that a pilot separation plant be built in Britain, and a pilot plant and a full-scale separation plant in North America. The panel finished its report on September 25, 1941. By this time Winston Churchill had already decided, as a result of the Maud Committee's work, to pursue the atomic bomb as a matter of urgency.[50]

The Maud Committee also played an important role in persuading the United States government to expand its nuclear research. American scientists had made key progress in some areas — notably the identification of plutonium by Glenn Seaborg and his colleagues at Berkeley in February 1941 — but the Committee on Uranium established by Roosevelt after Einstein's letter had proved to be ineffective. The Maud Report, with its conclusion that an atomic bomb could be built before the war was over, provided a powerful argument for expanding research and influenced the thinking of key American scientists.[51]

On October 9, 1941 Vannevar Bush, director of the Office of Scientific Research and Development, outlined the results of the Maud Committee's work to Roosevelt, and explained what needed to be done in the United States. Roosevelt gave Bush the authority to speed up the American effort in every possible way, in order to discover whether a bomb could be made. On the same day he wrote to Churchill to suggest that the American and British projects "be coordinated or even jointly conducted."[52] But the British government, conscious of its lead, responded coolly to this proposal and wanted only informal collaboration. The United States now pursued research with great urgency, and soon outstripped the British effort. Once they were ahead, the Americans did not see why they should disclose the results of their work to the British. The informal collaboration between the two countries broke down, and it was only in August 1943, when Roosevelt and Churchill met in Quebec, that British participation in the Manhattan project was arranged. Most of the physicists working on isotope separation and fast-neutron bomb calculations in Britain now went to the United States.[53]

Roosevelt authorized an all-out effort to build the atomic bomb in June 1942. Because construction on a huge scale was needed, the project was placed under the control of the Army, with Colonel Leslie R. Groves of the Army Corps of Engineers in charge. The United States pursued both the plutonium and the uranium-235 routes to the atomic bomb.[54] Fermi and his group achieved a self-sustaining chain reaction in a uranium-graphite pile at the University of Chicago in December 1942, by which time design of plutonium production piles had already begun.[55] These were later constructed at Hanford in Washington, where a chemical plant was also built to separate the plutonium from the irradiated uranium. Four different methods of isotope separation were investigated: gaseous diffusion, electromagnetic separation, thermal diffusion, and the centrifuge method. A huge gaseous diffusion plant was built at Oak Ridge in Tennessee, and electromagnetic and thermal-diffusion separation plants were also constructed nearby; the centrifuge method was not used for production. The plutonium and uranium-235 bombs were designed and fabricated at Los Alamos Laboratory in New Mexico, which was set up in the first months of 1943. The whole enterprise was a demonstration of the technological and industrial power of the United States, and of its commitment to be the first to build the atomic bomb.

The British and American projects were driven largely by the fear that Nazi Germany would build an atomic bomb, and thereby acquire a weapon of devastating power for use against the Allies. But the German nuclear project remained fragmented. Research continued in 1940 and 1941 along very much the same lines as in Britain, the United States, and the Soviet Union. "Even though the American research had been qualitatively superior to that conducted in Germany," writes Mark Walker in his study of the German nuclear project, "their German colleagues had performed the same sort of experiments, had made the same type of calculations, and had come to similar conclusions as the Allies."[56] But Germany did not embark on an all-out effort to build an atomic bomb. In June 1942, the month in which Roosevelt authorized the Manhattan project, Heisenberg conveyed to members of the German High Command that wartime Germany could not produce an atomic bomb.[57] He gave Albert Speer, the Minister for Armament and War Production, the impression that the bomb would take too long to build to have "any bearing on the course of the war."[58]

Heisenberg's motives in giving this advice remain contoversial; there is, besides, no agreement about the extent of his understanding of how a bomb might be made. But whatever the attitude or knowledge of the German scientists, the link between the bomb and the war was an important one in the decision to start a nuclear project. The British in 1940 and 1941 faced the prospect of a long war to defeat Germany, and were fearful that the balance of military power might be tipped decisively in Germany's favor if it acquired this new and terrible weapon. This was the context in which the Maud Committee worked. When the committee concluded that an atomic bomb might be built within two and a half years, it was apparent that the bomb might have an impact on the war, for there was no expectation that Germany would be defeated before then. The same was true for the United States, especially after the Japanese attack at Pearl Harbor on December 7, 1941. In Germany, however, the strategic outlook was different. The rapid German victories of 1940 and 1941 held out the promise of a short war, in which an atomic bomb would play no role. By 1942 the situation was less hopeful, but there had been no Maud Committee to provide a reasoned argument that a bomb could be built in less than three years. It did not appear, therefore, that an atomic bomb could affect the outcome of the war.[59]

IV

In 1941 British scientists had advanced farther than anyone else in their understanding of the feasibility of an atomic bomb. In the same year the Soviet government began to receive detailed information about British progress. On September 25, 1941 Anatolii Gorskii (codename Vadim), the NKVD resident in London, transmitted to Moscow information about a secret meeting that had been held nine days earlier to discuss the Maud Report.[60] Gorskii listed several points made in that discussion. It was quite possible, he reported, that a uranium bomb could be developed within two years; and a fusing mechanism for the bomb could be designed within several months. Three months earlier the Metropolitan Vickers Company had been given a contract for the design of a 20-stage machine (but Gorskii failed to point out that this was for isotope separation), and Imperial Chemical Industries had received a contract for the production of uranium hexafluoride. Finally Gorskii reported that the Chiefs of Staff Committee had decided at its meeting on September 20 to start immediate construction of a "factory for producing uranium bombs."[61]

This information was evidently drawn from one of the meetings that the Defence Services Panel of the Cabinet Scientific Advisory Committee held to discuss the Maud Report.[62] Eight days later Gorskii informed Moscow Center about the Scientific Advisory Committee's report to the War Cabinet; Gorskii had received a copy of this report. The Soviet government now knew that Britain had decided to build an atomic bomb, that British scientists estimated that it would take between two and five years to do this, and that Britain had decided to build a gaseous diffusion separation plant in North America.[63] It also had important details about the methods the British were intending to use to obtain uranium-235 and to build a bomb.

The source of this information was almost certainly John Cairncross, the "Fifth Man" of the "Cambridge Five," who had been recruited as a Soviet agent by Guy Burgess while he was an undergraduate at Cambridge in the 1930s.[64] Cairncross had entered the Foreign Office, but had then moved to the Treasury. In 1941 he was private secretary to Lord Hankey, Minister without Portfolio in the War Cabinet and chairman of the Cabinet Scientific Advisory Committee.[65] Hankey had chaired the Defence Services Panel that reviewed the work of the Maud Committee. Cairncross would have had access to the material contained in Gorskii's two reports. In his first message Gorskii wrote that he was sending a report from "List" about a meeting chaired by "Boss," who is identified in the document as Hankey. The use of the word "boss" seems to confirm that Cairncross provided Gorskii with the information.

It is not likely that the source was Klaus Fuchs, who also supplied information to Moscow at about this time. Fuchs had been an active communist in Germany, and went to Britain in 1933, at the age of twenty-one, to escape arrest. After completing his PhD in physics at the University of Bristol he worked in Edinburgh for a while. In May 1941 Rudolf Peierls invited him to come to Birmingham and once he had received his security clearance Fuchs began research on the theory of gaseous diffusion; he also did some work on evaluating the critical size and efficiency of an atomic bomb. After the German invasion of the Soviet Union, Fuchs decided to inform the Soviets about the atomic bomb, and before the end of 1941 made contact with Semen Kremer, a military intelligence officer who was secretary to the military attaché at the Soviet embassy in London.[66]

Fuchs had about six meetings with his Soviet control, an experienced agent named Ursula Kuczynski, before leaving for the United States with the British mission to the Manhattan project in December 1943.[67] He handed over all the reports he had written, which dealt mainly with the gaseous diffusion process. He told the Soviet Union that work on isotope separation was being actively pursued in Britain, and that a small pilot unit was being built in North Wales to test the principle of the process. He reported that similar work was being done in the United States and that the two countries were collaborating.[68] Fuchs is unlikely, however, to have been the source of information that Gorskii sent to Moscow in September and October 1941. There is no reason to suppose that he had access to the Maud Report or to the report of the Cabinet Scientific Advisory Committee. Besides, he worked with the GRU, the Chief Intelligence Directorate of the General Staff, not the NKVD. Given the rivalry that existed between these two organizations, it is unlikely that Gorskii, the NKVD resident, transmitted Fuchs's information to Moscow.

The information supplied by Gorskii had no immediate effect on Soviet policy. It arrived in Moscow less than a month before the great panic in the middle of October when most of the Soviet government was evacuated to Kuibyshev and thousands fled the city. The British decision to build an atomic bomb that would not be ready for two to five years doubtless

seemed a great deal less urgent than the effort to stop the Germans from
seizing Moscow in the next few weeks. It is not surprising that the
information about British plans did not have any immediate effect on
Soviet policy.

It was not until March 1942 that the Soviet leaders responded to the
information that was coming from Britain. Beria sent a memorandum to
Stalin and the State Defense Committee recommending that steps be taken
to evaluate this information.[69] Beria's memorandum was based largely on
the Maud Report. Peierls had estimated the critical mass of uranium-235 at
10 kilograms, it said, and Professor Taylor had calculated that this would
produce an explosion equivalent to 1,600 tons of TNT. Work was already
being done on an industrial method for separating the isotopes of uranium,
and Imperial Chemical Industries had estimated that a 1,900-stage separation plant would be needed, which would cost £4.5–5 million. The
memorandum concluded that the British High Command thought that the
problem of the atomic bomb was solved in principle, and that the efforts of
the best scientists and the biggest companies in Britain were being directed
to building an atomic bomb.

Beria recommended two steps. The first was to create an authoritative
Scientific-Consultative body attached to the State Defense Committee.
This should coordinate, study, and direct the research of all Soviet scientists
and research establishments working on the question of the atomic energy
of uranium. The second was to acquaint eminent specialists on a secret basis
with the intelligence materials so that they could assess those materials and
use them in an appropriate way. The memorandum then noted that
Skobel'tsyn, Kapitsa, and Professor Slutskii of the Ukrainian Physicotechnical Institute had worked on nuclear fission. Since none of these three
men had in fact done research on fission, it appears that Beria was better
informed about the British project than about Soviet research.[70]

Beria's memorandum showed that the Soviet government had received
a very full account of the work of the Maud Committee, and of its effect
on British policy. The NKVD had begun to receive intelligence about
American nuclear research in Sepember 1941, but this was not of the same
quality.[71] Beria's memorandum was written in March 1942, a month earlier
than Flerov's letter to Stalin. The Maud Report, besides providing the basis
for the British decision to build an atomic bomb and leading to a speed-up
of American work, also set in motion the consultations that resulted in the
initiation of the Soviet nuclear project.

V

The consultative body that Beria called for does not appear to have been set
up, but the government did consult scientists about the feasibility of an

atomic bomb in the following months, and before the end of 1942 Stalin took the decision to restart nuclear research. This research finally got under way early in 1943. The sequence of events between March 1942 and the beginning of 1943 cannot be established precisely on the basis of existing evidence, but a general picture can be given of the discussions that led to the renewal of nuclear research.

This was a very difficult time for the Soviet Union. Although the German advance had been stopped on the outskirts of Moscow in December 1941, the country was still in mortal danger. Buoyed up by the Red Army's success at Moscow, Stalin launched an ill-advised and poorly coordinated offensive in the early months of 1942, and this soon ground to a halt. The *Wehrmacht* regained the initiative, and in the summer pushed east towards Stalingrad, and south into the Caucasus. Sevastopol' finally fell to German forces at the beginning of July. German forces pressed towards Stalingrad, and on August 23 broke through to the Volga. The atmosphere in Moscow that summer was one of real crisis: Russian civilization seemed now to be in deadly danger.[72] On July 28 Stalin issued his severe Order No. 227 – "Not a step backward!" – which said that the country was in a desperate situation, and forbade any further retreat.[73]

This was the context in which the government consulted scientists, and it evidently affected the advice the scientists gave. In May "government organs" (often a euphemism for the NKVD) asked the Academy of Sciences whether there was any real basis for the practical utilization of atomic energy, and how plausible it was that other countries might be building an atomic bomb. This request was passed on to Khlopin, who gave a cautious assessment, stating that the only evidence that other countries were working on an atomic bomb was the secrecy that had enveloped nuclear research abroad.[74] This reply suggests that he had not been shown the intelligence about the British project.

Other scientists were similarly cautious when they were consulted about indications of German interest in an atomic bomb. In April 1942 a Colonel I.G. Starinov came to see S.A. Balezin, Kaftanov's senior assistant at the Scientific-Technical Council, and gave him a German officer's notebook that had been captured on the southern shore of Taganrog Bay, on the Sea of Azov. The notebook contained a list of materials needed for building an atomic bomb and calculations of the amount of energy that a critical mass of uranium-235 would release. Starinov, an NKVD officer and specialist on mine warfare, had been given the notebook by the staff of the 56th Army but could make nothing of it.[75] Balezin sent translations of the notebook to Aleksandr Leipunskii and to General G.I. Pokrovskii, an explosives expert, asking whether they thought that the Soviet Union should start work on an atomic bomb. Both replied that the Soviet Union should not do so, and Leipunskii wrote that when the country was under such incredible pressure it would be wrong to throw away millions of roubles on something that would take at least ten, and more probably fifteen or twenty years to bear results.[76]

But Flerov's letter to Stalin, which had been passed on to Kaftanov, suggested that Leipunskii and Pokrovskii might be wrong. Kaftanov and Balezin believed that it would be wise, in view of the evidence of German interest in the atomic bomb, to initiate a Soviet nuclear project; evidently they did not know of the intelligence about the British project. Kaftanov recalls that he consulted Ioffe, whom he had known since the late 1920s, and that Ioffe agreed that an atomic bomb was possible in principle. The two men sent a short letter to the State Defense Committee recommending that a nuclear research center be created.[77]

Balezin has given a somewhat different account of these events. He recalls that after receiving the scientists' assessments of the German notebook, he drafted a letter to Stalin in which he said that materials received from military intelligence pointed to intensive nuclear research in Germany and recommended that similar work be started without delay in the Soviet Union. Kaftanov signed the letter, and the two men agreed not to mention the negative reports they had received from the scientists. Two or three days later Kaftanov was summoned by Stalin. There was some opposition to the proposal, but Kaftanov defended it.[78] There was a risk of failure, he acknowledged, and the project might cost 20 or 100 million roubles, but the risk of doing nothing was greater. Stalin agreed to the proposal.[79] It is impossible to assign a precise date to this meeting, but it appears to have taken place before Flerov was summoned to Moscow from the southwestern front in the middle of July. By that time, Flerov has written, the decision to renew nuclear research had already been taken.[80] Flerov and Balezin discussed what should be done. It was evident that a nuclear project could have one of two goals: to build a Soviet bomb, which seemed unrealistic because of the time and effort it would take; or to determine the feasibility of a bomb and the danger that Germany would build one, which could be done relatively quickly and cheaply.[81] In August Flerov went to Kazan' to renew his work on neutron multiplication.[82]

The government continued its consultations with scientists. In the summer or autumn of 1942 Ioffe, Kapitsa, Khlopin, and perhaps Vavilov and Vernadskii too were called to Moscow to discuss the renewal of nuclear research.[83] In the middle of September Kurchatov was brought to Moscow for discussions, probably with Balezin and Kaftanov.[84] One of the main questions to be settled was whom to put in charge. Kaftanov talked to Ioffe, but Ioffe, who was sixty-three, declined on grounds of age and recommended Kurchatov and Alikhanov as candidates for the position.[85] Kurchatov, according to Kaftanov, had the reputation of not being able to concentrate his energies on one project, but was strongly backed by Ioffe. Alikhanov, who was a corresponding member of the Academy, was better known as a physicist. Kurchatov and Alikhanov came to Moscow from Kazan' on October 22. Alikhanov "was dying to take charge of this work," Balezin has written, but Kurchatov "produced on us a very pleasant impression, which cannot be said of Alikhanov."[86] Kaftanov and Balezin recommended Kurchatov for the position.[87]

Before returning to Kazan' at the beginning of December, Kurchatov prepared a memorandum on the renewal of nuclear research and drew up a list of likely participants. Among the first names on that list were Alikhanov, Kikoin, Khariton, and Zel'dovich.[88] Kurchatov traveled to some of the cities to which research institutes had been evacuated, to see who might be available for work on the uranium problem. In Sverdlovsk he visited Kikoin in his laboratory at the Urals Physicotechnical Institute. "Later it became clear," Kikoin recalled, "that he had the mission of sounding out the possibility of drawing me into a new research topic."[89]

Kurchatov returned to Kazan' on December 2, 1942, the day that Enrico Fermi achieved a chain reaction in his nuclear pile in Chicago. Kurchatov was now wearing a beard, which made him look like an Orthodox priest, and when his friends teased him about it he said that he would not shave it off until "Fritz" had been beaten.[90] Henceforth "the beard" (*boroda*) became his nickname. He was undergoing a "profound spiritual reorientation" at the time, according to his friend Anatolii Aleksandrov, who talked to him at length when he returned to Kazan'. His new responsibility weighed heavily on him: he wondered why a more prominent physicist like Ioffe or Kapitsa had not been put in charge, and worried that his own lack of authority as a physicist would hinder the project.[91]

The discussions with Kaftanov did not settle the future of nuclear research or finalize Kurchatov's appointment. In September or October 1942, according to his own recollection, Mikhail Pervukhin, Deputy Premier and People's Commissar of the Chemical Industry, was shown the intelligence material on foreign atomic research by Molotov.[92] Stalin wanted to know, said Molotov, what Pervukhin thought should be done with these reports. Pervukhin recommended that physicists be shown this material and asked their opinion of it. Molotov, however, told Pervukhin to ask the leading physicists what they knew about foreign research, and to find out what research was being done in the Soviet Union; in other words, the scientists were not to be shown the intelligence material.[93]

On January 9, 1943 Kurchatov returned to Moscow. With Alikhanov and Kikoin he now had his first meeting with Pervukhin. Pervukhin's background was very different from Kurchatov's. He had joined the Bolshevik Party in 1919, at the age of fifteen. He had been trained as an electrical engineer, and had risen rapidly in industry during the purges. He was by all accounts an intelligent and competent man. Kurchatov told Pervukhin that nuclear physics pointed to "the possibility of realizing an instantaneous chain reaction in uranium-235 with the release of enormous

energy." It was possible, he said, that German scientists were trying to build
an atomic bomb, and that the Nazis might therefore get their hands on a
weapon of terrible destructive power. The scientists at the Physicotechnical
Institute had discussed this danger more than once among themselves, he
said, and were worried by the secrecy that had descended on nuclear
research in Germany. He supported Flerov's proposal to restart work on
the uranium problem, but could not judge whether it was possible to do so
in the difficult wartime conditions.[94]

Pervukhin asked Kurchatov, Alikhanov, and Kikoin to write him a
memorandum about the organization of research on nuclear physics, isotope separation and nuclear piles. The three men completed the memorandum quickly and Pervukhin passed it on to Molotov with the
recommendation that the physicists' proposals be taken seriously. A few
days later Pervukhin and Kurchatov were instructed to work out measures
for renewing research, and Kurchatov was asked to write a memorandum
about the feasibility of an atomic bomb and the length of time it would take
to build one.[95]

It was about this time that Kurchatov first met Molotov, who now made
the final decision about Kurchatov's appointment as scientific director of
the nuclear project. "I was entrusted with responsibility for this research,"
Molotov later recalled,

with finding the kind of person who would be able to realise the creation of an
atomic bomb. The Chekists [i.e. the NKVD] gave me a list of reliable physicists
who could be depended on, and I made the choice. I summoned Kapitsa, the
Academician. He said we were not ready for that, and the atomic bomb was not
a weapon for this war, but a matter for the future. Ioffe was asked – his attitude to
this was also unclear. In short, I was left with the youngest, Kurchatov, who was
not known to anyone. . . . I summoned him, we had a talk, he made a good
impression on me.[96]

At the suggestion of Pervukhin and Kurchatov, the State Defense Committee adopted a special resolution in February 1943 on the organization of
research into the utilization of atomic energy. Pervukhin and Kaftanov
were made responsible for supervising the project and providing support
for it. A new laboratory was to be established in which all nuclear research
would be concentrated; there were to be no parallel institutions. On March
10 Kurchatov was confirmed as scientific director of the project.[97]

The uranium problem had now been put in the hands of the Leningrad
physicists. Khlopin had been consulted in 1942, but it is clear that he and
Vernadskii were unhappy with the way things were going. "How are
things with uranium? . . . What state is the Uranium Commission in? It
seems to me that it ought now to act," Vernadskii wrote to Fersman in
November 1942. "Khlopin has written to me that Ioffe went to the
government with some kind of memorandum in this connection, completely ignoring the Academy's effort."[98]

On January 15, 1943 Khlopin sent a letter full of hurt pride to Kaftanov and to Ioffe, from whom he had learned of the State Defense Committee's decision to renew work on the uranium problem. Khlopin complained that he had received no definite instructions from Ioffe or from the State Defense Committee, and insisted that "the solution of the task placed by the GKO [State Defense Committee] before the Academy of Sciences cannot be given without the basic participation in this work of the Radium Institute of the USSR Academy of Sciences, which has been entrusted to me, and of myself personally."[99] He outlined the research that he thought was needed. The central problem, in his view, was isotope separation, and he claimed for the Radium Institute a major role in carrying out this work.

Vernadskii too was much exercised about the uranium problem. He evidently did not know of the measures now being taken, for on March 13, 1943 he sent a memorandum to the president of the Academy, arguing that the Uranium Commission should be revived in view of the possible military uses of uranium, and because the country would need new sources of energy for economic reconstruction after the war. He saw signs, he wrote, that work on atomic energy was being done by the Soviet Union's allies as well as by its enemies. It was a matter of the "first state importance" to direct the Uranium Commission's activity to finding reserves of uranium. "The state of our knowledge," he wrote, "is the same as it was in 1935. Our huge bureaucratic apparatus has proved powerless."[100] Two days later he wrote to the Academy president again, complaining that "unfortunately Ioffe does not understand or pretends not to understand that for the use of atomic energy it is first necessary to find uranium ore in sufficient quantity. I think that this problem may be solved in one summer campaign. So far as I know, Fersman and Khlopin are of the same opinion."[101]

The decision to start a nuclear project was taken while the battle of Stalingrad was being fought. When Kurchatov was called to Moscow on October 22, the Red Army was trying desperately to hold on to the city. On November 19 the Red Army launched its counteroffensive, with the aim of encircling and trapping the German forces at Stalingrad. When Kurchatov went to Moscow on January 9, 1943 for his meeting with Pervukhin, the Red Army was tightening the noose, and the German forces surrendered on February 2. Stalingrad demonstrated the resilience of the Soviet state, the courage of the Red Army's troops, and the skill of its commanders. There were still hard battles and bloody campaigns to be fought, but the *Wehrmacht* no longer seemed invincible, and confidence in Allied victory grew.

The Soviet plan for the counteroffensive at Stalingrad carried the codename "Uran", which is usually translated as "Uranus" but can equally well be translated as "uranium." One Soviet writer has described it as "hardly accidental" that the counteroffensive should carry this name, given that it was planned at about the same time as the decision was taken to restart work on the uranium problem.[102] Whether accidental or not, the connection between the two events is not entirely fanciful. The victory at Stalingrad, by virtue of its contribution to the defeat of Nazi Germany, marked the beginning of the Soviet Union's emergence as a world power, while the nuclear project was later to provide the Soviet Union with one of the key instruments, and one of the most potent symbols, of power in the postwar world.

What was the connection between the war and the bomb in Stalin's decision? The consultations in 1942 showed that many scientists were skeptical about the advisability of starting a nuclear project, on the grounds that a Soviet atomic bomb could not be built in time to affect the outcome of the war. In January 1943 Kurchatov spoke to Pervukhin of the danger that Germany might build an atomic bomb, but he also expressed doubts about the possibility of even renewing research in Soviet wartime conditions. The small project Stalin initiated in 1943 could not lead quickly to a Soviet bomb. It is possible, though improbable, that Stalin believed otherwise in 1942. But certainly by the spring of 1943, when the fortunes of war had turned, it is extremely unlikely that Stalin thought a Soviet bomb could affect the outcome of the war with Germany.

Besides, the Soviet Union was receiving intelligence about the German atomic project, doubtless from sources in Germany, but also from its agents in Britain. British intelligence had an excellent source on the German project in Paul Rosbaud, a science editor at the Springer publishing house in Berlin, who supplied reliable information about the state of German nuclear research in 1942.[103] By the spring of 1943 the British government, after receiving confirmation of Rosbaud's report, began, in the words of the official history of British wartime intelligence, "to feel increasingly reassured in relation to Germany's nuclear research programme."[104] Klaus Fuchs became involved in 1942 in making assessments of German progress in nuclear research. Before Fuchs left for the United States at the end of 1943, the information that he transmitted to Moscow had "confirmed," in the words of the KGB officer who was Fuchs's control in London after the war, "that, first, the corresponding research in Hitler's Germany had reached a dead-end; second, that the USA and Britain were already building industrial facilities to make atomic bombs."[105] This suggests that in 1943 Stalin should have known enough about the progress of research in other countries not to regard the Soviet atomic project as crucial to the outcome of the war with Germany. The project he started is best understood as a rather small hedge against future uncertainties.

VI

In February 1943 Kurchatov was not sure that an atomic bomb could be built or, if it could, how long it would take. He told Molotov that there was a great deal that was unclear to him. "Then I decided to give him our intelligence materials," recalled Molotov; "our intelligence people had done a very important thing. Kurchatov sat in my office in the Kremlin for several days studying those materials. Some time after the battle of Stalingrad, in 1943."[106] There is no evidence that any of the other nuclear scientists had seen this material. Khlopin's letter to Ioffe in January 1943 suggests that he had not been shown it; so too does Vernadskii's correspondence. The government had apparently consulted the scientists in 1942 without letting them see material that had a crucial bearing on the decision that was being discussed.

Kurchatov studied the intelligence materials at the beginning of March, after his return from Murmansk where he had been sent for some weeks by the Navy to help with demagnetizing the ships of the Northern Fleet.[107] On March 7 he wrote an extensive memorandum for Pervukhin about the material he was shown. This memorandum, which he wrote by hand for reasons of secrecy, reveals what he learned from the intelligence material at the very outset of the project.[108]

Kurchatov was very impressed by what he saw, all of which concerned Britain. It had "huge, inestimable significance for our state and science," he wrote.

On one hand, the material has shown the seriousness and intensity of research in Britain on the uranium problem; on the other, it has made it possible to obtain very important guidelines for our research, to bypass many very labor-intensive phases of working out the problem and to learn about new scientific and technical ways of solving it.

Kurchatov discussed the material under three headings, the first of which was isotope separation. Soviet scientists had concluded, he wrote, that the centrifuge would be the most effective method of separation. The British preference for gaseous diffusion was unexpected, but the information about British work would make it necessary to include gaseous diffusion in the Soviet plan along with the centrifuge.

The material on gaseous diffusion, noted Kurchatov, provided a very thorough, detailed analysis of all the stages of the process proposed by Simon. This work had not yet been checked by Soviet theoreticians, but it appeared to have been done by a group of major scientists. It would be possible to reconstruct completely the plans for the machine and the factory on the basis of the material that had been received. This would make it possible "to bypass the initial stage, to begin here in the Union a new and very important direction for resolving the problem of isotope separation."[109]

British research, Kurchatov wrote, showed that thermal diffusion would not be very effective for isotope separation because it required enormous amounts of energy; this was confirmed by a study Zel'dovich had just done at Kurchatov's request. The British had concluded that the centrifuge method would not be effective for the separation of large quantities of uranium-235; but a final conclusion could be drawn, Kurchatov noted, only after the apparatus now being developed by Lange's laboratory had been tested. The material indicated that the mass-spectrographic and evaporation methods were unsuitable for separating uranium isotopes; this was being explored by the work of Artsimovich and Kornfel'd. Kurchatov listed a number of technical details about Simon's machine that it would be important to know.[110]

The second section dealt with the "problem of nuclear explosion and burning." Here the most interesting thing, in Kurchatov's view, was the confirmation that a chain reaction was possible in a mixture of uranium and heavy water. Soviet scientists, wrote Kurchatov, had come to the conclusion that this would be impossible. The problem was not the theoretical calculations done by Khariton and Zel'dovich, but the cross-section data they had to work with.[111] Because they lacked powerful cyclotrons and large quantities of heavy water, Soviet physicists had been unable to measure the thermal-neutron capture cross-section of heavy hydrogen. Now the experiments which Halban and Kowarski had done in Cambridge indicated that a chain reaction could take place in a uranium–heavy water system. The experimental method, wrote Kurchatov, was superior to calculations that involved several intermediate steps. Soviet physicists were not in a position to repeat the Halban–Kowarski experiment because there were only 2–3 kilograms of heavy water in the country. It was important therefore to know what further work Halban and Kowarski had done, and in particular to know whether they had gone to the United States, as the intelligence material suggested they would do, and whether they had done experiments in a laboratory with large supplies of heavy water.

In this section Kurchatov pointed to two other issues that were to prove important for the Soviet project. The first had to do with the design of a nuclear "boiler."[112] All the published research, Kurchatov noted, had been based on homogeneous mixtures of uranium and moderator. Might not fission be more likely, he asked, if the uranium were distributed in the moderator in blocks of an appropriate size? It would be desirable to know what kind of system Halban and Kowarski had used, and what kind of system was being used in the United States. This is the first evidence in Soviet writings of the idea of a heterogeneous system, which had occurred to Fermi, to Kowarski, and to German scientists in 1939.

The second issue was to prove more significant, because it suggested an alternative route to the atomic bomb. "In part of the material devoted to the problem of nuclear explosion and burning," wrote Kurchatov, ". . . there are very important remarks about using as the material for a bomb the element with mass number 239 which ought to be obtained in a uranium boiler as a result of the absorption of neutrons by uranium-238."[113] Kurchatov had been aware of the possibility that a nuclear chain reaction might produce a transuranic element that was fissionable. Soviet physicists had been very interested in the June 1940 paper by McMillan and Abelson reporting on the production of element 93. McMillan and Abelson had written that this element would decay to form an isotope of element 94, with mass number 239. The intelligence material indicated that this element might be used instead of uranium-235 in a bomb.

The third section of Kurchatov's memorandum dealt with the physics of the fission process. Here there was less material of interest. Kurchatov was gratified to discover, however, that Frisch had confirmed the phenomenon of spontaneous fission, which had been discovered by Flerov and Petrzhak. Because of spontaneous fission, Kurchatov wrote, it is impossible to keep the whole "bomb charge of uranium" in a single place. The uranium has to be divided into two parts, which at the moment of explosion have to be brought together with a high relative velocity. "This means of setting off a uranium bomb is considered in the material," Kurchatov noted, "and is also not new for Soviet physicists. An analogous approach was proposed by our physicist G.N. Flerov; he calculated the necessary velocity for bringing the two halves of the bomb together, and the results he obtained are in good agreement with those in the material."[114]

Kurchatov concluded by saying that the material he had seen had forced him to reconsider his views on many questions and to decide on three new directions of research: isotope separation by gaseous diffusion; a chain reaction in a mixture of uranium and heavy water; investigation of the characteristics of element 94. The material showed that the time needed for solving the uranium problem was significantly less than Soviet scientists, who did not know what was being done abroad, had thought. He had the impression, based on a careful study of the material, that it was genuine, and not designed to mislead Soviet scientists. This was a particularly important point, he noted, because Soviet scientists, owing to the lack of a technical base, were not in a position to check many of the results. Although there were some doubtful conclusions in the material, he wrote, these appeared to be the fault of the British scientists, not of the source.

Just over two weeks later, on March 22, Kurchatov wrote another memorandum to Pervukhin. This is a crucial document because it marks the point at which Kurchatov decided that the plutonium path to the bomb was the most promising one. The intelligence material he had seen made occasional reference to the possibility that a uranium boiler might produce material that could be used in a bomb instead of uranium-235. "Bearing these remarks in mind," he wrote, "I attentively looked through the last of the works published on transuranic elements (eka-rhenium-239 and eka-osmium-239) [i.e. elements 93 and 94, or neptunium and plutonium] by the Americans in *Physical Review* and was able to determine a <u>new</u> direction in the solution of the whole uranium problem. . . . <u>The prospects of this direction are unusually attractive</u>."[115] If eka-osmium possessed the same qualities as uranium-235, Kurchatov wrote, it could be produced in a uranium boiler and used as the active material in an "eka-osmium bomb." In that case it would be possible to avoid the whole problem of isotope separation.

This path to the bomb would make sense only if eka-osmium-239 were really analogous to uranium-235. No work had been done in the Soviet Union on elements 93 and 94, Kurchatov wrote. Everything that was known had been done by McMillan at Berkeley, using the world's most powerful cyclotron, and McMillan's last publiction had been in *Physical Review* on July 15, 1940. Kurchatov wrote that Soviet scientists would not be able to study the qualities of eka-osmium before the summer of 1944, when the Soviet cyclotrons would be restored and started up. It was therefore very important to learn what was known in the United States about elements 93 and 94. Kurchatov listed four key questions – does element 94 fission with fast or slow neutrons; if it does, what is its fission cross-section (separately for fast and slow neutrons); does spontaneous fission take place in element 94, and what is the half-life with respect to this process; what transformations does element 94 undergo over time? Kurchatov provided a list of the laboratories in the United States where the corresponding work might have been done. The Radiation Laboratory at Berkeley stood at the top of the list.[116] Pervukhin sent Kurchatov's memoranda to the NKVD. Gaik Ovakimian, deputy chief of the foreign department of the NKVD's Chief Directorate for State Security, was instructed to pass on Kurchatov's questions to agents abroad.[117]

Kurchatov's two memoranda of March 1943 are of critical importance in the history of the Soviet atomic project. They show that Kurchatov had already begun to organize research, assigning particular questions to his colleagues to study, especially on the methods of isotope separation. They also show how Soviet research was hampered by the lack of supplies (uranium, heavy water) and equipment (the cyclotron). In these memoranda Kurchatov can be seen choosing the path that will lead to the first Soviet bomb. It became clear to him in March 1943 that the plutonium path to the bomb might well get round the terribly complex problem of isotope separation. He did not, however, know yet of Fermi's success in Chicago, for he wrote in his memorandum of March 22 that it was still unclear whether a natural uranium-graphite system (which is what Fermi had built) was possible.

The tone of Kurchatov's memoranda is revealing. There is no gloating about obtaining information that Western governments were trying to keep secret; nor is there any bitterness at the fact that the war had speeded up research in Britain and the United States, but slowed it down in the Soviet Union. Kurchatov does not attempt to belittle the achievements of British and American scientists, or to magnify the work of his own colleagues. His excitement at learning of what was being done abroad comes through, along with his admiration for the quality of the research. The memoranda create the impression of an intelligent man who was able to get to the key questions without letting personal feelings interfere.

At about this time Molotov asked Kurchatov, "Well, how are the materials?" Molotov did not understand anything in the intelligence material, he later said, but he knew that it had come from good, reliable sources. Kurchatov replied: "Wonderful materials, they fill in just what we are lacking." Molotov recalled that he introduced Kurchatov to Stalin. Kurchatov "received every kind of support," Molotov later claimed, "and we began to be guided by him. He organized a group, and it turned out well."[118] But this claim raises two questions: what kind of priority did the nuclear project now receive? What understanding did the Soviet leaders have of the significance of the atomic bomb?

CHAPTER FIVE

Getting Started

I

ON APRIL 12, 1943, following the decision of the State Defense Committee to initiate a nuclear project, the Academy of Sciences issued a secret instruction setting up a new laboratory for Kurchatov. This was known as Laboratory No. 2 because the authorities did not want its name to reveal its function.[1] Although it was formally part of the Academy of Sciences, Laboratory No. 2 was in effect subordinate to Pervukhin and to the Council of People's Commissars. Pervukhin was the government official with whom Kurchatov now had most dealings; Kaftanov faded into the background.

Kurchatov wrote a memorandum on "The Proton, the Electron and the Neutron" for Pervukhin, to give him a basic understanding of atomic structure.[2] In the following month he wrote a longer report on the "Uranium Problem" which outlined the way in which the discovery of radioactivity had led to greater understanding of atomic structure, and described the development of particle accelerators and their role in nuclear physics.[3] This report also reviewed the state of knowledge about nuclear chain reactions in June 1941, when Soviet research had been brought to a halt. In this report Kurchatov made only brief reference to the atomic bomb, writing that a fast-neutron chain reaction in a block of uranium-235 would lead to a "very powerful explosion." But this would depend, he wrote, on the "solution of the unbelievably complex technical task of separating a large quantity of this isotope from ordinary uranium."[4] At least several kilograms of pure uranium-235 would be needed; estimates of the critical mass varied, he noted, from two to forty kilograms. Kurchatov referred briefly in his report to element 94, but he did not mention that it might be used instead of uranium-235 as the active material in a bomb.[5]

Kurchatov wrote this report after reviewing the intelligence from Britain. The report was strongly influenced by what he had learned, for it devoted special attention to the different possible types of nuclear pile, in which element 94 might be produced.[6] Kurchatov did not make this latter

point, however; he made no direct reference to the information he had
obtained from intelligence. This suggests that his report was intended as a
primer not only for Pervukhin, but for others in the government too. Very
few people had access to, or knowledge of, the intelligence material. After
writing his March 7 memorandum, Kurchatov gave his rough notes to
Pervukhin's assistant, A.I. Vasin, to be destroyed.[7] In the coming years he
had to obtain special permission to show any of the intelligence reports
from abroad to his fellow scientists. At the same time he had to make use
of the information he had acquired, without letting his colleagues know
where it had come from. This he did by proposing promising lines of
research, and by suggesting ideas in meetings and seminars. In his March
22 memorandum, for example, he wrote that no one knew he was writing
it, but that Alikhanov and Kikoin were familiar with the arguments it
contained.[8]

Kurchatov met with his closest colleagues – Khariton, Flerov,
Zel'dovich, Kikoin, Alikhanov, and Leipunskii – in the "Moskva" hotel in
Moscow, to decide upon the main lines of research.[9] He himself took
charge of the design and construction of an experimental pile which would
produce samples of element 94 for chemical and physical analysis.[10] The
first decision he had to make was what kind of pile to build. In his April
report to Pervukhin he estimated that 15 metric tons of heavy water and 2
metric tons of natural uranium would be needed for a heavy water pile, and
500–1,000 metric tons of graphite and 50–100 metric tons of uranium for
a uranium-graphite system.[11] By the beginning of July he had chosen
graphite as the moderator, even though a heavy-water pile would require
far less uranium. The main reason for this choice was that graphite would
be easier to obtain than heavy water: the Soviet Union had electrode plants
where graphite was produced, whereas the heavy water pilot plant, which
had been planned before the war at the nitrogen plant in Chirchik in
Tajikistan, had not been completed. Production of heavy water would
have to be organized, and this could be done only "in the very distant
future."[12] Kurchatov took direct charge of the work on the uranium-
graphite system, with one of his former students, I.S. Panasiuk, as his chief
assistant.[13] The task of building a heavy water pile was assigned to
Alikhanov, who was reluctant to work under Kurchatov; work on this
system did not begin in earnest until after the war.[14]

Kurchatov lacked the uranium he needed for experiments. All he could
do was ask the theoreticians in Laboratory No. 2 to investigate the design
of a pile. Isai Gurevich and Isaak Pomeranchuk worked out a theory for a
heterogeneous pile in which uranium lumps are distributed in the graphite
moderator in a lattice configuration.[15] This arrangement decreases the
chance of resonance absorption by uranium-238 because neutrons are less
likely to encounter uranium atoms while they are slowing down and
particularly vulnerable to such absorption. Zel'dovich and Pomeranchuk

developed a theory of the moderation and absorption of neutrons in graphite, and on this basis devised a method for measuring the purity of graphite.[16] This work was done in 1943. In January 1944 Pomeranchuk developed a theory of exponential experiments in which key measurements could be made even before the whole pile was assembled.[17]

Kurchatov knew that it would take years to create the experimental pile. In March 1943 he asked Leonid Nemenov, who had worked on the cyclotron at Ioffe's institute before the war, to build a cyclotron and to obtain trace quantities of element 94 as quickly as possible. He gave Nemonov sixteen months to do this, and sent him and P. Glazunov, an engineer from Ioffe's institute, to Leningrad to retrieve the generator which had been built for the *Fiztekh* cyclotron.[18] Armed with letters from Pervukhin to Andrei Zhdanov, the Leningrad party secretary, Nemenov and Glazunov flew to Leningrad with over one hundred parcels from colleagues for relatives in the besieged city. The worst of the siege was now over, for in January 1943 the Red Army had managed to open up a precarious rail line from the city to what Leningraders called "the mainland." But the people of Leningrad had suffered terribly and had been greatly weakened by hunger.

Nemenov and Glazunov collected the parts for the cyclotron. They prepared the generator and rectifier for shipment, and dug up copper pipes and brass plates that had been buried in the grounds of the institute when the staff had been evacuated to Kazan'. They found the 75-ton electromagnet at the Elektrosila plant, which was only three kilometers from the front line. With the help of soldiers assigned to them by the military command, they loaded all the equipment on to two goods wagons for transport to Moscow. Since the newly opened railway line passed through an area that came under German fire, Nemenov and Glazunov left the city by plane.[19]

On his return to Moscow, Nemenov began to assemble the cyclotron. There was still much to do: the acceleration chamber had to be designed and built; a cooling system had to be devised for the magnet windings; forgings had to be made for the magnet at the "Hammer and Sickle" plant in Moscow. But at last the assembly was completed and the cyclotron produced a deuteron beam at 2 a.m. on September 25, 1944 – two months later than Kurchatov had wanted. Nemenov telephoned Kurchatov, who was at a meeting with Boris Vannikov, the People's Commissar for Munitions. Kurchatov came to see the cyclotron in operation and afterwards took the cyclotron group back to his house for champagne. On the following day the irradiation of uranyl nitrate in the cyclotron began and continued until December 1945.[20]

The irradiated material was sent to the laboratory of Kurchatov's younger brother Boris, who had joined Laboratory No. 2 in the middle of 1943.[21] Boris Kurchatov managed to separate element 93 in the first half of 1944, and then turned his attention to element 94. He placed a flask with uranium peroxide in a barrel of water, which acted as a moderator, and in the center of the flask he put a radium-beryllium neutron source, which he left there for about three months. Then he reprocessed the irradiated uranium and separated a preparation with alpha-activity. This was how the first trace quantities of element 94 were obtained, in October 1944. Not until 1946 did Boris Kurchatov separate the first plutonium (as element 94 was now called) from uranium irradiated in the cyclotron.[22]

Kurchatov did not assign the task of chemical separation to his brother alone. He faced the problem of mending his relations with Khlopin, and decided to draw him into the project by asking the Radium Institute to develop a method for separating element 94 from irradiated uranium.[23] Kurchatov did not "try to settle accounts" with Khlopin, according to Flerov, but always showed him "signs of attention, respect for his knowledge and authority . . . Kurchatov always underlined Khlopin's services as the creator of our radiochemistry." Kurchatov here showed his skill in dealing with people, and the animosity between the two men disappeared.[24]

Isotope separation was included in the initial plan for Laboratory No. 2, but little was achieved during the war. Kikoin was made responsible for this part of the project.[25] He organized research into various methods. Lange continued his work on the centrifuge and in 1944 Kikoin and he built a 5-meter-long experimental centrifuge at Laboratory No. 2. This was noisy, however, and broke at the resonance frequency of rotation. Lange moved to Sverdlovsk, and Kikoin began to focus on the gaseous diffusion method. At the end of 1943 Kurchatov asked Anatolii Aleksandrov to organize research on thermal diffusion. In 1944 Artsimovich joined the laboratory to head the work on electromagnetic separation.[26]

Laboratory No. 2 grew slowly. Kurchatov had been given 100 Moscow passes, since special permission was required to live in Moscow; he also had the right to demobilize people from the Red Army.[27] At first the laboratory was housed in the Seismological Institute on Pyzhevskii Lane in the center of Moscow. It soon took over part of another institute on Bol'shaia Kaluzhskaia as well. As the laboratory grew, Kurchatov looked for a place where it could expand. He found a suitable site in Pokrovskoe-Streshnevo, to the north-west of the city, close to the Moscow river. Work had already started there on a new building for the All-Union Institute of Experimental Medicine, and since this area was then outside the city there was plenty of room to grow. Kurchatov took over the unfinished institute, buildings were added, and in April 1944 the laboratory moved into its new premises.[28] There were 74 people working in Laboratory No. 2 on April 25, 1944. Twenty-five of these were scientists, among them Alikhanov, Kikoin, Pomeranchuk, Flerov, Nemenov, Boris Kurchatov, V.A. Davidenko, and the mathematician S.L. Sobolev.[29] These were mainly people with whom Kurchatov had worked before.

When he had been asked to take charge of the "uranium problem," Kurchatov wondered whether he had enough authority as a scientist for this position. Elections to the Academy were to be held in September 1943. When it became clear that Alikhanov would be voted into the vacancy for a physicist, Ioffe and Kaftanov asked the government to create an additional vacancy for Kurchatov. The new position was created, and Kurchatov became an Academician in September 1943, without passing through the intermediate state of corresponding membership.[30] Kurchatov's election was opposed by some senior physicists such as Frenkel' and Tamm, and caused bewilderment more generally: "it seemed that his scientific merits were not so great that he should be elected a full member of the Academy," one physicist recalled in his memoirs.[31]

II

The most serious problem for Kurchatov was to obtain uranium and graphite for his pile. At the beginning of 1943 he had only a "motley selection" of small quantities of uranium, "not of the highest purity, in the form of pieces of uranium and powdered uranium and its oxides."[32] This was far less than the 50–100 metric tons that he had estimated, in his April memorandum to Pervukhin, he would need for a uranium-graphite pile. He would have 1–2 metric tons of uranium at his disposal in 1943, he wrote in July 1943 to Pervukhin, but it was quite unclear how long it would take to accumulate 50 metric tons.[33]

Pervukhin and Kurchatov brought Khlopin to Moscow to report on the country's known reserves, which were insignificant by comparison with what Kurchatov needed.[34] When Fersman had reported to the Uranium Commission in November 1940 on the expedition that he and Khlopin had made to Central Asia, he had said that 10 metric tons of uranium could be extracted each year by 1942–3; at that rate it would take five to ten years for Kurchatov to obtain the uranium he needed for his pile.[35] In 1943, after Khlopin's report, the government instructed the People's Commissariat of Non-Ferrous Metallurgy to obtain 100 metric tons of pure uranium metal as soon as possible.[36] This order had little effect; "as soon as possible" meant in practice low priority, since high-priority orders would have to be fulfilled by a specific date.

In May 1943 Kurchatov asked N.P. Suzhin and Zinaida Ershova at the Institute of Rare and Fine Metals to provide him with various uranium compounds and uranium metal, and in every case his requirements for chemical purity were unprecedentedly high. The first pure ingot of uranium metal, about one kilogram, was produced in Ershova's laboratory at the end of 1944, with a commission headed by Pervukhin in attendance.[37] Kurchatov was still a long way from obtaining the uranium he needed.

In August 1943 Kurchatov asked A.I. Vasin, Pervukhin's assistant, for help in obtaining graphite.[38] He soon received 3.5 metric tons of graphite from the Moscow Electrode Factory.[39] Graphite has to be extraordinarily pure to be used as a moderator, and tests soon showed that impurities of ash and boron in the graphite made its capture cross-section too big by orders of magnitude. When Kurchatov pressed the factory to eliminate the impurities, he was told he was asking for the impossible. With the help of physicists from Laboratory No. 2 the factory developed a suitable production process. In a tent on the grounds of the laboratory tests were done to assess the purity of successive batches of graphite. Only by the end of the summer of 1945 did graphite of the right purity for a nuclear pile begin to become available.[40]

At the end of January 1943 the Soviet government sent a request to the Lend-Lease Administration in Washington, DC for 10 kilograms of uranium metal, and 100 kilograms each of uranium oxide and uranium nitrate. General Groves approved this request, for fear that refusal would alert the Soviet Union to the American project or excite curiosity in Washington. The uranium compounds – but not the metal – were flown to the Soviet Union early in April.[41] Early in 1943 the Soviet Purchasing Commission submitted another request, this time for about 220 kilograms each of uranium oxide and uranium nitrate. This order was flown to Alaska for transhipment to the Soviet Union in June 1943.[42] In April 1943 General Groves granted the Soviet Purchasing Commission an export license for 10 kilograms of uranium metal. The Soviet commission was not able to find what it wanted and had to be content with acquiring one kilogram of impure metal at the beginning of 1945. A later request by the Soviet Commission for eight long tons each of uranium chloride and uranium nitrate was turned down.[43] In November 1943 the Soviet Union acquired 1,000 grams of heavy water in the United States, and a further 100 grams in February 1945.[44]

The amounts of uranium acquired from the United States would have been useful for experiments in Laboratory No. 2.[45] There is, however, no evidence that this uranium ever reached Kurchatov.[46] Certainly Kurchatov's need for uranium remained urgent. V.V. Goncharov, a chemical engineer who joined Laboratory No. 2 in 1943, has written that in 1945 the laboratory had only 90 kilograms of uranium oxide and 218 kilograms of metallic powder, and that these had been brought from Germany.[47] It is possible that the Soviet government acquired the uranium from the United States for the production of steel alloys for arms, and not for the atomic project.

In 1943 Dmitrii Shcherbakov, who had been a member of the Uranium Commission, wrote a memorandum on Soviet uranium deposits and the measures needed to exploit them.[48] He noted that the deposits in Central Asia had been inadequately studied. The first thing to do, therefore, was to explore them intensively and to begin mining. Organizing the search for uranium in the rest of the country was more difficult. Shcherbakov was certain that radioactive minerals could be found outside Central Asia, but

Soviet geologists had no criteria for deciding where to look. The only way was to take account of known uranium deposits at home and abroad, and to identify the kinds of geological conditions in which uranium might be found. On the basis of a survey of existing uranium deposits, Shcherbakov drew up a list of guidelines for uranium prospecting.

In 1943 some of the Academy of Sciences' branches were instructed to look for radioactive ores, and new finds of uranium were reported in Kirgizia in December.[49] On October 2, 1943 a commission organized by the government's Committee on Geological Affairs met to review plans for uranium exploration in 1944. Vernadskii, who had now returned to Moscow, took part in this meeting, along with Khlopin and Vinogradov. A permanent consultative bureau, with Vernadskii and Khlopin among its members, was set up to coordinate exploration and research, and to make recommendations for expanding the supply of uranium.[50] Progress was slow, however, for in May 1944 Vernadskii wrote to the head of the Committee on Geological Affairs to complain that he had "not received from you, in spite of your promise, news of the results of the pumping-out of Tiuia-Muiun. Money was allocated in sufficient quantity, there is ore, why the delay? This ought to have been done long ago"[51] All of this suggests that uranium exploration was receiving low priority from the government. In 1944 Shcherbakov advanced the idea of "exploration on a broad front," but it was not until September 1945 that field expeditions began full-scale exploration, and then they concentrated on the Fergana Valley in Central Asia.[52]

Kurchatov was frustrated by the slow progress of the project. On September 29, 1944 — four days after the cyclotron had gone into operation — he wrote to Beria to express his unhappiness at the way things were going. The letter is worth quoting in full:

In the letter Comrade M.G. Pervukin and I wrote to you, we informed you of the state of work on the uranium problem and of the colossal development of this work abroad.

In the course of the last month I have been making a preliminary study of new, very extensive materials (about 3,000 pages of text) concerning the uranium problem.

Studying [these materials] has shown once again that abroad there has been created around this problem a concentration of scientific and engineering-technical forces on a scale unseen in the history of world science, and that this concentration has already achieved the most valuable results.

But in our country, in spite of great progress in developing the work on uranium in 1943–1944, the state of affairs remains completely unsatisfactory.

The situation with raw materials and questions of separation is particularly bad. The research at Laboratory No. 2 lacks an adequate material-technical base. Research at many organizations that are cooperating with us is not developing as it should because of the lack of unified leadership, and because the significance of the problem is underestimated in these organizations.

Knowing that you are exceptionally busy I nevertheless decided, in view of the historic significance of the uranium problem, to bother you and to ask you to give instructions for the work to be organized in a way that corresponds to the possibilities and significance of our great state in world culture.[53]

Kurchatov was clearly unhappy with the support he was receiving from Molotov. If he found that other organizations would not cooperate with him effectively, that was because the Soviet leadership was not treating the uranium problem as a matter of high priority. Kurchatov was especially distressed by the gap between the Soviet project and the Manhattan project. He was in a better position than anyone else to understand how wide this gap really was.

III

At the end of 1942 Peter Ivanov, an official at the Soviet consulate in San Francisco, asked George Eltenton, a British engineer who had worked at the Institute of Chemical Physics in Leningrad and was now living in the Bay Area, if he could obtain information about the work of the Radiation Laboratory in Berkeley.[54] Eltenton sought help from Haakon Chevalier, a close friend of J. Robert Oppenheimer, one of the leading Berkeley physicists (though not at the Radiation Laboratory), who had just been appointed to head the Los Alamos laboratory. Early in 1943 Chevalier had a brief conversation with Oppenheimer, in which he told him that Eltenton had means of getting technical information to the Soviet Union. Oppenheimer made it quite clear that he would have nothing to do with such transactions.[55]

Ivanov tried to obtain information about the research at the Radiation Laboratory. The counterintelligence corps of the Manhattan project suspected several scientists of passing information to the Soviet consulate, and arranged for them to be dismissed from the laboratory or drafted by the Army and placed in nonsensitive posts. It brought no charges, however.[56] Further evidence of Soviet espionage was discovered in the course of 1943 and 1944. At the Metallurgical Laboratory in Chicago employees suspected of providing the Soviet Union with information were summarily dismissed, but once again no charges were brought. The counterintelligence corps also feared that information had been passed on about the design of the gaseous diffusion isotope separation plant at Oak Ridge.[57]

In July 1943 Kurchatov wrote another memorandum to Pervukhin about intelligence on the Manhattan project. It is evident from this memorandum that the Soviet Union had received extensive information about the progress of the United States effort. Kurchatov reviewed a list of 286 reports on various topics: methods of isotope separation; the uranium–heavy water and uranium-graphite piles; transuranic elements; and the chemistry of uranium. The information obtained from the United States was not very detailed, however, and not as complete as the reports from Britain in 1941–2. "These materials . . . provide only a short exposition of general research results," wrote Kurchatov about the intelligence on the uranium-graphite pile, "and do not contain very important technical details." "It is extremely necessary," he wrote, "to obtain detailed technical material on this system from America."[58] It is not apparent from this memorandum whether Kurchatov knew in July 1943 about Fermi's success in achieving a self-sustaining chain reaction in a uranium-graphite pile in Chicago the previous December.

In the same memorandum Kurchatov commented on the intelligence about American research on elements 93 and 94. This, he wrote, contained fairly detailed information about the physical qualities of the two elements, including the slow-neutron fission cross-section of element 94. There was, moreover, a reference to the work of Glenn Seaborg and Emilio Segrè at Berkeley on the fast-neutron fission of element 94. "By its characteristics in relation to the action of neutrons," he wrote, "this element is like uranium-235, for which fission by fast neutrons has not yet been studied. Seaborg's data for eka-osmium-94-239 are thus of interest also for the problem of making a bomb out of uranium-235. Obtaining information about the results of the research by Seaborg and Segrè is therefore especially important for us."[59]

Towards the end of his memorandum Kurchatov noted that "here in the Union research on the uranium problem (of course, on a wholly inadequate scale as yet) is being conducted along most of the lines along which it is developing in the United States."[60] Only in two areas was this not true: the heavy water–uranium pile, and the separation of uranium isotopes by electrolysis. The first of these areas required serious attention, in Kurchatov's view, but the latter did not appear very promising.[61]

In December 1943 Klaus Fuchs arrived in New York as a member of the British Diffusion Mission. He stayed in New York for nine months, working on the theory of the gaseous diffusion separation process. He knew that a large plant was being built, though he did not know that it was at Oak Ridge in Tennessee. He was now controlled by the NKGB, not the GRU. He gave his new courier, Harry Gold, general information about the barriers, which are a key element in the diffusion process, and told him that these would be made of sintered nickel powder, though he could not give him any of the technical details. He handed over all the reports prepared in the New York Office of the British Diffusion Mission.[62] During his stay in New York, Fuchs later confessed, he "still had no real knowledge of the pile process, or of the significance of plutonium."[63] Nevertheless, thanks to the information he had provided, Kurchatov and

Kikoin knew that the United States had selected gaseous diffusion to separate uranium-235 on a large scale. They also had a general picture of the design of the plant, and of the problems that had to be overcome in constructing it. This information evidently influenced Kikoin's decision to concentrate on gaseous diffusion, rather than the centrifuge, as the primary method for large-scale separation. This may not have been a good decision, since the centrifuge later proved to be a more efficient method of separation.

By the beginning of 1945 Soviet intelligence had a clear general picture of the Manhattan project. In February 1945 V. Merkulov, the People's Commissar of State Security, wrote to Beria that research by leading British and American scientists had shown that an atomic bomb was feasible, and that there were two main problems to be solved in making it: production of the necessary quantity of fissionable material – uranium-235 or plutonium; and the design of the bomb. An isotope separation plant was being built in Tennessee, and plutonium was being produced at Hanford, in the state of Washington. The bomb itself was being designed and built at Los Alamos, where about 2,000 people were employed. Two methods of detonating the bomb were being developed: the gun-assembly, and implosion. The first test of a bomb could be expected in two or three months. Merkulov also provided some very general information about uranium deposits in the Belgian Congo, Canada, Czechoslovakia, Australia, and Madagascar.[64]

Soviet intelligence also received information about the Anglo-Canadian wartime project, the most important element of which was the design and construction of a heavy water pile. The source of this information was Alan Nunn May, a British physicist who had joined the nuclear team at the Cavendish Laboratory in 1942 and was later sent to work at the Montreal Laboratory. In the spring of 1945 May gave the Soviet embassy in Ottawa a written report on what he knew about atomic research. He later said that he had done this to ensure "that development of atomic energy was not confined to the U.S.A."[65] In the first week of August 1945 he handed over microscopic amounts of uranium-235 – a slightly enriched sample – and uranium-233.[66] The samples of uranium-235 and uranium-233 were flown to Moscow at once.[67] In March 1945 Kurchatov had written in one of his memoranda to Pervukhin that it was exceptionally important to obtain several tens of grams of highly enriched uranium.[68] What May supplied fell far short of that.

IV

In 1943 Kurchatov began to assemble a group of physicists and engineers to work on the design of the atomic bomb. He asked Khariton to head this group. Khariton at first refused because he wanted to continue his work on

mines and anti-tank weapons, which would help in the war against
Germany. But Kurchatov was persistent, Khariton later recalled, and told
him that "you can't overlook the time when victory will be behind us, and
we ought to be concerned about the future security of the country too."[69]
Khariton, moreover, was attracted because "it was a completely new, and
so also a very interesting thing," and agreed to join the project, while
continuing to work at the same time for the People's Commissariat of
Munitions.[70] Kurchatov's choice surprised some people, because Khariton,
with his gentle and civilized manner, did not fit the prevailing image of a
Stalinist manager. Kurchatov's choice showed his skill in picking people,
for Khariton was to prove an effective scientific director of the weapons
program.[71] Khariton was thirty-nine at the time, a year younger than
Kurchatov. The two had known each other since 1925, and now they
worked together very closely, without strain or rivalry.

The bomb group did what it could to investigate the conditions under
which an explosive fission chain reaction would take place in uranium-235
and element 94, but it was severely hampered by the lack of basic data.
Khariton and his colleagues did not know the fast-neutron cross-sections
of uranium-235 and element 94. Experiments were done to study the
gun-assembly method of detonating a bomb. Vladimir Merkin, under
Khariton's direction, did experiments with two rifles firing at each other,
and used high-speed photography to analyze the way in which the bullets
impacted. Similar experiments were done later with 76 mm guns in a small
barn that was built near the laboratory. For help with this work Kurchatov
turned to Boris Vannikov, the People's Commissar for Munitions, who
handed the problem over to a special weapons institute.[72]

The work of the bomb group was transformed by information from the
United States in the early months of 1945. Klaus Fuchs had been sent to Los
Alamos in August 1944 as part of the British team, and put to work on
implosion.[73] In the summer of 1944 it had become clear at Los Alamos that
the gun-assembly method of creating a supercritical mass of active material
would not work for plutonium. It was discovered that one of the isotopes
of plutonium – plutonium-240 – had a very high rate of spontaneous
fission. If the gun-assembly method were used, spontaneous fission was
likely to cause predetonation; the explosion would begin before the active
material was fully compressed and then fizzle out. The subcritical masses
had to be brought together much more rapidly than was possible with the
gun assembly. This could be done by implosion: conventional high explosives would be placed around the active material, and the blast from these
explosives would be directed inward, squeezing the material until it
reached criticality and detonated.[74]

Detonating the plutonium bomb was the hardest problem Los Alamos
had to solve, according to Rudolf Peierls, who was a member of the British
team at the laboratory.[75] Fuchs worked on the difficult problem of calcu-

lating the implosion method, and this put him at the center of the work on this new approach to the design of an atomic bomb. In February 1945, when he visited his sister in Boston, he gave Harry Gold a report on the design of the plutonium bomb.[76] According to Fuchs's later confession, he

reported the highly spontaneous fission rate of plutonium and the deduction that a plutonium bomb would have to be detonated by using the implosion method rather than the relatively simple gun method which could be used with U-235. He also reported that the critical mass for plutonium was less than that for U-235 and that about five to fifteen kilograms would be necessary for a bomb. At this time the issue was not clear as to whether uniform compression of the core could be better obtained with a high explosive lens system, or with multipoint detonation over the surface of a uniform sphere of high explosives.[77]

This was an extremely significant report, and Fuchs supplemented it with more detailed information when he met Harry Gold again.

At their next meeting, which took place in Santa Fe in June 1945, Fuchs gave Gold a report which he had written in Los Alamos so that he could check his figures with the relevant files. In this report Fuchs, according to his confession,

fully described the plutonium bomb which had, by this time, been designed and was to be tested at "Trinity". He provided a sketch of the bomb and its components and gave all the important dimensions. He reported that the bomb would have a solid plutonium core and described the initiator which, he said, would contain about fifty curies of polonium. Full details were given of the tamper, the aluminum shell, and of the high explosive lens system.[78]

Fuchs informed Gold that the Trinity test was expected to produce an explosion equivalent to 10,000 tons of TNT, and told him when and where the test would take place. In his report he mentioned that there were plans to use the bomb against Japan if the test proved successful.[79]

In a memorandum written on March 16, 1945 Kurchatov reviewed intelligence material on "two possibilities, which we have not yet considered." The first was the possibility of using uranium-hydride-235 (uranium-235 mixed with hydrogen) as the active material in a bomb, instead of metallic uranium-235. Kurchatov was skeptical about this idea, but withheld final judgment until "after serious theoretical analysis of the question has been done." He was much more interested in the second possibility, implosion. "There is no doubt," he wrote, "that the implosion method is of great interest, correct in principle, and ought to be subjected to serious theoretical and experimental analysis."[80]

Three weeks later, on April 7, 1945, Kurchatov wrote another report which is clearly a response to the information provided by Klaus Fuchs in February. Kurchatov's earlier memorandum, of March 16, seems to have been written in response to information provided by someone else, possibly by David Greenglass, a machinist who worked in the laboratory of George Kistiakowsky, head of the explosives division at Los Alamos. Greenglass later confessed to providing the Soviet Union with information about the high-explosive lens designed for use in implosion, and his testimony was the basis for the charge of espionage brought against Julius and Ethel Rosenberg in 1951.[81] From Kurchatov's memorandum of April 7 it is clear that the information from Fuchs was more important than the material Kurchatov had reviewed three weeks earlier. It had "great value," Kurchatov wrote. The data about spontaneous fission were "exceptionally important." The data on the fission cross-sections of uranium-235 and plutonium-239 for fast neutrons of various energies had enormous significance, since they made it possible to define in a reliable manner the critical dimensions of an atomic bomb. Soviet physicists had come to the same conclusions as American physicists about efficiency, he wrote, and had formulated the same law, whereby the efficiency of the bomb is proportional to the cube of the amount by which the bomb's mass exceeds the critical mass.[82]

Most of the material reviewed by Kurchatov in this memorandum concerned implosion. Although Soviet physicists had only recently learned about implosion, "all its advantages over the gun-assembly method have already become clear to us." The intelligence provided very valuable information about the propagation of the detonating wave in the explosive, and about the process of compression of the active material. It also indicated how symmetry could be obtained in the implosion; how unequal action of the explosive wave might be avoided by an appropriate distribution of the detonators and the application of layers of different kinds of conventional explosive. "I would consider it necessary," Kurchatov wrote at the end of this section of his memorandum, "to show the appropriate text (from p. 6 to the end, excluding p. 22) to Professor Iu.B. Khariton."[83]

Kurchatov's memoranda confirm Fuchs's importance as a spy. They also reveal that the Soviet Union had other sources of information in the Manhattan project. Anatolii Iatskov, who – under the name of Anatolii Iakovlev – was Harry Gold's NKGB case officer in New York, has said that at most one half of his network of agents was uncovered by the FBI.[84] It is clear, for example, that someone was passing on information about the work of Seaborg and Segrè at Berkeley. But the available evidence suggests that Fuchs was by far the most important informant in the Manhattan project.[85]

V

The Red Army's advance into Central Europe brought important benefits for the atomic project. At the end of March 1945 the Czechoslovak government in exile, headed by President Edvard Beneš, traveled from

London to Moscow, on its way home to Prague. While it was in Moscow it signed a secret agreement giving the Soviet Union the right to mine uranium ore in Czechoslovakia and transport it to the Soviet Union.[86] The uranium mines at Jachymov (Joachimsthal) near the border with Saxony had been the world's main source of uranium in the early part of the century. Before World War II the mines had yielded about 20 metric tons of uranium oxide a year. During the war there was some production, but the mine was then closed.[87] Soviet intelligence had learned that Britain wanted to mine the uranium in Czechoslovakia.[88] This no doubt enhanced the Soviet interest in an agreement with the Czechoslovak government.

The Beneš government, probably unaware of the value uranium had now acquired, agreed to deliver the existing Czechoslovak stock and future production of uranium ore to the Soviet Union alone.[89] The Soviet Union was to control both the mining and the transportation, and was to pay a price equal to the cost of mining the ore, plus 10 per cent for commercial profit. This was the standard Soviet method for pricing raw materials, but the low price was later to cause resentment in Czechoslovakia.[90]

Access to Czechoslovak uranium was important, but greater benefits were to come from the occupation of Germany. In May 1945 a special Soviet mission went to Germany to study the German atomic project. This was the Soviet equivalent of the "Alsos" group that General Groves had formed to determine precisely how much the Germans knew about the atomic bomb.[91] It was also part of a much broader effort by the Soviet Union to exploit German science and technology.[92]

The Soviet nuclear mission was organized by Avraamii Zaveniagin, who was to play an important role in the atomic project.[93] Zaveniagin was an NKVD colonel-general and one of Beria's deputy people's commissars at the NKVD. Zaveniagin had joined the Party in 1917, at the age of sixteen, and worked for the Party until he was sent to the Moscow Mining Academy, from which he graduated in 1930. In the mid-1930s he organized the Metallurgical Combine in the new city of Magnitogorsk, one of the biggest construction projects of the decade. In 1937 he was sent to establish a mining and metallurgical combine at Noril'sk, above the Arctic Circle, where most of the work was done by prisoners. In 1941 he became Beria's deputy at the NKVD, where he helped to manage the NKVD's vast network of penal camps.[94] Zaveniagin was regarded by the scientists who worked with him as pragmatic and intelligent; "a man of great intelligence – and an uncompromising Stalinist," wrote Andrei Sakharov in his memoirs.[95]

The Soviet mission consisted of two or three dozen scientists, including Kikoin, Khariton, Flerov, Artsimovich, Nemenov, and Golovin. The leading scientists were put into the uniforms of NKVD lieutenant-colonels. Kurchatov did not take part in the mission: "You are not thinking of the future, of what our descendants will say, if they know that Kurchatov was in Berlin," he said to Flerov, who urged him to come to Germany.[96] Kurchatov may have feared that the NKVD would look to German rather than to Soviet scientists to play the key part in the Soviet project. This would have been, in his eyes, an insult to Soviet science.

The Soviet scientists soon discovered that they had little to learn from German nuclear science.[97] German scientists had not separated uranium-235, nor had they built a nuclear pile; nor had they progressed very far in their understanding of how to build an atomic bomb. The Soviet mission found, besides, that the leading German nuclear scientists – Otto Hahn and Werner Heisenberg among them – had fallen into Western hands. Ten of the most prominent men were interned by the British at Farm Hall, near Cambridge.[98]

Some German scientists, however, decided not to flee the Red Army. Among them was Baron Manfred von Ardenne, "a very able technician . . . and first-rate experimenter," who had a private laboratory in Berlin-Lichterfelde and had built a prototype electromagnetic isotope separation machine.[99] Another was Gustav Hertz, who had received the Nobel Prize with James Franck in 1925 for experiments about electron–atom collisions which played an important part in the development of the quantum theory. Hertz, who had also developed the gaseous diffusion process for isotope separation, had worked for the Siemens Company since 1935. Peter-Adolf Thiessen, head of the Kaiser Wilhelm Institute of Physical Chemistry in Berlin, who had been in charge of chemical research and development in the Third Reich, also went to the Soviet Union.[100] So too did Nikolaus Riehl, director of research at the Auer Company, and the chemist Max Volmer.[101]

Paul Rosbaud, who had given Britain crucial information about German science during the war, wrote in September 1945 to Samuel Goudsmit, chief scientific adviser to the Alsos group, about the motives of these scientists.[102] Rosbaud had extensive contacts in the German scientific community and had spoken to several of those who decided to work for the Soviet Union. Gustav Hertz explained to him that while some of his friends in the United States might be able to arrange for him to work there, "this is of course uncertain, besides American physics has made such great progress that I cannot be there of any help, people know more there about the things I was working on for the last years and I don't want to accept any charity."[103]

Peter-Adolf Thiessen, who had been a Nazi since the 1920s, told Rosbaud that

the only chance . . . German science in the future has would be to collaborate as closely as possible with Russia. He was sure that German scientists will play in the future a leading role in Russia, especially those who have some knowledge in secret weapons, which are in preparation but not yet ready develloped [sic]. His opinion was, that Germany, her scientists, engineers, skilled workmen, and her potential will be in the future the decisive factor, the nation, which has Germany on her side will be invincible.[104]

Other scientists had more mundane motives. Some, like Heinz Barwich, needed work and a livelihood, while others, like Max Steenbeck, found themselves in internment camps and were glad of the chance to return to scientific research.[105] The German scientists were taken to the Soviet Union in May and June 1945, along with their laboratory equipment.[106] They were held, in comfortable conditions, in *dachas* outside Moscow, and were not immediately assigned specific tasks.[107]

It was not German scientists or laboratory equipment, however, but German uranium that was the most important find for the Soviet mission. Khariton and Kikoin managed, after much detective work, to track down over 100 metric tons of uranium oxide that had been hidden away. Kurchatov later told Khariton that this had saved a year in building the first experimental pile.[108] United States intelligence later estimated that the Soviet Union had obtained between 240 and 340 tons of uranium oxide in Germany and Czechoslovakia at the end of the war.[109]

The United States and Britain tried to prevent the Soviet Union from deriving any benefit from Germany for its atomic project. The internment of German scientists was partly motivated by the desire to prevent them from falling into Soviet hands. Other steps were taken too. On March 15, General Groves asked the US Army Air Force to bomb the Auer Company plant in Oranienburg, north of Berlin. This plant had manufactured thorium and uranium metals for the German atomic project, and was in the Soviet zone of occupation. "Our purpose in attacking Oranienburg was screened from Russians and Germans alike," Groves remarked complacently in his memoirs, "by a simultaneous and equally heavy attack upon the small town of Zossen, where the German Army's headquarters were situated."[110] But the Soviet authorities were not deceived by this, for Nikolaus Riehl gathered from Soviet officers that they suspected why the plant had been bombed.[111] In April 1945 Groves arranged for an Anglo-American group to remove 1,200 tons of uranium ore, the bulk of the German stock, from a salt mine near Stassfurt, which was due to fall within the Soviet zone of occupation.[112] This uranium would have been enormously useful to the Soviet project.

The Soviet atomic project did gain a longer-term benefit from the Soviet occupation of East Germany, where it acquired uranium deposits that were to prove even more valuable than those in Czechoslovakia. Uranium had been found in south-west Saxony, on the northern slopes of the Erzgebirge mountains, to the south of which lay the Czech deposits at Jachymov. This uranium had not been mined, and Groves apparently did not know of the existence of these deposits. Nor did the Soviet authorities know at the end of the war how extensive the deposits were, but they soon became the most important source of uranium for the Soviet project.[113]

VI

In an article written in November 1942 but not published until many years later Vernadskii expressed his belief that the war would mark the start of a new era:

in the storm and in the tempest the noosphere is being born. A new state of life, which has been in preparation for millennia and about which utopians have dreamed, will become a reality, when wars – i.e. organized killings, when hunger and malnutrition can disappear comparatively quickly from our planet.[114]

Vernadskii's evolutionary optimism was linked with the "growth of scientific free thought and popular labor." He argued for the creation of an association of Soviet scientific workers – scholars, physicians, and engineers – which would exercise an influence on Soviet politics, and he called for much closer cooperation with scientists in other countries, and especially in Britain and the United States.[115]

In a letter to the president of the Academy in March 1943 Vernadskii wrote that "it seems to me that we need to enter into much closer contact with American scientists . . . I consider that at the present time American scientific organization and scientific thought stand at the forefront. We must turn for help to America in reconstructing after the depredations of Hitler's vandals."[116] Vernadskii hoped to travel to the United States at the end of the war to visit his son and daughter. His wife had died in February 1943, and he now had no immediate family in the Soviet Union. His request to travel was turned down, however, on the grounds that it would be too dangerous in wartime, and on January 6, 1945 – exactly seven months before the bombing of Hiroshima – he died in Moscow of a brain hemorrhage at the age of eighty-one.[117]

With his broad intellectual and political interests, and his courage and integrity in the pursuit of truth and justice, Vernadskii was the very model of a member of the Russian intelligentsia. In an essay on Igor' Tamm, Evgenii Feinberg has written that

in late nineteenth century Russia there existed something of fundamental importance – a solid, middle-class, professional intelligentsia which possessed firm principles based on spiritual values. That milieu produced committed revolutionaries, poets and engineers, convinced that the most important thing is to build something, to do something useful.[118]

Andrei Sakharov quotes this passage in his memoirs, and describes himself as fortunate in having come from a family that embodied these values.[119] Vernadskii came from the same tradition. He showed great courage in his commitment to intellectual freedom and justice. He was also persistent in trying to do something useful, as is clear from his interest in atomic energy. And he did not lose sight of the great responsibility that atomic energy would place on the human race.

Kapitsa too wanted to reestablish contact with foreign scientists. In October 1943 he wrote to Niels Bohr, who had just escaped to Britain from Nazi-occupied Denmark, to invite him to the Soviet Union. "I want to let you know," he said, "that you will be welcome in the Soviet Union where everything will be done to give you and your family a shelter and where we now have all the necessary conditions for carrying on scientific work. Even the vague hope that you might possibly come to live with us," he added, "is most heartily applauded by all our physicists: Ioffe, Mendelshtam, Landau, Vavilov, Tamm, Alihanov, Semenov and many others."[120] Kapitsa had obtained permission from Molotov to send this letter. In writing to Molotov Kapitsa had stated that Bohr was well disposed to the Soviet Union, and had visited it three times. "I think that it would be very good and correct," he wrote, "if we were to offer hospitality here in the Union to him and his family for the period of the war."[121] There is no reason to suppose that Kapitsa or Molotov intended Bohr to work on the atomic project. Bohr's presence would do Soviet physics good, as Kapitsa no doubt realized, and would lay the basis for international ties after the war.

Kapitsa argued that scientists had a role to play in securing international peace. In a speech to the third Anti-Fascist Meeting of Soviet Scientists in June 1944 he said that now, with the end of the war in sight, "our task, the task of all scientists, must not be limited to gaining a knowledge of nature in order to harness it for the benefit of mankind in peaceful construction. It is my opinion that scientists must also take an active part in the establishment of a sound and lasting peace."[122] Soviet scientists, said Kapitsa, shared many of the aspirations of foreign scientists for the "cultural evolution of human society," but they also had the experience of building a new society, and had witnessed "the conformance between real life and the teachings on society begun by Marx and continued by Lenin and Stalin."[123] If scientists could play as significant a role in social affairs as they had in the war effort, they could "help public spirited people and statesmen to lead their countries along a sounder path, each in accordance with the peculiarities of the country concerned."[124]

At the end of the war Soviet leaders supported the aspirations of Soviet scientists for closer contact with colleagues from abroad.[125] In June 1945 the Academy of Sciences held a special congress to celebrate its 220th anniversary, with over a hundred scientists from outside the Soviet Union taking part. For obvious reasons none of the leading nuclear scientists came, apart from Frédéric and Irène Joliot-Curie, though Oppenheimer, Chadwick, Peierls, Cockcroft and others had been on the invitation list.[126] At a reception in the Kremlin, attended by Stalin, Molotov made a short speech promising the "most favorable conditions" for the development of science and technology and for "closer ties of Soviet science with world science."[127]

Kapitsa spoke at the congress, declaring that there was really no such thing as Soviet science or British science; there was only one science, devoted to the betterment of human welfare. This celebration, he said, showed that the Soviet Union intended to play a leading role in international science. It would increase the number of its scientific publications in Russian, English, and French, and would organize and participate in more international congresses and scientific exchanges.[128]

The Academy clearly felt that it now had the opportunity to recreate the international ties that had been broken in the mid-1930s. On April 13, 1945 the president and academician-secretary of the Academy wrote to Georgii Malenkov, the Central Committee secretary responsible for science, to seek permission to send seven scientists to the United States for periods of several months. Three of the scientists – A.I. Alikhanian, G.D. Latyshev, and V.I. Veksler – were to spend six months each studying cyclotrons in Berkeley, Boston, and Washington. Two others – Artsimovich and A.A. Lebedev[129] – were to study American work in electron optics for six months. The other two scientists were to learn about luminescence and telescope reflectors. The request was supported by the Central Committee staff and forwarded to Molotov, who wrote on it on May 29: "This should be decided in the Central Committee Secretariat. In my view, it can be permitted, but the exit of all seven should hardly be simultaneous – better to break them up into 2–3 groups."[130] Although he showed characteristic suspicion of the scientists, Molotov believed at the end of May 1945 that it would be possible to send physicists to the United States for research in nuclear physics.

Molotov's recommendation appears to reflect the attitude of the Soviet leaders to nuclear research in the summer of 1945. The Soviet project had made slow progress during the war. Kurchatov's letter to Beria had not produced the desired effect; there is no evidence of any response to it. The problem of uranium supply was still being tackled slowly, and the project was not reorganized. It is true that research was expanding. A new institute, NII–9 (*Nauchno-issledovatel'skii institut No. 9*: Research Institute No. 9) was set up before the end of the war to work on the metallurgy of uranium and plutonium.[131] The occupation of Germany brought new equipment, uranium, and scientists. But the Soviet leadership did not treat the project as an urgent priority. The German scientists were not put to work quickly, for example. The transition had yet to be made from theoretical research and laboratory work to the creation of an atomic industry.[132]

In May 1945, the month in which Germany surrendered, Pervukhin and Kurchatov wrote to Stalin to urge that the project be speeded up. "Matters connected with the solution of the atomic problem," Pervukhin later recalled,

for several reasons caused by the war, were going slowly. Therefore in May 1945 Igor' Vasil'evich Kurchatov and I wrote a memorandum for the Politburo of the Central Committee and Comrade I.V. Stalin in which we briefly elucidated the position with the atomic problem and expressed alarm at the slow development of the work.[133]

Pervukhin and Kurchatov proposed that extraordinary measures be taken and that the nuclear project be given "the most favorable and advantageous conditions" in order to speed up the research and development work and the organization of "atomic industry enterprises."[134]

There is no evidence of any response to this memorandum. Stalin, Beria, and Molotov were well informed about the Manhattan project, yet showed no urgency about expanding the Soviet effort. Why not? One explanation, given by the KGB officer Iatskov, is that Beria did not believe the intelligence reports. "From the very beginning," Iatskov has written, Beria

suspected disinformation in these reports, thinking that the enemy was trying to draw us in this way into huge expenditures of resources and effort on work which had no future. . . . Beria retained his suspicious attitude to the intelligence even when work on the atomic bomb was in full swing in the Soviet Union. L.R. Kvasnikov has recounted that once when he was reporting to Beria on the latest intelligence data, Beria threatened him: "If this is disinformation, I'll put you all in the cellar."[135]

Beria may have communicated to Stalin and Molotov his suspicion of the intelligence reports. This suspicion was compounded by the Soviet leaders' distrust of Soviet scientists. How could Stalin, Beria, and Molotov be sure that Kurchatov was not deceiving them? They understood nothing of the science and technology involved, and other scientists had said that a bomb could not be built for a very long time. The discovery that Germany had not come close to building an atomic bomb may have reinforced the Soviet leaders' skepticism.

Whatever the reasons, it is clear that – in spite of Fuchs's report that the United States was planning to test the bomb on July 10, and to use it against Japan if the test was successful – neither Stalin, Beria, nor Molotov understood the role that the atomic bomb would soon play in international relations.[136] If they had seen the connection between the bomb and foreign policy, they would surely have provided Pervukhin and Kurchatov with more active support. Their failure to do so suggests that the atomic bomb had no reality for them in the summer of 1945, that they had no conception of the impact it was about to have on world politics.

CHAPTER SIX

Hiroshima

I

AT 5.30 A.M. ON JULY 16, 1945 the United States tested an atomic bomb in the desert at Alamogordo in New Mexico. This was a plutonium bomb, which employed the complex implosion method; the simpler gun-assembly uranium-235 bomb was judged not to need a test before it was used. The Alamogordo test was a triumphant success. It produced a greater than expected explosive yield equivalent to about 20 kilotons of TNT.[1] Five weeks later, on August 20, the State Defense Committee in Moscow adopted a decree setting up new organizations to direct the Soviet atomic project. It was in this five-week period that Stalin realized the strategic importance of the atomic bomb and launched a crash program to build a Soviet bomb.

The Alamogordo test took place on the day before the opening of the Potsdam conference, at which Churchill, Stalin, and Truman were to discuss the postwar settlement. At 7.30 p.m. on July 16, Henry L. Stimson, the US Secretary of War, who was in Potsdam for the summit meeting, received a telegram from Washington to say that the test had taken place that morning and had been successful. Five days later he received a detailed report from General Groves conveying some of the tension and relief – but above all the awe – that those present at the test had felt.[2] This powerful and eloquent document produced a profound effect in Potsdam. Stimson read it that afternoon to Truman who was immensely pleased. Truman was "tremendously pepped up by it," Stimson wrote in his diary, "and spoke to me of it again and again when I saw him. He said it gave him an entirely new feeling of confidence." The next morning Stimson took the report to Churchill, who exclaimed upon reading it that "this is the Second Coming in Wrath."[3] "The bomb as a merely probable weapon had seemed a weak reed on which to rely," Stimson realized, "but the bomb as a colossal reality was very different."[4]

Truman now decided to inform Stalin about the bomb. After the plenary session on July 24 he approached Stalin as the latter was about to leave the conference room. Truman casually mentioned to him "that we had a new weapon of unusual destructive force."[5] He did not say, however, that this was an atomic bomb. According to Truman's memoirs, Stalin said "he was glad to hear it and hoped we would make 'good use of it against the Japanese'."[6] Truman's account may not be accurate, however. Anthony Eden, the British Foreign Secretary, who with Churchill was watching intently from a few feet away, wrote in his memoirs that Stalin had merely nodded his head and said "Thank you," without further comment.[7] Stalin's interpreter, V.N. Pavlov, who translated Truman's remark, has confirmed Eden's account, but recalls that Stalin merely gave a slight nod of the head, without saying thank you.[8]

Truman and Churchill were convinced that Stalin had not understood that Truman was referring to the atomic bomb.[9] They were probably mistaken. Stalin knew more than they suspected about the Manhattan project, and it is likely that he had been informed that the test was scheduled for July 10. He also knew about Soviet nuclear research.[10] It is very probable that he realized what Truman was referring to, if not immediately, then very soon thereafter.[11] "On returning home from the session," Marshal Zhukov wrote in his memoirs,

Stalin, in my presence, told Molotov about his conversation with Truman.

"They're raising the price," said Molotov.

Stalin gave a laugh, "Let them. We'll have to have a talk with Kurchatov today about speeding up our work."

I realized that they were talking about the creation of the atomic bomb.[12]

"It is hard to say what [Truman] thought, but it seemed to me that he wanted to dumbfound us," Molotov recalled many years later. " 'Atomic bomb' was not mentioned, but we guessed at once what he had in mind."[13] It has been reported that Stalin contacted Kurchatov from Potsdam to tell him to speed up work on the bomb; but that claim has been disputed by one of Kurchatov's colleagues, on the grounds that more than a telephone call was needed to speed things up.[14]

Stalin, it seems clear, knew that Truman was speaking of the atomic bomb. What is less clear is what he understood the significance of Truman's remark to be. There are two possibilities. The first is that he still did not attribute great importance to the bomb; the second is that he now grasped that the bomb was a major factor in international relations. In either case his reaction would have been the same. His lack of response could indicate a failure to understand the full import of Truman's remark; or it could have been a deliberate attempt not to appear concerned, for fear of acknowledging Soviet backwardness and conveying an impression of weakness.

The latter interpretation is the one that Zhukov and Molotov suggest. There are, however, no contemporary documents to support it. It may be

wondered whether, in view of Stalin's failure to grasp the strategic importance of the bomb on the basis of the wartime intelligence, Truman's
remark did indeed inspire in him a new understanding of its significance.
In any event, the impact of the American atomic bomb on Soviet policy
did not become apparent until after Hiroshima.

II

The exchange between Truman and Stalin at Potsdam was the result, on
the American side, of considerable discussion about the effect of the bomb
on relations with the Soviet Union. Niels Bohr had tried to persuade
Churchill and Roosevelt to tell Stalin about the bomb. Bohr had escaped
from Nazi-occupied Denmark in September 1943 and had spent some
months at Los Alamos as a member of the British team.[15] He had been
astonished by the progress that had been made. He was afraid that if
political differences caused a breakdown in the wartime alliance, a nuclear
arms race would ensue. But he also believed that the bomb presented an
opportunity, because the need for cooperation to deal with the danger of
an arms race might form the basis for a new approach to international
relations. The United States and Britain should inform the Soviet Union of
the existence of the Manhattan project before the bomb was a certainty and
before the war was over. Only in this way might Stalin be convinced of the
need for international control of atomic energy, and persuaded that the
United States and Britain were not conspiring against the Soviet Union.[16]

Bohr's thinking was influenced by his high regard for Soviet physics. He
had visited the Soviet Union, and had had contact with several Soviet
physicists, especially Kapitsa and Landau.[17] He knew of Soviet research on
fission. His suspicion that Soviet physicists might be working on the bomb
was reinforced when he received Kapitsa's letter inviting him to come to
the Soviet Union. Bohr collected the letter at the Soviet embassy in
London in April 1944, on his return from the United States. He wrote a
warm but noncommittal reply to Kapitsa, after consulting the British
security authorities.[18] Kapitsa's letter convinced him that it was urgent to
inform Stalin about the bomb.

Bohr won support for his ideas from some leading advisers to Churchill
and Roosevelt.[19] But when he saw Churchill at No. 10 Downing Street in
May 1944, the meeting was a disaster. Churchill was vehemently opposed
to telling Stalin about the atomic bomb. He told Bohr that the bomb
would not change the principles of war, and that the postwar problems
could be handled by Roosevelt and himself.[20] Roosevelt, on the other
hand, seemed very receptive when Bohr saw him at the White House in
August. After this meeting Bohr drafted a letter to Kapitsa describing the
Manhattan project in very general terms and arguing the case for international control of atomic energy. He held himself ready to go to the

Gustav Hertz (who went to the Soviet Union at about this time). The Franck Report stressed the danger of an arms race and argued against using the bomb in Japan.[34] Oppenheimer and his colleagues on the scientific panel rejected the suggestion of a demonstration: "we can propose no technical demonstration likely to bring an end to the war; we see no acceptable alternative to direct military use."[35] On June 21 the Interim Committee reaffirmed its previous recommendation that the bomb be used at the earliest opportunity, without warning, and against a war plant surrounded by homes or other buildings most susceptible to damage.[36]

The committee also discussed the international control of atomic energy. Bush and Conant circulated to the committee the memorandum they had written for Stimson in September 1944.[37] Byrnes, who was a member of the committee, was impressed by their estimate that the Soviet Union could catch up with the United States in three or four years. General Groves told the committee that the Soviet Union would need twenty years to build the bomb, because it was backward in science and technology and lacked uranium. A panel of industrialists said that the Soviet Union would need between five and ten years.[38] Byrnes concluded from these discussions that the American monopoly might last for between seven and ten years. This confirmed his belief that the bomb would give the United States a diplomatic advantage for a significant period.[39]

Bohr had continued to press his views in Washington in 1945, and at the end of April he told Vannevar Bush that the United States should approach the Soviet Union before using the bomb. This argument was now echoed in the Interim Committee. At the meeting on May 31 Oppenheimer argued that "we might say [to the Russians] that a great national effort had been put into this project and express a hope for cooperation with them in this field."[40] General George C. Marshall, the Army Chief of Staff, even suggested that two prominent Soviet scientists be invited to the Alamogordo test. But Byrnes expressed the fear that if Stalin were told about the bomb he would want to become a partner in the project. Byrnes argued that the best policy was to make sure that the United States stayed ahead in production and research, while at the same time making every effort to improve political relations with the Soviet Union.[41] On June 6 Stimson told the President that the Interim Committee had decided that the project should not be revealed to the Soviet Union or to anyone else until the bomb had been used against Japan.[42] Two weeks later, however, the committee reversed its position. It recommended that the President inform Stalin at their forthcoming meeting at Potsdam that the United States was working on this weapon and expected to use it against Japan; he should also say that he knew that the Soviet Union was working on the bomb. The President, the committee added, "might say further that he hoped this matter might be discussed some time in the future in terms of insuring that the weapon would become an aid to peace."[43] Truman ignored most of this advice at Potsdam when he informed Stalin about the bomb.

The deliberations of the Interim Committee provide crucial evidence on the thinking behind American policy. By asking how, not whether, the atomic bomb should be used against Japan, the committee proceeded on the assumption that the bomb would be used against Japan when it was ready. This was an assumption that Truman had inherited from Roosevelt and, as Barton Bernstein has argued persuasively, it was an assumption that neither he nor the senior members of his administration questioned.[44] The fact that there was extensive discussion within the administration about the impact of the bomb on relations with the Soviet Union should not obscure the fact that the primary motive for using the bomb against Japan was to bring the war to a speedy end.

Members of the administration did recognize, however, that the bomb could be a powerful diplomatic instrument in relations with the Soviet Union. This function of the bomb became increasingly important, in their minds, as serious disagreements arose between the United States and the Soviet Union about the future of Europe. Stimson noted in his diary on May 14 that American economic power and the atomic bomb were "a royal straight flush and we mustn't be a fool about the way we play it"; on the following day he described the bomb as a "master card."[45] On June 6 he discussed with Truman the possibility of negotiating quick protocols with the Soviet Union in return for taking it into partnership in atomic energy: Poland, Romania, Yugoslavia, and Manchuria were the disputes that they hoped might be settled in this way.[46] The discussion was inconclusive, however, and no clear strategy was devised for using the bomb to win concessions from the Soviet Union.

III

Whatever Stalin may or may not have understood at Potsdam, the bombing of Hiroshima and Nagasaki on August 6 and 9 demonstrated in the most dramatic and pointed way the destructive power and strategic importance of the atomic bomb. It was Hiroshima that brought the atomic bomb squarely into Soviet strategic calculations. Before Potsdam the Soviet leaders had failed to see the connection between the bomb and foreign policy. After Hiroshima the connection could no longer be ignored. Stalin's conception of the strategic importance of the bomb was affected by the way in which it was used in Japan; it is therefore necessary to look at Hiroshima in the context of Soviet policy in the Far East.

The Soviet Union had signed a neutrality pact with Japan in April 1941, and Stalin strove to keep that pact in force as long as the fate of the Soviet Union hung in the balance in Europe. Soviet policy changed, however, once the defeat of Germany was in sight. In October 1943 Stalin promised Secretary of State Cordell Hull that the Soviet Union would join the war against Japan after Germany's defeat, and he repeated this assurance to Roosevelt and Churchill in November at the Teheran conference. Stalin told his allies in October 1944 that the Soviet Union would attack Japan about three months after the defeat of Germany, as long as the necessary arms and equipment had been stockpiled and the political terms clarified.[47]

The terms for Soviet entry into the war were settled between Stalin, Roosevelt, and Churchill at the Yalta conference in February 1945. Stalin wanted: (a) preservation of the status quo in Outer Mongolia (i.e. communist rule and independence from China); (b) restoration of rights lost by Russia in the Russo-Japanese war of 1904–5 (recovery of southern Sakhalin, internationalization of the port of Dairen, and restoration of the lease of Port Arthur as a Soviet naval base; joint Soviet–Chinese operation of the Chinese Eastern Railway and the South Manchurian Railway, with safeguards for the preeminent interests of the Soviet Union); (c) annexation of the Kurile islands. Neither Roosevelt nor Churchill objected to these terms. The provisions concerning Outer Mongolia and the ports and railways required the consent of China, which did not take part in the Yalta conference. Roosevelt promised to take steps to obtain agreement from Chiang Kai-shek, the Chinese Nationalist leader, but Stalin asked him not to inform Chiang of the agreement until the movement of Soviet troops to the Far East had been completed.[48] Stalin promised to enter the war within two or three months of Germany's defeat, and to conclude a treaty of friendship and alliance with China.

The willingness of Roosevelt and Churchill to grant Stalin's demands indicates just how anxious they were to have Soviet help in defeating Japan. The US Chiefs of Staff had concluded on the eve of the Yalta conference that, while Soviet participation was not essential, it would be desirable to have "Russian entry at the earliest possible date consistent with her ability to engage in offensive operations."[49] United States military planners hoped that the Red Army would tie down the Japanese Kwantung Army in Manchuria, thereby preventing the movement of those forces to the home islands to counter an invasion. They did not expect that Soviet entry would relieve the United States of the need to invade Japan. On May 25, less than three weeks after Germany's surrender, Truman ordered preparations to be made for an invasion of Japan on November 1.[50]

After the Yalta conference the Soviet General Staff began to plan seriously for the war with Japan.[51] Several different options were considered. One of these was invasion of the home islands. This was tempting because it would give the Soviet Union a voice in the postwar development of Japan, but it was difficult from a military point of view because it would require cooperation with Allied navies, which were still far from Japan, and it would entail great losses by Soviet forces. On the General

Staff's advice, Stalin decided that the Red Army's chief mission should be to rout the Kwantung Army in Manchuria in the shortest possible time, and then to smash the Japanese forces on southern Sakhalin and the Kurile islands.[52] On April 5 the Soviet government announced that it would not renew the Soviet-Japanese neutrality pact, which was due to expire in 1946.[53]

The General Staff calculated that significant superiority in manpower and equipment would be needed to defeat the Kwantung Army quickly. Between April and early August 1945 more than half a million troops were transferred a distance of almost 10,000 kilometers from the European theater to the Far East.[54] In May a special Far Eastern High Command was established; Marshal A.M. Vasilevskii, former Chief of the General Staff, was soon named Commander-in-Chief.[55] On June 26–27 Stalin discussed preparations for the war with Japan with members of the Politburo and the High Command.[56] On June 28 Stalin and General A.I. Antonov, Chief of the General Staff, ordered the Trans-Baikal and 1st Far Eastern Fronts to be ready to attack by July 25, and the 2nd Far Eastern Front to be ready by August 1.[57]

In spite of this order, however, it was not clear when the Soviet Union would enter the war. Stalin had told Truman's emissary, Harry Hopkins, on May 28 that Soviet forces would be ready to attack on August 8 but that entry into the war would depend on China's acceptance of the Yalta Agreement.[58] On July 10 Molotov implied, in conversation with T.V. Soong, the Chinese Foreign Minister, that the Soviet Union would declare war on Japan by late August. He could not name the exact date, he said, because it depended on transportation and supply.[59]

Stalin had begun talks about the Yalta Agreement with T.V. Soong on June 30. The Nationalist government was unwilling to accept the agreement as it stood. The Nationalists regarded Outer Mongolia as part of China, and resented the idea that the Soviet Union could have "preeminent" interests in Chinese railways; there was disagreement also over the arrangements for control of the port of Dairen.[60] Stalin pressed the Chinese to accept the agreement, arguing that the Soviet Union and China had a common interest in countering Japan. He explained that the Soviet Union wanted to strengthen its strategic position in the Far East. "Japan will not be ruined even if she accepts unconditional surrender, like Germany. Both of these nations are very strong," he said. "After Versailles, all thought Germany would not raise [sic]. 15–20 years, she recovered. Same would happen with Japan even if she is put on her knees."[61] The Soviet Union needed the Kurile islands, he said: "We are closed up. We have no outlet. One should keep Japan vulnerable from all sides, north, west, south, east, then she will keep quiet."[62] He complained about the lack of satisfactory ports in the Soviet Far East, and said that it would take twenty or thirty years to build up the necessary facilities. That was why the Soviet Union needed Chinese ports. "We need Dairen and Port Arthur for 30 years," he said, "in case Japan restores its forces. We could strike at her from there. Japan will raise again like Germany."[63]

As long as the Truman administration wanted Soviet entry, it had an incentive to press the Chinese to accept the Yalta Agreement. By the summer of 1945, however, Soviet policy in Europe made Soviet participation in the war against Japan appear less attractive to some members of the administration. Averell Harriman, the ambassador in Moscow, was very skeptical about the desirability of Soviet entry, and he urged Soong, who reported to him regularly on the progress of his talks with Stalin and Molotov, to stand firm.[64] After the Alamogordo test Soviet entry into the war appeared not only less desirable, but also less urgent.[65] Byrnes, believing that prolonged Sino–Soviet talks would delay Soviet entry, cabled Soong from Potsdam to advise him not to give way to the Soviet Union on any point.[66] "It is quite clear," noted Churchill on July 23, "that the United States do not at the present time desire Russian participation in the war against Japan."[67] In spite of the reservations among his advisers, however, Truman did not seek to withdraw from the Yalta Agreement.

Whether or not they knew of changing Western attitudes, the Soviet leaders feared that Britain and the United States might conclude the war with Japan before the Soviet Union was able to enter. The secret *Bulletin of the Central Committee Information Bureau* reported in its issue of July 1, 1945 that reactionary circles in Britain wanted a compromise peace with Japan in order to prevent the Soviet Union from strengthening its influence in the Far East. The same question, it noted, was being raised in American newspapers and journals as well.[68] Stalin was afraid that if the war ended before the Soviet Union entered, the United States and Britain would renege on the Yalta Agreement, which was contingent upon Soviet participation in the war. "Stalin was leaning on our officers to start military actions as soon as possible," Nikita Khrushchev later recalled. "Stalin had his doubts about whether the Americans would keep their word. . . . What if Japan capitulated before we entered the war? The Americans might say, we don't owe you anything."[69]

Stalin was aware that Japan was now in a hopeless position and that some elements in the Japanese government were seeking to end the war. In February 1945 the Japanese government had put out very tentative feelers to Iakov Malik, the Soviet ambassador in Tokyo. In April it had made another approach to Malik, but had once again elicited a noncommittal response. In June the former Prime Minister Koki Hirota offered Malik some specific concessions to Soviet interests in the Far East as a token of the Japanese desire for good relations. Malik reported these exchanges to Moscow, but gave no indication to Hirota that Moscow was interested. On July 8 Molotov, with Stalin's approval, instructed Malik to avoid giving the Japanese any pretext for presenting these talks as negotiations. "Hirota's proposals," Molotov wrote, "testify to the fact that, as its military situation deteriorates, the Japanese government is willing to make ever greater concessions in the effort to prevent our intervention in the war in the Far East."[70] The Soviet leaders showed no sign of being tempted by the Japanese overtures, however. There was more to be gained from participation in the war on the allied side than from a diplomatic volte-face.

The Japanese government made a new and more determined approach in July when it decided to send another former Prime Minister, Prince Konoye, to Moscow with a letter from the Emperor seeking Soviet mediation in ending the war. On July 13, four days before the start of the Potsdam conference, the Japanese ambassador in Moscow asked the Soviet government to receive Prince Konoye; five days later he was told that the Soviet government could not give a definite reply because it was not clear what the purpose of Prince Konoye's mission was.[71] At Potsdam Stalin informed his allies of the Japanese approaches and of the Soviet response; his policy, he told Truman, was to lull the Japanese.[72] The Japanese overtures suggested that Japan was growing increasingly desperate, and might soon surrender. Stalin wanted Soviet forces to be ready as soon as possible. On July 16, the day before the Potsdam conference opened, he had telephoned Vasilevskii to ask whether the date of the attack could be brought forward ten days, but Vasilevskii had replied that that was impossible, because more time was needed to make Soviet forces ready.[73] Stalin told Truman that Soviet forces would be ready to come into the war by the middle of August, and General Antonov, the Chief of the General Staff, made a similar statement to the Allied Chiefs of Staff.[74] On July 25 and again on July 30 the Soviet Foreign Ministry told the Japanese ambassador that the Soviet government could not yet answer the Japanese request to send Konoye to Moscow.[75]

Soviet preparations for entry into the war continued during the Potsdam conference. Stalin told General Antonov that the United States now possessed a new bomb of great destructive power. According to General Shtemenko, chief of the Operations Department of the General Staff, neither Stalin nor Antonov understood the significance of the bomb; at any rate they did not give the General Staff new instructions for the war against Japan.[76] On August 3, after his return to Moscow, Stalin received a report from Marshal Vasilevskii informing him that preparations for the war were nearing completion, and asking him to launch the attack no later than August 9–10, so that advantage could be taken of favorable weather.[77]

On July 26, during the Potsdam conference, Truman, Churchill, and Chiang Kai-shek had issued a joint declaration threatening prompt and utter destruction to Japan if the Japanese government did not proclaim "the unconditional surrender of the Japanese armed forces."[78] Stalin was not consulted about this declaration, and Molotov tried unsuccessfully to delay its publication, fearing no doubt that it might bring about a Japanese surrender before the Soviet Union entered the war.[79] But Japan did not surrender. Prime Minister Suzuki informed the press that his government intended to ignore the Potsdam Declaration.[80] "In the face of this rejection," Stimson later recalled, "we could only proceed to demonstrate that the ultimatum had meant exactly what it said."[81]

On August 6 a United States B-29 bomber took off from Tinian Island and delivered a gun-assembly uranium-235 bomb on Hiroshima at 8.15 a.m., local time. The explosive yield was equivalent to about 13 kilotons of TNT. The effect was devastating. Virtually everything within a radius of 500 meters of the explosion was incinerated. Buildings as far as 3 kilometers away were set ablaze. A thick cloud of smoke mushroomed into the sky to a height of 12,000 meters. Death was instantaneous for some; for others it was much slower. By the end of the year 145,000 people are estimated to have died from the effects of that one bomb; five years later the number of deaths resulting from the bomb had reached 200,000.[82]

IV

The official Soviet reaction to the bombing of Hiroshima was muted. *Izvestiia* and *Pravda* carried a brief Tass report summarizing Truman's statement that an atomic bomb with more destructive power than 20 kilotons of TNT had been dropped on Hiroshima. Tass noted that Britain and the United States had been working jointly on the bomb since early 1940, and reported Truman's comment that at its height the project had employed 125,000 people. Truman's warning that the United States would completely destroy Japan's capacity to wage war was cited. So too were his plans to set up an Atomic Energy Commission in the United States, and to take steps to ensure that atomic energy could be used to safeguard world peace.[83]

Hiroshima produced a greater effect in Moscow than the Soviet press coverage suggests. Alexander Werth, who was the *Sunday Times* correspondent in Moscow from 1941 to 1948, wrote that

the news [of Hiroshima] had an acutely depressing effect on everybody. It was clearly realized that this was a New Fact in the world's power politics, that the bomb constituted a threat to Russia, and some Russian pessimists I talked to that day dismally remarked that Russia's desperately hard victory over Germany was now "as good as wasted".[84]

Svetlana Alliluyeva, Stalin's daughter, went to her father's *dacha* on the day after Hiroshima to find that "he had his usual visitors. They told him that the Americans had dropped the first atom bomb over Japan. Everyone was busy with that, and my father paid hardly any attention to me."[85]

At 4.30 p.m. Moscow time on August 7, Stalin and Antonov signed the order for the Red Army to attack the Japanese forces in Manchuria on the morning of August 9, local time. The negotiations with the Chinese had not been completed, but it was urgent for the Soviet Union to enter the war, in case Japan surrendered. On the following day, August 8, Molotov summoned the Japanese ambassador to the Kremlin for 5 p.m. The ambassador went expecting to receive a reply to his request that Prince Konoye be allowed to come to Moscow. Molotov, however, informed him that the Soviet Union would consider itself to be in a state of war with Japan from August 9.[86] Shortly after this meeting, at 00.10 a.m. on August 9, local time (i.e. 6.10 p.m. on August 8 in Moscow) the Red Army attacked the Japanese forces in Manchuria with more than 1.5 million troops, 26,000 guns and mortars, 5,500 tanks and self-propelled artillery pieces, and 3,900 combat aircraft.[87] The Red Army achieved surprise and mounted a high-speed offensive along a number of different axes.[88] The Kwantung Army, which had been stripped of its best troops and equipment for other theaters, was weaker than Soviet intelligence had anticipated and no match for the Red Army.

Later on the evening of August 8 Stalin and Molotov received Averell Harriman and George Kennan, Minister Counselor at the US embassy, in the Kremlin. Stalin told the Americans that Soviet forces had just crossed into Manchuria and were making rapid progress.[89] Things in general were going much better than he had anticipated, Stalin said. When Harriman asked him what effect he thought the atomic bomb would have on the Japanese, Stalin replied that "he thought the Japanese were at present looking for a pretext to replace the present government with one which would be qualified to undertake a surrender. The bomb might give them this pretext." Stalin was well aware that the Japanese government was looking for a way out of the war, and he may have feared that the bombing of Hiroshima would lead to a quick surrender. Although he had intended to enter the war within a matter of days, the dropping of the atomic bomb appears to have precipitated his decision to attack on August 9.

Stalin told Harriman that Soviet scientists had tried to build an atomic bomb, but had not succeeded in doing so. In Germany they had found a laboratory where German scientists had apparently been working on the atomic bomb, but without any real success. "If they had found it," said Stalin, "Hitler would never have surrendered." Britain, he added, had made no progress, even though it had excellent physicists. Harriman replied that Britain had pooled its knowledge with the United States, but that it had required enormous installations, and an expenditure of $2 billion, to carry the project through to completion.[90] Harriman told Stalin that "if the Allies could keep it [i.e. the atomic bomb] and apply it for peaceful purposes it would be a great thing." Stalin agreed, and said "that would mean the end of war and aggressors. But the secret would have to be well kept."

On the surface the conversation between Stalin and Harriman was quite straightforward. But the subtext seems clear enough, even from the formal language of Kennan's dispatch. Stalin: we have entered the war, in spite of your attempt to end it before we did so. Harriman: the atomic bomb will end the war; we have it, and it was very expensive to build; it will have a great impact on postwar international relations. Stalin: Japan was about to surrender anyway, and the secret of the atomic bomb might be hard to keep. Harriman realized at about this time that the bomb had not been a secret for the Soviet leaders when Molotov, in the course of a conversation about Japan and the bomb (perhaps at this meeting on August 8), "looked at me with something like a smirk on his face and said, 'You Americans can keep a secret when you want to.' "[91]

Stalin was very guarded in his conversation with Harriman. He gave no hint of annoyance at not being informed about the bomb; nor did he give any indication of feeling threatened by the United States' possession of this new weapon. He may have taken a certain sly satisfaction in knowing much more than Harriman supposed. But that was surely little consolation. He must have regretted now that more had not been done during the war to support the atomic project. There was an unsettling parallel between the Soviet Union's entry into World War II and the conclusion of the war. The German attack had surprised Stalin, in spite of the many reports he had received of Hitler's intention. The atomic bomb also caught Stalin by surprise, in spite of the detailed intelligence the Soviet Union had obtained about the Manhattan project. Hiroshima was not as immediately threatening as the German attack, but its consequences for the Soviet Union were potentially dangerous.

Stalin now took immediate steps to set the Soviet atomic project on a new footing. In the middle of August he had discussions with Kurchatov and Boris Vannikov, the People's Commissar of Munitions.[92] On August 20 the State Defense Committee adopted a decree setting up a special committee to direct "all work on the utilization of the intra–atomic energy of uranium."[93] This committee was to be chaired by Beria. The same decree established the First Chief Directorate to manage the atomic project. Vannikov was appointed chief of this organization. Kurchatov remained as scientific director of the project.

The creation of the Special Committee was followed by immediate signs of activity. On August 22 the director of military intelligence in Moscow cabled Colonel Zabotin, the military attaché in Ottawa and head of a GRU spy ring: "Take measures to organize acquisition of documentary materials on the atomic bomb! The technical process, drawings, calculations."[94] Other intelligence residents doubtless received similar instructions. On August 23, M.I. Ivanov, consul at the Soviet embassy in Tokyo, arrived in Hiroshima with one of the military attachés to obtain a first-hand impression of the destruction that the atomic bomb had caused.[95] By September most of the German scientists had been set up in two institutes on the coast of the Black Sea to work on isotope separation.[96] In September a special commission was formed under the leadership of P. Ia. Antropov,

one of Vannikov's deputies at the First Chief Directorate, to go to Central
Asia to speed up the mining of uranium ore.[97] In the same month Iakov
Malik sent Moscow a report prepared by officials from the embassy in
Tokyo who had visited Hiroshima. Along with this report he sent articles
from the Japanese press describing the effects of the atomic bombs. This
material was circulated to Stalin, Beria, Malenkov, Molotov, and Anastas
Mikoian, the People's Commissar of Foreign Trade.[98]

V

In Tokyo the initial reaction to the bombing of Hiroshima was confused.
It was not until the following day that it became clear that a single bomb
had destroyed the whole city. When Truman announced, on August 6,
that it had been an atomic bomb, the Japanese military dismissed his claim
as propaganda and played down the damage that had been done, as well as
the destruction that might be expected in the future. Not until August 10,
the day after the bombing of Nagasaki, did Japanese government experts
agree that the United States had indeed destroyed Hiroshima with an
atomic bomb.[99]

In his careful study of Japan's decision to surrender, Robert Butow notes
that the effect of Soviet entry into the war on August 9 was all the more
staggering because it followed the destruction of Hiroshima. "In spite of
the element of personal danger which still remained," he writes,

the [Japanese] proponents of peace were prepared to act boldly. In short, they
recognized in the atomic bomb and the Soviet entry into the war not just an
imperative need to give in but actually a supreme opportunity to turn the tide
against the die-hards and to shake the government loose from the yoke of military
oppression under which it had been laboring so long.[100]

The advocates of peace in Japan had now to act more boldly not only
because the Red Army was advancing rapidly, but also because the Soviet
attack destroyed all hope of using Soviet good offices to bring the war to
an end.

At 11.02 a.m. local time on August 9 the United States exploded a
plutonium bomb over Nagasaki. The explosive yield was 21 kilotons.
Once again the effects were terrible. By the end of the year over 70,000
people, it is now estimated, had died from that one bomb.[101] When news
of the destruction of Nagasaki reached Tokyo, a bitter debate took place in
the government about the terms on which Japan might sue for peace. The
peace party was willing to surrender if the Emperor's prerogatives as a
sovereign ruler were maintained; the militarists sought other conditions.
Early on the morning of August 10 the Emperor, in an unprecedented act,
sided with the peace party and expressed his will that the Potsdam Declaration be accepted on the single condition that the Emperor's role be

preserved. This decision was communicated to the Allies on the same day. The Allied reply, which insisted that the Emperor be subject to the Supreme Commander of the Allied Powers, evoked renewed debate in Tokyo. Finally, on August 14, the Emperor decided to accept the Allied terms. On August 16 the Imperial General Headquarters ordered Japanese troops to stop fighting at once.[102]

In Manchuria the war continued for several days more. On August 19 General Yamada, Commander-in-Chief of the Kwantung Army, signed the act of surrender. The Red Army had made rapid progress, occupying northern China as far south as the Liaotung peninsula, as well as northern Korea, southern Sakhalin and most of the Kurile islands, by the time the formal act of unconditional surrender was signed by Japan on September 2. The Soviet Union had strengthened its strategic position in the Far East. Stalin declared publicly that "the surrender means that southern Sakhalin and the Kurile islands will pass to the Soviet Union, and from now on will not serve as a means for isolating the Soviet Union from the ocean or as a base for Japanese attacks on our Far East."[103]

But Stalin had hoped for more. On August 16 he wrote to Truman asking that Soviet forces be allowed to accept the surrender of Japanese forces on the northern half of the island of Hokkaido. This proposal had particular significance for Russian public opinion, he wrote, because Japanese forces had occupied the Soviet Far East in 1919–21. Two days later Truman replied rejecting this request and repeating that Japanese forces would surrender to the United States on all the main islands of Japan, including Hokkaido.[104] Stalin, however, was reluctant to give up the idea of landing Soviet forces on Hokkaido. On August 19 Marshal Vasilevskii ordered the 1st Far Eastern Front, whose forces were just about to take southern Sakhalin, to occupy the northern half of Hokkaido as well as the southern Kuriles. On August 21 Vasilevskii sent the Soviet forces a detailed plan for this operation – indicating that the General Staff had planned for this eventuality. On August 22, however, Vasilevskii rescinded the order to occupy Hokkaido, though the occupation of the southern Kuriles went ahead. Stalin had evidently concluded that the attempt to land forces on Hokkaido would cause a political row – and perhaps even an armed clash – with the United States.[105] The order rescinding the attack on Hokkaido stated: "To avoid the creation of conflicts and misunderstanding with respect to the allies, it is categorically forbidden to send any ships or planes at all in the direction of the island of Hokkaido."[106] Stalin chose to be satisfied with securing the concessions he had obtained at Yalta.

Stalin had already decided, by the time of the formal Japanese surrender on September 2, to organize a high-priority atomic project. There is no evidence of any discussion in the political leadership – at this time or later – about the wisdom of this decision. It was assumed that if the United States had the atomic bomb, the Soviet Union needed to have it too. But building the atomic bomb was, as Harriman had pointed out, an expensive undertaking. This was especially so for a country whose economy was in ruins after a bitter and destructive war. Yet Stalin did not stint the project. At about this time he told Kurchatov, "If a child doesn't cry, the mother doesn't know what he needs. Ask for whatever you like. You won't be refused."[107]

Stalin now understood that a new factor had entered into international relations. That factor could be seen in different ways. The United States had used the bomb to bring the war to an end as quickly as possible. American historians have generally seen the desire to end the war quickly as the primary motive for dropping the atomic bomb, and pressure on the Soviet Union as a secondary, though reinforcing, motive.[108] In Soviet minds, however, ending the war quickly could be interpreted as being, in itself, directed against Soviet interests. Stalin had feared that the war with Japan would be over before the Soviet Union could enter and secure its strategic interests in the Far East. From his conversation with Harriman it is clear that Stalin thought Hiroshima might lead to a quick surrender. It is possible – even likely – therefore that he believed that Truman had used the atomic bomb with the intention of thwarting Soviet purposes in the Far East.

The Soviet Union attacked Japan before the negotiations with the Chinese had been completed. Stalin had told Hopkins that the Soviet Union would not enter the war until the treaty with China was signed. This statement should not be taken too seriously, however. Stalin was determined to enter the war, and the timetable for entry was dictated more by the preparation of Soviet forces than by the talks with the Chinese. The Sino-Soviet Treaty of Friendship and Alliance was signed on August 14. The treaty did not incorporate all the demands that the Soviet Union had put forward in the negotiations. The hurried entry into the war may have meant that Stalin got less than he hoped for, but the Treaty did endorse all the basic provisions of the Yalta Agreement, including the independence of Mongolia from China.[109]

The bomb was important in a broader context too. Stalin is reported to have told Kurchatov and Vannikov in the middle of August that "Hiroshima has shaken the whole world. The balance has been destroyed."[110] The balance of power which was taking shape at the end of World War II had been upset by this new and terrible weapon. Hiroshima had demonstrated the power of the bomb and American willingness to use it. Stalin wanted to restore the balance by acquiring a Soviet bomb as quickly as possible. The scientists told him that that would take five years.[111] In the meantime the United States would enjoy a monopoly of the atomic bomb.

In his memoirs Andrei Gromyko, who was ambassador to the United States in 1945, recalls a conversation in which Stalin discussed the atomic bomb with Molotov, F.T. Gusev, the ambassador to Britain, and Gromyko himself. Gromyko writes that the conversation took place during the Potsdam conference, but there are reasons to doubt the accuracy of Gromyko's memory on that count.[112] The content of the exchange nevertheless rings true. Stalin, according to Gromyko, said that Washington and London doubtless hoped that the Soviet Union would take a long time to build the bomb. During that time, Stalin continued, they would use their atomic monopoly to impose their plans for Europe, and for the rest of the world, on the Soviet Union. But "no," said Stalin, "that will not be." Whether or not this account is true, it does formulate what appears to have been Stalin's concern, that the atomic bomb had altered the balance of power and would enable the United States to shape the postwar settlement to its own advantage.

The atomic bomb was not only a powerful weapon; it was also a symbol of American power. Stalin had pursued his policy of industrialization under the slogan, "Catch up and overtake." As the most powerful symbol of American economic and technological might, the atomic bomb was *ipso facto* something the Soviet Union had to have too. Stalin's decision to make an all-out effort to build a Soviet bomb fell squarely into the pattern of innovation discussed in Chapter 1: the Soviet Union was following the technological path mapped out by the advanced capitalist countries. Stalin had not taken the atomic bomb seriously until Hiroshima had shown in the most dramatic way that it could be built. The Soviet Union now mobilized its resources to catch up. These reasons for building the bomb – to restore the emerging balance of power, and to acquire a new and potent symbol of power – would have existed even if Niels Bohr's advice to inform Stalin had been followed. The bomb would still have affected the balance of power, and would still have been a symbol of the economic and technological might of the state. Stalin would still have wanted a bomb of his own.

CHAPTER SEVEN

The Post-Hiroshima Project

I

LAVRENTII BERIA made his career in the police apparatus in Georgia and Azerbaidzhan in the 1920s. Stalin brought him to Moscow in 1938, at the height of the great purge, as deputy to N.I. Ezhov, the head of the NKVD. Within a few months Ezhov disappeared and Beria took his place.[1] Stalin's daughter, Svetlana Alliluyeva, has portrayed Beria as her father's "evil genius," who exploited Stalin's self-doubt and trusting nature to establish and maintain influence over him.[2] It is true that Beria was a cunning intriguer, who manipulated his control of the police to increase his own power. But he was Stalin's creature, and retained his power because he was useful to the "Boss." "He was afraid of Stalin," one of the industrial managers who worked for him during the war has written, "afraid of his anger, afraid of losing his trust and favor."[3]

"A talented organizer, but cruel, ruthless," was Molotov's judgment on Beria.[4] All the leaders signed lists of people to be arrested and shot, but Beria also took part in torturing his victims. Beria was undoubtedly cruel, but he was also able. His effectiveness derived in large measure from his control of the police. An order from any Politburo member carried great authority, but an order from Beria was a matter of life and death: "just one remark like 'Beria has ordered . . .' worked absolutely without fail."[5] It was not an aberrant or eccentric act, therefore, to put him in charge of the atomic project, but an indication of the project's central importance for the Soviet leadership. Beria now worked through a powerful apparatus – though perhaps not of the kind that Academician Rozhdestvenskii had in mind when he spoke at the March 1936 session of the Academy of Sciences.[6]

Beria chaired the Special Committee on the Atomic Bomb, which the State Defense Committee had set up on August 20.[7] Two other powerful political figures were members of the committee: Georgii Malenkov, one of the Central Committee secretaries, and Nikolai Voznesenskii, head of

Gosplan, the State Planning Committee. Three industrial managers –
Vannikov, Zaveniagin, and Pervukhin – were members. The two scientists
on the committee were Kurchatov and Kapitsa. NKVD General V.A.
Makhnev, who headed the committee's secretariat, was also a member.
There were no military men on the committee. The Special Committee
took the most important decisions on the atomic project: it reviewed
proposals from Vannikov and Kurchatov, and prepared documents for
Stalin's signature.[8] Beria was supposed to report every week to Stalin on the
progress of the project.[9]

Two other organizations were set up to manage the project on a day-to-
day basis. The First Chief Directorate of the Council of People's Commissars was responsible for establishing and managing the mines, industrial
plants, and research establishments of the atomic industry.[10] Vannikov was
put in charge, with Zaveniagin, Pervukhin, and several other leading
managers, as his deputies. A Scientific-Technical Council (sometimes
called the Technical Council) was set up in the First Chief Directorate.
This was chaired by Vannikov; Pervukhin, Zaveniagin, and Kurchatov
were appointed his deputies. The council, which consisted of industrial
managers and scientists (Kikoin, Alikhanov, Ioffe, and Kapitsa were among
its first members) advised on the most important scientific and technical
decisions.[11]

Beria did not work through these organizations alone. He had his own
representatives – known as "plenipotentiaries of the Council of People's
Commissars" – at each of the nuclear plants and research establishments.
These were normally NKVD generals, who had offices near the office of
the institute or plant director. They reported to Beria on what was going
on at the installation to which they were assigned. Some of them were
helpful to the director of the installation, others were merely a threatening
presence.[12] The NKVD was a pervasive element in the administration of
the project. It was responsible for security, which was exceptionally stringent. Its camps and prisons provided construction workers for the atomic
industry and miners for the uranium mines.[13]

Beria set up a special "Department S" in the NKGB to coordinate the
distribution and evaluation of intelligence materials that were obtained.
This department was headed by Pavel Sudoplatov and his deputy, Leonid
Eitingon, who had arranged the assassination of Trotskii. (In 1946 these
two men were put in charge of a special service of the MGB (Ministry of
State Security) to carry out assassinations in the Soviet Union and abroad.)[14]
Sudoplatov later wrote that "we had daily working contact with Academi-
cians Kurchatov, Kikoin and others, and also with Generals Vannikov,
Zaveniagin. The comrades I have named were pleased with our informa-
tion."[15] In September 1945 Iakov Terletskii, a competent physicist from
Moscow University, was appointed scientific adviser to Department S. He
was able to evaluate the intelligence materials, summarize them, and report

on them to Kurchatov and his colleagues.[16] The intelligence materials were apparently no longer shown directly to Kurchatov.

The expanded project saw an influx not only of NKVD officers, but also of industrial managers. These men were members of the technical intelligentsia that had been created in the Stalin years to carry through the policy of industrialization. Vannikov and his colleagues at the First Chief Directorate were all in their forties in 1945, and most had acquired their technical education after some years of party work. They were promoted rapidly during the purges, and in the war played key roles in organizing arms production. Vannikov, for example, was born in Baku in 1897 and joined the Party in 1919. He did underground Party work before attending the Moscow Higher Technical School, the country's leading school of engineering. After graduating in 1926 he was made director of a defense plant in Tula. In 1937 he became Deputy People's Commissar of the Defense Industry. Two years later, when the Defense Industry Commissariat was broken up into four separate commissariats, he became People's Commissar of Armament.[17]

The role of men like Vannikov was to fulfill orders coming from above. They worked under intense pressure, and passed this pressure on to their subordinates. They did not enjoy political or personal security. Vannikov was put in prison early in June 1941, after a dispute with Zhdanov and Stalin about artillery production. In the desperate opening days of the war Stalin ordered him to write a memorandum on arms production, and soon he was taken from prison directly to Stalin's office in the Kremlin. Stalin sent him back to his old commissariat as deputy to Dmitrii Ustinov, the new People's Commissar. In the following year Vannikov was put in charge of a new People's Commissariat of Munitions, where his work was overseen by Beria, who had special responsibility for the armament, munitions, and tank industries during the war.[18]

Vannikov, Zaveniagin, and Pervukhin were very competent men. Vannikov, according to Khariton, was a superb manager and a fine engineer, very witty and good with people.[19] Zaveniagin and Pervukhin, as was noted earlier, were regarded by those who worked with them as extremely capable. Like the other managers who joined the project, they had played a major role in turning the Soviet Union into an industrial power and in producing arms and equipment for the victory over Nazi Germany. In the 1930s they had executed the policy of "catching up and overtaking" the West. Now they faced the same task again, in a new and difficult form.

Vannikov was dismayed by the responsibility he had been given. Early in September 1945 he said to Vasilii Emel'ianov, whom he had just asked to head the scientific-technical directorate at the First Chief Directorate:

Yesterday I met the physicists and the radiochemists from the Radium Institute. For the present we are still speaking different languages. Or more precisely, they are speaking while I blink; the words sound Russian, but I am hearing them for the first time, they're not in my vocabulary.[20]

Vannikov had to organize a new industry on the basis of what the scientists told him, even though he did not understand what they were saying. "We engineers," he said to Emel'ianov,

are used to touching everything with our hands and seeing everything with our eyes, and in extreme cases a microscope will help. But here it is powerless. It makes no difference, you won't see the atom, and even less will you see what is hidden inside it. And on the basis of this invisible and intangible thing we have to build factories, and organize industrial production.[21]

When Emel'ianov asked Vannikov what he should do first, Vannikov stared at him and said "You think that I know everything? If only it were so! Why then would I need so many deputies?"[22]

Kurchatov organized seminars to explain the uranium problem to the industrial managers. At one of these sessions Kikoin gave a report on isotope separation. When he had finished, Viacheslav Malyshev, one of the industrial managers drawn into the project, turned to Emel'ianov and asked, "Did you understand anything?" Emel'ianov whispered that he had understood a little, whereupon Malyshev sighed and said that he had understood virtually nothing – much to the relief of Emel'ianov, who had understood nothing either.[23] Kurchatov evidently sensed this, for he put questions to Kikoin to draw him out in a manner intelligible to the industrial managers. This was Emel'ianov's first meeting with Kurchatov, and he was impressed by Kurchatov's appearance – his spade-shaped black beard and his bright eyes – and by his open manner, which made Emel'ianov feel quite at ease.[24]

The task the managers faced was to convert a laboratory project into a whole industry. Uranium had to be found, and isotope separation plants built, as well as reactors for plutonium production. All of this entailed considerable planning and organization. Kurchatov, Kikoin, Alikhanov, Khariton, and Artsimovich were summoned to meetings in the Kremlin, in the NKVD headquarters on Lubianka Square, and in the People's Commissariat of Munitions, to explain what the atomic bomb was, and what the Soviet Union needed to do to make it.[25] The work that Kurchatov and his colleagues had done during the war provided the basis for the expanded project. But there was much to do in the first months: people to be recruited, sites found for the new installations, a research and development strategy defined.

The Manhattan project had proved successful, and the Soviet Union possessed a great deal of information about it. Soviet technical choices were strongly influenced by what the Americans had done. This was evident in the choice of isotope separation methods, but it was clearest of all in the design of the first Soviet bomb. In June 1945 Klaus Fuchs had provided a detailed description of the plutonium bomb: a list of the components and of the materials from which they were made, all the important dimensions, and a sketch of the design. He provided further information in September. On October 18, 1945 Merkulov, the head of the NKGB, sent Beria a report describing in detail the design of the plutonium bomb. This report, which was evidently based upon the information that Fuchs had supplied, described the components of the bomb, the materials from which they were made, and their dimensions.[26] Khariton later commented that it was detailed enough to enable a competent engineer to produce a blueprint for the bomb.[27]

When they studied the information Fuchs had supplied, Kurchatov and Khariton decided to use it for the design of the first Soviet bomb. Stalin wanted a bomb as soon as possible. It made sense therefore to use the American design, since that was available. Everything in the report had to be checked, of course: all the same calculations had to be done, and all the theoretical and experimental work. Only a very few people knew of the intelligence material. Apart from one or two men, the scientists and engineers who built the first Soviet bomb did not know that they were producing a copy of the American design.[28]

II

Not everyone was happy with the way in which the project was being organized. On October 3, 1945 Kapitsa wrote to Stalin asking to be allowed to resign from the Special Committee and the Technical Council.[29] Kapitsa was in good standing with the regime at this time. During the war he had developed a new method for producing liquid oxygen for the metallurgical and chemical industries, and had been put in charge of a Chief Directorate for Oxygen under the Council of People's Commissars. In May 1945 he had been made a Hero of Socialist Labor, the highest civilian honor.[30] Now he explained to Stalin that he wanted to resign from government work because of Beria's "unacceptable" attitude to scientists. When he invited Kapitsa to join the atomic project, Beria had "simply ordered his secretary to summon me to his office," wrote Kapitsa.

What was at issue, in Kapitsa's mind, was not good manners, but the larger question of the position of scientists in society. "There was a time," Kapitsa wrote, "when the Patriarch stood alongside the Emperor; the Church was then the repository of culture. The Church is becoming obsolete and the patriarchs have had their day, but the country cannot manage without leaders in the sphere of ideas." Only science and learning could provide the basis for technological, economic, and political progress. "You personally, like Lenin," he wrote to Stalin, "are moving the country forward as a scholar and a thinker. The country has been exceptionally fortunate to have such leaders, but that may not always be so. . . . Sooner or later we will have to raise scientists and scholars to the rank of patriarch." Only then would scientists serve their country with enthusiasm: "it is time for comrades like Comrade Beria to begin to learn respect for scientists." The time had not yet come, Kapitsa concluded, for "close and fruitful collaboration between politicians and scientists." Since he could not be a patriarch, he would prefer to remain a monk, and to resign from the Special Committee.

Stalin did not reply to this letter. Kapitsa wrote again on November 25, setting out more fully his objections to the way in which the atomic project was being organized.[31] The path that had been chosen, he wrote, was not the quickest or cheapest route to the bomb. The United States had spent $2 billion to build the most powerful weapon of war and destruction. That was equivalent to about 30 billion roubles, and the Soviet Union could hardly afford that much in the coming 2–3-year period of reconstruction. The Soviet Union had one advantage, Kapitsa wrote; it knew that the bomb could be built, while the Americans had had to take a risk. But Soviet industry was weaker, and had been distorted and destroyed by the war; the Soviet Union had fewer scientists, and their working conditions were worse; the American scientific base and scientific instruments industry were stronger. These handicaps did not mean that the Soviet Union should lay down its arms. "Although it will be difficult," Kapitsa wrote, "we must in any event try to make the A.B. [atomic bomb] quickly and cheaply. But not by the path we are now following, which is completely unmethodical and without a plan. . . . We want to retry everything the Americans did rather than try to follow our own path. We are forgetting that to follow the American path is beyond our means, and will take a long time."[32]

Kapitsa proposed his own approach. A two-year research program should be organized to find a cheaper and quicker way to make the bomb. During that time the industrial base should be made ready, because it was clear in general terms what would be needed. The scientific base should be strengthened in this period too, by improving the welfare of scientists, raising the standard of higher education, and organizing the production of scientific instruments and chemical reagents. There was great enthusiasm for the bomb among scientists and engineers, Kapitsa wrote, but this had to be harnessed properly. A commander-in-chief who wanted to take a fortress might receive many proposals about how to do it, but he would not tell each of his generals to do it in his own way. He would choose one plan, and one general to execute it. That was how the Soviet Union should solve the problem of building the bomb: concentrate its resources on a limited front and along a well-chosen axis.

There was, according to Kapitsa, one condition that had to be met if the Soviet Union was to build the bomb quickly and independently, and that was "greater trust between scientists and political figures."[33] This was an old problem, Kapitsa noted, and although the war had done much to resolve it, it would disappear only when there was greater respect for the scientist and for science. He had found that he was listened to only when he had been put in charge of the Chief Directorate for Oxygen; Kapitsa the administrator commanded more attention than Kapitsa the scientist with a world reputation. The same thing was happening with the atomic bomb. The opinions of scientists were treated with skepticism, and ignored in practice. "Comrade Vannikov and the others from the Technical Council," he wrote, "remind me of the citizen in the joke, who, not believing the doctors, drank all the mineral waters in Essentuki one after the other, in the hope that one of them would help."[34]

Kapitsa's criticism of the Special Committee was even more pointed. "Comrades Beria, Malenkov, and Voznesenskii," he wrote,

conduct themselves in the Special Committee like supermen. In particular Comrade Beria. It is true, he has the conductor's baton in his hand. That's fine, but all the same a scientist should play first violin. For the violin sets the tone for the whole orchestra. Comrade Beria's basic weakness is that the conductor ought not only to wave the baton, but also to understand the score. In this respect Beria is weak.[35]

Beria could handle the job of building the atomic bomb if he gave it time and energy. But he was too self-assured, in Kapitsa's view. Kapitsa wanted Beria to learn some physics. It was not enough to sit in the chairman's seat and cross out words in draft decrees; that was not what directing the project meant. The exchanges between Beria and Kapitsa in the Special Committee had evidently become unpleasant. When Kapitsa told Beria, "You do not understand physics, let us scientists decide on these questions," Beria responded that Kapitsa did not understand anything about people.[36] In this letter Kapitsa repeated his request to be allowed to resign from the Special Committee and the Technical Council.

Kapitsa's letter raises two important questions. The first is whether the Soviet Union could have followed a cheaper and quicker path to the bomb, as Kapitsa urged. It is unclear what Kapitsa had in mind, or whether he had anything very specific in mind at all. Kapitsa's argument no doubt seemed unconvincing to Beria, who appears to have feared that the intelligence about the Manhattan project might contain disinformation, but was also suspicious of Soviet scientists and their recommendations. The Soviet Union wanted the bomb as soon as possible, and was prepared to pay virtually any price to obtain it. It made sense to exploit the intelligence information about the Manhattan project rather than search for a new Soviet way to build the bomb. It also made sense to pursue redundant paths to the bomb, rather than adopt a single plan of attack. If the Soviet leaders had not wanted the bomb urgently, or had been more concerned about the cost, it would have been sensible for them to follow Kapitsa's advice.

Although this might have been cheaper, there was no guarantee that it would be quicker.

The second question raised by Kapitsa was the role of scientists in directing the project. Kapitsa wanted Beria to learn physics, and urged that scientists take a leading role in management. He recommended to Stalin that the signature of a scientist be attached to each protocol of the Special Committee and to the decrees of the various directorate chiefs. He urged that "scientific commissars" be appointed, to ensure that officials acted in "scientifically literate" way.[37]

Something like this arrangement did emerge. Kurchatov, as scientific director, ensured that decisions were "scientifically literate," and he became a kind of "scientific commissar" to Beria and Vannikov. Other scientists were appointed as scientific directors for different parts of the project, and there played a similar role, on a smaller scale. In spite of Kapitsa's misgivings – and perhaps because of his criticism – scientific advice and political authority were effectively combined. Beria was, by the account of scientists who worked with him, an efficient and competent administrator. Khariton found him correct in his attitude to scientists, and helpful in providing them with what they needed.[38] Sakharov regarded him as a terrible man, but an able administrator.[39] It is testimony to Kurchatov's extraordinary qualities as an organizer that he was able to work for Beria, collaborate with Vannikov and Zaveniagin, and retain the confidence and loyalty of his scientific colleagues.

Beria was not an easy person to work for. At the end of his November letter to Stalin, Kapitsa attached a postscript: "I wish Comrade Beria to be acquainted with this letter, for it is not a denunciation, but useful criticism. I would have told him all this myself, but it's a great deal of trouble to get to see him."[40] When Beria saw the letter he telephoned Kapitsa and asked him to come to see him. Kapitsa refused, saying that "If you wish to speak to me, then come to the institute." Beria came, bringing a double-barreled gun as a present for Kapitsa.[41] Kapitsa and Beria did not resolve their differences, however, and Kapitsa left the atomic project on December 19.[42] The letters make it clear that his withdrawal was motivated not by moral or political opposition to building the bomb, but by his unhappiness with Beria's attitude to scientists, and with the policy of copying the United States.[43] He was unwilling, he wrote to Stalin, to be a blind subordinate, executing a policy with which he did not agree.

Kapitsa was troubled by another issue: the effect of the bomb on science, and on international scientific contacts. At the Academy celebration in June 1945 he had expressed the view that there was no such thing as Soviet science or British science, only international science; and he had argued the year before that scientists should take an active part in establishing a sound and lasting peace.[44] On October 22, 1945 he wrote to Niels Bohr, who had now returned to Denmark, that in our days the danger exists that scientific discoveries, held in secret, may serve not humanity as a whole, but could be used in the egoistical interests of individual political and national groups. Sometimes I wonder what ought to be the correct position of scientists in such cases. I would very much like to discuss this problem with you personally at the first opportunity.[45]

On the day before Kapitsa wrote this letter, Bohr had written to Kapitsa expressing similar sentiments. He sent Kapitsa two articles he had recently published in *The Times* and *Science*, arguing for an open world.[46] "No control [of atomic energy] can be effective," he had written in *The Times*, "without free access to full scientific information and the granting of the opportunity of international supervision of all undertakings which, unless regulated, might become a source of disaster." To Kapitsa he wrote: "I shall be most interested to learn what you think yourself about this all-important matter which places so great a responsibility on our whole generation."[47]

Bohr had not given up his hope that scientists might come together to discuss the implications of the atomic bomb. Now that the existence of the bomb was no longer a secret, he was free to write to Kapitsa. His letter suggests that he wanted to see whether it might be possible to arrange a meeting between Soviet and Western scientists to discuss the implications of the atomic bomb. It is evident that Kapitsa too wished to discuss the atomic bomb with Bohr. But instead of a meeting between Bohr and Kapitsa, something bizarre happened. Beria sent Iakov Terletskii, the scientific adviser to the NKGB's Department S, to Copenhagen to see Bohr in November. Beria's aim was not to encourage an international dialogue between scientists, but to ask Bohr for information about the bomb. Bohr, who was correct and careful in dealing with secret matters, gave Terletskii very general answers to his questions and key Danish intelligence as well as British and American authorities informed about the visit.[48]

Terletskii believed that Beria had sent him to Copenhagen in order to "to put pressure in some way on our scientists, with whom they were angry for somehow slowing things down. . . . They had used these [intelligence] materials badly and hadn't made the bomb in time."[49] This is plausible. It is unlikely that Stalin, Beria, and Molotov took upon themselves responsibility for the failure to speed up the atomic project during the war; they no doubt blamed the scientists. But the episode is strange, nonetheless. Did Beria hope to persuade Bohr to collaborate with the Soviet project in some way? Did he hope to obtain technical information about the bomb? Terletskii's mission seems to show an enormous lack of confidence, on Beria's part, in both the intelligence materials and the Soviet scientists.

This episode may have contributed to the rift between Kapitsa and Beria. Kapitsa may have felt that Beria had abused his, Kapitsa's, relationship with Bohr; Beria may have thought that Kapitsa's international contacts had proved worthless for the project. On December 18 Kapitsa wrote to Molotov with the main points of an article he wanted to publish on the situation "created in world science in connection with questions of atomic energy."[50] The central point of the article was that secrecy was ineffective, and harmful to science. The success in harnessing atomic energy, he wrote, marked the opening of a new era in human culture. Its main significance was that it gave the human race a powerful source of energy. To see atomic energy only as a means of destruction was as trivial and absurd as to regard electricity primarily as a source of energy for the electric chair. American scientists and engineers had done remarkable pioneering work, but the path they had taken could not be regarded as the shortest or the most economical. "It is therefore quite natural," he wrote, "that already more effective ways connected with the technical utilization of atomic energy are emerging, and various possibilities of utilizing it."[51]

It was not yet clear, wrote Kapitsa, how effective atomic bombs would be. Only a fraction of the enormous potential energy of the bomb was released in the blast wave, which was less powerful than expected. A large part of the energy was "lost" in radiation. This radiation incinerated many houses and people in Japan. But "if the Japanese had lived not in 'cardboard houses' and had not been caught by surprise, the number of casualties would have been significantly smaller because one can protect oneself from most of the radiation released by the explosion of an atomic bomb."[52] These facts, he wrote, indicated that the main significance of atomic energy lay in its peaceful applications. The secrecy that now surrounded atomic energy had placed scientists in an absurd position: instead of sharing their findings with colleagues abroad, they had to rediscover what had already been discovered. This was the most unhealthy way for world science and technology to develop. But there was a common law of development for human culture, and secrecy would not stop the development of science and technology in a country where that development had already attained the appropriate level.

Kapitsa sought Molotov's permission to publish this article. Molotov sent the outline to Beria, after writing on top of the first page: "In my view Kapitsa may be permitted to publish such an article." Three days later, on December 21, Molotov wrote on the same document: "Inform Comrade Kapitsa over the telephone that in my view he had better wait with this matter." Kapitsa was informed of this decision on December 25. It seems clear that Beria had decided that Kapitsa should not publish this article. On December 19 Kapitsa was relieved of his position in the atomic project.[53]

Kapitsa did not fall into disfavor at once. Stalin wrote to him on April 4, 1946, in reply to a recommendation from Kapitsa that a certain book be published. This was one of only two letters that Stalin wrote to Kapitsa, and it read in full:

I have received all your letters. In your letters there is much that is instructive – I am thinking of meeting you some time and talking about them. As far as the book by L. Gumilevskii, *Russian Engineers*, is concerned, it is very interesting and will be published soon.[54]

Beria was apparently disturbed – as indeed Stalin may have intended – by the prospect of a meeting between Stalin and Kapitsa. He asked Stalin for permission to arrest Kapitsa, but Stalin refused, saying, "I will remove him for you, but don't you touch him."[55] Beria, presumably with Stalin's connivance, now organized an elegant intrigue; he set up a special commission, which condemned the oxygen production process that Kapitsa had devised. In August 1946 Stalin signed a decree dismissing Kapitsa from the directorship of his institute, and appointing Anatolii Aleksandrov in his place.[56] Kapitsa was now forced to conduct research at his *dacha* outside Moscow, where he set up a small laboratory. He had fallen into disfavor, but still depended on Stalin's protection. He may have owed his survival to Stalin's desire to show Beria who was really in charge. This was a precarious position, and especially difficult for someone who insisted that Soviet leaders should respect the authority of science and of scientists.

III

On August 8, 1945, two days after Hiroshima, the Politburo instructed Gosplan to prepare the Five-Year Plan for 1946–50.[57] The country had suffered terribly in the war. Twenty-six or 27 million Soviet citizens had been killed, according to the best estimates available today.[58] Twenty-five million were left homeless. Large industrial centers like Leningrad, Khar'kov, and Stalingrad were in ruins. The Soviet Union faced an immense task of reconstruction.[59] This was the context in which the atomic project had to be organized.

The new Five-Year Plan gave particular attention to technological progress, and for the first time there was a separate Technical Plan. On November 6, 1945, in a speech marking the 28th anniversary of the October Revolution, Molotov declared that economic policy now had to pay "paramount attention" to technological progress:

We ought to equal the achievements of modern world technology in all branches of industry and the national economy and provide the conditions for the greatest possible advance of Soviet science and technology. The enemy hindered our peaceful, creative work. But we will make up for everything, as necessary, and we will achieve the prosperity of our country. We will have atomic energy too, and much else. [*Stormy prolonged applause. All rise.*][60]

This was the first official announcement that the Soviet Union had an atomic project of its own.

The plan for new technology consisted primarily of military projects. "Without fear of exaggeration," a Russian historian has written, "one can say that at that time all the basic forces of science were concentrated on those directions on which the defense potential of the USSR depended."[61] Besides the atomic project, particular attention was paid to radar, rocketry, and jet propulsion. A.G. Zverev, the People's Commissar of Finances at the time, has written of the preparation of the Five-Year Plan that "in connection with the uneasy international situation and the beginning of the 'Cold War' expenditures on defense were not reduced as much as we had calculated. And besides, the rapid progress of military technology required significant resources."[62] Most of this additional expenditure was connected with the atomic bomb: the atomic project itself; the rockets which were intended ultimately to deliver atomic bombs to their targets; radar to enhance defenses against a possible atomic air attack; and jet propulsion, which was used first in air defense interceptors.

The radar, rocket, and jet propulsion programs provide striking support for the argument, which Kapitsa put forward in his November 25 letter to Stalin, that lack of trust in science and scientists (and, one might add, engineers) hampered technological progress in the Soviet Union. In all three cases pioneering research had been curtailed by the political authorities, and resumed only when it had become clear that other countries were developing these technologies.

The Soviet Union began to work on radar in the early 1930s, at about the same time as Britain, Germany, and the United States. Radar systems were developed, and some entered production before 1941, but progress was not as fast as the supporters of radar had hoped. There were practical and theoretical obstacles to be overcome, and there was some skepticism among scientists and in the military; besides, the Soviet radio industry had difficulty producing the necessary equipment. The purges too had a very negative effect on the development of Soviet radar.[63]

It was only during the war that the importance of radar was understood by the political authorities. In July 1943 the State Defense Committee set up a Council on Radar, with Malenkov as chairman, to coordinate research and development and expand the output of equipment. Copies were produced of the radar systems supplied by the United States, Britain, and Canada under Lend-Lease.[64] A Chief Directorate for Radar was set up in the People's Commissariat of the Aviation Industry, and one of the instrument-making plants was converted to radar production.[65]

At the end of the war the Council on Radar sent a special commission to Germany to examine on-site radar installations and the German electronics industry. The commission prepared detailed technical reports, which, together with studies of British and American radar, provided the basis for postwar radar development. German radar specialists were brought to the Soviet Union and assigned to Soviet factories.[66] The council drew up a three-year plan for radar development, and this was approved by the government in July 1946.[67] The Soviet Union had a considerable lag to make up: an American intelligence assessment in 1946 put it at least ten years behind the United States in radar development.[68] By early 1946, however, the Soviet Union had laid the basis for a large-scale radar development program.

Missile development followed a similar pattern. Missile research in the 1930s sprang from two traditions: military interest in rockets as an extension of artillery, and interest in outer space, symbolized above all by the great theorist of space flight, K.I. Tsiolkovskii. The Reactive Research Institute (RNII: *Reaktivnyi Nauchno-issledovatel'skii Institut*), which was established in 1933, worked on powder rockets and their launch platforms, liquid-propellant rocket motors, ramjets, and cruise missiles.[69] M.N. Tukhachevskii, Chief of Armament of the Red Army in the early 1930s, saw that rockets, by delivering projectiles of any power and range, might play an important role in the high-speed offensive operations that he thought would dominate modern warfare.[70]

Missile development suffered greatly when leading figures – including Tukhachevskii – were arrested and shot in the Great Purge. Sergei Korolev, who was to head the missile program after the war, was arrested but escaped death; after a spell at the notorious Kolyma camp, he was sent to work in the *sharashka* (a design bureau staffed by prisoners) headed by the aircraft designer A.N. Tupolev.[71] Valentin Glushko, who was to develop large liquid-propellant rocket engines after the war, was arrested and sent to an aircraft engine factory in Moscow to work on rocket boosters for aircraft.[72] The closer war seemed, the less interest the military and political leadership had in long-term missile development: Korolev was told by his interrogator that "your pyrotechnics and fireworks are not only not needed by our country, but are harmful to it."[73] The most successful outcome of the prewar work was the "Katiusha" rocket artillery, which was widely used in the war, to great effect.[74]

Soviet interest in rockets did not revive until 1944, when Germany attacked London with the V-1 air-breathing missile and the V-2 ballistic rocket. The first V-1 attack took place on June 13, 1944 while the first V-2 strike was launched in September.[75] If Soviet intelligence had information about the German missile program before these attacks, the information had no effect on Soviet policy. After the German attacks on London, however, Soviet design bureaus began to direct their work towards the development of long-range missiles. In October Korolev submitted to the People's Commissariat of the Aviation Industry a draft plan of "Necessary Measures for Organizing Work on Long-Range Missiles."[76] At about the same time A.M. Isaev's design bureau switched its attention from rocket engines for aircraft to rocket engines for missiles.[77]

In April 1945 a state commission, consisting of military officers, officials, scientists, and engineers, was sent to Germany to collect information about the German program. This commission, which included Korolev and Glushko, spent the second half of 1945 and much of 1946 in Germany. Most of the leading German rocket scientists had fled to the West, taking their papers with them. The commission set up a number of research centers in the Soviet zone of occupation, and enlisted the help of middle-level German specialists. The commission prepared a 13-volume "Collection of Materials on the Study of Captured Reactive Technology."[78] It was decided, however, to transfer rocket research and development from Germany to the Soviet Union. By the middle of 1946 a network of research institutes, design bureaus, and factories was being set up in the Soviet Union to develop long-range missiles.

Jet propulsion had a less dramatic history than radar or rocketry. It had been overshadowed in the aircraft industry by the interest in rocket planes and rocket boosters for aircraft. By the end of the war, however, developments in Germany and Britain showed that jet propulsion was a more promising technology than rocket boosters. A.M. Liul'ka had started work on the design of a turbojet engine in 1937, but had not been able to complete it before the outbreak of war.[79] He returned to jet propulsion in 1944, but he soon discovered, by examining a captured Messerschmitt-262, that the Germans had made greater progress. In December 1945 several meetings were held in the Central Committee and the government to discuss the future of Soviet aviation. At one of these meetings Stalin rejected a proposal by the People's Commissar, A.I. Shakhurin, to put the Messerschmitt-262 jet fighter into production, and decided that Soviet designs should be developed instead. On April 24, 1946 the Iak-15 and MiG-9 fighters, using German JUMO-004 and BMW-003 jet engines, made their first flights. Shakhurin was soon replaced and sent to prison.[80]

These three cases support Kapitsa's argument that suspicion of scientists and engineers was a major reason for the Soviet Union's poor record in developing technologies that were new in principle. It was not the quality of Soviet scientists and engineers that explained this pattern, but the social and political conditions in which they worked. Soviet ideas did not receive full support until and unless they had been proved by Western experience. During the war Germany, Britain, and the United States had made progress in atomic energy, radar, rocketry, and jet propulsion. It was now clear that these technologies would have an enormous impact on warfare, and that was why they were included in the postwar Five-Year Plan.

IV

On January 25, 1946 Stalin summoned Kurchatov. The two men met for an hour, with Molotov and Beria present. Although there is some evidence that Stalin and Kurchatov had met before, in 1943 and in August 1945, this is the first well-documented meeting between them. Kurchatov made some notes after the conversation. His main impression, he wrote, was "the great love of Comrade Stalin for Russia and V.I. Lenin, about whom he spoke in connection with his great hope for the development of science in our country."[81]

Stalin rejected the argument, which Kapitsa had advanced, that the Soviet Union should try to find its own, cheaper path to the atomic bomb. He told Kurchatov that "it was not worth engaging in small-scale work, but necessary to conduct the work broadly, with Russian scope, that in that connection the broadest all-round help would be provided. Comrade Stalin said that it was not necessary to seek cheaper paths." Stalin said also that he was anxious to improve the scientists' living conditions, and to provide prizes for major achievements – "for example, for the solution of our problem," Kurchatov wrote. Stalin "said that our scientists were very modest and they sometimes did not notice that they live poorly . . . our state has suffered very much, yet it is surely possible to ensure that several thousand people can live very well, and several thousand people better than very well, with their own *dachas*, so that they can relax, and with their own cars."

Stalin stressed that it was essential for the atomic project to move forward "decisively." It was necessary also to use Germany in every possible way, he said, since it had people, equipment, experience, and factories. He asked Kurchatov what benefit the atomic project had derived from German scientists; Kurchatov, however, did not record how he answered this question. Nor did he reveal how he had responded to another enquiry. "A question was asked about Ioffe, Alikhanov, Kapitsa, and Vavilov, and about the utility of Kapitsa's work," he wrote in his notes. "Misgivings were expressed: who were they working for, and to what were their activities directed – the good of the Motherland or not?" This question provides striking evidence of the Soviet leaders' distrust of Soviet scientists.

Stalin directed Kurchatov at this meeting to build the bomb quickly, and not to count the cost. Kurchatov was asked to set out in writing the measures needed to speed things up, and to indicate which other scientists should be drawn into the project. Whether the meeting marked a new phase in the project or merely reaffirmed the general approach which had already been adopted is not clear. The latter seems more likely, in view of Kapitsa's complaint to Stalin, in his letters of October 3 and November 25, 1945, that the strategy which was being adopted for building the atomic bomb was a very costly one. Stalin impressed upon Kurchatov that the project should proceed without regard to cost. He also conveyed to him that the state would now invest heavily in science, but that it expected practical results from this investment and political loyalty from scientists.

On February 9, 1946, just over two weeks after his meeting with Kurchatov, Stalin gave a speech in the Bolshoi Theater in which he underlined the importance of science. "I do not doubt," he said, "that if we render the proper help to our scientists they will be able not only to catch up, but also to overtake in the near future the achievements of science beyond the borders of our country."[82] In March significant pay rises for scientists were announced; the science budget for 1946 was three times greater than that for 1945.[83]

In his Bolshoi Theater speech Stalin charted the course of postwar Soviet policy. He claimed that his prewar policies had enabled the Soviet Union to defeat Germany. The war had been "a kind of examination for our Soviet order, for our state, for our government, for our communist party," he declared.[84] Victory had shown the superiority of the Soviet social order, but victory would not have been possible if the country had not been prepared for war. The basic task of the new Five-Year Plan was "to restore the prewar level of industry and agriculture and then to surpass that level on a more or less significant scale.[85] "We must strive," he said,

to ensure that our industry can produce each year up to 50 million metric tons of iron, up to 60 million metric tons of steel, up to 500 million metric tons of coal, up to 60 million metric tons of petroleum. *Only on that condition can we consider that our Motherland will be guaranteed against all contingencies. That will take, I dare say, three new Five Year Plans, if not more. But this must be done, and we ought to do it.*[86] [Emphasis added]

Although he promised that particular attention would be given to the production of consumer goods and to raising living standards, Stalin made it clear that economic policy would return to the prewar pattern of priority for heavy industry, in order to prepare the country for the contingency of war.[87] The new Five-Year Plan gave priority to the advanced technologies that had emerged from World War II – to radar, rockets, jet propulsion and the atomic bomb.

CHAPTER EIGHT

The Premises of Policy

I

IN HIS SPEECH IN THE BOLSHOI THEATER on February 9, 1946 Stalin claimed that World War II had not been an accident, or the result of mistakes by political leaders. The war had happened, said Stalin, "as the inevitable result of the development of world economic and political forces on the basis of modern monopoly capitalism."[1] Lenin had argued in 1916 that World War I was an imperialist war, which had its origins in the rivalry between capitalist states for raw materials and markets.[2] Stalin paraphrased Lenin's theory of imperialism. "Marxists have more than once declared," he said,

that the capitalist system of world economy is fraught with the elements of a general crisis and military clashes, that in view of this the development of world capitalism in our times proceeds not in a smooth and balanced forward movement, but through crises and military catastrophes.[3]

The uneven development of capitalist countries, he continued, leads to situations in which some countries think that they are ill-provided with raw materials and markets, and take up arms to redress the situation. A periodic redistribution of raw material supplies and markets in line with the shifting economic weight of different countries might make it possible to avoid war. But that was impossible in the capitalist world economy. World War II, like World War I, had resulted from a crisis of the capitalist system of world economy. Yet World War II had been different, because it was also an anti-Fascist war of liberation, one of the aims of which had been the restoration of democratic freedoms. This aspect had been greatly strengthened, Stalin claimed, by the Soviet Union's entry into the war.[4]

By opening his speech with Lenin's theory of imperialism, Stalin indicated that this was still the relevant framework for analyzing international relations. He implied that because capitalist states still existed, war could be expected in the future. He claimed that his prewar policies had prepared the Soviet Union for war, and he made it clear that those policies would have to be continued in order to prepare the country for a future war.

Nikolai Voznesenskii, the head of Gosplan, made the same point when he outlined the new Five-Year Plan to the Supreme Soviet on March 16. "We should not forget," he said, "that monopoly capitalism is capable of giving rise to new aggressors."[5] "The Soviet people," Voznesenskii said at another point in his speech, "wishes to see its armed forces even stronger and more powerful, in order to guarantee the country against all contingencies and stand on guard over peace."[6]

Stalin's image of postwar international politics was rooted in Lenin's theory of imperialism, but it was strongly influenced also by international relations between the two world wars. He made several comments at the end of the war indicating that he thought the postwar period would resemble the interwar years. In Tehran in November 1943 he warned Roosevelt and Churchill several times that Germany might rise again in fifteen or twenty years.[7] In October 1944 he told Churchill that Germany should be deprived of the possibility of revenge: "otherwise every twenty-five or thirty years there would be a new world war."[8] In April 1945, during a dinner in his *dacha*, he told the Yugoslav communist, Milovan Djilas that Germany would be on its feet in another twelve or fifteen years. At one point during the dinner "he got up, hitched up his trousers as though he was about to wrestle or to box, and cried out emotionally, 'The War will soon be over. We shall recover in fifteen or twenty years, and then we'll have another go at it.' "[9]

Stalin drew a direct analogy between the interwar years and the postwar period when he told T.V. Soong in July 1945 that Germany had recovered within fifteen to twenty years of the Treaty of Versailles; Germany and Japan, he said, would rise again.[10] In his February 1946 speech he said that it would take at least three five-year plans to prepare for "all contingencies." All of this suggests that he anticipated a new world war after an interval similar to that between the two world wars. Moreover, a new world war would originate, in Stalin's conception, in the rivalry between the imperialist powers, including Germany and Japan, which would by that time have risen from defeat. He did not foresee the hegemonic position that the United States would come to occupy in the capitalist world.[11]

But Stalin did not expect war in the short term. This is clear from his policies of industrial conversion and demobilization, which began in May and June 1945 and continued steadily during 1946 and 1947. On May 26, 1945, little more than two weeks after Victory Day, the State Defense Committee ordered the gradual conversion of industry to civilian production. Conversion was not easy, however, and military production declined much more rapidly than civilian production grew: defense output fell 68 per cent from the first to the fourth quarter of 1945, while civilian production rose only 21 per cent. Total industrial production in 1945 was 12 per cent lower than in 1944, and in 1946 it fell by almost 17 per cent compared with 1945.[12]

In June 1945 the Supreme Soviet adopted a law on demobilization, and by the end of the year the Red Army, which numbered 11.365 million in May, had been cut by over 3 million men. Demobilization continued during 1946 and by the end of 1947 the armed forces had been reduced to 2.874 million troops.[13] The shift to a peacetime footing was at least partially reflected in the defense budget, which fell from 137.8 billion roubles in 1944 to 128.2 billion in 1945, 73.6 billion in 1946 and 66.3 billion in 1947 (at 1946 prices it would have been 55.2 billion).[14]

Stalin's confidence that a major war was not imminent rested upon three considerations. The first was that the Soviet Union had emerged from the war a more secure and more powerful state. Stalin and the other leaders argued in their speeches in late 1945 and early 1946 that the Soviet Union's victory over Germany and Japan had greatly strengthened its international position. Its "historic borders" had been restored. No longer would southern Sakhalin and the Kurile islands constitute a barrier to Soviet access to the Pacific Ocean, or serve as a base for Japanese aggression. A "free and independent" Poland would ensure that Germany did not have a springboard for attacking Soviet Union. Germany, Italy, and Japan had been removed "for a period" from the list of great powers. Soviet leaders asserted, moreover, that by defeating Germany and liberating half of Europe from Nazism, their country had strengthened its international authority. "Important problems of international relations," declared Molotov on February 6, 1946, "cannot nowadays be settled without the participation of the Soviet Union or without heeding the voice of the country. The participation of Comrade Stalin is regarded as the best guarantee of a successful solution of complicated international problems."[15]

Stalin reportedly expressed the same view in private. Shortly after the war a map showing the Soviet Union's new borders was brought to his *dacha*. Stalin pinned it to the wall. " 'Let's see what the result is for us,' " he said.

"In the North everything is in order, fine. Finland committed a great offense against us, and we have moved the border back from Leningrad. The Baltic coast – an age-old Russian territory! – is ours again, the Belorussians are all now living together with us, the Ukrainians are together, the Moldavians are together. In the West everything is fine." And at once he went to the Eastern borders. "What have we here? . . . The Kurile islands are ours now, all of Sakhalin is ours, see how good it is! And Port Arthur is ours, and Dairen is ours" – Stalin drew his pipe across China – "and the KVZhD [Chinese Eastern Railway] is ours. China, Mongolia – everything is in order. But here I don't like our border," said Stalin pointing south of the Caucasus."[16]

Whatever the accuracy of this story, it merely repeats in more colorful terms what Soviet leaders were saying in public. Their concept of power and security was very largely a territorial one. "I saw it as my task as Minister of Foreign Affairs to extend as much as possible the bounds of our Fatherland," Molotov told an interviewer many years later.[17] Stalin and Molotov had used the pact with Germany to expand Soviet territory in 1939 and 1940, and those acquisitions had now been consolidated. Seen in that light, Soviet security had been greatly enhanced.

The second consideration was that popular war-weariness would restrain bellicose leaders in Britain and the United States. This was the argument that Stalin used to dismiss war as "very unlikely" in March 1946, when he criticized Churchill for his "Iron Curtain" speech. Speaking in Fulton, Missouri, Churchill had warned of Moscow's increasing control over Eastern and Central Europe, and had called for an Anglo-American "fraternal association" to resist Soviet expansion.[18] Stalin denounced Churchill's speech as "a dangerous act, calculated to sow discord between the allied states and hamper their cooperation."[19] He accused Churchill of calling for war against the Soviet Union, and recalled that after World War I Churchill had helped to organize intervention by capitalist powers to suppress the Bolshevik regime. "I do not know," said Stalin, "whether Mr Churchill and his friends will succeed in organizing after the second world war a new campaign against 'Eastern Europe'. But if they do succeed – which is very unlikely because millions of 'simple people' are standing guard over peace – then one can say with certainty that they will be beaten, just as they were in the past, 26 years ago."[20] A week later Stalin made his position on the likelihood of war even clearer: "I am convinced that neither nations nor their armies are seeking a new war – they want peace and are striving to ensure peace. . . . I think that 'the present fear of war' is caused by the actions of some political groups, who have taken up propaganda for a new war and are thus sowing seeds of discord and uncertainty."[21]

The third factor affecting Stalin's assessment of the likelihood of war was his knowledge that the United States had few atomic bombs in 1945. Molotov later recalled that at Potsdam he and Stalin "understood that [the Americans] were not in a position to unleash war, they had only one or two bombs."[22] Marshal Zhukov said in an interview in 1955 that the United States had had only five or six atomic bombs in the immediate postwar period, and that these did not have decisive significance.[23] Klaus Fuchs informed the Soviet Union in September 1945 that the United States had very few bombs.[24] One of the reasons for the urgency of the Soviet project is that Stalin wanted to acquire a Soviet bomb before American atomic forces grew large enough to pose an overwhelming threat to the Soviet Union. Fuchs was asked several times, after his return to Britain in the summer of 1946, about the United States rate of production, and the stockpile of atomic bombs.[25] It is apparent, however, that Stalin did not regard the nuclear threat as immediate in 1945–6.

II

On November 27, 1945 Harriman cabled to Washington an assessment of the effect of the atomic bomb on Soviet policy. The Soviet Union, he wrote, had been able to obtain defense in depth at the end of the war by disregarding the interests and desires of other people. But

suddenly the atomic bomb appeared and they recognized that it was an offset to the power of the Red Army. This must have revived their old feeling of insecurity. They could no longer be absolutely sure that they could obtain their objectives without interference.[26]

Harriman based this assessment not only on his own impressions, but also on a conversation with George Andreychin, an old Comintern agent, who had paid him a visit at Spaso House, the ambassador's residence. The Kremlin leaders had been shocked by the bomb, Andreychin said, because it exposed the Soviet Union's comparative weakness, and it was to conceal that weakness that they were now being so aggressive.[27]

On December 3 the British ambassador, Sir Archibald Clark Kerr, wrote to the Foreign Secretary with a similar analysis. The victory over Germany had made the Soviet leaders confident that national security was at last within their reach. "Then plumb came the Atomic Bomb," he wrote. "At a blow the balance which had now seemed set and steady was rudely shaken. Russia was balked by the west when everything seemed to be within her grasp. The three hundred divisions were shorn of much of their value."[28]

This assessment echoed Stalin's remark to Vannikov and Kurchatov that Hiroshima had destroyed the balance of power, but it exaggerated the sense of immediate military insecurity that the bomb aroused in the Soviet leadership. Stalin did not believe that war was likely in the short term; nor, as will be seen in a later chapter, did he believe that Soviet divisions had lost their value. The immediate threat he saw was not military, but the threat of atomic diplomacy. He was afraid, as he had explained to Gromyko and Gusev, that the United States would try to use its atomic monopoly to impose a postwar settlement.

This raises an interesting analytical question. How could the atomic bomb affect the balance of power when the United States, as Stalin knew, did not possess a real atomic capability? The United States had a very small number of bombs – the stockpile was nine in mid-1946 – and no desire to go to war. Yet the bomb was a political reality for Stalin. How is the difference between military capability and political effect to be explained? In an essay on the symbolic nature of nuclear politics Robert Jervis has argued that in the 1970s and 1980s the United States acquired nuclear weapons that were militarily useless in order to demonstrate resolve and political will.[29] The same kind of argument can be made about the effect of the atomic bomb in the early postwar years. The disjunction between military capability and political effect can be explained in terms of the bomb's symbolic meaning. It symbolized the immense power – not only the military, but also the economic and technological power – of the United States. It was the "scepter of state power," as the novelist Vasilii Grossman aptly put it.[30]

The symbolism of the atomic bomb had a pervasive effect on international politics in 1945–6, even though the bomb did not pose a real military threat to the Soviet Union at the time. Stalin tried to counter this symbolic power by treating the bomb as unimportant, and by showing that the Soviet Union would not be intimidated. The danger of the bomb, from Stalin's point of view, was that the United States would adopt a more confident and aggressive policy towards the Soviet Union, in the hope of extracting concessions.[31] The Soviet response, in the months after Hiroshima, was to try to disabuse the United States of the idea that this would be an effective policy.

The Truman administration certainly expected that the bomb could be used to influence Soviet policy, but it did not know exactly how that could be done. Troubled by Soviet behavior at Potsdam, Stimson had written a memorandum to Truman during the conference, arguing that international control of atomic energy would be impossible as long as a police state like the Soviet Union was a major force in the international control agency; the Soviet desire to participate in atomic development should therefore be used to bring about democratic change in that country.[32] By September 11, however, Stimson had been convinced by Harriman that the atomic bomb could not be used to induce internal change in the Soviet Union, and he now argued, in another memorandum to the President, that the United States and Britain should tell the Soviet Union that they wanted an agreement to control and limit the use of the atomic bomb as an instrument of war, and to direct atomic energy towards peaceful purposes. To do otherwise – to negotiate with "this weapon ostentatiously on our hip" – would, he warned, only increase Soviet suspicion and distrust.[33]

Truman's new Secretary of State, James Byrnes, did not share Stimson's doubts. Byrnes went to the London meeting of the Council of Foreign Ministers, which opened on September 11, 1945, confident that the bomb would strengthen his hand. The council had been established at Potsdam to prepare peace treaties with Germany and its allies. There were many issues in dispute between the three great powers, and Byrnes believed that the atomic bomb would help him in the negotiations.[34] "His mind," wrote Stimson in his diary on September 4, "is full of his problems with the coming meeting of foreign ministers and he looks to have the presence of the bomb in his hip pocket, so to speak, as a great weapon to get through the thing."[35] Byrnes did not want to use the bomb overtly. He instructed his delegation to avoid any mention of it, in the belief that the reality of the bomb would by itself make the Soviet Union more tractable.[36]

Soviet policy at the end of August had been conciliatory in Eastern Europe, agreeing to the postponement of elections in Hungary and Bulgaria.[37] It was at the London meeting in September 1945 that the new Soviet tactic was unveiled. Molotov came to the London meeting with the bomb on his mind. Atomic energy was not on the formal agenda, but Molotov raised the issue himself, at a reception on the third day of the conference. When Byrnes approached him and asked when he was going to stop sightseeing and get down to business, Molotov enquired whether Byrnes had "an atomic bomb in his side pocket." "You don't know southerners," Byrnes replied, "we carry our artillery in our pocket. If you don't cut out all this stalling and let us get down to work, I'm going to pull an atomic bomb out of my hip pocket and let you have it." Molotov and his interpreter laughed at this remark which, though offered as banter, put into words the threat that Stalin and Molotov feared.[38] Molotov evidently wished to laugh off the American bomb. Later that evening, at the embassy, Molotov proposed a toast, "Here's to the Atom Bomb! We've got it."[39]

If the bomb made Byrnes stand firm, it made Molotov stubborn. Molotov found Byrnes unyielding when he pushed for a control commission for Japan, with Soviet participation, and pressed the Soviet claim to trusteeship over Libya. Molotov, in turn, resisted Western attempts to influence the complexion of the governments in Romania and Bulgaria. Moreover, although he accepted a British suggestion that the French and Chinese foreign ministers be allowed to take part in the discussions, he changed his mind ten days later and asked for them to be excluded. Appeals from Truman and Attlee to Stalin failed to change the Soviet position, and the conference ended on October 2 without agreement.[40]

At a formal dinner during the conference Molotov said that "of course we all have to pay great attention to what Mr Byrnes says, because the United States are the only people making the atomic bomb."[41] But pay attention to Byrnes was what Molotov conspicuously and pointedly declined to do. He behaved as though his overriding concern was to show that the Soviet Union would not be intimidated, or forced into concessions, by the American atomic monopoly. If this was indeed his goal, he succeeded brilliantly. Byrnes now realized that the Russians were, in his own words, "stubborn, obstinate, and they don't scare."[42] Truman too was impressed by the bomb's failure to influence Molotov, and worried about the rapid rate of US demobilization. When his budget director, Harold Smith, told him that "you have an atomic bomb up your sleeve" he replied: "Yes, but I am not sure it can ever be used."[43]

Molotov's success in London was bought at a high price. The London meeting set the seal on his reputation as "Mr Nyet." The *Manchester Guardian* wrote that "during his stay in London Mr Molotov has recklessly squandered the vast credit of good will towards Russia which accumulated in this country during the war."[44] Lord Halifax, the British ambassador in

Washington, reported to the Foreign Office that, as a result of Soviet intransigence at the London meeting, "thoughtful-minded Americans and especially those just right of Centre, felt themselves reluctantly drawn towards the conclusion that there were two great ideological *blocs* in the world."[45]

In the Soviet Union too warnings were sounded about the breakdown of collaboration. An editorial in *Izvestiia* on October 5 declared that collaboration would be shaken unless the United States and Britain changed their attitude to existing agreements.[46] Later in the same month Stalin told Harriman that the Soviet Union might pursue a "policy of isolation." Harriman thought that the element of unilateralism in Soviet policy had already increased since the London conference.[47] Frank Roberts, Minister at the British embassy in Moscow, reported in the same month that the atomic bomb had "probably increased already existing Soviet suspicions of the outside world."[48]

On November 6 Molotov, in the speech in which he announced that the Soviet Union would have "atomic energy, and much else," warned against the attempt to use the bomb as an instrument of power politics:

It is necessary to speak about the discovery of atomic energy and about the atomic bomb, whose use in the war with Japan showed its huge destructive force. . . . *At the present time there can be no large-scale technological secrets that can remain the property of any one country or any one narrow group of countries. Therefore the discovery of atomic energy must not encourage . . . enthusiasm for using this discovery in a foreign-policy power game.*[49] [Emphasis added]

These last two sentences point to the two major goals of Soviet atomic policy at the time: to break the American monopoly, and in the meantime to ensure that the United States did not derive political benefit from that monopoly.

In November the atomic bomb assumed a new role in Soviet–American relations. On November 11–15 Truman held talks with Clement Attlee and the Canadian Prime Minister, Mackenzie King, in Washington on the international control of atomic energy.[50] At the end of their meeting the three men stated that they wished to prevent the use of atomic energy for destructive purposes and encourage its use for peaceful ends. They favored the dissemination of fundamental scientific research, but not "of the specialised information regarding the practical application of atomic energy," before effective and enforceable safeguards against its military use were established.[51] They called for a commission under the United Nations to study how atomic weapons might be eliminated and atomic energy put to peaceful uses.

This statement made no mention of the Soviet Union, but a week later Byrnes decided to raise the issue of atomic energy with Moscow. Byrnes was anxious to end the impasse caused by the London meeting, and decided to use the bomb as an inducement rather than an implied threat. On November 23 he proposed a meeting of the United States, British, and Soviet foreign ministers in Moscow in December. He directed his staff to prepare a proposal on the international control of atomic energy. Nikolai Novikov, the Soviet chargé d'affaires in Washington, cabled Moscow that the offer to discuss international control of atomic energy

represents a new tactical approach in relation to the USSR, the substance of which can be reduced to the following: on the one hand, to use the atomic bomb as a means of political pressure to oblige the Soviet Union to accept [Washington's] will and to weaken the position of the USSR in the United Nations, Eastern Europe and so on, but on the other hand, to accomplish all of this in such a form as to somewhat ameliorate the aggressive character of the Anglo-Saxon alliance of "atomic powers."[52]

Molotov quickly agreed to the meeting.[53] When Byrnes placed atomic energy at the top of the agenda, Molotov moved it to the bottom. This, wrote Byrnes later, "was just his way of informing me that he regarded the subject as one of little importance."[54] In London Molotov had sought to defuse the bomb as a political threat; now he tried to devalue it as political inducement.

To Byrnes's surprise the question of atomic energy was settled in Moscow without much difficulty.[55] Molotov agreed to co-sponsor, at the first session of the General Assembly of the United Nations in January 1946, a resolution to establish a commission to make proposals on the international control of atomic energy.[56] Molotov insisted that the commission be under the direction of the Security Council, in which the Soviet Union had a veto, and not of the General Assembly; Byrnes accepted this point.[57] The Soviet Union had nothing to lose by accepting Byrnes's proposal; rejection, on the other hand, might push the United States and Britain into closer cooperation, and indicate that the Soviet Union was really worried by the American monopoly. Stalin and Molotov can hardly have expected much benefit from the UN Commission. The Western allies had not informed them of the bomb when all three powers were fighting Germany: why expect them to reveal secrets now?

At dinner in the Kremlin on Christmas Eve Molotov returned to the tactics he had employed in London. James Conant had been brought to Moscow by Byrnes as adviser on atomic energy; Conant hoped to meet some of the Soviet nuclear scientists, but the Soviet authorities did not permit this. Molotov proposed a toast to Conant, saying (according to Conant's diary) "that after a few drinks perhaps we could explore the secrets I had and if I had a bit of the atomic bomb in my pocket to bring it out."[58] As all stood up to drink the toast, Stalin broke in, apparently in anger. "Here's to science and American scientists and what they have accomplished. This is too serious a matter to joke about," he said. "We must now work together to see that this great invention is used for peaceful ends."[59]

Charles Bohlen, who was a member of the American delegation, wrote later that "we saw Stalin abruptly change Soviet policy, without consulting his number-two man. The humiliated Molotov never altered his expression. From that moment on, the Soviet Union gave the atomic bomb the serious consideration it deserved."[60] But Stalin had taken the atomic bomb seriously since Hiroshima, and must certainly have approved Molotov's tactics for dealing with atomic diplomacy. Stalin's rebuke may indicate that he took the threat of atomic diplomacy less seriously than Molotov did, or – more probably – that he thought that Molotov, whose stubbornness he sometimes found infuriating, was being too dogged in his pursuit of the "bomb in the pocket" line.[61] If this was a humiliation for Molotov, as Bohlen suggests, then Stalin doubtless took pleasure in that too.

The Soviet government was pleased with the Moscow meeting. In his memoirs Novikov writes that the "principled and firm position of the Soviet government," demonstrated at the London meeting, had "forced the Western powers to reject the tactic of head-on pressure and to seek mutually acceptable solutions on the most important questions of the postwar period."[62] This new approach, he believed, was apparent at the Moscow meeting. Byrnes agreed to recognize the Bulgarian and Romanian governments in return for token changes in their cabinets; he also agreed to set up a toothless Allied Council for Japan, in which the Soviet Union would be represented. Byrnes failed to obtain assurances from the Soviet Union that it would withdraw its troops from northern Iran, which it had occupied during the war, or to clarify Soviet intentions toward Turkey. Stalin wrote to Truman to say that he was pleased with the results of the meeting.[63]

Truman did not share Stalin's satisfaction. He was irritated by Byrnes's failure to keep him informed about the course of the negotiations, and unhappy with the results of the meeting. Byrnes, he wrote in his memoirs, "had taken it upon himself to move the foreign policy of the United States in a direction to which I could not, and would not, agree."[64] On January 5, 1946 he wrote a stiff letter reprimanding Byrnes and complaining about Soviet policy. He insisted that the governments in Romania and Bulgaria should not be recognized until radically changed; he regarded it as an outrage that the Soviet Union was keeping troops in Iran and stirring up rebellion there; and he was convinced that the Soviet Union intended to invade Turkey and seize the Black Sea straits. "Unless Russia is faced with an iron fist and strong language another war is in the making," he wrote. "I'm tired," he concluded, "of babying the Russians."[65]

Truman's hardening attitude reflected a shift in official American opinion. Washington was increasingly frustrated by its dealings with the Soviet Union, and puzzled by Soviet unwillingness to cooperate on

American terms, especially in view of the American atomic monopoly.[66] In February 1946, after Stalin's speech in the Bolshoi Theater, a long telegram arrived from George Kennan. The Soviet Union, by its very nature, wrote Kennan, was "committed fanatically" to the belief that it could have no permanent *modus vivendi* with the United States, and that Soviet power could be secure only if the internal harmony of American society was disrupted and the international authority of the United States broken. This telegram answered the question that preoccupied the Truman administration: why was the Soviet Union so difficult to deal with? Besides, the answer it gave explained the difficulty in terms of the nature of the Soviet Union, and not of American policy. It expressed very eloquently the view that was taking shape in Washington.[67]

Novikov noticed that the political atmosphere in Washington had worsened when he returned from Moscow in February 1946. It became even tenser, in his view, after Churchill's "Iron Curtain" speech on March 5.[68] At just this time a serious crisis arose in United States–Soviet relations. In 1942 the Soviet Union and Britain had deployed troops in Iran to prevent that country from falling into German hands. At the end of 1945 Washington and London began to worry that the Soviet Union might not withdraw its forces from northern Iran, as it had agreed to do at Teheran in 1943 and at the London meeting of foreign ministers in September 1945.[69]

The deadline for withdrawal of Soviet forces was March 2, 1946. On that date Soviet troops were still in Iran, and Washington feared that Stalin intended to annex the Iranian province of Azerbaijan. The United States had already made clear its concern to the Soviet government, and had supported a firm Iranian position in the negotiations with Moscow. Now Byrnes sent a stiff note to Moscow and, when no reply was received, made the note public. Moscow quickly promised to pull its forces out of Iran by early May. Truman later recollected that he had issued an atomic ultimatum, and claimed that it was this that had forced the Soviet Union to withdraw its forces. This was not so, however. The Truman administration issued no ultimatum, much less an atomic one. It did, however, engage in firm and skillful diplomacy, which resolved the crisis.[70]

February and March 1946 marked a turning point in United States policy toward the Soviet Union. American attitudes had hardened to the point where cooperation and agreement were now much more difficult. The atomic bomb did not cause the deterioration in relations. There were serious issues in dispute between the Soviet Union and the Western Allies before Hiroshima. Nevertheless, the failure of the London conference, which took place under the shadow of the bomb, marked an important stage in the breakdown of cooperation. Byrnes felt that the bomb allowed him to adopt a tough and demanding position in London; Molotov evidently felt that the bomb required a tough and demanding Soviet position in return. Atomic diplomacy – the hope on the one side, the fear on the other, that the bomb would prove to be a powerful political instrument – contributed to the failure of the London conference, and to the deterioration of US–Soviet relations.

III

On January 24, 1946 the United Nations General Assembly adopted a resolution establishing an Atomic Energy Commission. In line with the agreement reached in Moscow, the commission was to make recommendations: on the exchange of basic scientific information; on the control of atomic energy to ensure its use for peaceful purposes; on the elimination of atomic weapons; and on "effective safeguards by way of inspection and other means to protect complying States against the hazards of violations and evasion."[71]

Byrnes appointed Dean Acheson, Undersecretary of State, to head a committee to advise him on the United States position. Acheson in turn established a board of consultants under David Lilienthal, chairman of the Tennessee Valley Authority. The Acheson–Lilienthal Report, as it became known, was written quickly and published in March, with a foreword by Byrnes.[72] The dominant influence in preparing this report was Oppenheimer, who had resigned as director of the Los Alamos laboratory and was a member of Lilienthal's board of consultants.[73] The report's basic idea was to place all dangerous activities under an international agency, while safe activities, such as research and the peaceful uses of atomic energy, were to be left under the control of individual states. The report defined as dangerous any activity that offered a solution to "one of the three major problems of making atomic weapons": the supply of raw materials; the production in suitable quality and quantity of plutonium and uranium-235; the use of these materials to make atomic weapons.[74] The international agency would conduct all the dangerous activities: it would control world supplies of uranium and thorium; it would construct and operate reactors and separation plants; it would also license and inspect activities in individual countries.

The Acheson–Lilienthal Report was a bold attempt to come to terms with the problem of international control, and it provided the basis for the United States position in the UN Atomic Energy Commission. Important new elements were added, however, by Bernard Baruch, who headed the US delegation. He insisted that states that contravened the agreement on international control should be punished; and that the right of veto possessed by permanent members of the Security Council should not "protect those who violate their solemn agreements not to develop or use atomic energy for destructive purposes."[75]

Baruch presented his plan to the UN Atomic Energy Commission on June 14, 1946. Five days later Gromyko presented the Soviet proposal, which called for an international convention banning the production, stockpiling, and use of atomic weapons. All existing atomic bombs were to be destroyed within three months of the conclusion of this convention. Within six months the signatory states were to enact legislation providing for punishment of any breach of the convention. Gromyko also proposed that two committees be established, one to discuss the exchange of scientific information, the other to examine methods of ensuring compliance with the convention.[76]

The Baruch plan and the Soviet proposal were based upon very different premises. The United States rejected the mere renunciation of the atomic bomb as inadequate, and judged international inspection to be an unsatisfactory mechanism for ensuring compliance with an agreement.[77] That was why it proposed the creation of a powerful international agency. The Soviet proposal, on the other hand, was modelled on prewar disarmament agreements, such as the 1925 Geneva Convention which banned the use of chemical weapons. Like those agreements, the Soviet proposal lacked provisions for inspection and control, and relied upon individual governments for enforcement. There was, besides, an important difference in phasing between the two proposals. The Soviet Union wanted the United States to ban the production and use of atomic weapons before arrangements had been made for policing such an agreement. The United States, for its part, wanted the Soviet Union to forgo the development of the atomic bomb, and accept the creation of a powerful international agency, before the United States surrendered its own atomic weapons.

By removing the right of veto, which had been included at Soviet insistence at the Moscow meeting, Baruch made it less likely that the Soviet Union would accept the United States proposal. But even the Acheson–Lilienthal Report, imaginative though it was, would have had little chance of acceptance, for it too would have left the Soviet Union at a disadvantage. More importantly, neither it nor the Baruch plan took into account the Soviet determination to acquire the atomic bomb. By June 1946 the Soviet project was proceeding at a rapid rate. Production of uranium metal for the first Soviet reactor had already begun. Sites were being prepared for a plutonium production reactor, a gaseous diffusion separation plant, and a weapons laboratory. The project was being pushed forward as fast as possible; it was not held back in the hope that agreement would be reached on international control.[78]

Given the premises of Soviet policy, it is very unlikely that Stalin or his colleagues believed that international control would be established. They did not expect help from the United States in building the bomb; nor did they expect the United States to give up its monopoly. On the contrary, they expected the United States to try to hold on to its monopoly for as long as possible, and to use it to put pressure on the Soviet Union. The Baruch plan contained a number of elements to reinforce this suspicion.[79] It called for an early survey of world reserves of uranium and thorium; this would entail inspection of Soviet deposits, which were of great interest to

United States intelligence. The Soviet Union was being asked to renounce the atomic bomb, and to agree to the establishment of a powerful international agency, before the United States yielded control over its own atomic bombs and atomic facilities. The Soviet government was afraid that the international agency would be dominated by the United States, which had more specialists on atomic energy than any other country.[80] If the veto were removed, as Baruch proposed, the United Nations would have the right to take action against the Soviet Union if it believed the Soviet Union was infringing the ban on nuclear weapons.

Soviet suspicions were not allayed by the United States' decision to detonate two atomic bombs on Bikini Atoll in the Marshall Islands in July 1946. The first test took place only two weeks after Baruch had presented his plan to the UN Commission, and each member of the commission, including the Soviet Union, was invited to send two observers to witness the tests. The Soviet observers were M.G. Meshcheriakov, a physicist from the Radium Institute, and S.P. Aleksandrov, a geologist who worked for the MGB. The first bomb was exploded on July 1 at a height of about 300 meters over a group of warships. The second on July 24 was detonated 10 meters below the surface of the sea.[81] These demonstrations had not been organized to coincide with the United Nations talks, but the Soviet press pointed to the incongruity between these tests and the US proposals. *Pravda* accused the United States of seeking to improve the atomic bomb, not to abolish it.[82]

The UN Commission discussed the Baruch plan and the Soviet proposal in the following months. A Scientific and Technical Committee, which comprised the scientific advisers to the delegations, prepared a report on verification of a ban on the production of nuclear weapons. The committee analyzed the different stages in producing atomic energy, and explored the elements of danger and the safeguards that might be erected against them. The two Soviet representatives on the committee, Dmitrii Skobel'tsyn and S.P. Aleksandrov, raised no objections to the committee's report, which was completed by early October.[83]

The Soviet scientists, however, felt themselves at a disadvantage in the committee. On October 12, 1946 Skobel'tsyn wrote to Beria and Molotov to urge that the Soviet Union take a more active stance in the UN Commission, instead of the "passive defense" it was now conducting.[84] The Soviet position was weak, he wrote, because it appeared to oppose the whole idea of verification and control. While the Baruch plan should be rejected, the Soviet Union should support a system of verification based on the following principles: atomic facilities should be subject to national ownership and national control; states should report to the international agency on the activities of their own facilities; the international agency should be permitted to inspect specific facilities to check on the reports submitted by governments to the international agency. Research should not be subject to verification and inspection. Only the activities of large facilities of the kind that now existed in the United States – and that would be built in the future in other countries – should be subject to inspection and control.

Skobel'tsyn's letter provides a clear picture of the Soviet attitude to the Baruch plan. "If the Baruch plan is accepted," Skobel'tsyn wrote,

then every independent activity in the development of atomic production in countries which have signed the agreement has to be curtailed and handed over to an international (in reality, probably, an American) organization. This international organization would then have to proceed to erect plants on our territory – in reality, above all, it would proceed to control [check on] our resources. *We reject such help and are determined to carry out by our own efforts all the research and preparatory work necessary for setting up atomic production in our country, as America did in the years of the war.*[85] [Emphasis added.]

Skobel'tsyn's proposal would allow the Soviet Union to catch up with the United States before becoming subject to inspection and control. For this reason, he wrote, the United States would probably be unwilling to accept the proposal, in which case "our position in the field of international 'atomic politics' would be stronger."[86] In the unlikely event of American acceptance the Soviet Union would gain significant advantages, he noted, since Soviet representatives would have access to atomic facilities in the United States.

In a speech to the UN General Assembly on October 29, 1946 Molotov attacked the Baruch plan as an attempt to secure a veiled atomic monopoly for the United States. But no country, he warned, could count on retaining such a monopoly. "Science and its exponents cannot be shut up in a box and kept under lock and key," he said. "It must not be forgotten," he declared,

that in response to the atomic bombs of one side atomic bombs, and perhaps something else as well, may be found on the other side, and then the final collapse of the calculations of certain self-satisfied but limited people will become more than obvious.[87]

What Molotov had in mind by "something else as well" was missiles.[88] Recalling this speech many years later, Molotov said that this statement had been his own idea, that he had not been instructed to make it. He felt, however, that something had to be said, because the bombs dropped on Japan

were, of course, not against Japan, but against the Soviet Union: see, remember what we have. You don't have the atomic bomb, but we do – and these are what the consequences will be if you stir. Well we had to adopt our tone, to give some kind of answer, so that our people would feel more or less confident.[89]

Stalin said to him afterwards, "My, you're strong."[90]

Molotov proposed to the General Assembly that atomic energy be dealt with in the framework of general disarmament. This proposal was likely to postpone agreement indefinitely, and indicates that Molotov did not seriously expect the bomb to be banned. In November Baruch began to press the UN Atomic Energy Commission to adopt a report on his plan, even though he knew that it would not be adopted unanimously. On December 30 the commission voted to approve the Baruch plan, with ten votes for, and the Soviet Union and Poland abstaining.[91] Since the Soviet Union had a veto in the Security Council, there was no danger that the United Nations would adopt the Baruch plan. Five days earlier Kurchatov's experimental reactor had gone critical, but this was kept secret at the time.

After the vote of December 30, 1946 the prospects for international control were remote, and they became dimmer as relations between the Soviet Union and its former allies continued to deteriorate. In June 1947, however, the Soviet Union made a new proposal, based on the ideas put forward by Skobel'tsyn the previous October. This proposal still called for an international convention banning atomic weapons and other weapons of mass destruction, but it now proposed the creation of an international control commission with the right to inspect "all facilities engaged in mining of atomic raw materials and in production of atomic materials and atomic energy." These facilities would not pass under international ownership and management as the Baruch plan had proposed, but would remain in national hands. Research establishments would not be subject to inspection.[92]

On the following day Bertrand Goldschmidt, scientific adviser to the French delegation, wrote to his colleagues in Paris that the new Soviet proposal was a concession by the Soviet Union and that it could have been important if it had been presented a year earlier.[93] By the summer of 1947, however, the international climate had worsened and the Soviet proposal did not receive serious consideration in the Atomic Energy Commission; it was formally rejected in April 1948. The new proposal was unacceptable to the United States: it fell far short of the kind of international control envisaged by the Baruch plan; and the activities of the International Control Commission would have been subject to veto by the council's permanent members. Although the Soviet Union was now willing to accept simultaneous conventions banning atomic weapons and establishing the International Control Commission,[94] it is unlikely that Beria or Molotov expected the new proposal, with its unchanged position on the veto, to be accepted by the United States. They may have calculated, as Skobel'tsyn had done in his letter, that the proposal would make the Soviet position look better and that, in the unlikely event of an agreement, the Soviet Union would be able to avoid inspection until it had created its own atomic industry.[95]

The change in Soviet policy was too little too late. Niels Bohr had hoped that the international community of physicists could draw the attention of political leaders to the danger that the atomic bomb presented to the human race, and that the common danger would persuade governments to cooperate. But the restoration of international scientific relations, which had seemed possible in the summer of 1945, did not take place. Scientists from the Soviet Union and the United States were not allowed to come together in the late 1940s to discuss the significance of the atomic bomb.[96] Only within the framework of the United Nations did discussions among scientists take place, and these discussions were severely constrained by government negotiating positions. Skobel'tsyn, for example, was kept on a very tight rein.[97] His letter nevertheless provides a small but interesting example of the way in which discussions among scientists could feed back into the formulation of government policy.

Would international control have been possible if Stalin had been informed about the atomic bomb before Hiroshima, as Niels Bohr had urged? Even if Stalin had been informed, he would still have wanted a bomb, I argued in Chapter 6. The real issue that Bohr had raised was how political leaders viewed the bomb: as an instrument of state policy, or as a common danger that would bring states together. To Stalin and Molotov it was clear that the United States wanted to use the bomb as an instrument of political pressure. Even if the Truman administration had eschewed all thought of atomic diplomacy, the bomb would have existed, and would have been seen by Stalin and Molotov as a factor in the balance of power.

Neither Truman nor Stalin saw the atomic bomb as a common danger for the human race, as Bohr had hoped. For Stalin the danger was not the atomic bomb as such, but the American monopoly of the bomb. The obvious solution to this problem, in Stalin's mind, was a Soviet atomic bomb. There was no questioning of this decision within the leadership and, once the decision had been taken, all public utterances were subordinated to the needs of Soviet policy. Some scientists published articles in the press about the atomic bomb, but these were explanations of the science and technology, not analyses of the broader implications of the bomb.[98] Stalin, according to Gromyko, commented in the course of some remarks about banning atomic weapons that "Of course, I did not touch on this question with Kurchatov. This is more a question of policy than of technology and science."[99] The place of scientists, in the Stalinist scheme of things, was to provide the state with what it needed, not to offer their views about foreign policy, or about the broader meaning of technological advances.

IV

In the latter years of World War II Stalin had a choice between three basic policies for the postwar period. He could pursue an insurrectionist policy by encouraging the communist parties in Western Europe and in Asia to seize power, and by helping them where possible with the Red Army.

There was some sentiment in support of this policy in Moscow, and some discussion of its feasibility.[100] This is not surprising, since it had obvious appeal for anyone interested in socialist revolution. No prominent figure in the leadership advocated it, however, and Stalin chose not to encourage revolution in Europe or Asia.[101] To have done so would have created a risk of war with the Western allies.

A second option was to pursue a policy of cooperation with the West. This was advocated by Maksim Litvinov, the People's Commissar of Foreign Affairs in the 1930s, who had been replaced by Molotov in May 1939, three months before the Nazi–Soviet pact. Litvinov was ambassador in Washington from December 1941 to the spring of 1943, when he was brought back to Moscow to a relatively unimportant post.[102] Litvinov wanted collaboration between the Soviet Union and the United States after the war, because he saw this as the only sound basis for peace.[103] In October 1944, however, he told the American journalist Edgar Snow that Britain was adopting its traditional balance-of-power policy in Europe and was unwilling to collaborate with the Soviet Union, which was now the strong power on the continent; and "we," he said, "are drifting more and more in the same direction," away from collaboration.[104] In June 1946 he told Richard Hottelet, the CBS correspondent in Moscow, that there had been "a return in Russia to the outmoded concept of security in terms of territory – the more you've got the safer you are." If the West acceded to Soviet demands, he said, "it would lead to the West being faced, after a more or less short time, with the next series of demands."[105] In February 1947 he told Alexander Werth that Russia could have cashed in on the goodwill it had accumulated during the war, but that Stalin and Molotov did not believe that goodwill provided a lasting basis for policy; "they had therefore grabbed all they could while the going was good."[106]

The transcript of at least one of these conversations was given to Stalin and Molotov by the Soviet police. Litvinov remained alive only by accident, Molotov later remarked.[107] It is possible, however, that Stalin left Litvinov alone not only to irritate Molotov, who detested him, but also to keep him in reserve in case he wanted to change Soviet policy; he could then produce Litvinov as a token of his desire for cooperation. Litvinov was dismissed from his position in the Ministry of Foreign Affairs on his seventieth birthday in July 1946, a month after his interview with Hottelet; he died at the end of 1951.[108]

Stalin rejected the policy advocated by Litvinov. He did not make collaboration with the United States the overriding goal of policy. That would have involved concessions in Germany and Eastern Europe that he was unwilling to make. He may have rejected it also on the grounds that a foreign policy of cooperation with the United States would not fit well with a domestic policy of reasserting the regime's control over Soviet society. According to the writer Konstantin Simonov, who met Stalin several times after the war to discuss cultural policy, Stalin feared a repeat of the Decembrist revolt of 1825: "he had shown Ivan to Europe and Europe to Ivan, as Alexander I had done in 1813–1814."[109] A policy of alliance with the Western powers might make it more difficult to tighten the regime's grip on Soviet life. Whatever the causal connection may have been, international tension went hand in hand with repression at home in Stalin's last years.

The policy Stalin pursued was one of *realpolitik*, within the framework outlined at the beginning of this chapter. Left-wing critics would later characterize it, correctly, as statist, because it treated states, rather than classes, as the primary actors in international relations, and because it put the interests of the Soviet state above those of international revolution. Stalin foresaw a difficult period in which capitalism would be wracked by crisis and war. He wanted to ensure that the postwar settlement enhanced Soviet power and security for the turbulent period that lay ahead. He rejected the analysis of Eugen Varga, the Hungarian director of the Academy of Sciences' Institute of World Economy and World Politics, who argued that the role of the state in capitalism had changed, and that as a result capitalism would develop in a more stable fashion than it had done in the interwar years.[110] Stalin lamented to Molotov that Russia "wins wars but does not know how to exploit the fruits of victory";[111] he was determined not to make the same mistake. The defeat of Germany and Japan had created the basis for a redistribution of power in the international system. Stalin wanted to consolidate Soviet territorial gains, establish a Soviet sphere of influence in Eastern Europe, and have a voice in the political fate of Germany and – if possible – of Japan. He sought unilateral guarantees of Soviet security, rather than security through cooperation.

Stalin and Molotov were prepared to be tough in pressing Soviet claims and stubborn in resisting Western pressure. But they did not want war with the West, and they understood that there were limits beyond which they should not go. Stalin's decisions not to land troops on Hokkaido and to withdraw Soviet forces from northern Iran show that he was unwilling to press Soviet claims beyond a certain point. This was evident too in Soviet policy toward Turkey. At the end of the war the Soviet Union sought to regain from Turkey territory that had been ceded by a weak Russia in 1921. It also asked for a revision of the 1936 Montreux Convention governing the passage of ships through the Turkish Straits between the Black Sea and the Mediterranean, and for a naval and military base in the Straits.

The Soviet Union put pressure on Turkey in the summer of 1945 by moving Soviet troops in Romania and Bulgaria close to the Turkish border.[112] At Potsdam the Western allies refused to grant Soviet claims, although they did accept that the Montreux Convention needed revision. The Soviet Union kept up the campaign of pressure against Turkey in

1945. In his letter of reprimand to Byrnes in January 1946 Truman expressed the fear that the Soviet Union intended to invade Turkey and seize the Straits.[113] On August 7, 1946 the Soviet Union formally requested a share in the defense of the Dardanelles, and argued that the Black Sea powers alone should determine a new regime for the Straits. This was interpreted in Washington as a move to obtain control of Turkey, and to open the way to a Soviet advance into the Persian Gulf and Suez Canal area. On August 19 Acheson, as Acting Secretary of State, informed the Soviet government that the Turkish Straits regime was of concern to the United States as a signatory of the Montreux Convention, and that Turkey should continue to be responsible for the defense of the Straits. US naval units were dispatched to the eastern Mediterranean. The Soviet Union dropped its claims.[114]

Many years later Molotov described the attempt to obtain joint Soviet–Turkish control of the Straits as a mistake. "Go on, apply pressure! For joint control," Stalin had told Molotov. When Molotov replied that they would not be given joint control, Stalin said to him, "You try."[115] "It is good that we retreated in good time," Molotov later commented, "or that would have led to a joint aggression against us."[116]

Stalin's choice of the postwar foreign policy line was not affected by the atomic bomb. The basic choice to pursue a realist, rather than a revolutionary or "liberal", foreign policy was made before the end of the war, and therefore before the atomic bomb had entered Stalin's strategic calculations.[117] The bomb did not lead to a reevaluation of the foreign policy line. Stalin and Molotov interpreted the significance of the bomb in terms of its effect on the balance of power and on the postwar settlement. The tactic they devised for dealing with it was to show that the Soviet Union would not be intimidated. This tactic, however, appears to have led to a quicker breakdown of cooperation than Stalin might have envisaged before August 1945. In that sense the bomb contributed to the collapse of the wartime alliance and the origins of the Cold War.

In September 1946 Nikolai Novikov, now the ambassador in Washington, wrote a memorandum that provides an interesting insight into the Soviet view of the role of the atomic bomb in US foreign policy.[118] Since Molotov instructed Novikov what to write, the result was, according to Novikov, a "report which could only conditionally be considered mine."[119] The United States, wrote Novikov, had emerged from the war more powerful than before, and was now intent upon world domination. Two of its main imperialist rivals, Germany and Japan, had been defeated, while the British Empire faced great economic and political difficulties. The Soviet Union was the main obstacle to American expansion. The Soviet Union, for its part, now enjoyed a much more solid international position than before the war. Soviet forces in Germany and other former enemy states were a guarantee "that those countries will not be used again for an attack on the USSR."[120] The Soviet Union carried great weight in international affairs, especially in Europe, and its growing political influence in Eastern and south-eastern Europe was inevitably regarded by American imperialists as an obstacle to their expansionist foreign policy.

Truman – "a politically unstable man with certain conservative tendencies"[121] – had turned away from the search for cooperation among the wartime allies. He had not yet responded to Churchill's call at Fulton for an Anglo-American military alliance, although he was clearly sympathetic to that idea, and maintained close military ties with Britain. Nevertheless, concluded Novikov, present-day relations between the United States and Britain could not last long, because they contained extreme contradictions. The most likely focus for this rivalry was the Middle East, where existing agreements between the United States and Britain might come unstuck.

The United States was trying to impose its will on the Soviet Union, and to limit or end Soviet influence in neighboring countries. Germany was a key element in this policy. The United States was not doing enough to democratize and demilitarize its zone of Germany, and might try to end the Allied occupation before these tasks had been carried out. This would open the way to a revival of imperialist Germany, which, Novikov asserted, the United States counted on using as an ally in a future war against the Soviet Union.

Speculation about war was rife in the United States, wrote Novikov. At public meetings and in the press, reactionaries were talking about war against the Soviet Union, and even calling for such a war "with the threat of using the atomic bomb."[122] This campaign was intended to put pressure on the Soviet Union and force it to make concessions, and also to create a war psychosis so that the government would be able to maintain a high level of military preparedness. These measures were not an end in themselves, argued Novikov. They were designed to create the conditions in which the United States could win the new war that the most bellicose circles of American imperialism were contemplating. No one, of course, could now determine when that war would take place. But the United States was building up its armed forces for a war against the Soviet Union, the main obstacle on the American path to world domination. Novikov did not present war as imminent, and implied that the immediate aim of American military power, including the atomic bomb, was to force the Soviet Union to accept the United States' plans for the postwar world.

Novikov's memorandum is rooted in the Leninist analysis of imperialism. He assumed that the United States was bent on world domination. Because Germany and Japan had been weakened by their defeat, and Britain was in decline, the Soviet Union was the main impediment to the expansion of American imperialism. It was inevitable, therefore, that the United States would try to undermine the Soviet Union and put pressure on it. Yet Novikov still expected inter-imperialist contradictions to come to the fore, and the Anglo–American alliance to break down as a result.

Novikov did not portray the atomic bomb as in any way shaping or transforming international relations, or as a preponderant element in the balance of power. Rather he presented it – as most commentators did – as a political instrument that the United States wanted to use to intimidate the Soviet Union.[123] Stalin made the same point on September 17, 1946, in one of his most important statements about the atomic bomb. There was no real danger of a "new war," he said. He did not think that Britain and the United States were trying to organize a "capitalist encirclement" of the Soviet Union, and he doubted that they could do so, even if they wanted to.[124] "Atomic bombs are meant to frighten those with weak nerves," he said, in reply to a question from Alexander Werth,

but they cannot decide the outcome of a war, since atomic bombs are quite insufficient for that. Of course, monopoly ownership of the secret of the atomic bomb creates a threat, but against it there exist at least two means: a) monopoly ownership of the atomic bomb cannot last for long; b) the use of the atomic bomb will be prohibited.[125]

Since the prospects for banning the use of the bomb were not good, Stalin was indicating that the Soviet Union intended to end the American atomic monopoly before long. His reference to weak nerves suggested that the Soviet Union did not have weak nerves, and that it would not be intimidated.

CHAPTER NINE

The Atomic Industry

I

AN ATOMIC INDUSTRY had to be established before the bomb could be built. This was a formidable task for a country that had suffered so much in the war. But Stalin wanted the bomb as soon as possible, and was prepared to disregard the cost. The building of the atomic bomb was the kind of task for which the Stalinist command economy was ideally suited. It resembled the huge construction projects of the 1930s – the steel city at Magnitogorsk, or Dneprostroi, the great dam on the Dnieper. It was a heroic undertaking for which the resources of the country could be mobilized, including the best scientists and industrial managers, as well as the slave laborers of the Gulag. The project was a curious combination of the best and the worst of Soviet society – of enthusiastic scientists and engineers produced by the expansion of education under Soviet rule, and of prisoners who lived in the inhuman conditions of the labor camps.

No good figures are available for the cost of the project, or for the number of people involved. Some indication of the project's size, however, is given by a 1950 Central Intelligence Agency report, which estimated that between 330,000 and 460,000 people were employed in it. Most of these – 255,000 to 361,000 – worked in mining in the Soviet Union (80–120,000) and in Eastern Europe (175–241,000); 50–60,000 worked in construction, 20–30,000 in production, and 5–8,000 in research.[1] The CIA estimated that about 10,000 technically qualified people – engineers, geologists, research scientists, and laboratory technicans – worked in the project.[2] Although these figures are estimates, they appear plausible, and certainly of the right order of magnitude. Many of these people, and in particular the miners and construction workers, were prisoners.

Anatolii Aleksandrov, who took over the Institute of Physical Problems from Kapitsa and was close to Kurchatov, has written that there were two kinds of managers in the project. There were those like Vannikov, Zaveniagin, and Pervukhin, who had great experience as organizers and were able to understand the technical issues quickly. There were others "who understood nothing of the matter, but all the time tried to display the power that had been given to them. Many of them understood the problem at the level of 'Will it explode, or not explode?' And I think that that is how Beria understood it, although, of course, all the information flowed to him."[3] The most important decisions had to go to Beria and Stalin, and to the Special Committee, for final approval, but it was Vannikov and Kurchatov who ran the project on a day-to-day basis.

Beria, as has been seen, had doubts about Soviet scientists, but he had to rely on Kurchatov. It is possible that he hoped to use the German scientists as a parallel team, which would compete with Kurchatov and his colleagues. That did not prove possible, however, except in some limited areas, because Soviet scientists were more advanced in their understanding of what needed to be done. The Manhattan project, on the other hand, did provide a model against which Soviet decisions could be assessed. It exercised a strong influence on the Soviet project not only because it had been successful, but because, in the political conditions of the time, Soviet scientists had to make a strong case if they wanted to do something different.

A Russian translation was made of *Atomic Energy for Military Purposes*, which the United States government had issued on August 12, 1945. This report, which was written by the Princeton physicist Henry D. Smyth, provided an extensive account of the Manhattan project, though it omitted the most sensitive information about the design of the bomb – implosion, for example, is not mentioned. The Russian translation was set in type by the middle of November, and published early in 1946 in an edition of 30,000.[4] The Smyth Report was distributed widely to scientists and engineers in the Soviet project. It provided them with an overall picture of what the United States had done. Along with the information from intelligence, it exercised an important influence on the technical choices made in the Soviet project.

Beria did not interfere in scientific or technical decisions. His role was to ensure that the project obtained the resources – the people, the materials, the information – that it needed, and to put pressure on those managing the project to build the bomb as quickly as possible. He visited the various institutes and plants, issuing threats and exuding an air of menace. Everyone understood that his threats were not idle; there were millions of victims to prove that. But Beria wanted the project to be a success, and he appears to have understood that arresting its managers would slow it down. During the war he had not made widescale arrests in the branches of industry he supervised.[5] So it was with the atomic project. He was intelligent enough to realize that he had to balance the repressive powers at his disposal against the need for competent management.

II

The first problem was to find uranium. This task could no longer be postponed. It was not made easier by the fact that the United States and Britain had set up a Combined Development Trust in June 1944 to gain control of world supplies of uranium and thorium. Chaired by General Groves, the trust had two aims: to procure enough uranium for the Manhattan project; and also to prevent other states – and in particular the Soviet Union – from acquiring uranium for their own projects.[6] Groves wrote to Stimson in November 1944 that "while it would be undesirable for any other government to have any stocks of the materials, it would be positively dangerous to permit any other government to secure in excess of one thousand tons of uranium oxide."[7]

During 1945 the Combined Development Trust signed agreements with Belgium, Brazil, and the Netherlands to prevent the supplies of uranium and thorium controlled by these states from falling into the hands of other countries.[8] On December 3, 1945 Groves informed Robert Patterson, Stimson's successor as Secretary of War, that the trust countries now controlled 97 per cent of the world's uranium output and 65 per cent of the world supply of thorium.[9] (Thorium is important because when thorium-232 absorbs neutrons it becomes thorium-233, which then decays to uranium-233, which is fissionable.) Large deposits of low-grade uranium were to be found, Groves wrote, in South Africa, which was part of the British Empire, and in Sweden which, although it had refused to sign a supply agreement, had promised not to export uranium.[10] The only countries with the resources and industrial power to challenge the dominant position of the United States and Britain in the near future were the Soviet Union and possibly Sweden. But "Russian resources of raw materials are far inferior to those of the Trust group of nations," he wrote, "and in all probability these could not be made available unless costs of production are completely disregarded."[11] Groves did not think that the Soviet Union would be able to obtain enough uranium for its project from the Jachymov mines in Czechoslovakia, and he aimed to deny it the possibility of obtaining uranium from elsewhere. Soviet intelligence was probably well informed about Groves's efforts by Donald Maclean, who was at the British embassy in Washington from May 1944 to the summer of 1948.[12]

Groves's estimate of Soviet uranium supplies was to prove mistaken, but in August 1945 the Soviet authorities had indeed reason to be concerned, for they did not know where they would get the uranium they needed. In spite of the government's order for 100 metric tons of uranium metal in 1943, only one kilogram had been produced by August 1945. The need for uranium was now very pressing. Uranium metal was needed for plutonium production reactors, and uranium in various forms was required for isotope separation. The uranium confiscated in Germany and Czechoslovakia at

the end of the war was useful, but far short of the total requirement. The
Soviet government did not yet know what Eastern Europe would be able
to supply. It knew even less about Soviet reserves. Dmitrii Shcherbakov's
1943 memorandum had produced only limited results.[13] Soviet geologists
had not studied the existing deposits very intensively, and they had,
moreover, no clear idea what other deposits might be found on Soviet
territory.[14] Uranium mining had not yet been organized on an industrial
scale.[15]

Urgent measures were now required. In September 1945 a commission
went to Central Asia to explore the uranium deposits and organize mining
there.[16] The commission was headed by P.Ia. Antropov, one of Vannikov's
deputies at the First Chief Directorate. Before the war Antropov had been,
successively, director of the Heavy Industry Commissariat's East Siberian
Geological Trust in Irkutsk, head of the Chief Directorate of the Zinc and
Lead Industry of the same commissariat, and first deputy People's Commissar of Nonferrous Metallurgy.[17] Antropov's commission, which included
Shcherbakov among its members, talked to the local geologists in Central
Asia and examined geological materials. Besides the old mine at Tiuia-
Muiun, deposits had been discovered before the war at Taboshary, Uigar-
Sai (Atbashi), Maili–Sai and other places in the region.[18] It was not easy,
however, to assess the extent of these deposits. At Taboshary, for example,
some geologists believed that the uranium was concentrated in two ore
bodies at a depth of no more than 100 meters, and that there was therefore
no point in further development of the mine. Others took the view that the
uranium ore ran to great depths, and that mining operations should be
extended. The only way to resolve this dispute was by further excavation,
which required investment.[19]

Antropov and Shcherbakov, under pressure to find uranium as quickly
as possible, decided to conduct exploratory excavations in an energetic
fashion at Taboshary. This proved to be the right decision. At other sites
Antropov adopted the same approach, arguing that further exploration
would lead to the discovery of additional reserves and of higher-quality ore.
He also organized extensive exploration in the areas around the deposits
that had already been identified. This led to the discovery of significant
new reserves.[20] Once Antropov's commission had made its initial survey,
permanent organizations were created to help Combine No. 6, which had
now been placed under the control of the First Chief Directorate. A
geological station and prospecting group were set up to help the combine
carry out exploration and prospecting, prepare geological maps of the
region, document the underground excavations, and study the distribution
and genesis of the ore deposits and the composition of the ore itself.[21]

In concentrating first on Central Asia, Antropov was following the
advice that Shcherbakov had given in his 1943 memorandum. But the
second step that Shcherbakov had recommended – prospecting for ura-

nium in the rest of the country – was more difficult. "For the sake of objectivity," Antropov wrote later, "it should be said that we all had a very poor conception of where and how to look for uranium ores."[22] Widely different views were now advanced. One leading mineralogist argued that uranium should be sought in the middle of the country. Kapitsa, who took part in these early discussions, argued that the first place to look for new deposits was in the north.[23]

Lacking clear guidelines, Antropov decided that it would be a mistake to restrict the search for uranium to any one type of geological formation. He therefore adopted Shcherbakov's "tactic of the broad front," and decided to prospect in large areas with different geological structure. At the end of 1947 the Ministry of Geology arranged special territorial expeditions to different parts of the country, and all other geological organizations were instructed to look out for uranium while pursuing their own work.[24] As soon as uranium was identified Antropov began mining operations at the site. By the end of 1948 mines had been started near Zheltye Vody in the Krivoi Rog region of the Ukraine; at Sillamäe in Estonia and at Slantsy in Leningrad province; near Piatigorsk in the Caucasus; and also in eastern Siberia, in the gold-producing areas along the Kolyma river.[25] In the Urals too, mines were opened up, and in 1948–50 rivers and lakes were studied as sources of uranium.[26] By 1948 the Soviet Union was also mining monazite from which thorium could be extracted and converted into the fissionable isotope uranium-233. Monazite was mined in the Altai mountains, the Urals, Siberia, the Kola peninsula, and the Caucasus.[27]

The conditions for mining in Central Asia were extremely difficult: "the uranium that was found was deposited in mountainous regions to which there were practically no approaches or roads."[28] The ore was taken to the processing plant operated by Combine No. 6 at Chkalovsk, near Leninabad, at the west end of the Fergana Valley.[29] The ore was leached with a mixture of nitric and sulfuric acid to produce a fairly pure uranium salt, which was then sent to the uranium plant at Elektrostal', near Moscow, for conversion into metal.[30] In the late 1940s another processing plant was built at Zheltye Vody in the Ukraine using the same process; other plants may have been built too.[31]

It was, however, Eastern Europe that provided most of the uranium in the early years. When the Soviet Union took over the uranium mines at Jachymov it also acquired ore that had already been mined but not removed from the site.[32] Mining operations were started soon thereafter, and extensive efforts, which began to yield results by the end of the decade, were made to find new deposits.[33] The Soviet zone of Germany soon became the most important source of uranium: southern and south-western Saxony contained rich deposits, which had been identified in 1943. Mining took some time to organize, however: equipment had to be assembled from the silver and cobalt mines in the region, and the layout of these mines had to be established; and transport, machinery, and special clothing had to be found. In July 1946 uranium mining began in the Erzgebirge and was soon extended to the Harz mountains, to the area around Plauen, Oelsnitz, and Bergen, and to the region around Goerlitz and Zittau. At first no attempt was made to use the silver, cobalt, bismuth, nickel and other ores that were mined along with uranium; these were merely thrown on waste piles, an indication of the priority being given to uranium. Plants were set up to concentrate the ore by mechanical and chemical means before it was shipped to the Soviet Union.[34] Uranium mines were set up in Bulgaria and Poland too. Exploitation of the uranium deposit mear Bukhovo in Bulgaria began in late 1945, and mining expanded later to other areas; in Poland mining began in 1947, in Lower Silesia. But these operations yielded much less uranium than those in Germany and Czechoslovakia.[35] The Soviet Union also started mining in Xinjiang province of China, which it controlled at the time.[36]

No figures have been published for Soviet uranium output, even for the early postwar years. The only figures available are estimates made at the time by the CIA and by individual analysts in the West. According to a 1950 CIA estimate, Soviet and East European mines produced some 70–110 tons of oxide a year in 1946 and 1947. It was only in 1948 that there was a significant increase in production.[37] No CIA estimates are available for the later years, but the CIA did conclude in 1950 that if "the Soviets . . . considered their uranium ore supply to be critically short" before the middle of 1948, "the supply of uranium ore is no longer critical, but is sufficient for their present needs."[38] This may have been a rather optimistic estimate, for uranium supply was still regarded as an urgent problem.[39]

The CIA estimated in 1950 that 45 per cent of Soviet uranium came from East Germany, 33 per cent from the Soviet Union, 15 per cent from Czechoslovakia, 4 per cent from Bulgaria, and 3 per cent from Poland.[40] These figures cannot be accepted without reservation, and the estimates for the Soviet Union are likely to be much less reliable than those for East Germany and Czechoslovakia, which were more accessible for intelligence operations. Nevertheless, the importance of East European uranium was confirmed in 1953 by Avraamii Zaveniagin, who noted that a "significant part" of the uranium for the Soviet project was obtained abroad, and called for urgent measures to expand the raw material base inside the Soviet Union.[41] In spite of the paucity of evidence, a general picture emerges: the Soviet Union had to adopt very determined and costly measures to acquire uranium for its nuclear project; it made a major effort to develop its own resources, but was forced to rely heavily on East European supplies in the immediate postwar years; and it was not until 1948 that the uranium supply bottleneck began to ease.

III

The task of producing uranium metal was given to Nikolaus Riehl, who had been responsible for the purification of uranium at the Auer Company in Berlin during the war. Riehl, who had been born in St Petersburg and spoke Russian fluently, had studied under Lise Meitner; he was "a good scientist and a very decent fellow (one of the list of the good ones)," according to Paul Rosbaud.[42] He had been brought to Moscow in June 1945, and assigned the task of uranium purification by Beria.[43] Zaveniagin chose Elektrostal', about 70 kilometers east of Moscow as the site for the uranium metal plant. This town took its name from a large electric steelworks that had been built by Germans in the 1930s. There was a munitions factory in which the uranium plant could be housed, and also workshops, a power station, a large automobile depot, and a supply of workers. Riehl was happy with this choice, because he believed that his work would be easier if he were close to Moscow.[44] All the equipment and machinery that had survived the American bombing raids and could be dismantled was shipped from the uranium purification plant at Oranienburg, just north of Berlin, to Elektrostal'.

At first it was decided (presumably by the Technical Council) to produce uranium metal by the methods of both Riehl and Zinaida Ershova, who had produced 1 kilogram of uranium metal at the Institute of Rare and Fine Metals in December 1944.[45] Riehl's method was judged to be quicker and simpler.[46] Production of uranium metal on a large scale nevertheless proved difficult. The production process consists of purification, reduction, and smelting, and it was the final stage that was ready for operation first. One night late in 1945 Riehl and his group smelted some uranium metal powder, which had been brought from Germany, in the newly installed furnace at Elektrostal'. They did this partly to test the process, partly to show the Soviet authorities that the Germans were not saboteurs or procrastinators.[47] By the end of 1945 the uranium plant was partially ready, but far behind the timetable that had been set by the government.[48] The atmosphere became tense and unpleasant, and at the beginning of the new year Zaveniagin arrived at the plant to speed things up. Using the full array of obscene and offensive expressions for which the Russian language is justly famous, he lectured the factory's managers in the most insulting way.[49] Things soon improved, however, when Riehl's group managed to produce several metric tons of uranium dioxide of sufficient purity for experiments that Kurchatov wanted to do.[50]

Although the plant was now in operation, the method for purifying uranium was causing a bottleneck. Riehl had chosen to remove the impurities from the uranium oxide by fractional crystallization. This was the method he had employed in Germany, but it was slow. When he received a copy of the Smyth Report (the Russian edition was published

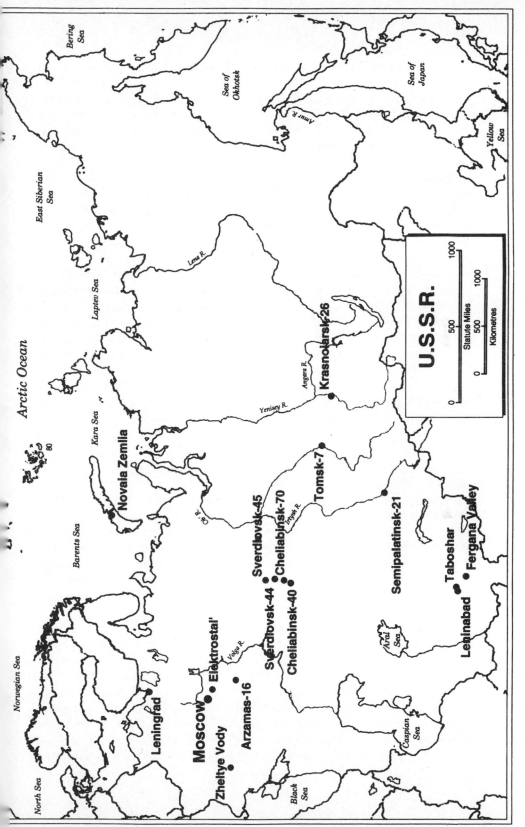

Soviet Nuclear Sites

early in 1946), he read it in one night and learned that the Americans had used an ether extraction method, which Riehl knew but had used only on a laboratory scale in the purification of rare earths. Riehl and his colleagues now said to themselves: "What the Americans can do, we can do too," and adapted the ether method for use on an industrial scale.[51] The process worked well for some years, and the throughput eventually reached almost one metric ton of uranium a day.[52]

Now, however, the metallurgical stage of the process caused delays. At first Riehl employed the calcithermal reduction method that the Degussa plant in Frankfurt had used, but this produced an unsatisfactory uranium powder with a considerable admixture of calcium.[53] One of the Soviet specialists asked Riehl why he did not use uranium tetrafluoride rather than uranium oxide, since the calcium fluoride, unlike calcium oxide, would melt, and metal rather than powder would result. In his memoir Riehl points to this advice as evidence that the Soviet Union was receiving information from spies, but in fact the Smyth Report mentions that the Americans used tetrafluoride, so that the question put to Riehl could well have been based on the Smyth Report.[54] Riehl took the hint, and the fluoride procedure was successfully adopted for production by one of Riehl's German colleagues, Dr. G. Wirths, and by the Russian chief engineer at the plant, Iu.N. Golovanov.[55] By September–October 1946 the Elektrostal' plant was delivering about 3 metric tons of uranium metal a week to Laboratory No. 2.[56]

IV

The next step on the road to the bomb was the experimental nuclear reactor that Kurchatov had been planning since early 1943. Kurchatov intended to use this reactor to produce samples of plutonium for chemical and physical analysis, to test materials for use in the production reactors, and to conduct experiments that would help in the design of those reactors. Although his responsibilities had expanded greatly after August 1945, Kurchatov himself took charge of building the experimental reactor. He headed the reactor group, which grew from 11 members in January 1946 to 76 by December.[57]

The reactor work at Laboratory No. 2 had been greatly hampered by the lack of graphite and uranium. It was only between May and August 1945 that the problem of producing graphite of the required purity was solved, and only at the end of the year that this graphite became available in quantity.[58] More than 500 metric tons of graphite were delivered during 1946, and all of this was tested for impurities at the laboratory.[59] In January 1946 the Elektrostal' plant began to deliver enough uranium, in the form of cylindrical metal slugs prepared to Kurchatov's specifications, for exponential experiments with different arrangements of uranium in graphite.

These experiments continued until March, and enabled Kurchatov and his group to calculate the best arrangement for the reactor. Kurchatov was also able to confirm that the uranium and graphite being supplied to the laboratory were of the right purity.[60]

In the summer of 1946 significant batches of uranium metal began to arrive at the laboratory from Elektrostal'. In August, however, the laboratory found that some of the uranium contained too high a concentration of boron.[61] Vannikov went to Elektrostal' to deal with the problem. His tone to the plant managers was polite but threatening, and the problem was soon solved. If the impurity had not been discovered, this uranium would have prevented the reactor from going critical, because boron is a strong absorber of neutrons.[62] Under the direction of A.P. Vinogradov, methods were developed for analyzing the impurities in uranium.[63] These methods were later adopted for quality control at the Elektrostal' plant.[64]

By June 1946 a special building had been erected on the grounds of Laboratory No. 2 to house the reactor. It was about 15 meters by 40, and the reactor itself was to be assembled in a pit 7 meters deep. There was a laboratory, which was protected from radiation by reinforced concrete walls and a thick layer of soil and sand. Entrance to the reactor was through a labyrinth made up of lead and blocks of paraffin and boric acid. Two independent substations supplied the electric power needed for controlling the reactor. Dosimeters were placed about the building to measure the level of radiation, and sirens and lights were installed on the building to warn if the level became dangerous.[65] In August, September, and October, Kurchatov and his group built four models of the reactor, using all the available uranium.

Experiments were conducted to determine the radius of the reactor core. This radius could not be determined theoretically because of variations in the purity of the graphite and uranium. The experiments showed that the core would have a radius of 3 meters, and that about 500 metric tons of graphite and 50 metric tons of uranium would be needed.[66] Assembly of the reactor began on November 15, 1946. The overall structure of the reactor was a cubic lattice of uranium embedded in a graphite sphere. The reactor was controlled by three cadmium rods that could be raised out of the core and lowered into it; cadmium is a strong absorber of neutrons and the presence of the rods in the reactor would prevent a chain reaction from developing. Through the center of the reactor there was a horizontal tunnel measuring 40 by 60 centimeters, in which materials and equipment could be placed for experimental purposes.[67]

On December 20, 1946, when the fiftieth layer was added to the reactor, it became clear that criticality would be achieved with 55 layers, instead of the planned 76. Kurchatov and his colleagues proceeded very carefully now that they were close to the critical state. At two o'clock in the afternoon of December 25 the fifty-fourth layer was added. Kurchatov asked all of those not directly involved in taking measurements to leave the building; he and five of his group remained.[68] At six o'clock in the evening the reactor went critical, with Kurchatov at the controls, and the first self-sustaining nuclear chain reaction took place in the Soviet Union, and indeed in Europe. Kurchatov remained at the controls until late that night, and ran the reactor up to 100 watts energy production before shutting it down.[69]

Once the reactor had started up, some of those who had worked on it hurried to the building to see it in operation. "It was for all of us an exciting and happy evening," one of those present has written. "We congratulated one another, with the restraint appropriate to the work situation, but warmly and sincerely."[70] Kurchatov, who had thought for more than six years about a nuclear chain reaction, was very happy at this success. "Atomic energy," he said, in the formal words that he used – or that were ascribed to him – on such occasions, "has now been subordinated to the will of Soviet man."[71] The start-up of the reactor marked the first import-ant milestone on the road to the bomb.[72]

Several days later Beria came to the laboratory for a special demon-stration of the new reactor. He stood at the control panel while Kurchatov raised the control rod. The clicks that registered the neutrons increased in frequency until they became a continuous wail, while the indicator on the galvanometer moved off the scale. The scientists present exclaimed, "It's started." But Beria, with evident disappointment, said, "Is that all? Nothing more? Can I go to the reactor?" Kurchatov stopped him, telling him that it would be dangerous for his health. The start-up of the reactor was far less impressive than the flight of a new airplane or the test of a new tank. Because there was so little to see at these "demonstrations," Beria could not be sure that Kurchatov was not pulling the wool over his eyes.[73]

The dimensions of the F-1 (Fizicheskii-1: Physical-1) reactor were roughly similar to those of the pile Fermi had built in Chicago in December 1942. Fermi's pile used 400 tons of graphite, 6 tons of uranium metal, and 50 tons of uranium oxide, while Kurchatov's used about 400 metric tons of graphite and 45.07 metric tons of uranium.[74] The similarity followed from the common desire of the two men to build a reactor as quickly as possible with graphite and natural uranium; no other explanation seems necessary, though the Smyth Report had provided a detailed de-scription of the design of the Chicago pile.[75] The Chicago pile was not operated at more than 200 watts, because of the radiation danger to people in and around the squash court where it was built.[76] Kurchatov wanted to produce plutonium, test materials, and conduct experiments, and he there-fore took steps to see that he would be able to operate his reactor at more than 200 watts, by shielding it and by providing for remote control. The F-1 reactor achieved 100 watts on the day it went critical and later (after more uranium and graphite had been added) was operated in short bursts at up to 3,800 kilowatts; it could be operated at several dozen watts over long periods.[77] In the early months of 1947 new layers of uranium and graphite were added to increase its power. When operated for comparatively long periods, it was controlled from a special control panel at a distance of 1–1.5 kilometers.[78]

Kurchatov had turned his attention to the production reactor long before the F-1 went critical. In May 1945 he had decided, probably on the basis of information from the United States, that the production reactor would be a uranium-graphite system.[79] This was the logical decision, given the inability of Soviet industry to supply heavy water in the near future.[80] The production of one gram of plutonium a day requires, as the Smyth Report pointed out, a reactor that can generate thermal power at the rate of 500–1,500 kilowatts.[81] Kurchatov and his colleagues faced the same problem the Americans had confronted in 1943: they had to design a reactor of the required capacity on the basis of a reactor that could operate only at a very much lower power level.

In January 1946 Kurchatov asked Nikolai Dollezhal', director of the Institute of Chemical Machine-Building, to help with the design of the production reactor. Dollezhal' had begun his career by designing heat and power stations and had later worked in various chemical engineering plants. When he looked at the preliminary design that had been prepared, he did not like it. It proposed a horizontal reactor in which the fuel and control rods would be inserted and withdrawn from the side; this was the type that had been built at Hanford. Dollezhal' suggested a vertical reactor instead, in which the rods could be loaded and unloaded under their own weight. By March 1946 he had a draft design ready, and in June he showed Kurchatov the drawings for it. At the same time a group in Leningrad was working on the design of a horizontal reactor. In July the Scientific-Technical Council decided, in a meeting that lasted 92 hours with only short breaks, to adopt Dollezhal's design. This decision was approved by the government in August, four months before the experimental reactor went critical.[82]

Dollezhal' assembled a design group at the Institute of Chemical Machine-Building. This group received higher pay and better ration cards than other members of the institute. Dollezhal' was given a government telephone, and a "plenipotentiary of the Council of Ministers" was appointed to his institute.[83] Kurchatov stayed in close touch. Every three or four days he came to the institute to see how the design was proceeding. "This allowed him to know everything in detail," according to Dollezhal', "to settle questions which proved unusual because of the novelty of the thing, and to take the appropriate decisions."[84] Although the first production reactor was, like the experimental reactor, a uranium-graphite system, its design presented many new problems. Its energy output was much greater, and it had therefore to be cooled when in operation. Water was to be the coolant, so pipes had to be inserted into the reactor to channel the water to where it was needed.

The uranium fuel had to be removed from the reactor so that the plutonium could be separated. It was therefore impractical to have the uranium embedded as lumps in the graphite. Fuel slugs which passed through the moderator would be much easier to load and unload, but were difficult to fabricate. These slugs, moreover, had to be sealed in some way against direct contact with the water, in order to protect them from corrosion. At Hanford the uranium slugs had been sealed or "canned" in protective aluminum jackets, and the Soviet designers adopted the same practice. Remote control had to be provided, so that the reactor could be operated, and the fuel slugs loaded and unloaded, safely. Special shielding had to be built to protect the reactor operators from radiation.[85]

The F-1 reactor proved to be extremely useful in seeking solutions to these problems. Thirty different lattices – with different spacing; with uranium slugs of different diameter; with water and without – were tested in the tunnel of that reactor, to see which arrangement was best. The uranium for the production reactor was checked in the experimental reactor, as was the aluminum for the canning and the fuel channels; quality control of the graphite was left to the graphite factories. The experimental reactor was used to investigate the shielding properties of various materials – water, concrete, earth, and screens of iron, lead, and paraffin – against neutrons and gamma-rays, and the results of these experiments were used in designing the shielding for the production reactor.[86] Experiments were also done in the reactor with animals to measure the effects of radiation.[87]

Kurchatov and Dollezhal' ran into many difficulties. There were problems with the fabrication of the uranium fuel slugs; in 1948 Fuchs was asked how uranium metal slugs were fabricated, but could not help.[88] The fabrication of aluminum tubes and the canning of the fuel slugs also caused headaches. Warned by the Smyth Report that the "canning problem" was one of the most difficult, Kurchatov had organized research at the beginning of 1946 in four different institutes on methods of sealing the fuel rods, and eventually a solution was found.[89]

V

The first production reactor was built in the Urals about 15 kilometers east of the town of Kyshtym, and about 80 kilometers north-west of the industrial city of Cheliabinsk. The site had been chosen by Zaveniagin before the end of 1945.[90] It was an area that Zaveniagin knew well because he had been selected in December 1937 to represent the Kyshtym district in the Supreme Soviet.[91] The new combine was called Cheliabinsk-40, in accordance with the Soviet practice of giving secret plants the name of a nearby city and a post-office box number. This was to be the Soviet equivalent of the American complex at Hanford.

Cheliabinsk-40 was built in an area of great natural beauty, among lakes, mountains, and forests. The site had practical advantages too: it was close to Lakes Irtiash and Kyzyltash, which could supply the vast quantities of water needed for cooling the reactor; it was in the region with the best electricity supply network in the war-devastated country; it was close to railways and roads, and to the industrial centers of the Urals which could provide many of the materials needed for construction; and it was in the interior of the country, and so less vulnerable to attack by enemy air forces.

Cheliabinsk-40 was built on land that before the October Revolution had been part of the Kyshtym Estates, which were the property of Baron Mellor Zakomelsky, a distant scion of the Romanov family. For some years before World War I the estates had been managed by an American firm, of which Herbert Hoover, the future US President, was a director. Hoover helped to develop copper mining and smelting at Kyshtym. "The Russian engineers were most able technical men but lacked training on the administrative side," he wrote in his memoirs. "There was instinctive camaraderie by which the Russians and Americans got along together."[92] After the revolution, however, the chemical and metallurgical operations on the estates had been shut down. Now Soviet engineers were building something incomparably greater than had existed before, a symbol this time not of Russian–American friendship, but of the profound political rivalry between the two countries.[93]

In the early months of 1946 roads were laid and the site was prepared for construction; digging of the foundations began in the summer. Zaveniagin put Iakov Rappoport, a major-general in the MVD, in charge of construction.[94] Rappoport had been one of the men responsible for building the White Sea Canal in the early 1930s, a notorious project in which hundreds of thousands of camp laborers had died.[95] Cheliabinsk-40 too was built by prisoners, with as many as 70,000 working on the site at one time.[96] In the autumn of 1946 the foundations for the main reactor building were laid, and by the end of 1947 the building was ready.[97]

By that time materials for the production reactor had begun to become available in quantity. In December a train left the Kazan' station in Moscow with everything needed for starting up the reactor, and with members of the reactor group on board.[98] Kurchatov and Vannikov moved to Cheliabinsk-40 early in 1948 to supervise the assembly of the reactor. Vannikov had just suffered a heart attack, and decided to live in a railway carriage at the site, in order to avoid the daily journey of more than 10 kilometers from the town where the workers and engineers were housed. Kurchatov decided to stay with Vannikov, and the two men spent most of the next year at Cheliabinsk-40.[99]

Kurchatov worked closely with Vannikov and Zaveniagin, and with the managers of the new complex, to get the reactor ready. The first director of Cheliabinsk-40 was E.P. Slavskii, one of Vannikov's deputies at the First Chief Directorate. Like most of Vannikov's other deputies, Slavskii had joined the Party early, in 1918. After serving as a commissar in the cavalry for ten years, he studied at the Moscow Institute of Nonferrous Metals and Gold, and then held various positions in the metallurgical industry, becoming director of the Urals Aluminum Plant during the war, and Deputy People's Commissar of Nonferrous Metallurgy in 1945.[100] At the end of 1947, however, B.G. Muzrukov, director of the Urals Machine-Building Plant, one of the main centers of tank production during the war, was brought in to head the whole complex. Muzrukov was a former naval officer who had been appointed to head the Urals plant in 1939, at the age of thirty-five.[101] The reasons for this change are unclear, but Slavskii stayed at Cheliabinsk-40 as chief engineer.[102]

Assembly of the reactor began in early March 1948.[103] Kurchatov made a speech. "Here, my dear friends, is our strength, our peaceful life, for long, long years," he said. "You and I are founding an industry not for one year, not for two . . . for centuries." He then quoted two lines from "The Bronze Horseman," Pushkin's poem about St Petersburg. In the poem Peter the Great stands on the bank of the Neva and decides to found a city that will threaten Sweden, which had recently defeated Russia in battle. "Here a town will be established," Peter says, "To spite our arrogant neighbor." "We still have enough arrogant neighbors, unfortunately," Kurchatov continued.

And to spite them [a town] will be founded. In time your town and mine will have everything – kindergartens, fine shops, a theater and, if you like, a symphony orchestra! And then in thirty years' time your children, born here, will take into their own hands everything that we have made. And our successes will pale before their successes. The scope of our work will pale before the scope of theirs. And if in that time not one uranium bomb explodes over the heads of people, you and I can be happy! And our town can then become a monument to peace. Isn't that worth living for![104]

By the end of May the basic assembly was complete.[105] Now it was time to test the instruments for monitoring the reactor and the mechanisms for controlling it.[106] The reactor was built underground in a concrete shaft with walls 3 meters thick, and these walls were surrounded by tanks of water. The reactor core contained 1,168 fuel channels, and had a diameter of 9.4 meters.[107]

At the beginning of June 1948 water was let into the pipes, and the uranium slugs were loaded into the fuel channels. This work went on around the clock, under the direction of Kurchatov, Vannikov, and the managers of Cheliabinsk-40. On June 7 Kurchatov began to withdraw the emergency rods and stopped the flow of water into the reactor. The reactor – known as "installation A" or "reactor A" or "Annushka" (a diminutive form of Anna) – went critical that evening and reached a power output of 10 kilowatts in the early hours of June 8. When Kurchatov announced that the physics of the reactor was in order, all those in the control room went up to him to offer their congratulations. "Further success will depend not only on physics," declared Kurchatov, "but on engineering, on technology."[108] After shutting the reactor down, Kurchatov ordered that more uranium be loaded.[109] At 8 p.m. on June 10, he started up the reactor with water in the pipes. Sitting at the controls, he ran the reactor up to 1,000 kilowatts. The final start-up began on June 19, and on June 22 the reactor reached the design level of 100,000 kilowatts.[110]

In July the reactor began to operate according to the plan for plutonium production.[111] Unexpected problems arose. The aluminum canning on the fuel slugs suffered severe corrosion and had to be replaced by aluminum oxidized in a different way. More seriously, the fuel slugs swelled up and wrinkles and lumps developed on the surface of the uranium; the slugs then became stuck in the discharge pipes. Beria's representatives suspected that this might be the result of sabotage, but Kurchatov pointed out that surprises were to be expected in the behavior of materials in intense neutron fields.[112] The reactor had to be shut down, the uranium taken out and studied, and the plutonium that had built up extracted. Changes were made in the design of the reactor, and the problem was solved.[113]

The second element at Cheliabinsk-40 was "installation B," the radiochemical plant in which the plutonium was separated from the uranium irradiated in the reactor. Kurchatov had assigned the task of developing the separation process to Khlopin and the Radium Institute.[114] Khlopin worked on this problem during the war, but it was only after the institute's return to Leningrad at the beginning of 1945, and especially after August, that the institute's best radiochemists and physicists began serious work on the separation process.[115]

The Smyth Report revealed that in the Manhattan project four types of method for chemical separation had been explored – volatility, absorption, solvent extraction, and precipitation – and that the Hanford separation plant had used a precipitation method.[116] The success of this process had "exceeded all expectations," according to the report, and had shown the choice to be the correct one, even though it had been based on a knowledge of plutonium chemistry gleaned from less than a milligram of that element.[117]

Khlopin set up several groups to investigate different methods of separating the plutonium[118] – perhaps the four listed in the Smyth Report. He believed that precipitation was the most promising method, partly no doubt because of the American experience, but also because he had done a great deal of work earlier in his career on the co-precipitation of radioactive elements, and had obtained the first Russian radium by this method in 1921. The first experiments had to be done with impulse quantities of neptunium and fission products because no plutonium was available.[119] On the basis of these initial experiments Khlopin and his

colleagues prepared a report in 1946 on the processing of irradiated uranium, for use by chemists and engineers in the project. By this time
Khlopin had provided some basic data for the design of the separation plant
at Cheliabinsk-40.[120]

It was not Khlopin, however, but Boris Kurchatov and a colleague at
Laboratory No. 2 who first succeeded in separating plutonium from uranium oxide that had been irradiated in the F-1 reactor. They did this
between April and August 1947, using a precipitation method. They
obtained two samples of plutonium, weighing 6.1 and 17.3 micrograms,
which were visible only under a microscope.[121] Even these tiny quantities
made it possible to begin research into the qualities of plutonium and its
compounds. An experimental semi-industrial plant was built at NII-9. This
produced the first Soviet plutonium on December 18, 1947. This sample
weighed less than a milligram, but in the following year two samples of
plutonium, each weighing milligrams, were produced by the pilot plant.[122]
Research continued into the methods of separation, but the presence of
continuing difficulties is suggested by the fact that Klaus Fuchs was asked
by his control about the solvent extraction process. He "knew hardly
anything of this, but was able to get some very limited information from
Harwell reports and passed this over, though he believed that this was of no
great significance."[123]

The basic feature of the separation plant at Cheliabinsk-40 was a canyon
consisting of a series of compartments with heavy concrete walls arranged
in a line and almost completely buried in the ground; the term "canyon,"
which was used at the plant, was taken from the Smyth Report.[124] Once
the aluminum canning had been removed, the fuel elements entered one
end of the canyon and were dissolved in nitric acid. Then they went
through various stages to remove the fission fragments that were to be
found in the uranium along with the plutonium.[125] The separation process
was based on slightly soluble sodium uranyl acetate precipitation from nitric
acid solutions of irradiated uranium.[126] Because the fission products were so
radioactive, the process had to be directed by remote control, and special
shielding provided for the plant operators. A tall chimney carried away the
radioactive xenon and radioactive iodine which were released in considerable quantity when the fuel slugs were dissolved.[127] The final process was
developed by B.A. Nikitin and A.P. Ratner of the Radium Institute,
because Khlopin was seriously ill and soon to die. The separation plant was
ready in December 1948, and began to produce plutonium early in the
following year.[128] Soviet accounts make it clear that mastering the plant
proved especially difficult, although they do not specify what the problems
were.[129]

The third element of the Cheliabinsk-40 combine was "installation V"
[the third letter in the Russian alphabet]; this was the chemical-metallurgical plant in which the plutonium from the separation plant was purified and
converted into metal for use in bombs. I.I. Cherniaev, director of the

Institute of General and Inorganic Chemistry, was responsible for developing the methods of purifying plutonium. A.A. Bochvar, director of NII-9,
was in charge of the metallurgy of plutonium. Vinogradov was "scientific
director of the problem of analytical control of the radiochemical and
chemical-metallurgical plants."[130] The plant was not ready at the beginning
of 1949, so a temporary "Shop No. 9" was set up.[131] On February 27, 1949
the shop received the first nitrate solutions of plutonium.[132] By the middle
of April pure plutonium dioxide was produced and transferred to the
metallurgical department, where it was converted into metal.[133] By June
there was enough plutonium for the first atomic bomb.[134] In August 1949
all production from the temporary Shop No. 9 was transferred to a specially
designed building.[135]

Construction of the Cheliabinsk-40 combine did not stop with the
making of the first atomic bomb. In the early 1950s new production
reactors were built: in September 1950 a second uranium-graphite system
came on line, and this was followed by two similar reactors in April 1951
and September 1952. In January 1952 a smaller reactor for isotope production was started up. A heavy water reactor was built at about the same
time.[136] Work on the production of heavy water had begun at the Chirchik
Nitrogen Combine in 1944, and the Institute of Physical Chemistry in
Moscow had started research on the physical chemistry of electrolytic cells
at about the same time.[137] In October 1945 the NKVD assembled a group
of German heavy water specialists at the Leuna works in Merseberg. This
group worked on the design of a heavy water plant until October 1946
when it was taken to Moscow and attached to the Institute of Physical
Chemistry. After 1948, however, the German scientists switched to other
work, since the Chirchik plant was now producing heavy water in large
quantities. In 1947 it had delivered its first large batch (200 liters) to
Moscow, where it was needed for the reactor that Alikhanov was building
at Laboratory No. 3. This reactor went critical in April 1949, with a power
output of 500 kilowatts thermal.[138] This served as a prototype for the heavy
water reactor at Cheliabinsk-40.[139]

VI

The United States had built three isotope separation plants in Tennessee
during the war. The first was an electromagnetic separation plant, which
supplied the uranium-235 for the Hiroshima bomb. A thermal diffusion
plant was built to produce feed material (i.e. partially enriched uranium) for
the electromagnetic plant. The last of the three plants to be completed –
the gaseous diffusion plant – became the primary supplier of uranium-235
for the American nuclear weapons program.[140]

The Soviet Union pursued all three methods after August 1945. Anatolii
Aleksandrov, who was in charge of the research on thermal diffusion,
wanted to abandon this line of research, but Kurchatov decided that it

should be continued, on the grounds that if some enrichment were needed of the uranium for the experimental reactor, thermal diffusion might provide the quickest method. It was not needed, however, and no thermal diffusion plant was built.[141] After August 1945 Kikoin began to work intensively with Sobolev and the theoretical physicist Ia.A. Smorodinskii on the theory of the gaseous diffusion process.[142] This involves the diffusion of uranium hexafluoride gas through a very large number of porous barriers so that the light isotope uranium-235, which passes more quickly through the barriers, becomes increasingly concentrated in the gas. Artsimovich, working with I.N. Golovin and G.Ia. Shchepkin, studied various possible methods of electromagnetic separation.[143] This process beams gaseous ions through a magnetic field; the ions will move in semicircular paths which will be different for the different isotopes; since the light ions will move in a smaller semicircle, a properly positioned collector will catch the light, but not the heavy, ions.

Early in 1946 sites were chosen for the gaseous diffusion and electromagnetic combines. The former was to be built in the central Urals, near the town of Neviansk, about 50 kilometers north of Sverdlovsk; it was given the code name Sverdlovsk-44.[144] The latter was to be built in the northern Urals, at Severnaia Tura, and called Sverdlovsk-45. Kikoin and Artsimovich were appointed scientific directors for these two plants.[145]

Considerable progress was made during 1946. Kikoin managed to produce porous barriers of sintered nickel powder; the first gas compressors were put into series production; uranium hexafluoride gas began to arrive in sufficient quantities; and some uranium was enriched in a small, experimental cascade (because the degree of enrichment at each stage is very slight, a "cascade" of many successive stages is needed). Artsimovich and his colleagues created the first ion source consisting of an electron beam traversing vaporized uranium tetrachloride, and with the help of an electromagnet brought from Germany directed a beam at the collector.[146]

Isotope separation was the aspect of the atomic project in which German scientists were most involved. Two separate institutes were set up, one under the direction of Gustav Hertz, the other under Manfred von Ardenne.[147] Both institutes were housed in sanatorium buildings on the Black Sea coast near Sukhumi, in Georgia; Hertz's institute was at Agudzheri, Von Ardenne's at Sinop. Although the two institutes were assigned the task of isotope separation, leading scientists seem to have been free to choose which method to work on.[148] As a result, several different lines of research were pursued.

Only a few Soviet scientists – and those not generally of the first rank – worked in Sukhumi at first.[149] But some of the leading Soviet scientists visited the institutes. In November 1945 Flerov came to lecture on the most important scientific problems of building uranium-235 and plutonium bombs.[150] Soon afterwards, Ioffe, Artsimovich, Kikoin, and

Sobolev visited Sukhumi.[151] German scientists were called to Moscow to attend meetings of the Technical Council where their work was discussed and their proposals assessed. None of them was assigned a role as important as that played by Nikolaus Riehl, but several did become involved in the development of the electromagnetic and gaseous diffusion processes. Max Steenbeck and Konrad Zippe did pioneering work on the ultracentrifuge separation method.

Max Steenbeck worked for Artsimovich at Laboratory No. 2 for about twelve to eighteen months in 1947–8.[152] Steenbeck, who had worked at the Siemens Company on a "whirling tube" rotating gas discharge, greatly admired Artsimovich for the clarity of his mind. Manfred von Ardenne's group in Sinop also worked on electromagnetic separation, but separately from Steenbeck. In 1949 the Technical Council adopted Von Ardenne's design for an ion source for the electromagnetic plant. Von Ardenne went to the Elektrosila plant in Leningrad to oversee the transition of the development work to an industrial scale.[153] Several of the German scientists worked on gaseous diffusion too, among them Gustav Hertz, Peter Thiessen, and Heinz Barwich.[154] Their work was apparently not an integral part of Kikoin's project, but done in parallel with it.

Things did not go smoothly for either the electromagnetic or the diffusion project. Artsimovich was unable to obtain ion sources with the required current.[155] The problems with the diffusion process were even more severe. Construction of the production plant was completed in 1948.[156] When operations began, however, nothing came out at the end of the final cascade, and in 1949 the degree of enrichment obtained was only 40 per cent, far less than the 90+ per cent needed for a bomb. Kurchatov asked Artsimovich to increase the enrichment. The 40 per cent enriched uranium was brought to Laboratory No. 2, and after a month of round-the-clock work Artsimovich and his group, using their experimental apparatus, managed to produce 400 grams of uranium enriched to 92–98 per cent.[157]

In November 1949 the German scientists were asked to help with the gaseous diffusion process.[158] Six Germans, including Hertz, Thiessen, and Barwich, were taken to Sverdlovsk-44. On the day after their arrival Vannikov and Kikoin briefed them on what had gone wrong. Kikoin explained that the plant was not achieving the expected level of enrichment – only 50–60 per cent instead of the required 90 per cent or more. Besides, he said, much of the uranium hexafluoride fed into the plant was disappearing. This conjured up the danger of losses through corrosion, but chemical analysis had not yet revealed why the uranium was being lost. Would the German scientists help?[159]

The diffusion plant at Sverdlovsk-44 was smaller than the American plant at Oak Ridge, and had a planned output of one kilogram of uranium-235 a day. Like the American plant, it was built in the shape of a giant U, covering many acres. It contained 6,000 compressors partitioned into sections consisting of 128 compressors each. The freshly painted compressors, barrier housings, and connecting pipes in air-conditioned rooms impressed the German scientists. They were struck by the speed with which this technically advanced plant had been built.[160]

The Germans worked in one cascade section which had been disconnected from the rest of the cascade. Thiessen experimented with passivation techniques to prevent corrosion, while Barwich measured and timed the disappearance of the uranium hexafluoride. The Germans, however, were unable to help. Beria came to the plant and gave Kikoin and his colleagues three months to solve the problem.[161] It was eventually discovered that the uranium was being lost inside the compressors. The rotors mounted inside the compressors had an armature of many iron laminations, and the interior laminations were moist and reacted with the uranium hexafluoride. This had not been discovered earlier because the outer laminations were quite dry.[162] With the help of A.N. Frumkin, a leading physical chemist, Kikoin's group found a way to deal with the problem.[163]

In 1950 Beria relieved Kikoin of his responsibilities as Kurchatov's deputy at Laboratory No. 2 so that he could devote all his efforts to the gaseous diffusion plant.[164] By the end of 1950 the problems at the plant had been resolved. Max Steenbeck, apparently catching wind of the difficulties with the diffusion process, had written to Beria to propose that a small centrifuge plant be built to "top off" the enrichment in the gaseous diffusion plant, and his proposal had been approved.[165] But in December 1950 the Technical Council criticized Steenbeck's proposal for the small centrifuge "topping plant," thereby effectively putting an end to that idea.[166] At about the same time the priority for electromagnetic separation was reduced. It was decided not to build a large-scale electromagnetic plant, and the small plant at Sverdlovsk−45, which had already been completed, was no longer treated as a top-priority project. These decisions suggest that alternatives to gaseous diffusion were not now needed so urgently.[167] In January 1951 Thiessen told Steenbeck that the corrosion problems at the gaseous diffusion plant had been solved.[168] In 1951 the gaseous diffusion plant began to produce uranium enriched to over 90 per cent with the light isotope.[169]

VII

The creation of the atomic industry was a remarkable feat, especially for a country whose economy had been devastated by the war. It showed that the Soviet Union had the scientists and engineers to create a whole new branch of industry. This was, moreover, not the only high-technology project being carried out in the Soviet Union at the time; the missile and radar projects also required highly skilled people. It is true that the Soviet

Union had a great deal of information about the Manhattan project, and that this information influenced the technical choices that were made. But this does not detract from the achievement of building the atomic industry in so short a time, for there is a great gap between knowing what should be done and actually building the plants.

The command-administrative system showed itself able to mobilize resources on a massive scale, and to channel them into a top-priority project. Stalin and Beria approved the costly strategy of pursuing alternative paths to the bomb. The principle of redundancy, which Kapitsa had criticized, was implemented in almost all parts of the project: plutonium and uranium-235; graphite and heavy water reactors; gaseous diffusion and electromagnetic isotope separation. This strategy shows that time was of the essence for Stalin.

The command-administrative system was effective in creating the atomic industry. But the system was a brutal one, and some of the costs it imposed should be noted here. First, the system made widespread use of prison labor. Most of the mining and construction appears to have been done by prisoners. They mined uranium in Central Asia and the other parts of the Soviet Union. They took part in the building of the new towns, plants, and institutes in the Urals, and in the building of the weapons laboratory at Arzamas-16.[170] Little has been published about the conditions in which the camp laborers worked and lived. Even Alexander Solzhenitsyn, in his encyclopedic *Gulag Archipelago*, has nothing to say about the uranium mines, and little about the prisoners who build the nuclear installations. Every three months, he writes, the prisoners in top-secret camps in the atomic industry

had to renew their pledges of "nondisclosure." But this was not the real trouble – the real trouble was that those released were not allowed to return home. The "released" prisoners were sent off in a large group in September, 1950 – to the Kolyma! Only there were they relieved of convoy and declared to be *a particularly dangerous special contingent*! They were dangerous because they had helped make the atomic bomb![171]

The lack of memoirs by inmates of the nuclear Gulag, or of evidence about their conditions of work, is therefore not an accident. Very few of these prisoners were set free, even after they had completed their sentences.[172]

More information is available about the uranium mines in the Soviet zone of Germany. The conditions of work were appalling, and the Soviet authorities drafted workers because they could not find enough volunteers. Labor exchanges were instructed to provide workers for the mines, and the police were ordered to enlist people who had no permanent employment.[173] Refugees from the Eastern territories of Germany which had now been absorbed into Poland were sent to the mines; so too were prisoners of war returning from the Soviet Union to those territories. Youth brigades were also organized.[174] By 1950 the uranium industry in the Soviet zone employed 150–200,000 people, according to the CIA.[175] The miners in Germany lived in barracks surrounded by barbed wire and guarded by MVD troops; they were punished if they tried to escape, though many apparently did.[176] Little attention was paid to medical consequences of working with uranium: protective clothing was inadequate, and many of the miners contracted lung cancer from exposure to radon gas. Accidents were not uncommon, and medical treatment was poor.[177] There is no reason to suppose that conditions in Soviet mines were any better. They are if anything likely to have been worse, since the mines were worked by prisoners rather than conscripted laborers. Those who died while working in the Soviet atomic industry camps were buried in communal graves.[178]

This leads to the second cost imposed by the command-administrative system. In the rush to build the bomb, health and safety were accorded low priority, though they were not neglected completely. In August 1948 the First Chief Directorate and the Ministry of Health worked out health norms and rules for those working at installations A and B at Cheliabinsk-40. Those norms were high by today's standards; they permitted a daily radiation dose of 0.1 rem over six working hours (about 30 rem a year). But even these norms were not complied with. The average dose received by workers at installation A (the reactor) in 1949 was 93.6 rem; at installation B (the chemical separation plant) the average dose was 113.3 rem in 1951.[179] No figures have been made available for the chemical-metallurgical plant, where direct contact with plutonium led to many occupational illnesses.[180] The situation there may have been much worse. Radiochemistry was particularly dangerous; a higher proportion of women, it should be noted, worked in this part of the project than in other areas.[181]

The first cases of radiation sickness appeared at Cheliabinsk-40 at the beginning of 1949. Soon thereafter one of the physicians wrote to Beria that the managers of Cheliabinsk-40 underestimated the danger of radiation to the workers, and additional measures were taken to improve the conditions of work.[182] The leaders of the atomic project did understand that radiation could be harmful, and this was evident in the design of the reactor and of the radiochemical plant. But they had a rather high estimate of the doses that could be tolerated. There was enormous pressure to build the atomic bomb, and the scientists, engineers, and technicians working in the project accepted the vital importance of this goal, and so were willing to expose themselves to high levels of radiation. "The danger of working in conditions of enhanced radiation impact were understood not only by the leaders, but by the rank-and-file workers," a later study notes. "However, they understood no less clearly that the country had to have atomic weapons, and that often forced them consciously to risk their safety."[183] The dangers were especially great in the early years when there were numerous problems to be resolved with the operation of new and untried technological processes. It was in these situations in particular that people received high doses of ionizing radiation.[184] Those who received high doses incurred a significant risk of chronic radiation sickness and cancer in later years. The situation at Cheliabinsk-40 began to improve only after 1953.

The third cost to follow from the construction of the atomic industry was the damage done to the environment. Between 1948 and 1951 76 million cubic meters of high-level and intermediate-level radioactive waste were discharged from Cheliabinsk-40 into the Techa–Iset–Tobol river system. It soon became apparent that people living along the banks of these rivers were suffering from exposure to the waste. In the summer of 1951 a survey revealed that the floodplain and bed of the Techa river were extensively contaminated, and that 124,000 people had been exposed to radioactivity without any warning. Ten thousand people were evacuated from the areas worst affected, and other settlements were supplied with water from new sources. The Techa river and its floodlands – about 8,000 hectares in all – were now excluded from use.[185] To rectify the situation a system of dams and reservoirs was constructed to isolate the river from the most contaminated areas. The first dam was build at the end of 1951 by prison labor.[186]

The Soviet Union is not the only country in which the atomic industry has harmed public health and the natural environment. But the intense pressure to build the bomb as quickly as possible diverted attention from these risks, and protests by those affected were not possible in the Stalinist system.[187] Even though there was no war, the nuclear arms race claimed its first Soviet victims in these years.

CHAPTER TEN

The Atomic Bomb

I

KLAUS FUCHS had provided a detailed description of the plutonium bomb in June 1945, but Khariton and his colleagues had to check everything for themselves, since they could not be sure that Fuchs's description was completely reliable. To investigate the implosion method they had to do repeated experiments with high explosives, and these could not be done at Laboratory No. 2 on the outskirts of Moscow. Kurchatov therefore decided to set up a branch of the laboratory in an isolated area, away from Moscow, where work on the design and development of the bomb could take place. Khariton was put in charge of the new organization, but he wanted to free himself from administrative responsibilities, in order to concentrate on scientific and technical problems. At Kurchatov's suggestion he approached Beria, who agreed to appoint an engineer as administrative director of the new organization, leaving Khariton as chief designer and scientific director. Beria chose General P.M. Zernov, Deputy People's Commissar of the Tank Industry, who had helped to organize the mass production of tanks during the war. Zernov was forty at the time, a year younger than Khariton. He and Khariton had not known each other before, but now they established a good working relationship.[1]

Vannikov suggested to Zernov and Khariton that they look at munitions plants for a suitable site for the new organization, which was to be known as KB-11 (*konstruktorskoe biuro-11*) or Design Bureau 11. In April 1946 Khariton and Zernov visited the small settlement of Sarov, about 400 kilometers east of Moscow, on the border of Gor'kii province and the Mordovian Autonomous Republic. Sarov had a population of 2–3,000 and a small factory which had produced projectiles for the 'Katiusha' rocket artillery during the war. Its great advantage was that it was situated on the edge of a large forest reserve, which provided room for expansion; and it was a beautiful spot. It was not too close to major lines of communication – and thus good from the point of view of security – but it was not too far from Moscow. Khariton and Zernov decided that this was the ideal location.[2] The town – or rather the carefully guarded "zone," which included the town and the research and development establishments — became known as Arzamas-16, after the city of Arzamas, 60 kilometers to the north. It was sometimes known as the "Volga office"; it was also — inevitably — referred to as "Los Arzamas."

In the center of Sarov were the remains of an Orthodox monastery which had flourished in the eighteenth and nineteenth centuries. St Serafim of Sarov, who was noted for his asceticism and his care for the people, lived there for fifty years until his death in 1833.[3] In 1903 Tsar Nikolai and his wife Aleksandra came to Sarov, along with tens of thousands of people, for Serafim's canonization. Nikolai and Aleksandra, who had four daughters, prayed for a son and heir. Their prayer was answered in the following year, when the Tsarevich Aleksei was born.[4] The Sarov monastery, which had 300 monks, was closed down by the communists in 1927. When Khariton and his group moved to Sarov, several churches were still standing, as well as the buildings in which the monks had had their cells. It was in these cells that the first laboratories were set up. Prisoners from a nearby labor camp built new laboratories and houses.[5]

The basic idea of the plutonium bomb was to squeeze, or implode, a subcritical mass of plutonium, thereby increasing its density and making it supercritical. This was to be done by surrounding a sphere of plutonium (and a natural uranium tamper which encased the plutonium) with high explosives so as to produce a shock wave that would travel inwards and compress the plutonium. The high velocity produced in this way would reduce the danger of predetonation and fizzle, while the compression of the plutonium would make it possible to obtain supercriticality with relatively little plutonium. At the very center of the bomb was an intense neutron source called the initiator. When the implosion compresses the plutonium, the compression lasts for only a few microseconds before the plutonium starts to expand again. The initiator was needed to ensure that the chain reaction would start at exactly the right moment.[6]

Fuchs's description had to be investigated in detail. Khariton's motto was: "We have to know ten times more than we are doing."[7] The design of the bomb, in other words, had to be understood in a profound way. Khariton assembled a "strong collective" to work on the bomb. The first people he recruited were those he knew from the Institute of Chemical Physics and from the munitions institute in which he had worked during the war.[8] Kirill Shchelkin, head of one of the laboratories at the Institute of Chemical Physics, moved to Arzamas-16 and became Khariton's first deputy. Shchelkin had worked on the detonation of gases and the structure of detonation waves.[9] The plutonium bomb required that the divergent detonation waves from the high explosives be converted, by means of a system of lenses, into a convergent spherical wave which would compress the plutonium from all directions and bring it into the supercritical state. Shchelkin took charge of the work on this problem.

Khariton was able to draw on a very strong school in the physics and chemistry of explosions and detonations, based largely in Semenov's Institute of Chemical Physics. A CIA report of 1949 commented that "the contributions of Soviet scientists to basic chemical, physical, and methematical theory of flames, explosions and detonations are regarded highly by US scientists."[10] One of the characteristic features of this school was close cooperation between theoretical and experimental physicists. Khariton had worked closely with Zel'dovich on the series of papers on fission chain reactions in 1939–41. Zel'dovich was one of the most versatile theoreticians of his generation. (When the English physicist Stephen Hawking met him in the 1980s, he said to him, "I'm surprised to see that you are one man, and not like Bourbaki" – a group of French mathematicians who published under one name.) Zel'dovich had worked on the theory of detonation before the war.[11] He was now appointed head of the theoretical department at KB-11. The chief members of his department were D.A. Frank-Kamenetskii, who came with him from the Institute of Chemical Physics, N.A. Dmitriev, and E.I. Zababakhin.[12] Zel'dovich and his colleagues studied how plutonium would behave under pressures of several million atmospheres, when temperatures of millions of degrees are generated and metals are as fluid as liquid. They also worked on calculations of critical mass.

One of the first people Khariton recruited was V.A. Tsukerman, who worked at the Institute for the Study of Machines. Tsukerman, who was blind and was helped in his work by his wife Z.M. Azarkh, had developed a method of using X-rays to analyze the way in which armor-penetrating shells exploded. During the war Khariton had seen the importance of this as a diagnostic tool in the study of conventional explosives, and in December 1945 he invited Tsukerman and his laboratory to join the work on the atomic bomb. Since X-rays reveal differences in density, they could show how the detonating wave moved through the high explosive, and investigate how the plutonium core would implode. In his new research Tsukerman had to "learn how to work with high pressures, cosmic velocities, to register processes lasting microseconds, to study the properties . . . of many different substances – metals, ionic compounds, minerals and rocks – under extremely high pressures."[13] He devised a system that used microsecond X-ray pulses to map the high-speed detonation processes and to analyze the implosion of iron, bronze, and other metals.

Calculations by Zel'dovich's group showed that the high explosives had to be detonated simultaneously in order to create a shock wave that would compress the plutonium. All the high explosives had to be detonated, moreover, in less than a microsecond. The best detonating caps in the Soviet Army could not meet this requirement. Intensive work was done at KB-11 for more than a year before V.S. Komel'kov was brought to the installation in 1948 to solve the problem. Komel'kov, who had worked in electrophysics, designed new detonating caps which could be fired synchronously.[14] The neutron initiator at the center of the bomb, which is needed to trigger the chain reaction at precisely the right moment, was the responsibility of Viktor Davidenko, who had joined Laboratory No. 2 in 1943 and later moved to Arzamas-16.[15]

In the summer of 1946 Khariton prepared a document called the Technical Assignment, which set out briefly the technical requirements for the atomic bomb – yield, dimensions, safety, etc. This document was signed by Zernov and Khariton, and sent to the government for approval.[16] It referred to both the uranium-235 and the plutonium bombs. This suggests that if problems had not arisen with the gaseous diffusion plant, the uranium-235 bomb might have been tested first. Although isotope separation proved to be more difficult than plutonium production, the design of the gun-assembly uranium-235 bomb was much simpler than that of the plutonium bomb. The scientists at Los Alamos had not thought it necessary to test the uranium-235 bomb before using it, but they had considered it essential to test the plutonium bomb. In the event, plutonium became available for the Soviet project before weapons-grade uranium.

In 1945 V.A. Turbiner, a designer and engineer, joined the project to head the design group. Early in 1946 Turbiner and his group prepared a technical drawing of the bomb, with the essential cross-sections in color (Turbiner did not know that the information had come from intelligence). Turbiner did not remain in charge of the engineering side of the design, however.[17] In July 1948 General N.L. Dukhov, a very experienced mechanical engineer, was brought to Arzamas-16 to take charge of the design and production of the basic elements of the bomb. Dukhov had been chief designer of the Kirov Tank Factory in the Urals during the war, and had designed the KV (Kliment Voroshilov) and IS (Iosif Stalin) heavy tanks.[18] He was now appointed deputy scientific director and deputy chief designer. Another engineer, V.I. Alferov, director of a plant that produced naval mines and torpedoes, was also recruited as a deputy to Khariton. Alferov had responsibility for the electrical systems in the bomb, and in particular for the firing system that would provide the impulse to operate the detonating caps.[19]

Khariton has argued that the information received from Fuchs did not lessen substantially the volume of theoretical and experimental work. Soviet scientists and engineers had to do all the same calculations and experiments, and the intelligence information could not ensure that they would obtain the correct results. At the end of 1948 or the beginning of 1949 two groups at KB-11 were given the task of measuring the velocity of the detonation products of the high explosives. This information was needed for calculating the pressure that would be brought to bear on the plutonium. One of these groups was headed by Tsukerman, the other by E.K. Zavoiskii, a first-class experimental physicist who had less experience with explosives. Tsukerman's group concluded that everything was in order, and that the necessary degree of compression would be obtained. But Zavoiskii's group, which finished its work later, concluded that the degree of compression would be insufficient, and that no nuclear explosion would take place. Kurchatov and Vannikov were informed, and Vannikov came to Arzamas-16, very worried by this disagreement. The two groups sat down together, and new experiments were done. It was discovered that Zavoiskii had used electrodes that were too thin in his diagnostic apparatus and had therefore underestimated the velocity of the products of the high explosives. Khariton later commented that this showed how important it was for Soviet scientists to understand and calculate everything themselves.[20]

The plutonium metal hemispheres were fabricated under Bochvar's direction at Cheliabinsk-40 in June 1949. They were then coated with nickel by Anatolii Aleksandrov, in order to make them safer to handle, and taken to Arzamas-16. When Zel'dovich saw the hemispheres, which were about 8–9 centimeters in diameter, he felt that a multitude of lives had been compressed into each gram: those of the prisoners who worked in the uranium mines and the installations of the atomic industry, as well as the potential victims of atomic war.[21]

At Arzamas-16 Flerov, who was a very skillful experimenter, conducted dangerous critical mass experiments in a small hut, guarded by a sentry, at some distance from other buildings. He had to check that the two plutonium hemispheres came close to the critical mass when brought together, so that when the plutonium sphere was compressed it would become supercritical. Flerov reported that the plutonium charge would be close to critical when surrounded by the uranium tamper.

Once these experiments had been done, the bomb was ready to be tested. Kurchatov assembled Khariton and those who had developed the main components and the equipment for monitoring the test. He asked each of them in turn whether they were ready to go to the test site. When they replied that they were, he said that he would report this to the government and ask for permission to test the bomb.[22]

At about this time the leading scientists and engineers were summoned to Moscow to report in person to Stalin on the preparations for the test. The scientists went into Stalin's office one by one to make their reports. Kurchatov was the first, followed by Khariton. This was Khariton's only meeting with Stalin. He made his report in the presence of Beria and Kurchatov. Stalin asked whether it would be possible to use the plutonium in the bomb to make two less powerful bombs, so that there would be one in reserve. Bearing in mind that the amount of plutonium in the bomb was right for that particular design – another design had been prepared at Arzamas-16 that required less plutonium – Khariton replied that that would not be possible.[23]

In his meetings with the designers of tanks, guns, and aircraft Stalin often asked detailed technical questions. But he showed no interest in the technical aspects of nuclear weapons. "When I was at meetings with Stalin, I had the impression that I bored him terribly," Kurchatov later told one of his close colleagues. "When I spoke to him, I did so briefly, finished quickly and fell silent as soon as possible. He never asked any questions about the technology." Stalin gave Kurchatov the impression that he thought he "was droning on like an annoying fly and wanted me to finish quickly."[24] Stalin did not ask Khariton any technical questions during their meeting. He did not launch into a disquisition on the dialectical nature of the concept of critical mass, as some reports have suggested; nor was he shown the plutonium charge, as others have written. He accepted without demur Khariton's answer about the impossibility of making two bombs from the plutonium charge that had been prepared for the first bomb.[25]

II

Lev Al'tshuler, who worked in Tsukerman's laboratory, moved to Arzamas-16 in December 1946. There was a narrow-gauge railway line that ran from Arzamas to Sarov, but Al'tshuler made the last part of the journey by bus:

We made this journey in a bus which had been thoughtfully provided with sheepskin coats. Past the windows flashed villages which recalled the settlements of pre-Petrine Russia.

On our arrival at the place we caught sight of the monastery churches and farmsteads, the forest, the Finnish houses nestling in the woods, the small engineering plant, and the inevitable companions of that period – the "zones" [prison camps] populated by representatives of all the regions of the country, all the nationalities. . . . The columns of prisoners passing through the settlement in the morning on their way to work and returning to the zones in the evening were a reality that hit you in the eyes. Lermontov's lines came to mind, about "a land of slaves, a land of masters."

Arzamas-16 was, Al'tshuler notes, at the epicenter of the "white archipelago" of atomic institutes and plants scattered about the country.[26]

Unlike the inhabitants of the "Gulag Archipelago," the scientists and engineers who lived in the "white archipelago" had privileged living conditions. They were protected as far as possible from the dreadful economic conditions of the war-torn country. Arzamas-16 was like paradise compared to half-starved Moscow, in Al'tshuler's view. Scientists and engineers "lived very well. Leading researchers were paid a very large salary for those times. Our families experienced no needs. And the supply of food and goods was quite different. So that all material questions were re-

moved."[27] Lazar Kaganovich, a member of the Politburo, complained in
1953 that the atomic cities were like "health resorts."[28]

These conditions reflected Stalin's belief that Soviet scientists, if they
were given the "proper help," would be able to overtake the achievements
of foreign science. Privileged though they were, however, the nuclear
scientists were surrounded by great secrecy and tight security. They could
not, of course, talk to unauthorized people about their work, and nothing
was published about the Soviet effort to build the atomic bomb. Within
the project secrecy was very strictly maintained. Reports were written by
hand, because typists were not trusted. If documents were typed – as, for
example, the Technical Requirement for the first atomic bomb – the key
words were written in by hand. Code words were used instead of scientific
terms in secret reports and laboratory notes; neutrons, for example, were
referred to as "zero points." Information was strictly compartmentalized.
During Andrei Sakharov's first visit to Arzamas-16 in 1949, Zel'dovich told
him "there are secrets everywhere, and the less you know that doesn't
concern you, the better off you'll be. Khariton has taken on the burden of
knowing it all."[29] The need for secrecy was so deeply instilled that some
people had recurrent nightmares about breaching security regulations; and
at least one suicide was attributed to anxiety about misfiled documents.[30]

Secrecy was reinforced by rigid security. Arzamas-16 was cut off from
the outside world. A zone of about 250 square kilometers was surrounded
by barbed wire and guards, and it was difficult in the early years to obtain
permission to leave the zone.[31] Khariton was accompanied wherever he
went by a bodyguard. (Kurchatov, Zel'dovich, and later Sakharov also had
bodyguards.) The security services had numerous informers in the project,
and encouraged denunciations. "Beria's people were everywhere,"
Khariton later remarked.[32] Once, when Khariton visited Cheliabinsk-40 to
see how work on the plutonium production reactor was progressing, he
attended a dinner to mark Kurchatov's birthday. After the dinner, at which
drink had been taken, Beria's representative said to Khariton: "Iulii
Borisovich, if only you knew how much they write against you!" And
although he added, "But I don't believe them," the point had been made:
there were plenty of accusations that Beria could use if he wanted to.[33]

As the date of the first atomic bomb test grew nearer, the political
climate in the country became increasingly oppressive. In August 1948
Lysenko achieved final victory over the geneticists, and in January 1949 a
campaign was launched against "cosmopolitans," a euphemism for Jews.
The number of denunciations increased. In Anatolii Aleksandrov's words,
"some new complications were characteristic of this period, incidentally –
a great number of 'inventors', including scientists, were constantly trying to
find mistakes, writing their 'observations' on this score, and their number
increased, the closer we came to completing the task."[34] Such "observations" would not have been confined to technical matters. Mistaken

technical choices were frequently explained in those days as the consequence of political error or disloyalty. Kurchatov was open to the accu-
sation that he had surrounded himself with colleagues who were Jewish, or
admired Western science too much, or had had strong links with the West.
Khariton was particularly vulnerable: he was Jewish, and he had spent two
years in Cambridge where he had worked closely with James Chadwick, a
key figure in the British nuclear project. Besides, both of his parents had left
Soviet Russia. His father had been expelled by the Soviet authorities, and
had worked in Riga as a journalist until 1940, when the Red Army
occupied Latvia. He was then arrested by the NKVD, and sent to the
camps or shot.[35] Khariton's mother lived in Germany in the 1920s with her
second husband, and later moved to Palestine.

Stalin and Beria wanted the atomic bomb as soon as possible, and they
had to rely on Kurchatov and his colleagues to make it for them. They gave
the scientists massive resources and privileged living conditions. Yet they
harbored a nagging suspicion of the nuclear scientists. After all, if Soviet
geneticists and plant breeders were trying to undermine Soviet agricultural
policy, as Lysenko charged, might not the physicists sabotage nuclear
policy? Aleksandrov, who was scientific director of the chemical separation
plant at Cheliabinsk-40 in 1949, was coating the plutonium hemispheres
with nickel when a group arrived that included Pervukhin, several generals
and the director of the plant. "They asked what I was doing," writes
Aleksandrov:

I explained, and then they asked a strange question: "Why do you think it is
plutonium?" I said that I knew the whole technical process for obtaining it and was
therefore sure that it was plutonium and could not be anything else! "But why are
you sure that some piece of iron hasn't been substituted for it?" I held up a piece
to the alpha-counter, and it began to crackle at once. "Look," I said, "it's alpha-
active." "But perhaps it has just been rubbed with plutonium on the outside and
that is why it crackles," said someone. I grew angry, took that piece and held it out
to them: "Feel it, it's hot!" One of them said that it did not take long to heat a
piece of iron. Then I responded that he could sit and look till morning and check
whether the plutonium remained hot. But I would go to bed. This apparently
convinced them, and they went away.[36]

Such episodes, according to Aleksandrov, were not unusual. Emel'ianov
recounts a similar incident. He once showed Zaveniagin a regulus of
plutonium, before the atomic test. "Are you sure that's plutonium?" asked
Zaveniagin, looking at Emel'ianov with fear. "Perhaps," he added
anxiously, "it's something else, not plutonium."[37]

The scientists were aware that failure would cost them dear, and knew
that Beria had selected understudies to take over the leading positions in
case of failure.[38] But although terror was a key element in Beria's style of
management, and a pervasive factor in the Stalinist regime, it was not this

that motivated the scientists. Those who took part in the project believed that the Soviet Union needed its own bomb in order to defend itself, and welcomed the challenge of proving the worth of Soviet science by building a Soviet atomic bomb as quickly as possible.

   According to Al'tshuler,

our consent [to work on the bomb] was determined, first, by the fact that we were promised much better conditions for research and second, by an inner feeling that our confrontation with a very powerful opponent had not ended with the defeat of Fascist Germany. The feeling of defenselessness increased particularly after Hiroshima and Nagasaki. For all who realized the realities of the new atomic era, the creation of our own atomic weapons, the restoration of equilibrium became a categorical imperative.[39]

Viktor Adamskii, who worked in the theoretical department at Arzamas-16 in the late 1940s, has written that

all scientists held the conviction – and it now seems right for that time – that the state needed to possess atomic weapons, that one could not allow one country, especially the United States, to hold a monopoly on this weapon. To the consciousness of performing a most important patriotic duty was added the purely professional satisfaction and pride from work on a splendid task in physics – and not only in physics. Therefore we worked with enthusiasm, without taking account of time, selflessly.[40]

Andrei Sakharov, who began work on thermonuclear weapons in 1948 and moved to Arzamas-16 in 1950, has said that "we (and here I must speak not only in my own behalf, for in such cases moral principles are formulated in a collective psychological way) believed that our work was absolutely necessary as a means of achieving a balance in the world."[41]

   In spite of the presence of informers and the threat of repression, a spirit of cooperation and friendship existed at Arzamas-16. "It was necessary to secure the defense of the country," Khariton later said. "In the collective of scientists there was quiet and intense work. Close cohesion and friendship . . . Although, of course, we had our sons of bitches."[42] Tsukerman and Azarkh write that "in the first, most romantic years of our work in the institute a wonderful atmosphere of good will and support was created around the research. We worked selflessly, with great enthusiasm and the mobilization of all our spiritual and physical forces."[43] It is striking how the apparatus of the police state fused with the physics community to build the bomb. In the 1930s the physics community – as was argued earlier – had enjoyed an unusual measure of intellectual autonomy, which was sustained by a set of social relationships. That autonomy was not destroyed by the creation of the nuclear project. It continued to exist within the administrative system that was set up to manage the project.

Before the war the nuclear scientists had paid close attention to research being done abroad, and had striven to show themselves as good as their foreign colleagues. The American atomic bomb presented a formidable challenge to Soviet scientists and engineers, who now sought to prove their own worth in this new competition. American priority may also have lessened the sense of responsibility that Soviet scientists felt in making this destructive weapon. They were responding to the American challenge, not initiating the atomic competition. They believed the Soviet Union needed its own atomic bomb in response. Discussion of moral qualms would of course have been very dangerous, and open opposition to the project doubtless fatal. Terror encouraged people to put such questions to one side and to immerse themselves in their work. In any event, scientists did not have to work on the bomb; they could refuse to join the project, and some did, including Sakharov before 1948.

In his memoirs Dollezhal', the chief designer of the first production reactor, discusses his own thoughts in 1946 when Kurchatov first drew him into the atomic project. Dollezhal' had regarded the bombing of Hiroshima as a "repulsive act of cynical antihumanism."[44] If that was so, did the Soviet Union have the right to make and use the same weapon? His answer to this was yes, on two grounds. First, making the weapon was not the same as using it against peaceful cities. The military and political leadership would choose the targets. And although Dollezhal' knew something of the terrible purge of 1937, "those affairs were internal – domestic, so to speak." The Soviet Union, as far as he knew, did not contravene the laws of war: unlike the Germans they had not destroyed the noncombatant population; unlike the Allies they had not carpet-bombed German cities. Dollezhal's second argument was that possession of the bomb did not necessarily mean that it would be used. All the main combatants in the war had had chemical weapons, but no one had employed them. That was because they feared retaliation. Hence the Soviet Union needed all the means of attack possessed by the aggressor, if it wanted to prevent such weapons from being used.

After the war, writes Dollezhal', cracks appeared in the foundation of the wartime alliance with the United States. Things that had not been spoken of in the critical moments of the war were now brought to light with merciless clarity: "the two systems were completely alien to each other ideologically – more than that, they were antagonistic, and the political trust generated by the wartime alliance was not long-lived or solid." The United States might declare the Soviet Union an enemy at any time in the future:

The security of the country and patriotic duty demanded that we create the atomic bomb. And these were not mere words. This was objective reality. Who would forgive the leadership of the country if it began to create the weapons only after the enemy had decided to attack? The ancients had a point when they coined the phrase "If you want peace, prepare for war."

From this reasoning Dollezhal' drew the conclusion that work on the bomb was morally justified. In his memoirs he writes that in a conversation early in 1946 he found that this was Kurchatov's position too.[45]

Whether or not Dollezhal's memory is accurate – he may be reading back into his 1946 attitude conclusions to which he came later on – his account is consistent with what other scientists have written about their general attitude to the project. Moreover, on two specific points Dollezhal's view was shared by other scientists at the time. It is apparent that others – Artsimovich and Khlopin, for example – were appalled by Hiroshima and Nagasaki.[46] And although people knew of the terror and the camps, they were not aware of the full extent of the crimes committed by Stalin and Beria. Al'tshuler later observed that "we knew nothing of those horrors of Stalinism which are today generally known. You can't jump out of your own time."[47]

The attitude of Soviet scientists was shaped, finally, by the war against Nazi Germany. The participants in the atomic project had either fought in the war or contributed to the war effort by designing or producing weapons. They had taken part in a bitter and destructive war to defend the Soviet Union and, whatever they may have thought of Stalin's regime or his policies, they believed that their cause was just. The war was hardly over before the atomic bomb posed a potential new threat to their country. They had taken up arms against the German invader, and now they worked to provide their country with its own atomic bomb. The atomic project was in some psychological sense a continuation of the war with Germany. In his memoirs Sakharov writes that he understood the terrible and inhuman nature of the weapons he was helping to build. But World War II had also been an inhuman affair. He had not been a soldier in that war, but "I regarded myself as a soldier in this new scientific war." Kurchatov, he notes, used to say they were soldiers, and this was not an idle remark.[48] He sometimes signed his letters and memoranda, "Soldier Kurchatov."

III

During the war Vernadskii and Kapitsa called for collaboration with Western scientists. It seemed as though their wish might be granted when Molotov, during the Academy celebration in June 1945, promised the "most favorable conditions" for closer ties between Soviet science and world science. The scientists' hopes were part of a broad desire among Soviet intellectuals for greater contact with the rest of the world.[49] They also reflected the widespread longing in the country for an easing of repression and a return to normal life. The war had restored the people's "pride and dignity," Sakharov later wrote: "We all believed – or at least hoped – that the postwar world would be decent and humane. How could it be otherwise?"[50]

Stalin dealt a blow to hopes of a normal life with his speech of February 6, 1946, which signaled a return to prewar economic policies and pointed to a dangerous period of international relations ahead. He soon made it clear that the relative intellectual tolerance of the war would be brought to an end. In August 1946 the Central Committee criticized the Leningrad journals *Zvezda* and *Leningrad* for publishing "ideologically harmful" works. The campaign for ideological orthodoxy now gathered momentum and in the course of 1947 "discussions" were organized in philosophy, economics, and biology. Militant critics attacked more moderate scholars and officials for subservience to Western ideas and a lack of ideological vigilance.[51]

The ideological campaign is associated with the name of Andrei Zhdanov, but it was Stalin who orchestrated it. The attack on Western ideas was part of Stalin's effort to tighten party control over the intelligentsia. In May 1947 Stalin told Simonov and two other writers that

if you take our middle intelligentsia, the scientific intelligentsia, professors, physicians, they have an insufficiently educated feeling of Soviet patriotism. They have an unjustified admiration for foreign culture. They all feel themselves to be still under age, not a hundred per cent, they have got used to thinking of themselves as eternal students. This is an obsolete tradition, it comes from Peter. Peter had good ideas, but soon there were too many Germans, that was the period of admiration for Germans. . . . First the Germans, then the French, there was admiration for foreigners. . . . A simple peasant will not bow for nothing, take his cap off, but these people do not have enough dignity or patriotism, do not understand the role that Russia plays.[52]

Stalin showed the writers a letter, which was soon published, condemning two Soviet scientists for sending a manuscript on the treatment of cancer to an American publisher.[53] The publication of this letter marked the beginning of a campaign against admiration for foreign culture.

The changing political climate had a profound effect on Soviet science. It offered Lysenko the opportunity to revive his fortunes. In the brief period of hope at the end of the war Lysenko's position had been weak, and in 1946 one of his main opponents, the geneticist N.P. Dubinin, had been elected a corresponding member of the Academy. But Lysenko now managed to link his crusade against genetics to the campaign for ideological purity. By clever political maneuvering, in which he portrayed his opponents as politically disloyal and in thrall to foreign ideas, he managed to win Stalin's support.[54]

In July 1948 Lysenko was summoned to a conversation with Stalin. He promised great improvements in agricultural output if he was allowed to defeat his scientific opponents and prevent their interference with his work. Stalin accepted Lysenko's argument. A special session of the Lenin All-Union Academy of Agricultural Sciences was hurriedly convened to review the situation in biology.[55] Lysenko's report to the meeting, which had been read and edited by Stalin himself, asserted that the science of genetics was incompatible with Marxism-Leninism, and that genetics was a bourgeois fabrication designed to undermine the true materialist theory of biological development.[56] Several speakers rejected Lysenko's claims, but Lysenko effectively silenced them by declaring, at the end of the conference, that "the Party Central Committee has examined my report and approved it."[57] To challenge Lysenko, in other words, was to challenge the party leadership. The Party – and more particularly Stalin – claimed ultimate authority in science, the right to say what constituted scientific truth. Thousands of geneticists and plant biologists were removed from their teaching and research positions. S.V. Kaftanov, who had advised Stalin to start an atomic project in 1942 and was now Minister of Higher Education, took an active role in this purge.[58]

Lysenko's victory gave heart to those who wanted to do for other disciplines what he had done for biology. In the next two years conferences were organized in physiology, astronomy, chemistry, and ethnography to root out foreign ideological influences: "cosmopolitanism" was attacked, and often ludicrous claims made for the priority of Russian and Soviet scientists and engineers in discovery and invention.[59] Physics too came under threat. Quantum mechanics and relativity theory had been the target for attacks by philosophers in the 1930s. A new controversy broke out in 1947, following the publication of an article by M.A. Markov of FIAN on epistemological problems in quantum mechanics.[60] Markov was attacked by the militant philosopher A.A. Maksimov for his stand on these issues, and especially for his espousal of Niels Bohr's concept of complementarity.[61] The editor of the journal in which Markov's article had appeared was removed from his post in 1948, and the Copenhagen school's interpretation of quantum mechanics was banished from the Soviet press for over a decade.[62]

Lysenko's triumph in August 1948 presented a far graver threat to physics than the ban on a particular interpretation of quantum mechanics. Within four months preparations were under way for an All-Union Conference of Physicists to discuss shortcomings in Soviet physics. The conference was to be organized by the Ministry of Higher Education, headed by Kaftanov, and by the Academy of Sciences, of which Sergei Vavilov was now president. On December 17 an organizing committee was set up with A.V. Topchiev, Deputy Minister of Higher Education, as chairman and Ioffe as his deputy.[63]

In a letter to Deputy Premier Kliment Voroshilov, Kaftanov outlined the shortcomings that the conference was supposed to remedy:

Physics is taught in many educational establishments without any regard to dialectical materialism. . . . Instead of decisively unmasking trends which are inimical to Marxism-Leninism, some of our scientists frequently adopt idealist positions, which are making their way into higher educational establishments through physics. . . . The modern achievements of physics do not receive consistent exposition on the basis of dialectical materialism in Soviet physics textbooks. . . . The role of Russian and Soviet scientists in the development of physics is treated in a completely inadequate way in textbooks; the books abound in the names of foreign scientists.[64]

It was proposed to invite 600 physicists to the Moscow "House of Scholars" for this conference, which was to be a kind of sequel to the 1936 conference on physics.[65] The latter was now criticized for having paid too little attention to ideology.

The organizing committee met forty-two times between December 30, 1948 and March 16, 1949. The meetings were attended not only by members of the committee but also by invited guests. The discussions were often sharp and bitter. Battlelines were drawn not only between physicists and philosophers, however. In the late 1940s the Soviet physics community was split into two groups – those from the Academy and those from Moscow University.[66] This split dated back to the mid-1930s when Vavilov began to build up FIAN as a powerful institute. As FIAN grew stronger, the situation at the university worsened. After the arrest in 1936 of B.M. Gessen, dean of the Physics Faculty, the faculty increasingly became dominated by physicists who were willing to resort to appeals to political authority in their academic and administrative disputes. A number of physicists, including Kapitsa and Ioffe, wrote to Molotov in 1944 to express their concern about the quality of teaching at the university and to ask him to appoint one of the leading physicists (Obreimov, Leontovich, or Fok) as dean of the faculty. Molotov did not take this advice, and the situation grew worse after the death of Leonid Mandel'shtam in 1944.[67] One by one members of Mandel'shtam's school – G.S. Landsberg, Igor' Tamm, S.E. Khaikin, M.A. Leontovich – left the university, which was taken over by a rather varied group of mediocre physicists. This group included some serious physicists such as D.D. Ivanenko and A.S. Predvoditelev, but also men like V.M. Kessenikh and V.F. Nozdrev, who made up for their lack of ability in physics with ideological vigilance.[68] What united the university physicists was disgruntlement that their work had not been given the recognition they thought it deserved. They were also annoyed that, in spite of strenuous efforts, they had not been drawn into the atomic project. Some of them were willing to resort to political charges to settle scores with the Academy physicists. The campaign against cosmopolitanism provided political cover for their accusations.[69]

The organizing committee discussed the ten papers that were to be presented at the conference. Vavilov was to deliver a paper "On Contemporary Physics and the Tasks of Soviet Physicists," and Ioffe "On Measures to Improve the Teaching of Physics in Technical Schools"; others were to speak on textbooks and ways to improve physics education. But the discussion in the committee ranged far beyond these apparently innocuous topics. The university physicists and their philosopher allies went on the attack, accusing the Academy physicists of spreading cosmopolitanism and idealism, of not citing Russian scientists, of avoiding honest arguments, of refusing to develop fundamental physics, and of spying for Germany. This last charge was leveled against Mandel'shtam, who had died five years earlier. But living physicists too came in for criticism. Ioffe, Tamm, and Markov, all of whom took part in committee meetings, were severely criticized. Frenkel' was a particular target, and his 1931 position on the irrelevance of dialectical materialism to physics was brought up against him. The absent Kapitsa was also attacked.[70]

Vavilov was in a difficult position. As a physicist he understood the absurdity of the charges made by the university physicists and their allies. As president of the Academy, however, he had to take part in a campaign that had been approved by the political authorities. He tried to balance these competing responsibilities but failed to satisfy the university physicists. The Academy physicists rejected the criticisms of quantum mechanics and relativity theory. They also rejected the criticisms of their attitude to Western science. If they did not cite the work of the university physicists more often, said Tamm, it was because they did not think they were very good. Landsberg accused Ivanenko of making citation of his work and that of his students the touchstone of a Soviet physicist's patriotism. The Academy physicists were willing to make token criticisms of the idealist philosophical views of some Western physicists. Under intense criticism Frenkel' admitted that in some of his works he had explained the ideas of the creators of quantum mechanics without criticizing them. On the key issues, however, the Academy physicists stood their ground.

In spite of the resistance of the Academy physicists, it is clear from the draft resolution which was prepared for adoption by the conference that the university physicists had official support. "For Soviet physics," the resolution said, "the struggle against kowtowing and grovelling before the West, and the education of a feeling of national pride, of faith in the inexhaustible powers of the Soviet people, have special significance. It is necessary to root out mercilessly every hint of cosmopolitanism, which is Anglo-American imperialism's ideological weapon of diversion." Criticism of specific physicists was also contained in the draft resolution. Landau and Ioffe were accused of "grovelling before the west"; Kapitsa of propagating "open cosmopolitanism"; Frenkel' and Markov of "uncritically receiving Western physical theories and propagandizing them in our country." Textbooks by Khaikin, Landau and Lifshits, Shpol'skii, and Frenkel' were condemned for popularizing foreign ideological concepts, and for not citing Russian authors frequently enough.[71]

It is hard to say what effect the conference might have had on Soviet physics. The draft resolution did not condemn quantum mechanics and relativity theory as such, so the conference might not have had as devastating an effect as the August 1948 meeting on biology. But it would have strengthened the position of the Moscow university physicists who, as a group, were narrow-minded, chauvinistic, and less able than the Academy physicists. Physics would have been drawn further into the realm of ideology, and disagreements and disputes would have been conducted more frequently in the language of Stalinist politics. The role of the philosophers as ideological policemen would have been strengthened. All this would have created a dangerous situation for Soviet physics.

The conference did not take place, however, and its possible effects must remain a matter for speculation. The last meeting of the organizing committee took place on March 16, 1949, and the conference was due to start on March 21. It was canceled between those dates. Only Stalin could have taken the decision to do this, and it appears that he canceled the conference because it might retard the atomic project. According to General Makhnev, head of the secretariat of the Special Committee on the Atomic Bomb, Beria asked Kurchatov whether it was true that quantum mechanics and relativity theory were idealist, in the sense of antimaterialist. Kurchatov replied that if relativity theory and quantum mechanics were rejected, the bomb would have to be rejected too. Beria was worried by this reply, and may have asked Stalin to call off the conference.[72]

A more circumstantial account, which does not contradict Makhnev's story, was given by Artsimovich, on the basis of a conversation with Beria after Stalin's death. According to Artsimovich, three leading physicists – Kurchatov may have been among them – approached Beria in mid-March 1949 and asked him to call off the conference, on the grounds that it would harm Soviet physics and interfere with the atomic project. Beria replied that he could not make a decision on this himself, but that he would speak to Stalin. Stalin agreed to cancel the conference, saying of the physicists, according to Beria, "Leave them in peace. We can always shoot them later."[73]

It was the atomic bomb that saved Soviet physics in 1949. Stalin was not so concerned about the condition of agriculture – he tolerated, after all, a desperate famine in the Ukraine in 1947 – and so it may not have mattered very much to him whether Lysenko was a charlatan or not. The nuclear project was more important, however, than the lives of Soviet citizens, so it was crucial to be sure that the scientists in the nuclear project were not frauds. For Beria, who was answerable to Stalin for the success of the project, it was important that the scientists should be politically reliable. But it was even more important that they should not be charlatans. Beria wanted the project to succeed and, in spite of the atmosphere of menace he created, he did not arrest any of the senior people in the project. For the same reason it was in his interest to resist those who wanted to do for physics what Lysenko had done for genetics.

The same logic can be seen in an episode that took place in 1951. A commission came to examine the level of political education at Arzamas-16. When Al'tshuler told the commission that he did not think Lysenko was right in his attack on classical genetics, it recommended that he be dismissed. Sakharov and Zel'dovich protested to Zaveniagin, who was visiting the installation, and Al'tshuler was allowed to remain. A year later the issue came up again. This time Khariton telephoned Beria, who asked, "Do you need him very much?" Khariton replied that he did, and that was the end of the matter.[74]

The cancellation of the March 1949 conference and the successful atomic test five months later were serious setbacks for the university physicists and the philosophers. But their criticism of cosmopolitanism and idealism did not stop, and physicists had to parry these attacks. Kurchatov was forthright in his views. Zel'dovich recalled that he was sitting in Kurchatov's office in the early 1950s when a telephone call came from an editorial board in Moscow asking whether they should publish an article attacking the theory of relativity. "Well, if that article is right," replied Kurchatov, "we can close down our business."[75] In 1952 some of the papers prepared for the March 1949 conference papers were published. The editors, headed by the philosopher A.A. Maksimov, complained that Soviet physicists lagged behind specialists in such fields as agrobiology and physiology – both of which had been thoroughly purged – in fighting against the survivals of capitalism in their own consciousness.[76]

A disjunction now existed in Soviet policy. Stalin had given support to Lysenko's argument that there was a fundamental difference between socialist science and capitalist science; at the same time Soviet physicists were building the plutonium bomb on the basis of the American design. Stalin had launched a campaign against kowtowing to the West, and against the denigration of Russian and Soviet science and technology; but it was the party leadership that took Western technology as the model and distrusted Soviet scientists and engineers. The Soviet Union was copying foreign technology in several areas (the atomic bomb, the V-2 missile, the B-29 bomber), but trying to hide that fact from its own people by trumpeting Soviet achievements. The campaign against foreign influence helped to create a political situation in which genetics was destroyed and physics put at risk. The Stalinist regime gave great importance to technology, and especially to military technology, but, unlike a technocracy, the regime did not accept the authority or autonomy of technical expertise.

The regime's fundamental logic was political: it claimed the right to say what constituted scientific truth and destroyed whole disciplines in the name of ideological orthodoxy.

Stalin did not destroy physics, because physics was needed to enhance the power of the state. Landau remarked that the survival of Soviet physics was the first example of successful nuclear deterrence. This comment had a serious point. What the bomb saved was a small island of intellectual autonomy in a society where the state claimed control of all intellectual life. Besides, the physics community saw itself in some significant sense as part of a larger international community, and was perhaps more closely linked with the West, in cultural terms, than any other part of Soviet society. Thus the atomic bomb, the most potent symbol of the hostility between the Soviet Union and the West, saved a community that constituted an important cultural and intellectual link between the West and the Soviet Union.

IV

By the summer of 1949 the "article" was ready for the test, which was to take place on the steppes of Kazakhstan.[77] A small settlement was built on the river Irtysh, about 140 kilometers north-west of the city of Semipalatinsk; this settlement was known as Semipalatinsk-21, and later as Kurchatov. The bomb was to be tested about 70 kilometers to the south. About a kilometer away from the settlement were laboratories in which the scientists could prepare their instruments and apparatus for measuring the results of the explosion. Most of this equipment had been developed and made at the Institute of Chemical Physics, where M.A. Sadovskii had played a key role.[78] In the evening, after the day's work, the men working at the test site went to the river to swim and fish.[79]

"Early every morning we went out in trucks to the working buildings near the test site," one of those who took part in the test has written:

Along the way there were neither houses nor trees. Around was the stony, sandy steppe, covered in feather-grass and wormwood. Even birds here were fairly rare. A small flock of black starlings, and sometimes a hawk in the sky. Already in the morning the intense heat could be felt. In the middle of the day and later there lay over the roads a haze, and mirages of mysterious mountains and lakes.

The road led to the test site, which was situated in a valley between two small hills.[80]

Preparation of the site had begun two years earlier. A tower 30 meters high had been erected, and beside it a workshop in which the final assembly of the bomb was to take place.[81]

Kurchatov and his colleagues not only wanted to learn whether the bomb would work, but also wanted to measure its effects: how destructive would it be? The United States had released little information about the effects of nuclear weapons, and Soviet intelligence had several times asked Klaus Fuchs for data from American detonations.[82] Now that they had their own bomb Soviet scientists would be able to study these effects for themselves. One-storey wooden buildings and four-storey brick houses were constructed near the tower, as well as bridges, tunnels, water towers, and other structures. Railway locomotives and carriages, tanks, and artillery pieces were distributed about the surrounding area. Instruments were placed in dug-outs near the tower, and above ground at greater distances; there were detectors to measure the pressure in the shock wave, ionization chambers to measure the intensity of the radiation, photomultiplier tubes to register radiation, and high-speed cameras. Animals were placed in open pens and in covered houses near the tower, so that the effects of initial nuclear radiation could be observed.[83]

A.I. Burnazian, Deputy Minister of Health and Chief of the Radiation Protection Service, was responsible for studying the effect of radiation on living organisms and for measuring the level of radioactivity after the test.[84] He procured two tanks which were to be equipped with dosimetric instruments and driven to ground zero immediately after the explosion. Burnazian wanted to remove the turrets and add lead shielding to give the crews greater protection, but the military protested that this would destroy the silhouette of the tanks. Kurchatov overruled the military, declaring that an atomic test was not a dog show, and that tanks were not poodles to be judged by their appearance and posture.[85]

Kurchatov came to the test site in May. He was to take charge of the test, in which thousands of people were involved in one capacity or another. Everyone was subordinate to him, including the army units, which were commanded by General V.A. Boliatko. Pervukhin was responsible for the preparation of the test site.[86] At the end of July Pervukhin came to the site to check on progress.[87] The tower was ready at the beginning of August. The workshop at its base had a traveling crane. Rails ran the whole length of the hall, with an entrance at one end for the trucks bringing the components of the bomb, and doors at the other end through which the carriage with the "article" would be moved on to the platform that would lift it to the top of the tower. Off the hall there were rooms where work was done on individual elements of the bomb. There was also a gallery which overlooked the hall.[88]

Pervukhin returned to Moscow to report that the test site was ready.[89] Following Soviet practice for tests of all kinds of weapons, a state commission was formed to monitor the test. Beria was chairman of this commission and arrived at the site with Zaveniagin in the second half of August. Beria inspected the work being done in the assembly hall, visited the command and observation posts, and reported to Stalin on the government line from the command post. On the following day Kurchatov announced that the test would take place on August 29, at 6 a.m.[90]

Beria's arrival served as a reminder that the test would pass judgment not only on the quality of the work that Kurchatov and his colleagues had done, but also on their personal fates. Pervukhin wrote later that "we all understood that in case of failure we would have to give a serious answer before the people."[91] Emel'ianov, who was also present at the test, made the same point more graphically when he told Heinz Barwich that if they had failed they would have been shot.[92] Khariton, who knew better than anyone else the work that had gone into the bomb, was confident that it would work.[93] Kurchatov made every effort to ensure that the test would go well. He had conducted two rehearsals before Beria's visit to make sure that everyone knew where he should be, and to check that the instruments and communications lines were in working order. He had also prepared a detailed plan for the final week, and this now went into effect. Beria came every day to the site, turning up unexpectedly to observe the final preparations. He spent much of his time in the hall, where the final assembly of the bomb took place.[94]

Beria, Kurchatov, Zaveniagin, Khariton, and Zernov watched the final assembly of the bomb; Vannikov had remained in Moscow, apparently because of illness. KGB General Osetrov looked on from the gallery above the hall. Shchelkin was responsible for arranging the high explosives. The bottom half of the uranium tamper was lowered into position by the crane, under the supervision of Dukhov. Dukhov then placed the first plutonium hemisphere into the tamper. Khariton took the initiator from Davidenko and placed it in the hollow at the center of the plutonium. Then the second plutonium hemisphere was placed on top of that, and the upper half of the uranium tamper. When Alferov had finished putting the lenses in position, the carriage on which the bomb – in fact the explosive charge, without the bomb casing – had been assembled was wheeled out through the door into the night and on to the platform of the lift. This was about 2 a.m. on August 29, nine eventful years to the day since Kurchatov, Khariton, Flerov, and Petrzhak had sent their plan for research on nuclear chain reactions to the Academy of Sciences.[95]

Beria and Kurchatov now left the tower, Beria to sleep in a cabin that had been built near the command post, Kurchatov to the command post itself. The platform, with Zernov standing beside the "article," was raised to the top of the tower, where Shchelkin, helped by the engineer G.G. Lominskii, took the detonators one by one from a box and inserted them into the openings in the side of the bomb, while his assistant removed the dampers that covered these openings.[96] Shchelkin then connected the detonators to the firing circuits. Flerov and Davidenko, on top of the tower, checked the counters that would measure the neutron background. When they had completed their work, they all left the tower. After receiving reports that there was no one in the area around the tower, General Osetrov lifted the guard and left the area.[97]

Two observation posts had been created, one 15 kilometers south of the tower for the military, the other 15 kilometers north of the tower for scientists. The command post was 10 kilometers from the tower, to which it was connected by a cable for transmitting the signal for detonation, and by lines for receiving information about the state of the "article." A two-room building had been erected, with the control panel and telephones to various points on the test site in one room, and telephones to the settlement and to Moscow in the other. Outside the building was an earthen wall, to deflect the shock wave. In the command post Kurchatov, Khariton, Shchelkin, Pervukhin, Boliatko, Flerov, and Zaveniagin waited for the test, as did Beria with his entourage.[98]

Kurchatov gave the order for the detonation. The control panel now began to work automatically. When everyone had assembled, Khariton went to the door, which was on the side opposite ground zero, and opened it slightly. This was quite safe because it would take about 30 seconds for the shock wave to reach the command post. When the hand on the clock which showed the countdown to the explosion reached zero, the whole area was lit for a short time by a very bright light. Khariton then closed the door until the shock wave had passed. Then everyone went outside. The cloud from the explosion was already rising.[99] This would soon form a mushroom cloud over the testing ground. Beria embraced Kurchatov and Khariton and kissed them on the forehead.[100] Those present congratulated one another on their success.[101] Shchelkin said later that he had not felt such joy since Victory Day in 1945.[102] Khariton said that "when we succeeded in solving this problem, we felt relief, even happiness – for in possessing such a weapon we had removed the possibility of its being used against the USSR with impunity."[103]

Komel'kov has provided a fine description of the scene from the northern observation post:

The night was cold and windy, and the sky was covered by clouds. Gradually the day broke. A sharp north wind was blowing. In the small room about twenty people were gathered, all huddled up. Gaps appeared in the low scudding clouds, and from time to time the field was lit by the sun.

Signals came from the central point. A voice from the control panel was carried over the communications network: "Minus thirty minutes." That meant the instruments had been turned on. "Minus ten minutes." Everything is in order. Without prearrangement, everyone went out of the building and began to watch. The signals could be heard out here too. In front of us, through the gaps in the low-lying clouds could be seen the toy tower and assembly shop, lit up by the sun. In spite of the multilayered cloud and the wind, there was no dust. Light rain had fallen during the night. Waves of fluttering feather-grass rolled away from us across the field. "Minus five" minutes, "minus three" minutes, "one," "thirty seconds," "ten," "two," "zero."

On top of the tower an unbearably bright light blazed up. For a moment or so it dimmed and then with new force began to grow quickly. The white fireball engulfed the tower and the shop and, expanding rapidly, changing color, it rushed upwards. The blast wave at the base, sweeping in its path structures, stone houses, machines, rolled like a billow from the center, mixing up stones, logs of wood, pieces of metal, and dust into one chaotic mass. The fireball, rising and revolving, turned orange, red. Then dark streaks appeared. Streams of dust, fragments of brick and board were drawn in after it, as into a funnel. Overtaking the firestorm, the shock wave, hitting the upper layers of the atmosphere, passed through several levels of inversion, and there, as in a cloud chamber, the condensation of water vapor began.

. . . A strong wind muffled the sound, and it reached us like the roar of an avalanche. Above the testing ground there grew a grey column of sand, dust, and fog with a cupola-shaped, curling top, intersected by two tiers of cloud and layers of inversion. The upper part of this étagère, reaching a height of 6–8 kilometers, recalled a cupola of cumulus storm-clouds. The atomic mushroom was blown away to the south, losing its outlines, and turning into the formless torn heap of clouds one might see after a gigantic fire.[104]

At another point on the testing ground, 10 kilometers from the tower, Burnazian waited with his tanks, behind one of the few hillocks on the steppe. The shock wave tossed the tanks like feathers, and one of the ionization chambers was damaged. Burnazian and his colleagues watched the radioactive cloud for some minutes, and then took their places in the tanks. They turned on their dosimetric instruments, put on gas masks and moved forward at full speed.[105]

"Literally ten minutes after the explosion," Burnazian has written,

our tank was at ground zero. In spite of the fact that our horizon was limited by the optics of the periscope, a fairly extensive picture of destruction nevertheless met our eyes. The steel tower on to which the bomb had been hoisted had disappeared together with the concrete foundation; the metal had vaporized. In place of the tower there yawned a huge crater. The yellow, sandy soil around had coagulated, turned to glass, and crackled eerily beneath the tracks of the tank. Molten lumps flew about in all directions like small pieces of shrapnel and radiated invisible alpha, beta and gamma rays. In the sector to which Poliakov's tank had gone an oil tank was on fire, and the black smoke added a touch of mourning to an already somber picture. The steel girders of a bridge were twisted into a ram's horns.[106]

After taking their measurements and collecting soil samples the tanks headed back. They soon met a convoy of light vehicles carrying Kurchatov and others to the site of the explosion. The convoy stopped to hear the report of Burnazian and his colleagues. Cameramen were filming Kurchatov in order to record the moment for history.[107] Burnazian's job was made easier by the fact that the radioactive cloud had been carried away over the unpopulated steppe, and that the areas visited by Kurchatov were not too badly contaminated by fission products. "We were well aware," he writes, "that the excitable test director would have risked penetrating to ground zero in a light vehicle even in the event of powerful radioactive contamination."[108]

When Kurchatov returned to the hotel he wrote a report by hand and sent it that day by plane to Moscow. Soviet measurements showed that the yield of the explosion had been the same, or perhaps slightly greater, than that of the American bomb tested at Alamogordo. It was equivalent, in other words, to about 20 kilotons of TNT, the yield specified in the design.[109] Analysis of the test results continued for another two weeks at the test site. Measurements were taken of the level of radioactivity, and analyses done of the radioactive soil. Aircraft traced the path of the radioactive cloud, and automobile expeditions were sent into the areas in which debris fell to earth in order to collect information about the contamination of the soil. Kurchatov held a special meeting to review the analyses and to formulate the main conclusions to be drawn from the test.[110]

On October 29 the Council of Ministers adopted a secret decree, signed by Stalin, granting honors and awards to those who had taken part in the atomic project. The decree was prepared by Beria. In deciding on who was to receive which award, Beria is said to have adopted a simple principle: those who were to be shot in case of failure were now to become Heroes of Socialist Labor; those who would have received maximum prison terms were to be given the Order of Lenin, and so on down the list. This story may well be apocryphal, but it nevertheless conveys the feeling of those in the project that their fate hinged on the success of the test.[111]

The highest honor – Hero of Socialist Labor – was given to a small number of the leading figures in the project. Along with the title they received large sums of money, ZIS-110 or Pobeda automobiles (Kurchatov and Khariton received the former car, the others the latter), the title of Stalin Prize Laureate of the first degree, and *dachas* at Zhukovka, outside Moscow (Kurchatov's *dacha* was in the Crimea). Their children received the right to education in any educational establishment at state expense, and they also received the right of free transport for themselves, their wives, and their children (until the age of majority) within the Soviet Union.[112] Five physicists became Heroes of Socialist Labor: Kurchatov, Khariton, Shchelkin, Zel'dovich, and Flerov. Mikhail Sadovskii was made a Hero of Socialist Labor for his work in preparing the instrumentation for the test. Dukhov and Alferov also received this award. Dollezhal', the chief designer of the production pile, and Bochvar, Vinogradov, and Khlopin, the scientists responsible for producing nuclear materials of the right quality, also became Heroes of Socialist Labor. Khlopin was now seriously ill and was to die in July 1950. Nikolaus Riehl was the only German to be made a

Hero of Socialist Labor, for his work on the purification of uranium and the fabrication of uranium metal. Several of the leading managers were also made Heroes of Socialist Labor, among them Vannikov, Zaveniagin, Pervukhin, Muzrukov, Zernov, and Slavskii.[113] Medals and prizes were awarded to other participants in the project.

It was clear to Soviet physicists, even before the August 1949 test, that the design of the plutonium bomb could be improved upon significantly. By the spring of 1948 experimental work on an alternative design had begun, and these experiments had shown that it was viable. In 1949 Zel'dovich, Zababakhin, Al'tshuler, and K.K. Krupnikov wrote a proposal with the calculations for a new design, which would be about half the weight of the plutonium bomb and have twice the explosive yield. V.M. Nekrutkin proposed a new way of achieving implosion, and this made it possible to reduce the diameter of the bomb significantly.[114] This new design was tested in 1951.

The first test took place on September 24, with Kurchatov once again in charge. The CIA concluded that this explosion

probably utilized only plutonium as the fissionable material (although a composite weapon cannot be excluded by the evidence). The efficiency of utilization of the plutonium was greater than that of the first explosion. . . . A study of the radioactive debris suggests that this explosion occurred on or slightly under the surface of the ground.[115]

The second test was held on October 18. The CIA concluded from an analysis of the debris that

both plutonium and uranium-235 were used as fissionable materials. The efficiency of utilization of the plutonium in the explosion has been determined to be about 35 per cent, but that of the other component has not been determined. The ratio of uranium-235 to plutonium was probably lower than that employed at present by the United States. If a model employing 7 kg of uranium-235 and 3.5 kg of plutonium is assumed, the yield would have been about 50 kilotons. This explosion did not occur close to the ground and the data are most consistent with an air burst.

This bomb used enriched uranium from the gaseous diffusion plant, which had finally begun to operate successfully at the end of 1950. The core consisted of both uranium-235 and plutonium, which makes it possible to use fissionable material more efficiently and thus to improve the yield-to-weight ratio of the core.[116] Soviet physicists assessed the yield at 40 kilotons.[117] The bomb was dropped by a Tu-4 bomber.[118] The plane was shaken twice in the air, once when it dropped its load, and then, with a sharper jolt, when the shock wave hit it. But everything turned out well: "henceforth," Komel'kov has written, "our air force could work with atomic bombs without fearing for the life of the crews."[119]

In December honors were distributed once again. Kurchatov became Hero of Socialist Labor for the second time; so too did Khariton. Kikoin, who was scientific director of the gaseous diffusion effort, also received this honor. At Kurchatov's laboratory, which since April 1949 had been called the Laboratory of Measuring Instruments of the Academy of Sciences (LIPAN: *Laboratoriia izmeritel'nykh priborov AN SSSR*), thirty people received Stalin prizes and 152 were given medals and honors.[120]

These awards were part of Stalin's policy of rewarding scientists for their services to the state. While they pointed to a change in the regime's attitude to science, they were not necessarily a good thing for science. Some scientists, Kapitsa among them, later complained that when scientists began to receive this kind of reward, science began to attract the wrong kind of people.

V

The Soviet test took place much sooner than the United States had expected. The US government had begun to gather intelligence about Soviet nuclear research by the spring of 1945, but was unable to obtain a clear picture of Soviet progress, which it consistently underestimated. In July 1948 Admiral R.H. Hillenkoeter, director of the Central Intelligence Agency, sent a memorandum to Truman stating that "the earliest date by which it is remotely possible that the USSR may have completed its first atomic bomb is mid-1950, but the most probable date is believed to be mid-1953."[121] This reflected the views of the intelligence community as a whole. A year later, on July 1, 1949, he repeated this estimate. This was less than two months before the Soviet test.[122]

The Soviet Union took about the same length of time as the United States to build the atom bomb. Kurchatov had been given five years to make the atomic bomb, and he had done so in four years from the initiation of the all-out project in August 1945. The United States took just over three years and nine months, from October 9, 1941, when Roosevelt made it clear to Vannevar Bush that he wanted the atomic project expedited in every possible way, to the Trinity test on July 16, 1945. The period between the first chain reactions (December 2, 1942 and December 25, 1946) and the first tests is even more strikingly similar: a difference of less than three weeks in two and a half years.

The Soviet test was an impressive achievement. It is true that the United States had shown that the bomb could be built, and that the Soviet Union had obtained a detailed description of the first American plutonium bomb. But the design of the bomb was not the only problem. An atomic industry had to be built to provide the materials for the bomb. This was an enormous undertaking in an economy that had been devastated by the war. Stalin gave the project the highest priority and did not allow the wretched state of the country to deflect him from his purpose. He told Kurchatov to organize the project "with Russian scope." Stalin was determined not only to have the atomic bomb, but to have it as quickly as possible. No effort was made to pare the cost of the project so that resources could be freed for other goals. Priorities were categorized in separate boxes, with no commensurability or trade-offs between them.

The Stalinist command economy was designed for precisely this purpose: to enforce the priorities of the leadership in a ruthless manner, no matter how pressing other claims on resources might be. Coercion was an intrinsic part of the system, and Beria was the logical person to put in charge because he was in a better position than anyone else to squeeze resources out of the war-damaged economy. But Stalin and Beria were fortunate to have Kurchatov as scientific director of the project. He had a clear sense of what needed to be done. He established good relations with Pervukhin, Vannikov, Zaveniagin, and the other managers. He was evidently able to work with Stalin and Beria. He retained the respect of his scientist colleagues even when he was exerting intense pressure on them to complete the project quickly. He was known affectionately as "the Beard" and sometimes (perhaps less affectionately) as "Prince Igor'." Willing to bear the responsibility that had been placed upon him, he did not try to pass it on to others. He was an excellent judge of abilities, and good at selecting people for positions in the project. It was he more than anyone else who ensured that the political leaders, managers, and scientists worked towards the same goal.

Working for Beria was not easy. Beria had chosen substitutes for the leading scientists before the first test. After the test, apparently irritated by Kurchatov's increased authority, he summoned Alikhanov and asked him if he would take over Kurchatov's position. Alikhanov refused, saying that he did not have Kurchatov's organizational abilities. Alikhanov told Kurchatov about this conversation, and assured him that he had turned down Beria's proposition.[123] Whether Beria really wished to replace Kurchatov, or merely to let him know who really had power, is not clear. The latter is more likely, since Beria was interested in the success of the project, and surely understood that Kurchatov was crucial to this.

The German contribution to the atomic project was small and limited. With one exception, German scientists did not play any role on the critical path to the plutonium bomb. The exception was Nikolaus Riehl's group, which produced uranium metal at a crucial stage of the project. But Zinaida Ershova had already produced some uranium metal, and it is difficult to imagine that Soviet scientists could not have devised a method for production on an industrial scale. Riehl may have saved the project weeks, or months at most. The German research on gaseous diffusion was parallel to what Soviet scientists were doing, and not central to the Soviet effort. Even when some Germans were asked to help with the diffusion plant, their contribution appears to have been minimal. German scientists did important work on the centrifuge, but that was not used on an industrial scale until the late 1950s.

The intelligence information – particularly that from Klaus Fuchs – was more important. Fuchs helped the nuclear project in two ways. He contributed to the setting up of the Soviet effort during the war; and he provided a detailed description of the design of the plutonium bomb. Fuchs's confession makes it clear that he gave little help with other stages of the plutonium route to the bomb:

Fuchs told me that during 1948 he did not pass to the Russian agent a great deal of information that was then in his possession as a result of his work at Harwell on the design and method of operation of plutonium production pile. He was surprised that very few questions were put to him on this subject . . .[124]

When Fuchs was asked about the fabrication of fuel rods, he was struck by the specificity of this question, and by the fact that "there were no questions about the recovery of uranium from its ore, the preparation of pure uranium complements or metals, canning techniques, dimensions of uranium rod or the preparation, purity and dimensions of graphite."[125]

Fuchs's information undoubtedly enabled the Soviet Union to build the atomic bomb more quickly than it could otherwise have done. Fuchs himself thought that he had saved the Soviet Union several years – though he added, on reflection, that he had speeded up the Soviet bomb "by one year at least."[126] But Fuchs, who had never been in the Soviet Union, knew almost nothing about the state of Soviet physics. The best-qualified estimates of the time that intelligence saved the Soviet Union have fallen into the range of one to two years.[127] This estimate seems plausible, though it is of course speculative. Edward Teller has argued that the Soviet Union might not have had the bomb for another ten years without Fuchs's help, because it required great ingenuity to devise the implosion mechanism. But this appears to underestimate the ability of the Soviet physicists, especially people like Khariton, Zel'dovich, and Shchelkin, who had worked on the physics of detonation and explosion before and during the war. Moreover, it ignores the fact that a bomb with uranium-235 was detonated in 1951, so that even if the Soviet physicists had not been able to devise the implosion method for plutonium, they would have been able to build a gun-assembly uranium-235 bomb by 1951.

Even with Fuchs's information, there was a great deal to do in designing and building the plutonium bomb. A comparison with the British project, which tested its first atomic bomb in 1952, is instructive. Britain had had nineteen scientists, including Fuchs, at Los Alamos during the war, but in 1946 the United States cut off the exchange of nuclear information. When the British government decided in 1947 to build an atomic bomb, British scientists were able to put together a working manual for duplicating the

American plutonium bomb. According to Margaret Gowing, this manual gave "a good idea of the manufacturing effort required for the bomb components and of the apparatus needed for testing."[128] Since the British team had included such outstanding physicists as Peierls and Frisch as well as Fuchs, this information was certainly more than Fuchs had provided to the Soviet Union. Nevertheless, the production and testing of the first British bomb was, in Gowing's words, "a complex task and the experts were conscious that the five years . . . given to 'provide a solution' was not long."[129]

The length of time the Soviet Union needed to develop the atomic bomb was determined more by the availability of uranium than by any other factor. As soon as uranium became available in sufficient quantity, Kurchatov was able to build and start up the experimental reactor. The first production reactor was built as soon as there was enough uranium for it. The physicists were ready to assemble and test the bomb as soon as plutonium had been extracted from uranium irradiated in the reactor and fabricated into two metal hemispheres. It was this path, rather than the design and development of the weapon itself, that determined how long it took the Soviet Union to build the bomb. Vernadskii and Khlopin had been right in 1940 when they stressed the importance of acquiring uranium; the great failure of the years 1943–5 was that more was not done to find uranium in the Soviet Union.

CHAPTER ELEVEN

War and the Atomic Bomb

I

THE ATOMIC PROJECT shows that Stalin took the bomb seriously, but it does not reveal how he understood its military and strategic significance. What difference did the bomb make to the military balance in the short term? What difference would it make in the longer term? How would it affect military strategy and the conduct of war? To answer these questions it is necessary to look at Stalin's military policy after World War II.

During the war with Germany Stalin came to rely on the professional expertise of the High Command. In August 1942, at the nadir of Soviet fortunes, he appointed Marshal Georgii Zhukov, the ablest of an outstanding group of commanders, as Deputy Supreme Commander-in-Chief. "From that moment," Zhukov later wrote, "Stalin almost never took decisions on questions of organizing operations without consulting me."[1] But after the war Stalin turned against Zhukov and reasserted his own authority in military affairs. Zhukov, who was Commander-in-Chief of the Group of Soviet Occupation Forces in Germany, was recalled to Moscow in March 1946 to become Commander-in-Chief of the Ground Forces. Shortly thereafter he attended a meeting of the Main Military Council. "Stalin came into the meeting hall," Zhukov wrote later. "He was gloomy, like a black cloud. Without saying a word, he took a paper out of his pocket and threw it to the secretary of the Main Military Council, General S.M. Shtemenko, and said 'Read it.'" The paper contained accusations against Zhukov by two officers who were being held in prison. Zhukov, they said, had claimed that he, and not Stalin, deserved most of the credit for the victory over Germany. He was supposed, moreover, to have had conversations directed against Stalin, and to have drawn to himself "a group of dissatisfied generals and officers."

When Shtemenko had finished reading, Stalin asked others to speak. Molotov, Beria, and Bulganin denounced Zhukov, but most of the military leaders said that they did not believe the charges. In June 1946 Stalin sent Zhukov to command the Odessa Military District and removed him from his position as candidate member of the Party Central Committee. In the following year the organs of state security arrested a group of generals and officers who had been associated with Zhukov. These men were tortured and forced to confess that they had taken part in a plot to overthrow Stalin. Beria, who was in charge of this affair, evidently wanted to arrest Zhukov, but Stalin told him that he did not believe that Zhukov could have been involved in a plot and refused to authorize his arrest. In February 1948 Zhukov was transferred to the Urals Military District, a further demotion.[2]

Stalin's treatment of Zhukov showed that he intended to assert tight control over the military. When the Defense and Navy Commissariats were combined in February 1946 to form the People's Commissariat (later Ministry) of the Armed Forces, Stalin remained as minister until March 1947. Even after resigning as minister, he retained his formal authority in military affairs as chairman of the Higher Military Council. His successor at the ministry was Nikolai Bulganin, a political officer who had become Stalin's deputy at the Defense Commissariat in November 1944. Bulganin knew little about military affairs, according to Zhukov, but served as Stalin's right hand in the military.[3] The General Staff, where Marshal A.M. Vasilevskii replaced Antonov as chief in March 1946, was the main repository of professional expertise, but it had to work within the confines of Stalin's views on strategy and war. "While Stalin was alive he completely monopolized all decisions about our defenses," Khrushchev recalled in his memoirs, "including – I'd even say especially – those involving nuclear weapons and delivery systems."[4]

Stalin assiduously cultivated his own image as a military leader. On Red Army Day, February 23, 1946, he published a letter in which he belittled Lenin's authority in military affairs ("Lenin did not consider himself a military expert"); argued that German military ideology, represented by Clausewitz, had not withstood the test of history ("it is ridiculous now to take lessons from Clausewitz"); and portrayed himself as a latter-day Kutuzov, whose retreat in the face of the German attack was patterned on the Russian withdrawal before Napoleon's armies in 1812.[5] Stalin presented the early retreats and disasters of the war as part of a planned strategy of active defense. In Order No. 55, issued on February 23, 1942, he had referred to the "permanently operating factors" which determine the outcome of war: the stability of the rear, the morale of the Army, the quantity and quality of divisions, the armament of the Army, and the organizing ability of the command personnel. He had contrasted these factors with the "transitory" element of surprise, thereby playing down the reverses of the first months of the war.[6]

Stalin did not abandon these principles after the war. He told Alexander Werth in September 1946 that atomic bombs "cannot decide the outcome of a war, since atomic bombs are quite insufficient for that."[7] Since Stalin wished to minimize the significance of the bomb, this statement cannot be taken as proof of his real views. But he had received several reports in 1945 and 1946 about the effects of atomic explosions, and although these drew attention to the destructive effects of the atomic bomb none of them portrayed it as a decisive weapon.

In September 1945 a small group from the Tokyo embassy visited Hiroshima to examine the destruction caused by the atomic bomb. After its return Iakov Malik, the ambassador, sent a report to Stalin, Beria, Molotov, Malenkov, and Mikoian, along with articles from the Japanese press. Malik wrote that

at the centre of the explosion, all wooden structures were burnt to ashes, and the roofs of brick houses were blown away or fell in, as did the floors. The shells of ferroconcrete buildings withstood the blast but the roofs, ceilings and floors were destroyed.

No damage was caused to highways; the wave blew away ferroconcrete bridge railings but wooden bridges were burnt down; river banks were not damaged. Neither streetcar tracks nor things buried in the earth were damaged. Big trees were blown away or burnt down. All life was destroyed by fire or otherwise within a range of up to 2 km.[8]

According to the Japanese press, Malik wrote, over 120,000 residents of Hiroshima had been killed or injured; in Nagasaki about 15,000 had been killed, and 20,000 injured.[9]

In their report the embassy officials wrote that "the atomic bomb and the destruction caused by it had an enormous effect on the population of Japan."[10] But because the bomb had been described by the Japanese government as one of the reasons for Japan's surrender, the Japanese press had gone out of its way "to exaggerate the destructive power of the bomb and the duration of the effects of the explosion. Rumour takes up and distorts press reports, even carrying them to the point of absurdity."[11] The Soviet officials returned to Tokyo with the chief of the Medical Service of the US Fifth Fleet, who told them that "after the explosion the area hit by the bomb was safe. He alleged that the Japanese greatly exaggerated the effectiveness of the bomb." The American physician also told them that "the effects of an atomic explosion were only dangerous for 24 hours."[12]

Soviet scientists did not have a good understanding of the destructive effects of nuclear explosions. Soviet intelligence asked Fuchs several times in the early postwar years for information about these effects. In the draft article he sent to Molotov in December 1945, Kapitsa wrote that it was not yet clear how destructive atomic bombs would be. It was possible, he claimed, to protect oneself from most of the radiation released by a nuclear explosion: if the Japanese had not lived in "cardboard houses," and had taken measures to protect themselves, the number of casualties would have been significantly smaller.[13]

This tendency to play down the effects of the bomb was reflected in two reports received by the Soviet government in 1946. Vannikov, Kurchatov, and Khariton prepared a memorandum for Molotov on the July 1946 detonations at Bikini Atoll. This memorandum drew on official US statements, as well as on the reports from Meshcheriakov and Aleksandrov, the Soviet observers at the tests. Meshcheriakov and Aleksandrov were not impressed by the first explosion, in which a plutonium bomb was detonated over a group of warships. They wrote of the "general disappointment with the results of the explosion." The ships had survived extremely well, and the "material results of the explosion proved to be insignificant compared with what had been expected here."[14] If the United States' purpose in staging the tests had been to impress the Soviet Union with the power of the bomb, it had failed to do so.

In August 1946 a mission from the Allied Control Council for Japan visited Hiroshima and Nagasaki. A Soviet intelligence officer who worked on the staff of the council described his impressions in a report to Moscow. The effects of the bomb should not be exaggerated, he wrote. Most of the people in Hiroshima had died for lack of medical assistance. Many of the casualties on the day of the bombing could be attributed to the lack of precautions: all offices, factories, schools were functioning as usual, and gas and electric stoves were on in apartment kitchens. That was why many people had been buried alive or burned in collapsed houses.[15]

Stalin's statement to Alexander Werth reflected the advice he was receiving as well as his desire to belittle the significance of the atomic bomb. It is possible, of course, that his advisers consciously told him what he wanted to hear, or that what they reported was shaped by their own hopes and fears. But because the scientists had little evidence to go on, it was not unreasonable for them to think that the destruction caused by an atomic bomb would be less in a Soviet than in a Japanese city, and to argue that casualties might be reduced significantly by precautions beforehand and medical treatment afterwards. It is a mistake to read our present understanding of the effects of nuclear weapons back into the context of 1946. Khariton later commented that "not all the consequences [of nuclear war] were taken into account then – we did not think of the possibility that humankind would perish."[16]

II

Soon after Hiroshima, military planners in Washington began to think about the way in which atomic bombs should be used in a war against the Soviet Union. The earliest list of targets for atomic attack was prepared on November 3, 1945 as part of an extensive study of the Soviet Union by the Joint Intelligence Staff of the Joint Chiefs of Staff (JCS).[17] By June 1946 the Joint War Plans Committee of the JCS had drawn up an interim plan, code-named "Pincher," which treated the bomb as a "distinct advantage" in the strategic air offensive against the Soviet Union.[18] This plan was not approved by the JCS or adopted as policy, but it indicates that military planners were thinking of using the atomic bomb against urban-industrial targets, in order to destroy the Soviet capacity to wage war. In the summer of 1947 the JCS concluded, after a careful evaluation of the 1946 Bikini tests, that atomic bombs could "nullify any nation's military effort and demolish its social and economic structures," and recommended that the United States should have "the most effective atomic bomb striking force possible."[19] The American stockpile was still small at the time when these studies were being done: on June 30, 1946 the United States had 9 atomic bombs; a year later it had 13 and in 1948 it had 56.[20]

The urgency of American military planning grew in 1948, however, and with it reliance on nuclear weapons. The communist coup in Czechoslovakia in February 1948 and the Berlin blockade in June marked a sharp deterioration in relations with the Soviet Union. In July 1948 Truman dispatched B-29 bombers to Europe. These were not modified to carry atomic bombs, but were intended nonetheless to demonstrate that the United States would defend Western Europe by nuclear attack if necessary.[21] On September 13, 1948 Truman told Secretary of Defense James Forrestal that he prayed he would never have to make such a decision, but that he would use atomic weapons "if it became necessary."[22] Three days later he endorsed a National Security Council paper which concluded that the United States must be ready to "utilize promptly and effectively all appropriate means available, including atomic weapons, in the interest of national security and must therefore plan accordingly."[23]

The atomic air offensive now became a crucial element in American strategy for a war against the Soviet Union. In May 1948 the JCS approved the Joint Emergency War Plan, "Halfmoon," which envisaged "a powerful air offensive designed to exploit the destructive and psychological power of atomic weapons against the vital elements of the Soviet war making capacity."[24] Truman rejected this plan and ordered that a plan based solely on conventional forces be prepared, for he still appears to have hoped that atomic weapons might be outlawed by international control. At the same time, however, he refused to countenance a defense budget that would allow the United States to maintain what the Joint Chiefs regarded as adequate conventional forces. As a result, American strategy came ultimately to depend on the atomic air offensive.[25] The Strategic Air Command (SAC), which had been established in March 1946 to conduct long-range offensive operations in any part of the world, now became the spearhead of American military power.

Not everyone was happy with the central role of the atomic bomb in war planning; the Navy, in particular, had misgivings because it feared that reliance on the bomb would diminish its own importance. In October 1948 Defense Secretary James V. Forrestal, himself a former Secretary of the Navy, asked the JCS to examine the impact on the Soviet Union if all the bombs were delivered. The Harmon Committee completed its report in May 1949 and concluded that the planned atomic attack on seventy Soviet cities would not, "*per se*, bring about capitulation, destroy the roots of Communism, or critically weaken the power of the Soviet leadership to dominate the people."[26] A successful strategic air campaign might result in 2.7 million deaths and reduce Soviet industrial capacity by 30–40 per cent, but it would not lead to the defeat of the Soviet Union. It would probably increase the will of the Soviet people to fight, the Harmon Report argued, and would not stop the advance of Soviet forces in Western Europe, the Middle East, or the Far East. Besides, by initiating the use of weapons of mass destruction, the atomic air offensive would "produce certain psychological and retaliatory reactions detrimental to the achievement of Allied war objectives."[27] In other words, an atomic attack could not by itself defeat the Soviet Union.

The Harmon Report did not, however, reject the atomic air offensive; it accepted that the atomic bomb was the only means of inflicting serious damage quickly on the Soviet capacity to wage war. Moreover, the report said, "from the standpoint of our national security, the advantages of its early use would be transcending. Every reasonable effort should be devoted to providing the means to be prepared for prompt and effective delivery of the maximum numbers of atomic bombs at appropiate target systems."[28] The report concluded that the United States was committed, for better or for worse, to an atomic strategy and should try to make that strategy as effective as possible.

Truman was increasingly convinced that the atomic bomb should indeed provide the central element in strategic policy. In July 1949 he told his advisers that "I am of the opinion we'll never obtain international control. Since we can't obtain international control we must be strongest in atomic weapons."[29] He was being warned, moreover, by political leaders in Europe, notably Churchill, that the threat of atomic retaliation was needed to deter a Soviet offensive against Western Europe. He was therefore receptive when the JCS, following the Harmon Report, requested a major expansion of nuclear weapons production. His willingness to meet this request was undoubtedly reinforced by the Soviet test in August 1949, and on October 19, less than seven weeks after the test, he approved the expansion.

The first mission assigned to SAC was to *disrupt* the Soviet capacity to make war. This was the same mission that strategic bombers had carried out against Germany. After the formation of NATO in April 1949 SAC was assigned an additional mission: to *retard* a Soviet advance into Western Europe. In the following year, soon after the Soviet test, SAC acquired a third mission: to *blunt* the Soviet capability to deliver an atomic offensive against the United States and its allies. This blunting mission had the highest priority because it had to be carried out quickly, before Soviet bombers got off the ground. The retardation mission was assigned second priority because it too had to be carried out before Soviet forces advanced into Western Europe. Disruption of Soviet industry was regarded as the least urgent task.[30]

These new missions, along with the military requirements that emerged from the Harmon Report, provided the rationale for larger and more diverse nuclear forces. Truman decided on two further expansions of nuclear production, in October 1950 and in January 1952.[31] The atomic stockpile had grown to 298 bombs by June 1950, and it now began to increase more rapidly – to 438 in 1951, to 832 in 1952, and to 1,161 in 1953.[32] This growth was accompanied by an increase in the number of nuclear delivery vehicles. Until 1948 SAC had only about 30 B-29s modified to drop atomic bombs, and all of these were based in New Mexico.[33] By December 1948 the number of nuclear-capable aircraft had grown to 60, and to 250 by June 1950; by the end of 1953 it had reached 1,000.[34] Most of these were medium bombers which could not strike the Soviet Union from the United States; only the B-36, of which SAC had 38 at the end of 1950 and 154 at the end of 1952, had intercontinental range.[35] SAC relied very heavily, therefore, on overseas bases. By the beginning of 1950 it had airfields in Britain, Iceland, Newfoundland, Alaska, Guam, and Okinawa, as well as bases in Bermuda, the Azores, Libya, and Saudi Arabia. This network was augmented during the Korean War: additional base rights were obtained from Canada in Newfoundland and Labrador, from France in Morocco, from Britain in Libya and Cyprus as well as Britain, from Denmark in Greenland, from Portugal in the Azores, and from Turkey at Adana.[36]

According to the SAC Emergency War Plan approved by the JCS in October 1951, strategic air operations would be launched about six days after the start of war. Heavy bombers flying from Maine would drop twenty bombs on the Moscow-Gor'kii region and return to Britain; medium bombers from Labrador would attack the Leningrad area with twelve bombs and return to British bases; medium bombers from Britain would fly along the edge of the Mediterranean and deliver fifty-two bombs in the industrial regions of the Volga and Donets basins, returning through Libyan and Egyptian airfields; medium bombers from the Azores would drop fifteen bombs in the Caucasus area and fly on to Saudi Arabia. Bombers from Guam would deliver fifteen bombs against Vladivostok and Irkutsk. Overseas bases were, therefore, a crucial element in the United States' strategic posture. General Hoyt S. Vandenberg, Chief of Staff of the Air Force, testified in December 1951 that if SAC did not have any overseas bases it would have to be "five or six times" stronger in order to perform the same missions.[37]

III

The military balance at the end of World War II was highly asymmetrical. The United States and Britain had strategic bomber forces, as well as large navies with aircraft carriers, which could strike the Soviet Union. The Soviet Navy and Air Force, which had been confined largely to support of the ground forces during the war, could not directly threaten the United States.[38] "The Soviet Union cannot attack the continental United States within the near future," the Joint Intelligence Committee of the US JCS pointed out in November 1945.[39] But in a war in Europe or on the mainland of Asia, the committee concluded, "the Soviets would enjoy a great preponderance in numbers of men against the United States or even against the United States, Great Britain and France."[40]

Soviet military planners were of course aware of the threat of an atomic air attack, and conscious also of the Soviet Union's inability to strike the United States. In late 1946 and early 1947 the General Staff prepared a "Plan for the active defense of the territory of the Soviet Union" for the Higher Military Council.[41] This plan assigned three main missions to the armed forces: "to ensure the reliable repulse of aggression and the integrity of the frontiers established by international agreements after World War II"; "to be prepared to repel an enemy air attack, including one with the possible use of atomic weapons." The third mission was assigned to the Navy, which was "to be prepared to repel possible aggression from the sea and to provide support for the Ground Forces operating in coastal regions."[42] According to this plan, the Air Forces and Air Defense Forces were to provide cover for the ground forces and to be constantly ready to repel a sudden air attack. The Navy was to support the ground forces by landing troops, covering coastal flanks and preventing enemy landings. Where possible, the Navy was to carry out independent missions to destroy enemy lines of communication, lay minefields, and cover important naval directions, but its primary mission was to support the ground forces.[43]

The ground forces were the spearhead of Soviet military power. After the setbacks and defeats of 1941 and 1942, the Red Army had emerged as a formidable force, which had driven the *Wehrmacht* out of the Soviet Union and Eastern Europe and had seized Berlin. The Army's 500 divisions were reduced to 175 after the war, but these remaining divisions were strengthened: the tank and mechanized divisions were allocated additional tanks and guns, while the infantry (rifle) divisions were reinforced with tanks, self-propelled guns, and motor transport. Their firepower and mobility were thus greatly enhanced.[44]

The Army was organized into three main elements: the repulsion or blocking army; the reserve of the Supreme High Command; and secondary forces which were maintained at reduced strength. The mission of the repulsion army was to "shatter the enemy in the border defense zone and to prepare the conditions for going over to the counteroffensive."[45] The reserve of the Supreme High Command was maintained in the interior of the country to be deployed as needed, once military operations had begun. This reserve was to join with the army of repulsion "to strike a destructive blow against the enemy's main forces, to inflict defeat on them, and to take part in the counteroffensive."[46] The secondary forces were to be ready to mobilize and to concentrate in designated areas near the front within 10–20 days.[47] According to US intelligence, about one-third of the Army's 175 divisions were maintained at cadre strength (less than 30 per cent of manning), one-third at partial strength, and one-third at full strength (over 70 per cent of manning).[48]

The operational plan for the Group of Soviet Occupation Forces in Germany (GSFG) provides a clear picture of the Army's missions in the early postwar period. According to this plan, which was approved on November 5, 1946, Soviet forces in Germany consisted of 17 ground force divisions, organized into four armies, as well as the 16th Air Army and other support groups. Apart from several regiments along the border, these forces were deployed at least 50 kilometers from the Western zones of occupation. The 3rd Shock Army and the 8th Guards Army, which were located behind this 50-kilometer security belt, had the mission of preventing the enemy from breaking through the main defensive belt before the 1st and 2nd Guards Mechanized Armies, deployed further to the east, were brought up.[49] There were other divisions stationed in Germany that could be quickly brought up to full strength.[50] With the support of the reserve of the Supreme High Command, these forces would launch the counteroffensive.

The Soviet posture in Europe after the war did not betray a real fear of imminent attack by the United States, or an urgent ambition to invade Western Europe; it was the posture of a state determined to consolidate its power on the territory that it now occupied, rather than expand that territory. Although the Western Allies demobilized more rapidly, the Soviet Union did not have overwhelming military superiority in Europe in the early postwar years. The Western powers had about 375,000 occupation troops in Germany and Austria in 1947–8, while other forces in Western Europe (excluding Britain) amounted to about 400,000.[51] In 1948 US intelligence estimated that the Soviet Union might have 700–800,000 men available for a surprise attack on Western Europe. This would not have provided the Soviet armed forces with anything like the kind of force ratios it considered desirable for large-scale strategic offensive operations.[52]

The Soviet posture was far from being unambiguously defensive, however. The Army's offensive capabilities were being improved by additional firepower and mobility, and it was ready to go over to the offensive quickly. The counteroffensive occupied a special place in Stalinist strategy.

"I think that a well-organized counteroffensive is a very interesting form of offensive," Stalin wrote in February 1946. He was referring to the "counteroffensive after a successful enemy offensive which has not, however, achieved decisive results, in the course of which the defender gathers his forces, goes over to the offensive and inflicts on the enemy a decisive defeat."[53] What he had in mind was the way in which the Red Army had gathered itself together after the disastrous setbacks of 1941 and 1942.

Writing several months after Stalin's pronouncement, Major-General N. Talenskii, one of the leading military theorists of the period, pointed to the battles of Moscow, Stalingrad, and Kursk as the start of the Soviet counteroffensive against Germany. Favorable conditions did not always exist for the offensive, wrote Talenskii, and sometimes it was necessary to conduct strategic defense, especially if the correlation of forces was unfavorable.[54] Stalin had discovered a new "historical law" that helped to explain the initial setbacks in the war with Germany: "aggressive nations, as nations that attack, are usually more prepared for a new war than peaceloving nations, which, being uninterested in a new war, are usually late in preparing for it."[55] In view of this, Talenskii wrote, the counteroffensive was of particular importance for a peaceloving country like the Soviet Union.

The counteroffensive was merely a variant of the offensive, which provided the main focus for Soviet military strategy. The General Staff regarded strategic defense as a "temporary form of strategic operation."[56] "It was proposed to conduct defensive operations in those cases when an attack was inexpedient or impossible," a Soviet military historian wrote, "when it was necessary to secure the offensive in other important directions or to win time. It was considered that defensive operations should create the conditions for going over to the counteroffensive."[57] Besides the plans for active defense, the General Staff drew up plans for offensive operations, which designated the forces to take part, the direction of the main blow, as well as the strategic tasks and the time in which they were to be completed.

These offensive plans have not been published, but their contents have been described in general terms.[58] They were based on the large-scale offensive operations the Red Army had conducted in the latter part of the war. Before attacking, Soviet forces would use artillery and air power for an hour or more to soften up the enemy. Air superiority was to be achieved by air strikes against enemy aircraft on their airfields, against weapons and fuel depots, and against radar installations. The ground forces were to move into action when the operation to win air superiority began, or shortly thereafter. Soviet forces were to advance rapidly and across a wide front. The ultimate aim of these operations was to achieve victory by destroying the enemy's forces.

IV

Ground force operations provided an element of continuity in military policy. But Stalin gave new priority to two elements of the Soviet Armed Forces – the Air Defense Forces and the Long-Range Air Force – that had important missions in connection with the atomic bomb. Strategic bombing was not a new concept for the Soviet Union. The Air Force's primary mission in the 1930s had been tactical support for ground force operations, but independent air operations against industrial and military targets in the enemy's rear had come to be regarded as important by the mid-1930s.[59] This commitment weakened later in the decade when some of the leading advocates of strategic bombing were arrested and shot. At the same time senior commanders concluded from the Spanish Civil War and from the Red Army's battles with Japanese forces at Lake Khasan and Khalkin-Gol that the Air Force would be most useful if deployed in support of ground forces.[60] The prevailing attitude was summed up by Marshal S.M. Timoshenko, the People's Commissar of Defense, when he assured the High Command at a meeting in December 1940 that "the decisive effect of aviation consists not in strikes on the deep rear, but in combined operations with troops on the battlefield."[61]

Strategic bombing played a small role in the Soviet war with Germany. The two countries used their air forces almost exclusively in support of ground operations. Soviet bombers made token raids on Helsinki and Berlin in 1941, and attacked the oilfields in Romania, but long-range bombers were used primarily in tactical roles and for transport.[62] Stalin was nevertheless impressed by the Anglo-American bombing campaign against Germany. In an effort to deflect Stalin's anger at the delay in opening the second front, Churchill sent him a "small stereoscopic machine" with a large number of photographic slides of the damage inflicted on German cities by the strategic bombing campaign.[63] At the Teheran meeting at the end of 1943 Stalin asked "innumerable and very intelligent questions" about American long-range bombers.[64] He made several formal requests for British and American four-engined heavy bombers, but these were refused.[65]

In 1944, however, Stalin had a stroke of luck. At the end of July a US Air Force B-29, running low on fuel after a mission over Manchuria, was forced to land near Vladivostok. In November two more B-29s crash-landed in Siberia after running out of fuel on raids against Japan, and a fourth crashed after the crew had bailed out.[66] The four-engined B-29, which had conducted its first bombing raid in June 1944, was the most advanced bomber in the world at the time: it had a speed of 584 km/h at 8,000 meters, and a range of about 6,100 kilometers with a bomb load of almost 5 metric tons.[67] Instead of returning the bombers to the United States, Stalin kept them so that they could be dismantled and studied by

Soviet designers.[68] Early in 1945 he ordered the aircraft designers A.N. Tupolev, S.V. Il'iushin, and V.M. Miasishchev to prepare designs for a four-engined bomber with a range of 3,000 kilometers.[69] In 1946, however, he decided to produce a copy of the B-29 instead. Tupolev was ordered to copy the airframe, and A.D. Shevtsov the engine.[70]

This sequence of decisions shows that Stalin had reassessed the importance of strategic bombing before Hiroshima. The leading historian of Soviet aircraft designs has written that

the war showed that the country needed a long-range high-speed strategic bomber, that the doubts and hesitations before the war about this type of aircraft . . . were only a temporary phenomenon and life had repudiated them.[71]

Hiroshima gave strategic bombing a new importance by showing how much destruction a single bomber could do with one bomb.

The new importance of strategic bombing was reflected in the build-up of the Long-Range Air Force (which is discussed below) and in the priority now given to air defense. The Air Defense Forces soon began to benefit from the research and development programs in jet propulsion and radar. The Iak-15 and MiG-9 jet fighters, which were powered by German engines, had their first flight tests in April 1946. Both planes entered service with the Air Defense Forces in limited numbers.[72] The second generation of jet interceptors soon followed, to meet the requirement for a fighter which could fly at about the speed of sound at very high altitudes, and stay airborne for an hour. The MiG-15 and the La-15 were powered by modified Soviet versions of the Rolls-Royce Derwent and Nene engines, which the Soviet Union bought from Britain in 1947. Stalin had been skeptical that Britain would sell these engines – "What kind of fool would be willing to sell his secrets!" he had reportedly said – but the British government agreed to the sale.[73] The MiG-15, which had its first test flight on December 30, 1947, was produced in very large numbers.[74] The La-15, which was designed by the Lavochkin bureau, entered series production in August 1948, though it was produced in smaller numbers than the MiG-15.[75] The third generation of interceptors – MiG-19 and Iak-25 – was produced in the early 1950s on the basis of Soviet jet engines.[76]

The Air Defense Forces also began to receive new anti-aircraft guns in 1947.[77] A 57 mm gun was built for targets up to an altitude of 5,000 meters, and a 100 mm gun was developed for targets up to 12,000 meters; 25 mm and 37 mm guns were to deal with low-flying planes.[78] The war had shown, however, that anti-aircraft artillery alone could not provide effective defense, and work was begun, with the help of German engineers, on the development of anti-air missiles. The first anti-aircraft missile training units were formed in 1952.[79]

Early-warning radars also received high priority.[80] There were two design groups, one working in the meter waveband, the other in the centimeter waveband. The first group designed the P-3a system, an improved version of the wartime P-3 radar.[81] The P-3a had a detection range of 130 kilometers and entered production in 1947. It was followed by the P-8 early warning radar, which underwent state trials in 1949 and 1950, and was widely deployed. The P-8 had an effective range of 150 kilometers, which could be increased to 250 kilometers with the addition of a special mast.[82] The P-10, a new radar system based largely on the P-8, was developed in 1951–3 and entered service soon afterwards. It had a similar effective range, but improved resolution and receiver sensitivity.[83] The first of the centimeter-band radars was the P-20 early-warning and acquisition radar, which passed its state trials in 1949 and was widely deployed with the Air Defense Forces, the Air Forces and the Navy.[84] It could define all three coordinates of targets with high accuracy and had an effective range of 190 kilometers.[85] Its range and resolving power were greater than those of the P-8, which was developed at about the same time, and it provided the basis for a series of early-warning radars developed in the 1950s.[86]

The Soviet High Command understood, on the basis of British and American strategy in World War II, that

independent operations by enemy strategic air forces against installations in the rear of the country would be a very important part of the conduct of the war as a whole. The enemy would conduct these operations with the aim of destroying the country's most important military-economic installations, disorganizing the rear and undermining the morale of the population.[87]

A meeting of senior air defense officers was held from February 27 to March 10, 1947 to discuss the problem of defending the interior of the country against air attack. This meeting resulted in a volume which analyzed the principles of air defense. In July of the same year an exercise was held in which all elements of the Air Defense Forces – interceptors, anti-air guns, radar, and early warning troops – took part.[88]

In July 1948 the National Air Defense Forces were converted into a separate service, on an equal footing with the Air Forces, the ground forces, and the Navy.[89] The country was divided for the purposes of air defense into a frontier zone and a zone of the interior. Responsibility for air defense in the frontier zone was given to the commanders of the military districts and to the Navy. Defense of the interior was the responsibility of the National Air Defense Forces.[90] Early-warning radars were first deployed to cover the approaches from the Baltic and Eastern Europe; by 1950 the radar net had been extended to the Pacific Ocean, and to the Caspian and Black Seas. Moscow was the most important target to defend, and the Moscow Air Defense District was the first to receive new equipment. The National Air Defense Forces tried to provide defense in depth, so that enemy planes could be intercepted long before reaching their targets. Fighter aviation was deployed in echelons, so that successive attacks could be made on incoming bombers, and anti-aircraft batteries were similarly deployed at various distances from the installations they were defending.[91]

Defense against strategic air attack was a matter not only for the Air Defense Forces, but for the Air Force as well. In the late 1940s and early 1950s the General Staff decided that "the antiair operations of the National Air Defense Forces would be complemented by strikes of the Long-Range Air Force and other means on the enemy's main airfields."[92] In other words, the Long-Range Air Force, like SAC, acquired a "blunting" mission.

V

There was very little discussion in the Soviet press of the military implications of the atomic bomb. The most substantial analysis was given by Major-General G.I. Pokrovskii, the explosives expert whom Balezin had consulted in 1942 about the feasibility of a uranium bomb. In a pamphlet published in 1946 Pokrovskii wrote that

atomic aviation bombs will be effective in destroying deep underground installations, large dams and hydroelectric plants, heavy naval vessels (especially when concentrated in narrow waters), and the most important transport junctions. On the other hand, against armies deployed over a wide area and dispersed and camouflaged in the appropriate way it will be more effective to use less concentrated forms of energy, i.e. conventional explosives.[93]

Pokrovskii calculated that world production of atomic bombs might reach as many as several hundred a year.[94] He noted, however, that uranium supplies were limited and atomic bombs expensive to produce.[95] These weapons would, therefore, have to be used as effectively as possible, and Pokrovskii's analysis suggested that they would be more effective in a strategic than in a tactical role, against targets in the enemy's rear rather than against his military forces in the field. This was an important conclusion and it guided military policy for the next five years.

In spite of Pokrovskii's pamphlet, the study of strategy in the military academies was devoted largely to assimilating the lessons of World War II, in accordance with Stalin's pronouncements.[96] The 1948 Field Regulations were based on the experience of the war and made no mention of atomic weapons.[97] In 1948 an Instruction was issued providing some information about the atomic bomb and its effects, and a short course on the bomb was organized at the General Staff Academy.[98] A special department of the Ministry of the Armed Forces, known as the 6th Directorate, was set up at about this time to deal with atomic affairs.[99] But information about the atomic bomb was not widely disseminated and did not have any apparent effect on the planning of military operations.[100] The classified journal *Voennaia Mysl'* confined its treatment of atomic warfare to commentaries on US strategy.

Brief though they are, these commentaries provide some insight into the Soviet understanding of the impact of the atomic bomb on military strategy. The commentators criticized the United States for exaggerating the role of strategic bombing in the defeat of Germany, and used the results of the US Strategic Bombing Survey to show that even in 1944 and 1945 strategic bombing had not made a decisive difference to the output of German industry.[101] The American advocates of strategic air power were said to be making a mistake in believing that one arm alone could win a war.[102] This criticism did not amount to a complete rejection of strategic bombing, but Soviet military analysts argued that strategic bombing alone could not lead to victory.

Military commentators played down the significance of the atomic bomb. In June 1949, for example, a Colonel M. Tolchenov argued that the atomic bomb was not as effective as some of its "apologists" claimed, and quoted an American admiral who was critical of the American reliance on air power. To be effective against the multimillion army of a powerful state, wrote Tolchenov, the enemy would need far more atomic bombs than any capitalist state could build.[103] In October 1951 a Colonel P. Fedorov argued, on the basis of data published in the American press, that the number of bombs dropped on Germany during the war was equal in effectiveness to about 330 atomic bombs, and that those bombs had not destroyed Germany's economic potential.[104] Consequently, he implied, the atomic bomb would not give the United States a decisive advantage over the Soviet Union.

In June 1950 Major-General of Tank Forces V. Khlopov argued, in a survey of American military doctrine, that in a war the United States would attack the most important Soviet military-economic and administrative-political centers in order to demoralize the population and the Army, and break their will to resist.[105] The United States would carry out these strategic air strikes in the first phase of the war, while mounting a blockade of the Soviet Union and its allies. The allies of the United States would try to wear down the forces of the Soviet Union and its allies, disorganize their rear, and shatter their morale. In the second phase of the war the United States would deploy its forces to defeat the enemy.

This strategy would be ineffective, Khlopov argued. Strategic bombing had not been all that successful during the war, and Soviet air defenses would be much more effective than Germany's had been. Besides, the ballyhoo about the atomic bomb was meant to frighten and blackmail people who had weak nerves. "There is not the slightest doubt," wrote Khlopov, "that the effect of using the atomic bomb against forces and equipment deployed and camouflaged over large areas at the front and in the rear will be far from that which was caused in the bombing of the Japanese cities with their dense population and their flimsy city buildings."[106] Furthermore, the American image of a future war was not realistic because the Soviet Union would carry out powerful air strikes with the "most modern" weapons to frustrate the movement and concentration of NATO forces. Soviet ground forces would be able to mount powerful large-scale, rapid offensive operations to deny the United States the springboard on which it hoped to concentrate its forces for the ground battles; and they would be able to do this before American reinforcements were transported across the Atlantic. "The war," wrote Khlopov, "will acquire in this case a completely different character from that which the representatives of military-political circles in the USA plan for it."[107]

Khlopov's article provides the clearest available Soviet discussion of the character of a future world war in the late Stalin years. The United States would launch an atomic air offensive, and this would be countered by Soviet air defenses and by strikes against United States air bases. Soviet ground forces would launch a counteroffensive in Europe, and perhaps also in the Middle East, to prevent the United States from using those regions as a springboard for attacking the Soviet Union. This image of a future war matches postwar military policy. The atomic bomb was seen as a strategic weapon which the United States would employ against targets in the rear, and not against forces in the field, where it would be relatively ineffective. The correct response to the atomic bomb therefore was air defense, coupled with strikes against United States air bases. The ground forces had to be ready for counteroffensives to prevent the United States from landing forces on the continent. If the United States were driven from the continent, it would find it much more difficult to mount a successful strategic bombing campaign.

Soviet military analysts naturally took their cue from Stalin, and in particular from his answer to Alexander Werth. The commentaries in *Voennaia Mysl'* might seem like an attempt to put a good face on a desperate situation. But the Soviet conception of a future war was very close to that elaborated in the war plans of the United States. For example, the "Offtackle" Emergency War Plan, which was approved by the Joint Chiefs of Staff in December 1949 and remained operative for two years, also envisaged a war in several phases. In the first three months the Soviet Union "was expected to launch offensives in Western Europe and the Middle East, an aerial bombardment of the British Isles, campaigns with limited objectives in the Far East, air-sea offensives against allied lines of communications, and selective air attacks upon North America."[108] Strategic bombing was not expected to stop these offensives. The Western allies would be too weak to hold Western Europe, and would have to try to secure the United Kingdom and hold on to North Africa and the Cairo–Suez area. The resulting situation would be like that of 1942–3. The Allies would carry out strategic bombing attacks, build up the United Kingdom as a major base, and begin to move outwards from the western Mediterranean and North Africa, with the aim of reentering the European continent.

World War III would be decided by campaigns reminiscent of those of 1944–5.[109]

Soviet and American military planners agreed in 1949–51 that the atomic air offensive would not win the war. This conclusion rested in part on the assumption that the United States did not yet have a sufficient number of bombs to be able to destroy the Soviet capacity to wage war. *Voennaia Mysl'* implied in October 1951 that more than 330 bombs would be needed to achieve this goal; American military planners calculated at the end of 1949, when the United States had about 200 bombs, that the 292 atomic bombs to be delivered under the "Offtackle" plan would be insufficient.[110] The similarity here is striking. Whether this was mere coincidence is unclear. Soviet intelligence prepared estimates of the number of bombs in the United States stockpile.[111] Since these have not been declassified, it is impossible to say how accurate they were, but Soviet leaders may have had a rough picture of the growth of the American stockpile.[112] Khrushchev, for example, refers in his memoirs to "several hundred" atomic bombs possessed by the United States in 1950.[113] Besides, it would have been possible to judge from the size of the Strategic Air Command roughly what number of bombs an atomic air offensive could deliver against the Soviet Union.

Soviet confidence was rooted partly in the belief that an effective military strategy was being devised to counter the atomic bomb. But the belief that the country could survive atomic war was also based on the Soviet Union's immense territory, plentiful manpower, and natural resources, as well as its dispersed industry.[114] In the first four months of the war with Germany millions of Soviet soldiers had been killed or taken prisoner, and the Soviet government had lost control of more than 60 per cent of its coal, iron, steel, and aluminum production facilities.[115] This was far worse than the damage the Harmon Report had calculated the atomic air offensive would inflict on the Soviet Union, yet the Soviet state had survived and gone on to defeat Germany. That victory buttressed Soviet confidence in the ability of the state to survive an atomic war.

The Soviet conception of a future war did not change in Stalin's last years, but an important shift of policy took place in 1949–50. Stalin decided to increase Soviet forces in Germany, to expand the Navy, and to build up the East European armies. These decisions reflected the growing tension in East–West relations. With the establishment of the North Atlantic Treaty Organization in April 1949, the United States was now formally committed to the defense of Western Europe, and the Western Allies began to build up their forces in Western Europe.[116]

Between the summer of 1949 and the spring of 1950 the Soviet Union added more than 80,000 men to GSFG, bringing the 3rd and 4th Guards Mechanized Armies up to more than 70 per cent of full strength.[117] The readiness of these forces was enhanced through increased discipline and a program of combat training that now included large-unit field maneuvers.[118] At the same time the Soviet Union began to reorganize the armed forces of Eastern Europe along Soviet lines, and to incorporate them into the Soviet order of battle. Marshal K.K. Rokossovskii, one of the great Red Army commanders in the war, was made Polish Minister of Defense in October 1949, and several other Soviet officers were appointed to leading positions in the Polish armed forces.[119] Conscription was introduced in Poland in 1949, leading to the creation of armed forces of 400,000 men.[120] In the Soviet zone of Germany the Alert Police (*Bereitschaftspolizei*), which had been set up in 1948, were reorganized in the autumn of 1949. Military training was intensified and recruitment stepped up. In March 1950 the Alert Police, which now numbered 50,000, were issued with Soviet military equipment, including tanks.[121] In 1950 1,000 Soviet advisers were sent to Czechoslovakia, where the armed forces were also reorganized along Soviet lines.[122] In the following year the Czechoslovak People's Army grew from 140,000 to 250,000 regulars and from 40,000 to 150,000 border guards and security troops.[123] At about the same time the Hungarian Army received a batch of new advisers from the Soviet Union.[124] These measures reflect a Soviet decision to strengthen the Soviet military power *vis-à-vis* Western Europe, and to integrate East European forces into the Soviet order of battle. By 1953 East European forces numbered more than one million.[125] The Soviet armed forces doubled in size from 2.874 million men in 1948 to 5.7 million men in 1955.[126] These measures enhanced the Soviet ability to occupy Western Europe in the event of war.

In 1950 Stalin decided to expand the Navy.[127] In He initiated a new shipbuilding program for cruisers, destroyers, escorts, and submarine chasers, as well as submarines.[128] In January 1950 he appointed Malyshev Minister of Shipbuilding, and in the following month he created a new Ministry of the Navy.[129] Stalin had decided that the Soviet Union needed more than a small coastal defense force. The Navy was to threaten NATO carrier groups and bases, and also to interdict supplies and troops coming from the United States to Europe during a war.[130] Khrushchev later referred to the decision to invest in the Navy as one of Stalin's biggest mistakes in military policy because it ignored the vulnerability of surface ships to destruction by nuclear weapons.[131]

Until the early 1950s Soviet military planning proceeded on the assumption that the atomic bomb was a strategic weapon to be used against targets in the rear, and not against forces in the field or at sea. As the earlier discussion of Soviet war plans has shown, ground force operations were planned without any reference to the atomic bomb. The first sign of a change came in 1951, when the commander of the Turkestan Military District, General Ivan Petrov, was ordered to prepare a large exercise to explore how ground force operations should be conducted when nuclear weapons were used.[132] Petrov's staff, who knew nothing about nuclear weapons, drew up a plan. This, however, was rejected by the General Staff and returned to Petrov in Tashkent with comments and suggestions. The Chief of the General Staff, General S.M. Shtemenko, sent a group of six officers to help Petrov prepare the plan. These men knew something about the characteristics of nuclear weapons, and a plan was finally prepared that satisfied the General Staff. The exercise proved helpful to those who were studying the effect of nuclear weapons on combat operations.[133]

This appears to have been the only exercise conducted before Stalin's death to explore the effect of nuclear weapons on combat. It is unclear precisely when in 1951 the exercise was held; perhaps in the autumn, the traditional period for maneuvers. The exercise was probably a response to the first signs of American interest in using nuclear weapons to stop offensive operations by Soviet conventional forces; it may also have been a response to discussions of the possible use of the atomic bomb in the Korean War. It did not signal a fundamental change in the Soviet conception of war. Stalin still did not regard nuclear weapons as decisive. In July 1952 he told the Italian Socialist leader, Petro Nenni, that the United States had the technological power, but not the human power, to wage war; it had the airplanes and the atomic bombs, but where would it find the millions of soldiers needed to wage a third world war? "It is not enough for America to destroy Moscow, just as it is not enough for us to destroy New York. We want armies to occupy Moscow and to occupy New York." From that point of view, Stalin said, the United States was weak. It would have to mobilize ground forces for a third world war in Europe and in Asia, but that was now more difficult than it had been, and would become even more difficult in the future.[134] Stalin took steps to ensure that Soviet forces could attack the United States. In the late 1940s he deployed the 14th Army on the Chukotka peninsula to land in Alaska in the event of war.[135]

Nevertheless, the Turkestan exercise formed part of a pattern of increasing military attention to the implications of atomic weapons for the conduct of war. In 1951 or 1952 an Instruction was issued on the effect of the atomic bomb on combat operations.[136] In 1952 a film of atomic explosions was shown in the military districts, accompanied by a short lecture on the atomic bomb.[137] In 1952 General Petrov moved from Tashkent to the Ministry of Defense in Moscow, and in April 1953 – the month after Stalin's death – he became head of the Chief Directorate of Combat and Physical Training. In this position he had special responsibility for working out new tactical and operational methods for atomic war.[138]

VI

Defense against atomic attack was a central focus of Stalin's military policy. Stalin strove also to develop the means to deliver atomic bombs against enemy targets. He reestablished the Long-Range Air Force in April

1946.[139] The Long-Range Air Force had only aircraft of prewar design; in 1947 it consisted of 1,800 aircraft − 1,000 Il-4s, 32 TB-7s, and the Li-2 transport, which was a Soviet version of the Douglas DC-3.[140] Neither the Il-4 nor the TB-7 had a combat radius of more than 2,000 kilometers. The Long-Range Air Force was therefore poorly equipped to carry out strategic bombing operations. Its chief mission in the late 1940s was to provide support for the ground forces.[141]

The first flight test of the Tu-4 (the Soviet copy of the B-29) took place in July 1947.[142] The new bomber had a range of 5,100 kilometers with a bomb load of 6–8 metric tons, and a flight speed of about 550 km/h at 10,000 meters.[143] It was not quite as good a plane as the B-29. Stalin authorized full production in 1948, even though there were still problems to iron out with the design.[144] More than a thousand Tu-4s were built over the next five or six years and some of these were modified to carry atomic bombs.[145]

The Tu-4 entered service with the Long-Range Air Force in 1948, but Soviet designers soon realized that it was becoming obsolete. Leonid Kerber, who worked in Tupolev's design bureau at the time, has written that in 1948–9 "it became clear to specialists that the era of piston-engined long-range bombers was coming to an end."[146] The maximum speed of these bombers was no greater than 600 km/h, so they were vulnerable to interception by jet fighters with a speed of 800–900 km/h.[147] At the end of 1948 or the beginning of 1949 the Ministry of Aircraft Production instructed Tupolev to begin work on a long-range jet bomber to replace the Tu-4.[148] Tupolev's main problem was to find the right engine. Only when he was satisfied that the Mikulin AM-03 engine would provide 8,000 kilograms of thrust did he proceed with development of the new bomber.[149] The Tu-88 − or Tu-16, as it was later called − was designed to carry nuclear bombs.[150] It had swept wings, a maximum speed of about 1,000 km/h, and could deliver 3 metric tons of bombs a range of 5,760 kilometers; it would thus have been able to carry the atomic bomb tested in 1951.[151] It began flight tests in April 1952 and entered series production in 1953. It made its first public appearance in the 1954 May Day flypast.[152]

In the early 1950s the Long-Range Air Force consisted of about 1,700 aircraft, organized into three air armies, two of which were stationed in the western part of the country, and one in the Far East at Vladivostok.[153] With the deployment of the Tu-4 in some numbers by the early 1950s, the Long-Range Air Force began to give special attention to the conduct of independent operations:[154] "methods were carefully worked out for delivering powerful air strikes against strategic targets in the deep rear, in the first place against strategic nuclear attack systems, military-economic potential, the system of state and military control, and groupings of forces."[155]

By the early 1950s the Long-Range Air Force had three missions. First, it was to damage the enemy's military-economic might and disrupt his war effort: bombers were to strike at defense plants, as well as at political and administrative centers.[156] Second, it was to strike naval bases, ports, railway junctions, and other targets in order to retard an enemy advance, or to disorganize enemy resistance to a Soviet offensive.[157] Third, it was to attack the air bases (and later, the missile sites) from which strikes – especially nuclear strikes – might be launched against the Soviet Union.[158] These missions corresponded roughly to the "disruption," "retardation," and "blunting" missions assigned to the US Strategic Air Command.

Most of the targets for the Long-Range Air Force's missions were located in Europe and Asia. This was obviously so for operations in support of the ground forces, but it was true of the other missions too. Since overseas bases played a crucial role in American war plans in the late 1940s and early 1950s, strikes by the Long-Range Air Force against these bases would help to blunt the United States atomic air offensive and to limit the damage that it could do to the Soviet Union. Given the Soviet concept of operations in the early 1950s, most of the important targets for the equivalent of the "retardation" mission – command-and-control systems, transport junctions – also fell within range of theater bombers. If NATO tried to build up Britain as a major base (as envisaged by the "Offtackle" plan) Britain would then become a particularly important target for bombing attacks.

Notwithstanding the importance of Europe and Asia as theaters of war, it was the United States that threatened the Soviet Union. Stalin was therefore determined to acquire some means of putting the United States under threat of attack. The Tu-4 could not strike the United States on a two-way mission, but it could have flown one-way missions against targets in Maine, or north-west of a line from San Diego to Lake Superior.[159] An inflight refueling system was devised to extend the range of the Tu-4, and a stripped-down version with larger fuel capacity was also developed.[160] But these were stopgap measures. In 1947 or 1948 the Air Force issued a requirement for a bomber with a range of 12–13,000 kilometers. On the basis of the Tu-4, Tupolev developed the Tu-85 bomber, which was powered by four piston engines, since the jet engines of the time did not have sufficient thrust to lift a heavy bomber into the air with all the fuel it needed for an intercontinental flight. The Tu-85 had a range of 8,500 kilometers with 20 metric tons of bombs, and 12,200 kilometers with 5 tons. Its speed was 665 km/h at an altitude of 10,000 meters. The first prototype performed well in its test flights in 1950.[161] It had the desired range, and a decision was taken to put it into production. The Air Force challenged this decision, on the grounds that piston-engined bombers were now vulnerable to jet interceptors. Tupolev finally accepted this argument, and production was cancelled; only two planes were produced.[162]

The decision was now taken to develop a jet-powered intercontinental bomber. During 1950 Stalin talked to several designers, pressing for the development of such a plane. He asked Tupolev to develop an intercontinental turbojet bomber, but Tupolev replied that he could not do so. When Stalin asked why an intercontinental bomber could not be built on the basis of the Tu-16, Tupolev replied that it would be impossible to achieve the required range with two Mikulin AM-03 engines. "Then put four engines on it, who's stopping you?" asked Stalin. Tupolev explained that simply increasing the number of engines would not help: turbojet engines needed too much fuel, and it was hard to see how the fuel requirement could be reduced. In spite of pressure from Stalin, Tupolev refused to undertake this project.[163] Tupolev was already at work on an intercontinental turbopropeller bomber, the Tu-95, which had its first flight test on November 11, 1952.[164] Problems with the engine delayed production, however, and it did not enter service until 1955. The Tu-95, which received the NATO designation "Bear", had a maximum speed of about 800 km/h at 12,500 meters, and a range of 12,550 kilometers with a bomb load of 11 metric tons.[165]

A turbopropeller bomber was not what Stalin wanted, however, for after Tupolev's refusal to build a turbojet bomber, he turned to Miasishchev, whose design bureau had been closed down in 1946. Miasishchev, who had designed long-range bombers as a member of Tupolev's *sharashka* during the war, had already been thinking about a jet-powered strategic bomber. With the help of his students at the Moscow Aviation Institute he had worked on the design of a high-speed, swept-wing strategic bomber with four jet engines.[166] The Air Force was very interested in this project, and at the end of 1950, after intensive discussions involving the Air Force and the Ministry of Aircraft Production, Stalin decided to give Miasishchev a new design bureau. The formal government decision was signed on March 24, 1951.[167]

Miasishchev organized his design bureau at the Fili Aircraft Plant in Moscow.[168] His new bomber, which was known as the 103M or the Mia-4, had its first test flight in January 1953, and in the following year it flew over Red Square in the May Day parade.[169] The 103M, which was called "Bison" by NATO, was powered by four Mikulin AM-03 engines. It had a speed of about 1,000 km/h, but its range was no more than about 9,000 kilometers, far short of the 16,000 kilometers that Stalin wanted.[170] Tupolev had been proved right about the impossibility of designing an intercontinental bomber with the AM-03 engine. The 103M was put into series production nonetheless, while Miasishchev worked to develop an in-flight refueling capability.[171] It entered service with the Long-Range Air Force in 1955, in small numbers.[172]

VII

Stalin did not look only to bombers to deliver nuclear weapons. Missiles received equally high priority. By the end of 1946 the foundations of the rocket program had been laid: a research and production base had been organized with the help of equipment brought from Germany; the first rocket units had been created in the Soviet Army; and a plan had been drawn up for rocket development. The director of the main rocket institute, NII-88, was General L.M. Gaidukov, who had headed the Technical Commission to Germany in 1945; Korolev was in charge of the design division.[173] It was to NII-88 that most of the German rocket scientists and engineers were brought in October 1946, though by May 1948 they had been concentrated in Branch No. 1 of the institute at Gorodomlia island in Kalinin province.[174] Conditions at NII-88 were difficult at first. Korolev did not have the design and research staff he needed. There were only sixty engineers in his division, and most of them had no experience with rockets or aircraft.[175] They spent much of the first year becoming familiar with the V-2 assembly line and the V-2 missiles that had been brought from Germany. The Germans helped them to assemble the missiles and the test and ground support equipment.[176]

The plan for rocket development drawn up at the end of 1946 had as its main aim the development of long-range missiles. In March 1947 Korolev, who had helped to prepare the plan, told his design team that they had been instructed to develop missiles "with a range many times greater" than that of the V-2, which had a maximum range of about 300 kilometers.[177] The Soviet military press had already noted that considerable increases in range were to be expected. In January 1947 Lieutenant-General of Artillery P.N. Kuleshov reported that the Germans had intended to develop a missile that would be able to strike the American continent from Europe.[178] The same concern about range was evident when Korolev asked Vasilii Emel'ianov, one of Vannikov's deputies at the First Chief Directorate, whether it would be possible to use nuclear fuel as a propellant in order to lift a missile out of the earth's gravitational pull.[179]

Korolev told his engineers in March 1947 how he intended to tackle the problem of range.[180] His idea was to reduce the weight of the missile by separating the nose cone from the body of the missile after the engine had shut off. He pointed out that the missile is subject to the greatest temperatures when it is moving at maximum speed, after the engine has stopped; when it is being boosted by the engine, on the other hand, the missile travels through the atmosphere on the active part of its trajectory at relatively slow speeds, and the temperatures are ten times lower than on the final stage of the passive part of the trajectory. If the nose cone were separated from the rest of the missile after the engine had stopped, it would be possible to reduce the missile's overall weight, since the body of the missile could then be designed to withstand only the lower temperatures of the boost phase. It would be possible to reduce the weight of the missile by doing without the stabilizers and the heat shield with which the V-2 was equipped, and to make the fuel tanks an integral part of the missile.[181] Korolev's approach had important advantages over the V-2, which was designed to fly from start to finish in one piece. His conception was not realized in full until 1953, but it nevertheless provided a goal for his engineers to work towards.[182]

This approach to the development of long-range missiles was too slow for Stalin. At a meeting of military leaders and rocket scientists in the Kremlin in April 1947 he demanded the rapid development of missiles that could strike the United States. According to one account, Stalin stressed the need for intercontinental — or, as he called them, transatlantic — missiles:

Do you realize the tremendous strategic importance of machines of this sort? They could be an effective straitjacket for that noisy shopkeeper Harry Truman. We must go ahead with it, comrades. The problem of the creation of transatlantic rockets is of extreme importance to us.[183]

Many specialists were skeptical of the possibility of developing a ballistic missile with a range of more than 1,000 kilometers.[184] NII-88 investigated cruise missiles in conjunction with institutes from the aircraft industry.[185] At RNII a group under M.V. Keldysh studied the theoretical possibility of building a stratospheric plane of the kind proposed by the German rocket scientist Eugen Sänger. This plane would be launched by a rocket to a height of tens or hundreds of kilometers and then skip along the top of the atmosphere until it finally came to land. Keldysh concluded that a rocket-plane with a range on the order of 12,000 kilometers could be built.[186]

In October and November 1947 Korolev supervised the first flight tests at the new missile testing site at Kapustin Iar, near the Caspian Sea. Several V-2s, which had been assembled in Russia from parts brought from Germany, were launched successfully by German crews and by Soviet crews trained in Germany. The Minister of Armament, Dmitrii Ustinov, the Commander of Artillery, Chief Marshal of Artillery N.N. Voronov, and Colonel-General M.I. Nedelin, Chief of Staff of Artillery, attended these tests.[187] The development of long-range missiles was viewed very much as an extension of artillery, and the artillery chiefs took part in the formulation of the early missile development plans, as well as in the flight testing of the missiles. The first missile units were formed on the basis of the Guards mortar units, which had used the "Katiusha" rocket artillery to great effect during the war.[188]

In 1947 Korolev started work on the R-1 and R-2 rockets. The R-1 (known as the *iedinichka*) was a Soviet version of the V-2, with the same design and performance characteristics. Korolev wanted to proceed directly to the development of a rocket with a range of 500–600 kilometers, but he was overruled. The decision was taken to produce the R-1, on the grounds that this would give industry and the military the opportunity to master the problems of producing and firing long-range rockets.[189] Flight tests took place from September to November 1948, and were used to study the methods of making ballistic calculations and of studying flight stability.

Further tests took place in 1949, and in the following year the R-1 entered service with the ground forces.[190]

From 1947 on, Korolev's team also worked on the R-2 rocket (the *dvoika*), which represented a significant advance on the R-1. Its weight was only 350 kilograms greater than that of the R-1, but it could deliver a payload of 1.5 metric tons over a distance of 600 kilometers, twice the range of the V-2 or R-1. The fuel tank was integral to the missile, but the liquid oxygen tank was not, because of uncertainty about how liquid oxygen would behave in flight. A mechanism was developed for separating the nose cone from the missile in flight, and this made it possible to replace some of the steel in the body of the missile with aluminum alloys, since the endurance requirements for the body of the missile were now less stringent. The weight of the engine was reduced, but its thrust was increased. The R-2 had a new guidance system, and proved to be more accurate than the V-2 or R-1. Its first flight tests took place in September and October of 1949, at Kapustin Iar. This missile entered service with the Army in 1951.[191]

The R-1 and R-2 were not equipped with nuclear warheads, and they may not have had much operational value, for they were not very accurate; their main function was to provide the Army's missile units – or "engineering units" as they were known – with the opportunity to become familiar with the new technology.[192] Missiles were, however, regarded as potential delivery vehicles for atomic weapons. In 1947 Stalin summoned Kurchatov to a meeting with Korolev, Voronov, and Nedelin, as well as Marshal of Artillery N.D. Iakovlev, Chief of the Chief Artillery Directorate of the Ministry of Defense.[193] Kurchatov's presence indicates that the possibility of atomic warheads for missiles was discussed. In 1948 Georgii Flerov directed a number of tests with the R-1 to see whether there was a danger that cosmic rays might initiate a chain reaction in a nuclear warhead at very high altitudes.[194]

The missile engines were developed by Valentin Glushko's design bureau, the GDL-OKB. Glushko's first designs were oxygen-alcohol liquid fuel engines, consisting of a single chamber, with turbopump fuel feed systems. The first design was the RD-100, which started its stand tests in May 1948 and was used to power the R-1 missile. This engine was developed on the basis of the "maximum use of proven technical solutions";[195] in other words, it was derived from the engine that powered the V-2. Work on an improved version of the RD-100, the RD-101, began at the same time. The RD-101 used a more concentrated fuel, and was modified in other ways too.[196] It powered the R-2 rocket. This pattern, in which each generation was developed by improving the preceding system, was characteristic of the approach that Korolev took as chairman of the Council of Chief Designers. Because he was under pressure to make rapid progress, he regarded the length of time it would take to build a system as

one of the decisive criteria for evaluating a new design. Technical continuity was an advantage because the existing production and experimental
base could then be exploited as fully as possible.[197]

Korolev began preliminary work on the R-3 missile in 1947.[198] This was
a single-stage ballistic missile, with an engine that would develop about 120
metric tons of thrust, compared with 25 metric tons for the V-2; Glushko's
design bureau had already begun work on this engine in 1947.[199] The new
missile was to have a launch weight of 70 metric tons and to deliver a
warhead weighing three metric tons a distance of 3,000 kilometers. (It
could carry the bomb tested in 1951.) It was to be transportable, like the R-
1 and R-2, and to be launched from a mobile launch platform.[200] The same
requirement, for a missile capable of delivering a 3-metric-ton warhead a
distance of 3,000 kilometers, was given to the German group on
Gorodomlia island in the spring of 1949. The Germans were now working
in isolation from the Soviet designers, who continued, however, to take an
interest in their technical ideas.[201]

In his draft design Korolev wrote that he regarded the R-3 as a stepping-
stone towards the development of an intercontinental missile:

a range equal to 3,000 km can be viewed only as the first stage that makes it
possible to solve certain problems envisaged in the requirement for the R-3.

The costs and the whole complex of technical measures necessary for attaining
the range of 3,000 km are so great that it would be unacceptable to isolate this
work from the prospects for further development.

Therefore for the following stage, capable of solving significantly greater tasks,
a range of the order of 8,000 km was projected with an increased payload.[202]

Work on the R-3 missile was abandoned in 1951, for by that time it had
become clear that it would be possible to proceed directly to the development of an intercontinental missile.

Three projects emerged from Korolev's work on the R-3 missile.[203] The
first was a single-stage missile designed on the basis of Korolev's initial
conception of a separable nose cone and integral fuel tanks. This was the
R-5 (the *piatiorka*), which had a range of 1,200 kilometers. It was first
flight-tested in March and April 1953.[204] The second was a "long-storage
rocket," with storable fuel. The R-1, R-2, and R-5 had to be fueled
immediately before launch. They were therefore not suitable for launch
from a submarine, or for tactical use on the battlefield, where they might
be destroyed if they could not be fired quickly. Work on the "long-
storage" R-11, which had a range of about 160 kilometers, began in 1952;
it was later deployed on submarines, and as a battlefield system.[205]

The third of Korolev's projects in the early 1950s was the intercontinental missile. Soviet missile specialists understood that a multi-stage missile
would probably be necessary for intercontinental ranges because the fuel

requirement made it impossible for a single-stage missile to attain the velocity needed for an intercontinental trajectory.[206] Various proposals for a multi-stage missile had been put forward – by the Russian pioneer Konstantin Tsiolkovskii, for example, and by the German rocket scientist, Hermann Oberth – but none of these seemed practicable. In 1947 M.K. Tikhonravov organized a group in the Research Institute of the Academy of Artillery Sciences to investigate the design of multi-stage, long-range, liquid-fuel rockets. By the end of 1947 he had prepared a preliminary report outlining his ideas for a composite rocket consisting of a "packet" of similar rockets joined together in parallel.[207] When Tikhonravov first presented his ideas in a lecture at his institute in July 1948 he met considerable opposition.[208] He argued that the rockets could be discarded in flight once they were no longer needed.[209] This idea, however, "evoked from many in the hall a stormy reaction of protest."[210]

The packet concept was nevertheless to play an important role in Soviet missile development. Korolev discussed it in December 1951 when he made a report on the prospects for developing ballistic missiles with a range of 5–10,000 kilometers. He concluded that a multi-stage missile could be built, using the packet concept.[211] In 1953 Korolev began work on the draft design of the R-7 (known as the *semiorka*), which employed the packet concept and was to become the world's first intercontinental ballistic missile.[212]

VIII

The atomic bomb occupied a central place in postwar military policy. Stalin gave high priority to defense against atomic attack and to the development of delivery vehicles for Soviet nuclear weapons. He did not, however, regard the bomb as a decisive weapon. He did not believe that it invalidated his thesis that the "permanently operating factors" would determine the outcome of war. Moreover, he saw the bomb as a strategic weapon to be used against targets in the rear, and did not regard it as an effective counterweight to ground forces or sea power. His build-up of the ground forces and his decision to expand the Navy are not signs that Stalin ignored the bomb, but they do indicate that he had a particular conception of the bomb and of its role in military strategy. Stalin did not think that the atomic bomb had ushered in a revolution in military affairs. Soviet military strategy drew heavily on the experience of the war with Germany. There was no radical shift in the Soviet conception of war.

The assumption that the atomic bomb would be used only against targets in the rear began to change in 1951–2, but the assumption that the bomb was not decisive continued to undergird military strategy. Stalin continued to minimize the destruction that an atomic war would bring. In October 1951 he said that an atomic war would destroy "tens and hundreds of thousands of the peaceful population."[213] He held to this view in spite of the rapid growth of the United States' atomic stockpile. By the summer of 1952 the United States had actually 832 bombs – far more than the 330 that *Voennaia Mysl'* had dismissed as insufficient to win a war. But the Soviet Union had now begun to acquire a nuclear force of its own, and it had, moreover, stepped up its efforts to provide defense against an atomic air attack. It was expanding its air defense network, and building up its offensive ground force capability, so as to be able to occupy Western Europe as quickly as possible in the event of war.

Stalin's conception of atomic war was, fortunately, never tested in practice, so no definitive judgment can be made about the military strategy he devised for waging it. There was, however, no guarantee that the destruction of Soviet cities in an atomic air offensive would not bring about the collapse of the Soviet regime; Stalin, as we shall see, appears to have harbored this fear in spite of his bravado. But during these years there was a striking similarity between Soviet and American assessments of a future war. In spite of the growing American arsenal, the US Air Force was pessimistic about its ability to defeat the Soviet Union in a single irreparable blow. In January 1952 General Hoyt Vandenberg, Air Force Chief of Staff, explained that

There are ways and means . . . of lessening the impact of the blow we have been and are now capable of delivering. The Soviet Union has been working to erect guards and take protective measures. As it takes these actions, the magnitude of our task grows. In light of this, I am convinced that the combat effectiveness of my forces from the standpoint of atomic warfare has tended to stand still, notwithstanding the gradual numerical increase in the size of the stockpile.[214]

The great success of Stalin's military policy was that it helped to persuade the United States that the atomic air offensive would not be decisive, and that war with the Soviet Union would be prolonged and difficult.

Stalin wanted to be able to threaten the United States with atomic weapons, just as the United States was able to threaten the Soviet Union. In pursuing this goal, however, he was confronted by the constraints of geography and technology. The Soviet Union did not have bases close to the United States from which to launch air or missile strikes. To pose a threat to the United States, Stalin had to have delivery vehicles with a genuine intercontinental range. This goal was beyond Soviet capabilities in the early postwar years. Most of the weapons systems designers were cautious men, unwilling and perhaps afraid to commit themselves to develop systems they did not believe could be built. Tupolev refused to yield to Stalin's pressure for a turbojet intercontinental bomber; Korolev insisted that one of the main criteria for choosing a design was the possibility of building it quickly. Miasishchev, who was by nature more ambitious in his technical ideas, accepted Stalin's challenge to build an intercontinental turbojet bomber but failed to produce what had been asked of him.[215] Nevertheless, by the time of Stalin's death the Soviet Union had made some progress towards acquiring an intercontinental nuclear capability.

CHAPTER TWELVE

The War of Nerves

I

STALIN BELIEVED AT THE END OF WORLD WAR II that postwar international relations would resemble those of the interwar period. Germany and Japan would rise from defeat. World capitalism would run into crisis, and sharp contradictions would emerge between the leading capitalist states. These contradictions would lead inevitably to a new world war. Since the Soviet Union would be drawn into this war, as it had been drawn into World War II, it had to be prepared. Exactly when or how the war would start was not clear, but it was clear that it would happen, probably after about twenty years, the interval of time between World War I and World War II.

The atomic bomb did not alter Stalin's conception of the postwar world. The bomb was, nevertheless, a factor which had to be taken into account in military strategy and foreign policy. War plans and military theory tell us something about the way in which the Soviet Union hoped to counter the United States atomic air offensive, and use its own nuclear weapons, in the event of war. They do not, however, reveal how Stalin assessed the impact of the atomic bomb on international relations. Stalin said very little about the bomb between 1946 and 1953, and what he did say was intended to create a particular impression. His statements have to be interpreted in the context of Soviet foreign policy.

After Hiroshima Stalin saw no immediate danger of war. Atomic diplomacy seemed to him the greater threat – atomic bombs were "meant to frighten those with weak nerves," he told Alexander Werth in September 1946 – and he took steps to show that the Soviet Union would not be intimidated. This remained the basic Soviet position as the Cold War took shape in 1947. The Soviet leaders regarded the Truman Doctrine and the Marshall plan as attempts to put pressure on the Soviet Union, and to weaken its influence in Europe, but they did not see these developments as the prelude to war.

When the British government decided in February 1947 that it could no longer supply aid to Greece and Turkey, Truman resolved to step into the breach. In his address to Congress on March 12, 1947 he framed the issue in a stark and dramatic way. "Totalitarian regimes imposed upon free peoples, by direct or indirect aggression, undermine the foundations of international peace and hence the security of the United States," he declared. The United States should "support free peoples who are resisting attempted subjugation by armed minorities or by outside pressures."[1]

Six days later, Nikolai Novikov, who had returned from Washington to Moscow to take part in a meeting of the Council of Foreign Ministers, discussed Truman's speech with Molotov. The speech showed, said Novikov, that the United States would support "reactionary regimes" in those countries where they existed, and would try to undermine the progressive regimes of Eastern Europe. Molotov replied with an ironical smile, Novikov writes in his memoirs. "The President is trying to intimidate us," Molotov said, "to turn us at a stroke into obedient little boys. But we don't give a damn. At the meeting of the Council [of Foreign Ministers] we will firmly pursue our principled line."[2]

Germany was the main topic at the Moscow meeting of the Council of Foreign Ministers, which lasted for six weeks in March and April 1947. No progress was made towards a peace settlement. General George Marshall, who had replaced Byrnes as Secretary of State in January, was worried by this situation, and alarmed by the attitude of Stalin, whom he met on April 15. Stalin described the talks on Germany so far as "only the first skirmishes and brushes of reconnaissance forces on this question." "It was necessary to be patient and not to become depressed," he added.[3] Marshall took this to mean that Stalin believed that Soviet interests were best served by political stalemate while the economic situation in Western Europe worsened. On his return to Washington Marshall asked George Kennan to work out a plan of action for Europe.[4]

Marshall first publicly mentioned the idea of large-scale economic assistance for Europe on June 5, 1947. There was as yet no detailed plan, for American aid was to be given in response to coordinated initiatives by the European governments. The Soviet Union was not excluded from participation, though neither Marshall nor Kennan believed that it would cooperate on terms acceptable to the United States.[5] Novikov cabled Moscow on June 9 that Marshall's proposal was a "perfectly clear outline for a West European bloc directed against us."[6] In spite of such suspicions, Molotov went to Paris at the end of June to discuss the plan with the British and French foreign ministers.[7] The Soviet Union was willing, he said, to cooperate in establishing what aid Europe needed and how that aid might be obtained from the United States.[8] It soon appeared, however, that Britain and France had no intention of agreeing to a plan that the Soviet Union would accept.[9] Molotov accused the British and the French of

seeking to create a new organization that would infringe upon the sover-
eignty of the European states: "it is now proposed to make the possibility
of any country's obtaining American credits dependent on its obedience to
the above-mentioned organization and its 'Steering Committee'."[10] He
then withdrew from the conference.[11]

Molotov recalled towards the end of his life that he had come to his
senses. "At first we in the Foreign Ministry wanted to propose to all the
socialist countries to take part," he said,

but we quickly surmised that that would be wrong. They were sucking us into
their company, but in a subordinate role. We would have been dependent on
them, but would clearly have got nothing, while we would have undoubtedly
been dependent. And even more so the Czechs, Poles, they were in a difficult
position. . . .[12]

Fear that the countries of Eastern Europe would come under American
hegemony lay behind Moscow's rejection of the Marshall Plan. Moscow
now instructed the governments of Eastern Europe to reject the plan as
well.[13]

In August 1947, after these developments, Novikov wrote a memorandum at Molotov's request.[14] The Marshall Plan, he argued, was formulated as a way of putting the Truman Doctrine into practice. It envisaged
the formation of an American–West European bloc directed against the
Soviet Union and the countries of Eastern Europe. After discussing the
ways in which the United States planned to attain this goal, Novikov
concluded that

the adoption of all these measures would make it possible to create a strategic ring
around the USSR, passing in the west through West Germany and the West
European countries, in the north through a network of bases on the northern
islands of the Atlantic Ocean, and also in Canada and Alaska, in the east through
Japan and China, and in the south through the countries of the Middle East and
the Mediterranean.

Molotov described this memorandum as a "useful document."[15]

The strategic situation had taken a turn for the worse. The United States
now had the initiative in Europe. Stalin decided to create a new organiza-
tion to coordinate the activities of the European communist parties.[16]
The founding meeting of the Communist Information Bureau (the
Cominform) was held in Szklarska Poręba, a spa near Wrocław, from
September 22 to 29, 1947. Delegates came from all the countries of Eastern
Europe apart from Albania, as well as from France and Italy, which had the
two largest communist parties in Western Europe.[17]

Zhdanov's report on the international situation was one of the key
postwar statements of Soviet foreign policy. He echoed the Truman
Doctrine by saying that there were now two diametrically opposed camps

in world politics: the imperialist and anti-democratic camp, which was preparing a "new imperialist war," and the anti-imperialist camp, which was struggling "against the threat of new wars and imperialist expansion."[18] American imperialism was searching for markets for its goods and capital, and using economic aid to extort concessions from other countries and to subjugate them; it was building up its military power, stockpiling atomic bombs, and building bases around the world.

The Soviet Union, the new democracies of Eastern Europe, and the working class in the capitalist countries stood in the way of American expansion, Zhdanov argued. Wicked and unbalanced politicians, like Churchill, were proposing a preventive war against the Soviet Union, and calling for the use of the "temporary American monopoly on atomic weapons" against Soviet people.[19] But the overwhelming majority of Americans did not want war and the sacrifices it would entail. Monopoly capital was trying to overcome the opposition to expansionism, but the warmongers knew that, because the Soviet Union had won immense popularity during the war, long ideological preparation would be needed before they could send their soldiers to fight the Soviet Union.

The Truman Doctrine and the Marshall Plan, Zhdanov asserted, were part of the policy of expansion aimed at bringing West European states under American control and at "restoring the power of imperialism in the countries of the new democracy and forcing them to reject close economic and political collaboration with the Soviet Union."[20] The Truman Doctrine was an attempt to intimidate the countries of Eastern and south-eastern Europe; the Marshall Plan aimed to lure them into a trap and shackle them with "assistance." Communists had to close ranks, and to lead all anti-Fascist freedom-loving forces in the struggle against the American plans for enslaving Europe.

Although he pointed to imperialist preparations for war, Zhdanov insisted that there was a huge distance between the desire to unleash a new world war and the possibility of doing so. "The peoples of the world do not want war," he asserted.[21] Imperialist agents were raising a ballyhoo about the danger of war in order to frighten those who were unstable or had weak nerves, and to obtain concessions by means of blackmail. The main danger for the working class was in underestimating its own strength and exaggerating the strength of the enemy. The "Munich policy" of appeasement had encouraged Hitler's aggression, and concessions to the American imperialists would have a similar effect.

Zhdanov's report, which had been approved by Stalin, struck a more militant tone than previous Soviet statements.[22] There were limits, however, to the degree of confrontation that Stalin sought. His aim was to put pressure on West European governments, not to bring the class war in individual countries to the point of revolution.[23] A wave of strikes swept France and Italy in October and November 1947, but the communist parties, which had recently been pushed out of coalition governments in those countries, had no success in turning these strikes against the Marshall Plan. In December Stalin, apparently worried that disorder might lead to civil war, indicated to the French and Italian communist leaders that they should restrain their supporters, and draw back from confrontation.[24]

In organizing the Cominform, Stalin rejected the idea – which he had tolerated after the war – that communist parties could act independently, each pursuing its own path to socialism.[25] He now took steps to consolidate the Soviet position in Eastern Europe by replacing coalition governments, whether genuine or bogus, with a communist monopoly of power. The most dramatic instance of this took place in Prague in February 1948 when the communists, who already formed part of the government, seized complete control.[26]

The same impulse to exercise control brought about the rift with Yugoslavia. The Yugoslav communists, who had come to power by their own efforts, had a self-assurance that other East European leaders lacked.[27] When Stalin learned in January 1948 that Yugoslavia had promised to send a division to Albania to guard the border with Greece, he sent a message to Belgrade warning that the "Anglo-Saxons" might use this as a pretext for military intervention to "defend" Albania's independence. A further message followed, with a more threatening tone: it was "abnormal" that Yugoslavia should take such a decision without consulting the Soviet Union or even informing it.[28]

Stalin summoned a Yugoslav delegation to Moscow. He made clear his opposition to insurrectionism, and declared that the revolution in Greece should be folded up. He also made it clear that Moscow was determined to control the foreign policies of its allies. At Soviet insistence, Molotov and Edvard Kardelj, the Yugoslav Foreign Minister, signed an agreement on consultation in foreign policy.[29] This did not settle the rift, however. At Szklarska Poręba the Yugoslavs had supported Moscow's view that communist parties had to act in concert. Now Yugoslavia found itself isolated in asserting the very principle of party autonomy that it had helped to undermine. On June 28, 1948 the Cominform expelled Yugoslavia and called on Yugoslav communists to overthrow Tito's regime. Stalin mistakenly believed that "healthy" (pro-Soviet) elements would replace Tito with someone more pliable.[30]

By the end of 1947 the Cold War had begun in earnest. In Moscow's view, however, there was no immediate danger of war. Zhdanov had ruled out this danger in his report to the Cominform meeting. The Central Committee did not consider war to be imminent, Malenkov told Pietro Nenni on November 25, 1947. The United States was not in a position to start a war, he said, but was conducting a cold war, a war of nerves, with the aim of blackmail. The Soviet Union would not be intimidated, and would persist with its policy. All the forces of peace had to be mobilized.

When the United States decided to start a war, said Malenkov, it would not declare it first, but would foment it in Europe by using Greece, De Gaulle if he came to power in France, De Gasperi in Italy, or Franco in Spain.[31]

Although postwar demobilization came to an end in 1947, Soviet military policy did not betray any fear that war was imminent. In December 1947 Viacheslav Malyshev was appointed deputy chairman of the Council of Ministers with special responsibility for military research, development, and production.[32] This suggests that some increase in military production and research and development was now planned, but there is no evidence of a build-up of forces in 1947 or 1948.[33] The Soviet leaders continued to regard the atomic bomb, in the short term at least, as a political rather than a military threat.

On November 6, 1947, in a speech to mark the thirtieth anniversary of the October Revolution, Molotov claimed that

a sort of new religion has become widespread among expansionist circles in the USA: having no faith in their own internal forces, they put their faith in the secret of the atomic bomb, *although this secret has long ceased to be a secret.*[34] [Emphasis added]

The timing of this remark was not dictated by any particular development in the atomic project; it was tied, rather, to the international situation following the formation of the Cominform. It was a move in the war of nerves, an attempt once again to disabuse the United States of the idea that it could gain political advantage from the bomb.

The Truman administration did not take Molotov's statement seriously and felt secure in its monopoly.[35] Moscow, however, seems to have believed that the statement carried some credibility. The secret bulletin of the Central Committee's information bureau reported that it had been treated as a sensation by the Western press. "The majority of reactionary politicians and journalists," it continued,

realizing that the broad masses of the people will certainly believe Comrade Molotov's statement, and that the imperialist camp has lost thereby one of its most powerful means for blackmailing people, try to prove that the Soviet Union, knowing the secret of the atomic bomb, has not yet mastered the "technology of production" in this area.[36]

II

The Berlin blockade of June 1948 was the first nuclear crisis of the Cold War. With the growing division of Europe the German question had moved increasingly to center stage. The Council of Foreign Ministers met in London in November–December 1947 to make another attempt to devise a German settlement. Once again Molotov pressed for reparations and for four-power control of the Ruhr, and argued for an all-German government that could negotiate a peace agreement with the Allies. Against the background of widespread strikes in Western Europe, however, Soviet proposals were regarded with suspicion by the United States and Britain, which feared that a unified Germany would fall prey to Soviet subversion.[37] The London meeting failed to produce agreement, and this failure reinforced the growing Western belief that a separate West German state should be created. In February 1948 delegates from the United States, Britain, and France, and later from the Benelux countries as well, met in London to discuss the situation in Germany. On March 6 they announced preliminary agreement on the formation of a West German government. Further discussions resulted on June 1 in the London Program on procedures and a timetable.[38] This effectively closed the door to a four-power settlement of the German problem.

The Soviet Union protested against these moves, arguing that they contravened the Potsdam agreement on the formation of a unified, democratic German state.[39] On March 20, 1948 Marshal V.D. Sokolovskii, Commander-in-Chief of the Group of Soviet Occupation Forces in Germany and the Soviet representative on the Allied Control Council, walked out of the council, declaring that the actions of the Western powers made it impossible for the council to continue its work.[40] On June 18 the Western powers informed the Soviet Union that a new currency – the Deutsche Mark – was to replace the Reichsmark in the western zones. Sokolovskii told the Western commanders that this was illegal and would complete the division of Germany. In retaliation, the Soviet Union introduced a new currency into all sectors of Berlin, whereupon the Western powers, on June 23, extended their currency reform to the western sectors of Berlin. On the following day the Soviet Union, claiming unspecified "technical difficulties," imposed a blockade of rail, road, and water routes to Berlin.[41]

Stalin was engaged in what George Kennan called a "kind of squeeze play."[42] He wanted to force the Western powers either to give up their moves towards a separate West German state, or to relinquish West Berlin. At dinner in his *dacha* on January 10, 1948, and again a month later in a meeting with Yugoslav and Bulgarian communist leaders, Stalin had "stressed that Germany would remain divided: 'The West will make Western Germany their own, and we shall turn Eastern Germany into our own state.'"[43] His main aim was to prevent the establishment of a West German state, but he may have regarded control over West Berlin as a more realistic goal by the summer of 1948. Khrushchev later commented that "when access to West Berlin was cut off the purpose was more or less clear. We wanted to exert pressure on the West to create a unified Berlin in a GDR [German Democratic Republic] with closed borders."[44]

Soviet policy had another, more general, purpose. Soviet leaders regarded relations with the West as a war of nerves, and were determined to show that they would not be intimidated. That was a recurrent theme in Soviet speeches, and it had been the central message of Zhdanov's report at the Cominform meeting. The attitude is nicely illustrated by a remark of Zhdanov's to Jacques Duclos, one of the French delegates at the Cominform meeting. After the Yugoslavs had criticized French communist policy at the end of the war, Zhdanov said: "I think that Duclos agrees that we are not trying to say that an insurrection was called for." But, he asked, "is it useful to disclose your own cards to the enemy? To say: I am unarmed. Then the enemy will say to you: good, I will beat you. The law of the class struggle is such that only the law of force counts."[45] Khrushchev suggested the same kind of attitude when he described the blockade in his memoirs as "prodding the capitalist world with the tip of a bayonet."[46] If the Western powers were able to set up a West German state unopposed, they would see the Soviet Union as a weak opponent and be encouraged to pursue a more active policy. It was important for the Soviet Union to take a stand.[47]

The blockade confronted the Western powers with a serious dilemma: if they acquiesced in it, they would suffer the political setback of giving up West Berlin. If they made concessions on Germany, that would disrupt their plans for postwar Europe. If they tried to remove the blockade by force, they would risk war. This does not mean that Stalin, in imposing the blockade, was willing to start a war. Alexander George and Richard Smoke have argued plausibly that the Berlin blockade was a "classical example of a low-risk, potentially high-gain strategy," because it could be controlled and reversed. "Soviet leaders were not committed to persisting in the blockade," they have written. "They could at any time find a solution to the 'technical difficulties' and open up ground access to West Berlin. Nor need the Soviets persist in the blockade if the Western powers threatened to overreact to it in ways that raised the danger of war."[48]

Andrei Gromyko, who was Deputy Foreign Minister at the time, later commented that "I believe that Stalin – of course nobody actually asked him directly – embarked on that affair in the certain knowledge that the conflict would not lead to nuclear war. He reckoned that the American administration was not run by frivolous people who would start a nuclear war over such a situation."[49] Stalin wanted to apply pressure to achieve his goals, but he did not want to precipitate war. Although his policy caused alarm in the West – as it was intended to do – it is clear in retrospect that he behaved cautiously, and in the end he was willing to forgo his goals in the interests of avoiding war.[50]

The Western powers organized an airlift of supplies to the western sectors of Berlin. Conceived at first as a temporary expedient, the airlift proved unexpectedly successful, and gradually the Western governments realized that they would be able to support their position in the city without resorting to arms. Now Stalin faced a choice between letting the airlift go ahead, thus forfeiting his political goals, and stopping the airlift, thereby increasing the risk of war. The Soviet Union had superior conventional forces in and around Berlin, but Stalin did not send up fighters to shoot down the Western transport aircraft, or to harass them; nor did he send up barrage balloons in the air lanes, or jam the Western air traffic control systems – steps he could have taken as part of a war of nerves.[51]

How was Stalin's calculation of risk affected by the atomic bomb? He certainly recognized that it was a powerful weapon. In January 1948 he had waxed enthusiastic about the bomb: "That is a powerful thing, pow-er-ful!" His expression as he said this, according to Milovan Djilas, was "full of admiration."[52] Yet the American atomic monopoly did not deter him from imposing the blockade in the first place. On July 15, however, the nuclear element in the crisis was boosted when Truman decided to deploy two bomber wings – sixty B-29s – to Britain. The bombers were officially described as going on a routine training exercise, but press reports, inspired by the administration, said that they were capable of carrying atomic bombs, and hinted that they did so.[53] The bombers were not in fact nuclear-capable, and no explicit threat was made against the Soviet Union; nor was any hint dropped that a nuclear attack might be made if the Soviet Union did not lift the blockade.[54] The transfer of the bombers nevertheless served as a reminder that the United States had the atomic bomb and the Soviet Union did not, and signified that the United States regarded the bomb as an appropriate instrument of policy. "Not coercion but deterrence was the vaguely conceived objective of the move: deterring the Russians from escalating in response to the airlift," writes Avi Shlaim in his careful study of the crisis.[55]

Stalin did not to try to stop the airlift. Whether his caution was induced by the implied threat of nuclear war is impossible to say with certainty. The Soviet press made no mention of the B-29s. Soviet leaders, however, did not need to be reminded about the American atomic monopoly. Only the month before, the Soviet embassy in Washington had made a formal protest about an article in *Newsweek* in which General George C. Kenney, Commander-in-Chief of Strategic Air Command, had written of plans to attack Soviet cities with atomic bombs.[56] The transfer of the B-29s may not in itself have been decisive;[57] it may have been the general fear of war with the United States that made Stalin cautious. But the bomb was, in Soviet eyes, a central element in American military power, and the element most capable of inflicting damage on the Soviet Union.

On the evening of August 2 Stalin, wearing his uniform as Generalissimo, received the American, British, and French ambassadors in the Kremlin.[58] He took an affable tone, perhaps because he still believed that the blockade would be effective. The "restrictive measures," he explained, were designed to prevent the economy in the Soviet zone of occupation from being upset by the introduction of the currency reform into the western sectors of Berlin. Because the Western powers were breaking Germany into two states, Berlin was no longer the capital of Germany. The Western powers had to realize that they had lost their legal right to be in Berlin, but this did not mean, he said, that the Soviet Union wanted to force their troops out of the city. The blockade could be lifted if two conditions were met: if the currency in the western sectors of Berlin were replaced by the currency used in the Soviet zone; and if an assurance were given that the London Program for the creation of a West German state would not be implemented until the representatives of the four countries had met and agreed on all the basic questions affecting Germany.[59]

This meeting did not break the stalemate; nor did a further meeting between Stalin and the ambassadors. Disagreement continued over the currency and the London Program. Talks dragged on. On September 4 Sokolovskii informed the other military governors that the Soviet Union would start air maneuvers in two days' time, and that these would extend into the air corridors and over Berlin. Nothing came of this threat to interfere with the airlift, but Sokolovskii's statement suggests that thought was given in Moscow to escalating the crisis.[60] Moscow tried to create an atmosphere of pressure and tension in Berlin, but it did not interfere directly with the airlift.

In January 1949 Stalin hinted in an interview that the Soviet position had shifted.[61] Informal soundings by the Truman administration led to negotiations, which resulted in a four-power agreement, on May 5, 1949, to end the blockade. Stalin had not prevented the creation of a separate West German state: the Federal Republic of Germany was established on September 1, 1949. Nor had he succeeded in dislodging the Western powers from Berlin. He did not, however, abandon the Soviet claim that the Western powers no longer had a legal right to be in Berlin; that issue remained, to be revived at a later time.

Stalin showed in the Berlin crisis that he was willing to put pressure on the West and to raise the level of tension. He showed also that he was aware that pressure and tension should not exceed certain limits. Molotov later emphasized the importance of limits in Stalin's policy:

Well, what does the "Cold War" mean? Aggravated relations. . . . They, of course, became hardened against us, and we had to secure what had been conquered. To make our own socialist Germany out of part of Germany, while Czechoslovakia, Poland, Hungary, Yugoslavia – they were in a fluid state, we had to introduce order everywhere. To squeeze the capitalist orders. That's the Cold War. Of course you have to know the limits. I think that in that respect Stalin kept very sharply within the limits.[62]

But if Stalin knew the limits to which he could go without provoking war, his pressure on the West helped to solidify the division of Europe into two blocs. Tension was an essential element in the "war of nerves," which was how Soviet leaders characterized their relationship with the West. But tension enhanced the cohesion of the West. With the formation of NATO in April 1949, the United States was committed to a military as well as an economic presence in Europe. By this time the Soviet Union had imposed tight control on the countries of Eastern Europe, with the important exception of Yugoslavia. The division of the continent had now congealed.

The Berlin blockade was the first nuclear crisis, and it gave new impetus to the nuclear competition between the United States and the Soviet Union. The atomic bomb came to occupy a central role in United States military strategy, while the deployment of B-29s to Britain signified an American nuclear commitment to the defense of Western Europe.[63] For the Soviet Union the Berlin blockade was not a nuclear crisis to the same degree. There were, however, several signs in 1948 that the American atomic threat was being taken more seriously. The National Air Defense Forces were established as a separate service, and the first Instruction on the atomic bomb was issued by the Ministry of the Armed Forces.[64] It is not clear whether these were a response to the Berlin crisis or – more probably – to the general trend of American military policy. But the crisis, at the very least, made these steps more urgent by its effect on United States policy.[65]

III

Stalin's communications with the Chinese communists in the spring and summer of 1949 throw interesting light on his attitude to nuclear weapons. In March or April Ivan Kovalev, Stalin's personal emissary to Mao Zedong, received information from a Chinese communist agent about "supersecret" American plans that had been found in Chiang Kai-shek's headquarters. These plans purported to describe the "Asian option" for a third world war, according to which the United States was to conclude a military alliance with Japan and Nationalist China. The United States would then land a 3-million-man army in China, the Japanese would revive the Imperial Army, and the Kuomintang would mobilize millions of Chinese soldiers. This general offensive was to be preceded by a sudden nuclear strike against more than one hundred targets in Manchuria, the Soviet Maritime Province, and Siberia. Once the Chinese People's Liberation Army (PLA) and the Soviet forces in the Far East had been defeated, the United States would organize an offensive in the general direction of the Urals.[66]

Kovalev was skeptical about this information – and it appears that the plans were a fabrication – but he passed the document on to Stalin nonetheless. When he dispatched further information of a similar kind to Moscow, "Comrade Filippov" (as Stalin was known in these communications) sent an answer, some time after late May 1949:

War is not advantageous to the imperialists. Their crisis has begun, they are not ready to fight. They frighten [us] with the atomic bomb, but we are not afraid of it.

The material conditions for an attack, for unleashing war, do not exist.

The way matters stand now, America is less ready to attack than the USSR to repulse an attack. That is how matters stand if one analyses them from the point of view of normal people – objective people.

But in history there are abnormal people. The US Secretary of Defense Forrestal [who committed suicide on May 22, 1949] suffered from hallucinations.

We are ready to repulse an attack.[67]

Stalin gave a similar assessment when a high-level delegation of Chinese communists visited Moscow in July and August 1949. He told Liu Shaoqi, the Politburo member who headed the delegation, that "the Soviet Union is now strong enough not to be frightened by the nuclear blackmail of the USA."[68] "A third world war was improbable," he said, according to the recollections of the Chinese interpreter,

if only because no one had the strength to start it. The revolutionary forces were growing, the peoples were more powerful than before the war. If the imperialists wanted to start a world war, preparations for it would take at least twenty years. If the peoples did not want a war, there would be no war. How long the peace would last depended on how hard we worked for it and how events would develop. We wanted to devote ourselves to building. Peace was most important. The thing to do was to safeguard peace for as long as possible. But who could be sure no madmen appeared on the scene?[69]

Stalin presented a confident face to the Chinese communists, whom he was eager to impress with Soviet strength; so eager indeed that Liu Shaoqi was shown a film that was said to be of a Soviet nuclear test. This was weeks before the first Soviet atomic bomb test took place.[70] Stalin told Liu that the Soviet Union would soon have weapons that were even more formidable.[71]

Stalin gave two main reasons for his confidence that war was not imminent. The first was that the United States was unlikely to attack because the Soviet Union was ready to repulse an attack. This judgment corresponded with Soviet and American assessments of the military balance in the summer of 1949.[72] The second reason was that people were not willing to fight another war, and that imperialist governments would find it difficult to make them fight.[73] Popular attitudes in the West had assumed an important place in Stalin's foreign policy. The peace movement had started in France in 1948, and the first World Congress of "Fighters for Peace" was held in Paris in April 1949.[74] The peace movement was a means for fostering popular opposition to Western policies: it called for a ban on nuclear weapons, and opposed NATO and German rearmament. It was closely controlled by the communist movement, and its positions were carefully coordinated with Soviet foreign policy.[75]

Stalin, for his part, was anxious to avoid war with the United States. "Stalin assessed the correlation of forces in the world soberly enough," Kovalev said, "and strove to avoid any complications that might lead to a new world war."[76] The Chinese communists had asked the Soviet Union to provide air and naval support for an attack on Taiwan. When Liu arrived in Moscow Stalin explained to him that the Soviet Union was not ready for war. He emphasized that the Soviet economy had suffered colossal damage during World War II, and that the country had been laid waste from its western borders to the Volga. Soviet military support for an attack on Taiwan, he said, would mean a collision with the American Air Force and Navy, and would create a pretext for unleashing a new world war. "If we, as leaders, do this," said Stalin, "the Russian people will not understand us. More than that. It could dismiss us. For underestimating its wartime and postwar misfortunes and efforts. For thoughtlessness . . ."[77]

"Of course," Kovalev comments, "these arguments of Stalin's about the Russian people smack of the demagogy so characteristic of this leader."[78] Certainly there was a demagogic element in Stalin's remark that the Russian people "could dismiss us." But this remark is particularly interesting because it recalls the toast Stalin made to the Russian people in May 1945, when he referred to the desperate situation in 1941–2 and the retreat of the Red Army. "Another people," he said, "could have said to the government: you have not justified our expectations, go away, and we will install another government which will conclude peace with Germany and guarantee us a quiet life."[79] That toast was demagogic too, but it was the closest Stalin ever came to acknowledging how close the Soviet regime was to collapse in 1941–2. The fear that the state would collapse in the event of war remained with Stalin, according to Khrushchev.[80] Stalin's comment that the Russian people "could dismiss us" provides an echo of that fear, a recognition that war might mean the end of the Soviet regime. It stands in sharp contrast to the confidence he tried to project to the Chinese leaders and to the world at large.

IV

The first Soviet atomic bomb test took place on August 29, 1949, but the world learned of it only three and a half weeks later, from the United States. On September 23 President Truman announced that the United States had "evidence that within recent weeks an atomic explosion occurred in the U.S.S.R."[81] Two days later the Soviet news agency Tass issued a statement noting that the Western press had published "numerous utterances which spread alarm among broad social circles." In this connection, it continued,

TASS is empowered to announce the following: In the Soviet Union, as is known, building work on a large scale is in progress – the building of hydroelectric stations, mines, canals, roads, which evoke the necessity of large-scale blasting work with the use of the latest technical means. Insofar as this blasting work has taken place pretty frequently in various parts of the country, it is possible this might draw attention beyond the confines of the Soviet Union.

As for the production of atomic energy, TASS considers it necessary to recall that already on November 6, 1947, the Soviet Minister of Foreign Affairs, V.M. Molotov, made a statement concerning the secret of the atom bomb, when he declared that this secret was already long ago nonexistent. This statement signified the Soviet Union already had discovered the secret of the atomic weapon and that it had this weapon at its disposal.

Scientific circles of the United States of America took this statement by V.M. Molotov for bluff, considering that the Russians could not possess the atomic weapon earlier than the year 1952. They were mistaken, however, since the Soviet Union possessed the secret of the atomic weapon in 1947. As for the alarm that is being spread on this account by certain foreign circles, there is not the slightest ground for it.

Tass went on to affirm that the Soviet government had not changed its "position in favor of the absolute prohibition of the use of the atomic weapon."[82]

This grotesque statement was prepared without the participation of the nuclear scientists, who thought it appalling.[83] It did not even acknowledge that there had been a test, and sought to convey the impression that the Soviet Union had possessed the atomic bomb since 1947. This deception was part of a pattern. Molotov's statement of November 6, 1947 had implied, without actually saying so, that the Soviet Union had the atomic bomb. The Bulgarian party leader, Georgii Dimitrov, had told Milovan Djilas in Moscow in February 1948 that "the Russians already had the atom bomb, and an even better one than the Americans', that is, the one exploded over Hiroshima."[84] The film of an atomic test shown to Liu Shaoqi was also intended to deceive. The Soviet Union was trying to create a false impression of its nuclear progress, and evidently intended to keep its first test secret. The Soviet Union made no announcement for four weeks, and then only in response to Truman's disclosure.[85]

The Soviet Union had been making a determined effort to end the American atomic monopoly: surely it would have wanted the world to know that it had succeeded? Why should it keep the test secret? There were two plausible motives. The first was fear that the United States would redouble its efforts to stay ahead in the arms race. Kurchatov had given this as a reason for secrecy when he told Anatolii Aleksandrov some years earlier that the only way to defend our country is to make up for lost time and create an atomic industry on a sufficient scale without attracting the attention of the outside world. And if we trumpet it everywhere, the USA will so speed up its work that we will not be able to catch up with it.[86]

This remained a powerful reason for secrecy in 1949. If the United States was complacent about Soviet progress, so much the better. Why frighten the Americans into increasing their efforts, especially when the Soviet Union still lagged behind? The Soviet test did indeed give new impetus to the American nuclear weapons program. In October 1949 Truman approved an expansion of atomic bomb production capacity.[87] More importantly, he decided to authorize the urgent development of the hydrogen bomb and on January 31, 1950 made this decision public.

The second motive was fear that the test might goad the United States into a more aggressive policy before the Soviet Union had acquired an effective atomic capability. The test would show that the Soviet Union was catching up more quickly than the United States expected, but also that it would be some time before the Soviet Union had a stockpile of atomic bombs. The United States might be tempted to adopt a more active policy. There was already a current of opinion in the United States and Britain in favor of preventive war. Churchill had called for "bringing matters to a head" before the American atomic monopoly was ended.[88] The Tass statement, with its assertion that the Soviet Union had had the atomic bomb in 1947 – an assertion that was repeated by political leaders in the following months – appears to reflect this fear. The Soviet Union made no attempt to reassure the United States by pointing out that it still lagged behind. On the contrary, it made misleading claims in order to appear more powerful, and more threatening, than it really was. Soviet leaders now claimed that the United States would no longer be able to escape the consequences of war, implying that the Soviet Union could now deliver nuclear strikes against the United States.[89] This suggests that it was the fear of a more aggressive American policy, rather than the danger of speeding up United States nuclear weapons development, that was the dominant reason for secrecy about the Soviet test.

Soviet fears on this score were not misplaced. On January 31, 1950 Truman directed the Secretaries of Defense and of State to reexamine national security policy "in the light of the probable fission bomb capability and possible thermonuclear bomb capability of the Soviet Union."[90] NSC 68, as the resulting report was known, was given to the President on April 7.[91] It presented an alarming picture. The Soviet Union was "widening the gap between its preparedness for war and the unpreparedness of the free world."[92] The Soviet possession of nuclear weapons had greatly intensified the Soviet threat to the United States, NSC 68 concluded. The Soviet nuclear threat is more immediate than had previously been estimated. In particular, the United States now faces the contingency that within the next four or five years the Soviet Union will possess the military capability of delivering a surprise atomic attack of such weight that the United States must have substantially increased general air, ground, and sea strength, atomic capabilities, and air and civilian defenses to deter war and to provide reasonable assurance, in the event of war, that it could survive the initial blow and go on to the eventual attainment of its objectives.[93]

NSC 68 did not have an immediate effect on United States policy, since its call for a sharp increase in the defense budget was unpopular in the government,[94] and the administration did not act upon it before the Korean War broke out on June 25, 1950. But the report did reflect a sense of deep foreboding in Washington now that the Soviet Union had acquired the atomic bomb.

Once the test had been made public, the Soviet press sounded a triumphant note. *Bol'shevik* published an article whose point was clearly conveyed by its title: "The Collapse of the Diplomacy of Atomic Blackmail." The Anglo-American imperialists, it argued, had based their foreign policy and their military strategy on the American atomic monopoly; now that the monopoly was ended, imperialist policy was in ruins.[95]

The same optimistic note was struck by Politburo member Georgii Malenkov in a speech given on November 6, 1949 to celebrate the 32nd anniversary of the October Revolution. The "adventuristic nature" of atomic diplomacy, one of the key elements in American policy, had now been revealed. Atomic diplomacy had been based on the "utterly false initial assumption" that the United States enjoyed a monopoly on the atomic bomb. But the Soviet government, said Malenkov, had "made no secret of the fact that it possessed atomic weapons."[96] The peace movement was growing in strength, and now had more than 600 million organized supporters. The horror and the sacrifices of the recent war were still fresh in people's minds, and this was why they were actively prepared to defend the cause of peace.[97]

If there should be a new world war, it would mean the end of imperialism:

What does the experience of history tell us? It tells us that the first world war unleashed by the imperialists led to the victory of the Great October Socialist Revolution in our country.

The experience of history further tells us that the second world war unleashed by the imperialists led to the establishment of the people's democratic system in a number of countries in Central and South-Eastern Europe and the victory of the great Chinese people.

Can there be any doubt that, if the imperialists start a third world war, it will mean the end, not of individual capitalist states, but of all the capitalist world.[98]

The United States would not escape unscathed in a future war: "the American people are beginning to realize that if the warmongers start a new slaughter, the grief of mothers, wives, sisters, and children will visit the American continent too. And it is a terrible grief. The warmongers will inevitably be suffocated and drowned in it."[99] Because of the successes of the socialist camp, the "camp of imperialism" was seized with alarm. But Malenkov did not conclude that this alarm was dangerous. "Let those doomed by history rage in fury!" he declared. "The greater the frenzy in the camp of the warmongers, the greater should be the calm and restraint in our camp of peace."[100]

Alongside this celebratory tone, however, a more somber note was also to be heard. In a report to a Cominform meeting in Hungary in the second half of November, Mikhail Suslov, Central Committee secretary responsible for ideology and relations with foreign communist parties, stressed that the imperialist camp was actively preparing for war.[101] Since the founding of the Cominform two years before, he said, the struggle between the two camps had become more intense, and the aggressiveness of the imperialist camp had increased. The American imperialists were organizing new blocs, raising their military expenditure, creating bases around the world, and turning West Germany and Japan into staging-grounds for an attack on the Soviet Union and the countries of the anti-imperialist camp.

But the imperialist camp, Suslov argued, was in disarray and growing weaker. The announcement that the Soviet Union possessed the atomic bomb since 1947 had "caused consternation and dismay in the camp of the imperialists and warmongers" and had "diminished its strength."[102] The peace movement was becoming a powerful political force. "The correlation of forces in the international arena," claimed Suslov, "has changed fundamentally and is continuing to change, in favor of the camp of peace, democracy and socialism."[103]

Unlike Malenkov, however, Suslov warned that the improving correlation of forces did not mean that the danger of war was receding. Such a conclusion would be "profoundly erroneous and harmful." "The experience of history," he said

teaches that the more hopeless the position of imperialist reaction, the more frantic it becomes and the greater is the danger of its launching military adventures.

The changing correlation of forces in the world arena in favor of the camp of peace and democracy drives the imperialist and warmongering camp into fresh outbursts of frenzied fury. The Anglo-American imperialists are counting on war to change the course of history, to resolve their external and internal contradictions and difficulties, to strengthen the positions of monopoly capital, and to achieve world domination.[104]

It was essential, argued Suslov, to be vigilant and united if the imperialists' plans were to be foiled.

Malenkov and Suslov gave two different views of the international situation in November 1949. Both argued that the balance of power was shifting in the Soviet favor. Malenkov drew confidence from this; Suslov concluded that the world was becoming more dangerous. This was a fundamental difference, which reflected two currents in Soviet thinking about international relations: the correlation-of-forces model which predicted that growing Soviet power would lead to a more peaceful world; and the hostility thesis, which argued that growing Soviet power would elicit a more aggressive policy from the capitalist states.[105] This difference evidently reflected disagreement within the leadership about the course that Soviet policy should now follow.[106] Stalin did not always have a clear position on foreign policy and sometimes allowed different points of view to emerge. Once he decided on his own position, however, there was no dissent. In this case it was Suslov's call for vigilance and unity, rather than Malenkov's appeal for calm and restraint, that provided the truer reflection of Stalin's own assessment of the international situation.[107]

The question of war and peace now cast a darker shadow than it had done in the previous four years. In 1949 and 1950 Stalin began a major military build-up: Soviet forces in Germany were increased; the East European armies were strengthened; a new naval shipbuilding program was launched; and Stalin put pressure on aircraft designers to develop an intercontinental turbojet bomber.[108] These programs would strengthen the Soviet ability to attack Western Europe in the short term but, even with the intense pressure that Stalin now applied, it would be some years before the new naval and bomber programs came to fruition.

In the meantime the situation was dangerous. Stalin "was afraid that the capitalist countries would attack the Soviet Union," writes Khrushchev, who moved from Kiev to take over the Moscow Party organization in December 1949.

Most of all, America. America had a powerful air force and, most important, America had atomic bombs, while we had only just developed the mechanism and had a negligible number of finished bombs. Under Stalin we had no means of delivery. We had no long-range bombers capable of reaching the United States, nor did we have long-range rockets. All we had was short-range rockets. This situation weighed heavily on Stalin. He understood that he had to be careful not to be dragged into a war.[109]

Khrushchev's memoirs, even allowing for their characteristic hyperbole, suggest that Stalin's view of the strategic situation was far from sanguine. Khrushchev was in a good position to know what Stalin's view was, since after his move to Moscow he was, along with Malenkov, Beria, and Bulganin, one of the leaders closest to Stalin. His account suggests that behind the confident statements of Soviet policy lay a sense of military inferiority, and anxiety about the possibility of war. Stalin is reported to have said to Kurchatov after the August 1949 test that "if we had been a year or a year and a half later with the atomic bomb, we would surely have felt it on ourselves."[110] It was of course better to have tested the bomb than not to have tested it. But the test did not remove all feeling of insecurity. The secrecy surrounding the atomic test, and the misleading claims that were made once the test had become public, tend to support Khrushchev's account because they indicate that Stalin did not believe that the atomic test had made the Soviet Union secure. On the contrary, the test heightened United States anxiety at a time when the Soviet Union had not yet acquired a significant atomic capability. Stalin appears to have agreed with Suslov that imperialism was becoming more frantic and more hostile.

Suslov's argument was classic Stalinism. At the plenary session of the Central Committee in February–March 1937 Stalin had claimed that the class struggle would intensify as socialism grew stronger.[111] This theory had provided ideological underpinning for the Great Purge. After the war Stalin had used the Cold War to enhance repression at home and to increase his control over Eastern Europe through the Cominform. During 1949 he tightened the screws still further, with the campaign against cosmopolitanism and the first trials of East European communist leaders on charges of spying for Anglo-American imperialism. The growing tension in international relations was used to justify the theory that the class struggle was becoming more intense.[112]

V

How different would Soviet foreign policy have been if the atomic bomb had not existed? Did the bomb deter the Soviet Union from doing things it would otherwise have done – for example, from invading Western Europe, or escalating the Berlin crisis? Did it compel the Soviet Union to do things it would not otherwise have done? How important a factor was it in Stalin's foreign policy?

There is little evidence to suggest that the United States was able to use the bomb to compel the Soviet Union to do things it did not want to do. Atomic diplomacy played no part in the withdrawal of Soviet forces from Iran in 1946, the example of compellence (to use the political science term) most frequently cited in the postwar period. There is more evidence for the *deterrent* effect of the atomic bomb, especially during the Berlin crisis, but even in this instance the case is not conclusive. There is no convincing evidence to show that the atomic bomb deterred a Soviet invasion of Western Europe in the first four years after the war. The United States did not have enough atomic bombs in the early postwar years to be able to prevent the Soviet Union from occupying Western Europe; and the Soviet leaders were aware of this. There is no evidence to show that Stalin intended to invade Western Europe, except in the event of a major war;

and his overall policy suggests that he was anxious to avoid such a war, and not merely because the United States possessed the atomic bomb.

Stalin's policy on the bomb was guided by two principles: the concept of the "war of nerves," and the idea of "limits." The first of these principles sprang from the assumption that the United States would use the atomic bomb to intimidate the Soviet Union, to wring concessions from it, in order to impose its own conception of the postwar order. Stalin had concluded after Hiroshima that atomic diplomacy rather than war was the immediate danger, and this assumption underpinned his policy until 1949. It was crucial therefore to show that the Soviet Union was tough, that it could not be frightened. This sometimes involved putting pressure on the West and raising international tension. Even if the Western powers did not yield, they would be forced to understand, as Byrnes had done in 1945, that the Soviet leaders were "stubborn, obstinate, and they don't scare." Stalin's conduct of the "war of nerves" had the great drawback of reinforcing the conviction of the Western powers that the Soviet Union was an aggressive expansionist power, and that they needed to defend themselves by forming NATO and building up their armed forces. This effect was not the result of a tactical miscalculation on the part of the Soviet leaders, but a consequence of the way in which they conceived of the nature of their relationship with the West.

The second principle – the concept of limits – acted as a brake on the war of nerves. Stalin did not want war with the West; he did not believe that the Soviet Union was ready for war. If the Soviet Union pursued a conciliatory and accommodating policy towards the West, it would appear weak, and its weakness would invite pressure and an aggressive Western policy. That was why he thought it necessary to conduct the war of nerves. But in the war of nerves it was crucial not to go too far, for fear of precipitating a real war. Hence the importance of limits. Soviet awareness of limits was evident in the Berlin crisis of 1948.

The bomb did not come into play only when discrete threats – explicit or implicit – were made by the United States. By symbolizing American might and Soviet backwardness, it cast a pervasive shadow over Soviet relations with the United States. It helped to shape the Soviet view of the nature of the relationship and of the appropriate policies to pursue. It was a crucial element in the war of nerves. It enhanced the American ability to strike the Soviet Union, and thereby affected the limits that restrained Soviet action. At the same time the bomb, by conjuring up the danger of intimidation, strengthened the incentive to appear tough and unyielding. Thus the bomb had a dual effect. It probably made the Soviet Union more restrained in its use of force, for fear of precipitating war. It also made the Soviet Union less cooperative and less willing to compromise, for fear of seeming weak.

1.   Vladimir Vernadskii and colleagues on an expedition to look for radioactive minerals in Central Asia in 1911.

2.   Abram Ioffe and his seminar. Ioffe is standing on the far right; Peter Kapitsa, Iakov Frenkel', and Nikolai Semenov are seated on the far left (left to right).

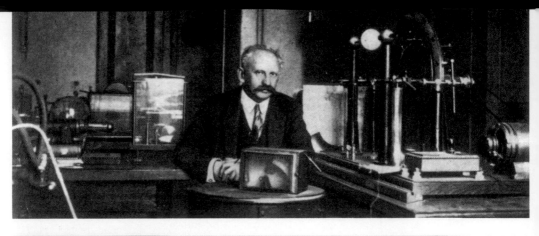

Доктор физики И.В.Курчатов (1936г.)

6. Igor Kurchatov, Baku, 1924.

7. Igor Kurchatov, 1936.

8. Abram Ioffe and Niels Bohr in the grounds of Ioffe's Institute, 1934.

3. Abram Ioffe in his laboratory in 1924.

4. Left to right: A.A. Chernyshev, Abram Ioffe, Paul Ehrenfest, Nikolai Semenov, Ivan Obreimov.

5. Left to right: Lev Landau, Evgeniia Kanegisser, V.A. Ambartsumian, unknown, N. Kanegisser, Matvei Bronshtein, in the 1920s.

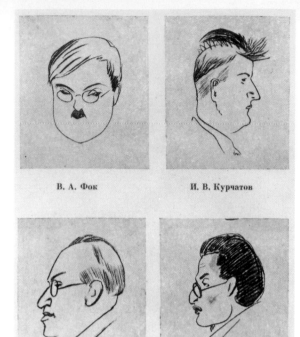

В. А. Фок

И. В. Курчатов

Я. И. Френкель

М. П. Бронштейн

9. Caricatures by N.A. Mamontov of participants in the 1933 conference on nuclear physics in Leningrad. Clockwise from top left to bottom left: Vladimir Fok, Igor Kurchatov, Matvei Bronshtein, Iakov Frenkel'.

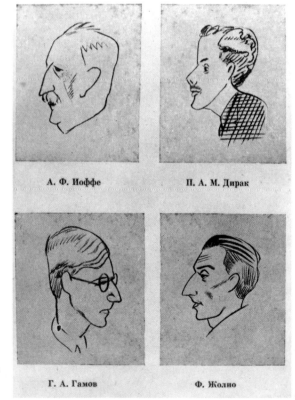

А. Ф. Иоффе

П. А. М. Дирак

Г. А. Гамов

Ф. Жолио

10. Clockwise from top left: Abram Ioffe, Paul Dirac, Frédéric Joliot, Georgii Gamov.

11. At the entrance to the Ukrainian Physicotechnical Institute, Khar'kov, 1930s: Front row, left to right: Lev Shubnikov, Aleksandr Leipunskii, Lev Landau, Peter Kapitsa; second row: B.N. Finkel'shtein, Olga Trapeznikova, Kirill Sinel'nikov, Iu.N. Riabinin.

12. Left to right: unknown, Igor Kurchatov, Abram Alikhanov, Vladimir Fok, at the Nuclear Physics Conference, Khar'kov, 1939.

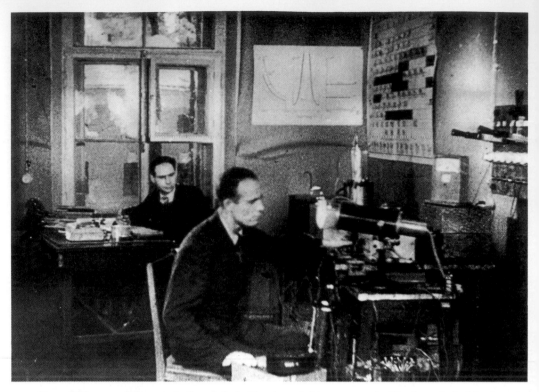

13.   Georgii Flerov and Konstantin Petrzhak, in Kurchatov's laboratory at the Physicotechnical Institute in Leningrad, 1939. At this period they were working on the experiments that led to the discovery of spontaneous fission in 1940.

14.   Lieutenant Georgii Flerov, 1942.

15. Page 12 of the letter sent by Georgii Flerov to Kurchatov in December 1941. The diagram shows Flerov's suggestion for bringing together two hemispheres of uranium-235 to cause a nuclear explosion.

16.   Vladimir Vernadskii and Aleksandr Fersman, 1940.

17.   Peter Kapitsa, 1939, on the right, with one of his
mechanics.

18.   Vitalii Khlopin.

19.   Top Row: Isaak Kikoin,
Iakov Zel'dovich, 1946, Igor
Kurchatov, 1943.

Middle Row: Abram
Alikhanov, Avraamii
Zaveniagin, Mikhail Pervukhin.

Bottom Row: Viacheslav
Malyshev, Igor Tamm.

20. Potsdam meeting, July 18, 1945. Left to right, row 1: Stalin, Truman, Gromyko, Byrnes, Molotov. In the second row, between Stalin and Truman, is Charles Bohlen.

21. The conference table at Potsdam, August 1, 1945. Stalin at the top in white jacket, with Molotov on his right. Truman at the right, with Byrnes on his right. Attlee at the lower left, with Bevin on his right.

(previous page)

22.   The tent in which graphite was tested for purity at Laboratory No. 2 in 1945.

23.   1946 Photograph of the building for the experimental reactor which went criticial on December 25, 1946.

24.   Iulii Khariton and Igor Kurchatov, late 1940s or early 1950s.

25.   On the left is Iulii Khariton, on the right is Kirill Shchelkin; in the center is Nikolai Shvernik, Chairman of the Presidium of the USSR Supreme Soviet (i.e. President of the Soviet Union) from 1946 to 1953. Stalin looks on from behind. The occasion appears to be the award of the honor, Hero of Socialist Labor, in 1949.

26.   Assembling the experimental reactor, 1946.

27.   Khrushchev, Beria, and Malenkov at Stalin's lying-in-state, March 1953.

28.   Igor Kurchatov and Iulii Khariton in Central Asia after the 1953 thermonuclear test.

29. Marshal Georgii Zhukov, hand on hip, at field exercises in the Carpathian Military District, 1950s.

30. Nikolai Semenov and Igor Kurchatov, near Moscow, 1954.

31. Igor Kurchatov, Abram Ioffe, and Anna Ioffe, and Marina Kurchatova, late 1950s.

32. Efim Slavskii, Boris Vannikov, Igor Kurchatov, late 1950s.

33. Sergei Korolev and Igor Kurchatov in the Kremlin, 1958.

34. Sergei Korolev, Igor Kurchatov, and Mstislav Keldysh, 1959.

35. Frédéric Joliot, Igor Kurchatov, Dmitrii Skobel'tsyn, Lev Artsimovich, and Abram Alikhanov, 1956.

36. The reactor building for the first nuclear power station, at Obninsk.

37. Arzamas-16, with the bell-tower of the Sarov monastery.

38. Andrei Sakharov and Igor Kurchatov, 1959.

39. Dmitrii Ustinov, Boris Vannikov, A.I. Efremov, and Viacheslav Malyshev.

40. Abram Alikhanov, Igor Kurchatov, Lev Artsimovich, and Frédéric Joliot-Curie, 1958.

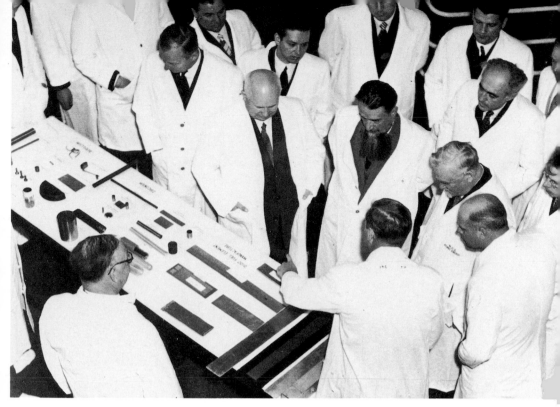

41. In the center are Khrushchev, Kurchatov, and Bulganin, on their visit to Harwell in April 1956. John Cockcroft is standing at the lower left with his back to the camera.

42. Iulii Khariton with a copy of the bomb detonated on August 29, 1949. Photograph taken in 1992.

43. Models of the first three Soviet nuclear weapons, from left to right: the "Layer Cake" tested on August 12, 1953; the 40-kiloton weapon tested in 1951; the first Soviet atomic bomb. The photograph shows the bomb casings; it was the explosive charges only that were tested. Photograph by V.I. Luk'ianov and S.A. Nazarkin, Museum of Nuclear Weapons, Arzamas-16.

44. Statue of Kurchatov in the town of Kurchatov, formerly Semipalatinsk-21.

45. The August 29, 1949 atomic bomb test.

46.   The August 12, 1953 hydrogen bomb test.

47.   The August 12, 1953 hydrogen bomb test.

48.　The superbomb test on November 22, 1955.

CHAPTER THIRTEEN

Dangerous Relations

I

ON DECEMBER 21, 1949 Stalin celebrated his seventieth birthday. He was now an old and tired man. Those who met him after the war and had not seen him for some years were struck by how much he had aged.[1] His decline grew more pronounced after he turned seventy. "Every year," Khrushchev recalls in his memoirs, "it became more and more obvious that Stalin was weakening mentally as well as physically. This was especially clear from his eclipses of mind and losses of memory."[2] His memory, which had always been formidable, began to falter. His suspicious nature, a central feature of his personality, became even more pronounced. "In his last years Stalin was not completely in control of himself. He did not believe anyone," said Molotov, whose wife Polina had been arrested in 1949.[3] On one extraordinary occasion in 1951 Stalin said to no one in particular, but in the presence of Khrushchev and Mikoian, "I'm finished. I trust no one, not even myself."[4]

Not only was 1949 the year of Stalin's seventieth birthday. It also marked a turning-point in Soviet foreign policy. In March Stalin appointed Andrei Vyshinskii as Foreign Minister in place of Molotov. Vyshinskii, who had been chief prosecutor in the show trials of the 1930s, was associated in Western minds with those grisly charades. When Molotov had replaced Litvinov as People's Commissar of Foreign Affairs ten years earlier, his appointment had cleared the way for the Nazi–Soviet Pact. Vyshinskii's appointment did not lead to anything so dramatic, though it did suggest that Stalin was not seeking to ingratiate himself with the West. Vyshinskii never became one of Stalin's inner circle, and Molotov remained Deputy Premier and continued to take part in key foreign policy meetings.[5]

Western scholars generally agree that Soviet foreign policy took a new direction in 1949, but there is no agreement about what that direction was. Some have argued that policy became more flexible, presaging the shift to peaceful coexistence in the mid-1950s.[6] Others contend that there was no

softening of Soviet policy before Stalin's death in March 1953, and that
Stalin's policy became, if anything, more rigid and aggressive.[7] This disagreement reflects the difficulty of understanding the last four years of
Stalin's life, a peculiarly opaque and ominous period of Soviet history. Yet
it is crucial to examine this period as carefully as possible to establish
whether Stalin's attitude to war and peace, and to the atomic bomb,
changed in the last years of his life.

II

In 1949 the Cold War in Europe had become a war of position; in Asia,
where the situation was much more fluid and dynamic, it was a war of
maneuver. Stalin had discouraged the Chinese communists from pressing
ahead with their revolution after World War II. "I did not believe that the
Chinese communists could win," he told Bulgarian and Yugoslav communist leaders in February 1948. "I was sure that the Americans would do
everything to put down an uprising."[8] Mao ignored Stalin's advice to come
to terms with Chiang Kai-shek. When Liu Shaoqi arrived in Moscow in
July 1949 Stalin made what was tantamount to an apology. "He had
underrated the potential of the Chinese revolution," he said, according to
the recollections of Liu's interpreter. "He did not think we were a match
for Chiang Kaishek's excellently equipped army of many million men
which had US backing while the Soviet Union was unable to help us. That
was why he had disagreed with any policy that led to war."[9]

Stalin was aware that communist success in China would be a strategic
shift of major proportions; that indeed was why he anticipated American
intervention. In May 1948 he told Ivan Kovalev that "if socialism is
victorious in China and our countries [i.e. China and the Soviet Union] go
along the same path, then the victory of socialism in the world can be
considered guaranteed. We will not be threatened by any contingencies."[10]
A Sino–Soviet alliance would be invincible. But the conditional clause in
Stalin's remark – "if . . . our countries go along the same path" – was
crucial. Stalin did not assume that Sino–Soviet relations would be smooth
with the communists in power. His relations with the Chinese party
leadership had not been easy, and Mao had become leader of the Party
by defeating Stalin's protégés in the 1930s.[11] Stalin's remark to Kovalev
was made a month before the Cominform expelled Yugoslavia, and in
December 1948, when Kovalev returned to Moscow to report on the
situation in China, Stalin asked about the Chinese attitude to the Yugoslav
issue: which side did they support?[12]

Stalin was still worried about the danger of American intervention in the
summer of 1949. The People's Liberation Army (PLA) had crossed the
Yangtze river in April 1949 and moved rapidly to occupy the south of
the country. In a telegram to Chinese leaders in June 1949, Stalin expressed
the fear that the Americans might intervene. Although Chinese commu-

nists had fought brilliantly, he wrote, the campaign was not yet over. The
"Anglo-Franco-Americans" were afraid that the approach of the PLA to
the borders of neighboring countries would create a revolutionary situation
in those countries and in the islands occupied by Chiang Kai-shek. The
imperialists might do anything, from imposing a blockade to starting a war
with China. There was a particular danger, Stalin noted, that Anglo-
American troops might be landed in the rear of the main PLA forces which
had now moved south. He recommended that the Chinese prepare their
campaign in the border areas with great care.[13]

In his conversations with Liu Shaoqi in July and August 1949 Stalin was
less cautious. He encouraged the Chinese communists to assume leadership
of revolutionary movements in Asia.[14] "The center of revolution . . . has
moved to China and East Asia," he said. "I say that you are already playing
an important role. . . . But at the same time I assert that the responsibility
laid upon you has grown even more. You ought to carry out your duty in
relation to the revolution in the countries of East Asia."[15] Liu had already
been arguing that China should provide ideological guidance for anti-
imperialist revolutions in the East. Encouraged by Stalin's words, he stated
this idea forcefully in November 1949 to a trade-unions conference in
Beijing. "The way which has been followed by the Chinese people," he
said, ". . . is the way which should be followed by the peoples of many
colonial and semi-colonial countries."[16]

Stalin had adopted a cautious attitude to the Chinese revolution, and had
avoided insurrectionism in Europe. Now, however, he was encouraging
the Chinese communists to support revolution in Asia. Why this shift in
policy? Was it because, as many people in the West feared, Soviet foreign
policy was about to become more active once the Soviet Union possessed
the atomic bomb?[17] But Stalin's remarks to Liu preceded the Soviet test;
and in any event, Stalin's reaction to the test was to conclude that the world
was a more hostile place, not to see it as safer for Soviet expansion. Stalin's
remarks are best understood in the strategic context of Asia. When Liu
asked whether China should join the Cominform, Stalin replied that the
situation in China was different from that in Eastern Europe. It might be
appropriate, he said, to organize a Union of East Asian Communist Parties,
with both the Chinese and Soviet parties as members.[18]

Stalin evidently believed that different policies should be pursued in Asia
and in Europe. He may have thought that the prospects for political gains
were greater in the fluid situation in Asia than in Europe, where the
continent was clearly divided in two. He may also have hoped that, by
aiding the revolutions in Malaya and Indochina, China would tie down
British and French forces, thereby slowing the build-up of NATO forces
in Europe.[19] It is possible, however, that Stalin's main goal in encouraging
Chinese support for revolution was to bring China into conflict with the
United States, thereby forestalling rapprochement between China and the
West. Stalin was anxious to secure a firm alliance with China; that would

constitute, in his view, a major shift in the strategic balance. Mao had gone out of his way in the summer of 1949 to make it clear that China was firmly in the Soviet camp.[20] But Stalin continued to harbor suspicions, and China was too big and independent to be dealt with in the same way as the countries of Eastern Europe. Conflict between China and the United States – especially if the United States decided to ally itself with the Nationalists on Taiwan, which the communists regarded as an integral part of China – would give China no option but to commit itself to the Soviet Union.[21]

On December 16, 1949 Mao arrived in Moscow by train to visit Stalin; he remained in the Soviet Union until February 17. The visit was a strange and fascinating affair.[22] Stalin and Mao were eager to conclude an alliance, but were exceedingly wary of each other. Stalin was unsure of Mao's intentions, and wanted to bind the new China to the Soviet Union; Mao was afraid that Stalin would not treat China as an equal.[23] Stalin did not come to the station to meet Mao. After a conversation with Stalin on the first evening Mao was left in virtual isolation at his *dacha* outside Moscow. Eventually, however, the situation improved, and the two men agreed to conclude a new treaty. Zhou Enlai, the Chinese premier, arrived in Moscow on January 20 to negotiate the terms of the treaty, which was signed on February 14, 1950 by Zhou and Vyshinskii, along with a number of secret agreements which preserved most of the gains Stalin had made in August 1945.

The new treaty replaced the one that Stalin had concluded with Nationalist China in August 1945. As before, the two governments undertook to prevent the resumption of aggression on the part of Japan or any other state collaborating with Japan. If either China or the Soviet Union were attacked by Japan or by a state allied with Japan, the other would "immediately render military and other assistance by all means at its disposal." The phrase "by all means at its disposal," which implies nuclear weapons, was added, after much discussion, at Zhou's insistence.[24] The focus on Japan was carried over from the August 1945 treaty. Japan's significance was now quite different, however. Like West Germany it was being converted into an ally of the United States. Suslov had claimed in November 1949 that the United States wanted to turn Japan into a staging-ground for war against the Soviet Union and China.[25] In January 1950 *Pravda* concluded from a speech by Secretary of State Dean Acheson that "the American imperialists have settled down in Japan and have no desire to leave it."[26] In the same month Stalin pushed the Japanese Communist Party to adopt a more militant stance on the issue of US occupation forces.[27]

III

The Sino–Soviet alliance set the stage for the Korean War, the most serious crisis of the first postwar decade. At the time it was widely assumed in the West that Stalin – emboldened by the first Soviet atomic test – had directed

North Korea to attack the South. Some historians have argued more recently that Stalin might not have known of North Korea's decision to unify the country by force. The issue is a crucial one for understanding Stalin's policy in the last years of his life, and in particular his attitude to war and peace.[28]

The Korean peninsula was occupied in 1945 by Soviet and American forces. In 1948 the Democratic People's Republic of Korea was set up north of the 38th parallel, in the area occupied by Soviet forces; the Republic of Korea was established in the south. When Soviet and American forces withdrew, they left behind two regimes, each of which aspired to reunify the peninsula under its own rule. Kim Il Sung, the North Korean communist leader, built the Korean People's Army (KPA) into a force that was significantly superior in troops and equipment to the South Korean Army. Kim calculated that the United States would not go to war over South Korea, and sought the agreement of Stalin and Mao for his goal of reunifying the country by force of arms.[29] He first raised the issue during a visit to Moscow in March 1949.[30]

Stalin took a cautious attitude to Kim's idea, but he did not reject it in principle. "Such a big matter in relation to South Korea . . . needs great preparation," he told Kim.[31] It was only when Kim visited Moscow in March–April 1950 that Stalin gave his final approval.[32] He was apparently now convinced by Kim's argument that South Korea would explode at the first push, and that "people's power" would be established in the South, as it had been in the North.[33] Stalin and Kim, according to Khrushchev, were "inclined to the view that if it could be done quickly (Kim Il Sung was certain that it would be done quickly), then intervention by the USA was excluded."[34] Mao concurred in this judgment. When Kim visited Beijing in May 1950 Mao told him he was certain that the Americans would not go to war "for such a small territory as Korea."[35] The United States would see this as an internal affair, to be settled by the Koreans themselves.[36]

Stalin told the Soviet leaders that they could not sidestep the "national question of a unified Korea," and none of them demurred.[37] This was hardly Stalin's only motive in approving Kim's plan, however, since he had been perfectly willing to rein in European communists when he opposed their policies. The recently declassified Chinese and Soviet documents do not reveal the strategic thinking behind Stalin's decision. He may have believed that the unification of Korea under communist rule would enable him to put greater political pressure on Japan, in line with his remark to T.V. Soong in 1945 that "one should keep Japan vulnerable from all sides, north, west, south, east, then she will keep quiet."[38] Besides, a unified, communist Korea would be an ideal staging-ground for the invasion of Japan in the event of war. But Stalin's main concern may have been the triangular relationship between the Soviet Union, China, and the United States. My colleagues Sergei Goncharov, John Lewis, and Xue Litai have argued that Stalin hoped that the invasion would provoke the United States into backing the Nationalist regime on Taiwan, thereby removing the danger that China might be tempted to align itself with the United States.[39]

Stalin ordered that all North Korean requests for arms and equipment be satisfied quickly. By June 25 the North enjoyed a significant military superiority over the South. According to a later Soviet estimate, the balance of forces favored the North 2:1 in troops, 2:1 in artillery pieces, 7:1 in machine-guns, 13:1 in sub-machine-guns, 6.5:1 in tanks, and 6:1 in aircraft. This was the kind of force ratio that Soviet military planners liked for offensive operations. Soviet advisers helped to prepare the operational plan for the Korean People's Army. The plan envisaged a North Korean attack, a rate of advance of about 15–20 kilometers a day, and conclusion of military operations within 22–27 days. At Kim Il Sung's request, June 25 was set as the date for the start of military operations.[40]

On the morning of Sunday, June 25, 1950 the Korean People's Army attacked the South. The initial operation was a great success, with the South Korean Army collapsing even more quickly than expected.[41] By the morning of June 28, North Korean forces occupied Seoul. But the opening campaign, although a stunning military success, did not achieve its political objective. The operational plan was based on the assumption that once the North attacked, communists in the South would rise up and overthrow the South Korean regime. There was, however, no uprising.[42] Moreover, by the time Seoul was taken, the United States had decided to intervene. The political premises on which Stalin had approved Kim's plan were proved to be utterly mistaken. Once again – as in his failure to anticipate the German attack in 1941 and his failure to grasp the importance of the atomic bomb before August 1945 – Stalin's judgment was shown to be far from infallible in international affairs.

As soon as news of the attack reached Washington, the Truman administration called a meeting of the United Nations Security Council to condemn North Korea. A resolution was adopted in the absence of Iakov Malik, the Soviet representative. The Soviet Union was boycotting the United Nations because the Nationalists still occupied the Chinese seat. Two days later, on June 27, Truman announced that he had ordered US air and sea forces to give cover and support to the South Korean Army, and that he had interposed the Seventh Fleet between Taiwan and the Chinese mainland. On June 30 he committed ground forces to Korea as well.[43]

On June 27 the Security Council adopted a second resolution, which called on UN members to give South Korea such help as it might need to repel the attack and restore peace. This resolution provided the legal basis for sending military forces to Korea under the flag of the United Nations. General Douglas MacArthur, the commander of US forces in Japan, was put in command of the UN forces, which were drawn largely from the United States. Once again Malik was absent from the Security Council when the vote was taken, though, as on the 25th, he could have vetoed the resolution had he been present. The Foreign Ministry wanted Malik to return to the Security Council for the debate, and prepared a directive instructing him to veto any resolution directed against North Korea or the Soviet Union. Stalin overruled the ministry's advice, even though Gromyko pointed out that, if the resolution were adopted, United States troops could be sent to South Korea under UN auspices.[44] Stalin did not give his reasons to Gromyko, but he may have wished to distance the Soviet Union from the war now that the United States had decided to intervene.

This interpretation receives support from the Soviet attitude in the early months of the war. Even after the United States' decision to intervene, Soviet statements treated the war in Korea as a civil war in which the Soviet Union would not become involved. When Malik returned to the Security Council in August he adopted a relatively conciliatory stance, and sought to promote peacemaking efforts. When the United States bombed the Rashin oil supply depot only 25 kilometers from the Soviet border with North Korea, the Soviet protest was unexpectedly mild. Moscow's position was noted in Washington, where it was regarded as a sign that the Soviet Union realized it had made a mistake, and was willing to write off its losses.[45]

United States intervention did not at first halt the North Korean advance, and by September UN forces had been driven back to a small area around the port of Pusan in the south-east of the peninsula. On September 15, however, General MacArthur transformed the military situation by landing forces at Inchon, to the rear of the Korean People's Army, close to the 38th parallel. On September 26 United States forces recaptured Seoul. Five days later, on October 1, the first South Korean forces crossed the 38th parallel into the North, and United States forces followed on October 7. The United States had now expanded the aims of the war beyond restoration of the status quo.

North Korea was now in a grim position. On September 29 – three days after the recapture of Seoul and two days before South Korean troops crossed the 38th parallel – Kim Il Sung and Pak Hon Yong, the leader of the South Korean communists, wrote to Stalin to ask for help. "We are full of resolve to overcome all the difficulties before us so that Korea will not be a colony and military staging-ground for the American imperialists," they wrote. But the situation was "extraordinarily difficult," and the KPA would not be able to stop the enemy if he decided to attack North Korea. "Therefore, dear Iosif Vissarionovich," the letter continued, "we cannot but ask for special help from you. In other words, at the moment when enemy forces cross to the north of the 38th parallel, we very much need direct military help from the Soviet Union." Kim and Pak apparently understood that they were unlikely to get the help they wanted, for they continued: "If for some reason that is impossible, then help us to create international volunteer units in China and in the other People's Democracies to provide military help for our struggle. We ask for your instructions on the proposal we have set out."[46] Kim wrote to Mao on October 1 to seek help from China.[47]

Kim was right not to expect direct military help from Stalin. According to Khrushchev, Stalin was very reluctant to become involved. He rejected the suggestion that Marshal Rodion Malinovskii, the Commander-in-Chief of Soviet forces in the Far East, be sent to Korea to organize military operations.[48] Later in October, when it looked as though Kim Il Sung would have to take refuge in the North Korean mountains, Stalin said "Well, what of it? Let the United States of America be our neighbors in the Far East. They will come there, but we will not fight with them. We are not ready to fight."[49]

Mao did not take such a detached view. When the Chinese Politburo met on October 1, he argued that China would have to intervene. Those who opposed entry pointed to China's industrial and military weakness, and to the regime's need to consolidate itself at home. Mao countered that a Sino–American war was only a matter of time, and that Korea was the most favorable battleground from the Chinese point of view. It would be much more difficult to fight in Vietnam or on the offshore islands. Korea provided "the most favorable terrain, the closest communication to China, the most convenient material and manpower backup . . . and the most convenient way for us to get indirect Soviet support."[50] The Politburo meeting lasted several days, but the decision to send Chinese People's Volunteers – in fact regular units of the PLA – to Korea was taken on October 2, five days before United States forces crossed the 38th parallel.[51]

Mao explained his decision in a telegram to Stalin on October 2.[52] The United States would become even more arrogant and aggressive if it defeated North Korea and occupied the whole country, he wrote, and this would be harmful for the East as a whole. Chinese forces should be able to destroy the armies of the United States and the other invaders, and to drive them out of Korea. China had to be prepared for a declaration of war by the United States, with attacks on Chinese cities and industrial bases. If Chinese forces could destroy the American forces in Korea, the Korean problem would be solved. Even if the United States then declared war on China, that war "will not escalate rapidly and will not last long."

The worst situation, wrote Mao, would be a military stalemate in Korea and an American declaration of war on China. That would undermine China's plans for economic reconstruction and spark the dissatisfaction of the "national bourgeoisie and other segments of the people (they are very afraid of war)." The Chinese leadership was worried by the effect of the American advance on the political situation in China. Their concern was not surprising, since the border with Korea was close to the centers of Chinese industrial and political power. Mao informed Stalin that he intended to send twelve divisions into North Korea. These forces would engage in defensive warfare while waiting for the delivery of Soviet weapons. The implication was clear: Soviet military assistance was needed if China was to carry out its goal of defeating the United States forces quickly; if China failed to do this, a stalemate would result, leading to a Sino–American war in which the Soviet Union might become embroiled, in line with its commitment under the Sino–Soviet Treaty. Mao's decision to intervene was thus predicated on extensive Soviet military aid. Stalin had already agreed to provide air support, and to equip Chinese ground force divisions.[53] On October 8 Mao issued the order for the Chinese People's Volunteers to enter North Korea under the command of Peng Dehuai.[54]

Zhou Enlai flew to the Soviet Union to settle the details of Soviet military aid. When he met Stalin in the Crimea on October 9, Stalin withdrew his promise of air support for Chinese forces. He insisted that the Soviet Air Force needed more time to get ready.[55] Zhou told Stalin that China might postpone the entry of its forces into Korea because it was not sure that the Chinese People's Volunteers could stop the UN forces without Soviet support. Stalin responded that he would be willing to speed up the training of Chinese pilots, and promised to provide equipment for twenty ground force divisions. He asked Zhou to tell Mao that if the United States forces defeated the North Koreans, Kim Il-Sung could set up a government in exile in north-east China.[56] Zhou cabled a report to Mao on October 10.[57]

Mao now put the decision to enter the war on hold. On October 12 he sent telegrams to Peng Dehuai and other commanders rescinding his earlier order to move into North Korea.[58] On the following day, however, Mao sent a telegram to Zhou saying that "after discussion with members of the Politburo, we have reached a consensus that the entry of our army in Korea is still to our advantage."[59] He explained that

If we don't send troops, the reactionaries at home and abroad will be swollen with arrogance when the enemy troops press on toward the Yalu river. Consequently, it is unfavorable to various parties, especially unfavorable to north-east China. The entire Northeast Frontier Force will be tied down and the power supply in South Manchuria will be controlled [by hostile parties]. In short, we hold that we should enter the war.

It is evident that anxiety about the political situation inside China played a crucial role in Mao's decision. The Commander of the North-east Military District, Gao Gang, reported in February 1951 that when the American troops advanced into North Korea, "workers were led astray by various rumors that the situation was unstable."[60] One hundred thousand people had been arrested and 40–50,000 shot, Gao Gang said, in order to eliminate the danger of counter-revolution.[61]

Mao did not mention the atomic bomb in his telegrams to Stalin. He had been even more outspoken than Stalin in playing down the significance of the bomb. As early as August 13, 1945, one week after Hiroshima, he had written: "Can atom bombs decide wars? No, they can't. Atom bombs could not make Japan surrender. Without the struggles waged by the people, atom bombs by themselves would be of no avail."[62] A year later he had said:

The atom bomb is a paper tiger which the US reactionaries use to scare people. It looks terrible, but in fact it isn't. Of course, the atom bomb is a weapon of mass slaughter, but the outcome of a war is decided by the people, not by one or two new types of weapon.[63]

By October 1950, however, the nuclear balance was very different from what it had been in 1946. The United States had over 300 bombs, which could inflict great damage on Chinese cities.

The Chinese leaders were of course aware that the United States might use the atomic bomb, either against Chinese cities, or against Chinese forces in the field. They reassured themselves with the same arguments they used to reassure their troops.[64] An official propaganda instruction, issued on October 26, 1950, argued that the bomb was not suitable for use in Korea, because the United States had too few bombs to think of using them against non-Soviet targets. Besides, it said, the utility of the bomb against Chinese targets would be limited by China's large size and population, while in Korea hostile forces would be too close to each other to make it possible to use the bomb effectively.[65] It is moreover possible that the Chinese leaders, if they believed the statements that the Soviet Union had had the bomb since 1947, thought that Soviet atomic capabilities were in fact greater than they were. In any event Chinese fears of the atomic bomb did not outweigh the reasons for entering the war – fear of the consequences inside China of the American presence in Korea; fear that the United States would use Korea as a staging-ground; and the belief that war with the United States was inevitable, and that Korea was the most advantageous place for China to wage it.

On October 19 Chinese forces began to cross the Yalu river into North Korea.[66] They took part in tactical skirmishes with South Korean and United States units, and then disappeared from American sight.[67] MacArthur did not take these clashes as a sign of serious Chinese intervention. When he launched his drive to the Yalu river on November 24, he was caught completely by surprise by a massive Chinese counteroffensive. The UN forces now had to retreat in disarray. On December 4 the Chinese took Pyongyang, and on December 26 they reached the 38th parallel. It began to look as though the UN forces might have to evacuate the peninsula.[68]

In November, after the Chinese entry into the war, Stalin committed Soviet Air Force units to Korea. The first of these were deployed in north-east China; by the end of the year there were two divisions stationed there.[69] Stalin may have been speaking the truth when he told Zhou Enlai that the Soviet Union needed time to provide air support; perhaps this was the earliest date on which such support could be organized. Alternatively, Stalin may have decided that he could not stand aside once China had entered the war. In any event, he took pains to hide Soviet involvement. Soviet airmen wore Chinese People's Volunteer uniforms, and were instructed to identify themselves as Russians living in China if they were caught by the enemy. They were forbidden to fly over the sea, or south of the line from Pyongyang to Wonsan, in order to minimize the chances of being taken prisoner if shot down.[70]

Stalin had miscalculated in supporting Kim's plan to unify Korea by force. There had been no uprising in the South, and the Americans, contrary to expectation, had decided to intervene. Stalin was apparently prepared to abandon Kim and to have him set up a government in exile in China, rather than have the Soviet Union drawn into war with the United States. Stalin's support for Kim was a miscalculation, not a sign that Soviet policy had been emboldened by the atomic bomb. Stalin's reaction to the American advance toward the Yalu river shows that he did not want war with the United States. But now, thanks to the success of the Chinese forces in Korea, the most dangerous moment in postwar Soviet–American relations had arrived.

IV

The Chinese counteroffensive made it "an entirely new war," MacArthur reported to Washington on November 28. He complained to the press that orders forbidding him to strike across the Chinese border put his troops under "an enormous handicap, without precedent in military history." Acheson believed that "we were closer than we had yet been to a wider war."[71] The CIA could not rule out that the Soviet Union might "already have decided to precipitate global war in circumstances most advantageous to itself through the development of general war in Asia."[72]

On November 30 Truman gave unsettling, and perhaps unwary, answers to a reporter, creating the impression that the atomic bomb might be used in Korea, at MacArthur's discretion.[73] Alarmed by these remarks, the British Prime Minister Clement Attlee flew to Washington, after consultations with the French Premier and Foreign Minister. He arrived on December 4, the day Chinese forces captured Pyongyang.[74] Attlee had learned before leaving London that Truman was not actively considering use of the bomb in Korea, and that the decision to use it would remain in the President's hands.[75] But Attlee, who had sent British troops to Korea, was concerned about the possible extension of the war to China. Britain had recognized the People's Republic of China, and favored a conciliatory policy, in the belief that this would encourage China to assert its independence from Moscow.[76] Attlee told Truman that the Allies "must not get so involved in the East as to lay ourselves open to attack in the West. The West is, after all, the vital part in our line against Communism." On December 10 Attlee cabled his Foreign Secretary that the British delegation had "shaken the American service chiefs by impressing on them the dangers of limited war with China."[77] Truman and Acheson were well aware of the connection between Europe and the war in Korea, and were not unhappy to have Attlee make that argument.[78]

On the evening of December 31, 1950 the Chinese launched a new offensive, crossing the 38th parallel into the South. They soon took Seoul, and their advance continued unchecked until January 25, when the US Eighth Army began a counteroffensive. MacArthur wanted to extend the war to China in order to retard the Chinese advance. Truman rejected this recommendation for fear that it would lead to Soviet involvement; but in spite of the dangers, the Truman administration was very close to expanding the war.[79] The tension in Washington eased only when General J. Lawton Collins, the Army Chief of Staff, who had gone to Korea to assess the situation on the ground, reported on January 17 that things were not as bad as MacArthur had made out.[80] Eight days later the Eighth Army ended its two-month retreat by launching an attack on the Chinese forces. Soon afterwards Peng Dehuai, Commander of the Chinese forces in Korea, went to Beijing to explain to Mao that the Korean War could not be won quickly.[81]

The crisis in December and January was the most dangerous point in postwar international relations. There was a real possibility that Truman would extend the war to China, and that Stalin would come under pressure to enter the war too. In the Berlin crisis Stalin had largely controlled the risks, and was able to decide how far to raise the tension and when to resolve the crisis by making concessions. But the Korean case was far more complicated. Some of Truman's advisers – most notably General MacArthur – wanted to extend the war to China. Stalin had to take Mao's wishes into account. This made for a complicated and dangerous set of relationships.

Stalin gave no indication in December or January that he wanted a settlement in Korea. He did not press – as it might have been logical to do – for a ceasefire along the 38th parallel. On the contrary, both he and Mao pursued an uncompromising line. On December 7 Gromyko, on instructions from the Politburo, cabled Vyshinskii, who was at the United Nations in New York:

Your proposal for a ceasefire in Korea we consider to be incorrect in the present situation when the American forces are suffering defeat and when the American side is more and more often proposing a ceasefire in Korea in order to win time and prevent the complete defeat of the American forces.[82]

This telegram suggests that the Soviet leadership expected the complete expulsion of US forces from Korea.

China took a similar line. A Chinese delegation had gone to New York in November to take part in Security Council deliberations on Korea. "We maintained our unalterable stand, neither expressing any desire to compromise, nor having any contact with the American authorities apart from openly denouncing the US acts of aggression," the head of the delegation, General Wu Xiuquan, wrote later. "What they could not get on the Korean battlefield, they could not get from us either. On the contrary, as the Chinese and Korean troops scored one victory after another, our stand in the UN became more and more firm."[83] The departure of the delegation from New York on December 19 underlined Beijing's lack of interest in a compromise. Indeed Mao was pressing hard, over the objections of Peng Dehuai, for Chinese forces to cross the 38th parallel. Stalin supported Mao, though he appears to have been more cautious than Mao in urging hot pursuit of the retreating UN forces.[84]

A crucial question here is why Stalin, if he was worried about the expansion of the war, did not back Peng Dehuai and press Mao to seek a ceasefire along the 38th parallel? Perhaps Stalin's support for Mao shows that he was not afraid that the war would be expanded. Alternatively, he may have thought that he could control the risks of expansion even if UN forces were driven from Korea. One of the interesting aspects of the crisis is that Stalin took several steps in December and January that can be interpreted as an attempt to deter the United States from expanding the Korean War by playing upon Western fears about the security of Europe. Donald Maclean, who was spying for the Soviet Union, had been appointed head of the American desk in the Foreign Office on November 1, 1950.[85] Maclean saw the briefing papers for Attlee's visit to Washington, and also the cabinet paper on the results of the meeting.[86] He was in a position to tell Moscow of Washington's assurances about the atomic bomb, and also of British anxiety about the vulnerability of Europe and of the differences between Britain and the United States. Maclean's reports would have made it clear that Attlee's main argument against expansion of the Korean War was the danger that this would leave Western Europe defenseless. Moscow appears to have concluded that the best way to prevent expansion of the war in Asia was to draw attention to the danger of war in Europe.

On December 15 the Soviet government presented sharp notes to the British and French governments attacking the proposed rearmament of West Germany as a violation of the Anglo–Soviet and Franco–Soviet treaties.[87] This gambit had the desired effect, Acheson concluded in his memoirs, for the atmosphere was "tinged with fear" at a meeting in Brussels a few days later to discuss the defense of Western Europe. The French Foreign Minister's assistant asked an American official, "Do you really think we are going to be in war in three months?"[88] Ernest Bevin, the British Foreign Secretary, was cautious too. He had been impressed by a warning from the British ambassador in Moscow that it might be just as grave a blunder to ignore Soviet warnings about the rearmament of Germany as it had been to ignore Chinese warnings about crossing the 38th parallel in Korea.[89]

Later in December Stalin asked Palmiro Togliatti, the leader of the Italian Communist Party who was in Moscow to recuperate from a serious operation, to take over as General Secretary of the Cominform. On December 24 Stalin told Togliatti that the international situation was getting worse, and that American imperialism was preparing new aggressive actions. Togliatti turned down Stalin's proposal on the grounds that he was needed in Italy.[90] Stalin summoned two of the Italian Party leaders to Moscow in the middle of January to explain his proposal. The international situation was serious, he said, and the Cominform had to be strengthened. At any moment there could be an international conflict, and a ban on communist parties in Western countries. Togliatti must not be taken prisoner by the enemy; he could continue to lead the Italian Party, but he would have to live abroad, perhaps in Czechoslovakia. The Italian Party leadership voted to support Stalin's proposal, but Togliatti persisted in his refusal, and returned to Italy in February.

This incident has been treated as a puzzling episode in the leadership politics of the Italian Communist Party.[91] The timing suggests, however, that it was connected to the international situation. It may be that Stalin believed that war in Europe was imminent. It is also possible that he wanted to communicate that danger to the Western powers. He may have believed that his conversations with the Italian Party leaders would be leaked to Western governments, which would then think that the Soviet Union was taking political steps to prepare for war. On December 24 the Viet Minh launched a new offensive against the French in Indochina. Whether or not it was ordered by Stalin, this campaign had a direct bearing on the situation in Europe because it affected France's ability to contribute forces to NATO. It added to the sense of crisis in Europe.[92]

In January Stalin summoned East European leaders to Moscow. Edward Ochab, a Central Committee secretary in the Polish Party at the time, later recalled that:

there was the Cold War, the conflict in Indochina, and the situation in Korea was becoming acute. Some representatives of people's democracies, including myself, Rakosi, Slansky, and Rokossowski, went to Moscow to discuss the problems of strengthening defense in socialist countries. Stalin, and in particular his military advisers, Marshals Vasilevsky and Sokolovsky, were of the opinion that, given the difficult international situation, the people's democracies, and Poland especially, ought to contribute more, in the name of common defense interests.[93]

On the next day bilateral meetings were held between the Soviet General Staff and each of the East European ministers of defense to review the obligations that Stalin's plan entailed for the countries concerned, and to settle what forces they should deploy in the theater of military operations.[94] "It was with a heavy heart that we accepted these 'suggestions' and their consequences," Ochab recalled later.[95] In the following month Czechoslovakia, Hungary, and Poland announced increases in their plans for industrial output; these increases were really in military production.[96] In this case too Stalin may have expected news of his preparations to leak to the West.[97]

Stalin's policy in December and January can be interpreted as an attempt to deter the United States from expanding the war in Asia by drawing attention to the Soviet threat to Europe. Although Stalin anticipated a new world war in the longer term, his policy since 1945 had shown that he wanted to avoid war with the United States. He had made this clear to North Korea and China in October 1950, and there is no reason why he should have changed his mind on that point between October and December. Hence it seems reasonable to conclude that his policy in December and January was designed to prevent expansion of the Korean War, even as he supported the decision to cross the 38th parallel.

This is speculation, but it makes sense of Stalin's policy. Pressure on Western Europe confronted the United States with the prospect that expansion of the war in Asia would leave Western Europe vulnerable to a Soviet attack. The "war of nerves" would push the West Europeans to argue more strongly against expansion of the Korean War. It might also exacerbate tensions among the Western Allies, and reinforce isolationist opinion in the United States.[98] A conciliatory policy, on the other hand, might only invite more pressure from the United States and, by showing that pressure worked, strengthen those who wanted to expand the war.[99] Stalin's policy was a continuation of the "war of nerves": the United States might be more likely to expand the war if China and North Korea sought an end to hostilities, because that would show that they were unable or unwilling to continue fighting.

Stalin also appealed to public opinion in the West. *Pravda* published his first interview for two years on February 16, 1951. Attlee had made a speech several days earlier criticizing the Soviet Union for building up its military forces and arming its satellites. "The result," Attlee had said, "is that there is this grave anxiety in the world."[100] Attlee was lying, Stalin said in his interview, in order to deceive the British people into supporting the "new world war being organized by the ruling circles of the United States." The war in Korea, he said, could end only in defeat for the "interventionists," because their cause was not just.

War could not be considered inevitable at present, Stalin said. The "aggressive forces" in Western countries could be held in check by the "peace-loving forces" in those countries. The peace movement had remained an important focus for Soviet policy, and Stalin offered it encouragement: "peace will be preserved and consolidated if the peoples will take the cause of preserving peace into their own hands and defend it to the end. War may become inevitable if the warmongers succeed in entangling the popular masses in lies, in deceiving them and drawing them into a new world war." The newly organized World Peace Council held its first meeting in February, in East Berlin, and focused on West German rearmament.[101]

In the spring of 1951 – after Truman had removed MacArthur from his command in April – the Truman administration began to think about bringing the war to an end by negotiation. Acheson sent George Kennan to hold informal talks with Iakov Malik at the beginning of June. The Soviet Union responded favorably to the American initiative, and armistice talks began on July 10, 1951. The most dangerous crisis of Stalin's last years had now passed. Although the war continued for another two years, there was a military stalemate on the peninsula. The Truman administration considered ways of breaking out of the stalemate by expanding the war, or by using nuclear weapons, but it did not come as close to doing so as it had in December 1950 and January 1951.

Stalin was in no hurry to reach a peace agreement. In August 1951 he rejected a proposal by Mao to bring in neutral states as observers, on the grounds that this would suggest that the "Chinese-Korean side" was more eager than the Americans for an armistice.[102] On November 19, 1951 he wrote to Mao that "we consider it correct that the Chinese-Korean side, while using flexible tactics in the negotiations, should continue to follow a firm line, without showing haste or revealing any interest in a speedy conclusion of the negotiations."[103] Stalin was quite content to let China and the United States remain at war, deepening their mutual hostility, and tying down US forces in Asia. In July 1952 Stalin told Pietro Nenni that there was a kind of equilibrium between the forces of war and the forces of peace. The war in Korea, he added, could not be settled by military means.[104]

V

In the last years of his life Stalin suffered from hypertension and arteriosclerosis. Early in 1952 his doctor, Vladimir Vinogradov, recommended that he follow a course of medical treatment and retire from all public activity.

Stalin was furious and would not allow Vinogradov to examine him again.[105] Yet anger at his physician could not cure his infirmities. Old age was very much on his mind, and he complained about it more and more. He went to his office less often, and reviewed lists of the issues to be decided, rather than the draft decisions themselves. Many important questions were left unresolved; there was a blockage at the center, as Stalin himself said.[106]

In October 1952 Stalin published *Economic Problems of Socialism in the USSR*. This disjointed and confusing pamphlet consists of his comments on a meeting held the previous November to discuss a draft textbook on political economy.[107] Part of the work is devoted to the question of war and peace. In this part Stalin answered an argument put forward by Eugen Varga at the November 1951 meeting. Stalin's comments can best be understood by looking at Varga's argument.

Varga had been a Comintern official in the 1930s, and Stalin had adopted some of his ideas. After World War II Varga put forward an analysis of world politics that was different from Stalin's. Varga argued that the capitalist state had acquired some capacity to manage the capitalist economy and to delay the kind of crisis that had shaken capitalism in the 1930s. Besides, Varga argued, the United States had achieved a hegemonic position in the capitalist world and would be able therefore to prevent intercapitalist rivalries from erupting into war. In retrospect this analysis looks far more prescient than Stalin's, but Varga was condemned for his views, and in 1948 the Institute of World Economy and World Politics, which he directed, was closed down.[108]

Varga nevertheless continued to advance his ideas. In a memorandum to the Central Committee he argued that (1) the bourgeoisie had learned from the two world wars that wars cause revolution; (2) the imperialist camp was turning into a single military alliance; (3) the bourgeoisie's interest in defense against socialism was stronger than its internal contradictions; (4) "it is extremely difficult to *imagine concretely* a new war among the imperialists."[109] These considerations, in Varga's mind, overruled Lenin's thesis that war was inevitable. This argument did not lead Varga to predict a war between capitalism and socialism. He believed that the balance of power was such that the risk for the imperialists in this type of war was very great; "the potential winnings do not match the risk of the destruction of the entire capitalist system."[110]

This was the argument that Stalin sought to refute in his *Economic Problems of Socialism in the USSR*. "Some comrades," he wrote, believed that wars between capitalist countries had ceased to be inevitable, but they were mistaken.[111] Although the United States seemed to have the other capitalist powers under control, it was wrong to think that "things can continue to 'go well' for 'all eternity.'" Britain and France would be compelled, by their search for cheap raw materials and secure markets, to break from the embrace of the United States and enter into conflict with it. Germany and Japan too would try to throw off the US "regime" and force their way to independent development.[112]

Although it was true in theory that the "contradictions between capitalism and socialism are stronger than the contradictions among the capitalist countries," this did not mean that a new world war would start as a clash between capitalism and socialism. The same situation had existed before World War II, wrote Stalin, yet that war had started not as a conflict between the capitalist world and the Soviet Union, but as a war between capitalist countries. There were two reasons why a new war would not start as a war between socialism and capitalism. First, war with the Soviet Union put at risk not only the supremacy of certain capitalist countries, but the very existence of capitalism itself. Second, capitalists were aware of the Soviet Union's peace policy and knew that it would not attack capitalist countries of its own accord.

Stalin drew a parallel between the interwar years and the period after World War II. Germany had risen to its feet within fifteen to twenty years after World War I. Britain and the United States had helped Germany to recover, in order to set it against the Soviet Union. But Germany moved first against the "Anglo–French–American bloc," and when Hitler attacked the Soviet Union those capitalist countries were compelled to enter into a coalition with the Soviet Union. "Consequently," concluded Stalin,

the struggle of the capitalist countries for markets and their desire to crush their competitors proved in practice to be stronger than the contradictions between the capitalist camp and the socialist camp. What guarantee is there, then, that Germany and Japan will not rise to their feet again, will not attempt to break out of American bondage and live their own independent lives? I think there is no such guarantee.[113]

In William Wohlforth's words, Stalin believed that "postwar world politics would be a grand, cataclysmic replay of prewar world politics."[114] Stalin had told Nenni in July that West Germany would prove less docile than the Americans imagined.[115]

Stalin next rejected the argument that the peace movement had rendered obsolete Lenin's inevitability-of-war thesis. The peace movement did not aim to overthrow capitalism and establish socialism, he wrote. If it succeeded, the peace movement would prevent a "*particular* war," preserve a "*particular* peace," but it would not be enough to eliminate the inevitability of wars between capitalist countries generally. It would not be enough, because, "for all the successes of the peace movement, imperialism will remain, continue in force – and consequently, the inevitability of wars will also continue in force. To eliminate the inevitability of war, it is necessary to abolish imperialism."[116] The peace movement was a useful instrument of policy, but it could not transform international politics.

Some Western commentators have taken Stalin's argument to mean that war between capitalism and socialism could be avoided.[117] But that is mistaken. Stalin argued, as he had done in February 1946, that World War II had its origins in interimperialist rivalry, and that a new world war might well engulf the Soviet Union again. The implication of Stalin's argument was that the Soviet Union had to be ready for war. This too was the point of his comments on the peace movement: since the peace movement could not abolish war in general, the Soviet Union could not weaken its military strength in favor of reliance on the peace movement. War was inevitable as long as imperialism existed. All the Soviet Union could do was build up its military strength and liquidate its enemies at home. This argument fitted in with Stalin's stress in the rest of this work on heavy industry, and his rejection of greater use of the market.

Economic Problems of Socialism in the USSR was published three days before the opening of the Nineteenth Party Congress in October 1952.[118] This was the first party congress in thirteen years. Malenkov gave the main report, in which he repeated the argument that World War I had led to Russia's leaving the capitalist system, and World War II to the creation of the socialist system. "There is every reason to assume," he continued, "that a third world war would bring about the collapse of the capitalist system." But it was Stalin who dominated the proceedings, even though he gave only a short speech. He sat alone on the right of the Presidium, listening to the speakers vie with one another in sycophancy; there was no one beside him, or behind him.[119]

On October 16, the day after the congress ended, Stalin gave a long and harsh speech to a plenary session of the new Central Committee. The main point of the speech (according to Konstantin Simonov, who had just become a candidate member of the Central Committee) was that

he was old, and that the time was approaching when others would have to continue doing what he had done, that the situation in the world was complex and a difficult struggle with the capitalist camp lay ahead and that the most dangerous thing in this struggle was to flinch, to take fright, to retreat, to capitulate. That was the main thing that he wished not only to say, but to instill into those present and that in its turn was connected with the theme of his own age and possible departure from this life.[120]

In stressing the dangers of retreat, fright, and capitulation, Stalin pointed to Lenin's fearlessness in the face of difficulties. And to drive home his point he made a furious attack on Molotov and Mikoian – two of the longest-serving members of the Politburo – for their lack of firmness, their cowardice and capitulationism.

Molotov and Mikoian were sitting behind Stalin, their faces white and lifeless. When Stalin had finished, they responded to his attack: "they tried to explain to Stalin their actions and deeds, to justify themselves, to tell him that it was not so, that they had never been cowards or capitulationists, and that they were not afraid of new clashes with the camp of capitalism and that they would not capitulate before it." They spoke like condemned men making their last speeches.[121]

The five-month period from the Nineteenth Congress to Stalin's death on March 5, 1953 was "difficult and strange," according to Simonov. Arkady Vaksberg has written that it was "pervaded by a terrifying atmosphere in which new catastrophes were anticipated on a far more nightmarish scale than anything that had gone before."[122] In November Stalin ordered the arrest of the leading Kremlin doctors, including his own physician, Vinogradov. Confessions were soon obtained by torture, and Stalin passed these around the leadership, saying "You are like blind kittens; what will happen without me? The country will perish because you do not know how to recognize enemies."[123] The doctors were accused of murdering Zhdanov, and attempting to kill other members of the leadership. Most were said to be working for Jewish organizations in the service of American intelligence; others to be British agents. Publication of these charges in January 1953 created a hysterical atmosphere in the country, with strong anti-Semitic overtones.

It appears that Stalin's intention was to have the doctors tried and hanged. Anti-Jewish pogroms would follow, and Jewish leaders would ask that the Jews be deported to Siberia for their own safety. Molotov's wife, Polina, who was Jewish, was to be charged as one of the leaders of an anti-Soviet conspiracy. This would provide a link to Molotov, who would undoubtedly have been arrested too. Mikoian and Voroshilov, both of whom Stalin suspected of being British agents, were likely victims as well. Beria too would perhaps have been caught up in the purge, since the security agencies were being accused of negligence in the Doctors' Plot.[124]

Whatever it was that Stalin had in mind, it seems clear that the country stood on the brink of catastrophe when he died. At home he appears to have been preparing a bloody purge. Abroad his policies had helped to create an extremely tense situation, and had drawn the Soviet Union into a costly arms race. The danger of war seemed close at hand, but Stalin was not seeking détente with the West.[125] Lt.-Gen. N.N. Ostroumov, who was deputy chief of the operations department of the Air Force Staff in 1952, has recalled that he and his colleagues believed that Stalin was actively preparing for war. This was evident, he has written, not only in military policy: "public consciousness was gradually being prepared, and the country purposefully made ready, for approaching trials – more precisely, for war."[126] Stalin had always been cautious in the use of force, and there is no reason to believe that he wanted war. But he had made serious miscalculations in the past, and old age had further warped his capacity for judgment. It is hard to see in the Stalin of those last months a man willing to come to grips with new ideas about war and peace in the nuclear age. Rather he appears to have been engaged in preparing the country – stabilizing the home front in his own capitalist fashion – for coming clashes with the brutal world.

CHAPTER FOURTEEN

The Hydrogen Bomb

I

STALIN'S DEATH was to have profound consequences for the Soviet Union and the world, but it was not immediately obvious that those consequences would be beneficial. Some people – even those who knew of at least some of the evil Stalin had done – felt a sense of loss and apprehension: what would happen now? Andrei Sakharov, who was working in Arzamas-16 at the time, wrote to his wife expressing the grief and confusion he felt at Stalin's death. "Afterwards I felt ashamed of this," he wrote many years later. "When trying to analyze myself, I think that at the time we associated Stalin's name, above all, with the cause which we thought to be the most important."[1] Sakharov recalled accepting – if only subconsciously – the argument that historic transformations such as the transition to communism entailed great suffering. More specifically, "I felt myself committed to the goal which I assumed was Stalin's as well: after a devastating war, to make the country strong enough to ensure peace."[2]

Not everyone felt the same way about Stalin's death. Lev Landau remarked to a colleague, "That's it. He's gone. I'm no longer afraid of him, and I won't work on [nuclear weapons] any more."[3] Landau was directing a computing group, which worked on calculations for nuclear weapons, at the Institute of Physical Problems. Landau's attitude to the Soviet regime had not been improved by the year he had spent in prison before the war. He had agreed to work on the nuclear project because he believed that it provided him with a measure of protection, but he regarded this work as a distraction from his real research. He quit the nuclear project in 1955.[4] Landau's attitude was the exception rather than the norm, and there was no exodus of scientists from the project. Indeed Stalin's death had little immediate effect on the project, which was now focused on the development of thermonuclear weapons.

Early in 1942 Enrico Fermi had suggested to Edward Teller that an atomic bomb might be used to ignite a hydrogen bomb, in which energy is released through the fusion of light nuclei (for example isotopes of hydrogen) as well as through the fission of heavy elements. The fusion of light elements takes place only at temperatures of tens of millions of degrees (as in the sun, whose energy comes from fusion); hence the fusion reaction is also called a thermonuclear reaction. Fermi and Teller understood from the outset that the explosive yield of such a bomb could be made indefinitely large and would depend only on the amount of thermonuclear fuel it contained.[5]

When the Los Alamos laboratory was established, work on the thermonuclear bomb – the superbomb or Super, as it was known – was one of its main tasks. Edward Teller was the chief advocate of the Super and headed a small theoretical group working on it. Teller's initial idea was to create a thermonuclear reaction in deuterium, a heavy isotope of hydrogen, but he soon realized that this was impracticable, because fusion of the deuterium nuclei would require a temperature of hundreds of millions of degrees. He concluded that it would be possible to ignite thermonuclear reactions with an atomic bomb only if tritium, a still heavier isotope of hydrogen, was used as well, because tritium ignites at tens, rather than hundreds, of millions of degrees. Tritium occurs rarely in nature, and is difficult and costly to produce. This lessened the promise of the superbomb as a wartime project. Besides, the development of the atomic bomb proved more difficult than expected, and so required almost all of the laboratory's resources. Although Teller worked almost exclusively on the Super, nearly everyone else at Los Alamos worked to develop the fission bombs.[6]

As work on the atomic bomb moved toward completion, scientists at Los Alamos, including Oppenheimer, supported the idea that vigorous development of the hydrogen bomb should begin once the war was over. A conference on the Super was held at Los Alamos in April 1946, with thirty-one participants including Teller and Klaus Fuchs. A report of the conference prepared in June concluded that "it is likely that a super-bomb can be constructed and will work," and stated that the objections which had been raised to the "Classical Super," the detailed design submitted to the conference, could be overcome.[7]

It was in 1946 that Soviet scientists began to work on the hydrogen bomb. In that year Gurevich, Zel'dovich, Pomeranchuk, and Khariton wrote a report on the "Utilization of the nuclear energy of light elements." This brief document surveyed some of the problems of designing a thermonuclear bomb, focusing in particular on the problem of igniting the thermonuclear reaction. "The nuclear reaction will proceed without being damped," they wrote, "only at very high temperatures of the entire mass." They pointed out that in principle it was possible to achieve "an explosion of an unlimited amount of the light element," and they proposed deuterium as the explosive material. They concluded that "it appears to us to be very essential to discover a system in which a single powerful pulse can initiate a nuclear detonation of an unlimited amount of matter."[8]

It is possible that the immediate stimulus for this report came from the realization that a thermonuclear bomb was possible in principle. The idea that a fission bomb might be used to initiate a thermonuclear explosion occurred independently to Soviet physicists. At the end of 1946 Iakov Frenkel', who had not been drawn into the nuclear project, wrote in a popular science magazine that

the possibility is not to be excluded that actinouranium (uranium-235) and plutonium will be used in the future as a kind of initiating material or detonator for the explosion of more stable elements, both heavy elements, which explode by means of fission, and also light elements, capable of exploding when combined with hydrogen or with one another.[9]

It seems more likely, however, that the 1946 report was a response to intelligence from the United States. The Soviet Union had begun to receive information about American work on the superbomb in 1946. On December 31 Kurchatov wrote to V.S. Abakumov, the Minister of State Security, that "the material with which Comrade Vasilevskii acquainted me today on . . . American work on the superbomb . . . is, in my opinion, probably true and of great interest for our work in this country."[10] Whatever the stimulus, the work was begun in the context of intense competition with the United States. Soon after the report by Gurevich *et al.* a small group was organized at the Institute of Chemical Physics in Moscow to investigate the hydrogen bomb. This group worked under the direction of Zel'dovich, who also headed the theoretical department at Arzamas-16.[11]

In his confession to Michael Perrin, Fuchs said that during 1947 Soviet intelligence asked him for any information he could provide about the "tritium bomb."[12] If Fuchs is correct about the date, the information received by Kurchatov in 1946 must have come from another source.[13] The reference to tritium in the question to Fuchs indicates that Soviet physicists had already concluded – either by themselves or with the help of intelligence material – that tritium would lower the ignition temperature for the hydrogen bomb.

Everything Fuchs knew about the hydrogen bomb came from his time at Los Alamos, where he had taken part in the April 1946 conference on the Super shortly before returning to Britain. According to his confession, Fuchs passed on information about

the T-D [tritium-deuterium] cross-section value before this was declassified, and he also gave all that he knew from his Los Alamos period on the methods for calculating radiation loss and the ideal ignition temperature. He also described the current ideas in Los Alamos when he left on the design and method of operation of a super bomb, mentioning, in particular, the combination fission bomb, the tritium initiating reaction and the deuterium one.[14]

Fuchs himself did not place a very high value on the information he gave to the Soviet Union. He told the FBI that "his information concerning the H-bomb work in the United States at the time he returned to England was . . . best described as a confused picture."[15]

Zel'dovich's group at the Institute of Chemical Physics apparently checked the intelligence information from the United States.[16] This would certainly not have provided a workable design for a hydrogen bomb, because these early American ideas were later shown not to work. Nevertheless, by the summer of 1948 Zel'dovich's group had done calculations for a specific design. In June of that year Kurchatov asked Igor Tamm, head of the theoretical department at FIAN, to analyze the calculations that Zel'dovich's group had done, to refine and extend those calculations, and to make an independent assessment of the whole design.[17]

Tamm was widely regarded by his colleagues as a "model of decency in science and public life."[18] Born in Vladivostok in 1895, he had grown up in the Ukraine, where his father was a city engineer. His parents sent him to the University of Edinburgh in 1913 to keep him out of revolutionary politics, but in 1914 he moved to Moscow University, where he became an active Menshevik. In the summer of 1917 he was a delegate to the first All-Russian Congress of Soviets; he was one of the Menshevik-Internationalists who opposed Russia's continued participation in the world war.[19] In 1919–20 he taught physics at the Tauridian University in Simferopol, where Iakov Frenkel' was also teaching and Vernadskii was rector. In 1922 Tamm came to teach at Moscow University, where he headed the department of theoretical physics from 1930 to 1941. In 1934 he organized the theoretical department at FIAN, and headed it until his death in 1971. In 1937 his brother was arrested and shot; so too was his boyhood friend, B.M. Gessen, the first dean of the physics faculty at Moscow University. At this period Tamm kept a bag ready to take with him in case he was arrested.[20] Tamm never lost his commitment to socialist ideals; and he never joined the Communist Party.

Kurchatov's request to Tamm to check the work of the Zel'dovich group marked a new stage in the project. Up to this point Kurchatov had relied on the Leningrad school of physics, drawing largely on people from Ioffe's institute and Semenov's Institute of Chemical Physics. By bringing Tamm into the project he began to involve the Moscow school, whose founding figure had been Leonid Mandel'shtam. Relations between the two schools had not always been easy and, besides, Tamm had spoken in favor of Alikhanov and not Kurchatov during the Academy elections in 1943. But Kurchatov needed a strong theoretical physicist to assess Zel'dovich's work, and he was not a man to let personal slights or resentment stand in the way of cooperation. Tamm agreed to accept Kurchatov's task, since he believed that it was important for the Soviet Union to have its own nuclear weapons.[21]

To carry out Kurchatov's assignment, Tamm recruited some of the younger physicists in his own department, including Andrei Sakharov, who was twenty-seven years old at the time, as well as Vitalii Ginzburg, S.Z. Belenkii, and Iurii Romanov.[22] Sakharov was the son of a well-known Moscow physics teacher. After graduating from Moscow University in 1942 he had worked at an arms plant in Ulianovsk, on the Volga. He returned to Moscow in 1945 to become a graduate student at FIAN under Tamm's supervision. Tamm's decency and independence of mind exercised an important influence on Sakharov's moral and political formation.[23]

Sakharov had been asked by Kurchatov to join the atomic project, but had declined to do so.[24] He did agree, however, to join Tamm's thermonuclear group. Like Tamm he was convinced that the Soviet Union needed nuclear weapons to restore the balance of power.[25] In an interview not long before his death in 1989 he repeated this view, saying that it was justified to build the hydrogen bomb, "in spite of the fact that we were giving the weapon into the hands of Stalin and Beria."[26] He also found the project challenging, and was attracted by its size and scope: "the interest here was caused by the nature of the problems, the possibility to prove what one can do, above all to oneself."[27]

Tamm and his colleagues found the design proposed by Zel'dovich's group unsatisfactory, and quickly moved beyond it. Before the end of 1948 Tamm's group had come up with an alternative design. In September Sakharov proposed the "First Idea," as he calls it in his memoirs.[28] The idea was to place alternate layers of thermonuclear fuel (deuterium, tritium and their chemical compounds) and uranium-238 in a fission bomb between the fissile material and the conventional high explosive. This would make a fission–fusion–fission reaction possible, since the high-energy neutrons from the deuterium-tritium reaction would fission the uranium-238. More importantly, the low heat conductivity of the uranium would reduce the heat loss from the bomb, and the fissioning of the natural uranium casing would compress the light elements several times, thereby speeding up the thermonuclear reaction.[29] Sakharov called this concept the "Layer Cake." It is similar to the "Alarm Clock" concept proposed by Edward Teller in late 1946, but not pursued further.[30] Sakharov makes it clear in his memoirs that he conceived of his "First Idea" independently. Tamm supported Sakharov's design as more promising than Zel'dovich's, and so too did Zel'dovich when he learned of it.[31] It was now agreed that Tamm's group should work on Sakharov's idea, not on the design proposed by Zel'dovich's group. For its part, Zel'dovich's group was to help with the work on Sakharov's design, while continuing to work on its own original proposal.[32]

A second important step was taken when Vitalii Ginzburg proposed in November 1948 that lithium deuteride – a compound of lithium-6 and deuterium – be used in the bomb, instead of deuterium and tritium. The merit of this proposal was that lithium deuteride, a chalklike solid, would be easier to handle than deuterium and tritium and their chemical compounds. More importantly, the lithium-6 would produce tritium when it was bombarded by neutrons in the course of the explosion. Sakharov refers to Ginzburg's proposal in his memoirs as the "Second Idea." Kurchatov realized its importance, and immediately took steps to organize the production of lithium deuteride.[33]

The Soviet Union had the basic design concept for a workable thermonuclear bomb before the end of 1948, well before its first atomic bomb test. The decision to develop the hydrogen bomb was seen as a logical next step and occasioned none of the soul-searching that took place in the United States.[34] After the test, according to Golovin,

everyone was longing for the holiday they had not had for five years. But before letting people go to their well-deserved rest, Kurchatov kept everyone for a week, let the excitement calm down, and directed them to the next stage - the creation of a hydrogen bomb.[35]

After a rest of two months, Kurchatov returned to work. The development of the hydrogen bomb was now a top priority for the Soviet Union.

II

Work on the superbomb proceeded slowly in the United States in the immediate aftermath of the war. Many of the Los Alamos scientists returned to the universities. Most of the laboratory's resources were devoted to improving fission weapons.[36] In the summer of 1948 Oppenheimer, who had left Los Alamos and was now chairman of the General Advisory Committee (GAC) of the Atomic Energy Commission (AEC), suggested that Los Alamos work on the development of a boosted fission weapon.[37]

The distinction between the boosted fission weapon and the superbomb is crucial in the history of the United States program. The boosted weapon is one in which a fission bomb is used to initiate a small thermonuclear reaction so that the neutrons from this reaction might increase the efficiency of the use of the fissile material. The idea of the superbomb, on the other hand, was to use a fission bomb to ignite a very large mass of thermonuclear fuel, in order to produce a very large explosive yield on the order of 1,000 times more powerful than the atomic bomb.[38] Oppenheimer had advocated the boosted fission bomb as early as 1944, on the grounds that it would provide "an experimentally possible transition from a simple gadget [a fission bomb] to the super and thus open the possibility of a not purely theoretical approach to the latter."[39] Now, in 1948, it was planned to proceed with this work at Los Alamos and to test a boosted weapon in 1951.[40] This test was conducted on May 24, 1951; it produced an explosive yield of 45.5 kilotons.[41]

By the time of the first Soviet atomic test in August 1949, "work on the super itself," writes Herbert York, "presented a very mixed picture." Theoretical calculations had cast serious doubt on the feasibility of the design discussed at the Los Alamos conference in April 1946.[42] In spite of Teller's continuing enthusiasm, there was little support in the AEC or at Los Alamos for a crash program. AEC chairman David Lilienthal wrote in July 1949 to the Military Liaison Committee, which linked the AEC and the Defense Department, that "in regard to thermonuclear assemblies, theoretical studies are continuing at a pace which does not interfere seriously with more urgent elements of the laboratory program."[43]

The Soviet atomic test transformed this situation. In Washington there was a general sense that some response was needed, and support for an all-out effort to build the Super soon developed. On October 5, 1949 Lewis Strauss, one of the members of the AEC, wrote to his fellow commissioners that "the time has come for a quantum jump in our planning (to borrow a metaphor from our scientist friends) . . . we should make an intensive effort to get ahead with the super."[44] One of the main arguments used by advocates of a crash program was that the Soviet Union might be ahead of the United States in developing thermonuclear weapons.[45] On October 17 Senator Brien McMahon, chairman of the Congressional Joint Committee on Atomic Energy, warned the AEC that "there is reason to fear that Soviet Russia has assigned top priority to development of a thermonuclear super-bomb. If she should achieve such a bomb before ourselves, the fatal consequences are obvious."[46] US intelligence had no evidence that the Soviet Union had given top priority to the Super, but the failure to anticipate when the first Soviet atomic test would take place had shown how fast the Soviet Union was progressing, and how little the United States knew. The argument that the Soviet Union might be working on the superbomb seemed plausible to advocates of a crash program.

Not everyone, however, was in favor of developing the Super. The GAC, at its meeting on the weekend of October 28–30, 1949 opposed its development. Although it was formally an advisory body, the GAC normally carried great weight on scientific and technical matters. Among its members were Harvard president James Conant, and Nobel prizewinners Enrico Fermi and I.I. Rabi, as well as Oppenheimer.[47] The GAC approved the build-up and diversification of fission weapons (including tactical weapons), endorsed preparation for radiological warfare, and supported the development of boosted fission weapons; but it unanimously opposed an all-out effort to develop the Super.[48] It pointed to technical and theoretical problems that stood in the way; questioned whether such a weapon would be cheaper than fission bombs in terms of damage area per dollar; and finally raised moral objections, on the grounds that the Super "carries much further than the atomic bomb itself the policy of exterminating civilian populations."[49]

The majority of the committee felt that the United States should make an unqualified commitment not to develop the Super, since this would be "in a totally different category from an atomic bomb" and might become a "weapon of genocide." They argued that the "extreme dangers to mankind inherent in the proposal wholly outweigh any military advantage that could come from this development."[50] Enrico Fermi and I.I. Rabi, on the other hand, took the position that an American commitment not to develop the Super should be made conditional on a similar renunciation on the part of the Soviet Union. "It would be appropriate to invite the nations of the world to join us in a solemn pledge not to proceed in the development or construction of weapons of this category," they wrote. "If such a pledge were accepted even without control machinery, it appears highly probable that an advanced stage of development leading to a test by another power could be detected by available means."[51]

Three of the five AEC commissioners, including the chairman, David Lilienthal, agreed with the GAC recommendation not to go ahead with the Super, while two opposed it. Lewis Strauss wrote to Truman on November 14 that the recent Soviet success with the atomic bomb showed that the hydrogen bomb was within the Soviet grasp, and that "a government of atheists is not likely to be dissuaded from producing the weapon on 'moral' grounds."[52] Senator McMahon was an equally forceful advocate. He sent a long and eloquent letter to the President on November 21 supporting development of the superbomb.[53] The Joint Chiefs weighed in on November 23 with a paper arguing that "possession of a thermonuclear weapon by the USSR without such possession by the United States would be intolerable."[54]

Truman set up a three-man committee to advise him on the issue. Secretary of State Dean Acheson chaired this committee; David Lilienthal and Secretary of Defense Louis Johnson were the other members.[55] Acheson was not persuaded by Oppenheimer's arguments, and asked "How can you persuade a paranoid adversary to disarm 'by example'?"[56] On January 31, 1950 the committee recommended that the United States go ahead with the Super, at least to the test stage. Later that day the President issued a statement saying that he had directed the Atomic Energy Commission to work "on all forms of atomic weapons, including the so-called hydrogen or super bomb."[57] On the following day the *New York Times* carried a four-column headline: "Truman Orders Hydrogen Bomb Built." The decision was applauded in Congress and in the press.[58]

Three days later Klaus Fuchs was arraigned in London. The FBI had begun a full-scale investigation of Fuchs in September 1949, on the basis of a message that the Soviet consulate in New York had sent to the KGB headquarters in Moscow in 1944; this message had recently been deciphered.[59] But it was only on January 27, 1950 that Fuchs made his confession to William Skardon of MI5, and only three days later that he revealed in detail to Michael Perrin, Deputy Director for Technical Policy of the UK Atomic Energy Authority, what he had told the Soviet Union. Although some United States officials may have known of the Fuchs investigation before Truman's January 31 decision, this knowledge does not appear to have played any role in that decision, or in the debate that preceded it.[60] Now, however, many people drew the conclusion that Fuchs had given the Soviet Union a head start in developing the hydrogen bomb. This lent added urgency to the Super, and undoubtedly contributed to Truman's secret decision on March 10, 1950 to accelerate the program by authorizing preparations not only for a test, but also for production of the weapon.[61]

When Truman made this decision, American scientists still did not know how to build a superbomb. The two basic problems were how to transfer the energy released by the exploding fission bomb to the thermonuclear fuel (the ignition problem), and how to ensure that the explosive fusion reaction (the thermonuclear burning) would be self-sustaining. There was some optimism that these two problems could be solved. Teller thought that the high temperature generated by the fission bomb could be used to ignite a thermonuclear reaction in a mixture of deuterium and tritium; and calculations that he and his group had done seemed to show that a self-sustaining thermonuclear reaction would take place in deuterium. The GAC had estimated in October 1949 that "an imaginative and concerted attack on the problem has a better than even chance of producing the weapon within five years."[62]

In the course of 1950, however, the mathematician Stanislaw Ulam showed that Teller's earlier calculations had been mistaken, and that a very large amount of tritium would be needed to ignite a self-sustaining thermonuclear reaction; this would make the Super a very expensive proposition. Further work by Ulam and Fermi cast doubt on whether or not a self-sustaining thermonuclear reaction could take place in deuterium. As a result of these calculations, the Super program was in extreme difficulty by the autumn of 1950. The "Classical Super", as the design discussed at Los Alamos in April 1946 was called, now looked impracticable. Teller was very worried.[63]

It was only in the early months of 1951 that Teller and Ulam found a way out of this impasse.[64] The Teller–Ulam solution was based on three ideas. The first was that the thermonuclear fuel should be not merely heated, but compressed in order to increase its density. Compression was the key, because it would make the fuel burn more quickly, thereby preventing heat loss in the fuel from proceeding more quickly than heat production.[65] The second idea was to use the X-rays from the fission explosion to compress the thermonuclear fuel; this was the concept of radiation implosion. The third idea was to separate the fission primary from the thermonuclear fuel package, and to use the bomb casing to channel and focus the radiation from the fission explosion in order to compress, or implode, the thermonuclear fuel. Because the fission primary is physically separate from the thermonuclear fuel, bombs of this kind are sometimes referred to as two-stage weapons.[66]

It was clear at once to American weapons scientists that the Teller–Ulam configuration made the superbomb feasible.[67] The first test of the concept took place on November 1, 1952 when a thermonuclear device was detonated on the Eniwetok atoll in the South Pacific. This was not a deliverable weapon, but a large and bulky assembly, weighing about 60 metric tons. The thermonuclear fuel was liquid deuterium, which had to be kept at temperatures colder than −250 degrees C, and therefore required a large refrigeration unit. The liquid deuterium was surrounded by uranium-238. The detonation, which was known as the Mike test, produced an explosive yield equivalent to 10 megatons of TNT. This was the first detonation to employ the principle that made the superbomb possible. It proved to be about 500 times more powerful than the first plutonium bombs, and almost 1,000 times as powerful as the bomb dropped on Hiroshima.[68]

In the spring of 1954 the United States tested six variants of the Super in the Pacific. The first and most powerful of these was detonated on Bikini atoll in the Bravo test on March 1. This was a deliverable bomb, and used lithium deuteride as its thermonuclear fuel. The yield of 15 megatons was greater than expected. A Japanese fishing-boat, which was about 80 miles from ground zero when the test took place, received a heavy dusting of radioactive debris. The twenty-three crew members soon contracted radiation sickness, and one of them died from it.[69]

III

The first Soviet atomic bomb had been a copy of the first American bomb. But the first Soviet hydrogen bomb was an original design, and the path of development pursued by the Soviet Union was different from that of the United States. Although Soviet physicists continued to investigate other designs, the main effort focused on the "Layer Cake" design. In the spring of 1950 Tamm's group moved from Moscow to Arzamas-16. Sakharov and Romanov went at the beginning of March, and Tamm himself in April; Ginzburg was not permitted to join them because his wife had been exiled to Gor'kii; Belenkii remained in Moscow because of illness.[70] There were now two theoretical groups at Arzamas-16, Zel'dovich's and Tamm's, and they competed in a spirit of friendly rivalry.[71]

Arzamas-16 was where the main theoretical and experimental work on the hydrogen bomb was done. But other institutes became involved too. There were two computing groups in Moscow, as well as one at Arzamas-16, working on the calculations for the new design. One of the Moscow groups was at the Institute of Applied Mathematics. The other, at the Institute of Physical Problems, was directed by Landau.[72] In other institutes – including his own laboratory – Kurchatov organized research on thermonuclear reactions and on the fission reactions caused by the high-energy neutrons that the thermonuclear reactions would release.[73]

Kurchatov also began, in the autumn of 1952, to prepare for radiochemical monitoring of the test. Soviet scientists wanted to be able to evaluate how effective the design was. Kurchatov asked N.A. Vlasov to study the reactions of deuterons (the nuclei of deuterium atoms) with lithium-6 and lithium-7. According to Vlasov,

in order to evaluate the intensity of the thermonuclear process and improve the design of the reactor, it is necessary to be able to find traces of the reactions. It is possible to use, for example, some radioactive indicator which is formed with the participation of fast deuterons. One of the suitable indicators was acknowledged to be radioactive beryllium-7, with a half life of 53 days.[74]

Beryllium-7 can be formed in the reactions of deuterons with both isotopes of lithium. In order to use it as an indicator it was essential to know the cross-sections for reactions of lithium with deuterons of different energies. This was Vlasov's assignment.[75] Since 1950 Kurchatov's brother Boris had been studying the fission reactions caused by high-energy neutrons and the fission products that would result from such reactions.[76] This work too was important for analyzing the test.

The production of lithium deuteride was organized at the same time. Heavy water, which contains deuterium atoms instead of hydrogen, provides a source for deuterium. Several different methods of producing deuterium were pursued, not all of them successful. Anatolii Aleksandrov recalls a meeting of the Special Committee at which deuterium production was discussed:

Several military. Kurchatov, Vannikov, Pervukhin, Malyshev, Zhdanov, Makhnev . . . Meshik (who was responsible for security, and was arrested later in the Beria case). I was put sitting on one side of Beria, on the other side was Makhnev. He makes a report: "Lavrentii Pavlovich, comrade Aleksandrov here proposes to build a factory for obtaining deuterium." It's as if Beria does not see me. He addresses only Makhnev: "And does comrade Aleksandrov know that an experimental plant has blown up?" He says: "Yes, he knows." "And comrade Aleksandrov is not removing his signature?" "No, he is not." I am sitting beside him – he could ask me! "And comrade Aleksandrov knows that if the factory blows up he will go to where Makar drives the calves?" [i.e. will be sent far away]

I can't contain myself: "I speak for myself." He turns to me: "You are not removing your signature?" "No, I'm not." The factory was built. Thank God it hasn't blown up yet.[77]

The process that produced the deuterium for the first Soviet thermonuclear weapons was designed at the Institute of Physical Problems.[78]

More than one path was likewise pursued to the separation of lithium isotopes. Lithium-6, which produces tritium upon reacting with neutrons, makes up only 7.4 per cent of natural lithium. Artsimovich's group was assigned the task of separating lithium-6 by the electromagnetic method.[79] Boris Konstantinov at the Leningrad Physicotechnical Institute devised a much cheaper and more effective chemical method of separation.[80] Konstantinov's method required a new plant, however, and there were delays in building it. In the summer of 1952 Beria reprimanded KGB General Nikolai Pavlov, the responsible official at the First Chief Directorate. "When we Bolsheviks want to get something done," said Beria, "we close our eyes to everything else (here Beria screwed his eyes shut, so that his face seemed even more frightening). Pavlov, you've lost your Bolshevik edge. We won't punish you now, and I hope you'll correct the error. But don't forget – we have plenty of room in our prisons."[81] One of the members of Artsimovich's group, P.M. Morozov, devised a way to separate the lithium isotopes by the electromagnetic method, and separated enough lithium-6 for the "Layer Cake" design.[82] Some of the lithium-6 was used to produce lithium deuteride, and some was irradiated to produce tritium for the bomb.

By the summer of 1953 preparations were well under way at the Semipalatinsk test site. The level of radioactivity had fallen, and after some treatment of the surface a 30-meter tower and a small workshop were erected there. As before, military equipment was placed around ground zero, and military-engineering works were erected. Underground structures were also built – including a kilometer of metro line – to test how well they would withstand the effects of the explosion. The control post was heaped up with earth and gravel, so that the shock wave would not demolish it. The observation post was moved to 20–25 kilometers away.[83]

At the last minute a serious hitch occurred. In their anxiety to get the bomb ready, the scientists had ignored the danger of fallout. It was only as the test approached that they realized that radioactive material spread by the explosion might damage the health of people living in the surrounding areas. Several teams were organized at the test site to calculate the effects of fallout with the help of the "Black Book," an American manual on nuclear weapons effects.[84] Calculations showed that a ground burst would produce large quantities of radioactive fallout, and that tens of thousands of people would have to be evacuated. Kurchatov, Malyshev, and Marshal

Vasilevskii, the military director of the test, had to decide whether to postpone the test for six months until an air drop could be arranged, or carry out the evacuation. They opted to evacuate the population from an area tens and even hundreds of kilometers from ground zero. The evacuation continued right up to the night before the test. Some of those evacuated were unable to return to their homes until the spring of 1954.[85]

Preparations for the test were made in an atmosphere of high tension. The urgency of the work on the hydrogen bomb had increased after the Mike test of November 1, 1952.[86] The strain on people at Arzamas-16 was further enhanced by Beria's sending two leading mathematicians, Mikhail Lavrent'ev and Aleksandr Iliushin, to the installation, apparently as potential replacements for Khariton and Shchelkin, should the test fail.[87] The nuclear project remained Beria's fiefdom after Stalin's death. After Beria's arrest on June 26, however, Malyshev was put in charge of the Ministry of Medium Machine-Building, as the First Chief Directorate was renamed.[88] In spite of Beria's arrest the test went ahead. On August 8 Malenkov declared in a speech to the Supreme Soviet that the United States did not have a monopoly on the production of the hydrogen bomb.[89] The "article" had not yet been hoisted on to the tower, and the surrounding population was still being evacuated. The scientists at the test site listened to Malenkov's speech on the radio in the lobby of their hotel. "Malenkov's remarks," Sakharov notes in his memoirs, "would have raised the level of tension if we had not already been keyed up to the maximum."[90]

Kurchatov was once again in charge of the test. By six o'clock on the morning of August 12, 1953 he was at the observation post and in communication with the control panel. When he received a report that everything was ready, he gave the order for the countdown.[91] V.S. Komel'kov has described the explosion:

the intensity of the light was such that we had to put on dark glasses. The earth trembled beneath us, and our faces were struck, like the lash of a whip, by the dull, strong sound of the rolling explosion. From the jolt of the shock wave it was difficult to stand on one's feet. A cloud of dust rose to a height of 8 kilometers. The top of the atomic mushroom reached a height of 12 kilometers, while the diameter of the dust of the cloud column was approximately 6 kilometers. For those who observed the explosion from the west, day was replaced by night. Thousands of tons of dust were lifted into the air. The huge mass moved slowly over the horizon. Observations of the cloud were made by airplanes, including those which were sent up to collect samples.[92]

The power of the explosion came close to the physicists' estimates. Malyshev reported by phone to Malenkov, who told him to congratulate and embrace Sakharov in particular.[93]

The test directors, dressed in special suits and equipped with dosimeters, drove out to near ground zero. Malyshev and Sakharov got out while the others remained in their vehicles, and walked over the glazed earth to the remains of the tower on which the bomb had been detonated. Where the tower had stood there was now a wide, plate-shaped depression. The metal tower and its concrete base had largely evaporated. A 5-kilometer-wide lake of glazed earth surrounded the point where the tower had stood. Tanks and weapons had been destroyed and tossed about; a railway engine was overturned; concrete walls had been crushed and wooden buildings burnt. Those present at the test were shocked to see helpless birds writhing in the grass, well away from ground zero. Wakened by the light from the test, they had taken off, only to have their wings scorched and their eyes burned out.[94]

The scene at ground zero has been described by N.A. Vlasov, who went out to the site on the third day after the test:

the general impression of a terrible and huge destructive force took shape already at a distance. Yes, the explosion had indeed been far more powerful than the explosion of the atomic bomb. The impact of it apparently transcended some kind of psychological barrier. The effects of the first atomic bomb explosion had not inspired such flesh-creeping terror, although they had been incomparably more terrible than anything seen in the still recent war.[95]

Kurchatov remained at the test site to analyze the test and write a report. On August 20 *Pravda* and *Izvestiia* announced that the Soviet Union had tested "one of the types of hydrogen bomb."[96]

The yield of the explosion was estimated by Soviet scientists at 400 kilotons, about 20 times greater than that of the first atomic bomb, and about 25 times smaller than that of the Mike test.[97] Unlike the Mike assembly, the Soviet device was – or rather could be made into – a deliverable bomb, since it had the same dimensions as the first atomic bomb.[98] It used lithium deuteride as well as tritium; the Americans first used lithium deuteride in 1954.

The "Layer Cake" design was not based on a principle such as the Teller–Ulam idea, which would make it possible to build a bomb with almost unlimited explosive power. It compressed the thermonuclear fuel, but not to the degree that the Teller–Ulam configuration made possible; and the design itself limited the amount of thermonuclear fuel that could be used. On the other hand, it was different from the boosted fission weapon tested by the United States in 1951. It used far more thermonuclear fuel – many kilograms as opposed to a few grams.[99] A much greater proportion of its explosive yield – about 15–20 per cent – came from thermonuclear reactions; about 90 per cent of the yield came from thermonuclear reactions or from the fission caused by high-energy neutrons generated by the thermonuclear reactions.[100] Sakharov believed that the "Layer Cake" design could be modified to yield an explosive power at least on the order of one megaton.[101]

The US government set up a committee chaired by Hans Bethe to evaluate the Soviet test. This committee soon estimated the yield of the explosion at about 500 kilotons. It concluded that Joe-4 – the United States named the Soviet tests Joe-1, Joe-2 etc. in honor of Stalin – was not a superbomb: its design was not capable of producing infinitely large explosive yields; it was more akin to a boosted fission weapon. The committee could not determine the precise dimensions or geometry of the bomb, though it concluded that it must have been a very unwieldy device.[102] It is now clear that the Bethe committee's evaluation was substantially correct, although the device was apparently not as large and cumbersome as the committee believed.

At the time neither Moscow nor Washington provided public information about the yield of the test, or about the design of the bomb. Although the official Soviet announcement said that the Soviet Union had tested "one of the types of hydrogen bomb," distinctions between different kinds of hydrogen bomb were not elaborated on in public, and remained obscure to many officials in both capitals. In Washington some officials argued that the Joe-4 test proved that Truman had been right to press ahead with the Super. Moscow had no interest in refuting this claim, in making itself appear less advanced – less powerful – than Washington wanted to portray it.[103]

There is little disagreement now about the nature of the "Layer Cake" design. It is, to some degree, a matter of taste whether one calls it a thermonuclear bomb or a boosted weapon.[104] It is important to note, however, that calling it a boosted weapon undervalues the significance it was given in the Soviet Union at the time. It was not seen, as the boosted weapon was in the United States, as a line of development largely distinct from the superbomb. This is clear from Sakharov's memoirs, and from the recollections of other participants in the project.[105] At the July 1953 Central Committee plenum Zaveniagin said:

The Americans built the atomic bomb, exploded it. After a certain time, with the help of our scientists and our industry, under the leadership of our government, we ended the USA's monopoly on the atomic bomb. The Americans saw that their advantage was lost and on Truman's instruction began work on the hydrogen bomb. Our people and our country are no less able than they are, we also started on this and as far as we can judge we think that we are not lagging behind the Americans. The hydrogen bomb is tens of times more powerful than an ordinary atomic bomb and its explosion will mean the end of a threatened second monopoly for the Americans, that is, it will be a most important event in world politics.[106]

The significance of the test, in Soviet eyes, was that it deprived the United States of the opportunity to create a second, thermonuclear, monopoly.

Tamm returned to FIAN. Sakharov remained at Arzamas-16 and took over leadership of Tamm's group.

The test was followed by a new round of honors. In December 1953 Sakharov, Zel'dovich, and Tamm were made Heroes of Socialist Labor. In 1954 the same honor was awarded to Kurchatov, Khariton, Aleksandrov, Konstantinov, Dukhov, Vannikov, Alikhanov, Landau, and Shchelkin. The achievement of the nuclear scientists was also reflected in the elections to the Academy of Sciences in October 1953. This was the first round of elections since 1946. Sakharov was elected to full membership of the Academy, at the early age of thirty-two, without passing through the intervening stage of corresponding membership. Tamm, Khariton, Kikoin, Aleksandrov, Vinogradov, and Artsimovich were also elected full members, while Ginzburg and Dukhov became corresponding members.

Not everyone was happy with these elections. The dean of the Physics Faculty at Moscow University wrote to Mikhail Suslov, Central Committee secretary responsible for science and ideology, that the Moscow University physicists had not been treated fairly.[107] One of the Moscow University physicists, S. Akulov, wrote to Khrushchev in October to denounce Tamm as politically unreliable and worthless as a physicist: he was a Menshevik, and related to traitors and spies, and not worthy of election to the Academy.[108] Political considerations of this kind had apparently prevented Tamm's election to full membership of the Academy in 1946. Now his contribution to building the hydrogen bomb protected him against such attacks.

IV

Washington had known nothing about Soviet work on the hydrogen bomb, but lack of knowledge had not assuaged anxiety. In mid-February 1950, less than three weeks after Truman's announcement authorizing development of the superbomb, the chairman of the Military Liaison Committee forwarded to the Secretary of Defense a memorandum that argued that "the thermo-nuclear weapon may be in actual production" in the Soviet Union.[109] In his covering letter, the chairman of the Military Liaison Committee wrote that since "there are areas in Russia not covered by our agents," CIA reports were "based on intelligence from an incomplete coverage of the Soviet Union." CIA estimates were likely, therefore, to represent "a minimum capability of the Soviet Union."[110]

Not everyone agreed with this approach. The Joint Atomic Energy Intelligence Committee, which was under the aegis of the CIA but included representatives from other intelligence agencies, commented somewhat caustically in July 1950 that in addition to the Soviet desire to build a thermonuclear bomb, "one must consider their capabilities with respect to the theoretical problems concerned, the engineering problems to be solved, and the production of critical materials."[111] It was impossible to say whether the Soviet Union could come up with a workable design, the Joint Committee concluded, because the United States did not yet know how to build a thermonuclear weapon: "our own program indicates that some new approaches may be necessary before the thermonuclear weapon is practical."[112]

Concerned though it was about Soviet work on the superbomb, the United States was unable to obtain information about Soviet progress. In December 1950 the Joint Committee reported that "there is no specific evidence that the Soviet atomic energy program is being directed toward the production of thermonuclear weapons."[113] In July 1951 the committee made a similar statement, though it added that, in light of the information supplied by Fuchs, "undoubtedly, the possibilities of developing such weapons are being extensively investigated in Soviet laboratories."[114] In January 1953 the committee still had no firm evidence of thermonuclear development in the Soviet Union. Analysis of the fallout from the 1951 Soviet tests had not identified either the high-energy neutrons or the particular radioactive isotopes that would be associated with the detonation of a boosted fission weapon or a superbomb.[115] As late as June 16, 1953, less than two months before the Joe-4 test, the CIA reported that "we have no evidence that *thermonuclear* weapons are being developed by the USSR."[116]

These bland assessments hide the considerable disagreement that existed among American scientists about the value of Klaus Fuchs's information to the Soviet Union, and about likely Soviet progress. The controversy about Fuchs began early, and was inevitably bound up with the argument over Truman's decision to proceed with a crash program to develop the superbomb. In May 1952 Hans Bethe sent Gordon Dean, chairman of the AEC, a brief history of the American thermonuclear program to make the point that Fuchs's information would have been of little value to Soviet physicists. "The theoretical work of 1950," he wrote, "had shown that every important point of the 1946 thermonuclear program had been wrong. If the Russians started a thermonuclear program on the basis of the information received from Fuchs, it must have led to the same failure."[117] Bethe also argued that the discoveries that had led to the promising designs being worked on in 1952 had been largely accidental: it could not be assumed that intensive work on those earlier ideas would lead in a straight-forward way to the Teller–Ulam concept. Consequently, while the Soviet Union might indeed be making a major effort to develop the hydrogen bomb, there were good reasons, in Bethe's mind, for thinking that it was not ahead of the United States.

In response to Bethe, Edward Teller argued that the Soviet Union might well have advanced much farther than the United States towards the development of a deliverable hydrogen bomb. He disputed Bethe's thesis that intensive work on the ideas of 1946 would not have led to the development of a workable design. He disagreed with Bethe's characterization of the discovery of the Teller–Ulam idea as "accidental": modifications to the earlier ideas, he argued, might have yielded practicable results. Teller argued that "radiation implosion is an important but not a unique device in constructing thermonuclear bombs." He went on to claim, moreover, that "the main principle of radiation implosion was developed in connection with the thermonculear program and was stated in a conference on the thermonuclear bomb, in the spring of 1946. Dr. Bethe did not attend this conference but Dr Fuchs did."[118] Teller was concerned that if Fuchs had communicated the idea of radiation implosion to Soviet scientists, they might have hit upon the Teller–Ulam configuration before Teller and Ulam did so.

Teller's fear that Fuchs had provided the Soviet Union with the radiation implosion concept proved to be unfounded. Fuchs told the FBI that it had been his idea to ignite the superbomb by implosion, but "that he did not furnish information concerning the ignition of the super bomb by the implosion process."[119] Fuchs did not understand the significance that implosion would have in the Teller–Ulam configuration; nor of course did Teller before about March 1951. Bethe was right to argue that Fuchs's information was of little help to Soviet physicists. The design developed by Zel'dovich's group in 1948 was apparently inspired by intelligence about Teller's early work, but it led nowhere.

Teller argued that Fuchs might have given the Soviet Union the advantage. Other scientists argued that the United States program to develop the superbomb might help the Soviet Union. In the autumn of 1952 a State Department Panel of Consultants on Disarmament, which was chaired by Vannevar Bush and included Oppenheimer among its members, argued for postponement of the Mike test and for a thermonuclear test ban. In making their case that a ban should be negotiated before the superbomb was tested they wrote that

it seems to us almost inevitable that a successful thermonuclear test will provide a heavy additional stimulus to Soviet efforts in this field. It may well be true that the Soviet level of effort in this area is already high, but if the Russians learn that a thermonuclear device is in fact possible, and that we know how to make it, their work is likely to be considerably intensified. *It is also likely that Soviet scientists will be able to derive from the test useful evidence as to the dimensions of the device.*[120] [Emphasis added]

Analysis of the radioactive debris from the Mike test could reveal two important things about the design of the superbomb. First, the high densities achieved in the thermonuclear fuel would leave tell-tale signs in the debris. Isotope analysis of the debris would show that the thermonuclear fuel had been greatly compressed. Second, the effect on the fission primary of the tremendous neutron flux produced by the thermonuclear reactions would depend on the distance of the primary from the thermonuclear fuel. Analysis of the debris could show that the fission primary was physically separate from thermonuclear fuel. Isotope analysis could make it clear, in other words, that Mike was a two-stage design. Analysis of the debris would not, however, reveal that radiation implosion was the mechanism used to compress the thermonuclear fuel.[121]

Soviet physicists had understood from the beginning the importance of compression. In their 1946 report Gurevich, Zel'dovich, Pomeranchuk, and Khariton had written that "the greatest possible density of deuterium is desirable, and this should be realized by using it under high pressure."[122] Compression of the thermonuclear fuel had been a key element in the "Layer Cake" design. But the "Layer Cake" was not a two-stage weapon. Analysis of the debris from the Mike test could have been useful to Soviet physicists in pointing to the idea of "staging" – assuming of course that they had not been aware of it before.

Early in 1990 Daniel Hirsch and William G. Mathews argued in an article in the *Bulletin of the Atomic Scientists* that Soviet scientists had managed to deduce the Teller–Ulam idea from a careful analysis of the debris from the Mike test.[123] When this article appeared, it caused some consternation among scientists who had taken part in the Soviet project. Khariton asked that a search be done of the files of those scientists who had been engaged in the detection and analysis of foreign nuclear tests. Nothing was found in those files to indicate that useful information had been obtained from analysis of the Mike test.[124] This was not because of self-denial. Sakharov and Viktor Davidenko collected cardboard boxes of new snow several days after the Mike test in the hope of analyzing the radioactive isotopes it contained for clues about the nature of the Mike device. One of the chemists at Arzamas-16 unfortunately poured the concentrate down the drain by mistake, before it could be analyzed.[125] Because the relevant radioisotopes have short half-lives, the analysis would have to be done soon after the test. It was only in the autumn of 1952 that Kurchatov began to make preparations for the radiochemical monitoring of the first Soviet hydrogen bomb test. In November 1952 the Soviet project was still poorly organized for obtaining and analyzing debris from nuclear tests. "The organization of our work was at that time at an insufficiently high level," Khariton has said, "and no useful results were obtained."[126]

V

The Mike test, although it gave an added urgency to Soviet work on thermonuclear weapons, did not alter its direction. Soviet scientists were already working intensively on the "Layer Cake," and exploring other possible designs. It would be a mistake to exaggerate the effect of the Mike test on the Soviet project. The "Layer Cake" remained the main focus of Soviet thermonuclear effort until the spring of 1954.

In November 1953, three months after the Joe-4 test, Malyshev asked Sakharov for a report on his conception of a second-generation weapon, its principles of operation, and its approximate specifications. Khariton and Zel'dovich were on vacation, so Sakharov wrote a brief report on his own. Two weeks later he was summoned to a meeting of the Central Committee Presidium (as the Politburo was now called), which decided that in the next two years the Ministry of Medium Machine-Building should develop and test the weapon that Sakharov had described. At the same meeting the Presidium approved development of the R-7 ICBM to carry this new weapon.[127]

At Arzamas-16 work proceeded on Sakharov's second-generation design, which was expected to lead to a significant increase in the yield of the weapon, perhaps to several megatons and certainly to at least one. By the spring of 1954, however, it had become clear that the modifications Sakharov had made to the design would raise its yield by very little.[128] It was at this time that Soviet physicists hit upon what Sakharov, in his memoirs, calls the "Third Idea." Iurii Romanov, a member of Sakharov's group at the time, has written that "in the early spring of 1954 . . . the ideas to which Ulam and Teller had come in 1951 were born."[129] Exactly how the Third Idea originated, or who made the greatest contribution, remains unclear.[130] A suggestion by Zaveniagin may have sparked off the process by which the Third Idea was formulated.[131] Something like it had been discussed before, but without result. It was only now that the idea emerged clearly in discussions between Sakharov and Zel'dovich and members of their theoretical groups.[132] There is no evidence to suggest that the American tests in the Pacific in March 1954 provided clues to the idea. According to Romanov, the basic idea came before those tests had been analyzed.[133]

Soviet scientists realized at once, as their American counterparts had done, that the Third Idea was very promising. In his memoirs Sakharov writes that

from the spring of 1954, the two theoretical departments (Zel'dovich's and my own) concentrated on the Third Idea. We devoted minimal thought and effort to the "classical" device; we recognized the risks of that neglect, but we were convinced that our strategy would pay off. Our resources were too limited to pursue both tracks aggressively.[134]

Khariton and Kurchatov approved the new direction, even though it meant disobeying the decree that the Presidium had issued at the end of 1953. When Malyshev learned of the new direction, he went to Arzamas-16 to persuade the physicists to concentrate on the "Layer Cake," and not to take the risk of trying out the new idea. In several stormy meetings he attempted to convince Kurchatov, Khariton, Sakharov, and Zel'dovich that they were wrong to focus on the Third Idea, but he did not succeed in making them change their minds. He was furious at Kurchatov, and arranged a severe party reprimand for him. This was rescinded later, after the Third Idea had proved successful and Malyshev was no longer minister.[135] Malyshev's opposition to the switch to the Third Idea is further indication that in 1953 and early 1954 the Soviet leadership regarded the "Layer Cake" as the main path of development in thermonuclear weapons.

An important development in 1953–5 was the increasing use of computers for the very complicated calculations required for thermonuclear weapons. Earlier calculations had been done by large teams of people – mainly women – using electric calculators. Work on the development of computers had begun in 1947, but in April 1949 the Council of Ministers issued a decree complaining that slow progress was delaying the development of new technology "in the field of nuclear physics, reactive technology, ballistics, electronics, gas dynamics etc."[136] Several different computers were developed in the early 1950s. The most important of these was the BESM, which started operation in 1952. By 1954 this was a fast and reliable machine, and was, according to one American specialist, "close to matching the performance of the IBM 701" introduced in 1954.[137] One of the first uses for Soviet computers was to do calculations for the thermonuclear bomb program.[138]

By November 1955 the two-stage weapon was ready for testing. In that month the Soviet Union conducted two thermonuclear tests at the Semipalatinsk test site. The first, which took place on November 6, was a test of the "Layer Cake" design, this time without tritium (though tritium was produced in the course of the explosion). According to a US intelligence report, the test was "an air burst of a boosted fission weapon using a U-235 core which obtained an energy yield of approximately 215kt. It was probably a weaponized version of the 1953 boosted configuration reduced to a more easily deliverable size."[139] This was a back-up device, in case the new two-stage design should fail.[140]

The test of the two-stage weapon was planned for just two weeks later, on November 20, 1955. The bomb was to be dropped from a Tu-16 bomber and detonated in the air in order to minimize the radioactive fallout. Kurchatov was once again responsible for the test, which proved to be a very tense and trying one. After the aircraft had taken off with the bomb on board, the test site was suddenly and unexpectedly covered by low cloud. The bomber crew could not see the mark on the ground that indicated ground zero; more importantly, the optical instruments would be unable to monitor the explosion. Kurchatov decided to call off the test.

The bomber now had to land with the bomb on board. The only place it could do so was at the airfield near Semipalatinsk. There was the danger that a crash or accident might cause the bomb to explode, with devastating consequences for the town. Kurchatov asked Sakharov and Zel'dovich what the risk was, and they stated in writing that it was very small. The airfield had iced over while the bomber was in the air, and an army unit from Semipalatinsk had to clear the runway. Kurchatov drove to the airfield and gave the order to land. He met the crew under the wing of the bomber, and congratulated them on a successful landing.[141]

The test took place two days later when the Tu-16, which was painted white to reflect the heat caused by the explosion, dropped the bomb. Sakharov, Zel'dovich, and some of the other leading scientists watched from a platform beside the laboratory building which served as the headquarters for the test, 70 kilometers from ground zero.[142] An hour before the drop Sakharov spotted the bomber rising into the air and recalled that for many peoples the color white symbolizes death. "I stood with my back to ground zero," he wrote in his memoirs,

and turned around quickly when the building and the horizon were illuminated by the flash. I saw a blinding yellow-white sphere swiftly expand, turn orange in a fraction of a second, then turn bright red and touch the horizon, flattening out at its base. Soon everything was obscured by rising dust which formed an enormous, swirling, gray-blue cloud, its surface streaked with fiery crimson flashes. Between the cloud and the swirling dust grew a mushroom stem, even thicker than the one that had formed during the first thermonuclear test. Shock waves criss-crossed the sky, emitting sporadic milky-white cones and adding to the mushroom image. I felt heat like that from an open furnace on my face – and this was in freezing weather, tens of miles from ground zero. The whole magical spectacle unfolded in complete silence. Several minutes passed, and then all of a sudden the shock wave was coming at us, approaching swiftly, flattening the feather-grass.[143]

The test was a success. The bomb was designed to have a yield of 3 megatons, but special measures were taken to reduce the yield by half for the test. Soviet scientists estimated the yield of the test explosion at 1.6 megatons.[144] The yield was not the main point, however. The significance of the test was that, as Sakharov wrote in his memoirs, it "had essentially solved the problem of creating high-performance thermonuclear weapons."[145] On November 26, Khrushchev, on a visit to India, announced that "our scientists and engineers have succeeded, with a relatively small quantity of the nuclear materials used, in obtaining an explosion whose power is equal to the explosion of several million metric tons of conventional explosives."[146] A year later Sakharov and Zel'dovich were again made Heroes of Socialist Labor.[147]

The satisfaction of technical achievement was tempered by dismay at two deaths caused by the explosion. Because of a temperature inversion at the test site, the shock wave had proved to be much more powerful than calculated. A young soldier was killed at a distance of dozens of kilometers when the trench he was in fell in and buried him. A two-year-old girl was killed in a village outside the test site. All the people of the village had been gathered into a bomb shelter, but when the explosion took place and the flash lit up the shelter through the open door everyone ran out, leaving the girl playing with bricks. The shelter fell in and killed her. Sakharov later recalled the horror he had felt. "This horror, I think," he said, "was felt not only by me, but by many others."[148]

On the evening of November 22 a celebration banquet was held in the house where Marshal of Artillery Mitrofan Nedelin, the director of the test, was living. Nedelin was Deputy Minister of Defense for Armament and became the first Commander-in-Chief of the Strategic Rocket Forces in December 1959. The banquet was attended by the leading scientists and military officers. Nedelin asked Sakharov to give the first toast. Sakharov said that he hoped that their "articles" would explode successfully over test sites, and never over cities.

This sentiment was surely unexceptionable, and indeed Khrushchev said the same thing in his speech in India four days later.[149] But Nedelin did not like what Sakharov had said, for he responded by telling the following story:

An old man wearing only a shirt is praying before an icon with a light in front of it. "Guide me and make me strong, guide me and make me strong." The old woman is lying on the stove and says from there, "You just pray for strength, old man, I can guide it in myself." Let's drink to growing strong.[150]

Sakharov found the story ominous. "I made no reply, but I was shaken inside. To some extent one can say . . . that this was one of the stimuli that made a dissident out of me."[151] The point of the story was clear. The scientists, engineers, and workers had created a terrible weapon, but would have no say in how it was used. That would be decided by the Party and military leaders. Sakharov of course had understood this before, but now it had been brought home to him in a crude and brutal way.[152]

The November 1955 test caused Sakharov to think more of his responsibility for the weapons he was creating. He feared that "this newly released force could slip out of control and lead to unimaginable disasters."[153] "The impressions from the tests were of a dual nature," he later said of the tests he observed.

On the one hand, let me repeat, there was a sensation of the tremendous scope of the project. On the other, when you see all of this yourself, something in you changes. When you see the burned birds who are writhing on the scorched steppe, when you see how the shock wave blows away buildings like houses of cards, when you feel the reek of splintered bricks, when you sense melted glass, you immediately think of times of war. . . . The very moment of the explosion, the shock wave which moves along the field and which crushes the grass and flings itself at the earth. . . . All of this triggers an irrational yet very strong emotional impact. How not to start thinking of one's responsibility at this point?[154]

In the following years Sakharov became increasingly concerned about the long-term biological consequences of nuclear tests and campaigned for a cessation of tests in the atmosphere.[155]

The superbomb test was also a turning-point for Kurchatov.[156] It had been a great strain. "One more test like those of 1953 and 1955, and I'm going to retire," he told Sakharov;[157] this was in fact the last weapons test he took charge of. After the test he and Khariton walked out to ground zero; Kurchatov was upset when he saw the mounds of earth that had been thrown up, even though the explosion had taken place more than 4 kilometers above ground.[158] He was still shaken when he returned to Moscow. Anatolii Aleksandrov has recalled a statement that Kurchatov made, perhaps after the 1953 test, but more probably in 1955. When Aleksandrov asked him what was wrong, he said: "Anatolius! That was such a terrible, monstrous sight! That weapon must not be allowed ever to be used."[159]

VI

In developing the atomic bomb, Soviet scientists had followed the American path. In developing the hydrogen bomb, they had blazed their own trail. Klaus Fuchs had not provided them with significant help; nor had they got the Third Idea from the Mike test. The 1953 and 1955 tests were a considerable achievement for Soviet science and engineering. The Soviet Union had lagged four years behind the United States in testing the atomic bomb. In August 1953 it had tested a deliverable hydrogen bomb, six months before the test of the first American superbomb; and even if one takes the view that that was not a "real" thermonuclear bomb, the November 1955 test of a superbomb came less than twenty months after the first American test of the equivalent weapon.

Herbert York, former director of the Livermore nuclear weapons laboratory, has argued that the United States could have deferred the decision to develop the superbomb without harming its relative military power. He argues that if the United States had not decided to develop the superbomb until after the Soviet test of August 1953, it would still have been able to test a multi-megaton superbomb in late 1955 or early 1956. He then points to a "most probable alternative" in which the Soviet Union, lacking the stimulus of the Mike test and the information that could be gleaned from it, would have tested a superbomb only in 1958 or 1959. The "worst plausible alternative" would be the same, except that the Soviet Union would test its first superbomb in November 1955. In other words, York claims that the GAC's advice not to go ahead with the superbomb would not have led to disaster for the United States.[160] Nothing in this chapter contradicts York's basic argument. The evidence presented here does suggest, however, that his "worst plausible alternative" was in fact far more plausible than he allows, because the Mike test was a much less important stimulus than he assumes.

Historians have continued to wonder whether, in launching an all-out program to develop the superbomb, Truman missed an opportunity to halt the arms race.[161] If the GAC's recommendation not to develop the hydrogen bomb had been accepted, would the Soviet Union have reciprocated? If the minority suggestion from Fermi and Rabi to seek a thermonuclear test ban had been acted upon, would an agreement have been possible? If the United States had decided in 1952, on the advice of the State Department Panel of Consultants on Disarmament, not to go ahead with the Mike test and to seek a thermonuclear test ban, what would have been the result?

In his memoirs Sakharov is very skeptical about the possibility that Stalin might have reciprocated American restraint in the development of thermonuclear weapons. In the late 1940s, he writes, Stalin and Beria "already understood the potential of the new weapon, and nothing could have dissuaded them from going forward with its development. Any US move toward abandoning or suspending work on a thermonuclear weapon would have been perceived either as a cunning, deceitful maneuver, or as evidence of stupidity or weakness."[162] In either case Stalin's reaction would have been the same. He would have pressed ahead with the hydrogen bomb in order to avoid a possible trap, or to exploit American stupidity. I find it hard to disagree with this judgment. Stalin in the last years of his life was profoundly distrustful of the United States and of its intentions. It is hard to imagine that he would have seen American restraint as evidence of good will, or as a sign that agreement was really possible.

The same argument applies to the 1949 and 1952 proposals for a ban on thermonuclear tests. These proposals did not require inspection, since it was assumed that a thermonuclear explosion could be detected beyond the borders of the country that carried it out. It is likely that in this case too Stalin would have seen either a trap or stupidity. He might have agreed to talks in the hope of influencing United States policy. But the political context was not propitious, especially after the outbreak of the Korean War, and serious negotiations would have required at least a minimum amount of confidence that an agreement was possible. It is hard to conceive of the ageing Stalin, who suspected his own colleagues of being spies and traitors, entering into talks in the expectation that a satisfactory agreement could be reached. Khariton, when asked whether a test ban might have been concluded while Stalin was alive, said no. He was just as skeptical about the possibility of a test ban as Sakharov about the possibility that American restraint might be reciprocated.[163]

The proposals from American scientists for mutual restraint and a formal test ban were based on the argument that the hydrogen bomb was qualitatively different from the atomic bomb, that it was a weapon of genocide and not of war. The proposals drew their force from a combination of scientific understanding and moral concern. But there is no evidence on the Soviet side that either the political leaders or the scientists had the same appreciation of what the hydrogen bomb meant.[164] Sakharov's whole outlook on the need to build more powerful weapons was, as he himself writes, akin to that of Edward Teller, not that of Oppenheimer. None of his colleagues appears to have thought differently. It was only after the death of Stalin, when repression eased, and after the first hydrogen bomb tests, which heightened scientists' understanding of what they had created, that signs can be observed of a new attitude to nuclear weapons.

CHAPTER FIFTEEN

After Stalin

I

THE DOMINANT FIGURES in the post-Stalin leadership were the men who had been closest to Stalin in his final years. Malenkov became chairman of the Council of Ministers. Khrushchev headed the Central Committee Secretariat and became First Secretary in September 1953. Beria was put in charge of the new Ministry of Internal Affairs (MVD), which combined the old ministry of that name with the Ministry of State Security (MGB). Bulganin, who had been replaced as Minister of the Armed Forces by Marshal A.M. Vasilevskii in 1949, took over the new Ministry of Defense, to which the Navy was once again subordinate; Zhukov was appointed First Deputy Minister of Defense and Commander-in-Chief of the Ground Forces.[1] At the Foreign Ministry Molotov, freed from Stalin's disfavor, replaced Vyshinskii.[2]

Malenkov, Beria, and Khrushchev all agreed that new policies were needed. Malenkov hinted as much in his speech at Stalin's funeral on March 9, 1953 when he put domestic policies at the top of the agenda.[3] On April 4 Beria's ministry announced that the charges brought against the Kremlin doctors were false, that their confessions had been extracted by torture, and that the case against them would be dropped.[4] The whole trend of policy was towards a relaxation of tension in Soviet society. The same was true of foreign policy. Immediate steps were taken to improve relations with Turkey, Yugoslavia, and Greece, and to bring the Korean War to an end.[5]

A power struggle soon broke out. Beria took the initiative in proposing reforms, perhaps because he wanted to show himself in a new light. The other leaders feared that Beria intended to amass for himself the kind of power that Stalin had possessed. Khrushchev organized a conspiracy. A group of soldiers headed by Marshal Zhukov arrested Beria at a meeting of the Presidium on June 26, 1953.[6] A special plenum of the Central Committee met at the beginning of July to denounce Beria as an agent of international imperialism and an enemy of the Party and the Soviet people.[7] Beria was tried in secret, and shot on December 23.

At the July plenum Malenkov accused Beria of taking the decision to test the hydrogen bomb without informing other members of the leadership.[8] Zaveniagin explained to the Central Committee that a draft government decision on the test had been prepared for Malenkov's signature. Beria had crossed out Malenkov's name and signed it himself. Zaveniagin went on to explain that the hydrogen bomb was a "question of world significance," and that the test would put an end to American hopes of a second nuclear monopoly. "And the scoundrel Beria," he concluded, "took the liberty of deciding such a question without the knowledge of the Central Committee."[9] This was not a trivial matter. There had been some anxiety that Beria might use the atomic bomb – or threaten its use – in a *coup d'état*.[10] On the day of Beria's arrest the Presidium abolished the Special Committee and renamed the First Chief Directorate the Ministry of Medium Machine-Building. Malyshev, one of Malenkov's men, was named minister, with Vannikov as his first deputy, and Zaveniagin as deputy minister.[11]

Malenkov, who was now the most powerful figure in the leadership, outlined his policies in a speech to the Supreme Soviet on August 8.[12] This was the speech that Sakharov and his colleagues listened to on the radio at Semipalatinsk. Malenkov wanted to give priority to improving the standard of living, and he proposed to do this by shifting investment from heavy to light industry, and by reforms in agriculture. The reordering of priorities at home was to be accompanied by a reduction of tension abroad.[13] The United States did not have a monopoly on the production of the hydrogen bomb, he said. He no doubt wanted to reassure his audience that his new policy would not endanger the security of the country.

Malenkov's policies did not command full support in the leadership. In September 1953 Khrushchev, whom some members of the Presidium regarded as more reliable than the "rightist" Malenkov, was chosen as First Secretary of the Central Committee.[14] Although Malenkov and Khrushchev shared the belief that change was needed, they disagreed on many specific issues. The conflict between them came to a head at the Central Committee plenum in January 1955. Khrushchev, who had been busily increasing his own power, accused Malenkov of seeking cheap popularity with his August 1953 speech.[15] Malenkov, he said, was not a "sufficiently mature and firm Bolshevik leader."[16] Malenkov resigned as chairman of the Council of Ministers on February 8, though he remained in the Presidium. Bulganin took over as chairman and Zhukov succeeded Bulganin as Minister of Defense.[17]

One year later, in February 1956, the Twentieth Party Congress took place. Khrushchev made a fierce attack on Stalin in a secret session of the congress. Even today, when the extent of Stalin's evil deeds is much more widely known than it was then, Khrushchev's speech remains a powerful indictment of Stalin's rule, and its impact at the time was stunning. Khrushchev described, in considerable detail, Stalin's purge of the Party in the 1930s, and criticized in vehement terms his leadership in the war with Germany.[18] But his rejection of Stalin's legacy was only partial. He did not question the policy of collectivization, or the dominant role of the Party in Soviet society. Khrushchev was still too much a product of the Stalin regime to cast it off entirely. DeStalinization remained a limited and sluggish process until the 1980s.

II

US intelligence estimated in November 1952 that the Soviet Union would have about 100 atomic bombs by the middle of 1953, though possibly as few as 50 or as many as 200.[19] Since no Soviet figures have been made public, it is impossible to say how accurate these estimates were. The start-up problems with the production reactors and the diffusion plant suggest that the number of bombs possessed by the Soviet Union at the time of Stalin's death was at or below the lower end of the CIA's estimate. It was only in 1953 that the first series-production bombs entered the arsenal.[20] This too tends to point to a stockpile smaller than 50 in mid-1953.

Whatever differences may have existed between Malenkov and Khrushchev, they did not slow the nuclear project. The pace of testing increased. There had been three nuclear tests before Stalin's death; there were sixteen between March 1953 and the end of 1955 (see table, p. 323). A new test site was organized in 1954 on the Novaia Zemlia archipelago in the Arctic Ocean. This was to be used for high-yield weapons tests and underwater explosions. The first test there – an underwater explosion – took place on September 21, 1955.[21] In 1955 a second weapons design bureau was established at Kasli, in Cheliabinsk province, about 40 kilometers from Kyshtym, in order to foster competition. The new laboratory, known as Cheliabinsk-70, was organized by a group from Arzamas-16. The first scientific director was K.I. Shchelkin, who had been Khariton's first deputy; the first director was Dmitrii Vasil'ev.[22] Plans were also afoot to create two new large centers for plutonium production, near Tomsk (Tomsk-7) and Krasnoiarsk (Krasnoiarsk-26).[23]

The new leadership continued the delivery vehicle programs initiated by Stalin. The Tu-16 medium bomber was deployed in large numbers with the Long-Range Air Force.[24] The intercontinental bombers proved less satisfactory, however, and provided only a rudimentary intercontinental capability when they entered service in 1955.[25] The Tu-95's cruising speed and altitude made it vulnerable to air defense. "It would be shot down long before it got anywhere near its target," Khrushchev noted in his memoirs. "Therefore it couldn't be used as a strategic bomber."[26] Miasishchev's bomber was no more successful because its range was too short. A modified

Soviet Nuclear Explosions 1949–55

Test Number	Date	Site	Comments
1.	Aug. 29, 1949	Semipalatinsk	Plutonium bomb; yield of about 20kt.
2.	Sept. 25, 1951	Semipalatinsk	Bomb used uranium-235 and plutonium; yield of about 40kt.
3.	Oct. 18, 1951	Semipalatinsk	Bomb dropped from Tu-4 bomber.
4.[1]	Aug. 1953	Semipalatinsk	Fission bomb.
5.	Aug. 12, 1953	Semipalatinsk	First thermonuclear bomb; yield of 400kt.
6–7.[2]	1953	Semipalatinsk	Fission bombs.
8.	Sept. 14, 1954	Totskoe	Medium-yield fission bomb detonated during troop exercise.
9–14.[3]	Sept.–Oct. 1954	Semipalatinsk	A series of fission bomb tests; one of these (on October 19th) was a fizzle.
15.[4]	July 29, 1955	Semipalatinsk	Fission bomb; yield of about 5kt.
16.	Aug. 2. 1955	Semipalatinsk	Fission bomb; yield of about 25kt.
17.	Sept. 21, 1955	Novaia Zemlia	Underwater burst; yield of about 20kt.
18.	Nov. 6, 1955	Semipalatinsk	Version of the "classical design" tested on Aug. 12, 1953; yield of about 215kt.
19.	Nov. 22, 1955	Semipalatinsk	First two-stage thermonuclear bomb; yield of 1.6 MT.

Sources: Most of the information is given in the text with the appropriate references. See also the following:

1 Although U.S. intelligence believed that the test of August 12, 1953 was the fourth Soviet test (hence the name Joe-4), Andrei Sakharov indicates that there was a fission bomb test earlier in August. Andrei Sakharov, Memoirs, New York: Alfred A. Knopf, 1990, p. 173.

2 Thomas B. Cochran et al., Nuclear Weapons Databook: Volume IV, Soviet Nuclear Weapons, New York: Ballinger, 1989, p. 349.

3 Ibid. The information on the fizzle is given in Iu.B. Khariton and Iu.N. Smirnov, "O nekotorykh mifakh i legendakh vokrug sovetskikh atomnogo i vodorodnogo proektov," in Materialy iubileinoi sessii uchenogo soveta tsentra, Moscow: Rossiiskii nauchnyi tsentr "Kurchatovskii institut," January 12, 1993, p. 51.

4 The data for tests 15–19 comes from "Intelligence Information for Use in the AFSWP Weapons Orientation Course (Advanced)" a memorandum prepared on February 15, 1956. National Archives, RG 218, Records of the U.S. Joint Chiefs of Staff, 1954–6, CCCS 334 JIC (12-28-55) Section 3. The yield for the November 22, 1955 test has been confirmed by Russian sources; the yields for the other tests have not been confirmed, though recent information suggests that the yield of the November 6 test was about 250kt.

version, with new engines and longer wings, still did not have the desired range.[27] According to A.N. Ponomarev, head of the Air Force's Scientific-Technical Committee in the postwar years,

everyone liked Miasishchev's M-201 bomber [as the new version was called], but you would not call it intercontinental in the full sense; the fuel supply was limited, and from the very beginning the designer had to rack his brains over inflight refuelling of the bomber.[28]

When Khrushchev complained that the 201M did not have a true intercontinental range, Miasishchev replied that it could bomb the United States and then land in Mexico. Khrushchev was not amused: "What do you think Mexico is – our mother-in-law? You think we can simply go calling any time we want? The Mexicans would never let us have the plane back."[29]

There were signs, however, that the investment in rocket development would pay off. At the end of 1953 the Presidium approved Korolev's proposal to develop the R-7 ICBM.[30] "Not too long after Stalin's death," Khrushchev recalls in his memoirs, "Korolev came to a Politburo meeting to report on his work. I don't want to exaggerate, but I'd say we gawked at what he showed us as if we were a bunch of sheep seeing a new gate for the first time."[31] Korolev was also developing the R-5 and R-11 missiles at this time.[32] The R-5, which had a range of over 1,000 kilometers, was called the first "strategic" missile; it was the first Soviet missile to carry a nuclear warhead.[33] (It was known in the West as the SS-3.) The R-11 missile, which had a range of 150 kilometers, was designed for surface launch from submarines, as well as for service with the ground forces as a mobile "operational-tactical missile." (The naval version was known in the West as the SS-N-3, and the ground forces version as SCUD.)[34]

These weapons programs show that the post-Stalin leadership remained firmly committed to the creation of a substantial strategic nuclear force. There was considerable continuity with the Stalin period. In 1954 a new design bureau for long-range missiles was set up, under the direction of Mikhail Iangel', who had worked with Korolev since 1950. Iangel' and Korolev had disagreed about rocket design, with Iangel' favoring rockets with storable fuel. The political leadership decided to give Iangel' his own bureau in Dnepropetrovsk.[35]

The post-Stalin leadership was also committed to defense against a nuclear attack. Deployment of a new air defense system around Moscow began in 1954. Over 3,000 R-113 anti-air missiles were deployed in two years, along with an extensive radar network.[36] This enormous investment shows that the leadership gave high priority to the defense of the capital. In the autumn of 1953 seven military leaders wrote to the Central Committee to point out that the United States would soon deploy ballistic missiles and to press for a Soviet anti-ballistic missile (ABM) system. A group was set up to study the problem, and it recommended that an experimental ABM system be built. In 1956 construction of an ABM testing ground began near Sary-Shagan, to the west of Lake Balkhash in Kazakhstan.[37]

III

The United States began to deploy tactical nuclear weapons in Europe in the early 1950s. Los Alamos had been working since 1948 to develop light low-yield weapons for use on the battlefield. The Korean War had given this work new impetus; so too had anxiety about NATO's ability to defend Western Europe against a Soviet conventional attack. In January 1952 the Joint Chiefs of Staff authorized the Supreme Allied Commander Europe, General Eisenhower, to begin planning for the use of atomic bombs by Navy tactical air units and by Air Force units which were soon to be stationed in Europe.[38] Tactical nuclear weapons soon began to be allocated to the defense of Western Europe, for delivery by aircraft, missiles, and guns.

The Soviet military followed the developments in NATO closely, and in 1953 and 1954 made a serious effort to adjust tactics and operational art to the nuclear battlefield.[39] The 1951 exercise in the Turkestan Military District indicates that some work had been done already, but it was in the autumn of 1953 that the problem was first tackled seriously. A field exercise was held in the Carpathian Military District to explore the "methods of conducting combat operations in conditions in which the 'enemy' uses nuclear weapons."[40] The exercise was directed by Marshal I.S. Konev, the district commander. Zhukov helped to prepare and conduct the exercise, while Kurchatov and Korolev served as consultants. Ministers of Defense from the socialist countries attended, as did Soviet marshals, and representatives from the military academies and the General Staff.[41] Before the exercise special days were set aside for commanders to study nuclear weapons. The troops were instructed in the effects of nuclear weapons and methods of defense against them. Officers and men were given psychological preparation for combat on the nuclear battlefield. Special emphasis was laid in field training on forced marches, encounter battles, attacking on the move, forcing water barriers, night operations with tactical air drops, and elimination of the effects of enemy weapons of mass destruction.[42]

Although the nuclear explosion was simulated, the Carpathian exercise marked a new stage in military policy. In November 1953 the Ministry of Defense ordered that all military personnel be instructed in the effects of atomic weapons, and in the tactics and techniques of combat on the nuclear battlefield.[43] Officers were to study the characteristics of the new weapons, and field-grade officers were also to study how atomic weapons might be used. (The main emphasis in this period, however, was on defense against nuclear weapons, not on their employment.) The ministry arranged a six-week course on nuclear weapons for 150 generals and officers.[44] Secret field and training manuals were issued, and in 1954 training for operations in nuclear conditions began in the military districts.[45] The post of Senior Officer of the Operations Department for Weapons of Mass Destruction was established in the staffs of all military districts.[46] The curricula of the military academies were changed to cover nuclear weapons and nuclear warfare, and articles about nuclear weapons appeared in the military press for the first time since 1947. During 1954, for example, *Voennaia Mysl'* carried detailed reports of American discussions of tactical nuclear weapons.[47]

Preparations began in the winter of 1953–4 for an exercise with a real nuclear detonation. This was held in September 1954 on a firing-ground near the village of Totskoe, in the province of Orenburg, then part of the South Urals Military District.[48] The United States had already conducted exercises in which troops had been exposed to nuclear detonations, but these were smaller in scale than the Totskoe exercise in which 44,000 troops took part.[49] The troops were commanded by General Ivan Petrov, who had directed the 1951 exercise in the Turkestan Military District and was now head of the Chief Directorate of Combat and Physical Training in the Ministry of Defense. Marshal Zhukov was in overall charge of the exercise.

The Ministry of Defense wanted to study the conditions and tactics of combat on the nuclear battlefield. Defenses of different kinds were erected on the firing-ground, from ordinary field defenses to fortified regions: trenches and bunkers, many of them covered; dug-outs with double doors; shelters for weapons and ammunition. When the soldiers arrived at Totskoe in the spring and summer they learned that they were to take part in a nuclear exercise and signed a statement that they would not talk about it for twenty-five years. They received instructions about how to defend themselves against the effects of a nuclear explosion. Zhukov was apparently worried that the precautions were making the troops afraid. "You have frightened people too much with your safety measures," he told the exercise commanders after a visit to see how preparations were going. "Now you'll have to 'unfrighten' them."[50] People from the villages within 7 kilometers of ground zero were evacuated; others living nearby were told what to do when the bomb exploded.

At 6.28 a.m. on September 14 a Tu-4 took off from an airfield 680 kilometers from Totskoe, with an atomic bomb on board. The plane was guided carefully to the target, and did not fly over towns; smoke fires were lit on the steppe to mark the flight path. The Tu-4 was accompanied by two Il-28 light bombers to ensure that it was on the right path. The crew had trained for a month, and had made thirteen training flights. (There was a reserve Tu-4, which had also made thirteen training flights.) Information

about the state of the bomb and the conditions in the bomb-bay –
temperature, humidity, etc. – was sent by radio to the command post.
Kurchatov, who had taken part in the preparations for the exercise, had
explained that an atomic bomb was a "living being," and that its state had
to be monitored during flight.[51]

Ground zero was marked with a large chalk cross. Weapons and equipment of all kinds were distributed round about; so too were scarecrows in
military uniform, sheep, dogs, cattle, and other animals. The trenches
for the attacking side were 5 kilometers from ground zero at the closest
point, while most of the trenches were 6–7 kilometers away; the trenches
for the defending side were 8 kilometers from ground zero. At 9.20 a.m.
Zhukov signed the order authorizing the release of the bomb. A state of
atomic alert was announced, and the troops took cover. At 9.33 the Tu-4
dropped a "medium-yield" atomic bomb from a height of 8,000 meters.
It exploded at a height of 350 meters, 280 meters from ground zero. The
explosion annihilated the oak forest around Ground Zero to a radius of
1–1.5 kilometers. Covered trenches and passageways were destroyed to a
distance of 500 meters; uncovered trenches to a distance of 1.2–1.3
kilometers. Bulganin and members of the High Command watched
the exercise from a distance of 15 kilometers; the Defense Ministers and
Chiefs of the General Staff from the socialist countries – including Peng
Dehuai and Zhu De from China – were also present. The shock wave blew
the hats off these senior officers; adjutants had to scurry about to retrieve
them.

Five minutes after the detonation the attacking forces began artillery
fire.[52] Twenty-one minutes later 86 Il-28 light bombers attacked the
defending side. Almost 700 high-explosive bombs were dropped in the
course of the exercise. According to one participant, "experienced officers,
who had taken part in the storming of Berlin, later said that they had not
seen anything like it."[53] Forty minutes after the detonation a special group
was sent to ground zero to monitor the level of radiation. When the
offensive began, the troops were not allowed to come closer than 500–600
meters to ground zero. After the exercise the troops returned to camp,
where they were checked with a radiometer, went to the bath-house and
changed their uniforms.

The exercise was conducted in frighteningly realistic conditions, according to those who took part. It was judged a success by the High Command:

All the missions that had been set were carried out. The nuclear strike, delivered
precisely against the designated targets, caused the damage that had been expected.
And the troop units, which took part in these exercises, went without fear into
the region of the atomic explosion, even to ground zero, overcame the zones
of radiation and carried out the missions that had been set for the units and
formations.[54]

At a meeting to analyze the exercise Bulganin spoke of the atomic bomb as an important means of enhancing firepower.[55] The officers who took part in the exercise were impressed by the power of the bomb, but they did not regard it as something so terrible as to make war unwageable.[56]

Since the late 1980s former soldiers who took part in the exercise have claimed that they developed serious illnesses as a result of exposure to radiation. In the Totskoe region there have been reports of a higher than normal incidence of cancer.[57] It is impossible, on the basis of the available evidence, to make a judgment about the damage caused to people's health by the exercise. It is clear that measures were taken to protect the troops and the villagers; but it is also clear that the High Command took a harsh view of what troops would face on the nuclear battlefield and wanted to create those conditions in the exercise.

The Totskoe exercise was filmed and studied carefully, and used as the basis for new field regulations.[58] The 1955 Field Regulations marked a turning-point in Soviet operational art and tactics, for they assumed that in a future war nuclear weapons would be used on the battlefield as well as against strategic targets.[59] NATO's introduction of tactical nuclear weapons did not cause the Soviet Army to abandon its plans for strategic offensive operations in the event of war. The Soviet response was to study how those operations could be conducted in conditions in which nuclear weapons were used.[60]

A banquet was held in an army tent after the exercise. Kurchatov presented to the marshals and generals some of the scientists who had been responsible for the development of nuclear science in the Soviet Union. This occasion marked the transfer of nuclear weapons from the Ministry of Medium Machine-Building to the armed forces.[61] The first series-production bombs had entered the arsenal in 1953, but the Ministry of Medium Machine-Building retained custody of them.[62] In the last months of 1954 nuclear weapons were first distributed to military districts.[63] Zhukov apparently pressed hard for the weapons to be transferred to the custody of the Defense Ministry, but did not get what he wanted.[64] (His relations with Malyshev were very bad, perhaps because of disagreement on this issue.)[65] A new Chief Directorate, staffed by military officers, was set up in the Ministry of Medium Machine-Building to handle nuclear weapons, but the weapons were still guarded by KGB troops. The issue of custody was not finally resolved until the late 1950s when the 12th Chief Directorate for Nuclear Weapons was established in the Ministry of Defense.

IV

Military strategy changed more slowly than tactics and operational art. The first signs of a revision of Stalinist orthodoxy came in September 1953, when Major-General N. Talenskii, editor of the classified journal *Voennaia*

Mysl', published an article "On the Question of the Character of the Laws of Military Science."[66] As its title suggests, this article was an abstract discussion of military science.[67] What made it significant was that it questioned the adequacy of the "permanently operating factors" as a guide to victory, and asserted the prerogatives of the military by defining the subject matter of military science as armed conflict (the preserve of the military) rather than the political character of war (the preserve of political leaders and ideologists).

The debate that followed Talenskii's article was brought to a close in April 1955 by an editorial in *Voennaia Mysl'*, which concluded that armed conflict, and not the political character of states, was the proper subject of military science; that the basic law of military science – as yet unformulated – was to be a law of victory; and that victory was to be achieved by means of a decisive defeat of the enemy in armed conflict.[68] The military were arguing, in other words, that victory had to be thought of in terms of military operations, and not only as the inevitable outcome of a historical process, which was how Malenkov, for example, had presented it in his November 1949 speech when he said that a third world war would lead to the collapse of the capitalist system.[69]

This discussion was important for the development of Soviet military thought, but it was remote from the specific problems of strategy. A more urgent note was sounded at the beginning of 1955 when Bulganin and Zhukov called at a meeting of senior officers for a profound study of "modern military technology and advanced military theory."[70] Bulganin told the High Command that they should pay serious attention to bourgeois military science, because imperialist armies, although they had a different class basis, used similar equipment, and because bourgeois military science reflected the experience of past wars.[71] An editorial in *Voennaia Mysl'* in February 1955 stressed that the officer corps needed a clear conception of what operations would be like in modern war, and that the troops had to be trained for the very tough conditions in which they would have to fight.[72]

Soviet military strategy was in serious need of revision because the nuclear threat to the Soviet Union had grown rapidly in the early 1950s. The United States stockpile grew from 832 nuclear weapons in 1952, to 1,161 in 1953, 1,630 in 1954, and 2,280 in 1955.[73] The Strategic Air Command had a network of bases from which medium bombers could strike the Soviet Union; and in June 1955 the intercontinental B-52 bomber entered service with SAC. In 1955 the Soviet nuclear stockpile was certainly very much smaller than the American. The Long-Range Air Force had a large number of obsolescent Tu-4s, and a small but growing force of medium-range Tu-16s. By mid-1955, the Long-Range Air Force had a small number of intercontinental bombers (perhaps 30), but these, as has been seen, were not regarded as satisfactory by the Soviet leadership.

In its first year in office the Eisenhower administration devised and announced the "New Look" strategy, which placed increasing reliance on nuclear weapons.[74] In the event of war, the Strategic Air Command would deliver a massive blow against the Soviet Union. A SAC briefing in March 1954 gives a good picture of how it intended to do this.[75] The optimum plan, in SAC's view, was one in which it deployed its tankers and bombers to overseas bases before attacking the Soviet Union. According to the briefing,

it was estimated that SAC could lay down an attack under these conditions of 600–750 bombs by approaching Russia from many directions so as to hit their early warning screen simultaneously. It would require about 2 hours from this moment until bombs had been dropped by using the bomb-as-you-go system in which both BRAVO [i.e. blunting] and DELTA [i.e. disruption] targets would be hit as they reached them. . . . The final impression was that virtually all of Russia would be nothing but a smoking, radiating ruin at the end of two hours.[76]

150 B-36s and 585 B-47s would be involved in such an attack. The B-47 did not have intercontinental range, and the B-36 could strike from bases in the United States only with a light load of bombs. Consequently the United States had to launch its attack from forward bases if it wanted to deliver a full strike against Soviet targets.

The main targets for the blunting mission were atomic energy installations (estimated at 25), airfields (estimated at 645), military headquarters, and government control centers.[77] The disruption mission targeted industries that were critical for the conduct of war: atomic energy, aircraft, POL [Petroleum–Oil–Lubrication], ammunition, steel, and electric power.[78] Early in 1955 the Defense Department's Weapons Systems Evaluation Group (WSEG) concluded that the currently planned atomic offensives against the Soviet Union would result in 77 million casualties in the Soviet bloc, of whom 60 million would die. Of the 134 major cities, 118 would be bombed, and between 75 and 84 per cent of the population in those cities would be killed.[79] These estimates were very much higher than those given in the Harmon Report of May 1949. New designs and growing stockpiles were making nuclear war a much more destructive affair.

As the SAC briefing shows, United States military planners believed that the most effective nuclear offensive was a single, massive blow covering the entire target set. The WSEG briefing makes clear that the ideal strike was a preemptive one, so that Soviet forces could be destroyed before they had the chance to deliver their nuclear weapons.[80] Truman and Eisenhower consistently rejected the option of preventive war, though it was discussed seriously within the government.[81] But a preemptive attack was not ruled out; indeed it was seen to be vital for the performance of the highest-priority mission, that of blunting a Soviet atomic attack.

Surprise attack was the central element in the reformulation of Soviet military strategy after Stalin's death. Stalin had called surprise a transitory factor in war, in order to play down the disaster of 1941. In the early 1950s the Long-Range Air Force was given the mission of striking United States strategic nuclear forces, and this implied preemption insofar as those forces would have to be destroyed on the ground. After Stalin's death the importance of surprise was acknowledged more openly in the military press, but the Stalinist orthodoxy still inhibited discussion of the need to counter a surprise attack. In February 1955, however, *Voennaia Mysl'* published an article, which it had earlier rejected, by Marshal of Armored Forces Pavel Rotmistrov advocating a preemptive strategy for the Soviet Union.[82]

Rotmistrov, a leading wartime tank commander who was now teaching at the General Staff Academy, argued that a surprise attack with atomic and hydrogen weapons could lead to significantly greater consequences than in past wars. Surprise had now become one of the decisive conditions for success not only in a battle or an operation, but also in the war as a whole. In some cases surprise attack with the massed use of nuclear weapons could lead to the rapid collapse of a state whose resistance was low as a result of radical faults in its social or economic structure, or because of an unfavorable geographical location. The United States and Britain were planning surprise attacks against the Soviet Union, Rotmistrov argued. Aggressors had often launched surprise attacks against other states in the past, and the Soviet Union could not ignore the lessons of history: "we should always be ready for preemptive actions against the perfidy of aggressors."[83] It was the duty of the armed forces, he wrote, "not to allow an enemy surprise attack on our country and, in the event of an attempt to carry one out, not only to repel the attack successfully, but also to inflict counterstrikes on the enemy [i.e. strikes launched on warning of an incoming attack] or even preemptive surprise strikes of terrible destructive force. The Soviet Army and Navy have everything necessary for this."[84]

Surprise now assumed a central role in Soviet military strategy. In the month after Rotmistrov's article an editorial in *Voennaia Mysl'* repeated his words that "we should always be ready for preemptive actions against the perfidy of aggressors."[85] It went on to criticize the Stalinist version of 1941. A revisionist historiography now began to appear, blaming Stalin for his failure to anticipate the German attack and to make the Red Army ready.[86] Zhukov had been Chief of the General Staff in 1941 and had witnessed the build-up of German forces with alarm; according to some recent accounts, he had urged Stalin to prepare for a preemptive strike.[87] The stress on preemption as Zhukov took over as minister is therefore not surprising.

The main reason, however, for the Soviet and American interest in preemption was the state of the strategic nuclear balance. For the United States, the threat of Soviet nuclear retaliation could be greatly reduced – or even eliminated – if Soviet nuclear forces could be destroyed on the ground. For the Soviet Union, the force of a United States attack could be greatly blunted if Soviet bombers could strike US bombers on their bases. The Soviet High Command was afraid of "going late," since it would then lose most of its nuclear forces and its ability to retaliate would be greatly reduced, if not destroyed completely. The strategic balance was unstable, in the sense that each side had a strong incentive to strike first if war seemed to be imminent.

In August 1955 Lieutenant-General S. Krasil'nikov, a veteran military theorist teaching at the General Staff Academy, provided a further glimpse into the post-Stalin revision of military strategy.[88] In the initial phase of the war each side would try to strike the other's air forces and nuclear weapons production facilities. Along with air defense, these strikes would provide the "most reliable method of guaranteeing the security of the rear and the freedom to conduct military operations at the front and at sea."[89] Ground and air force operations would be combined with

powerful systematic strikes by strategic aviation against the basic military–economic centers and communications nodes of the enemy countries, with continuous strenuous struggle by submarines, surface ships, and air forces against his sea communications and with other forms of struggle with the aim of disrupting the enemy's economic power and weakening his will to resist.[90]

Krasil'nikov argued for powerful strikes against the enemy's economy as well as his armed forces, "for then the military power of the enemy country or bloc of countries will be like a candle burning at both ends."[91] In other words, Soviet nuclear strikes, like those of the US Strategic Air Command, would be aimed at both "blunting" and "disruption" targets.

Serious thought was now being given to the implications of nuclear weapons for the conduct of war. The goal of military strategy was still to win a war by destroying the enemy's forces, but the initial period of war had assumed a new importance, and preemption was seen as a desirable, even necessary, strategy. Although the military knew that nuclear weapons were immensely destructive, they still regarded them as instruments of war, not as machines that made war impossible. Nuclear weapons might knock some small, densely populated countries out of the war in its opening stages, but the Soviet Union, with its vast territory and dispersed population, would not suffer such a fate, as long as it took the proper precautions. In Krasil'nikov's view, nuclear weapons alone would not decide the outcome of the war.

Krasil'nikov pointed out that nuclear weapons would change the re-lationship between the services, and this was already happening by the time his article was published. Khrushchev decided to abandon Stalin's naval shipbuilding program, which he regarded as "one of his [Stalin's] biggest errors" in military policy.[92] Khrushchev, supported – or inspired – by Zhukov, believed that nuclear weapons had made surface ships obsolete. He cut naval shipbuilding, in spite of the opposition of Admiral Kuznetsov, Commander-in-Chief of the Navy.[93] Large surface warships were particularly affected, and priority in the Navy was shifted to submarines, land-based aviation, and light surface ships.[94]

There was disagreement too about the implications of nuclear weapons for the ground forces. Some officers argued that larger forces were needed because divisions could now be easily destroyed; others claimed that fewer troops were needed because their firepower was enhanced by nuclear weapons. Zhukov and Khrushchev took the latter position. In August 1955 the government announced that it would cut the armed forces by 640,000 men by the end of the year. This was the first of several steps to reduce the armed forces from the bloated size of 5.7 million troops they had reached in 1955.[95]

V

In his speech at Stalin's funeral Malenkov said that the Soviet Union would pursue a policy following from the "Leninist-Stalinist position on the possibility of the long-term coexistence and peaceful competition of two different systems – the capitalist and the socialist."[96] In spite of the ritualistic bow to Lenin and Stalin, these words pointed to a new direction in policy. Stalin had indeed spoken of the possibility of peaceful coexistence between socialism and capitalism, but *only* if certain conditions were met.[97] He held out peaceful coexistence as something that might follow large concessions by the West – though he would surely then have asked for more concessions, as Litvinov had warned. Stalin's conception of the international situation after World War II, his expectation of a new world war within fifteen or twenty years, his military preparations in the early 1950s, his reaffirmation of the inevitability of war, and his speech to the October 1952 plenum of the Central Committee – all of this ran counter to the idea that socialism and capitalism could coexist peacefully over the long term.

Stalin's successors made immediate changes in foreign policy. The most pressing issue they faced was the Korean War. By May 1952 agreement had been reached at the armistice talks on all points except the repatriation of prisoners. The United States insisted that repatriations be voluntary; the communist side wanted all Chinese prisoners repatriated, regardless of their wishes. In October 1952 the armistice talks broke down on this point.[98] When Zhou Enlai came to Moscow for Stalin's funeral, he had conversations with the Soviet leaders about the situation in Korea. On behalf of the Chinese government he proposed that the Soviet Union help to bring the war to an end. In the words of an official Soviet account written thirteen years later, "this position of the Chinese coincided with our position too."[99] In the same month Moscow sent a special envoy to Pyongyang to discuss steps to end the war. By this time "the [North] Koreans exhibited a clear desire for a speedy end to military operations."[100]

On March 19, 1953, exactly two weeks after Stalin's death, the Soviet Council of Ministers approved a draft letter to Mao and Kim. "It would be wrong to continue the line on [the Korean War] which has been followed until recently," the letter said, "without introducing into that line those changes which correspond to the present political moment and which spring from the deepest interests of our peoples."[101] The letter set out a series of steps, which were taken by the three communist governments in the following weeks. On March 28 Peng Dehuai and Kim Il Sung wrote to General Mark Clark, the Commander-in-Chief of the United Nations forces in Korea, accepting a proposal he had made, in a letter of February 22, for the exchange of sick and wounded prisoners.[102] Two days later Zhou Enlai proposed that all other prisoners who were unwilling to be repatriated should be transferred to a neutral state, until the problem was sorted out.[103] Kim Il Sung issued a statement supporting Zhou's proposal. On April 1 Molotov gave his support to the statements by Zhou and Kim.[104]

Zhou's proposal was regarded in Washington as a significant concession, but it was not acceptable as it stood because the prisoners who were unwilling to be repriated might have to spend the rest of their lives in the countries to which they were transferred.[105] When the armistice talks resumed at the end of April, there was much haggling over voluntary repatriation. Washington now applied pressure to bring the negotiations to an end. On May 21 Secretary of State John Foster Dulles, who was visiting India, informed Prime Minister Nehru that "if armistice negotiations collapsed, the United States would probably make a stronger rather than a lesser military exertion and that this might well extend the area of conflict."[106] Dulles hoped that this message would reach Beijing. On May 25, on instructions from Washington, the chief UN negotiator at the armistice talks presented a modified proposal to his communist counterparts, and explained that this was the United Nations' final position.[107] At the same time General Clark wrote to Kim and Peng that the United States would not continue to talk for much longer.[108] On May 28 the United States ambassador in Moscow, Charles Bohlen, told Molotov that the latest proposal was "a most serious and important" one.[109]

It did not come as a surprise to the Soviet leaders that Zhou's proposal of March 28 had not resulted directly in an end to the war. The final paragraph of the March 19 letter to Mao and Kim made it clear that further steps would be needed:

Of course we cannot now foresee all the steps and measures the governments of the USSR, PRC, and DPRK will have to take. However, if full agreement is reached between our governments on the conduct of the general line on this question – and we have complete confidence that it will be – then it will be possible to agree on the rest as things develop.[110]

The communist governments decided to accept the UN proposals on voluntary repatriation. On June 3 Molotov told Bohlen that "the path to the successful conclusion of the armistice talks has been mapped out."[111] On June 4 the Chinese and North Korean negotiators told the UN side of their decision, and on June 8 an agreement was drawn up. The armistice was signed on July 27.

Eisenhower and Dulles both claimed to believe that it was the threat to use the atomic bomb that elicited concessions from China and North Korea.[112] This is doubtful, however. There was a general shift in Soviet foreign policy after Stalin's death.[113] The new leadership moved quickly on several fronts to reduce international tension. Their motives for doing so were varied: to create the conditions for domestic reform; to secure a breathing-space during the post-Stalin transition; to reduce the risk of world war; to expose and exploit contradictions among the Western powers. Different leaders may have had different goals in mind, but it was clear that none of these goals could be attained without an end to the war in Korea; that was why the new leaders had moved at once to revive the armistice talks. If Dulles's hint to Nehru in May did speed up the conclusion of the war – and that is doubtful, because Nehru denied that he had passed on Dulles's warning[114] – it did so by nudging Moscow, Beijing, and Pyongyang further along a path they had already chosen to travel.

Malenkov noted that the Korean War had been "fraught with the threat of the most serious international complications" in his speech on August 8. "There is a certain improvement in the international situation," he said. "After a long period of growing tension, some relaxation of the international atmosphere has begun to be felt for the first time in the postwar years."[115]

VI

The term "peaceful coexistence" began to appear in leadership statements during the "election campaign" for the Supreme Soviet early in 1954. On February 11, 1954 the Central Committee's Appeal to Voters emphasized that the Party's foreign policy of peace and friendship with all peoples had been formulated by Lenin, "who pointed to the possibility of a prolonged peaceful coexistence of two different economic systems – socialist and capitalist."[116] In March some of the political leaders, including Khrushchev, spoke of peaceful coexistence in their election addresses.[117]

Molotov avoided the term "peaceful coexistence." It was a "slippery expression," he explained many years later.[118] He was opposed to it because it made the Soviet Union look as though it was asking for peace: "but to ask for peace means to show one's weakness. And to show one's weakness before the strong is politically disadvantageous, inadvisable. It won't do for Bolsheviks."[119] More fundamentally, it was a confusing concept and cast doubt on the need to overthrow imperialism: if imperialism and socialism could keep to themselves, "Then, pray, what are we living for?"[120] It was an illusion to think that communism could be reached by way of peaceful coexistence: "We ought to preserve peace, but if we, besides fighting for peace and delaying war, if we also believe that it is possible to get to communism that way, then that is deception from the point of view of Marxism, self-deception, and deception of the people."[121]

In spite of Molotov's misgivings, "peaceful coexistence" soon became a standard term in the Soviet political lexicon. It was a significant innovation, as Molotov's criticism indicates. By asserting that capitalism and socialism could coexist for a long time, the new leaders were rejecting Stalin's vision of another world war within fifteen to twenty years of the end of World War II. "Peaceful coexistence" was defined as the alternative to nuclear war, as the policy that had to be followed if nuclear war was to be avoided. Khrushchev, for example, writes in his memoirs that the main issue for Mao was "not peaceful coexistence but how to prepare for war and to defeat our enemies in war."[122] Peaceful coexistence did not mean ideological coexistence, however, nor did it entail renunciation of the struggle with imperialism. But that struggle had to be conducted in such a way as to avoid nuclear war.

"Peaceful coexistence" raised important questions about war and peace. Could it last forever, or was a new war to be expected later rather than sooner? If there were a war, what would its outcome be? Malenkov addressed this last question on March 12, 1954. In a statement that was to prove controversial in the leadership and harmful to his own political prospects, he said that

it is not true that humanity is faced with a choice between two alternatives: either a new world war, or the so-called Cold War. The peoples are vitally interested in a durable strengthening of peace. The Soviet government stands for further weakening of international tension, for a stable and durable peace, decisively opposes the Cold War, since that policy is the policy of preparing a new world war, which with modern weapons means the end of world civilization.[123]

Some Western commentators have interpreted this statement as acceptance of nuclear deterrence; Dinerstein, for example, writes that Malenkov "implied very strongly that peace was assured because all would lose by the destruction of civilization."[124] But Malenkov was making a different argument – not that peace was *assured* because everyone would lose by world war, but that peace was *essential* because everyone would lose. Although this statement had long-term implications for military policy, it had no immediate bearing on nuclear weapons programs. Malenkov's aim was to underscore the need to pursue peaceful relations with the West.

This position was very different from the view Malenkov had propounded in November 1949 and again in October 1952, that a new world war would mean the end of the capitalist system. Why had he changed his position? One possibility is that he had made the earlier statements because he was ordered to do so by Stalin. There is some evidence, as was seen in Chapter 12, that Malenkov favored a less confrontational policy than that pursued by Stalin after 1949. Beyond that, however, there is nothing to suggest that in 1949 and 1952 he had had the same view of the consequences of nuclear war that he expressed in 1954. A second and more likely explanation is that he changed his assessment of nuclear war between 1952 and 1954 as a result of the development of thermonuclear weapons.

Malenkov made his statement twelve days after the Bravo test on the Enewetak Atoll, which produced an explosive yield of 15 megatons. This test made an enormous impression on public opinion around the world. In a letter to Eisenhower on March 9 Churchill gave a somber assessment of its implications. Protection would now be impossible, "except for small Staff groups"; several million people would be obliterated by four or five hydrogen bombs; radioactive fallout could extinguish human life over very large areas. Human minds recoiled from realizing these facts, he wrote, but "the few men upon whom the supreme responsibility falls . . . have to drive their minds forward into these hideous and deadly spheres of thought."[125] It is possible that in his statement of March 12 Malenkov too was responding, if somewhat less eloquently, to the demonstration in the Pacific of the terrible destructiveness of thermonuclear weapons.

At the end of March Malyshev, Kurchatov, Alikhanov, Kikoin, and Vinogradov wrote an article entitled "The Dangers of Atomic War and President Eisenhower's Proposal," which gave a very stark picture of the consequences of nuclear war.[126] (The main purpose of the article was to respond to Eisenhower's "Atoms for Peace" proposal, which will be discussed in the next chapter.) The United States had announced two hydrogen bomb tests in March, Malyshev and his colleagues wrote. Thermonuclear reactions made possible an unlimited increase in the destructive power of the bomb, they noted. One multi-megaton thermonuclear bomb could "destroy all the apartment houses and buildings within a radius of 10–15 kilometers, i.e. destroy all the structures on the ground of a city with a multimillion population."[127] Nuclear weapons could be delivered against targets thousands of kilometers away, and since "defense against such weapons is in practice impossible, it is clear that the mass use of atomic weapons will lead to devastation of the belligerent countries."[128] Calculations showed that if the existing stockpiles of atomic weapons were used in war they would create "on a significant part of the surface of the earth doses of radiation and concentrations of radioactive materials that are biologically harmful for the life of people and plants." The rate of production of atomic bombs was such that in a few years there would be enough "to create on the whole globe conditions impossible for life." "The explosion of about a hundred large hydrogen bombs," they added, "would lead to the same result." "One cannot but acknowledge," they concluded, "that over the human race there hangs the threat of an end to all life on earth."[129]

This remarkable document is open and explicit about the consequences of nuclear war. There is nothing here about the destruction of capitalism and the victory of socialism. This document supported Malenkov's position that a new world war would mean the end of world civilization. One of the chief authors – Malyshev – was Malenkov's protégé; and the article was written shortly after Malenkov's controversial statement, at a time when Malenkov was apparently being criticized in the leadership for what he had said. Malyshev sent the draft article to Malenkov, Khrushchev, and Molotov on April 1, 1954, with the suggestion that it be published under the names of Academicians Nesmeianov, Ioffe, Skobel'tsyn, and Oparin, who "are well known abroad and not connected with our subject."[130] It was not published, however, and it failed to save Malenkov.

Malenkov had gone further than his colleagues in the leadership found acceptable. Six weeks after his statement, on April 27, he reverted to the old formula, asserting that

if . . . aggressive circles, setting their hopes on atomic weapons, were to decide on folly and wished to test the power and strength of the Soviet Union – then it cannot be doubted that the aggressor would be crushed by the same weapons, and that such an adventure would lead to the collapse of the capitalist social system.[131]

Khrushchev said much the same thing in a speech on the same day. It seems that pressure had been put on Malenkov to change his position. At the Central Committee plenum in January 1955 Khrushchev criticized Malenkov's statement about the end of world civilization as "theoretically mistaken and politically harmful."[132] Malenkov's statement had confused comrades abroad and at home, who had taken it as an expression of the Central Committee's line. It was a harmful statement, said Khrushchev, because it was "capable of giving rise to feelings of hopelessness about the efforts of the peoples to frustrate the plans of the aggressors."[133]

Molotov was even more outspoken on the same point. "A communist should not speak about the 'destruction of world civilization' or about the 'destruction of the human race,'" he said at the plenum, "but about the need to prepare and mobilize all forces for the destruction of the bourgeoisie."[134] "How can it be asserted," he asked, that civilization could perish in an atomic war? . . . Can we make the peoples believe that in the event of war all must perish? Then why should we build socialism, why worry about tomorrow? It would be better to supply everyone with coffins now. . . . You see to what absurdities, to what harmful things, mistakes on political issues can lead.[135]

Molotov disliked the concept of peaceful coexistence because it implied that peace was more important than the struggle against imperialism. But Malenkov had gone further: if socialism could not emerge victorious from a world war, then it was clear that priority had to be given to avoiding war. This was anathema to Molotov, for he saw it as tantamount to abandoning the communist cause.

In March 1955, one month after his resignation from the chairmanship of the Council of Ministers, Malenkov's thesis was subjected to a sustained attack in *Kommunist*, the Party's leading theoretical journal. In an editorial entitled "The Peoples Decide the Fate of Peace and Civilization" *Kommunist* argued that even though recent tests had shown a great increase in the destructive power of nuclear weapons, a thermonuclear war would not destroy world civilization. The fate of humankind was not to be decided by science and technology; it depended on the character of social relations, on the state and level of the class struggle, on the outcome of the struggle between progressive forces and the forces of reaction. No weapon, not even the hydrogen bomb, could alter the laws of social development.[136]

The paper that Malyshev had sent to Khrushchev, Malenkov, and Molotov gave no support at all for the kind of argument that *Kommunist* advanced. Kurchatov and his colleagues had brought the dangers of nuclear war clearly and explicitly to the attention of the leadership. There is evidence that they had done so on other occasions too. Many years later Khrushchev described his reactions on receiving a full briefing about nuclear weapons in September 1953. "When I was appointed First Sec-retary of the Central Committee," he said

and learned all the facts about nuclear power I couldn't sleep for several days. Then I became convinced that we could never possibly use these weapons, and when I realized that I was able to sleep again. But all the same we must be prepared. Our understanding is not sufficient answer to the arrogance of the imperialists.[137]

Kurchatov would have been the obvious person to brief Khrushchev. If Anatolii Aleksandrov is correct in saying that Kurchatov returned to Moscow shaken by the August 1953 test, then he appears to have conveyed his feelings to Khrushchev.

The reason why Khrushchev rejected Malenkov's position – apart from political opportunism – was not that he had an alternative analysis of nuclear war. He refused to acknowledge it because to do so would have damaging political and ideological consequences. That was the burden of the criticisms leveled against Malenkov. There appears now to have been a dual — even a schizophrenic — attitude to nuclear war in the Soviet leadership: a recognition of its destructive consequences for the Soviet Union as well as the West, and an official position that nuclear war would mean the end of capitalism.

VII

With Malenkov defeated, Khrushchev took the initiative in foreign policy. In May 1955 he decided that the Soviet Union should sign the Austrian State Treaty, which provided for the withdrawal of occupation forces and laid the basis for Austrian neutrality.[138] In June he and Bulganin visited Yugoslavia to restore relations with Tito. Molotov, who was still Foreign Minister, was opposed to these policies. He argued that the Soviet Union should not sign the Austrian State Treaty unless there was a settlement in Germany.[139] Nor did he agree with the attempt to renew party-to-party ties with Yugoslavia. He told the Central Committee plenum at the beginning of July that it lowered Soviet prestige to say that it had made mistakes in the past. He considered the Yugoslav leaders "traitors, anti-Marxists, degenerates who had slid over to the camp of the social democrats." Molotov was roundly criticized at the plenum by other members of the Presidium. "Molotov is living only in the past, inspired by the anger which accumulated in him during that Soviet–Yugoslav quarrel," said Mikoian. Bulganin called him a "hopeless dogmatic." Molotov remained in the post of Foreign Minister for another year, but his influence was greatly diminished.[140]

One of the initiatives taken by the Soviet Union in the spring of 1955 was a set of disarmament proposals put forward on May 10. Disarmament talks since 1946 had had a largely ritualistic character for all the great powers. Soviet proposals were designed to portray the Soviet Union as the bastion of peace in the world. There is no evidence that Stalin expected disarmament. After Stalin's death there were signs of a shift in Soviet thinking. At first the Soviet Union held to its old positions: a prohibition on nuclear weapons; reduction of one-third in the conventional forces of the five permanent members of the Security Council; and elimination of military bases on the territory of foreign countries.[141] These elements were all unacceptable to the Western powers. But in its proposals of May 10, 1955 the Soviet Union adopted a new approach, incorporating some of the ideas put forward by Britain and France in previous months. It abandoned the idea of proportional reductions in conventional forces and accepted the ceilings that Britain and France had proposed; it agreed that control should be permanent, and that the international control organ's inspectors should have "unimpeded access at all times to all objects of control"; it proposed that control posts be established at large ports, railway junctions, main motor highways, and airfields on the territory of all the countries concerned, in order "to see to it that there is no dangerous concentration of land, air or naval forces" for a surprise attack. The Soviet Union also proposed a ban on nuclear weapons tests.[142]

There were still elements in these proposals that were unacceptable to the Western powers – the elimination of foreign military bases, for example. But the proposals marked a major shift in Soviet policy, and looked like an attempt to move beyond the rhetoric of disarmament to a position from which agreements might be reached. A.A. Roshchin, who helped to draw them up, has written that "in essence they represented acceptance by the USSR of the proposals of the Western states."[143] It is impossible to say how much flexibility there was in the proposals, or how great a desire for agreement, because they never became the subject of negotiation. The initial response from the British and French was favorable, but the United States soon made its opposition clear, and the earlier Western proposals were withdrawn.[144] "For us who had worked out the proposals of May all this was incomprehensible," writes Roshchin.[145] In a report prepared on July 7, 1955 on possible Western positions at the forthcoming Geneva summit meeting, the Committee of Information attached to the Foreign Ministry, which coordinated intelligence assessments, noted that the May 10 proposals had "put the USA in an exceptionally difficult position"; the United States, it concluded, did not want to discuss these proposals at Geneva because it did not want to reject them without advancing new ones of its own.[146]

The Geneva conference, which lasted from July 18 to 23, was the first summit meeting since Potsdam. It took place in what was called the "spirit of Geneva" – the improved international atmosphere that followed the signing of the Austrian State Treaty. Bulganin was the formal head of the Soviet delegation, which included Khrushchev (its real head), Molotov, and Zhukov. Eisenhower led the United States delegation; Anthony Eden, who was now Prime Minister, headed the British delegation; and Edgar Faure, the French Premier, was chief of the French delegation. Little progress was made on the four main topics discussed – European security, Germany, disarmament, and East–West contacts – and no formal agreements were concluded.[147] Bulganin reiterated the Soviet interest in a nuclear test ban, but elicited no interest from the Western governments.[148]

The most dramatic event at the Geneva conference was Eisenhower's proposal that each country provide the other with "a complete blueprint of our military establishments" and "ample facilities for aerial reconnaissance." This, Eisenhower said, would reassure both sides that neither was preparing a "great surprise attack." Khrushchev eventually accepted overflights over Eastern Europe as a way of providing reassurance against surprise attack, but he rejected overflights over the Soviet Union as an attempt to spy on the Soviet Union, no doubt fearing that they would merely expose Soviet weakness and enable the United States to identify targets for a surprise attack.[149] Eisenhower had not expected the "Open Skies" proposal, as it became known, to be accepted by the Soviet Union. It gained great support in the West, however, and trumped the Soviet proposals of May 10, 1955 in the game of disarmament.

In spite of the lack of specific agreements, the Geneva summit was particularly important in one respect. It provided the leaders of the Soviet Union and the Western powers with the first indication that they shared a common understanding of nuclear weapons and nuclear war. Eisenhower took pains to impress on the Soviet leaders how destructive nuclear weapons were. At dinner one evening he told Bulganin "with great earnestness" that the development of modern weapons was such that the country which used them "genuinely risked destroying itself. Since the prevailing winds went east to west and not north to south, a major war would destroy the Northern Hemisphere."[150] He made the same point in a meeting with Zhukov, his old comrade-in-arms in the war against Nazi Germany. "Not even scientists," he said, "could say what would happen if two hundred H-bombs were exploded in a short period of time, but if atmospheric conditions were right, the fall-out might destroy entire nations and possibly the whole northern hemisphere." Zhukov agreed with the President, saying that "if on the first day of war the United States dropped three or four hundred bombs on the Soviet Union and they would do the same, it would be impossible to say what would happen to the atmosphere under those conditions." He was "unqualifiedly for total abolition of weapons of this character."[151] Eisenhower returned to Washington believing that, as he said in a television broadcast, "there seems to be a growing realization by all that nuclear warfare, pursued to the ultimate, could be practically race suicide."[152]

Eden drew very much the same conclusion from the Geneva conference. He had begun to take this view in 1954. "My conversations with the Soviet leaders, from 1954 onwards," he writes in his memoirs,

convinced me that they had clearly estimated the strategic changes created by nuclear weapons. World conflict meant mutual destruction, which they did not intend to provoke. This I first sensed in our discussion over Indo-China at Geneva in 1954. It was not paraded, but it was felt.[153]

The Geneva summit in July 1955 had been useful in that respect. "Each country present learnt that no country attending wanted war and each understood why. The Russians realized, as we did, that this situation had been created by the deterrent power of thermo-nuclear weapons."[154]

Khrushchev returned from Geneva satisfied with the meeting. He had gone to Geneva with a sense of apprehension that the Western powers would apply strong pressure. "We returned to Moscow from Geneva knowing that we hadn't achieved any concrete results," he recalls in his memoirs. "But we were encouraged, realizing now that our enemies probably feared us as much as we feared them. . . . They now knew that they had to deal with us honestly and fairly, that they had to respect our borders and our rights, and that they couldn't get what they wanted by force or by blackmail."[155] It is perhaps not fanciful to believe that Khrushchev saw Eisenhower's homilies on nuclear war as evidence that the West was now as anxious as the Soviet Union to avoid such a war.

In December 1955 the Committee of Information wrote a report on Western attitudes to war and peace. It noted that a shift had taken place over the previous three years: those who favored peaceful settlement of disputes were now in a stronger position than in 1952. There were various reasons for this, the report explained, including Soviet efforts to lower international tension, and the decline of British and French power in Asia and Africa. But the growth of Soviet power had also made a difference:

The regrouping of forces in bourgeois circles in the basic capitalist countries was speeded up by the announcement that the Soviet Union had conducted tests [sic] of a hydrogen bomb in August 1953, which meant the loss by the United States of its monopoly on hydrogen weapons. Influential circles of the bourgeoisie, especially in West European countries, came to the conclusion that the development of thermonuclear weapons, strategic aviation, and intercontinental missile weapons made it pointless for the Western bloc to pursue a policy of creating a decisive military advantage over the countries of the socialist camp.[156]

Soviet power received a boost on November 22 when the first Soviet superbomb was tested. On November 26 Khrushchev told an audience in Bangalore that he hoped these bombs would never be used in war. "Let these bombs lie," he said, "let them get on the nerves of those who would like to unleash war. Let them know that war cannot be unleashed, because if you start a war, you will get the proper response."[157]

Two months later, at the Twentieth Party Congress, Khrushchev rejected the idea that war was inevitable. Soviet leaders laid great stress at the congress on peaceful coexistence. "Either peaceful coexistence or the most destructive war in history," Khrushchev said in the main report to the congress. "There is no third way."[158] Other leaders echoed this, though Molotov entered a note of caution by stressing that the Soviet Union had to make sure that the capitalist powers accepted peaceful coexistence too.[159] Peaceful coexistence implied that a new world war was not inevitable, but it was only at the Twentieth Party Congress that this was formally acknowledged. Wars had been inevitable when imperialism was an all-embracing world system, Khrushchev said. But now there existed a world socialist system which possessed the moral and material means to prevent aggression. "As long as capitalism survives in the world," said Khrushchev, the reactionary forces representing the interests of the capitalist monopolies will continue their drive towards military gambles and aggression, and may try to unleash war. But war is not fatally inevitable. Today there are mighty social and political forces possessing formidable means to prevent the imperialists from un-leashing war and, if they actually try to start it, to give a smashing rebuff to the aggressors and frustrate their adventurist plans.[160]

The Soviet Union was now strong enough – thanks in part to those "formidable means," nuclear weapons – to deter war. Khrushchev rejected the position that Stalin had taken in 1952, in his *Economic Problems of Socialism in the USSR*.[161]

Stalin had not allowed the atomic bomb to alter his conception of international relations. Nuclear weapons, however, did shape the way in which his successors thought about East–West relations. It was the danger of nuclear war, above all, that led them to adopt the policy of peaceful coexistence; and it was the deterrent power of Soviet nuclear weapons that made it possible for them to declare that war was "not fatally inevitable." But there were limits to the changes they were willing to make. They did not adopt the position Malenkov had espoused in 1954, that world civiliz-ation would perish in a new world war. On the contrary, several leaders – including Malenkov – asserted that if there were a world war, socialism would emerge victorious. Mikoian, for example, declared that "a hydrogen and atomic war could lead to great destruction, but it could not lead to the annihilation of humankind or its civilization. It will annihilate an obsolete and pernicious system – capitalism in its imperialist stage."[162] This was an important position, because it provided the ideological underpinning for Soviet military strategy. War might not be inevitable, but neither was it impossible. Moreover, if it occurred it would end in victory for socialism. The goal of military strategy, therefore, was victory in a world nuclear war. This ideological position precluded the adoption of a more limited policy, such as minimum deterrence.

By the end of 1955 the nuclear balance between the United States and the Soviet Union was unstable, in the sense discussed above. A stable relationship of mutual deterrence, based on the possession by both sides of assured retaliatory capabilities, would not be firmly established for another ten years. Nevertheless, a kind of existential deterrence had come into being. The Soviet leaders and the leaders of the United States understood how terrible a nuclear war would be, and each side believed that the other understood this too. On this basis they shared the conviction that neither would start a nuclear war. This conviction did not preclude the develop-ment of military strategies designed to achieve victory in the event of war. It did not put an end to the search for military advantage, or to the arms race that this search generated. Nor did it prevent either side from attempt-ing to use nuclear threats for political purposes. (Indeed Khrushchev, emboldened by the growth of Soviet nuclear power and his awareness of Western anxieties, soon took the offensive in the "war of nerves" by embarking on a spectacular career of missile diplomacy; this proved, however, no more successful than American efforts at atomic diplomacy.) Nevertheless, the shared understanding that nuclear war was ultimately unacceptable had now become a basic premise in the management of the East–West rivalry. This was a crucial restraining factor during a period in which the strategic nuclear balance was unstable and the ideological and political competition remained intense.

CHAPTER SIXTEEN

The Atom and Peace

I

THIS BOOK HAS ALREADY HAD TWO ENDINGS: the November 1955 superbomb test, which marked a new stage in nuclear weapons development, and the renunciation in February 1956 of the inevitability-of-war thesis, which marked a new stage in thinking about war and peace in the nuclear age. This chapter provides a third ending. Its substantive focus is the use of atomic energy for peaceful purposes, but it also deals with themes raised in the first chapter and discussed at intervals during the book – technological innovation, the physics community as a sphere of intellectual autonomy in Soviet society, and physicists as a transnational community.

After the first atomic bomb test Kurchatov raised the issue of atomic power with Nikolai Dollezhal', chief designer of the first plutonium production reactor. "One job has been done, and done not badly," he said to Dollezhal'. "We got a result with the bomb a year earlier than we had calculated. Now another job can be undertaken: the peaceful utilization of the energy of the atom. Have you any thoughts on that score?"[1] Kurchatov had been interested in using atomic energy to generate electric power since 1939–40. Once the bomb was tested he took the initiative in suggesting that a small nuclear electric power station be built to explore the feasibility of nuclear power.

Kurchatov and Dollezhal' favored a reactor with graphite moderator and water coolant, the same kind of system as the first plutonium production reactor.[2] By 1949 other types of reactor had been investigated as well. Alikhanov had built a heavy water reactor; research had been done on a gas-cooled reactor at the Institute of Physical Problems, under Aleksandrov's direction.[3] And in Obninsk, 100 kilometers south of Moscow, two types of system had been investigated: a reactor with a beryllium oxide moderator and helium coolant; and a fast-breeder reactor.[4] Early in 1950 the Scientific-Technical Committee of the First Chief Directorate selected the graphite system for the power station, partly because it was expected to be more efficient at converting thermal energy into electric power, and partly on the grounds that it could be built more quickly and more cheaply.[5]

In June 1950 the Scientific-Technical Council also approved a proposal from Aleksandr Leipunskii for the development of an experimental fast-breeder reactor.[6] Fast reactors were an appealing idea in 1950, when uranium was in short supply, and they were being developed in the United States and Britain as well. The basic idea was to surround a core of fissionable material with natural uranium, so that fast neutrons emitted by the core would convert the natural uranium into plutonium, which could be extracted for use either as reactor fuel or for weapons. Leipunskii calculated that a system with a 12-metric-ton core of uranium enriched to 14 per cent, and a blanket of 60 metric tons of natural uranium, would generate about 300 megawatts of electric power and produce 140–160 grams of plutonium-239 a day; liquid metal was to be used as the coolant.[7] In 1955 Leipunskii built a small experimental reactor, the BR-1, with a thermal power output of a few dozen watts; in the following year he built the BR-2 experimental reactor with 100 kilowatts thermal output.[8]

Kurchatov and Dollezhal' decided that their atomic power plant should have an electrical output of 5,000 kilowatts. This figure was chosen because a turbogenerator of that power already existed and could be used in the power station. Calculations showed that a thermal output of 30,000 kilowatts would be needed to produce 5 megawatts of electric power. The reactor would produce steam at a temperature of over 200 degrees and a pressure of 12 atmospheres to power the turbine. It would use uranium enriched to 3–5 per cent.[9]

In March 1951 Kurchatov handed over scientific direction of the atomic power station to Dmitrii Blokhintsev, director of the laboratory at Obninsk. Kurchatov was preoccupied with the thermonuclear weapons program, and felt that he could not devote the necessary time to the power reactor. He continued to follow its progress closely, however, and intervened on specific issues. Without his interest and support, work on the power reactor would not have continued, for there was opposition to the reactor on the grounds that it would not be economical.[10] Leading officials in the nuclear program regarded it as "no more than a concession to [Kurchatov], a question of prestige."[11] The power reactor did not divert significant resources from weapons development.

The power reactor, in spite of the conservatism of its design, presented many new engineering problems, the most difficult being the design and fabrication of the fuel elements. It finally achieved criticality on May 9, 1954. On June 26, in Kurchatov's presence, steam was fed to the turbogenerator, and on the following day electric power was supplied to the surrounding neighborhood. (The reactor was mentioned in the press for the first time on July 1, when *Pravda* carried a brief government announcement on its first page; this did not reveal where the reactor was located.)[12] It was some months, however, before the reactor could achieve full power, because leaks developed in the stainless steel control channels, allowing water to seep into the graphite stacking. This changed the reactivity of the system, and created a potentially explosive situation. Replacing the channels with others of the same design made no difference. One of the top ministry officials told Blokhintsev that the atomic power plant was no use. Blokhintsev was unwilling to wait months for the fabrication of new and stronger channels. On October 13, 1954 he allowed the reactor to reach full power; and on that day the turbine generated 5,000 kilowatts of electric power.[13]

While working on the Obninsk power plant, Dollezhal' continued to design plutonium production reactors. He also began work on a new concept, a reactor that could be used for both electric power and plutonium production. In his memoirs he describes the basic idea:

The energy which is born in the womb of the reactor is used only partially in transforming the chemical elements, in transferring them from one cell of Mendeleev's table to another. A significant part of the energy, discharged in the form of heat, proves to be worthless. The water which washes the uranium slugs, cooling them, is itself heated and flows free, into the reservoir where it cools down naturally. Is that not a barbarism, to throw away energy where it could be made useful to the national economy? In principle it looked quite clear how the heat should be utilized: to circulate the water . . . in a closed loop, so that while it is cooling it can do something useful and then be used again for cooling.[14]

The simplicity of this idea was only apparent, however, since a compromise had to be found between the two functions of power generation and plutonium production.[15]

Dollezhal's concept proved to be very controversial, and many voices were raised to criticize his idea, as well as the specific design he proposed. In the end, however, the Ministry of Medium Machine-Building decided to proceed with the reactor, which went into operation in 1958. It was known as the I-2 (Isotope-2, or Ivan the Second), and later as the EI-2 (Energy, Isotope-2) reactor. It was built not at Kyshtym, but near the city of Tomsk at Tomsk-7, and was known as the "Siberian" reactor. It generated 100,000 kilowatts of electricity. Several other reactors were added, bringing the electrical output of the Siberian power station up to 600,000 kilowatts. But power production was the secondary function of these reactors; plutonium production was their primary purpose.[16]

II

On December 8, 1953 Eisenhower made his "Atoms for Peace" speech to the United Nations. This speech was the product of lengthy consideration in Washington. The process had begun with a recommendation from Robert Oppenheimer for greater openness about the growing danger posed by nuclear weapons.[17] This element is present in Eisenhower's speech, which stressed the dangers of nuclear weapons and nuclear war. "Even a vast superiority in numbers of weapons," said Eisenhower, "and a consequent capability of devastating retaliation, is no preventive, of itself, against the fearful material damage and toll of human lives that would be inflicted by surprise aggression." He spoke of the "probability of civilization destroyed" – language echoed by Malenkov three months later.[18]

Eisenhower was not content merely to stress the dangers of the nuclear arms race. The main point of his speech was to urge that atomic power be made to serve "the arts of peace."[19] Governments should "begin now and continue to make joint contributions from their stockpiles of normal uranium and fissionable materials to an International Atomic Energy Agency," under the aegis of the United Nations. The agency would be responsible for the impounding, storage, and protection of the fissionable and other materials; it would also "devise methods whereby this fissionable material would be allocated to serve the peaceful pursuits of mankind."[20] In this speech Eisenhower was pursuing several purposes vis-à-vis the Soviet Union. One was to engage it in a cooperative undertaking. Another was to improve the relative American position: the United States had much larger stockpiles of fissionable materials than the Soviet Union had, and could more easily contribute materials to an international agency.

The Soviet response to the speech was cautious. Two weeks after it the Soviet government said it was ready to engage in private talks on bringing the arms race to an end, but it pointed, rightly, to two flaws in the President's proposal.[21] First, governments were to allocate only a small part of their stockpiles of atomic materials to peaceful purposes; this meant that they could continue to produce nuclear weapons. Second, there was nothing in the proposal to prevent an aggressor from using nuclear weapons.[22] The Soviet Union, for its part, proposed that states possessing nuclear weapons make a solemn commitment not to use them, on the lines of the 1925 Geneva protocol forbidding the use of chemical and bacteriological weapons. Whether such an agreement would have prevented the growing production of nuclear weapons or the use of those weapons is doubtful. It was, in any event, unacceptable to the United States, since the threat to use nuclear weapons was a key element in the foreign policy of the Eisenhower administration.

In the early months of 1954 Dulles and Molotov met several times to discuss the "Atoms for Peace" proposal.[23] At their meeting in Geneva on April 27 Molotov handed Dulles a long note, which added a new objection to the earlier ones: that it was "possible for the very application of atomic energy for peaceful purposes to be utilized for increasing the production of atomic weapons." It drew attention to the fact that the use of atomic energy for electric power converted "harmless atomic materials" into "explosive and fissionable materials." "Such a situation," it continued, "not only fails to lead to a reduction of the stocks of atomic materials utilized for the manufacture of atomic weapons, but also leads to an increase of these stocks without any limitations being applied either to the constantly increasing production of these materials in individual states or to production by the International Agency itself."[24]

This note reflected the advice that the Soviet leadership was receiving from its scientists. Malyshev, Kurchatov, Alikhanov, Kikoin, and Vinogradov made this argument in the draft article that Malyshev sent to Khrushchev, Malenkov, and Molotov on April 1, 1954.[25] They wrote that "the development of the industrial use of atomic energy by itself does not only not exclude, but leads directly to, an increase of military atomic potential." This is because nuclear fission, on which the generation of atomic power is based, produces new substances such as plutonium, uranium-233, and tritium, which "are themselves powerful atomic explosives." The use of atomic power on a large scale could therefore provide materials for atomic and hydrogen bombs. (Indeed, at just this time Dollezhal' was designing a reactor that would produce plutonium as well as generate electricity.) Atomic power would not save the world from the danger of nuclear war.[26]

Dulles was disheartened by the Soviet memorandum of April 27. His conversation with Molotov on May 1 was no more to his liking. Molotov pressed the point that the "Atoms for Peace" proposal might increase the danger of nuclear war. When Dulles asked him what he meant, Molotov replied that "parallel with the peaceful use of atomic materials, as in power plants, it was possible concurrently to increase the production of material needed to produce atomic bombs."[27] Dulles did not understand this point, and answered lamely that "he would seek out a scientist to educate him more fully."[28] It was beginning to become clear that "Atoms for Peace" made it necessary to devise safeguards to ensure that the spread of atomic power did not encourage the spread of nuclear weapons.

Dulles left his meeting with Molotov under the impression that the Soviet Union would not go any further unless the United States agreed to renounce the use of nuclear weapons. On September 22, however, Gromyko told Bohlen that the Soviet Union was willing to continue discussions.[29] On November 29 Moscow agreed that a ban on the use of nuclear weapons should not be a prerequisite for negotiations on the peaceful uses of atomic energy; it also accepted a United States proposal that experts from the two countries study the danger that nuclear power might lead to larger stockpiles of fissionable materials and the production of more atomic weapons.[30]

On December 4 the UN General Assembly unanimously approved a resolution expressing the hope that an International Atomic Energy

Agency would be established without delay. It also called for an international conference on the peaceful uses of atomic energy to be held under the auspices of the United Nations. This conference, which had been proposed by I.I. Rabi to Lewis Strauss, the chairman of the US Atomic Energy Commission, was to be the first practical result of the "Atoms for Peace" proposal.[31] The conference was to explore the possibility of international cooperation in developing the peaceful uses of atomic energy, to study the development of atomic power, and to consider possible areas of cooperation such as biology, medicine, and fundamental science.[32] The conference was to be held in Geneva in August 1955.

The Soviet Union now took several steps to indicate its interest in the peaceful use of atomic energy. On January 14, 1955 it informed the United Nations that it would give a paper on the Obninsk power station at the Geneva conference.[33] Four days later it announced that it would help China, Poland, Czechoslovakia, Romania, and East Germany develop nuclear research for peaceful purposes.[34] Between April and June the Soviet Union concluded nuclear cooperation agreements with these countries. Under these agreements it promised to help with the construction of research reactors, particle accelerators, radiochemical laboratories, and the training of scientists; to collaborate on specific problems and on the development of instruments; to discuss research plans and the plans for the peaceful uses of atomic energy; and to exchange experience in the production of radioactive isotopes.[35] The Soviet Union agreed to supply these countries with natural uranium, thorium, uranium-235, uranium-233, plutonium, tritium, and heavy water in quantities needed for physical and radiochemical research.[36]

Washington was afraid that Moscow was seeking to appear cooperative only to impede genuine collaboration. But this fear proved unfounded. After initial hesitation, the Soviet Union took an active role in arranging the conference in Geneva. An Advisory Committee was set up, under the chairmanship of the Indian physicist Homi Bhabha, to help the United Nations organize the conference. I.I. Rabi, John Cockcroft, and Bertrand Goldschmidt were the representatives from the United States, Britain, and France. The Soviet representative was Dmitrii Skobel'tsyn, who had become director of FIAN in 1951 on the death of Sergei Vavilov.[37] Soviet participation was increased when Sergei's son, Viktor Vavilov, was appointed deputy secretary-general of the conference. Dag Hammarskjold, Secretary-General of the United Nations, was pleasantly surprised by the degree of cooperation he got from Skobel'tsyn and Vavilov.[38]

In July 1955 the Soviet Union took a further step towards cooperation when Bulganin stated, during the opening session of the Geneva summit meeting, that the Soviet Union was willing to take part in the discussions about the proposed International Atomic Energy Agency. He promised that the Soviet Union would deposit 50 kilograms of fissionable material with the agency as soon as it was established. (This was a token amount, which would have a negligible impact on Soviet weapons programs.) The agency was finally set up in 1957, with Soviet participation, to encourage the peaceful application of atomic energy and to establish and administer safeguards designed to ensure that activities supported by the agency did not contribute to the military use of atomic energy.[39]

Although Skobel'tsyn was the Soviet representative on the Advisory Committee for the Geneva conference on the peaceful uses of atomic energy, it was Kurchatov who directed the Soviet preparations. Kurchatov believed that Soviet nuclear physics was suffering from unnecessary secrecy and from the lack of contact with Western physicists.[40] He wanted not merely token participation, but a large and serious Soviet delegation. He decided on the topics of the Soviet papers, commented on most of them, and discussed some of them in detail with their authors.[41] He took an active part, for example, in preparing the paper on the Obninsk power station, which was to be given by Blokhintsev.[42] This was to be the first meeting of Soviet and Western nuclear scientists since the 1930s, and Kurchatov was determined that Soviet science should give a good account of itself. The Soviet Union, like the other participating states, declassified a great deal of material relating to nuclear physics and reactor technology for the conference.[43] Over 1,000 papers were presented at the conference, and 102 of these were Soviet.

On Kurchatov's initiative the Academy of Sciences held a meeting on the peaceful uses of atomic energy in the first week of July 1955. This was a rehearsal for the Geneva conference, which opened four weeks later.[44] The Central Committee Presidium approved the Academy meeting only on June 14, and it therefore had to be arranged rather hastily.[45] Scientists from all over the world were invited, but it was chiefly those from Eastern Europe and the Scandinavian countries who came. The highlight of the meeting for foreign visitors was a tour of the Obninsk power station.[46]

The Geneva conference on the peaceful uses of atomic energy opened on August 8 and lasted for two weeks. "Russian scientists made, in general, an excellent impression on their Western colleagues," Laura Fermi wrote in her book on the conference.[47] Blokhintsev was very pleased with the reception of his report on the Obninsk power plant.[48] He later recalled that when Walter Zinn, the American reactor specialist, shook his hand after the talk, it occasioned a round of applause: "such a handshake at that time was a real sensation."[49] Vladimir Veksler's lecture, in which he announced that the world's most powerful particle accelerator was nearing completion at Dubna, also created a major impression.[50] Cockcroft noted that "individual Russian scientists such as Blokhintsev, Vinogradov, Markoff, Veksler were first class."[51] Lewis Strauss told the National Security Council in October that "in the realm of pure science the Soviets had astonished us by their achievements, notably with the photographs they exhibited of their new cyclotron." "It was now perfectly clear," he said, "that [the Russians] could be described in no sense as technically backward."[52]

Kurchatov was pleased with the outcome. "International meetings are essential," he said. "We learned a lot. Doubts have been dispelled, mutual mistrust has disappeared. We learned our weak sides."[53] He told the Twentieth Party Congress in February 1956 that "we received great satisfaction from the fact that the reports of our scientists and engineers at that conference won high marks from the world scientific community."[54]

The most significant aspect of the conference, however, was not that Soviet scientists made a good impression – important though that was for Kurchatov and his colleagues – but that the international scientific community was being reconstituted after a twenty-year interval caused by repression in the Soviet Union and Germany in the 1930s, by World War II, and by the nuclear arms race. The Geneva conference was the first occasion in a very long time that Western scientists could speak at length to Soviet scientists.[55] Some of the older delegates, like Peierls, Weisskopf, Cockcroft, and Bohr, had met Soviet scientists in the 1930s, but most of those taking part were too young to have had such contact.

Veksler, in a talk given after the conference, remarked that "the debates were friendly in tone . . . the scientists of the world easily found a common language." Rabi commented that, if Veksler's impressions were shared by other Soviet scientists, "I am satisfied with the results of the Conference in helping to reestablish the worldwide community and communion of scientists."[56] Cockcroft made the same point when he wrote, in a report for the Foreign Office, that the conference "has brought together East and West after a long period of separation in the Physical Sciences . . . and has done a great deal to re-establish the normal pattern of communication in the scientific world."[57]

The Geneva conference was followed immediately by a meeting on safeguards, to which Moscow had agreed the previous November. The aim of the meeting, which began on August 22 and lasted for five days, was to devise technical methods to prevent nuclear fuel made available for reactors under the auspices of the International Atomic Energy Agency from being diverted to the manufacture of weapons. The Soviet delegation was headed by Skobel'tsyn, and the United States delegation by Rabi. Four other countries took part – the United Kingdom, Canada, France, and Czechoslovakia.[58] The United States proposed that fissionable materials supplied to other countries be tagged by spiking them with energetic gamma emitters (radioactive cobalt for plutonium-239, and uranium-232 for uranium-235); this would make it possible to monitor where the fuel went, and how it was used. Skobel'tsyn was skeptical about this proposal and asked probing questions about its feasibility. The Soviet Union made no proposal of its own, however, and the meeting ended inconclusively. The problem of ensuring that the peaceful uses of atomic energy remained peaceful was proving to be more difficult than the Eisenhower adminstration had appreciated at first.

This was the first meeting in which members of the newly reconstituted international scientific community engaged in formal talks about arms control. It had been easy for scientists to find a common language in discussing nuclear science at Geneva, and many scientists believed that it would be easier for scientists than for political leaders to bridge the East–West political divide in other areas too. It is in this period that the Pugwash movement had its origins. This brought Soviet and Western scientists together to discuss nuclear weapons and disarmament.[59] This attempt to use the internationalism of science to address the common danger presented by nuclear weapons was what Niels Bohr had had in mind in 1944. Talks between scientists from East and West, in both government and unofficial meetings, were now to become an increasingly important element in the search for ways to manage and control the nuclear arms race.

III

In spite of its earlier misgivings, the Soviet Union was now committed to international collaboration. It had signed agreements with the socialist countries in the early months of 1955. During the Geneva conference in August 1955 Veksler visited CERN (Conseil Européen pour la Recherche Nucléaire) to explore the possibility of collaboration. This large research center been set up three years earlier outside Geneva by the countries of Western Europe.[60] According to Soviet physicists, however, CERN was not interested in collaborating with Soviet scientists.[61] Kurchatov proposed the creation of an "Eastern Institute," a counterpart of CERN in which the Soviet Union would participate along with the socialist countries. The government agreed, and in March 1956 the Joint Institute of Nuclear Research was established at Dubna, on the basis of two laboratories that already existed there. The title "Eastern Institute" was dropped because for China, North Korea, and Mongolia the institute was not "eastern."[62]

The Soviet Union's nuclear relationship with China showed just how interconnected the peaceful and the military uses of atomic energy were. Notwithstanding Mao's assertion that the atomic bomb was a "paper tiger," Chinese leaders had shown considerable interest in nuclear weapons. The Soviet Union, however, was not eager for China to build its own bomb. During the Totskoe exercise in September 1954 the Commander-in-Chief of the Soviet Air Force instructed one of his aides to explain to the Commander-in-Chief of the Chinese Air Force that China did not need the bomb because it had the Soviet Union's protection.[63] On January 15,

1955, however, Mao finally decided that China should build its own atomic bomb.[64]

The Chinese decision was a response to American threats, explicit and implicit, to use nuclear weapons against China.[65] It also betrayed a lack of faith in the ability or willingness of the Soviet Union to use its nuclear weapons to defend Chinese interests. China nevertheless expected Soviet help in building up its nuclear research base. On January 17, two days after the Chinese decision, the Soviet Council of Ministers decided to help China and other socialist countries develop nuclear research for peaceful purposes. Three days later the Soviet Union and China signed an agreement to undertake joint exploration for uranium in China; China agreed to sell any surplus uranium to the Soviet Union.[66] On April 27, 1955 the two countries signed an agreement under which the Soviet Union was to supply China with an experimental nuclear reactor, a cyclotron, and the "necessary quantity of fissionable material."[67] In the next few years hundreds of young Chinese scientists received training in nuclear physics at Dubna.[68] Although the Soviet Union was not yet committed to helping China build its nuclear industry and research facilities – that agreement came only in August 1956[69] – it knew that China had decided to build its own bomb and that Soviet assistance would help it towards that goal; after all, the wartime cyclotron and the first experimental reactor had been significant milestones on the Soviet path to the bomb.[70] Khrushchev connived at Chinese nuclear ambitions in the mid-1950s. Thus began a turbulent and complex nuclear relationship.

IV

The success of the Soviet nuclear project gave Soviet science immense prestige not only abroad, but at home too. Stalin and Beria had regarded the scientists with suspicion and mistrust, but the development of the atomic and hydrogen bombs gave the scientists a new standing in the regime. Kurchatov now enjoyed great authority in the upper reaches of the Party and government. "Such was our confidence in him," Khrushchev writes in his memoirs, "that we let him go around by himself in England, calling on physicists and visiting laboratories. . . . It should go without saying that so remarkable a man, so great a scientist, and so devoted a patriot would deserve our complete trust and respect."[71]

By the mid-1950s there existed in the Soviet Union – and in the rest of the world – a great sense of optimism about science and technology in general, and about atomic energy in particular.[72] The successes of the nuclear project seemed to show that the Soviet Union could indeed make technological progress. In words that recalled Vernadskii's reaction to the discovery of nuclear fission, Bulganin spoke at the Central Committee plenum of July 1955 of an impending scientific-technical revolution:

Science and technology are developing along the path of ever greater mastery of high and superhigh speeds, pressures and temperatures. The summit of the contemporary stage of the development of science and technology is the discovery of the methods of obtaining and utilizing intraatomic energy. We stand on the threshold of a new scientific-technical and industrial revolution, far surpassing in its significance the industrial revolutions connected with the appearance of steam and electricity.[73]

The Soviet leadership now put great hope in science and technology to provide not only for the defense of the country, but also for its economic development.

Scientists and officials were keenly aware, however, of the backwardness of Soviet science and technology. In July 1952, after the publication of excerpts from Stalin's *Economic Problems of Socialism in the USSR*, Kapitsa had written to Stalin lamenting the poor state of Soviet science. The most important technological developments based on new discoveries in physics – shortwave technology including radar, television, all forms of jet propulsion, the gas turbine, atomic energy, isotope separation, accelerators – had all been made abroad, he wrote, and adopted by the Soviet Union only when other countries had recognized their importance. What was worse, the basic ideas for some of these technologies had been born in the Soviet Union, but had not found favorable conditions for development. Kapitsa cited as examples radar, the gas turbine, and his own method for producing oxygen. And of nuclear physics he wrote:

I remember the exceptionally small attention that nuclear physics received here in the Union before the war. . . . True, we have now begun work in this field, and are making up for lost time. But how much better it would have been if we had been leaders in the field of nuclear physics and had had the atomic bomb sooner than others. I think it is perfectly possible that our scientists working in nuclear physics, with their creative abilities and knowledge, could have solved the problem of the atomic bomb completely independently and earlier than others, if they had not been distracted and had been boldly helped.[74]

Kapitsa deplored the way in which science was subordinated to practical needs. Was it not now time to raise the level of Soviet science by tackling basic research, he asked, just as Stalin had taken time off from the affairs of state to think profoundly about the economic laws of socialism?[75]

The state of Soviet science and technology became a matter of discussion after Stalin's death. Kapitsa was not alone in his concerns. The situation in biology was understood by many to be disastrous. Even in a field like nuclear physics, which had been well supported by the state, the Soviet Union lagged behind the West, in the opinion of Soviet physicists. There was also disquiet in the government about the state of Soviet technology. Malyshev spoke of the Soviet Union's scientific-technical backwardness, and of the tendency to technological stagnation in the economy.[76] In late 1954 and early 1955 the Soviet leadership organized several meetings of designers, engineers, factory directors, and institute directors to discuss technological progress and the introduction of scientific discoveries into industrial production.[77] On the basis of these discussions the government took steps to speed up technological progress: it established the State Committee for New Technology (with Malyshev in charge) and the Institute of Scientific-Technical Information, and it created the position of Deputy Minister for New Technology in the industrial ministries.[78]

Far more was needed, however, than administrative reforms to solve the problems of Soviet science and technology. Kapitsa, who had been released from virtual house arrest in August 1953 and restored as director of the Institute of Physical Problems in January 1955, wrote several penetrating letters to Khrushchev on the state of Soviet science. The most important issue he raised was the weakness of the Soviet scientific community.[79] Scientists had been "beaten" so often that they were afraid to think for themselves, he wrote. It was bureaucrats who evaluated a scientist's work rather than other scientists; and the excessive secrecy surrounding research made it impossible for the Soviet scientific community at large to form its own judgments. Moreover, now that scientists received high wages and privileges, science was attracting people who were seeking advancement by bureaucratic means and blocking real scientists: these "weeds" were threatening to strangle science.

The only remedy for these defects, in Kapitsa's view, was a healthy climate for scientific opinion. Two conditions were needed. The first and more important was related to the natural desire of scientists for free discussion: scientists should not be afraid to express their opinions, even if those opinions were going to be rejected. It was particularly harmful to decree scientific truths, as the Science Department of the Central Committee had done. "A scientific idea should be born and grow strong in the struggle with other ideas," Kapitsa wrote, "and only thus can it become a truth."[80] The second condition was that the leadership should take account of scientific opinion. The organization of scientific life should be based on the opinions formed in the process of public discussion. The situation in biology, Kapitsa complained, was a direct consequence of the failure to observe this second condition; the leadership had not heeded the views of the scientific community.

After Stalin's death scientists did try to remove the worst consequences of Stalin's rule, and physicists sought to extend their own intellectual autonomy to other fields. Individual scientists wrote to the political leadership about the situation in biology. When these letters failed to produce any effect, Leningrad biologists decided to write a collective letter, even though "it was known that the authorities took a very negative attitude to collective letters."[81] In the autumn of 1955, 300 biologists signed a 23-page letter to the Central Committee calling for a disavowal of the August 1948 session on biology and for the revival of genetics. Physicists and chemists supported this initiative. Twenty-four of them – including Artsimovich, Ginzburg, Zel'dovich, Kapitsa, Landau, Sakharov, Tamm, Flerov, and Khariton – wrote a letter to the Central Committee drawing attention to the harm that the situation in biology was doing to Soviet science as a whole.[82]

Kurchatov supported the initiative of the 300 biologists. Neither he nor A.N. Nesmeianov, the president of the Academy of Sciences, could sign the letter from the physicists and chemists, since they were members of the Central Committee, to which the letter was addressed. They did meet Khrushchev, however, to discuss the letter, and to try and persuade him to adopt the measures it proposed. But Khrushchev, who fancied himself an expert in agriculture, became indignant and called the letter scandalous.[83] This episode showed that there were limits to the authority of scientists, even the authority of someone like Kurchatov. Party leaders still claimed the right to adjudicate what counted as science, and what as pseudoscience. The situation in biology improved somewhat in the mid-1950s, but Lysenko regained some of the lost ground later in the decade.[84]

The only thing wrong with the letter of the 300, in Kapitsa's view, was that its signatories were expecting the Central Committee to issue another decree on biology, but now saying something different. "It would have been more correct," Kapitsa wrote to Khrushchev in December 1955, "if the letter had appeared in print, and an honest discussion had been organized."[85] It was not up to the Central Committee to make a judgment on biology, even if it was the correct judgment. Kapitsa put the issue clearly: where was scientific authority – the right to say what constitutes scientific truth – to reside? In the Party, or in the scientific community? In the mid-1950s there was, in spite of Khrushchev's continued support for Lysenko, a gradual shift in the relationship between scientific truth and political authority. The scientific community was claiming more autonomy for itself, and pushing back the Party's claim to be able to say what was science and what was pseudoscience. Militant "philosophers" lost their role as ideological watchdogs. The Party was not willing, however, to cede completely its claim to authority in science.[86]

V

Scientists sought greater intellectual freedom inside the Soviet Union. They were also eager to reestablish contact with colleagues abroad. This was evident at the Geneva conference on the peaceful uses of atomic energy. It was even clearer in the initiative Kurchatov took to establish international collaboration in the field of controlled fusion. Soviet work in this area began in June or July 1950, when Andrei Sakharov was asked to comment on a proposal that Oleg Lavrent'ev, a young sailor serving in the Far East, had sent to the government about the possibility of using controlled thermonuclear reactions for power generation. Sakharov found the proposal impracticable, but it stimulated his own thinking, and he decided to explore the possibility of using a static magnetic field to create and confine a high-temperature deuterium plasma. When Tamm returned to Arzamas-16 from Moscow in August he was taken with Sakharov's ideas, and the two men worked together on the magnetic thermonuclear reactor (MTR), a term that Tamm coined for their project.[87]

Kurchatov was informed of this work in November 1950. He studied the initial results carefully for two months, and then decided to write a report proposing a broad expansion of this research. At the end of January 1951 he brought together a group of leading nuclear physicists (including Khariton, Zel'dovich, Tamm, Sakharov, Golovin, Artsimovich, and Meshcheriakov) to discuss this proposal. Once this group had approved the proposal, Kurchatov prepared a draft government decree and sent it to Beria for Stalin's signature.[88]

Beria had not responded to Kurchatov's proposal when news arrived in April 1951 of the claim by the Argentinian dictator Juan Peron that the Austrian scientist Ronald Richter had achieved a controlled thermonuclear reaction in a laboratory in Argentina. This claim caused alarm in Moscow. Richter had worked in Manfred von Ardenne's laboratory during the war, and Von Ardenne, Gustav Hertz, and Max Steenbeck were summoned to Moscow for consultations. Von Ardenne told Zaveniagin not to take the matter seriously, because Richter was unable to tell fantasy from reality; Peron's claim did indeed prove to be unfounded.[89] In spite of Von Ardenne's assurances, Peron's statement speeded up Soviet work. Beria quickly called a meeting of the Special Atomic Committee in his Kremlin office to discuss controlled fusion. Tamm and Sakharov spoke to the committee. Kurchatov proposed Mikhail Leontovich to head the theoretical work and Artsimovich the experimental work. He asked for approval to set up a council on the MTR, to be chaired by himself, with Sakharov as his deputy. On May 5, 1951 Stalin signed the decree.[90]

Although controlled fusion came to be regarded as a potential civilian application of nuclear energy, the initial impetus for this research was military. A fusion reactor would have important military uses. It would produce large amounts of neutrons that could be used to produce fissionable materials for use in bombs or in reactors. It could also be used to produce tritium for thermonuclear bombs.[91] Research on controlled fusion in the Soviet Union, as in the United States, was regarded as a natural concomitant of the effort to build thermonuclear weapons.[92] As more reactors were built to produce fissionable materials and tritium, the military applications of controlled thermonuclear reactions seemed less urgent. In the euphoria generated by the Geneva conference on the peaceful uses of atomic energy, it began to seem unreasonable to keep all the work on controlled fusion classified.[93]

At the end of 1955 Kurchatov decided that the whole controlled fusion project would have to be put on to a new footing. In December 1955, shortly after the superbomb test, he organized a conference on the MTR, attended by about 150 scientists. Artsimovich and Leontovich spoke about the results they had achieved so far. Kurchatov drew other people – from Khar'kov and from Leningrad – into this work, but he came to the conclusion that international collaboration was needed if progress was to be made. In his speech to the Twentieth Party Congress in February 1956 he said that Soviet scientists would like to work on controlled fusion with scientists from all countries of the world, including American scientists, "whose scientific and technical achievements we value highly."[94]

The opportunity to lay the basis for international collaboration came when Khrushchev asked Kurchatov to accompany himself and Bulganin on their visit to Britain in April 1956. Eden had issued the invitation to the Soviet leaders during the Geneva summit meeting the previous July. In his memoirs Khrushchev explains that he had three purposes in mind in taking Kurchatov along: "first, he would elevate the prestige of our delegation; second, he would allow us to establish useful contacts with the Western scientific community; and third, taking him with us would be a welcome demonstration of trust towards our own intelligentsia."[95] Khrushchev also invited Tupolev, the aircraft designer to join the delegation. After dinner at No. 10 Downing Street on April 19 Khrushchev introduced "Academician Kurchatov who makes our hydrogen bomb" and "Academician Tupolev . . . who produces the plane that delivers it" to Churchill.[96] This was a subtle form of atomic diplomacy. Khrushchev doubtless hoped that the presence of Kurchatov and Tupolev would serve as a reminder of the growing strategic nuclear might of the Soviet Union.

Kurchatov wanted to use his visit to Britain – his first journey abroad – to open the way to collaboration in controlled fusion. This work was still classified in Britain and the United States, the two other countries engaged in serious research in this area. He prepared two lectures for Britain, one on nuclear power, the other on Soviet research on controlled fusion. He gave a great deal of thought to the latter lecture, relying heavily in its preparation on Artsimovich, but drawing on others as well, including Tamm and Sakharov.[97] According to Golovin, who was involved in the fusion research,

Kurchatov discussed and corrected the text with great pleasure and great taste, worrying not only about the comprehensibility of the exposition, but also taking care that the lecture should impress the English, correspond to English traditions, and take account of the peculiarities of the English national character. For he had not simply to communicate certain information, but to lay the basis for further long-term collaboration.[98]

Kurchatov hoped that by breaching the barrier of secrecy and showing the high standard of Soviet research he would lay the ground for collaboration.

On April 20 Kurchatov had lunch at the Athenaeum in London with John Cockcroft, director of the Atomic Energy Research Establishment at Harwell. "I had not met Kurchatov before but was greatly impressed by his intelligence and by his eagerness to talk about collaboration in Atomic Energy work," Cockcroft wrote later.[99] They had a very animated discussion at the top of the Athenaeum staircase. Kurchatov suggested that he lecture at Harwell, and Cockcroft agreed to arrange this; the lecture had not been included in the program beforehand. On the following day Kurchatov visited Harwell with Khrushchev and Bulganin. On April 25 he returned there alone to deliver his lecture. Cockcroft was not present at the lecture, since he had to fly to the United States for a conference on declassification.[100]

Kurchatov spoke to an audience of about 350 people. English texts of his two lectures had been prepared as pamphlets, and these were handed out to the audience. Kurchatov first made some brief remarks on the development of power reactors in the Soviet Union.[101] Then he proceeded to the second, and more remarkable, part of his lecture. This described Soviet experiments with high-temperature discharges in deuterium gas as one approach to controlled fusion.[102] The research described by Kurchatov was very well received at Harwell and by physicists more generally; one of the Harwell physicists wrote that it "adds considerably to scientific knowledge," and that "the experiment has been very beautifully performed."[103] A brief note about the lecture was sent to Eden on the following day.[104] The Foreign Office cabled the embassy in Washington on April 27:

All claims believed. This is the first published work on nuclear reactions in a gas discharge plasma. . . . Experiments carried out with care and considerable insight on hydro-magnetic and gas discharge physics.[105]

In the United States four scientists, including Edward Teller, were called to Washington to advise the members of the Atomic Energy Commission on the importance of Kurchatov's lecture. The four men "unanimously concluded that Kurchatov was apparently talking about genuine Russian accomplishments. . . . There was no question in their minds on the point that the statements made are impressive."[106]

Kurchatov's visit to Britain produced the effect he desired. His lecture made an impact not merely because of the quality of the research it reported, but because the Soviet Union had decided to declassify unilaterally this area of research. "The circumstances of the lecture were sensational," said a former director of classification at the US Atomic Energy Commission. "At Harwell, scientists of a nominally free nation were given a public lecture by a representative of a totalitarian nation on fusion for peace."[107] By the time of the second Geneva conference on the peaceful uses of atomic energy in 1958, research on controlled fusion had been declassified in the West as well as the Soviet Union, and was one of the main topics at the conference.[108] "Kurchatov broke the spell by his celebrated lecture at Harwell," wrote Cockcroft.[109]

Kurchatov produced an extremely favorable impression on his British hosts. Malcolm Mackintosh, one of the British interpreters, provided an attractive portrait of Kurchatov shortly after his visit. This is worth quoting because it confirms the impression of intelligence, self-confidence, and personal charm conveyed by the memoirs of Kurchatov's Soviet colleagues. Kurchatov displayed a lively interest in conditions of life in Britain, and in the things he saw on his trip. "He had a very enquiring mind, and would never leave a subject until he had satisfied himself that he understood it fully," Mackintosh wrote.

Kurchatov was an extremely pleasant companion. He was always courteous and well-mannered, never ruffled, and always had a friendly word for everyone. He enjoyed his popularity and prestige, and, like Tupolev, considered himself indispensable to the Soviet Union. His first demand each morning was for a translation of any British press references to himself, and he was half-amused, half-flattered at the description "father of the Soviet hydrogen bomb." He had a very high regard for British progress in nuclear physics, and spoke again and again in most favorable terms of Sir John Cockcroft, particularly after he was invited to read a paper at Harwell. Kurchatov spoke little of his own work, on the plea that he could not explain his ideas to a layman.

Mackintosh reports that "Kurchatov considered privately that the conception of science overstepping national frontiers was inadmissible at the moment. He himself was a Russian first and a scientist second."[110]

There is a parallel between Kurchatov's attitude to science and that of his teacher, Abram Ioffe. Both believed that science should serve the Soviet state; no one had done more than Kurchatov to put into practice Ioffe's slogan that physics was the basis of future technology. But both regarded science as an international enterprise, and both undertook to restore disrupted scientific relations with the West – Ioffe after the Revolution and Civil War, Kurchatov after the worst period of the Cold War. During the twenty years when almost all contact with Western scientists had been severed, the consciousness of being part of a broader community remained intact among Soviet physicists.

Kurchatov had not forgotten his teacher. In May 1955 he – along with Aleksandrov, Alikhanov, Artsimovich, Kikoin, Semenov, and Khariton – had written to Khrushchev asking that Ioffe be awarded the title of Hero of Socialist Labor on his 75th birthday for his services to Soviet physics. Ioffe had been forced by the Soviet authorities to resign as director of his institute in 1950, just before his 70th birthday; and on his 70th birthday – an occasion normally celebrated festively by Soviet scientists – he alone was allowed to speak, and then only to engage in self-criticism.[111] In their letter

Kurchatov and his colleagues pointed out that half the physicists who were members of the Academy were representatives of Ioffe's school.[112] Their request was granted, and Ioffe became a Hero of Socialist Labor in 1955, just over thirty years after he had made his speech on "Science and Technology" at the opening of his institute's new building in February 1923.

Soviet physics flourished, as Ioffe had hoped it would. The nuclear project protected Soviet physics, and this had a broader social and political significance. The conditions that Kapitsa had argued, in his letter to Khrushchev, were necessary for a healthy scientific community – willingness to speak out, and decisions based on the community's opinion – were also conditions required for democracy, or at least for a "public sphere" in which public opinion could be formed, and decisions taken, on the basis of open discussion. The scientific community was in a poor state by the time of Stalin's death – it had been "beaten" too often and was threatened by "weeds," to use Kapitsa's language – but it had enjoyed more autonomy than other parts of Soviet society under Stalin's rule. This was especially true of physics. The physics community was an island of intellectual autonomy in the totalitarian state. The scientific community – and especially the physics community – was, for all its failings, the closest thing to civil society in the Stalinist regime. The scientist – or at least scientists like Frenkel', Kapitsa, Tamm, Vernadskii, and later Sakharov – was the nearest approximation to a citizen that could be found in Soviet society. The scientist as citizen was a figure of great significance for the society as a whole. In providing protection for Soviet physics, the bomb had done something more: it had helped to protect a small element of civil society in a state that strove for totalitarian control over the life of society.

Conclusion

FOR FORTY YEARS the Soviet–American nuclear arms race dominated world politics, yet much of the competition was hidden from public view. It was nuclear weapons above all that made the Soviet Union a super-power, but the Soviet nuclear establishment was shrouded in secrecy. In the early years of the Cold War Western governments – and citizens – knew very little about Soviet nuclear policy; the ordinary Soviet citizen knew even less. Only recently has it become possible to write about Soviet nuclear policy as the product of individual decisions taken in particular circumstances. I have tried to provide a coherent – though inevitably incomplete and provisional – analysis of Stalin's nuclear policy in those terms. I have tried also to set it squarely in both its international and Soviet contexts.

The central theme of the book is the development of Soviet nuclear weapons. Political scientists have studied the dynamics of the Soviet-American nuclear arms race, and the role of international as well as domestic factors in explaining the weapons decisions on either side. This book shows that it would make no sense to treat the Soviet nuclear project solely in terms of an "internal dynamic," rooted in the structures and values of Soviet society. In the 1930s Soviet nuclear scientists were part of an international community, competing with research groups in other countries to make discoveries and win recognition for their work. The Soviet wartime nuclear project was started in response to intelligence about the nuclear projects in Britain and the United States. After Hiroshima rivalry with the United States provided the Soviet nuclear project with its dynamism.

This does not mean that domestic factors were unimportant in explaining Soviet nuclear policy. There were aspects of the Soviet regime that predisposed it to accept the challenge of a nuclear arms race. The most important of these was the conception that the Communist Party had of the Soviet Union as a socialist state leading the world from capitalism to communism. Stalin at the end of World War II foresaw a new world war in twenty or thirty years' time, and believed that this would complete the transition to socialism on a global scale. Stalin viewed the atomic bomb in the context of preparations for a new world war; but he also wanted the bomb in order to resist political pressure from the United States.

There were also aspects of the regime that explain how and when the nuclear challenge was taken up. Although official ideology regarded the West with hostility and suspicion, the policy of "catch up and overtake" focussed attention on Western technological development as the path to be followed. This policy reflected a deep-rooted consciousness of backwardness *vis-à-vis* the West, and a determination to overcome that backwardness. The atomic bomb was a powerful symbol of the United States' position as the economic and technological leader of the world. It was therefore a natural goal for the policy of "catch up and overtake" to pursue.

The tendency to copy Western technology was, as Kapitsa pointed out in letters to the Kremlin, reinforced by the Soviet leaders' distrust of Soviet scientists and engineers; innovative proposals from Soviet scientists tended not to be taken seriously unless and until they were validated by Western experience. If Stalin, Beria, and Molotov had had greater trust in Soviet scientists, they might have had a clearer appreciation of the remarkable intelligence they received about the atomic bomb during World War II. They might then have had a better grasp, before August 1945, of the role that the bomb was to play in international relations.

The failure to understand the bomb's significance increased the shock of Hiroshima. Stalin immediately put the nuclear project on a new footing. He took the bomb seriously, not because he heeded the advice of Soviet scientists, but because the United States had demonstrated the power of the bomb at Hiroshima and Nagasaki. Studies of Soviet technology have shown that the command economy placed great obstacles in the way of technological innovation. After Hiroshima, however, Stalin used the command economy to mobilize resources for the atomic project. This was the kind of large-scale, high-priority project for which the command economy had been created. But success came at a price. In the race to build the bomb Stalin gave low priority to health, safety, and the environment. The consequences soon became apparent at Cheliabinsk-40, and are still evident in the former Soviet Union. The accident at the Chernobyl nuclear power plant in 1986 has been blamed by many observers on the secrecy and lack of public accountability characteristic of the command economy.

Along with the atomic project, Stalin initiated projects to develop radar, rockets, and jet propulsion. He made a major commitment of resources to military technology, thereby placing a heavy burden on the war-damaged Soviet economy. He involved the Soviet Union in a nuclear arms race with a state that was economically and technologically much more powerful. This decision, which was taken without any apparent discussion of the alternatives, had fateful consequences. The causes of the Soviet Union's collapse were doubtless many, but one of them was surely the economic and political burden of the military-industrial complex. A different foreign policy after the war – along the lines that Litvinov suggested, for example – might have enabled the Soviet Union to establish a more cooperative relationship with the United States and to avoid at least some of the costs of the arms race. But Stalin appears to have given no serious consideration to such a policy. It would not have fitted easily with his conception of postwar international politics, or with his wish to reestablish tight control over Soviet society after the war.

The first Soviet atomic bomb was a copy of the American plutonium bomb tested at Alamogordo in July 1945. Espionage played a key role in the atomic Soviet project, and its role would have been even greater if the Soviet leaders had paid more heed to the intelligence they received during the war. The best estimates suggest, however, that the Soviet Union could have built a bomb by 1951 or 1952 even without intelligence about the American bomb. There already existed in the Soviet Union strong schools of physics and radiochemistry, as well as competent engineers. Soviet nuclear research in 1939–41 had gone a long way toward establishing the conditions for an explosive chain reaction. It was because Soviet nuclear scientists were so advanced that they were able to make good use of the information they received from Britain and the United States about the atomic bomb. Soviet scientists showed their ability by developing thermo-nuclear weapons independently. Although the Soviet Union did receive information about American research on thermonuclear weapons, this information was misleading rather than helpful. The nuclear project was a considerable achievement for Soviet science and engineering.

The relationship between scientists and the political system is the second major theme of the book. That relationship was changed by the nuclear project. Stalin regarded scientists and engineers with suspicion, fearing that they might be wreckers or saboteurs, and claimed for himself the right to say what constituted valid science. Physics survived, however, as a sphere of intellectual autonomy, in spite of the repression of physicists in the 1930s. The hopes that existed at the end of World War II for a more liberal intellectual climate were not fulfilled, but physics was protected by the bomb from the terrible obscurantism of Stalin's last years. The survival of physics pointed to a profound cultural contradiction in Stalinism, between the effort to make the Soviet Union a powerful state vis-à-vis the rest of the world and the urge to exercise complete control over the life of society at home. The Soviet nuclear project shows not that science and totalitarian-ism are compatible, but that totalitarian regimes have to allow some zones of intellectual autonomy in the society if they are to reap the benefits of science.

After Stalin's death, nuclear scientists – and Kurchatov in particular – enjoyed unprecedented authority among the political leaders. The physics community tried, with only limited success, to extend its own relative intellectual autonomy into other areas of Soviet life. It was an embryonic civil society, though that term was not used then. Physicists wanted to see their own norms of discussion reflected more widely in scientific and political life. In the most unexpected way, it appeared that science might fulfill the hopes of those like Vernadskii who believed that it was in and of itself a cultural value, a rationalizing and democratic force in society. These hopes were not fully realized in the post-Stalin years, however. The Soviet bureaucracy pressed heavily on the scientific community, and the Party did what it could to discourage scientists from thinking critically about politics and public life.

After the mid-1950s scientists did, however, play important public roles. The most important public figure was of course Sakharov, who continued to work at Arzamas-16 until 1968. Alexander Solzhenitsyn has written that Sakharov was a "miracle," who emerged among the "swarms of corrupt, venal, unprincipled intelligentsia."[1] In his Memoirs Sakharov rejects this description of himself, and of the people he worked with. Sakharov was an exceptional man, who inherited the best traditions of the Russian intelligentsia from his family; but the physics community also contributed to his moral and political formation. In the opening sentences of his 1968 essay, *Reflections on Progress, Peaceful Coexistence, and Intellectual Freedom,* he wrote that

the views of the author have been formed in the milieu of the scientific-technical intelligentsia, which shows great anxiety about the questions of principle and the concrete questions of humankind's future. In particular, this concern feeds upon consciousness of the fact that the scientific method of directing politics, economics, art, education, and military affairs has not yet become a reality. We consider "scientific' that method which is based on a profound study of facts, theories and views, presupposing unprejudiced and open discussion, which is dispassionate in its conclusions.[2]

In calling for the norms of scientific discussion to be transferred to public life, Sakharov was taking science as the model for politics, echoing the tradition which regarded science as a force for rationality and democracy. After the publication of this essay in the West Sakharov was forced to quit secret work. Although his life now took a very different turn, he never rejected his former colleagues – though some of them gave in to political pressure to reject him – and was clearly aware of the influence that they had had on his own development.

The third theme of the book – the effect of nuclear weapons on international relations – is closely linked to the weapons decisions, and to the relationship between science and politics. Stalin took the atomic bomb very seriously after Hiroshima. He expected the postwar world to resemble that of the interwar years, and decided therefore to invest heavily in the new weapons technologies that had emerged during World War II. He did not expect a major war in the short term, nor did he fear an imminent nuclear attack on the Soviet Union. But he did fear that the United States would try to use its atomic monopoly to shape the postwar settlement. He therefore devised a tactic to counter the political effect of the atomic bomb. That tactic consisted in showing that the Soviet Union would not be intimidated. The atomic bomb did not cause Stalin to alter his conception of international relations or to change the basic direction of Soviet foreign policy, but the steps he took to counter the threat of atomic diplomacy did contribute to the breakdown of the wartime alliance, and to the tensions of the Cold War.

The atomic bomb occupied a central place in Stalin's military policy. He gave priority in the immediate postwar period to measures that would lessen the effect of a nuclear strike against the Soviet Union: he built up Soviet air defenses, and enhanced the Soviet capacity to conduct strategic offensive operations in Europe. He pressed at the same time for the development of delivery vehicles for Soviet nuclear weapons. It was important for the Soviet Union to be able to strike the forward bases in Europe, Africa, and Asia, from which the United States might launch a nuclear attack. Stalin was also determined to acquire, as soon as possible, the intercontinental systems that would enable the Soviet Union to hold the United States at risk.

The first Soviet atomic bomb test in August 1949 did not create a stable East-West nuclear balance. The American discovery of the test appears indeed to have made the situation more dangerous in Stalin's eyes. His reaction was not to seek détente with the West, but to pursue a more active policy in Asia in order to bind China to the Soviet Union; this policy further heightened international tension. Stalin resisted the idea that the Soviet Union should adopt a more moderate policy. His successors, how-ever, acted quickly to seek a relaxation of tension, placing new emphasis on peaceful coexistence between capitalism and socialism.

Although he conducted a war of nerves with the Western powers, Stalin clearly wanted to avoid war with the United States. He succeeded in convincing the Western powers that the Soviet Union could not be intimidated, and in making them treat the Soviet Union with caution. But the United States committed itself to the defense of Western Europe in response to Stalin's policy, and the Western powers built up their armed forces. At the time of Stalin's death the Soviet Union was apparently on the verge of a new blood purge at home, and faced a dangerous situation abroad. Stalin was cautious and cunning in the conduct of foreign policy, but his policy was a disaster when judged in broad terms. It was not only that he made serious mistakes – in not heeding the warnings about a German attack in 1941; in failing to understand the significance of the atomic bomb before Hiroshima; and in miscalculating the effect of North

Korea's attack on the South in 1950 – but more importantly, he committed the Soviet Union to a path of militarized development from which his successors were unable to escape. The institutions he created before and after the war – the command economy, the defense industry including the nuclear and missile sectors, the large military establishment – came to play a powerful role in Soviet politics after his death, creating a stronger "internal dynamic" in foreign and defense policy.

Stalin did not allow nuclear weapons to shake his conception of international relations. It was only after his death that nuclear weapons began to affect the conceptual underpinnings of Soviet foreign policy. The concept of peaceful coexistence acquired substance, and Khrushchev renounced Lenin's thesis that war was inevitable among capitalist states. Soviet scientists pointed out, after the explosion of thermonuclear weapons, that nuclear war might destroy all human life. The political leadership accepted that nuclear war would be immensely destructive, but insisted, for ideological reasons, that it would destroy only capitalism, not civilization as a whole. The result was a confused – and confusing – assessment of nuclear war. Military doctrine pointed to the need to prepare to fight and win a nuclear war, but by the end of 1955 Soviet leaders understood that a Soviet-American nuclear war was, at some fundamental level, unacceptable, and realized that Western leaders understood this too. Western leaders had come to the same realization. This shared understanding was to be a stabilizing factor in the dangerous years ahead.

It was in the mid-1950s too that the international physics community was reconstituted, and that scientists from East and West began to meet, in official as well as informal settings, to search for ways of managing the nuclear arms race. Many scientists shared the belief, which Niels Bohr had expressed during World War II, that the international contacts of physicists would help to moderate interstate rivalry. The consciousness of being part of an international community had remained strong among Soviet physicists, in spite of the fact that there had been almost no personal contact for twenty years with Western colleagues. This consciousness was reflected in Kurchatov's bold initiative at Harwell in April 1956 to establish international collaboration in research on controlled fusion. After his return from Britain Kurchatov focussed on controlled fusion, and had less to do with weapons development. He supported Sakharov's efforts in 1958 to persuade Khrushchev not to renew nuclear weapons tests. He died on February 7, 1960, sitting on a park bench talking to Khariton about a forthcoming trip to France. He was buried in a place of honor in the Kremlin wall.

The years from 1945 to 1955 were a formative period in international relations. It was then that the Cold War took shape and the infrastructure was created in the United States and the Soviet Union for developing and building vast arsenals of nuclear weapons. One of the recurrent questions in the historiography of this period is whether things could have taken a different course, whether there were missed opportunities to avoid or end the nuclear arms race. I have been skeptical in this book about the possibility that changes in American policy would have elicited significant shifts in Soviet policy. Bohr was fundamentally right, to my mind, when he argued that nuclear weapons were a common danger confronting the human race, but neither Truman nor Stalin viewed the atomic bomb primarily in that way. If Stalin had been informed officially about the Manhattan project before Hiroshima, he would still have wanted a bomb of his own; and although he might have been less suspicious of American atomic diplomacy, that is by no means certain. I have argued also that there was no plausible missed opportunity to avoid the development of thermo-nuclear weapons, because Stalin would not have reciprocated American restraint.

The question of missed opportunities is generally asked about American policy, but it can, in principle, be raised with respect to Soviet policy too. Could Stalin have adopted a policy that would allow the Soviet Union to acquire nuclear weapons, but not involve it in a dangerous and costly arms race? It is possible, I think, to imagine the Soviet Union pursuing a more cooperative relationship with the United States, along the lines suggested by Litvinov. Such a policy might well have prevented the Cold War, or at least moderated the intensity of Soviet-American rivalry. But it would have involved concessions in Eastern Europe that Stalin was not willing to make. Besides, it would have required of Stalin a different conception of international relations, and a different attitude to the American atomic monopoly.

All attempts to imagine alternative courses of postwar international relations run up against Stalin himself. It is difficult to think counterfactually about this period without assuming Stalin away. His malevolent and suspicious personality pervades the history of these years. If ever personality mattered in politics, it surely did so in the Soviet Union under Stalin. His death resulted in a significant relaxation of tension in the Soviet Union and abroad, but the patterns that had been set in the early postwar years remained strong. The Soviet Union and the United States took new steps to manage their nuclear relationship, but the arms race continued apace.

The period discussed in this book was a tragic one for the people of the Soviet Union, and the title "Stalin and the Bomb" might seem to promise a tale of unrelieved horror. Horror there certainly is in this history – war and repression on a brutal scale, as well as the creation of weapons of mass destruction. But this is also a story of intellectual integrity and civic courage. And in these years there was a growing consciousness, in both the Soviet Union and the West, that the human race faced a common danger in the threat of nuclear war; this awareness provided the indispensible basis for joint efforts to prevent nuclear war and to bring the nuclear arms race under control. This is therefore a study not only of horror but also of hope, of the common desire, even at a time of bitter ideological and political rivalry, to ensure the survival of the human race in face of the nuclear danger.

Bibliographical Note

I HAVE PIECED THIS HISTORY together from different sources of varying quality. For the first three chapters there are many contemporary documents, and also excellent works by Russian historians of science. There are fine studies of American, British, French, and German nuclear research in this period, and these provide the context in which I have analyzed Soviet work.

Sources on the Soviet wartime project are less satisfactory, but I was able to use an important set of documents relating to atomic espionage. The KGB made these documents available to the Institute of the History of Science and Technology, which prepared them for publication in its journal *Voprosy istorii estestvoznaniia i tekhniki*, 1992, no. 3. The issue was withdrawn from publication, however, at the insistence of the Russian government, on the grounds that information in two of the documents might contribute to nuclear proliferation. The whole set of documents has been quoted in the Russian press, and I have used it extensively in this book; I have not, however, quoted the data that caused the Russian government to withdraw the journal from publication.

There is an extensive literature on the relationship between the atomic bomb and American foreign policy at the end of World War II. This provided the context for examining the impact of the bomb on Soviet policy. The sources on the Soviet side are far from satisfactory. Decision-making on nuclear matters was highly centralized under Stalin, and the relevant papers (whatever they may be) have not been declassified. Besides, public utterances were themselves part of the political game, and cannot be taken at face value. Furthermore, Soviet foreign policy in the postwar period is being reassessed in the light of new archival materials. This makes it particularly challenging to examine the impact of the bomb on Soviet foreign policy. Nevertheless, enough new evidence has come to light from Russian and from Chinese sources to make it possible to provide a new assessment of the bomb's effect on Stalin's policy.

In writing about the effect of the bomb on Soviet military policy I have benefited from the research on American nuclear policy. New Soviet sources have become available, especially on specific issues like weapons development and the Totskoe exercise. On some crucial questions – Soviet force levels and the military build-up of 1949–50, for example – the Soviet sources are very fragmentary. I have made use of United States intelligence reports when Soviet data are lacking, but these reports are not likely to be wholly reliable. This is an area that would benefit greatly from new sources from Soviet archives.

I have made considerable use of memoirs by, and interviews with, Soviet participants in the nuclear project, especially in my analysis of the development of the atomic and hydrogen bombs. The quality of the memoirs varies, as might be expected. Censorship and self-censorship detract from the value of memoirs published before the late 1980s; only then did it become possible to mention Beria's name, for example. Nevertheless the memoirs are an important source and provide a great deal of information that cannot be found elsewhere. I have used these sources carefully, and cross-checked wherever possible.

The sources available for the study of Soviet nuclear history are growing, as Russian archives open up. I have been able to use archival materials on Soviet science and on Soviet foreign policy. I am grateful to archivists and librarians in Russia, Britain, and the United States for their help.

The following archives and libraries are referred to in the notes:

ARAN *Arkhiv Rossiiskoi Akademii Nauk* (Archive of the Russian Academy of Sciences), Vernadskii papers

AVP *Arkhiv Vneshnei Politiki* (Archive of the Russian Ministry of Foreign Affairs)

United States Army War War College Library, Carlisle Barracks, Pennsylvania

Butler Library, Columbia University, New York, Russian Archives

HIA Hoover Institution Archive, Victor Hoo Papers and Sander Papers

HSTL Harry S. Truman Library, Independence, Missouri, PSF (President's Secretary's Files)

Library of Congress, Harriman Papers

NA United States National Archives, Washington DC

Niels Bohr Library, American Institute of Physics, New York, Bohr Correspondence, Goudsmit Papers

PRO Public Record Office, London

Pusey Library, Harvard University, Conant Papers

RTsKhIDNI *Rossiiskii Tsentr Khraneniia i Izucheniia Dokumentov Noveishei Istorii* (Russian Center for the Storage and Study of the Documents of Contemporary History)

TsKhSD *Tsentr Khraneniia Sovremennoi Dokumentatsii* (Storage Center for Contemporary Documentation)

Yale University Library, Stimson Diary

The following abbreviations are also used in the notes:

DBPO Documents on British Policy Overseas, published by Her Majesty's
    Stationary Office, London in various volumes and various years

FRUS Foreign Relations of the United States, published by the United
    States Government Printing Office, Washington DC in various volumes
    and various years

FBIS Foreign Broadcast Information Service

Notes

Introduction

1. Among the most valuable are Raymond Garthoff, *Soviet Strategy in the Nuclear Age*, London: Atlantic Books, 1958; Herbert Dinerstein, *War and the Soviet Union*, New York: Frederick A. Praeger, 1959; Thomas W. Wolfe, *Soviet Strategy at the Crossroads*, Cambridge, Mass.: Harvard University Press, 1964.

2. Richard Hewlett and Oscar Anderson, Jr., *The New World: A History of the US Atomic Energy Commission Vol. 1, 1939–1946*, Berkeley: University of California Press, 1990, Richard G. Hewlett and Francis Duncan, *Atomic Shield: A History of the US Atomic Energy Commission Vol. 2, 1947–1952*, Berkeley: University of California Press, 1990 (these volumes were originally published in 1962 and 1969); Richard G. Hewlett and Jack M. Holl, *Atoms for Peace and War, 1953–1961*, Berkeley: University of California Press, 1989; Margaret Gowing, *Britain and Atomic Energy*, London: Macmillan, 1964; Margaret Gowing (assisted by Lorna Arnold) *Independence and Deterrence: Britain and Atomic Energy 1945–1952, Vol. 1: Policy Making, Vol. 2: Policy Execution*, London: Macmillan, 1974; McGeorge Bundy, *Danger and Survival*, New York: Random House, 1988; Spencer Weart, *Scientists in Power*, Cambridge, Mass.: Harvard University Press, 1979; John Wilson Lewis and Xue Litai, *China Builds the Bomb*, Stanford: Stanford University Press, 1988. A very useful general history is Bertrand Goldschmidt, *The Atomic Complex: A Worldwide Political History of Nuclear Energy*, La Grange Park: American Nuclear Society, 1982 (originally published in France in 1980).

3. For obvious reasons there is not an extensive literature in English on the history of the nuclear project. The pioneering work was Arnold Kramish, *Atomic Energy in the Soviet Union*, Stanford: Stanford University Press, 1959; see also George Modelski, *Atomic Energy in the Communist Bloc*, Melbourne: Melbourne University Press, 1959. I published two articles on this history: "Entering the Nuclear Arms Race: The Soviet Decision to Build the Atomic Bomb," *Social Studies of Science*, May 1981, pp. 159–97, and "Soviet Thermonuclear Development," *International Security*, Winter 1979–80, pp. 192–7. Steven Zaloga's *Target America* (Novato: Presidio Press, 1993) draws on some of the latest evidence.

4. The literature is voluminous. See, for example, Colin Gray, "The Arms Race Phenomenon," *World Politics*, October 1971; Dieter Senghaas *Rüstung und Militarismus*, Frankfurt am Main: Suhrkamp, 1972; the essays in *Daedalus*, 1975, no. 3; the review essay by Harvey Sapolsky, "Science, Technology, and Military Policy," in I. Spiegel-Rösing and D. de S. Price, *Science, Technology and Society. A Cross-Disciplinary Perspective*, London and Beverly Hills: Sage, 1977, pp. 443–71; Matthew Evangelista, *Innovation and the Arms Race*, Ithaca: Cornell University Press, 1988. A particularly valuable study is Donald Mackenzie, *Inventing Accuracy: A Historical Sociology of Nuclear Missile Guidance*, Cambridge, Mass.: MIT Press, 1990.

5. On Soviet technological performance see R. Amann, J. Cooper, and R.W. Davies (eds) *The Technological Level of Soviet Industry*, New Haven: Yale University Press, 1977; R. Amann and J. Cooper (eds) *Industrial Innovation in the Soviet Union*, New

Haven: Yale University Press, 1982; Joseph Berliner, *The Innovation Decision in Soviet Industry*, Cambridge, Mass.: Harvard University Press, 1976; Arthur Alexander, *Decisionmaking in Soviet Weapons Procurement*; Santa Monica: Rand Corporation, 1978; David Holloway, "Technology and Political Decision in Soviet Armaments Policy," *Journal of Peace Research*, 1974, no. 4.

6. Evangelista, *op.cit.*

7. See, for example, Kendall E. Bailes, *Technology and Society under Lenin and Stalin*, Princeton: Princeton University Press, 1978; Bruce Parrott, *Politics and Technology in the Soviet Union*, Cambridge, Mass.: MIT Press, 1983; Loren R. Graham, *Science in Russia and the Soviet Union: A Short History*, Cambridge: Cambridge University Press, 1993; Alexander Vucinich, *Empire of Knowledge*, Berkeley: University of California Press, 1984.

8. See, for example, David Joravsky, *The Lysenko Affair*, Cambridge, Mass.: Harvard University Press, 1970; Zhores Medvedev, *The Rise and Fall of Trofim Lysenko*, New York: Columbia University Press, 1969.

9. The best work in English is Paul Josephson, *Physics and Politics in Revolutionary Russia*, Berkeley: University of California Press, 1991.

10. Apart from works already cited see, for example, Gar Alperovitz, *Atomic Diplomacy*, 2nd edn, New York: Penguin, 1985; Martin Sherwin, *A World Destroyed*, New York: Vintage Books, 1977; various writings by Barton J. Bernstein, especially "Roosevelt, Truman, and the Atomic Bomb, 1941–1945: A Reinterpretation," *Political Science Quarterly*, Spring 1975.

11. Among general works see especially Bundy, *op.cit.*; Robert Jervis, *The Meaning of the Nuclear Revolution*, Ithaca: Cornell University Press, 1989; John Lewis Gaddis, *The Long Peace*, New York: Oxford University Press, 1987; Kenneth Waltz, "Nuclear Myths and Political Realities" *American Political Science Review*, September 1990, pp. 731–45; John Mueller, *Retreat from Doomsday: The Obsolescence of Major War*, New York: Basic Books, 1989.

1. Ioffe's Institute

1. Petrograd was the name of the former capital, St Petersburg, in the years 1914–24.

2. M.S. Sominskii, *Abram Fedorovich Ioffe*, Moscow-Leningrad: Nauka, 1964, pp. 244–6.

3. *Ibid.* N.N. Semenov, *Nauka i obshchestvo*, 2nd edn, Moscow: Nauka, 1981, pp. 348–52.

4. See Alexander Vucinich, *Science in Russian Culture. A History to 1860*, Stanford: Stanford University Press, 1963; and *Science in Russian Culture, 1861–1917*, Stanford: Stanford University Press, 1970.

5. See David Joravsky, *Soviet Marxism and Natural Science, 1917–1932*, London: Routledge and Kegan Paul, 1961.

6. Quoted in A.V. Kol'tsov, *Lenin i stanovlenie akademii nauk kak tsentra sovetskoi nauki*, Leningrad: Nauka, 1969, p. 26.

7. Quoted by Kendall E. Bailes, *Technology and Society under Lenin and Stalin*, Princeton: Princeton University Press, 1978, p. 49.

8. Robert Lewis, *Science and Industrialization in the USSR*, London: Macmillan, 1979, pp. 6–7.

9. Alexander Vucinich, *Empire of Knowledge. The Academy of the Sciences of the USSR (1917–1970)*, Berkeley: University of California Press, 1984, ch. 2; Loren R. Graham, *The Soviet Academy of Sciences and the Communist Party, 1927–1932*, Princeton: Princeton University Press, 1967, pp. 25–7; M.S. Bastrakova, *Stanovlenie sovetskoi sistemy organizatsii nauki (1917–1922)*, Moscow: Nauka, 1973, pp. 124–5.

10. N.I. Bukharin and E. Preobrazhensky, *The ABC of Communism*, Baltimore: Penguin Books, 1969, p. 449.

11. Kol'tsov, *op.cit.*, pp. 141–2, 226; Paul Josephson, *Physics and Politics in Revolutionary Russia*, Berkeley: University of California Press, 1991, pp. 48–55.

12. Lewis, *op.cit.*, pp. 1–5.

13. A dielectric substance is substance that is capable of sustaining an electrical stress, i.e. an insulator.

14. Ioffe's life before 1917 is described in Sominskii, *op.cit.*, pp. 1–192.

15. This is taken from a draft of the letter he sent to Röntgen in August or September 1906. See A.F. Ioffe, *Vstrechi s fizikami*, Leningrad: Nauka, 1983, pp. 125–6.

16. Sominskii, *op.cit.*, p. 70.

17. *Ibid.*

18. *Ibid.*, pp. 39–41.

19. A.F. Ioffe, "Moia zhizn' i rabota," in his *O fizike i fizikakh*, Leningrad: Nauka, 1977, p. 239. This was first published in 1933 as a pamphlet.

20. On the elections see Sominskii, *op.cit.*, pp. 186, 194. The Academy has two levels of membership: full (Academician), and corresponding membership. Election to the Academy was a great honor and carried

significant privileges in the way of housing, food supplies, etc.

21. Sominskii, *op.cit.*, p. 450.
22. *Ibid.*, p. 191ff.
23. Sominskii, *op.cit.*, pp. 190–201, 237ff.; *Organizatsiia nauki v pervye gody sovetskoi vlasti (1917–1925). Sbornik dokumentov*, Leningrad: Nauka, 1968, pp. 233–55.
24. *Erenfest-Ioffe. Nauchnaia perepiska 1907–1933 gg.*, 2nd edn, Leningrad: Nauka, 1990, p. 274.
25. Sominskii, *op.cit.*, pp. 214–30.
26. V.Ia. Frenkel', "Piat'desiat let fiziko-tekhnicheskomu institutu im. A.F. Ioffe AN SSSR," *Uspekhi fizicheskikh nauk*, 1968, no. 3, p. 534.
27. *Ibid.*
28. Letter of 19 June 1922, in J.W. Boag, P.E. Rubinin, and D. Shoenberg (eds), *Kapitza in Cambridge and Moscow*, Amsterdam: North-Holland, 1990, p. 152.
29. Sominskii, *op.cit.*, pp. 283–311.
30. Quoted *ibid.*, p. 299.
31. *Organizatsiia nauki*, p. 244.
32. Sominskii, *op.cit.*, p. 246; *Organizatsiia nauki*, pp. 245–6; R.A. Lewis, "Industrial Research and Development in the USSR 1924–1935," PhD thesis, University of Birmingham, 1975, pp. 75–8.
33. Sominskii, *op.cit.*, pp. 256–7; V.D. Esakov, *Sovetskaia nauka v gody pervoi piatiletki*, Moscow: Nauka, 1971, p. 158; A.P. Grinberg and V. Ia. Frenkel', *Igor' Vasil'evich Kurchatov v fiziko-tekhnicheskom institute*, Leningrad: Nauka, 1984, pp. 20–5.
34. Josephson, *op.cit.*, pp. 127–30 gives an account of the Institute's research program.
35. Sominskii, *op.cit.*, pp. 351–78; Frenkel', *loc.cit.*, pp. 529–68; *Nauchno-organizatsionnaia deiatel'nost' akademika A.F. Ioffe. Sbornik dokumentov*, Leningrad: Nauka, 1980 documents 27, 28.
36. Sominskii, *op.cit.*, pp. 264–74, 379–86; Esakov, *op.cit.*, pp. 157–63; *Nauchno-organizatsionnaia deiatel'nost'*, pp. 110–28; Lewis, *Industrial Research and Development*, pp. 133–5.
37. "Ob industrializatsii strany i o pravom uklone v VKP(b)," I.V. Stalin, *Sochineniia*, Vol. 11, Moscow: Gospolitizdat, 1950, p. 248.
38. Quoted in Bruce Parrott, *Politics and Technology in the Soviet Union*, Cambridge, Mass.: MIT Press, 1983, p. 28.
39. Antony C. Sutton, *Western Technology and Soviet Economic Development, 1930–1945*, Stanford: Hoover Institution Press, 1971.
40. Parrott, *op.cit.*, p. 34.

41. From a speech given in 1931, J.V. Stalin, *Problems of Leninism*, Moscow: Foreign Languages Publishing House, 1947, p. 213.
42. He had extensive contact with Lunacharskii, V.V. Kuibyshev, G.K. Ordzhonokidze, and S.M. Kirov, the Leningrad Party Secretary. V.Ia. Frenkel', "Abram Fedorovich Ioffe," *Uspekhi fizicheskikh nauk*, 1980, no. 1, pp. 35–6.
43. Esakov, *op.cit.*, pp. 164–7; Sominskii, *op.cit.*, p. 352ff.
44. Quoted in Esakov, *op.cit.*, pp. 165–6.
45. *Ibid.*, p. 166.
46. See Ioffe's letter of December 27, 1932 to Ehrenfest, in *Erenfest-Ioffe.*, pp. 298–301.
47. There are two important articles by V.P. Vizgin: "Martovskaia (1936 g.) sessiia AN SSSR: Sovetskaia fizika v fokuse," *Voprosy istorii estestvoznaniia i tekhniki*, 1990, no. 1, pp. 63–84; "Martovskaia (1936 g.) sessiia AN SSSR: Sovetskaia fizika v fokuse. II (arkhivnoe priblizhenie)," in the same journal 1991, no. 3, pp. 36–55. See also V.Ia. Frenkel', "K 50–letiiu martovskoi sessii Akademii Nauk SSSR (1936 g.)," *Chteniia pamiati A.F. Ioffe 1985*, Leningrad: Nauka, 1987, pp. 63–86.
48. "Nauka i proizvodstvo," *Izvestiia*, March 14, 1936, p. 3.
49. *Izvestiia Akademii Nauk SSSR. Seriia fizicheskaia*, 1936, no. 1–2, p. 21. This issue of the journal contains a report of the Academy Session.
50. *Ibid.*, pp. 24–6.
51. *Ibid.*, p. 21.
52. *Ibid.*, p. 23.
53. *Ibid.*
54. *Ibid.*, pp. 76–7.
55. *Ibid.*, pp. 60–63.
56. *Ibid.*, p. 93. The speaker was B.N. Finkel'shtein.
57. *Ibid.*, p. 129.
58. *Ibid.*, pp. 83–7. The *Manchester Guardian*'s science correspondent, J.G. Crowther, was echoing a widespread Soviet view when he wrote in 1936 that "the variety of the researches at the Leningrad Physical Technical Institute, which has been for a long period a foundation of the institute's value, is now, perhaps, tending to produce one avoidable weakness. Greater concentration on fewer lines of research would probably produce discoveries of still more profound importance. Many of the highly gifted young physicists there tend to fly after the latest exciting world discovery, and add a few embellishments to it, and then turn to the next and add something to that." J.G. Crowther, *Soviet Science*, London: Kegan

Paul, 1936, p. 75.

59. *Izvestiia Akademii Nauk*, pp. 83–7.
60. *Ibid.*, p. 151.
61. *Ibid.*, p. 153.
62. *Ibid.*, p. 157.
63. *Ibid.*, p. 60.
64. R.A. Lewis, "Some Aspects of the Research and Development Effort in the Soviet Union, 1924–1935," *Science Studies*, 1972, no. 2, p. 164.
65. Bailes, *op.cit.*, pp. 69–140.
66. See, for example, Joseph S. Berliner, *The Innovation Decision in Soviet Industry*, Cambridge, Mass.: MIT Press, 1976; R. Amann, J. Cooper, and R.W. Davies (eds), *The Technological Level of Soviet Industry*, New Haven and London: Yale University Press, 1977; R. Amann and J. Cooper (eds), *Industrial Innovation in the Soviet Union*, New Haven and London: Yale University Press, 1982.
67. Vizgin, *loc.cit.*, 1990, no. 1, p. 75.
68. Vizgin, *loc.cit.*, 1991, no. 3, pp. 50–51.
69. K. Bauman, in "Soveshchanie v Narkomtiazhprome o nauchno-issledovatel'skoi rabote," *Sotsialisticheskaia rekonstruktsiia i nauka*, 1936, no. 8, p. 142.
70. *Ibid.* For the background to this meeting see Parrott, *op.cit.*, pp. 66–7.
71. Sominskii, *op.cit.*, pp. 274–9; *Nauchnoorganizatsionnaia deiatel'nost'*, pp. 92–3, 313.
72. *Izvestiia Akademii Nauk*, pp. 402–9.
73. Sominskii, *op.cit.*, pp. 277–8.
74. Graham, *op.cit.*, pp. 80–153.
75. Joravsky, *op.cit.*, pp. 233–71.
76. See David Holloway, "Scientific Truth and Political Authority in the Soviet Union," *Government and Opposition*, 1970, no. 3, pp. 345–67; and "Innovation in Science – the Case of Cybernetics in the Soviet Union," *Science Studies*, 1974, no. 4, pp. 299–337.
77. N. Semenov, "Nauka ne terpit subektivizma," *Nauka i zhizn'*, 1965, no. 4, p. 43.
78. See Josephson, *op.cit.*, pp. 247–75.
79. Three physicists who found it impossible to adjust were A.K. Timiriazev, N.P. Kasterin, and V.F. Mitkevich. See G.E. Gorelik, "Obsuzhdenie 'Naturfilosofskikh ustanovok sovremennoi fiziki' v Akademii Nauk SSSR v 1937–1938 godakh," *Voprosy istorii estestvoznaniia i tekhniki*, 1990, no. 4, pp. 17–31.
80. Joravsky, *op.cit.*, pp. 275–95; Josephson, *op.cit.*, pp. 225–46.
81. Quoted in V.Ia. Frenkel', "Zhar pod peplom," *Zvezda*, 1991, no. 9, p. 141.
82. See the marvelous portrait of Frenkel' by his son, *ibid.*, no. 9, pp. 129–48, and no. 10, pp. 129–42.
83. Josephson, *op.cit.*, pp. 247–75.
84. Vizgin, *loc.cit.*, 1991, no. 3, p. 43. This discussion of the January meeting of the organizing committee is taken from *ibid.*, pp. 43–6.
85. One famous exchange did take place, however. Igor' Tamm responded to a question put by V.F. Mitkevich, one of the old physicists who could not come to terms with relativity theory, by saying that there were questions to which no intelligent answer could be given; for instance, what color is the meridian that passes through Pulkovo? Red or green? Mitkevich responded: "I ask my ideological opponents, what color is their meridian? The color of my meridian is clear enough to everyone here. I think it is clear enough to everyone what color Professor Tamm's meridian is. But what is not clear is what color the meridian of Ioffe and Vavilov is: red or green?" Vizgin, *loc.cit.*, 1991, no. 3, p. 49.
86. The one exception in physics was relativistic cosmology, which raised rather general philosophical questions.
87. David Joravsky, *The Lysenko Affair*, Cambridge, Mass.: Harvard University Press, 1970.
88. E.V. Shpol'skii, *Ocherki po istorii razvitiia sovetskoi fiziki 1917–1967*, Moscow: Nauka, 1969, pp. 5–29; Vucinich, *Science in Russian Culture, 1861–1917*, p. 393.
89. D.D. Gulo and A.N. Osinovskii, *Dmitrii Sergeevich Rozhdestvenskii*, Moscow: Nauka, 1980; and A.M. Prokhorov (ed.), *Akademik L.I. Mandel'shtam. K 100–letiiu so dnia rozhdeniia*, Moscow: Nauka, 1979.
90. *Organizatsiia nauki*, p. 146.
91. Crowther, *op.cit.*, p. 146.
92. Prokhorov, *op.cit.*, pp. 5, 22, 215. He made important contributions in a number of fields. He and his colleague G.S. Landsberg, somewhat before Raman and independently of him, discovered the "Raman effect" for which Raman received the Nobel Prize in 1930, but they were slow to publish their results and so lost their priority.
93. *Ibid.*, pp. 23, 232.
94. These descriptions are taken from N.M. Reinov, *Fiziki – uchitelia i druz'ia*, Leningrad: Lenizdat, 1975, p. 9; V.Ia. Frenkel', "Piat'desiat' let", p. 529; V.M. Tuchkevich, "Kolybel' sovetskoi fiziki," *Priroda*, 1969, no. 6, p. 3; Sominskii, *op.cit.*, p. 335.
95. Sominskii, *op.cit.*, p. 451.
96. *Izvestiia Akademii Nauk*, p. 25; Frenkel', "Ioffe," p. 41.
97. V.Ia. Frenkel', *Iakov Il'ich Frenkel'*, Mos-

cow-Leningrad: Nauka, 1966, p. 239. Frenkel' spent the academic year 1930–31 at the University of Minnesota.

98. *Izvestiia Akademii Nauk*, p. 25; Sominskii, *op.cit.*, p. 508. Kapitsa to Niels Bohr, November 15, 1933, in P.L. Kapitsa, *Pis'ma o nauke*, Moscow: Moskovskii rabochii, 1989, pp. 25–6.

99. Arnosht (Ernest) Kol'man, *My ne dolzhny byli tak zhit'*, New York: Chalidze Publications, 1982, p. 176. Bukharin was attending the second International History of Science Congress in London. Kol'man says that Stalin entrusted Bukharin with this mission. Kol'man was a member of the delegation and accompanied Bukharin to Cambridge. Ioffe was also a member of the delegation to the History of Science Congress. The papers the Soviet delegation gave had a significant influence on a group of left-wing British scientists (J.D. Bernal and Joseph Needham among others) and affected their thinking about the role of science in society. Thus Bukharin and his colleagues earned a footnote in British intellectual history. See Gary Werskey, *The Visible College*, London: Allen Lane, 1978, pp. 138–49. The Soviet papers were published in *Science at the Cross Roads: Essays by N.I. Bukharin and Others*. With a new foreword try Joseph Needham and a new introduction by P.G. Werskey, 2nd edn, London: Frank Cass, 1971. The most influential paper was that by Boris Hessen (or Gessen) on Isaac Newton. On Hessen see Loren R. Graham, "The Sociopolitical Roots of Boris Hessen: Soviet Marxism and the History of Science," *Social Studies of Science*, 1985, Vol. 15, pp. 705–22.

100. An excellent essay on Kapitsa's life and work is given by David Shoenberg in Boag *et al.*, *op.cit.*, ch. 1. See p. 54 ff. for the work of the new institute.

101. Kapitsa, *op.cit.*, p. 121. Some of Kapitsa's letters have been published in Boag *et al.*, *op.cit.*

102. Kapitsa, *op. cit.*, pp. 43, 54, 56, 76, etc.

103. Robert Conquest, *The Great Terror: A Reassessment*, New York: Oxford University Press, 1990, p. 485.

104. Interviews with Victor Weisskopf, August 15, 1980, Rudolf Peierls, October 7, 1980.

105. David Shoenberg, "Forty Odd Years in the Cold," *Physics Bulletin*, January 1978, p. 18.

106. Josephson, *op.cit.*, p. 308.

107. Sominskii, *op.cit.*, pp. 607–10; Lidiia Chukovskaia, *Zapiski ob Anne Akhmatove*, Vol. 1, Paris: YMCA-Press, 1976, pp. 7–8, 210–11. Bronshtein was Chukovskaia's husband. See G.E. Gorelik and V.Ia.

Frenkel', *Matvei Petrovich Bronshtein*, Moscow: Nauka, 1990. V.V. Kosarev, "Fiztekh, Gulag i obratno," in V.M. Tuchkevich (ed.), *Chteniia pamiati A.F. Ioffe 1990*, St Petersburg: Nauka, 1993, pp. 105–77.

108. Semenov, *op.cit.*, p. 344; Reinov, *op.cit.*, pp. 35–6; Interview with Lady Peierls, March 12, 1984.

2. Nuclear Prehistory

1. Frederick Soddy, *The Interpretation of Radium*, New York: G.P. Putnam's Sons, 1909, pp. 249–50.

2. V.I. Vernadskii, *Izbrannye sochineniia*, vol. 1, Moscow: izd. AN SSSR, 1954, p. 623.

3. *Ibid.*, p. 628.

4. The only biography in English is Kendall E. Bailes's *Science and Russian Culture in an Age of Revolutions. V.I. Vernadsky and his Scientific School, 1863–1945*, Bloomington: Indiana University Press, 1990. Bailes provides a very sympathetic account of Vernadskii's early life in particular. I.I. Mochalov's biography *Vladimir Ivanovich Vernadskii*, Moscow: Nauka, 1982 is based on extensive use of Vernadskii's papers and gives a detailed account of his early life. Vernadskii's role in Russian scientific life before the October Revolution is discussed in Alexander Vucinich, *Science in Russian Culture, 1861–1917*, Stanford: Stanford University Press, 1970, pp. 411 ff., 477 ff.

5. L.L. Zaitseva and N.A. Figurovskii, *Issledovaniia iavlenii radioaktivnosti v dorevoliutsionnoi Rossii*, Moscow: izd. AN SSSR, 1961, pp. 186–207; S.A. Pogodin and E.P. Libman, *Kak dobyli sovetskii radii*, 2nd edn, Moscow: Atomizdat, 1977, p. 48.

6. Pogodin and Libman, *op.cit.*, p. 65.

7. *Ibid.*, pp. 25–6, 31–2.

8. Vernadskii, *op.cit.*, p. 628.

9. This was formed in the Commission for the Study of Natural Productive Forces (KEPS: Kommissiia po izucheniiu estestvennykh proizvoditel'nykh sil), which Vernadskii had helped to organize during the war to help industry exploit Russia's natural resources. Pogodin and Libman, *op.cit.*, pp. 65–9; Mochalov, *op.cit.*, pp. 205–8; M.S. Bastrakova, *Stanovlenie sovetskoi sistemy organizatsii nauki (1917–1922)*, Moscow: Nauka, 1973, pp. 47ff, esp. p. 52.

10. Pogodin and Libman, *op.cit.*, pp. 78–82. In the early 1920s radium cost 250,000 roubles a gram; after the discovery of uranium deposits in the Belgian Congo, the price fell to 150,000 roubles. (*Ibid.*, p. 155.) The dollar price in 1914 was $180,000 a gram, but this

fell to under $100,000 in the early 1920s. (Edward R. Landa, "The First Nuclear Industry," *Scientific American*, 1982, November, p. 192.) At the Brest-Litovsk negotiations in 1918 the German government asked for the radioactive residues and ore deposits. (Pogodin and Libman, *op.cit.*, p. 85.)

11. Pogodin and Libman, *op.cit.*, pp. 87–113. Because of the low quality of the ore and the absence of fuel, Khlopin had to use a fractional precipitation method rather than fractional crystallization. See B.P. Nikol'skii and V.R. Klokman, "Akademik V.G. Khlopin u istokov sovetskoi radiokhimii," in *Akademik V.G. Khlopin: Ocherki, Vospominaniia sovremennikov*, Leningrad: Nauka, 1987, pp. 29–30.

12. Vladimir Vernadsky, "The First Year of the Ukrainian Academy of Sciences (1918–1919)," *The Annals of the Ukrainian Academy of Arts and Sciences in the US, Inc.*, vol. 11, 1964–8, no. 1–2 (31–2), p. 14.

13. *Ibid.*

14. This draws on the account by Vernadskii's son: G.V. Vernadskii, "Bratstvo 'Priiutino'," *Novyi Zhurnal*, 96, 1969, pp. 153–71. Mochalov (*op.cit.*, pp. 221–32) gives a rather different account in which he stresses Vernadskii's continuing concern for science and education in Russia, and his view that the Bolsheviks were doing their best to foster learning. See also Bailes, *op.cit.*, p. 147.

15. Pogodin and Libman, *op.cit.*, pp. 129–31; Mochalov, *op.cit.*, pp. 236–9; *Organizatsiia nauki v pervye gody sovetskoi vlasti (1917–1925). Sbornik dokumentov*, Leningrad: Nauka, 1968, pp. 165–73.

16. Mochalov, *op.cit.*, p. 238.

17. V.I. Vernadskii, *Ocherki i rechi I*, Petrograd: Nauchnoe khimikotekhnicheskoe izdatel'stvo, 1922, p. ii.

18. See Bailes, *op.cit.*, pp. 161–2, 187–93; and Mochalov, *op.cit.*, pp. 246–9.

19. V.I. Vernadskii, "Po povodu kriticheskikh zamechanii Akad. A.M. Deborina," *Izvestiia Akademii Nauk SSSR. Otdelenie matematicheskikh i estestvennykh nauk*, 1933, p. 401. This is Vernadskii's reply to the philosopher A.M. Deborin, who attacked him, writing that "the whole worldview of V.I. Vernadskii is . . . deeply hostile to materialism and to our contemporary life, to our socialist construction." ("Problema vremeni v osveshchenii Akad. Vernadskogo," *Izvestiia AN SSSR. Otdelenie matematicheskikh i estestvennykh nauk*, 1932, p. 568.) In the Stalin period

accusations of this kind could lead to political repression. In his reply Vernadskii called himself a philosophical skeptic: "this means that I consider that not one philosophical system (including our official philosophy) has commanded that general degree of assent which science (and only in several specific areas) can command." Vernadskii, "Po povodu," p. 406. On Vernadskii's role during the reform of the Academy see Loren Graham, *The Soviet Academy of Sciences and the Communist Party, 1927–1932*, Princeton: Princeton University Press, 1967, pp. 99–102, 132–8.

20. He wrote on behalf of Lichkov and other repressed people to V.M. Molotov, L.P. Beria and others. See V.I. Vernadskii: "Iz pisem raznykh let," *Vestnik Akademii Nauk SSSR*, 1990, no. 5, pp. 76–125. In the late 1930s he sent a letter to the Presidium of the Supreme Soviet to seek the release of a colleague who had been arrested. "I consider myself morally obliged to speak with complete frankness to the end," he wrote. "At this time many people have found themselves in Simorin's position without real guilt on their part. We cannot close our eyes to this." Lev Gumilevskii, *Vernadskii*, 2nd edn, Moscow: Molodaia gvardiia, 1967, p. 214. Vernadskii received no reply to his letter, but continued to correspond with Simorin. The fact that an Academician was corresponding with him helped Simorin who was given work in the camp hospital. (*Ibid.*)

21. A.L. Ianshin, "Uchenie V.I. Vernadskogo o biosfere i perekhode ee v noosferu," in V.I. Vernadskii, *Filosofskie mysli naturalista*, Moscow: Nauka, 1988, p. 498.

22. V.I. Vernadskii, "Neskol'ko slov o noosfere," *ibid.*, p. 509. This article was written in 1944.

23. Most of the text is in Vernadskii, *Filosofskie mysli naturalista*, pp. 20–195, but some important sections were published only in *Voprosy istorii estestvoznaniia i tekhniki*, 1988, no. 1, pp. 71–9. These sections contain a discussion of dialectical materialism.

24. On the democratic character of science see Vernadskii's "Nauchnaia mysl' kak planetnoe iavlenie," in his *Filosofskie mysli*, p. 95.

25. On Khlopin see V.M. Vdovenko, *Akademik V.G. Khlopin. Nauchnaia deiatel'nost'*, Moscow: Gos. izd. lit. v oblasti atomnoi nauki, 1962. See also *Radievyi institut imeni V.G. Khlopina*, Leningrad: Nauka, 1972, and *Akademik V.G. Khlopin: Ocherki*.

26. Pogodin and Libman, *op.cit.*, pp. 114ff.,

122, 133–6, 179–80. E. Libman, "Radii," in *Nauka i Zhizn'*, 1939, no. 6, p. 55, says that the Tiuia-Muiun mine was recently put into "temporary conservation," and that new mines had replaced it, but it is not clear what those mines might have been. Shimkin quotes a 1936 Soviet source which says that Soviet needs are covered by radium extracted from the Ukhta waste waters and the Tiuia-Muiun ore. (Demitri B. Shimkin, *Minerals. A Key to Soviet Power*, Cambridge, Mass.: Harvard University Press, 1953, p. 149.)

27. Pogodin and Libman, *op.cit.*, p. 177.

28. Vernadskii diary, March 2, 1932. ARAN 518–2–17, p. 20. See also V.R. Polishchuk, "Sud'ba professora I.Ia. Bashilova," in M.G. Iaroshevskii (ed.), *Repressirovannaia nauka*, Leningrad: Nauka, 1991, p. 355.

29. E.V. Shpol'skii, *Ocherki po istorii razvitiia sovetskoi fiziki 1917–1967*, Moscow: Nauka, 1969, p. 54.

30. D.D. Gulo and A.N. Osinovskii, *Dmitrii Sergeevich Rozhdestvenskii*, Moscow: Nauka, 1980, pp. 89–91. This episode had a curious sequel. A garbled version of Rozhdestvenskii's work seems to have inspired a report that appeared in December 1920 in the London weekly paper *The Nation* (November 20, 1920, p. 274), which wrote that "a radiogram from Moscow announced the other day that a Russian scientist had at last discovered the whole secret of atomic energy. If that news were true, the man who held that secret could smile at our labors to extract coal and harness waterfalls." This article was apparently shown to Lenin backstage in the Bolshoi theater during the Eighth Congress of Soviets, and sparked off a conversation about atomic energy. (See E. Drabkina, "Nevozmozhnogo net," *Novyi Mir*, 1961, no. 12, pp. 6–10.) One of those who took part in this conversation was the Bolshevik publicist I.I. Skvortsov-Stepanov who later wrote, in a book on electrification to which Lenin contributed a foreword, that "the practical, industrial application of the achievement (the discovery of radioactivity) will not be slow in coming." (Quoted in Pogodin and Libman, *op.cit.*, p. 9.) What Lenin thought about the report that a Russian scientist had "discovered the whole secret of atomic energy" is not recorded.

31. Gulo and Osinovskii, *op.cit.*, p. 92; S.E. Frish, *Skvoz' prizmu vremeni*, Moscow: Politizdat, 1992, p. 87.

32. Gulo and Osinovskii, *op.cit.*, pp. 88–97. It did save lives, however, for

Rozhdestvenskii survived only thanks to the special rations he received as chairman. Letter to author from Gennady Gorelik, March 26, 1993. See also "Nachalo atomnykh issledovanii," *Priroda*, 1967, no. 11, pp. 33–4. The physics department of the Radium Institute made little progress. Mysovskii, its head, worked on the development of high-voltage particle accelerators, but did not get beyond the construction of models of different machines. On this early work see V.V. Igonin, *Atom v SSSR*, Saratov: izd. Saratovskogo universiteta, 1975, p. 139 ff.

33. Igonin, *op.cit.*, p. 176 ff.; Margaret Gowing, *Britain and Atomic Energy, 1939–1945*, London: Macmillan, 1964, pp. 17–18.

34. D.D. Ivanenko, "Model' atomnogo iadra i iadernye sily," in B.M. Kedrov (ed.), *50 let sovremennoi iadernoi fizike*, Moscow: Energoatomizdat, 1982, pp. 18–52, esp. 22–4.

35. N.A. Perfilov, K.A. Petrzhak, and V.P. Eismont, "Ot radioaktivnosti k fizicheskim osnovam atomnoi energetiki," in *Ocherki po istorii razvitiia iadernoi fiziki v SSSR*, Kiev: Naukova Dumka, 1982, p. 29. Vernadskii diary, February 11, March 15, 17. ARAN 518–2–17, pp. 5, 33, 35, 36.

36. On the nuclear group set up in 1932, see M.S. Sominskii, *Abram Fedorovich Ioffe*, Leningrad: Nauka, 1964, pp. 361–2. For the grant of 100,000.roubles see Ioffe's report for 1933 in *Nauchno-organizatsionnaia deiatel'nost' akademika A.F. Ioffe*, Leningrad: Nauka, 1980, p. 85.

37. V.Ia. Frenkel', "Pervaia vsesoiuznaia iadernaia konferentsiia," in *Chteniia pamiati A.F. Ioffe 1983*, Leningrad: Nauka, 1985, p. 77.

38. For the proceedings see M.P. Bronshtein et al. (eds), *Atomnoe iadro*, Leningrad, Moscow: Gosudarstvennoe tekhniko-teoreticheskoe izdatel'stvo, 1934; see also A.P. Grinberg and V.Ia. Frenkel', *Igor' Vasil'evich Kurchatov v Fiziko-tekhnicheskom Institute*, Leningrad: Nauka, 1984, pp. 125–9; Ivanenko, *loc.cit.*, pp. 33–7.

39. Sominskii, *op.cit.*, pp. 362–3; *Vklad akademika A.F. Ioffe v stanovlenie iadernoi fiziki v SSSR*, Leningrad: Nauka, 1980, pp. 13–14.

40. Iu.B. Khariton, speech on the hundredth anniversary of Ioffe's birth, in A.F. Ioffe, *Vstrechi s fizikami*, Leningrad: Nauka, 1983, p. 242.

41. A.F. Ioffe, "Nad chem rabotaiut sovetskie fiziki," in his *O fizike i fizikakh*, Leningrad: Nauka, 1977, pp. 135–6. Among Soviet

physicists only Landau seems to have had an inkling as to how atomic energy might be harnessed. The German physicist Rudolf Peierls went on a walking tour in 1934 with Landau and one of his friends who was an engineer. The engineer asked one day: "What is all this one hears about nuclear energy? Is that all science fiction, or is this a real possibility?" Landau replied that "it is difficult, you see, because there are reactions in which one can release energy from nuclei, but with charged particles it is very inefficient; they lose their energy on the way. Neutrons are different; they don't lose energy. But at the present the only way we know of making neutrons is by bombardment with charged particles, so we are back to the same problems. But if one day somebody finds a reaction initiated by neutrons that releases secondary neutrons, one is all set." (Peierls in Roger H. Stuewer, ed., *Nuclear Physics in Retrospect*, Minneapolis: University of Minnesota Press, 1979, p. 79.)

42. A.P. Aleksandrov, "Gody s Kurchatovym," *Nauka i zhizn'*, 1983, no. 2, p. 12. In 1932 Bukharin attended a lecture by George Gamow on nuclear reactions and energy production in the sun. After the lecture Bukharin offered to put the entire electric power of the Moscow industrial district at Gamow's disposal for a few minutes one night a week so that he could send it through a very thick copper wire impregnated with small "bubbles" of lithium-hydrogen mixture, and thus produce a controlled thermonuclear reaction. "I decided to decline the proposal," wrote Gamow later, "and I am glad I did because it certainly would not have worked." George Gamow, *My World Line*, New York: Viking Press, 1970, p. 121.

43. L.V. Mysovskii, "Vystuplenie," *Izvestiia AN SSSR. Seriia fizicheskaia*, 1936, no. 1–2, p. 333.

44. I.E. Tamm, "Zakliuchitel'noe slovo," *ibid.*, pp. 346–7. There was some discussion of the feasibility of atomic energy in the organizing committee for the session. Frenkel' and Ioffe pointed to the possibility that the energy in the nucleus would be released in the not too distant future. Rozhdestvenskii argued that it was more than a century away. V.P. Vizgin, "Martovskaia (1936 g.) sessiia AN SSSR: Sovetskaia fizika v fokuse. II (arkhivnoe priblizhenie)," *Voprosy istorii estestvoznaniia i tekhniki*, 1991, no. 3, pp. 41–2.

45. I.N. Golovin, *I.V. Kurchatov*, 3rd edn, Moscow: Atomizdat, 1978, pp. 5–14;

Grinberg and Frenkel', *op.cit.*, pp. 8–9. An interesting picture of the university at the time is given in letters by Iakov Frenkel'; see V.Ia. Frenkel', *Iakov Il'ich Frenkel'*, Moscow-Leningrad: Nauka, 1966, pp. 53–97.

46. See Kurchatov's autobiography in V.Ia. Frenkel' (ed.), *Fiziki o sebe*, Leningrad: Nauka, 1990, p. 311.

47. Golovin, *op.cit.*, pp. 15–20; Grinberg and Frenkel', *op.cit.*, pp. 9–19.

48. On Ioffe's institute in the mid-1920s see Golovin, *op.cit.*, pp. 21–5; Grinberg and Frenkel', *op.cit.*, pp. 20–31; N.N. Semenov, *Nauka i obshchestvo*, 2nd edn, Moscow: Nauka, 1981, pp. 338–69; A.P. Aleksandrov, "Acad. A.F. Ioffe and Soviet Science," *Soviet Physics: Uspekhi*, September 1980, p. 527.

49. Quoted in Lev Kokin, *Iunost' akademikov*, Moscow: Sovetskaia Rossiia, 1970, p. 97.

50. N.M. Reinov, *Fiziki – uchitelia i druz'ia*, Leningrad: Lenizdat, 1975, p. 35.

51. Aleksandrov, "Gody s Kurchatovym," p. 11.

52. Grinberg and Frenkel', *op.cit.*, pp. 32–46; Golovin, *op.cit.*, pp. 25–30.

53. Grinberg and Frenkel', *op.cit.*, pp. 47–61.

54. Iu.B. Khariton, "Nezabyvaemoe," in A.P. Aleksandrov (ed.), *Vospominaniia ob Igore Vasil'eviche Kurchatove*, Moscow: Nauka, 1988, p. 78.

55. A.I. Alikhanov, "Zhizn', otdannaia nauke," in Aleksandrov, *op.cit.*, p. 54.

56. V.Ia. Frenkel' and B.G. Gasparian, "Akademik A.I. Alikhanov," *Voprosy istorii estestvoznaniia i tekhniki*, 1982, no. 2, pp. 75–84.

57. *Vospominaniia ob akademike L.A. Artsimoviche*, Moscow: Nauka, 1981, p. 5; Sominskii, *op.cit.*, p. 274.

58. S.N. Vernov, N.A. Dobrotin, G.T. Zatsepin *et al.* (eds), *Dmitrii Vladimirovich Skobel'tsyn*, Moscow: izd. AN SSSR, 1962.

59. Reinov, *op.cit.*, pp. 54, 56.

60. I.K. Kikoin, "On prozhil shchastlivuiu zhizn'," in his *Rasskazy o fizike i fizikakh*, Moscow: Nauka, 1986, p. 88.

61. Reinov, *op.cit.*, pp. 44–50; Golovin, *op.cit.*, pp. 19–21.

62. Golovin, *op.cit.*, p. 20.

63. Lucie Street (ed.), *I Married a Russian. Letters from Kharkov*, New York: Emerson Books, 1947, p. 29. The Englishwoman's name was Edna Cooper. This is a rather strange book, but undoubtedly authentic. It was compiled during the war from letters written in the 1930s, which were not intended for publication.

64. Interview with I.N. Golovin, November 15, 1990.

65. Grinberg and Frenkel', *op.cit.*, pp. 62–74; I.V. Kurchatov, *Izbrannye trudy v trekh tomakh. Tom 2: Neitronnaia fizika*, Moscow: Nauka, 1983, pp. 6–7.

66. Kurchatov established this first for bromine-80. Grinberg and Frenkel', *op.cit.*, pp. 74–80; see also A.P. Grinberg, "K istorii izucheniia iadernoi izomerii," *Uspekhi fizicheskikh nauk*, December 1980, no. 4, pp. 663–78.

67. Interview with Maurice Goldhaber by Gloria Lubkin and Charles Weiner, January 10, 1966, p. 27; Niels Bohr Library, American Institute of Physics, New York.

68. Boris Volodin, "Povest' ob Igore Vasil'eviche Kurchatove," in *Puti v neznaemoe, sbornik 16*, Moscow: Sovetskie pisateli, 1982, p. 72. This consists of interviews with I.I. Gurevich and G.N. Flerov.

69. Alikhanov, *loc.cit.*, p. 55; Grinberg and Frenkel', *op.cit.*, pp. 82–3.

70. Volodin, *loc.cit.*, p. 72. In spite of Kurchatov's collaboration with Mysovskii, the supply of neutron sources – ampoules of radon mixed with beryllium – was inadequate. Ioffe had complained about this in his report for 1933. The situation did not improve, however, for at the March 1936 session Mysovskii stated that research was being hampered by the shortage of radioactive materials. Tamm agreed, saying that "the shortage of radium has an extremely harmful effect on [our work] and slows it down." Tamm, *loc.cit.*, p. 346. The session proposed that the government be asked to release radium to the nuclear laboratories.

71. Vernadskii diary, February 16, 1932. ARAN 518–2–17, p. 5; Vernadskii chronology, May 15, 1942. ARAN 518–2–52, p. 244.

72. V.I. Vernadskii, "Vystuplenie," *Izvestiia Akademii Nauk SSSR. Seriia fizicheskaia*, 1936, no. 1, pp. 330–1. Tamm's suggestion about the cyclotron was made in the outline of his paper, which had been circulated before he spoke. When he spoke he withdrew this proposal and said only that some arrangement should be made whereby the cyclotron could most effectively be used by the country's leading nuclear physicists; but this did not mollify Vernadskii.

73. Grinberg and Frenkel', *op.cit.*, p. 85.

74. *Ibid.*, pp. 84–95.

75. I.Kh. Lemberg, V.O. Naidenov, and V.Ia. Frenkel', "Tsiklotron Fiziko-tekhnicheskogo instituta im. A.F. Ioffe AN SSSR (k 40-letiiu so dnia puska)", *Uspekhi fizi-*

cheskikh nauk, 1987, November, p. 499.

76. *Vklad akademika A.F. Ioffe*, pp. 15–17.

77. Lemberg *et al.*, *op.cit.*, p. 8.

78. Volodin, *loc.cit.*, p. 78.

79. *Ibid.*, pp. 77–8. A.B. Migdal, G.N. Flerov, L.I. Rusinov, I.S. Panasiuk, L.A. Artsimovich, Ia. I Frenkel', M.P. Bronshtein, A.I. Alikhanov, and D.V. Skobel'tsyn also took part. M.G. Meshcheriakov, K.A. Petrzhak, and Gurevich came from the Radium Institute. After the discovery of fission Iu.B. Khariton and Ia.B. Zel'dovich from the Institute of Chemical Physics came too.

80. Ernest O. Lawrence Papers, Bancroft Library, U.C. Berkeley, Banc MSS 72/117c, carton 17, folder 38; Frenkel' to Lawrence, Sept. 14, 1934; Lawrence to Kurchatov, October 1, 1934.

81. Grinberg and Frenkel', *op.cit.*, pp. 125–36; Igonin, *op.cit.*, pp. 26–37.

82. Sominskii, *op.cit.*, pp. 381–2; I.V. Obreimov, in *Vospominaniia ob A.F. Ioffe*, Leningrad: Nauka, 1973, pp. 50–53; *Nauchno-organizatsionnaia deiatel'nost'*, pp. 110–18. Among those he sent to Khar'kov were I.V. Obreimov, A.I. Leipunskii, L.V. Shubnikov, L.V. Rozenkevich, V.S. Gorskii, Sinel'nikov, and Ivanenko.

83. *Vospominaniia ob A.F. Ioffe*, Leningrad: Nauka, 1973, p. 53; Grinberg and Frenkel', *op.cit.*, pp. 63, 67–8, 84.

84. See Ioffe's letters of March 1929 and of November 30, 1931, in *Erenfest-Ioffe: Nauchnaia perepiska 1907–1933 gg.*, 2nd edn, Leningrad: Nauka, 1990, pp. 285, 294.

85. Alexander Weissberg, *The Accused*, New York: Simon and Schuster, 1951, pp. 67, 155; Street, *op.cit.*, *passim*; O.N. Trapeznikova, "Vospominaniia," in L.V. Shubnikov, *Izbrannye trudy. Vospominaniia*, Kiev: Naukova dumka, 1990, p. 280; A.I. Leipunskii, *Izbrannye trudy. Vospominaniia*, Kiev: Naukova dumka, 1990, p. 11.

86. Weissberg, *op.cit.*, p. 157.

87. *Ibid.*, pp. 49–53, 157–8; Street, *op.cit.*, pp. 133, 145; Leipunskii, *op.cit.*, p. 9.

88. R.A. Lewis, "Industrial Research and Development in the USSR 1924–1935," PhD dissertation, University of Birmingham, 1975, p. 135, shows that in 1934 UFTI's budget was 1,981,000.roubles, compared with 786,000 roubles for Ioffe's institute; Lewis (*ibid.*) gives a total staff figure of 230 in 1935, including 42 scientists. In a letter to Rutherford on January 31, 1936 Leipunskii gives a manpower figure of 450 (Rutherford Collection, Cambridge University Library).

89. Weissberg, *op.cit.*, pp. 157–8; Trape-

znikova, *loc.cit.*, pp. 277–91.

90. Victor Weisskopf, letter to author, May 13, 1993.

91. Weissberg, *op.cit.*, p. 158.

92. Street, *op.cit.*, pp. 263–4.

93. *Ibid.*, p. 276.

94. Interview with Weisskopf, August 15, 1980.

95. Weissberg, *op.cit.*, is devoted to the purge in the institute.

96. Weissberg, *op.cit.*, p. 364. Arthur Koestler drew upon the testimony of Weissberg's wife in writing *Darkness At Noon*, New York: Macmillan, 1941.

97. P.L. Kapitsa, *Pis'ma o nauke*, Moscow: Moskovskii rabochii, 1989, pp. 174–5.

98. *Ibid.*, p. 179; Lev Landau, "Derzat' rozhdennyi," *Komsomol'skaia pravda*, July 8, 1964, p. 4. See also G.E. Gorelik, "Moia antisovetskaia deiatel'nost' . . . ," *Priroda*, 1991, no. 11, pp. 93–104.

99. Arthur Koestler, "Introduction," in Weissberg, *op.cit.*, p. xi; on Shubnikov see his *Izbrannye trudy*. *Vospominaniia*, Kiev: Naukova dumka, 1990.

100. Weissberg, *op.cit.*, pp. 505–6; V.V. Kosarev, "Fiztekh, gulag i obratno," in *Chteniia pamiat A.F. Ioffe 1990*, St Petersburg: Nauka, 1993 gives a detailed account of the Khar'kov affair on pp. 127–37.

101. G.E. Gorelik, "Predistoriia FIANa i G.A. Gamov," Moscow: Institut istorii estestvoznaniia i tekhniki, preprint no. 41, 1990.

102. I.M. Frank, "Nachalo issledovanii po iadernoi fizike v FIAN," *Uspekhi fizicheskikh nauk*, 1967, no. 1. p. 12; L.V. Levshin, *Sergei Ivanovich Vavilov*, Moscow: Nauka, 1977, pp. 171–97, esp. 184–6.

103. Levshin, *op.cit.*, pp. 198–204; see also P.A. Cherenkov, "Sluzhenie nauke," in *Sergei Ivanovich Vavilov. Ocherki i vospominaniia*, Moscow: Nauka, 1981, pp. 193–5. Vavilov had died in 1951.

104. Frank, *loc.cit.*, p. 16.

105. Levshin, *op.cit.*, p. 191.

106. E.L. Feinberg, "Vavilov i vavilovskii FIAN," in *Sergei Ivanovich Vavilov*, p. 252.

107. *Ibid.*

108. Ia.G. Dorfman in *Vospominaniia ob A.F. Ioffe*, p. 98.

109. *Vklad akademika A.F. Ioffe*, p. 28.

110. "Khronika," *Vestnik Akademii Nauk SSSR*, no. 11–12, 1938, p. 129.

111. *Ibid.*

112. Vernadskii diary, November 29, 1938. ARAN, 518–2–19, p. 8.

113. Rudolf Peierls, Interview with Charles Weiner, August 1969, New York: Niels Bohr Library, American Institute of Physics,

p. 17.

114. *Nauchno-organizatsionnaia deiatel'nost'*, pp. 247, 249.

115. *Ibid.*, p. 254.

116. Feinberg, *loc.cit.*, p. 252.

117. Interview with Weisskopf, August 15, 1980.

118. A.F. Ioffe, *O fizike i fizikakh*, p. 62.

119. *Vklad akademika A.F. Ioffe*, p. 24. It specifically mentioned the Alikhanov brothers, Veksler, Cherenkov, and Frank, but not Kurchatov.

3. Reacting to Fission

1. Margaret Gowing, *Britain and Atomic Energy, 1939–1945*, London: Macmillan, 1964, pp. 25–6; Iu B. Khariton, "Khimicheskie i iadernye razvetvlennye tsepnye reaktsii," in A.P. Aleksandrov (ed.), *Voprosy sovremennoi eksperimental'noi i teoreticheskoi fiziki*, Leningrad: Nauka, 1984, p. 31.

2. O. Hahn and F. Strassmann in *Die Naturwissenschaften*, vol. 27, January 1939, p. 11; reprinted in Hans G. Graetzer and David L. Anderson (eds), *The Discovery of Nuclear Fission*, New York: Van Nostrand, 1971, p. 47.

3. Otto R. Frisch, *What Little I Remember*, Cambridge: Cambridge University Press, 1979, p. 116.

4. See Robert H. Stuewer, "Bringing the News of Fission to America," *Physics Today*, October 1985, pp. 49–56; Spencer R. Weart, *Scientists in Power*, Cambridge, Mass.: Harvard University Press, 1979, p. 63; research on fission during 1939 is surveyed in Louis A. Turner, "Nuclear Fission," *Reviews of Modern Physics*, 1940, no. 1, pp. 1–29.

5. Golovin writes that a letter from Frédéric Joliot-Curie to Ioffe informed Soviet physicists of the discovery of nuclear fission, I.N. Golovin, *I.V. Kurchatov*, 3rd edn, Moscow: Atomizdat, 1978, p. 45. G.N. Flerov writes that "we first learned of the new phenomenon from the work of Joliot-Curie." G.N. Flerov, "Vsemu my mozhem pouchit'sia u Kurchatova," in A.P. Aleksandrov (ed.), *Vospominaniia ob Igore Vasil'eviche Kurchatove*, Moscow: Nauka, 1988, p. 63. It appears that the story of the letter from Joliot-Curie is a myth. Interview with Golovin, October 15, 1992.

6. He and his colleagues published a series of papers on fission products in the course of 1939; the first of these papers was submitted for publication on March 7. V.V. Igonin, *Atom v SSSR*, Saratov: izd. Saratovskogo universiteta, 1975, pp. 405–10.

7. L.V. Komlev, G.S. Sinitsyna, and M.P. Koval'skaia, "V.G. Khlopin i uranovaia problema," in *Akademik V.G. Khlopin: Ocherki, vospominaniia sovremennikov*, Leningrad: Nauka, 1987, p. 39.

8. *Pis'ma V.G. Khlopina k V.I. Vernadskomu*, Moscow-Leningrad: izd. Akademii Nauk SSSR, 1961, p. 54; A.E. Polesitskii, "Issledovanie deleniia atomnykh iader," *Nauka i zhizn'*, 1940, no. 5–6, p. 39.

9. Ia.I. Frenkel', "Elektrokapilliarnaia teoriia rasshchepleniia tiazhelykh iader medlennymi neitronami," *Zhurnal eksperimental'noi i teoreticheskoi fiziki*, 1939, no. 6, pp. 641–53; see also Igonin, *op.cit.*, pp. 388–95.

10. L.I. Rusinov and G.N. Flerov, "Opyty po deleniiu urana," *Izvestiia AN SSSR: seriia fizicheskaia*, 1940, no. 2, pp. 310–14; A.P. Grinberg and V.Ia. Frenkel', *Igor' Vasil'evich Kurchatov v fiziko-tekhnicheskom institute*, Leningrad: Nauka, 1984, pp. 97–9; Volodin, "Povest' ob Igore Vasil'eviche Kurchatove," in *Puti v neznaemoe*, Collection 16, Moscow: Sovetskie pisateli, 1982, pp. 93–7. On the French work see Weart, *op.cit.*, pp. 83–6. These measurements were not accurate. The real figure is about 2.5.

11. Flerov, *loc.cit.*, p. 64.

12. Abraham Pais, *Niels Bohr's Times*, Oxford: Clarendon Press, 1991, pp. 456–7. Richard Rhodes, *The Making of the Atomic Bomb*, New York: Simon and Schuster, 1986, pp. 282–7 gives a good account of the genesis of Bohr's hypothesis.

13. Barton J. Bernstein, "Introduction," in Spencer R. Weart and Gertrud Weiss Szilard (eds), *Leo Szilard: His Version of the Facts*, Cambridge, Mass.: MIT Press, 1978, p. xxix.

14. L.I. Rusinov and G.N. Flerov, "Opyty po deleniiu iadra," *Izvestiia AN SSSR. Seriia fizicheskaia*, 1940, no. 2, pp. 310–14; Grinberg and Frenkel', *op.cit.*, p. 99; Igonin, *op.cit.*, pp. 414–16. Rusinov and Flerov did not really provide experimental confirmation of Bohr's conclusion. Rather their experiment showed that resonance neutrons (i.e. neutrons of energy higher than thermal) do not cause fission in uranium-238. They argued that it was implausible that thermal neutrons would cause fission in uranium-238 if neutrons with higher energy did not do so; hence thermal fission must belong to uranium-235. Letter from Rudolf Peierls to author, October 10, 1986.

15. See Vernadskii's comment on the delays in receiving journals. V.I. Vernadskii diary, August 24, 1940. ARAN, 518-2-20, p. 15.

16. Iu.B. Khariton and Z.F. Val'ta, "Okislenie

parov fosfora pri malykh davleniiakh," in Aleksandrov (ed.), *Voprosy*, and Khariton, *loc.cit.*, pp. 9–16, 28–32.

17. A.P. Aleksandrov *et al.*, "Iulii Borisovich Khariton," in Aleksandrov (ed.), *Voprosy*. Khariton's dissertation topic was "On the calculation of scintillations produced by alpha-particles." See V.Ia. Frenkel' (ed.), *Fiziki o sebe*, Leningrad: Nauka, 1990, p. 437.

18. Iu.B. Khariton, "Fizika – eto moia zhizn'," *Pravda*, February 20, 1984, p. 8.

19. On Khariton's work in this area see Ia.B. Zel'dovich, "Iulii Borisovich Khariton i nauka o vzryve," in Aleksandrov (ed.), *Voprosy*, pp. 32–7.

20. B. Konovalov, "Iakov Borisovich Zel'dovich," in *Schast'e tvorcheskikh pobed*, Moscow: Politizdat, 1979, pp. 84–96.

21. Perrin had published his paper in May 1939. Gowing, *op.cit.*, p. 28.

22. Konovalov, *loc.cit.*, p. 89.

23. Ia.B. Zel'dovich and Iu.B. Khariton, "K voprosu o tsepnom raspade osnovnogo izotopa urana," *Zhurnal eksperimental'noi i teoreticheskoi fiziki*, 1939, no. 12, pp. 1425–7.

24. In the main body of the paper they stated that a chain reaction might be possible in pure uranium, but not in uranium oxide; in a note added while the paper was in press they concluded, on the basis of Bohr and Wheeler's work, that it would not be possible in pure uranium. *Ibid.*, p. 1427.

25. Ia.B. Zel'dovich and Iu.B. Khariton, "O tsepnom raspade urana pod deistviem medlennykh neitronov," *ibid.*, 1940, no. 1, pp. 29–36.

27. Emilio Segrè, *Enrico Fermi: Physicist*, Chicago: University of Chicago Press, 1970, p. 112; Rhodes, *op.cit.*, pp. 298–301; Weart, *op.cit.*, pp. 111–12.

28. Zel'dovich and Khariton, "O tsepnom raspade," p. 36. This paper provided a formulation of the "four-factor formula" for nuclear chain reactions. This formula was discovered independently by several groups in 1939.and 1940, but the formulation by Zel'dovich and Khariton was one of the earliest. Their paper was received by the journal on October 22, 1939, and published in the first issue of 1940. Joliot's group derived more or less the same formula in the same month, October 1939, but did not publish it because the war had started; they deposited it in a sealed envelope in the archives of the Academy of Sciences on October 30. Spencer Weart, "Secrecy, Simultaneous Discovery, and the Theory of Nuclear Reactors," *American Journal of Phys-*

ics, 1977, no. 11, pp. 1052, 1055.

28. G.Kh. Frank-Kamenetskii, "O nekotorykh voprosakh fiziki atomnogo iadra," *Priroda*, 1940, no. 5, p. 28.

29. I.N. Golovin, "The First Steps in the Atomic Problem in the USSR," Paper presented at a conference on "Fifty Years With Nuclear Fission," Washington, DC, April 1989, p. 5.

30. A.I. Leipunskii, "Delenie iader," *Izvestiia AN SSSR: Seriia fizicheskaia*, 1940, no. 2, p. 298.

31. Herbert F. York, *The Advisors: Oppenheimer, Teller and the Superbomb*, San Francisco: W.H. Freeman, 1976, p. 29. The other two versions of Tamm's remark are: "Have you heard the news? Khariton and Zel'dovich have calculated that a uranium bomb is possible in principle." (Sergei Snegov, *Tvortsy*, Moscow: Sovetskaia Rossiia, 1979, p. 157.) Also: "Do you know – Khariton and Zel'dovich have already calculated that out of approximately 10 kilograms of uranium-235 it is possible to make such a destructive bomb that its explosion will destroy the whole of the Moscow province." (I.N. Golovin and Iu.N. Smirnov, *Eto nachinalos' v zamoskvorech'e*, Moscow: Kurchatov Institute of Atomic Energy, 1989, p. 3.) This last version is wrong because Khariton and Zel'dovich did not calculate the critical mass for uranium-235 until 1940. I.N. Golovin is the source for all three versions.

32. A.F. Ioffe, "Tekhnicheskie zadachi sovetskoi fiziki i ikh razreshenie," *Vestnik Akademii Nauk SSSR*, 1939, no. 11–12, p. 141.

33. Kapitsa, "O nauchnoi fantastike," *Detskaia literatura*, April 4, 1940, p. 22. This was a conversation, held some time in 1939, about science fiction with staff members from the journal *Children's Literature*.

34. Flerov, *loc.cit.*, pp. 65–8; Grinberg and Frenkel', *op.cit.*, pp. 101–3.

35. "V otdelenii fiziko-matematicheskikh nauk," *Vestnik Akademii Nauk SSSR*, 1940, no. 6, pp. 56, 60. K.A. Petrzhak and G.N. Flerov, "Spontannoe delenie urana," *Zhurnal eksperimental'noi i teoreticheskoi fiziki*, 1940, no. 9–10, pp. 1013–17; *Doklady Akademii Nauk*, 1940, no. 6, pp. 500–1.

36. *Physical Review*, series 2, vol. 58, no. 1, July 1, 1940, p. 89. The note reads as follows: "With 15 plates ionization chambers adjusted for detection of uranium fission products we observed 6 pulses per hour which we ascribe to spontaneous fission of uranium. A series of control experiments

seem to exclude other possible explanations. Energy of pulses and absorption properties coincide with fission products of uranium bombarded by neutrons. No pulses were found with UX and Th. Mean lifetime of uranium follows ten to sixteen or seventeen years." See also K.A. Petrzhak and G.N. Flerov, "Spontannoe delenie tiazhelykh iader," in *50 let sovremennoi iadernoi fiziki*, Moscow: Energoatomizdat, 1982, esp. pp. 105–9. On Kurchatov's attitude to authorship see Flerov, *loc.cit.*, pp. 68–9.

37. Volodin, *loc.cit.*, p. 96.

38. Ia.B. Zel'dovich and Iu.B. Khariton, "Kinetika tsepnogo raspada urana," *Zhurnal eksperimental'noi i teoreticheskii fiziki*, 1940, no. 5, p. 477.

39. *Ibid.*

40. *Ibid.*, p. 479.

41. *Ibid.*, p. 482.

42. Ia.B. Zel'dovich, *Izbrannye trudy: chastitsy, iadra, vselennia*, Moscow: Nauka, 1985, p. 26.

43. Bernstein, *loc.cit.*, pp. xxv–xxviii gives an excellent overview of this period of Szilard's life.

44. Weart and Szilard, *op.cit.*, p. 54.

45. Weart, *op.cit.*, pp. 79–87; Spencer R. Weart, "Scientists with a secret," *Physics Today*, 1976, no. 2, pp. 23–30.

46. Weart, *op.cit.*, pp. 88–91.

47. Gowing, *op.cit.*, pp. 34–7.

48. Mark Walker, *German National Socialism and the Quest for Nuclear Power, 1939–1949*, Cambridge: Cambridge University Pres, 1989, pp. 17–20; Weart, "Scientists," pp. 28–9.

49. Weart, *op.cit.*, pp. 130–7.

50. Weart and Szilard, *op.cit.*, pp. 84–5; Richard G. Hewlett and Oscar E. Anderson, Jr., *The New World: A History of the United States Atomic Energy Commission: Vol. I, 1939–1946*, Berkeley: University of California Press, 1990, pp. 14–24.

51. Weart, "Scientists," pp. 29–30.

52. As noted in Chapter 2, the Academy of Sciences decided to set up a Commission on the Atomic Nucleus at the end of 1938, but this does not appear to have taken a very active role in planning and coordinating work on fission. Its main purpose was to reorganize nuclear physics within the Academy.

53. Francis Perrin, in the paper that had stimulated Khariton and Zel'dovich's interest in nuclear fission, had tried to calculated the amount of uranium needed to sustain a chain reaction, and had concluded that it was about 40 metric tons, or 12 if the uranium was surrounded by a neutron reflector

made of iron or lead. Weart, *op.cit.*, pp. 93–5.

54. The text is in Gowing, *op.cit.*, pp. 389–93. Frisch and Peierls wrote a second memorandum of a more general nature. The text is in Ronald W. Clark, *Tizard*, London: Methuen, 1965, pp. 215–18. Both Frisch and Peierls have written about the memorandum. See Frisch, *op.cit.*, pp. 126–7; Rudolf Peierls, *Bird of Passage*, Princeton: Princeton University Press, 1985, pp. 152–6.

55. Gowing, *op.cit.*, p. 42. There is continuing controversy about how much Heisenberg really really understood about the design of an atomic bomb. See Thomas Powers, *Heisenberg's War: The Secret History of the German Bomb*, New York: Alfred A. Knopf, 1993.

56. William L. Laurence, *Men and Atoms*, New York: Simon and Schuster, 1959, pp. 37–43.

57. *New York Times*, May 5, 1940, pp. 1, 51.

58. Laurence, *op.cit.*, p. 47.

59. Mochalov, *Vladimir Ivanovich Vernadskii*, Moscow: Nauka, 1982, pp. 330–1. Vernadskii, of course, knew about nuclear fission already. In a letter to his friend Lichkov in June 1939 he had written about the "break-up of uranium atoms" and about the possibility of chain reactions that would release much more energy than ordinary radioactive processes. *Perepiska V.I. Vernadskogo s B.L. Lichkovym 1918–1939*, Moscow: Nauka, 1979, p. 236.

60. Mochalov, *op.cit.*, p. 331.

61. "Ispol'zovanie vnutriatomnoi energii," *Izvestiia*, June 26, 1940, p. 4; Mochalov, *op.cit.*, pp. 331–2.

62. Mochalov, *op.cit.*, pp. 332–3. The comment in brackets can be found in Kendall E. Bailes, *Science and Russian Culture in an Age of Revolutions. V.I. Vernadsky and his Scientific School, 1863–1945*, Bloomington: Indiana University Press, 1990, p. 171.

63. Vernadskii Collection, Russian Archives, Butler Library, Columbia University, New York: Correspondence – Vernadskii, Vladimir and Natal'ia, George and Nina Vernadskii, 1940.

64. Komlev *et al.*, *loc.cit.*, pp. 40–1.

65. Vernadskii and Khlopin sent a similar memorandum to the Academy of Sciences on the same day, making the same arguments about the need to keep abreast of other countries, but adding some new recommendations. The Academy should tell the Commission on Isotopes and the Commission on the Atomic Nucleus (both Academy bodies) to decide which insti-

tutions and which people should work on isotope separation, and what funds and raw materials would be needed for this work. A conference on uranium exploration should be organized in the autumn of 1940, and a conference on radioactivity in the winter of 1940–41. Uranium salts should be provided to the institutes already working on uranium, and additional sums be given to the Radium Institute and to Vernadskii's Biogeochemical Laboratory. Mochalov, *op.cit.*, pp. 334–5.

66. *Ibid.*, p. 335.

67. *Ibid.*

68. *Perepiska*, p. 31.

69. V.I. Vernadskii, chronology, July 16, 1940. ARAN 518-2-49, p. 3.

70. "Khronika," *Vestnik Akademii Nauk SSSR*, 1940, no. 8–9, p. 103.

71. V.S. Emel'ianov, *S chego nachinalos'*, Moscow: Sovetskaia Rossiia, 1979, pp. 181–2. This account is based on minutes of the meeting quoted by Emel'ianov.

72. *Ibid.*, p. 182.

73. *Ibid.*, pp. 182–3. In his diary for August 24, 1940 Vernadskii refers to discussions in the Central Committee about the uranium question. Vernadskii diary, ARAN 518-2-20, p. 15.

74. Komlev *et al.*, *loc.cit.*, p. 42.

75. Vernadskii wrote in March 1939 that the reserves at Tiuia-Muiun had still not been clarified, and that the real significance of other uranium deposits in Central Asia remained unclear. V.I. Vernadskii, "Otzyv o dissertatsii V.G. Melkova 'Mineralogiia urana Tabosharskogo mestorozhdeniia'," March 26, 1939. TsKhSD f. 5, op. 17, d. 409, pp. 44–6.

76. Emel'ianov, *op.cit.*, p. 183.

77. This plan is referred to by various sources, e.g. Golovin, *op.cit.*, p. 50, and A.P. Aleksandrov, "Iadernaia fizika i razvitie atomnoi tekhniki v SSSR," in *Oktiabr' i nauchnyi progress*, vol. 1, Moscow: Novosti, 1967, p. 195. Only Sergei Snegov, in *Prometei raskovannyi: povest' ob Igore Kurchatove*, Moscow: Detskaia literatura, 1980, pp. 101–3 provides excerpts from it. This documentary novel may seem an unconventional source, but it was based on numerous interviews, and people who were close to Kurchatov have recommended it to me as a source. Most of what Snegov writes is confirmed in other memoirs, and there is no reason to doubt the accuracy of the excerpts he provides from the plan prepared by Kurchatov and his colleagues.

78. Flerov, *loc.cit.*, p. 65.

79. Komlev et al., loc.cit., pp. 43, 44.
80. It may be that in an unpublished portion of the document there is discussion of the possibility of an atomic bomb, but it is hard to see why that should not have been published.
81. Ia.B. Zel'dovich and Iu.B. Khariton, "Delenie i tsepnoi raspad urana," Uspekhi fizicheskikh nauk, 1940, no. 4, p. 353.
82. Komlev et al., loc.cit., p. 45.
83. Ibid.
84. Flerov describes Kurchatov's relations with Khlopin as "complex and competitive, with perhaps some personal jealousy on Khlopin's side, as well as a concern that the Radium Institute should occupy the leading role in this area," see Volodin, loc.cit., p. 86. On Kurchatov's working at the Radium Institute see Grinberg and Frenkel', op.cit., p. 87.
85. Komlev et al., loc.cit., pp. 45–6.
86. The description "very lively" comes from I.K. Kikoin, "On prozhil schastlivuiu zhizn'," in his Rasskazy o fizike i fizikakh, Moscow: Nauka, 1986, p. 86; on the specific points raised in the discussion see E. Lifschitz, "Report on the Nuclear Physics Conference," Journal of Physics (Moscow), 1941, no. 3, p. 283.
87. Kurchatov, "Delenie tiazhelykh iader," Uspekhi fizicheskikh nauk, 1941, no. 2, pp. 159–69.
88. Protactinium (Pa) has an atomic number of 91. Pa-231 is fissionable with neutrons of less than 1 MeV.
89. Kurchatov, loc.cit., p. 169.
90. Golovin, loc.cit., pp. 5–6.
91. On the memorandum see Flerov, loc.cit., p. 70, and Kikoin, loc.cit., p. 87. It is not clear whether this was ever sent. The logic of the discussion at the Moscow conference suggests that it was not.
92. A.F. Ioffe, Nekotorye problemy sovremennoi fiziki, Moscow: Gossotsekizd., 1941, pp. 13–15. This is the text of a public lecture given on November 23, 1940. Ioffe is quoted by I.V. Obreimov as saying in this prewar period that "if the mastery of rocket technology is a matter for the next fifty years, then the use of intra-atomic energy is a matter for the next century." Vospominaniia ob A.F. Ioffe, Leningrad: Nauka, 1973, p. 47.
93. Mochalov, op.cit., p. 337; D.I. Shcherbakov, Zhizn' i deiatel'nost', Moscow: Nauka, 1969, p. 280.
94. Komlev et al., loc.cit., p. 47. Shcherbakov wrote later that the expedition's report played a "significant role in subsequent

practical measures." D.I. Shcherbakov, Izbrannye trudy, Vol. 2, Moscow: Nauka, 1969, p. 214.
95. Drawing on the Bohr–Wheeler theory they wrote that "when uranium-235 is bombarded by neutrons the capture of a neutron, with a probability that does not differ from unity, leads to fission." Ia.B. Zel'dovich and Yu.B. Khariton, "The Mechanism of Nuclear Fission (Part II)," Soviet Physics Uspekhi, March 1983, p. 286.
96. Ibid. See also the introductory essay in Ia.B. Zel'dovich, Izbrannye trudy: Khimicheskaia fizika i gidrodinamika, Moscow: Nauka, 1984, p. 29. This is the source for the neutron reflector. The three men did write a paper in May 1941, but it was not published: "Pamiati I.I. Gurevicha," Kurchatovets, December 1992, p. 6.
97. Zel'dovich and Khariton, "The Mechanism of Nuclear Fission (Part II)," p. 286.
98. This was the second part of a two-part paper on the mechanism of fission. The first part was published in the September 1941 issue of Uspekhi fizicheskikh nauk, which was sent to press on July 15. The next issue of the journal did not appear until 1944, by which time it was considered inappropriate to publish the second part, which appeared in Uspekhi fizicheskikh nauk only in 1983.
99. The critical mass of a sphere of uranium-235 at normal density, without a reflector, is approximately 52 kilograms. Thomas B. Cochran, William B. Arkin, Milton M. Hoenig, Nuclear Weapons Databook: Volume 1, US Nuclear Forces and Capabilities, Cambridge: Ballinger, 1984, p. 24.
100. Frisch and Peierls wrote that "a sphere with a radius of less than about 3 cm could be made up in two hemispheres, which are pulled together by springs and kept separated by a suitable structure which is removed at the desired moment" (Gowing, op.cit., p. 391). The suggestion by Khariton and Zel'dovich may have been similar. See the discussion of Flerov's design in Chapter 4.
101. Iu.B. Khariton, "K voprosu o razdelenii gazov tsentrifugirovaniem," in Aleksandrov, Voprosy, pp. 78–80. In writing this paper Khariton had nitrogen, not uranium, in mind.
102. Interview with Khariton, March 12, 1988. Golovin, op.cit, p. 40. Golovin writes that the letter was sent to the Commissariat of Heavy Industry, but that no longer existed in 1940. Also see Iu.B. Khariton, "Nachalo," in A.E. Shilov (ed.), Vospominaniia ob Akademike Nikolae

Nikolaeviche Semenove, Moscow: Nauka, 1993, p. 38.

103. A proposal entitled "On the utilization of uranium as an explosive and as a poisonous agent" was sent to the People's Commissariat of Defense by V.A. Maslov and V.S. Shpinel' of the Ukrainian Physicotechnical Institute in October 1940. The proposal was sent around various departments in the Defense Commissariat, which decided early in 1941 that it was premature to think of using atomic energy in the Red Army. In fact the design did not even approach a workable concept. See Iu.B. Khariton, and Iu.N. Smirnov, "O nekotorykh mifakh i legendakh vokrug sovetskikh atomnogo i vodorodnogo proektov," in *Materialy iubileinoi sessii uchenogo soveta tsentra*, Moscow: Kurchatovskii Institut, 1993, p. 41. V. Babaev and E. Gudkov, "Atomnaia bomba: Khar'kovskii proekt," *Nedelia*, no. 22, 1990, pp. 14–15.

104. Mochalov, *op.cit.*, p. 338; A.P. Aleksandrov, "Gody s Kurchatovym," *Nauka i zhizn'*, 1983, no. 2, p. 17; M.G. Pervukhin, "U istokov uranovoi epopei," *Tekhnika – molodezhi*, 1975, no. 6, p. 17.

105. Bohr Correspondence, Niels Bohr Library, American Institute of Physics, New York. Bohr's reply is dated December 23, 1940.

106. V.G. Khlopin, "Prevrashchenie elementov i periodicheskii zakon," *Zhurnal obshchei khimii*, 1941, no. 12, p. 1067.

107. Grinberg and Frenkel', *op.cit.*, pp. 87–95. The foundation for the cyclotron building was laid on September 22, 1939, but work was held up during the winter of 1939–40 by the war with Finland, when work on civilian projects was stopped. By February 1941, however, the magnet, which had a polar diameter of 1.2 meters was undergoing trials at the Elektrosila plant in Leningrad.

108. D. Alkhazov and A. Murin, "O metode razdeleniia izotopov s pomoshchiu lineinogo uskoritelia," *Doklady AN SSSR*, 1941, no. 3, pp. 204–5; Mochalov, *op.cit.*, p. 337; A.E. Brodsky, "Partial Separation of Uranium Light Isotope by Thermodiffusion," *Acta Physicochemica*, 1942, no. 3–4, pp. 225–7.

109. See Khariton's comment at the November 1940 nuclear conference. "Report on the Nuclear Physics Conference," *Journal of Physics*, no. 3, 1941, p. 283.

110. V.S. Shpinel', "Kak razdeliaiut izotopy," *Nauka i zhizn'*, 1941, no. 6., p. 35.

111. I.S. Panasiuk, "Eto bylo v 1938–1946 godakh," in M.K. Romanovskii (ed.),

Vospominaniia ob akademike I.V. Kurchatove, Moscow: Nauka, 1983, p. 23.

112. Mochalov, *op.cit.*, p. 337.

113. Vernadskii diary, May 16, June 15, 1941. ARAN 518–2–20, p. 64; 518–2–21, p. 1 verso; Vernadskii chronology, 1941. ARAN 518–2–50, p. 7 verso.

114. Vernadskii diary, May 16, 1941. ARAN 518–2–20, p. 64.

115. *Ibid.*, June 1, 1941. ARAN 518–2–20, p. 70. Vernadskii was not on bad terms with all physicists. He became very friendly with Mandel'shtam, whom he much admired, during the war. His opinion of Ioffe remained low. He regarded him as a "careerist, less talented and great than he thinks." Khronologiia, May 25, 1942. ARAN 518–2–52, p. 311.

116. Snegov, *op.cit.*, p. 216.

117. *Ibid.* Leipunskii was a member of the Ukrainian, not the Soviet, Academy of Sciences.

118. I. Golovin and R. Kuznetsova, "'Dostizheniia est'?'," *Pravda*, January 12, 1988, p. 3.

119. Volodin, *loc.cit.*, p. 94.

120. Edwin McMillan and Philip H. Abelson, "Radioactive Element 93," *Physical Review*, 1940, no. 57. p. 1185. Several references to this paper appeared in the writings of Khlopin, and of Khariton and Zel'dovich in 1941. Zel'dovich and Khariton refer to it in the second part of their paper on the mechanism of fission, *loc.cit.*, p. 286, and Khlopin in his March 1941 lecture, *loc.cit.*, p. 1065.

121. Snegov, *op.cit.*, p. 219. I have heard another explanation: that Stalin did not want one of the first Stalin prizes to be awarded to a discovery that had no practical value.

122. Bohr Correspondence, *loc.cit.*

4. Making a Decision

1. A.I. Mikoian, "V pervye mesiatsy velikoi otechestvennoi voiny," *Novaia i noveishaia istoriia*, 1985, no. 6, pp. 95–6; S.P. Ivanov (ed.), *Nachal'nyi period voiny*, Moscow: Voenizdat, 1974, pp. 209–13.

2. K.A. Meretskov, *Na sluzhbe narodu*, Moscow: Politizdat, 1968, p. 202.

3. Alexander Werth, *Russia at War, 1941–1945*, London: Pan Books, 1964, pp. 132–3.

4. On this period see John Erickson, *The Road to Stalingrad*, Vol. 2, New York: Harper and Row, 1975, pp. 13–49.

5. Ivanov, *op.cit.*, pp. 211–13; Dmitrii Volkogonov, *Triumf i tragediia*, 2nd edn, Book 2, Moscow: Novosti, 1990, pp. 125–

48; G.K. Zhukov, *Vospominaniia i razmyshleniia*, 10th edn, Vol. 1, Moscow: Novosti, 1990, pp. 341–71.

6. Ivanov, *op.cit*, pp. 206, 212; John Erickson, "Threat Identification and Strategic Appraisal by the Soviet Union, 1930–1941," in Ernest R. May (ed.), *Knowing One's Enemies*, Princeton: Princeton University Press, 1984, pp. 417–22.

7. Mikoian, *loc.cit*, p. 103. Volkogonov, *op.cit*., pp. 154–69.

8. Khrushchev's Secret Speech, in N.S. Khrushchev, *Khrushchev Remembers: volume I*, Harmondsworth: Penguin, 1977, p. 614.

9. N.S. Khrushchev, *Khrushchev Remembers: The Glasnost Tapes*, Boston: Little, Brown, 1990, p. 101; Robert Conquest, *Stalin: Breaker of Nations*, New York: Viking, 1991, p. 239.

10. Mikoian, *loc.cit*, pp. 96–7; Volkogonov, *op.cit*., pp. 168–70.

11. Werth, *op.cit*., pp. 164–8.

12. On the early Soviet setbacks see Erickson, *op.cit*., pp. 136–222.

13. B.V. Levshin, *Sovetskaia nauka v gody velikoi otechestvennoi voiny*, Moscow: Nauka, 1983, pp. 13–14.

14. Ibid., p. 44; Kaftanov, "Organizatsiia nauchnykh issledovanii v gody voiny. Beseda s professorom S.V. Kaftanovym," *Voprosy istorii estestvoznaniia i tekhniki*, no. 2, 1975, pp. 25–6; Kaftanov, "Po trevoge. Rasskaz upolnomochennogo gosudarstvennogo komiteta oborony S.V. Kaftanova," *Khimiia i zhizn'*, 1985, no. 6, pp. 16–17. See also Bruce Parrott, *Politics and Technology in the Soviet Union*, Cambridge, Mass.: MIT Press, 1983, pp. 111–12.

15. V.M. Tuchkevich and V.Ia. Frenkel', "Fiziko-tekhnicheskii institut imeni A.F. Ioffe v gody voiny," *Voprosy istorii estestvoznaniia i tekhniki*, 1975, no. 2, pp. 13–23.

16. Levshin, *op.cit*., p. 66.

17. A.P. Grinberg and V.Ia. Frenkel', *Igor' Vasil'evich Kurchatov v fiziko-tekhnicheskom institute*, Leningrad: Nauka, 1984, pp. 137–8.

18. *Ibid.*, pp. 138–45; B.A. Tkachenko, *Istoriia razmagnichivaniia korablei sovetskogo voenno-morskogo flota*, Leningrad: Nauka, 1981, pp. 81–7, 96–7.

19. B.M. Vul, "FIAN – oborone rodiny," *Vestnik Akademii Nauk SSSR*, 1975, no. 4, pp. 35–6.

20. Levshin, *op.cit*., pp. 197, 210, 211. Khariton worked for one of the institutes of the Commissariat of Munitions.

21. A.K. Val'ter, "Fizikotekhnicheskii institut akademii nauk USSR," in *Uchenye Khar'kova k godovshchine osvobozhdeniia rodnogo goroda*, Khar'kov: izd. "Sotsialistichna Kharkivshchina", 1944, pp. 51–2.

22. L.V. Komlev, G.S. Sinitsyna, and M.P. Koval'skaia, "V.G. Khlopin i uranovaia problema," in *Akademik V.G. Khlopin: Ocherki, vospominaniia sovremennikov*, Leningrad: Nauka, 1987, p. 48.

23. V.I. Vernadskii, "Korennye izmeneniia neizbezhny . . . ," *Literaturnaia gazeta*, March 16, 1988, p. 13.

24. Letter of July 15, 1941 from Vladimir to George Vernadskii. Vernadskii Collection, Russian Archives, Butler Library, Columbia University, New York; Correspondence Vernadskii, V.I. and Natal'ia to George and Nina Vernadskii 1941.

25. Vernadskii, *loc.cit*. See also the first section of a memorandum that Vernadskii wrote in November 1942: V.I. Vernadskii, "Ob organizatsii nauchnoi raboty," *Priroda*, 1975, no. 4, pp. 35–6.

26. *Vestnik Akademii Nauk SSSR*, 1941, no. 9–10, pp. 9–10. See also the discussion in Arnold Kramish, *Atomic Energy in the Soviet Union*, Stanford: Stanford University Press, 1959, pp. 40–44.

27. *Vestnik Akademii Nauk*, p. 10.

28. Boris Volodin, "Povest' ob Igore Vasil'evich Kurchatove," in *Puti v neznaemoe. Pisateli rasskazyvaiut o nauke, Sbornik 16*, Moscow: Sovetskie pisateli, 1982, pp. 104–5; I.N. Golovin, *I.V. Kurchatov*, 3rd edn, Moscow: Atomizdat, 1978, pp. 56–7; I.N. Golovin and N.N. Smirnov, *Eto nachinalos' v zamoskvorech'e*, Moscow: Kurchatov Institute of Atomic Energy, 1989, p. 4. The precise date is unclear, but it must have been between December 17 and 23. These dates are given on Flerov's pass (copy in author's possession).

29. Golovin and Smirnov, *op.cit*., p. 4.

30. P.T. Astashenkov, *Akademik I.V. Kurchatov*, Moscow: Voenizdat, 1971, p. 177.

31. Copy in author's possession.

32. He also dismissed a proposal, which he said Alikhanov had made, to use a chain reaction to obtain 100.kilograms of artificial radioactive elements, on grounds of cost and difficulty. This suggests that Alikhanov had seen the possibility of using fission chain reactions to produce a fissionable material like plutonium.

33. The latter was later shown not to work.

34. This suggests that Flerov was aware of cal-

culations other than those done by Zel'dovich and Khariton.

35. Flerov did not know which isotope fissioned spontaneously. It is in fact uranium-238 that undergoes spontaneous fission, which does not, therefore, present a problem for a uranium-235 bomb. Spontaneous fission is, however, a serious problem in the design of a plutonium bomb.

36. This mechanism is the same as that suggested by Khariton and Zel'dovich. See p. 67.

37. Astashenkov, *op.cit.*, p. 177.

38. Golovin, *op.cit.*, p. 57. Kurchatov kept this letter in his desk until his death.

39. G.N. Flerov, "Vsemu my mozhem pouchit'sia u Kurchatova," in A.P. Aleksandrov (ed.), *Vospominaniia ob Igore Vasil'eviche Kurchatove*, Moscow: Nauka, 1988, p. 71.

40. *Ibid.*, pp. 71–2. Volodin, *loc.cit.*, p. 105.

41. Flerov, *loc.cit.*, p. 72.

42. Golovin and Smirnov, *op.cit.*, pp. 4–5. The date of the letter is not given in the source.

43. The full text of the actual letter has not come to light. I draw on a draft that Flerov made, which was published in part in Mikhail Chernenko, "100,000 tonn dinamita, ili proshu ispravit' orfografiiu," *Moskovskie novosti*, April 17, 1988, p. 16.

44. *Ibid.* A.B. Migdal was a theoretical physicist from Ioffe's institute.

45. *Ibid.*

46. Kaftanov, "Po trevoge," p. 6. S.A. Balezin, who was Kaftanov's deputy, says that Flerov's letter was passed on to no other government agency, and not to the Scientific-Technical Council, S.A. Balezin, "Rasskaz professora Balezina," *Khimiia i zhizn'*, 1985, no. 6, p. 19. But Kaftanov has written in other places too that Flerov's letter was given to him (see "Organizatsiia," pp. 28–9), and there seems to be no reason to disbelieve him; Balezin may not have known about the letter at the time.

47. Margaret Gowing, *Britain and Atomic Energy, 1939–1945*, London: Macmillan, 1964, p. 394. The Maud Reports – there was one on the use of uranium for a bomb, and one on its use as a source of power – are reprinted, along with their appendices, by Gowing, pp. 394–436. For a description of the work of the committee see *ibid.*, pp. 45–89.

48. *Ibid.*, p. 432.

49. *Ibid.*, p. 105.

50. *Ibid.*, p. 106. On the work of the Defence Services Panel see pp. 97–106.

51. *Ibid.*, pp. 115–22; Richard G. Hewlett and Oscar E. Anderson, Jr., *The New World: A History of the United States Atomic Energy Commission, Vol. 1 1939–1946*, Berkeley: University of California Press, 1990, pp. 32–49.

52. Gowing, *op.cit.*, p. 123.

53. On the Quebec Agreement see *ibid.*, pp. 164–77, 439–40.

54. Hewlett and Anderson, *op.cit.*, pp. 73–4.

55. "Pile" was the American term for what later became known as a reactor.

56. Mark Walker, *German National Socialism and the Quest for Nuclear Power, 1939–1949*, Cambridge: Cambridge University Press, 1989, p. 172.

57. David Irving, *The German Atomic Bomb*, New York: Simon and Schuster, 1967, p. 120; Thomas Powers, *Heisenberg's War: The Secret History of the German Bomb*, New York: Alfred A. Knopf, 1993, pp. 146–50.

58. Albert Speer, *Inside the Third Reich*, New York: Macmillan, 1970, p. 226.

59. Walker, *op.cit.*, pp. 173–5.

60. The head of the espionage organization (the residency) in a Soviet embassy or consulate abroad is known as the resident. On Gorskii see Christopher Andrew and Oleg Gordievsky, *KGB: The Inside Story*, New York: Harper Collins, 1990, pp. 293–4.

61. The text of Gorskii's message is given in "U istokov sovetskogo atomnogo proekta: Rol' Razvedki, 1941–1946 gg," *Voprosy istorii estestvoznaniia i tekhniki*, 1992, no. 3, pp. 107–8.

62. Compare the text of Gorskii's telegram with Gowing, *op.cit.*, p. 99.

63. "U istokov," p. 108.

64. Andrew and Gordievsky, *op.cit.*, pp. 216–17. The other four were Philby, Maclean, Burgess, and Blunt.

65. *Ibid.*, p. 279.

66. Norman Moss, *Klaus Fuchs: The Man Who Stole the Atom Bomb*, London: Grafton Books, 1987, pp. 38–42; Robert C. Williams, *Klaus Fuchs: Atom Spy*, Cambridge, Mass.: Harvard University Press, 1987, pp. 35–63.

67. Williams, *op.cit.*, p. 61.

68. *Statement of Klaus Fuchs to Michael Perrin*, January 30, 1950, in a letter of March 2, 1950 from J. Edgar Hoover to Admiral Souers, pp. 1–2, HSTL, PSF.

69. "U istokov," pp. 109–11. The document given in this source is only a draft of the memorandum actually sent, which may therefore be different.

70. Skobel'tsyn worked on cosmic rays, Kapitsa on low-temperature physics, and Slutskii was a specialist at UFTI in radio-

engineering. Beria in the memorandum mistakenly referred to Slutskii as Slutskin.

71. A.A. Iatskov, "Atom i razvedka," in "U istokov," p. 104.

72. Werth, op.cit., pp. 442–72.

73. The order, which was read out to troops at the time, was not published until 1988. A. Shcherbakov, "Nachal'nikam politupravlenii frontov i okrugov i nachal'nikam politotdelov armii," Voenno-istoricheskii zhurnal, 1988, no. 8, pp. 78–9.

74. Levshin, op.cit., p. 106.

75. Kaftanov, "Po trevoge," p. 7; Balezin, loc.cit., p. 18. I. Starinov, Proidi nezrimym, Moscow: Molodaia gvardiia, 1988, pp. 110, 123, 128–9. Starinov's account of what the notebook contained is more modest, but he did not understand the contents. He just refers to formulae. There is no obvious explanation for the presence of a German officer with a notebook like this traveling between Mariupol and Taganrog.

76. Kaftanov, "Po trevoge,", p. 7; Balezin, loc.cit., p. 19.

77. Kaftanov, "Po trevoge," p. 8.

78. Various government agencies were asked for their views on this proposal, and their replies were passed on to Kaftanov. The proposal did not meet with unanimous support. Gosplan, the State Planning Commission, which was no doubt worried about the resources that the project would require, was among its opponents. Ibid.

79. Kaftanov, "Po trevoge," p. 8. Balezin's version of the meeting with Stalin, at which he seems not to have been present but about which he doubtless heard from Kaftanov, is essentially the same as Kaftanov's. "And how much will this cost?" asked Stalin. Kaftanov replied that it would cost 20 million roubles for a start. "And what will we gain from this?" Stalin asked, and then answered his own question. "We may gain nothing. But?" He looked at Kaftanov, who added "It's worth risking." Stalin gave his approval, Balezin, loc.cit., p. 19.

80. Quoted in A.S. Balezin et al., Stepan Afanas'evich Balezin, Moscow: Nauka, 1988, p. 33.

81. Ibid.

82. Levshin, op.cit., p. 106; Astashenkov, op.cit., pp. 34–5.

83. Golovin, op.cit., p. 58 names Ioffe, Khlopin, Kapitsa, and Vernadskii; Balezin, loc.cit., p. 19 mentions Vavilov, Vernadskii, and Ioffe. See also I. Golovin and R. Kuznetsova, " 'Dostizheniia est'?'," Pravda, January 12, 1988, p. 3. There is no reference to such consultations in Vernadskii's diary.

84. Aleksandrov, op.cit., p. 461. According to Golovin and Kuznetsova, Ioffe had recommended to Pervukhin that Kurchatov be brought to Moscow, ibid.

85. Kaftanov, "Po trevoge," p. 8; Balezin, loc.cit., p. 19.

86. Balezin, quoted in A.S. Balezin et al., op.cit., p. 170.

87. Kaftanov, "Po trevoge," pp. 8–9; Balezin, loc.cit., pp. 19–20.

88. Golovin and Kuznetsova, loc.cit., p. 3.

89. I.K. Kikoin, "On prozhil schastlivuiu zhizn'," in his Rasskazy o fizike i fizikakh, Moscow: Nauka, 1986, p. 86.

90. There was a popular song of the time: "When we've driven Fritz away, we'll have time to shave."

91. Golovin, op.cit., p. 59; A.P. Aleksandrov, "Gody s Kurchatovym," Nauka i zhizn', 1983, no. 2, p. 18.

92. This meeting is placed in the spring by A.I. Ioirysh, I.D. Morokhov, and S.K. Ivanov, A-Bomba, Moscow: Nauka, 1980, p. 377. M.G. Pervukhin, "Pervye gody atomnogo proekta," Khimiia i zhizn', 1985, no. 5, p. 62, places it in September–October. In another article Pervukhin places this meeting in the autumn. See his "U istokov uranovoi epopei," Tekhnika-molodezhi, 1975, no. 6, p. 17.

93. Ioirysh et al., op.cit., p. 377; Pervukhin, "Pervye gody," p. 62.

94. M.G. Pervukhin, "Vydaiushchiisia uchenyi i talantlivyi organizator," in M.K. Romanovskii (ed.), Vospominaniia ob akademike I.V. Kurchatove, Moscow: Nauka, 1983, pp. 6–7.

95. Ibid.; and Pervukhin, "Pervye gody," p. 62.

96. Sto sorok besed s Molotovym: iz dnevnika F. Chueva, Moscow: Terra, 1991, p. 81.

97. The February decision has not been published. Some idea of the contents is given by Pervukhin, "Pervye gody . . . ," p. 63. The date is given as February 11 by Golovin, op.cit., pp. 60–61. V.V. Goncharov gives the date as February 15. See his Pervye (osnovnye) etapy resheniia atomnoi problemy v SSSR, Moscow: Kurchatov Institute of Atomic Energy, 1990, p. 2. The chronology in Aleksandrov, op.cit., p. 461 gives March 10 as the date of Kurchatov's appointment as scientific director.

98. Vernadskii to Fersman, November 27, 1942, in Pis'ma V.I. Vernadskogo A.E. Fersmanu, Moscow: Nauka, 1985, p. 227. It is likely that it is the letter that Ioffe and Kaftanov sent to the State Defense Committee that Vernadskii has in mind. This seems to confirm Kaftanov's account of his

and Ioffe's approach to Stalin. Earlier in the same month Vernadskii had written a memorandum about the organization of scientific research, in which he had urged that the Uranium Commission be revived and turned into a flexible organization. He sent this memorandum to V.L. Komarov, the president of the Academy of Sciences. See V.I. Vernadskii, "Ob organizatsii nauchnoi raboty," *Priroda*, 1975, no. 4, p. 37.

99. Komlev *et al.*, *loc.cit.*, p. 48. The text of this letter can be found *ibid.*, pp. 48–52.

100. I.I. Mochalov, *Vladimir Ivanovich Vernadskii*, Moscow: Nauka, 1982, p. 355; the comment about the bureaucratic apparatus is to be found in Kendall E. Bailes, *Science and Russian Culture in an Age of Revolutions*, Bloomington: Indiana University Press, 1990, p. 174.

101. Mochalov, *op.cit.*, p. 355; Levshin, *op.cit.*, p. 111; Bailes, *op.cit.*, p. 174. On April 27 the president, V.L. Komarov, wrote in reply that he had forwarded Vernadskii's memorandum on the Uranium Commission to the Council of People's Commissars. Mochalov, *op.cit.*, p. 356.

102. Iu.V. Sivintsev, *I.V. Kurchatov i iadernaia energetika*, Moscow: Atomizdat, 1980, p. 13.

103. Arnold Kramish, *The Griffin*, Boston: Houghton Mifflin, 1986, pp. 126–32. R.V. Jones, *Reflections on Intelligence*, London: Heinemann, 1989, p. 284.

104. F.H. Hinsley, *British Intelligence in the Second World War*, Vol. 2, New York: Cambridge University Press, 1981, p. 122.

105. A.S. Feklisov, "Podvig Klausa Fuksa," *Voenno-istoricheskii zhurnal*, 1990, no. 12, pp. 24, 25.

106. *Sto sorok besed*, p. 81.

107. Tkachenko, *op.cit.*, pp. 163–4.

108. "U istokov," pp. 111–16.

109. *Ibid.*, p. 112.

110. Among these were the size of the clearances between the moving and non-moving parts of the machine; the material out of which the membranes, through which the uranium hexafluoride was pressed, were made; whether stable lubricants had been found against hexafluoride. *ibid.*

111. These calculations had evidently been done since August 1940, for Kurchatov's plan had included research on a uranium–heavy water system as one of its main elements.

112. This was the British term for what later bacame known as a reactor. The Russian term *kotel* (boiler) appears to have been taken from the British term. I have found no use of it before this memorandum.

113. "U istokov," p. 114.

114. *Ibid.*, pp. 114–15.

115. *Ibid.*, pp. 116–18; the quotation is from p. 116. Kurchatov's emphasis.

116. *Ibid.*, p. 118.

117. *Ibid.*, p. 100. How well this was done is not clear. Fuchs later commented that the questions he was asked in 1942 and 1943 "were very few and were sometimes so garbled as to be almost meaningless." *Statement of Klaus Fuchs*, p. 2. Fuchs was being operated by the GRU at the time, and that may have made a difference.

118. *Sto sorok besed*, p. 82.

5. Getting Started

1. Pervukhin and Kurchatov had asked for a new institute, but were told that a laboratory was more appropriate, because Kurchatov had not directed an institute before. M.G. Pervukhin, "Pervye gody atomnogo proekta," *Khimiia i zhizn'*, 1985, no. 5, p. 68; S.V. Kaftanov, "Po trevoge. Rasskaz upolnomochennogo gosudarstvennogo komiteta oborony S.V. Kaftanova," *Khimiia i zhizn'*, 1985, no. 6, p. 9. I. Golovin and R. Kuznetsova, "'Dostizheniia est'?'," *Pravda*, January 12, 1988, p. 3. Laboratory No. 2 was given the rights and status of an institute by the Academy in February 1944. A.P. Aleksandrov (ed.), *Vospominaniia ob Igore Vasil'eviche Kurchatove*, Moscow: Nauka, 1988, p. 461. For an explanation of the name Laboratory No. 2 see *Vklad akademika A.F. Ioffe v stanovlenie iadernoi fiziki v SSSR*, Leningrad: Nauka, 1980, pp. 30–31.

2. I.V. Kurchatov, *Izbrannye trudy v trekh tomakh, tom 3, Iadernaia energiia*, Moscow: Nauka, 1984, pp. 9–19.

3. *Ibid.*, pp. 20–57.

4. *Ibid.*, pp. 52, 53.

5. *Ibid.*, pp. 49, 50.

6. "Pile" became the common term in English for reactor, before the term "reactor" was adopted. I use it instead of "boiler" for the period up to 1945; after that I use "reactor".

7. "U istokov sovetskogo atomnogo proekta: rol' razvedki," *Voprosy istorii estestvoznaniia i tekhniki*, 1992, no. 3, p. 116.

8. *Ibid.*, p. 118.

9. I.N. Golovin and Iu.N. Smirnov, *Eto nachinalos' v zamoskvorech'e*, Moscow: Kurchatov Institute of Atomic Energy, 1989, p. 6.

10. M.G. Pervukhin, "U istokov uranovoi epopei," *Tekhnika-molodezhi*, 1975, no. 6, p. 17.

11. Kurchatov, *op.cit.*, p. 56.

12. I.V. Kurchatov and I.S. Panasiuk, "Stroitel'stvo i pusk pervogo v Sovetskom Soiuze uran-grafitivogo kotla s samorazvivaiushcheisia tsepnoi reaktsiei," in Kurchatov, op.cit., p. 74. See also Kurchatov's July 4, 1943 memorandum for Pervukhin, where the same reasoning is given. "U istokov," p. 121.

13. The most complete discussion of the early research on the uranium-graphite system is to be found in I.F. Zhezherun, Stroitel'stvo i pusk pervogo v Sovetskom Soiuze atomnogo reaktora, Moscow: Atomizdat, 1978. Flerov continued to work on the possibility of a natural–uranium–light water system, but soon abandoned this idea as unfeasible. Ibid., pp. 62–5.

14. On Alikhanov's attitude, see Nadezha Kozhevnikova, "Baloven' zhestokoi epokhi," Sovetskaia kul'tura, April 14, 1990, p. 15; on his research see Iu.G. Abov, "Abram Isaakovich Alikhanov – Direktor ITEFa," in A.P. Aleksandrov (ed.), Akademik A.I. Alikhanov, Vospominaniia, pis'ma, dokumenty, Leningrad: Nauka, 1989, p. 77.

15. Zhezherun, op.cit., p. 34; I.I. Gurevich, "Isaak Iakovlevich Pomeranchuk," and A.D. Galanin, "O rabotakh I.Ia. Pomeranchuka po fizike iadernykh reaktorov," in L.B. Okun' (ed.), Vospominaniia o I.Ia. Pomeranchuke, Moscow: Nauka, 1988, pp. 44–5, 230–34.

16. Kurchatov and Panasiuk, loc.cit., p. 74. Golovin has pointed out that this theory differed from the theory proposed by Eugene Wigner in the United States. I.N. Golovin, "The First Steps in the Atomic Problem in the USSR," Paper presented at Conference "Fifty Years with Nuclear Fission," Washington, DC, 1989, p. 10.

17. Zhezherun, op.cit., p. 79; Galanin, loc.cit., pp. 243–4. See also Golovin's comments on this work in his "First Steps" paper; Soviet results were different from those obtained in the US.

18. Leonid Nemenov, "Poslezavtra nachnem obluchenie . . . ," Tekhnika-molodezhi, 1975, no. 6, pp. 18–21; and his "The Past Becomes History," Soviet Atomic Energy, 1978, no. 1, pp. 13–18 (originally in Atomnaia energiia, 1978, no. 1, pp. 17–22). Nemenov was the son of the man who had founded the X-ray Institute from which Ioffe's institute had split in 1921.

19. On this whole episode see Nemenov, "Poslezavtra". On the opening of the rail line see Harrison Salisbury, 900 Days. The Siege of Leningrad, New York: Da Capo Press, 1985, pp. 547–50.

20. Nemenov, "Poslezavtra," pp. 20–21; Aleksandrov, Vospominaniia, p. 461.

21. Nemenov, "The Past," p. 18.

22. Boris Kurchatov, "Nekhozhenymi putiami," Tekhnika-molodezhi, 1975, no. 12, pp. 16–18; Nemenov, "Poslezavtra," p. 21. Kurchatov determined the half-life of the substance he found to be 31,000 years; the half-life of plutonium, he later learned, is 24,300 years.

23. Z.V. Ershova, "Moi vstrechi s akademikom V.G. Khlopinym," in Akademik V.G. Khlopin: Ocherki, vospominaniia sovremennikov, Leningrad: Nauka, 1987, pp. 112–14. B. Nikol'skii and G. Petrzhak, "Ot radiia k plutoniiu," Tekhnika-molodezhi, 1976, no. 1, p. 37. The institute was also assigned an important role in developing methods for extracting uranium from the ore, and for refining it.

24. Boris Volodin, "Povest' ob Igore Vasil'eviche Kurchatove," in Puti v neznaemoe, Collection 16, Moscow: Sovetskie pisateli, 1982, pp. 86–7.

25. Golovin, loc.cit., p. 9.

26. On Artsimovich see Iu.A. Khramov, Fiziki. Biograficheskii spravochnik, 2nd edn, Moscow: Nauka, 1983, p. 21. On the centrifuge method see A.P. Aleksandrov (ed.), Voprosy sovremennoi eksperimental'noi i teoreticheskoi fiziki, Leningrad: Nauka, 1984, p. 81; and I.N. Golovin, interview, October 19, 1992. On thermal diffusion see A.P. Aleksandrov, "Gody s Kurchatovym," in his Vospominaniia, pp. 37–8.

27. Kaftanov, "Po trevoge," p. 9; S.A. Balezin, "Rasskaz professora Balezina," Khimiia i zhizn', 1985, no. 5, p. 20.

28. I.N. Golovin, I.V. Kurchatov, 3rd edn, Moscow: Atomizdat, 1978, pp. 63–6; Balezin, loc.cit., p. 20; V.V. Goncharov, Pervye (osnovnye) etapy resheniia atomnoi problemy v SSSR, Moscow: Kurchatov Institute of Atomic Energy, 1990, p. 3.

29. Goncharov, op.cit., p. 23. According to A.R. Striganov, there were 120 people in the laboratory in July 1944. See his "I.V. Kurchatov – Kommunist," in Aleksandrov, Vospominaniia, p. 394.

30. Kaftanov, "Po trevoge," p. 8; Iu.B. Khariton, "A.F. Ioffe i I.V. Kurchatov," Uspekhi fizicheskikh nauk, Vol. 139, March 1983, p. 395.

31. S.E. Frish, Skvoz' prizmu vremeni, Moscow: Politizdat, 1992, p. 315.

32. V.I. Merkin, "Reshaiushchii eksperiment Kurchatova," in Aleksandrov, Vospominaniia, p. 271. The first experiments to

test a heterogeneous pile were done with tungsten rods instead of uranium. See Golovin, *loc.cit.*, pp. 8–9.

33. "U istokov," p. 120.

34. Pervukhin, "Pervye gody," p. 63.

35. See p. 66.

36. Pervukhin, "Pervye gody," p. 63.

37. Zinaida Ershova, Miriam Pozharskaia, and Vladimir Fomin, "Milligrammi – eto nemalo," *Tekhnika-molodezhi*, 1976, no. 2, pp. 48–9.

38. I.S. Panasiuk, "Eto bylo v 1938–1946 godakh," in M.K. Romanovskii (ed.), *Vospominaniia ob akademike I.V. Kurchatove*, Moscow: Nauka, 1983, p. 24.

39. Three graphite plants had been set up in the Soviet Union in 1938, but these could not meet the needs of Soviet industry, and during the war between 4,000 and 6,000 tons were imported each year from the United States. See CIA, *National Intelligence Survey: USSR, Section 73, Atomic Energy*, January 1951, pp. 73–17, 73–18.

40. Panasiuk, *loc.cit.*, pp. 25–6; Merkin, *loc.cit.*, pp. 271–3; Goncharov, *op.cit.*, pp. 9–13.

41. A summary of these transactions may be found in: Joint Committee on Atomic Energy, US Congress, *Soviet Atomic Espionage*, Washington, DC: US Government Printing Office, 1951, pp. 185–92. More detailed evidence is presented in US Congress, House Committee on Un-American Activities, *Hearings Regarding Shipment of Atomic Material to the Soviet Union during World War II*, Washington, DC: US Government Printing Office, 1950; see esp. p. 941.

42. *Soviet Atomic Espionage*, p. 187; *Hearings Regarding Shipment*, p. 941.

43. *Soviet Atomic Espionage*, p. 189; *Hearings Regarding Shipment*, pp. 942, 950, 1043–6.

44. *Soviet Atomic Espionage*, p. 189; *Hearings Regarding Shipment*, pp. 942, 950, 1043–6.

45. In their 1947 report on the uranium-graphite pile Kurchatov and Panasiuk wrote that "when about 220 kg of the purest uranium oxide became available, we conducted experiments with a layer of uranium intersecting a graphite prism." Kurchatov and Panasiuk, *loc.cit.*, p. 76. The date of this report is given in Zhezherun, *op.cit.*, p. 137. These experiments made it possible to calculate some of the key conditions for a chain reaction. But these experiments do not appear to have been conducted until 1945, when graphite of the right purity became available.

46. No one I talked to knew of uranium coming to the laboratory in this way.

47. Goncharov, *op.cit.*, p. 5. It is not clear what happened to the 1–2 metric tons of uranium Kurchatov expected to get in 1943. See above, p. 100.

48. F.I. Vol'fson, N.S. Zontov, and G.R. Shushaniia, *Dmitrii Ivanovich Shcherbakov*, Moscow: Nauka, 1987, pp. 49–54; D.I. Shcherbakov, "Avtobiograficheskie ocherki (konspektivno)," in his *Zhizn' i deiatel'nost' 1893–1966*, Moscow: Nauka, 1969, p. 281.

49. *Ibid. Moscow News*, an English-language weekly newspaper, reported on December 29, 1943, p. 3, that deposits of uranium-bearing ores had been found recently in Kirgizia (which is where Tiuia-Muiun is). The report made no mention of the possible use of uranium in the production of atomic energy. In the same year scientists at the Ukrainian Physicotechnical Institute began to work on the development of instruments for uranium exploration. Viktor Ivanov, "Po sovetam Kurchatova," *Tekhnika-molodezhi*, 1975, no. 10, p. 20.

50. B.V. Levshin, *Sovetskaia nauka v gody velikoi otechestvennoi voiny*, Moscow: Nauka, 1983, p. 112.

51. *Ibid.*

52. Shcherbakov, *loc.cit.*, p. 281. Shcherbakov organized research into the metallogenesis and geochemistry of uranium at the All-Union Institute of Mineral Resources. According to the CIA mining began in the Fergana Valley in 1944, and before the end of the year this operation was put under the control of an organization known as Combine No. 6. CIA, *op.cit.*, pp. 73–2.

53. The letter is reproduced in I.N. Golovin, "Kurchatov – uchenyi, gosudarstvennyi deiatel', chelovek," in *Materialy iubeleinoi sessii uchenogo soveta tsentra 12 ianvaria 1993 g.*, Moscow: Rossiiskii nauchnyi tsentr Kurchatovskii institut, 1993, pp. 24–5.

54. Haakon Chevalier, *Oppenheimer: The Story of a Friendship*, New York: George Braziller, 1965, pp. 53–5, 90–91. Philip M. Stern with Harold P. Green, *The Oppenheimer Case*, New York: Harper and Row, 1969, pp. 43–5.

55. Oppenheimer and Chevalier later gave different versions of this conversation, assigning different degrees of explicitness to Chevalier's approach, but all versions agree that Oppenheimer rejected the approach. Stern, *op.cit.*, pp. 43–4; Barton J. Bernstein, "The Oppenheimer Loyalty-Security Case Reconsidered," *Stanford Law Review*, July 1990, Vol. 42, no. 6, pp. 1383–484.

56. Vincent C. Jones, *Manhattan: The Army and*

the Atomic Bomb, Washington, DC: Center of Military History, United States Army, 1985, pp. 263–4; Stern, *op.cit.*, p. 47; Joint Committee on Atomic Energy, US Congress, *op.cit.*, pp. 171–82.

57. Jones, *op.cit.*, pp. 265–6; Joint Committee on Atomic Energy, *op.cit.*, pp. 163–70.

58. "U istokov," p. 119.

59. *Ibid.* This work had been done by Seaborg and Segrè in July 1941. See Richard G. Hewlett and Oscar E. Anderson, Jr., *The New World: A History of the United States Atomic Energy Commission: Vol. 1, 1939–1946*, Berkeley: University of California Press, 1990, pp. 41–2.

60. "U istokov," p. 120.

61. *Ibid.*

62. *Statement of Klaus Fuchs to Michael Perrin*, January 30, 1950, in a letter of March 2, 1950 from J. Edgar Hoover to Admiral Souers, HSTL, PSF, pp. 2–3. On Fuchs's activities in this period see Norman Moss, *Klaus Fuchs: The Man Who Stole the Atom Bomb*, London: Grafton, 1987, pp. 49–61; Robert C. Williams, *Klaus Fuchs: Atom Spy*, Cambridge, Mass.: Harvard University Press, 1987, pp. 64–74.

63. *Statement of Klaus Fuchs to Perrin*, p. 3.

64. "U istokov," pp. 120–22.

65. *The Report of the Royal Commission, 27th June 1946*, Ottawa: Controller of Stationery, 1946, p. 455. See also Margaret Gowing, *Independence and Deterrence: Britain and Atomic Energy, 1945–1952, Vol. 2, Policy Execution*, London: Macmillan, 1974, pp. 138–44. It is not clear whether May had provided atomic information to the Soviet Union before 1945.

66. *Royal Commission*, pp. 450, 455. "The U-235 was a slightly enriched sample," he later confessed, "and was in a small glass tube and consisted of about a milligram of oxide. The U-233 was about a tenth of a milligram and was a very thin deposit on a platinum foil and was wrapped in a piece of paper" (Alan Moorehead, *The Traitors*, New York: Scribner, 1952, p. 37). May also reported that the output of uranium-235 amounted to 400 grams daily at the magnetic separation plant at Clinton, and that the output of element 94 was probably twice as great. Some graphite piles capable of producing 250 grams a day were planned. *Royal Commission*, p. 450.

67. Robert Bothwell and J.L. Granatstein (eds), *The Gouzenko Transcripts: The Evidence Presented to the Kellock-Taschereau Royal Commission of 1946*, Ottawa: Deneau Publishers, 1982, p. 145.

68. "U istokov," p. 123.

69. V. Gubarev, "Fizika-eto moia zhizn'," *Pravda*, February 20, 1984, p. 8. This article is based on an interview with Khariton. See also A.P. Aleksandrov *et al.*, "Iulii Borisovich Khariton," in Aleksandrov (ed.), *Voprosy*, p. 7.

70. Gubarev, *loc.cit.*, p. 7. Interview with Khariton, July 16, 1992.

71. Ia.B. Zel'dovich and B. Konovalov, "Imia veka daet nauka," in A.N. Sinitsyn (ed.), *Geroi vdokhnovennogo truda*, Moscow: Politizdat, 1983, p. 259.

72. Golovin, *op.cit.*, pp. 67–8.

73. Statement to Perrin, pp. 3–4; Williams, *op.cit.*, pp. 75–91.

74. Margaret Gowing, *Britain and Atomic Energy, 1939–1945*, London: Macmillan, 1964, pp. 263–4.

75. Rudolf Peierls, "The Bomb that Never Was," *New York Review of Books*, April 22, 1993, p. 7.

76. Statement to Perrin, p. 3; Hugh H. Clegg and Robert J. Lamphere, memorandum to the director of the FBI, June 4, 1950, pp. 18–23. HSTL, PSF.

77. *Statement to Perrin*, p. 4.

78. *Ibid.*

79. *Ibid.*; Clegg and Lamphere, *loc.cit.*, pp. 24–5.

80. "U istokov," pp. 122–3.

81. Joint Committee on Atomic Energy, *op.cit.*, pp. 60–144; Ronald Radosh and Joyce Milton, *The Rosenberg File. A Search for the Truth*, New York: Holt, Rinehart and Winston, 1983, pp. 184–7. My analysis does not make any assumption about the controversial matter of whether one or both of the Rosenbergs were spies. Two former KGB men have claimed that the Rosenbergs did spy for the Soviet Union, but not on the atomic bomb. Natalia Gevorkian, "Razvedchiki byvshimi ne byvaiut," *Moskovskie novosti*, 1993, no. 1, p. 4. Another American couple, Morris and Leontina Cohen, was deeply involved in atomic espionage, according to KGB sources. (See the articles by V. Chikov in *Armiia*, Nos 18, 19, 20, 1991.) The Cohens vanished in 1950 after Klaus Fuchs' arrest. They reappeared in Britain, where they were convicted of spying in 1961; in Britain they used the names Helen and Peter Kroger.

82. "U istokov," pp. 123–4.

83. *Ibid.*

84. Michael Dobbs, "How Soviets Stole U.S. Atom Secrets," *Washington Post*, October 4, 1992, p. A1.

85. According to Iatskov, another scientist at

Los Alamos provided secret information to the Soviet Union. This man, who has been described as having the code name "Perseus," has not been identified. *Ibid.* Kurchatov's memoranda suggest, however, that whatever information Perseus provided, it was not as valuable as that supplied by Fuchs.

86. Jiri Kasparek, "Soviet Russia and Czechoslovakia's Uranium," *The Russian Review*, 1952, no. 2, pp. 98–9. Letter from Eugen Loebl to the author, July 18, 1982. In 1947 Loebl headed a Czechoslovak trade delegation that tried, unsuccessfully, to get the Soviet Union to pay world prices for Czechoslovak uranium.

87. Norman Naimark, "The Soviet Occupation of Germany, 1945–1949, manuscript, 1993. Demitri B. Shimkin, Minerals: A Key to Soviet Power," Cambridge, Mass.: Harvard University Press, 1953, p. 148. The figures for prewar production do not always agree. See *Minerals Yearbook 1946*, Washington, DC: US Bureau of Mines, p. 1228, which gives a lower figure for prewar production.

88. This was noted in Merkulov's letter to Beria of February 28, 1945. "U istokov," p. 122.

89. Kasparek, *loc.cit.*, p. 98. See also Edward Taborsky, *President Edvard Beneš*, Stanford: Hoover Institution Press, 1981, p. 145, and Eugen Loebl, *My Mind On Trial*, New York: Harcourt Brace Jovanovich, 1976, p. 70.

90. Kasparek, *loc.cit.*, pp. 102–3. Loebl, *op.cit.*, p. 73.

91. See Samuel A. Goudsmit, *Alsos*, New York: Henry Schuman, 1947.

92. See Naimark, *op. cit.*

93. Andreas Heinemann-Grüder, "Die Sowjetische Atombombe," Berlin: Arbeitspapiere der Berghof-Stiftung für Konfliktforschung, 1990, pp. 22–3.

94. *Bol'shaia Sovetskaia Entsiklopediia*, 3rd edn, Vol. 9, Moscow: Sovetskaia Entsiklopediia, 1972, p. 326.

95. Andrei Sakharov, *Memoirs*, New York: Alfred A. Knopf, 1990, p. 136. In a volume on repressed science in the Soviet Union, V.R. Polishchuk writes that Zaveniagin "stood out sharply among the other leaders of that department [the NKVD] by virtue both of his level of education and his ability to value the people entrusted to him, if only pragmatically, as useful workers." Polishchuk, "Sud'ba professora I.Ia. Bashilova," in M.G. Iaroshevskii (ed.), *Repressirovannaia nauka*, Leningrad: Nauka, 1991, p. 361.

96. Interview with Flerov, October 18, 1989.

97. Interview with Khariton, July 16, 1992.

98. The house was bugged; the transcripts have been published in *Operation Epsilon: The Farm Hall Transcripts*, Berkeley: The University of California Press, 1993.

99. Goudsmit, *op.cit.*, pp. 164–5.

100. CIA, *German Scientists at Sukhumi, USSR*, OSI/SR-2/49, published October 31, 1949 *passim*. HSTL, PSF.

101. Nikolaus Riehl, "10 Jahre im goldenen Käfig: Erlebnisse beim Aufbau der Sowjetischen Uran-Industrie," unpublished manuscript. I am grateful to Ulrich Albrecht for making this available to me. A. Neibauer, "Nemetskii khimik i sovetskii atomnyi proekt posle 1945 g: Maks Vol'mer," *Voprosy istorii estestvoznaniia i tekhniki*, 1991, no. 4, p. 24.

102. Niels Bohr Library, American Institute of Physics, New York, Goudsmit Papers, Box 1, folder 25.

103. *Ibid.* Paul Rosbaud, Memorandum of September 1945, p. 4. Hertz told Hans Bethe after the war that the reason he had chosen to go to the Soviet Union was that there were so many knowledgeable scientists in the United States that his abilities would be better appreciated by the Soviet authorities. Interview with Bethe, April 20, 1979.

104. *Ibid.*, p. 1.

105. Heinz Barwich, *Das Rote Atom*, Munich and Berne: Scherz Verlag, 1967, p. 21; Max Steenbeck, *Impulse und Wirkungen*, Berlin: Verlag der Nation, 1977, pp. 163–79.

106. CIA, *German Scientists*, p. 3.

107. Rosbaud, *loc.cit.*, pp. 5–6.

108. Interview with Khariton, July 16, 1992.

109. This estimate may of course be too high. CIA, Joint Atomic Energy Intelligence Committee, *Status of the Soviet Atomic Energy Program, 4 July 1950*, CIA/SCI–2/50, p. 1. HSTL, PSF.

110. Leslie R. Groves, *Now It Can Be Told*, New York: Harper, 1962, pp. 230–1.

111. Riehl, *loc.cit.*, pp. 8–9.

112. Groves, *op.cit.*, pp. 236–9.

113. Naimark, *op. cit.* See also Nikolai Grishin, "The Saxony Uranium Mining Company (Vismut')," in Robert Slusser (ed.), *Soviet Economic Policy in Postwar Germany*, New York: Research Program on the USSR, 1953, pp. 127–55.

114. V.I. Vernadskii, "Ob organizatsii nauchnoi raboty," *Priroda*, 1975, no. 4, p. 36.

115. *Ibid.*

116. Quoted by Kendall E. Bailes, in his *Science and Russian Culture in an Age of Revolutions*, Bloomington: Indiana University Press, 1990, p. 177.

117. I.I. Mochalov, *Vladimir Ivanovich Vernadskii*, Moscow: Nauka, 1982, p. 397.

118. E.L. Feinberg, "Epokha i lichnost'," in his *Vospominaniia o I.E. Tamme*, Moscow: Nauka, 1986, p. 225.

119. Sakharov, *op.cit.*, pp. 128–9.

120. Kapitsa to Bohr, October 28, 1943, US National Archives, RGFF, MED TS folder 11; on the context see Gowing, *op.cit.*, p. 350.

121. P.L. Kapitsa, *Pis'ma o nauke*, Moscow: Moskovskii rabochii, 1989, p. 207.

122. *Third Anti-Fascist Meeting of Soviet Scientists, Moscow, June 1944*, Moscow: Foreign Languages Publishing House, 1944, pp. 17–18.

123. *Ibid.*, p. 21.

124. *Ibid.*, p. 22.

125. The Council of People's Commissars issued a decree on January 21, 1945 on measures to mark the 220th anniversary of the Academy of Sciences. RTsKhIDNI, f. 17, op. 125, ed. khr. 359, p. 5.

126. *Ibid.*, p. 65.

127. Quoted by Alexander Vucinich, *Empire of Knowledge*, Berkeley: University of California Press, 1984, p. 206. For a Western description of the congress see Eric Ashby, *Scientist in Russia*, Harmondsworth: Penguin Books, 1947, pp. 126–45.

128. Ashby, *op.cit.*, pp. 136–7. Kapitsa's speech was not published in the Academy's journal *Vestnik Akademii Nauk*.

129. A physicist at the State Optical Institute.

130. RTsKhIDNI, f. 17, op. 125, ed. khr. 362.

131. Interviews with Golovin, October 19, 1992 and Khariton, July 16, 1992.

132. In the spring of 1945 Kurchatov instructed Vladimir Merkin to start work on the design of a pile that would produce plutonium in quantities large enough for a bomb. Merkin, *loc.cit.*, pp. 267–9; M.G. Pervukhin, "U istokov uranovoi epopei," *Tekhnika-molodezhi*, 1975, no. 7, p. 25. (This is a continuation of the article with same title cited earlier.) But to build such a pile large quantities of uranium would be needed, as well as a major construction effort.

133. Pervukhin, "Pervye gody," p. 64.

134. *Ibid.*

135. Iatskov, "Atom i razvedka," in "U istokov," p. 105.

136. Kurchatov was informed on July 2 that the test would take place on or about July 10. "U istokov," p. 134.

6. Hiroshima

1. For a detailed description of the test see Richard Rhodes, *The Making of the Atomic Bomb*, New York: Simon and Schuster, 1986, pp. 617–78.

2. Richard G. Hewlett and Oscar E. Anderson Jr., *The New World: A History of the United States Atomic Energy Commission, Vol. 1, 1939–1946*, Berkeley: University of California Press, 1990, p. 389; Martin Sherwin, *A World Destroyed*, New York: Vintage Books, 1977, contains the report, pp. 308–14.

3. Henry L. Stimson, *Diary*, July 21, 1945. Deposited at Yale University.

4. Henry L. Stimson and McGeorge Bundy, *On Active Service in Peace and War*, New York: Harper and Brothers, 1948, p. 637.

5. Truman, *Memoirs. Vol. 1: 1945, Year of Decisions*, New York: Signet Books, 1965, p. 458.

6. *Ibid.*

7. Anthony Eden, *The Reckoning*, Boston: Houghton Mifflin, 1965, p. 635.

8. V.G. Trukhanovskii, *Angliiskoe iadernoe oruzhie*, Moscow: Mezhdunarodnye otnosheniia, 1985, p. 23. Andrei Gromyko, who was nearby when Truman made his remark to Stalin, writes in his memoirs that Truman said that the United States intended to use the new weapon against Japan, and that Stalin said "Thank you for the information." A.A. Gromyko, *Pamiatnoe*, Book I, 2nd edn, Moscow: Politizdat, 1990, p. 272. None of the American or British participants in the conference has suggested that Truman told Stalin about his intention to use the bomb in Japan.

9. Herbert Feis, *The Atomic Bomb and the End of World War II*, Princeton: Princeton University Press, 1971, p. 102; John Wheeler-Bennett and Anthony Nicholls, *The Semblance of Peace*, London: Macmillan, 1972, p. 372.

10. M.G. Pervukhin, "U istokov uranovoi epopei," *Tekhnika – molodezhi*, 1975, no. 7, p. 24.

11. There is some evidence that Soviet intelligence learned of the test within a day or two of its taking place. I.N. Golovin, in an interview. See Oleg Moroz, "Nikogda ne dolzhno byt' primeneno!," *Literaturnaia gazeta*, July 25, 1984, p. 10.

12. G.K. Zhukov, *Vospominaniia i razmyshleniia, tom 3*, 10th edn, Moscow: Novosti, 1990, p. 334.

13. *Sto sorok besed s Molotovym: iz dnevnika F. Chueva*, Moscow: Terra, 1991, p. 81.

14. Gromyko, *op.cit.*, p. 276; V.V. Goncharov, *Pervye (osnovnie) etapy resheniia atomnoi problemy v SSSR*, Moscow: Kurchatov Insti-

tute of Atomic Energy, 1990, p. 4 suggests that this may be wrong.

15. This account is based on Margaret Gowing, *Britain and Atomic Energy, 1939–1945*, London: Macmillan, 1964, pp. 346–66; and on Aage Bohr, "The War Years and the Prospects Raised by the Atomic Weapons," in S. Rozental (ed.), *Niels Bohr*, Amsterdam: North-Holland, 1967, pp. 191–214.

16. Bohr's views are set out in memoranda of July 3, 1944 and March 24, 1945. Excerpts from these are reproduced in his Open Letter to the United Nations, which he wrote in 1950. See Rozental, *op.cit.*, pp. 342–6.

17. V.Ia. Frenkel', "Nil's Bor i sovetskie fiziki," in *Nil's Bor i nauka xx veka*, Kiev: Naukova dumka, 1988, pp. 16–27.

18. Gowing, *op.cit.*, p. 350; Rhodes, *op.cit.*, p. 529.

19. Among them Sir John Anderson, the minister responsible for the British nuclear effort, Lord Cherwell, Churchill's science adviser, and Supreme Court Justice Felix Frankfurter, a close friend of Roosevelt's. Gowing, *op.cit.*, pp. 354–8.

20. This is based on an account by R.V. Jones, quoted in Rhodes, *op.cit.*, p. 530.

21. Gowing, *op.cit.*, pp. 357–8.

22. See his memorandum of July 3, 1944, in Rozental, *op.cit.*, p. 343.

23. Gowing, *op.cit.*, p. 447.

24. Hewlett and Anderson Jr., *op.cit.*, pp. 329–30; Sherwin, *op.cit.*, pp. 121–8; the memorandum may be found *ibid.*, pp. 286–8. Conant had given thought since May to the issue of international control of atomic energy, and had written a memorandum on May 4, 1944 on this question.

25. Sherwin, *op.cit.*, pp. 129–34; Hewlett and Anderson, *op.cit.*, pp. 334–5.

26. Stimson and Bundy, *op.cit.*, pp. 615–16.

27. Barton J. Bernstein, "Roosevelt, Truman, and the Atomic Bomb, 1941–1945, A Reinterpretation," *Political Science Quarterly*, 1975, no. 1, pp. 34ff. is particularly helpful on this transition.

28. Truman, *op.cit.*, p. 104.

29. *Ibid.*

30. Hewlett and Anderson, *op.cit.*, pp. 344–5; Sherwin, *op.cit.*, pp. 167–70.

31. Gowing, *op.cit.*, p. 447.

32. On the assumptions which underpinned the atomic policy that Truman inherited see Gowing, *op.cit.*, pp. 367–8; Sherwin, *op.cit.*, pp. 143–6; Bernstein, *loc.cit.*, pp. 34–6.

33. Hewlett and Anderson, *op.cit.*, pp. 356–8. The notes of the meeting are in Sherwin, *op.cit.*, pp. 295–304; the quotations are taken from p. 302.

34. On the Franck Report see Alice Kimball Smith, *A Peril and a Hope. The Scientists' Movement in America, 1945–47*, Chicago and London: University of Chicago Press, 1965, pp. 41–52; the text of the report is given on pp. 560–72.

35. Hewlett and Anderson, *op.cit.*, pp. 365–9. The recommendations of the science panel are given in Sherwin, *op.cit.*, pp. 304–5; the quotation comes from p. 305.

36. Hewlett and Anderson, *op.cit.*, p. 369.

37. *Ibid.*, p. 353; the text of the memorandum may be found in Sherwin, *op.cit.*, pp. 286–8.

38. Hewlett and Anderson, *op.cit.*, pp. 354, 359–60.

39. James F. Byrnes, *Speaking Frankly*, New York and London: Harper and Brothers, 1947, pp. 260–61.

40. Sherwin, *op.cit.*, p. 300; Hewlett and Anderson, *op.cit.*, p. 357.

41. See Sherwin, *op.cit.*, p. 301.

42. Hewlett and Anderson, *op.cit.*, p. 360; Stimson, *Diary*, June 6, 1945.

43. Bernstein, *loc.cit.*, p. 40. Hewlett and Anderson, *op.cit.*, p. 369.

44. Bernstein, *loc.cit.*, pp. 36–7.

45. Stimson, *Diary*, May 14.and 15, 1945.

46. *Ibid.*; Bernstein, *loc.cit.*, pp. 41–2.

47. Wheeler-Bennett and Nicholls, *op.cit.*, pp. 344–8.

48. *Ibid.*, pp. 348–52; V.L. Israelian, *Diplomatiia v gody voiny, 1941–1945*, Moscow: Mezhdunarodnye otnosheniia, 1985, pp. 354–8.

49. Quoted by Wheeler-Bennett and Nicholls, *op.cit.*, p. 349. See also John Lewis Gaddis, *The United States and the Origins of the Cold War, 1941–1947*, New York: Columbia University Press, 1972, pp. 78–80.

50. Feis, *op.cit.*, p. 7.

51. *Istoriia vtoroi mirovoi voiny*, Vol. 11, Moscow: Voenizdat, 1980, p. 187.

52. S.P. Ivanov, "Iz opyta podgotovki i provedeniia Man'chzhurskoi operatsii 1945 goda," *Voennaia mysl'*, 1990, no. 8, pp. 42–3; M.V. Zakharov, *Finale*, Moscow: Progress Publishers, 1972, pp. 54–5.

53. Israelian, *op.cit.*, p. 412.

54. N.V. Eronin, "O strategicheskoi peregruppirovke sovetskikh vooruzhennykh sil na dal'nevostochnyi teatr voennykh deistvii letom 1945 g." and S.T. Mazhorov, "Nekotorye voprosy, sviazennye s razgromom militaristskoi Iaponii v 1945 g.," in *Pobeda SSSR v voine s militaristskoi Iaponiei i poslevoennoe razvitie vostochnoi i iugo-vostochnoi Azii*, Moscow: Nauka, 1977, pp. 44–7, p. 206.

55. *Istoriia*, p. 193.

56. Boris N. Slavinsky, "The Soviet Occupation of the Kurile Islands and the Plans for the Capture of Northern Hokkaido," *Japan Forum*, April 1993, pp. 97–8.

57. *Ibid.*, p. 199; Zakharov, *op.cit.*, pp. 89, 95. A report by Marshal Malinovskii (prepared on Stalin's instruction) on June 18 proposed August 20–25 for the start of the offensive. Col.-Gen. S. Shtemenko, "Iz istorii razgroma Kvantunskoi armii," *Voenno-istoricheskii zhurnal*, 1967, no. 4, pp. 65–6.

58. W.A. Harriman and E. Abel, *Special Envoy to Churchill and Stalin, 1941–1946*, New York: Random House, 1975, p. 471.

59. Hoover Institution Archive, Victor Hoo Papers, Box 2, File "Sino-Soviet Relations, 1945–46," p. 24. These are notes taken at the talks in July and August 1945.

60. *Ibid.*, pp. 2–5.

61. *Ibid.*, p. 2.

62. *Ibid.*, p. 6.

63. *Ibid.*, p. 36.

64. Harriman and Abel, *op.cit.*, p. 483. For a Soviet analysis of the talks see A.M. Ledovskii, *Kitaiskaia politika SShA i sovetskaia diplomatiia, 1942–1954*, Moscow: Nauka, 1985, pp. 90–108.

65. Bernstein, *loc.cit.*, pp. 44–6.

66. Byrnes, *op.cit.*, p. 205.

67. John Ehrman, *Grand Strategy, Vol. 6: History of the Second World War, UK Military Series*, London: Her Majesty's Stationery Office, 1956, p. 292.

68. *Biulleten' Biuro informatsii TsK VKP(b): Voprosy vneshnei politiki*, 1945, no. 13, July 1, pp. 1–6. RTsKhIDNI f. 17, op. 128, t. 1, d. 50.

69. N.S. Khrushchev, *Khrushchev Remembers: The Glasnost Tapes*, Boston: Little Brown, 1990, p. 81.

70. "Za kulisami tikhookeanskoi bitvy (iapono-sovetskie kontakty v 1945 g.)," *Vestnik Ministerstva Inostrannykh Del SSSR*, October 15, 1990, no. 19 (77), p. 53. This issue contains Soviet documents relating to the Japanese approaches to the Soviet Union.

71. *Ibid.*, p. 54; Robert J.C. Butow, *Japan's Decision to Surrender*, Stanford: Stanford University Press, 1954, pp. 112–26; Israelian, *op.cit.*, p. 415.

72. Feis, *op.cit.*, p. 80.

73. A.M. Vasilevskii, *Delo vsei zhizni*, Moscow: Politizdat, 1974, p. 513. Vasilevskii writes that Stalin could not have known of the Alamogordo test when he telephoned, and that the call must have been prompted by general military-political considerations.

74. *Sovetskii Soiuz na mezhdunarodnykh konferentsiiakh perioda velikoi otechestvennoi voiny 1941–1945 gg. Tom VI. Berlinskaia (Potsdamskaia) konferentsiia*, Moscow: Politizdat, 1980, p. 43. Truman noted in his Potsdam Diary for July 17 that Stalin had said August 15. HSTL, PSF. On July 24 General A.I. Antonov, the Chief of the General Staff, assured the Allied Chiefs of Staff that the Soviet Union would be ready to start operations in the latter half of August, though the exact date would depend on completion of the negotiations with the Chinese. See Truman, *op.cit.*, p. 422. This is slightly different from what Stalin had told Truman.

75. Butow, *op.cit.*, p. 128; Feis, *op.cit.*, p. 104; "Za kulisami," pp. 54, 55.

76. Shtemenko, *The Soviet General Staff at War, 1941–1945*, Book I, Moscow: Progress Publishers, 1985, p. 431.

77. *Ibid.*

78. Feis, *op.cit.*, pp. 105–7.

79. *Ibid.*, p. 106; Israelian, *op.cit.*, p. 439.

80. Butow, *op.cit.*, p. 148.

81. Stimson and Bundy, *op.cit.*, p. 625.

82. Rhodes, *op.cit.*, p. 734.

83. "Zaiavlenie Trumena o novoi atomnoi bombe," *Izvestiia*, August 7, and *Pravda*, August 8, 1945, on p. 4 in each. The yield at the time was thought to be about 20 kilotons, but was later recalculated at about 13 kilotons.

84. Alexander Werth, *Russia at War, 1941–1945*, London: Pan Books, 1964, p. 925.

85. Svetlana Alliluyeva, *20 Letters to a Friend*, Harmondsworth: Penguin Books, 1968, p. 164.

86. "Za kulisami," p. 55.

87. Shtemenko, *op.cit.*, pp. 435–8.

88. See, for example, the discussion in S.P. Ivanov (ed.), *Nachal'nyi period voiny*, Moscow: Voenizdat, 1974, pp. 281–301.

89. Cable from Kennan to Washington, DC, August 8, 1945, Library of Congress, Harriman Papers, Box 181.

90. *Ibid.*

91. Harriman and Abel, *op.cit.*, p. 491.

92. Werth, *op.cit.*, p. 926, gives the date of the meeting as August 7, but this seems too soon after Hiroshima. Soviet sources put it in the middle of August. See, for example, A. Lavrent'ieva in "Stroiteli novogo mira," *V mire knig*, 1970, no. 9, p. 4. It was certainly before August 20.

93. "Delo Beriia," *Izvestiia Tsk KPSS*, 1991, no. 1, p. 145.

94. *The Report of the Royal Commission to investigate the facts relating to and the circumstances*

surrounding the communication, by public officials and other persons in positions of trust of
secret and confidential information to agents of a
foreign power, Ottawa: Controller of Stationery, June 1946, p. 452. Soviet intelligence
operations were hampered by the defection
of Igor Gouzenko, a cipher clerk at the
Embassy in Ottawa, in September 1945.
The materials Gouzenko gave the Canadian
government showed that the Soviet Union
was engaged in atomic espionage.

95. M.I. Ivanov, Iaponiia v gody voiny. Zapiski
ochevidtsa, Moscow: Nauka, 1978, pp. 228–
34.

96. Andreas Heinemann-Grüder, Die sowjetische
Atombombe, Berlin: Berghof-Stiftung für
Konfliktforschung, Arbeitspapiere no. 40,
1990, p. 40.

97. F.I. Vol'fson, N.S. Zontov, and G.R.
Shushaniia, Petr Iakovlevich Antropov,
Moscow: Nauka, 1985, p. 30.

98. This material is published in "The Hiroshima and Nagasaki Tragedy in Documents," International Affairs, 1990, no. 8, pp.
122–38.

99. Butow, op.cit., p. 152.

100. Ibid., p. 158.

101. The Committee for the Compilation of
Materials on Damage Caused by the Atomic
Bombs in Hiroshima and Nagasaki, Hiro-
shima and Nagasaki: The Physical, Medical,
and Social Effects of the Atomic Bombings, New
York: Basic Books, 1981, p. 114.

102. Butow, op.cit., pp. 166–209.

103. "Obrashchenie predsedatelia soveta
narodnykh komissarov SSSR k narodu,"
September 2, 1945, in USSR Ministry of
Foreign Affairs, Sovetsko-amerikanskie
otnosheniia vo vremiia Velikoi Otechestvennoi
voiny 1941–1945, Tom 2, Moscow: Politizdat,
1984, pp. 497–8.

104. Perepiska predsedatelia Soveta Ministrov SSSR
s Prezidentami SShA i Prem'er-ministrami
Velikobritanii vo vremia velikoi otechestvennoi
voiny 1941–1945.gg., Vol. 2, Moscow:
Politizdat, 1986, pp. 285–7; Herbert Feis,
Contest over Japan, New York: Norton,
1967, pp. 19–20.

105. Boris Slavinskii, "Sovetskii desant na
Khokkaido i Iuzhnye Kurily," Izvestiia,
May 12, 1992, p. 6. For a fuller version see
Slavinsky, loc.cit., pp. 95–114. See also N.G.
Kuznetsov, Kursom k pobede, 3rd edn,
Moscow: Voenizdat, 1989, p. 484. According to Slavinsky (loc.cit., p. 98), the idea of
occupying northern Hokkaido had been
discussed at the Politburo meeting on June
26–27. Khrushchev and Marshal Meretskov
had supported the idea. Voznesenskii,

Molotov, and Zhukov had opposed it.
Molotov had said that it would be seen by
the Allies as a flagrant violation of the Yalta
Agreement.

106. According to Volkogonov, Stalin gave the
order to prepare to embark the 87th infantry
corps for a landing on Hokkaido on August
23. But the order to embark did not come
on August 25 when southern Sakhalin was
liberated. Finally he gave the order not to
land on Hokkaido. General S.P. Ivanov,
Chief of Staff of Soviet forces in the Far
East, passed on the order quoted above.
Dmitrii Volkogonov, Triumf i tragediia,
Book II, 2nd edn, Moscow: Novosti, 1990,
p. 410.

107. A.P. Aleksandrov, "Kak delali bombu,"
Izvestiia, July 22, 1988, p. 3.

108. Sherwin, op.cit., pp. 165–238. For the most
authoritative discussion of the decision, see
Bernstein, loc.cit. This seems to be a more
persuasive argument than that of Gar
Alperovitz in his Atomic Diplomacy: Hiroshima and Potsdam, 2nd edn, New York:
Penguin Books, 1985. Alperovitz's book is
important in pointing to the connection
between the bomb and American policy
towards the Soviet Union.

109. For the text of the treaty, see J.A.S.
Grenville, The Major International Treaties,
1914–1973, London: Methuen 1974, p. 237.
See also Hoo Papers, loc.cit.

110. Lavrent'ieva, loc.cit., p. 4.

111. I.N. Golovin, I.V. Kurchatov, 3rd edn,
Moscow: Atomizdat, 1978, p. 71.

112. Gromyko, op.cit., p. 276.

7. The Post-Hiroshima Project

1. S. Mikoian, "Sluga," Komsomol'skaia pravda,
February 21, 1988, p. 4. This article is based
on evidence from Anastas Mikoian, Beria's
colleague in the Soviet leadership.

2. Svetlana Alliluyeva, 20 Letters to A Friend,
Harmondsworth: Penguin Books, 1968,
esp. pp. 75, 122.

3. V.N. Novikov, "Shefstvo Berii," in Beriia:
konets kar'ery, Moscow: Politizdat, 1991,
p. 237.

4. Sto sorok besed s Molotovym: iz dnevnika F.
Chueva, Moscow: Terra, 1991, p. 255.

5. Mikoian, loc.cit.

6. See p. 19.

7. "Delo Beriia . . . ," Izvestiia TsK KPSS,
1991, no. 1, p. 145.

8. I.N. Golovin, "The First Steps in the
Atomic Problem in the USSR." Paper pre-
sented at Conference "Fifty Years with
Nuclear Fission," Washington, DC, April

1989, p. 12.

9. Dmitrii Volkogonov, *Triumf i tragediia*, Book II, 2nd edn, Moscow: Novosti, 1990, p. 484.

10. Golovin, "First Steps," p. 11; Interview with I.N. Golovin, October 21, 1990.

11. Golovin, "Rossiiskii nauchnyi tsentr – Kurchatovskii institut," unpublished paper, pp. 10–11.

12. Interviews with Golovin, October 19, 1992, and Iu.B. Khariton, July 16, 1992.

13. Towards the end of 1945 Beria suggested to Kurchatov and Kikoin that Laboratory No. 2 be transferred to the NKVD, and all the scientists put in uniform. It was Kikoin who had the presence of mind to reply that this was a bad idea, because it would be easier to recruit scientists for an Academy institution than for the NKVD. Beria accepted this argument, and dropped the matter. Interview with Golovin, October 21, 1990.

14. "Kremlevskie palachi i nyne sredi nas," *Trud*, July 25, 1992, p. 3. This article quotes a letter from Sudoplatov to the Central Committee in 1966 seeking rehabilitation. On Sudoplatov and Eitingon see Christopher Andrew and Oleg Gordievsky, *KGB: The Inside Story*, New York: Harper Collins, 1990, pp. 168–71, 309. The NKGB became the MGB in March 1946; in that month all the People's Commissariats were renamed ministries.

15. "Kremlevskie palachi," p. 3.

16. Interview of Ia.P. Terletskii with A.V. Andreev, May 19, 1993.

17. *Bol'shaia Sovetskaia Entsiklopediia*, 3rd edn, Vol. 4, Moscow: Sovetskaia Entsiklopediia, 1971, p. 291. Vannikov's memoirs about the prewar years have been published in *Znamia*, 1988, nos 1 and 2.

18. B.L. Vannikov, "Zapiski narkoma," *Znamia*, 1988, no. 1, p. 133; Novikov, *loc.cit.*, p. 228.

19. Interview with Khariton, July 16, 1992.

20. V.S. Emel'ianov, *S chego nachinalos'*, Moscow: Sovetskaia Rossiia, 1979, p. 153.

21. *Ibid.*, p. 154.

22. *Ibid.*, p. 158.

23. *Ibid.*, p. 196.

24. *Ibid.*, p. 198.

25. Golovin, "Rossiiskii nauchnyi tsentr," p. 9.

26. "U istokov sovetskogo atomnogo proekta: rol' razvedki," *Voprosy istorii estestvoznaniia i tekhniki*, 1992, no. 3, pp. 126–9.

27. Interview with Khariton, July 16, 1992.

28. Golovin, "Rossiiskii nauchnyi tsentr," pp. 16–17; interview with Khariton, July 16, 1992.

29. P.L. Kapitsa, *Pis'ma o nauke*, Moscow:

Moskovskii rabochii, 1989, pp. 232–5. All quotations in the next two paragraphs are taken from this source.

30. On Kapitsa's work in this area, see J.W. Boag, P.E. Rubinin, and D. Shoenberg (eds), *Kapitza in Cambridge and Moscow*, Amsterdam: North-Holland, 1990, pp. 65–6.

31. Kapitsa, *op.cit.*, pp. 237–47.

32. *Ibid.*, p. 239.

33. *Ibid.*, p. 242.

34. *Ibid.*, p. 243.

35. *Ibid.*

36. *Ibid.*, p. 244.

37. *Ibid.*, p. 245.

38. Interview with Khariton, March 12, 1988.

39. Interview with A.D. Sakharov, June 15, 1987.

40. Kapitsa, *op.cit.*, pp. 246–7.

41. *Ibid.*, p. 247.

42. P.L. Kapitsa, "Pis'mo Molotovu," *Vestnik Ministerstva Inostrannykh Del SSSR*, 1990, no. 10, p. 58.

43. Kapitsa reiterated these objections in a letter to Khrushchev of September 22, 1955, Kapitsa, *op.cit.*, pp. 312–13.

44. See pp. 113–14.

45. Kapitsa, *op.cit.*, p. 236.

46. Bohr, "Energy from the Atom," *The Times*, August 11, 1945, p. 5; and his "A Challenge to Civilization," *Science*, October 12, 1945, pp. 363–4.

47. Bohr Correspondence, Niels Bohr Library, American Institute of Physics, New York.

48. Thomas Powers, *Heisenberg's War: The Secret History of the German Bomb*, New York: Alfred A. Knopf, 1993, p. 474. Statement by Aage Bohr Niels's son, April 27, 1994. Aage Bohr took part in the conversations with Terletskii.

49. Terletskii, interview with A.V. Andreev, May 19, 1993.

50. Kapitsa, *loc.cit.*, p. 61. A photocopy of Kapitsa's letter is reproduced on pp. 61–3.

51. *Ibid.*, p. 61.

52. *Ibid.*

53. *Ibid.*, pp. 58–9.

54. Kapitsa, *op.cit.*, pp. 257–8.

55. *Ibid.*

56. *Ibid.*, pp. 271–2.

57. *Istoriia kommunisticheskoi partii sovetskogo soiuza*, Vol. 5, Book II, Moscow: Politizdat, 1980, pp. 129–30.

58. Volkogonov, *op.cit.*, p. 418; G.F. Krivosheev (ed.), *Grif sekretnosti sniat*, Moscow: Voenizdat, 1993, p. 128.

59. V.I. Anufriev, *V pervuiu poslevoennuiu . . .*, Moscow: Mysl', 1983, pp. 9–10; Alec Nove, *An Economic History of the USSR*,

Harmondsworth: Penguin Books, 1972, pp. 287–8.

60. V.M. Molotov, "Doklad V.M. Molotova na torzhestvennom zasedanii moskovskogo soveta 6-go noiabria 1945 g.," *Pravda*, November 7, 1945, p. 1.

61. V.S. Lel'chuk, *Nauchno-tekhnicheskaia revoliutsiia i promyshlennoe razvitie SSSR*, Moscow: Nauka, 1987, p. 83.

62. A.G. Zverev, *Zapiski ministra*, Moscow: Politizdat, 1973, p. 227.

63. On the early history of Soviet radar see M.M. Lobanov, *Razvitie sovetskoi radiolokatsionnoi tekhniki*, Moscow: Voenizdat, 1982, pp. 16, 26, 61–2. See also John Erickson, "Radio-location and the Air Defense Problem: the Design and Development of Soviet Radar, 1934–40," *Science Studies*, 1972, no. 2, pp. 241–63.

64. Steven J. Zaloga, *Soviet Air Defence Missiles*, Coulsden: Jane's Information Group, 1989, pp. 3–7.

65. A.I. Shakhurin, *Kryl'ia pobedy*, 3rd edn, Moscow: Politizdat, 1990, p. 250.

66. Irina Radunskaia, *Aksel' Berg – chelovek xx veka*, Moscow: Molodaia gvardiia, 1971, p. 226; A. Fedoseev, *Zapadnia*, Frankfurt am Main: Possev-Verlag, 1976, pp. 105–6; Lobanov, *op.cit.*, pp. 162–5.

67. Lobanov, *op.cit.*, p. 158.

68. Central Intelligence Group, *Soviet Capabilities for the Development and Production of Certain Types of Weapons and Equipment*, ORE 3/1, October 31, 1946, p. 2. HSTL, PSF.

69. *Kosmonavtika*, Moscow: Sovetskaia Entsiklopediia, 1985, pp. 332–3.

70. V.P. Glushko, *Rocket-Engines GDL-OKB*, Moscow: Novosti, 1975, p. 11.

71. G.A. Ozerov, *Tupolevskaia sharaga*, 2nd edn, Frankfurt am Main: Possev-Verlag, 1973, pp. 34–5.

72. V.P. Glushko, *Razvitie raketostroeniia i kosmonavtiki v SSSR*, Moscow: Mashinostroenie, 1987, p. 30; V.S. Lel'chuk, *Nauchno-tekhnicheskaia revoliutsiia i promyshlennoe razvitie SSSR*, Moscow: Nauka, 1987, p. 80.

73. Ozerov, *op.cit.*, p. 34.

74. *Kosmonavtika*, pp. 157–8.

75. Frederick I. Ordway III and Mitchell R. Sharpe, *The Rocket Team*, New York: Thomas Y. Crowell, 1979, pp. 180, 195.

76. B.V. Raushenbakh (ed.), *Iz istorii sovetskoi kosmonavtiki*, Moscow: Nauka, 1983, p. 225.

77. Mikhail Arlazorov, *Doroga na kosmodrom*, 2nd edn, Moscow: Politizdat, 1984, p. 100. On July 13, 1944 Churchill wrote to Stalin asking for information from the missile testing ground at Debice in Poland, which would soon fall into the hands of the Red Army. Churchill believed that even though the Germans would remove or destroy their equipment, much might be learned by examining the site. He asked Stalin to give orders that the equipment and machinery at Debice be preserved, and that British specialists be allowed to examine them. Stalin asked Churchill for the location of Debice, and promised to do all he could to meet Churchill's request. For this exchange see *Perepiska predsedatelia soveta ministrov SSSR s prezidentami SShA i prem'er-ministrami Velikobritanii vo vremia velikoi otechestvennoi voiny 1941–1945 gg.*, Vol. 1, Moscow: Politizdat, 1986, pp. 276–81. Stalin sent a group of Soviet specialists to Debice. There they collected what they could, including a V-2 combustion chamber, and parts of the fuel tanks, and brought them back to the Soviet Union where they were studied and analyzed. Only then were British specialists taken to Debice, where they found more rocket parts, in spite of the fact that the area had already been combed by Soviet engineers. These finds too were studied in Moscow, before being sent to Britain. B. Konovalov, "U sovetskikh raketnykh triumfov bylo nemetskoe nachalo," *Izvestiia*, March 4, 1992, p. 3. On the British mission see Ordway and Sharpe, *op.cit.*, pp. 153–9.

78. Konovalov, *loc.cit.*, p. 3. This was the first of a series of articles based on the reminiscences of B. Chertok, who took part in the work of the Soviet commission in Germany. See also Raushenbakh, *op.cit.*, p. 225. For a full account of the activities of the commission see Norman Naimark, "The Soviet Occupation of Germany, 1945–1949," manuscript, 1993.

79. A.N. Ponomarev, *Sovetskie aviatsionnye konstruktory*, 3rd edn, Moscow: Voenizdat, 1990, pp. 284–8.

80. A.S. Iakovlev, *Sovetskie samolety*, Moscow: Nauka, 1979, pp. 138–9; Shakhurin, *op.cit*, pp 247–8; V.B. Shavrov, *Istoriia konstruktsii samoletov v SSSR, 1938–1950.gg.*, Moscow: Mashinostroenie, 1978, pp. 296–99, 313–14. On Shakhurin's arrest see "Delo Beriia," p. 175.

81. The quotations in the following paragraphs are drawn from Kurchatov's notes on the meeting. This document is in the archive of the Kurchatov Institute of Atomic Energy, reference N 185 of February 18, 1960. I am grateful to the Institute for permission to quote this document. It is possible that this is the same meeting referred to by

Aleksandrov; see p. 132. For references to Kurchatov's earlier meetings with Stalin see above, pp. 95, 132.

82. I.V. Stalin, "Rech' na predvybornom sobranii izbiratelei Stalinskogo izbiratel'nogo okruga goroda Moskvy, 9 February 1946," in Robert H. McNeal (ed.), *I.V. Stalin, Works, Vol. 3, 1946–1953*, Stanford: Hoover Institution, 1967, p. 19.

83. Lel'chuk, *op.cit.*, pp. 82–3; A.G. Zverev, *Gosudarstvennyi biudzhet SSSR na 1946 god*, Moscow: Gosfinizdat, 1946, p. 21.

84. Stalin, *loc.cit.*, p. 4.

85. *Ibid.*, p. 19.

86. *Ibid.*, pp. 19–20. In 1960 65 million metric tons of steel were produced, as well as 513 million metric tons of coal and 148 million metric tons of petroleum.

87. There was some disagreement among both party leaders and economic planners about the relative priority to give to heavy as opposed to light industry, but no one argued for a radical shift of priorities. See Timothy Dunmore, *The Stalinist Command Economy*, London: Macmillan, 1980, pp. 99–102; Bruce Parrott, *Politics and Technology in the Soviet Union*, Cambridge: MIT Press, 1983, pp. 82–7.

8. The Premises of Policy

1. I.V. Stalin, "Rech' na predvybornom sobranii izbiratelei Stalinskogo izbiratel'nogo okruga goroda Moskvy, February 9, 1946," in Robert H. McNeal (ed.), *I.V. Stalin, Works, Vol. 3, 1946–1953*, Stanford: Hoover Institution, 1967, p. 2.

2. V.I. Lenin, *Imperialism: the Highest Stage of Capitalism*, Moscow: Foreign Languages Publishing House, 1947.

3. Stalin, *loc.cit.*, p. 2.

4. *Ibid.*, pp. 3–4.

5. N.A. Voznesenskii, *Piatiletnyi plan vosstanovleniia i razvitiia narodnogo khoziastva SSSR na 1946–1950 gg.*, Moscow: Gospolitizdat, 1946, p. 13.

6. *Ibid.*, p. 12.

7. FRUS, *The Conferences at Cairo and Tehran*, pp. 510–11; 532; 553–4.

8. Martin Gilbert, *Winston S. Churchill. Vol. 7: Road to Victory, 1941–1945*, Boston: Houghton Mifflin, 1986, p. 995.

9. Milovan Djilas, *Conversations with Stalin*, Harmondsworth: Penguin Books, 1963, p. 91. Djilas comments that "there was something terrible in his words: a horrible war was still going on. Yet there was something impressive, too, about his realization of the paths he had to take, the inevitability that

faced the world in which he lived and the movement that he headed" (*ibid.*).

10. Hoover Institution Archive, Victor Hoo Papers, Box 2, File "Sino-Soviet Relations, 1945–46," p. 2. See also p. 49.

11. William Curti Wohlforth, *The Elusive Balance*, Ithaca and London: Cornell University Press, 1993, provides an excellent discussion of Soviet conceptions of the postwar order, on pp. 59–137.

12. S.G. Strumilin (ed.), *Ekonomicheskaia zhizn' SSSR, Kniga pervaia, 1917–1950*, 2nd edn, Moscow: Sovetskaia Entsiklopediia, 1967, pp. 378, 384, 389, 399; *Istoriia vtoroi mirovoi voiny 1939–1945*, Vol. 11, Moscow: Voenizdat, 1980, p. 348, and Vol. 12, Moscow: Voenizdat, 1982, p. 166.

13. *50 let vooruzhennykh sil SSSR*, Moscow: Voenizdat, 1968, pp. 474, 479; *Istoriia kommunisticheskoi partii Sovetskogo Soiuza*, Vol. 5, Book II, Moscow: Politizdat, 1980, p. 14; V.N. Donchenko, "Demobilizatsiia sovetskoi armii i reshenie problemy kadrov v pervye poslevoennye gody," *Istoriia SSSR*, 1970, no. 3, p. 98. The figure of 2.874 million was given by Khrushchev in 1960; no figure was given by the Soviet authorities at the time. Contemporary Western estimates put the size of the Soviet armed forces at about 4 million. See Thomas W. Wolfe, *Soviet Power and Europe, 1945–1970*, Baltimore: Johns Hopkins University Press, 1970, pp. 10–11, and Matthew Evangelista, "Stalin's Postwar Army Reappraised," *International Security*, Winter 1982–83, pp. 111–20.

14. The Soviet military budget in those years covered much the same as Western military budgets, though it does not seem to have covered all military R&D. See Frank Doe, "Understanding the Soviet View of Military Expenditures," in Joint Economic Committee, US Congress, *Soviet Military Economic Relations*, Washington, DC: US Government Printing Office, 1983, pp. 160–61. The point about price changes at the end of 1946 is made in A.G. Zverev, *Gosudarstvennyi biudzhet SSSR na 1947 god*, Moscow: Gosfinizdat, 1947, p. 15.

15. The quotation is taken from V.M. Molotov, "Speech at a Meeting of Voters of the Molotov Electoral Area, Moscow," in his *Problems of Foreign Policy*, Moscow: Foreign Languages Publishing House, 1949, p. 28. The other arguments were advanced by Molotov, "Doklad V.M. Molotova na torzhestvennom zasedanii moskovskogo Soveta 6-go noiabria 1945 g.," *Pravda*, November 7, 1945; Stalin, in his February

9, 1946 speech, *loc. cit.*; Voznesenskii, *op.cit.*, pp. 12–13; and in "Obrashchenie tsentral'nogo komiteta vsesoiuznoi kommunisticheskoi partii (bol'shevikov)," *Bol'shevik*, 1946, no. 2, esp. p. 3.

16. *Sto sorok besed s Molotovym: iz dnevnika F. Chueva*, Moscow: Terra, 1991, p. 14.

17. *Ibid.*

18. Martin Gilbert, *Winston S. Churchill. Vol. 8, Never Despair*, Boston: Houghton Mifflin, 1988, pp. 197–203.

19. Stalin, "Otvet korrespondentu *Pravdy*," in McNeal, *op.cit.*, p. 43.

20. *Ibid.*

21. Stalin, "Otvety na voprosy g-na E. Gil'mora," in McNeal, *op.cit.*, p. 4.

22. *Sto sorok besed*, p. 81.

23. "Beseda Marshala Sovetskogo Soiuza G.K. Zhukova," *Krasnaia Zvezda*, February 13, 1955, p. 2.

24. Hugh H. Clegg and Robert J. Lamphere to the director of the FBI, June 4, 1950, p. 26. This memorandum reports on the interviews Clegg and Lamphere had with Fuchs in May and June 1950. See also Robert J. Lamphere and Tom Shachtman, *The FBI–KGB War*, New York: Random House, 1986, pp. 164–6. Fuchs also provided figures for United States production of uranium-235 (about 100 kilograms a month) and of plutonium (about 20 kilograms a month); this would have allowed the United States to produce between 30 and 40 bombs a year. If the Soviet Union estimated the size of the United States stockpile on the basis of Fuchs's figures, it would have overestimated its size because the United States produced atomic bombs much more slowly than these figures imply.

25. Fuchs's statement to Michael Perrin, in a letter from J. Edgar Hoover to Admiral Souers, March 2, 1950, p. 5. HSTL, PSF.

26. FRUS 1945, v, p. 923.

27. W. Averell Harriman and Elie Abel, *Special Envoy to Churchill and Stalin, 1941–1946*, New York: Random House, 1975, p. 519.

28. FRUS 1945, ii, p. 83.

29. Robert Jervis, "The Symbolic Nature of Nuclear Politics," in his *The Meaning of the Nuclear Revolution*, Ithaca: Cornell University Press, 1989, pp. 174–225.

30. Vasilii Grossman, *Zhizn' i sud'ba*, Paris: L'Age d'Homme, 1980, p. 535.

31. Andrei Gromyko, who was at the Potsdam conference, said many years later that members of the Soviet delegation noticed a change in Truman's behavior during the conference; he began to take a more active part in the discussions, and was more willing to counter Stalin's arguments. Only later did they realize that it was the atomic bomb that had given him new confidence. "Poslednee interv'iu," *Ogonek*, 1989, no. 30, p. 7.

32. Henry L. Stimson and McGeorge Bundy, *On Active Service in Peace and War*, New York: Harper and Brothers, 1948, pp. 638–41.

33. *Ibid.*, pp. 642–6; the quotation is taken from p. 644.

34. John Lewis Gaddis, *The United States and the Origins of the Cold War, 1941–1947*, New York: Columbia University Press, 1972, pp. 264–5.

35. Stimson Diary, September 4, 1945. Deposited at Yale University.

36. Gregg Herken, *The Winning Weapon*, New York: Alfred A. Knopf, 1980, pp. 45–9.

37. Gar Alperovitz has argued that Stalin made these concessions as a result of the bombing of Hiroshima. Gar Alperovitz, *Atomic Diplomacy: Hiroshima and Potsdam*, 2nd edn, New York: Penguin Books, 1985, pp. 253–64. There is no direct evidence for this. The concession in Hungary was a minor one, and in line with Soviet policy in that country. See Charles Gati, *Hungary and the Soviet Bloc*, Durham, NC: Duke University Press, 1986, p. 21. Soviet concessions in Bulgaria were limited; the Western demand that the government in Sofia be changed was resisted by the Soviet Union. See Alperovitz, *op.cit.*, p. 263.

38. Herken, *op.cit.*, p. 48.

39. Deborah Welch Larson, *Origins of Containment*, Princeton: Princeton University Press, 1985, p. 223.

40. *Perepiska predsedatelia soveta ministrov SSSR s prezidentami SShA i prem'er-ministrami Velikobritanii vo vremia velikoi otechestvennoi voiny 1941–1945 gg.*, Vol. 2, Moscow: Politizdat, 1986, pp. 290–92.

41. Quoted by Daniel Yergin, *Shattered Peace*, Boston: Houghton Mifflin, 1977, p. 132. At another point Molotov jested, when the Western powers were reluctant to accede to the Soviet demand for the former Italian colony of Tripolitania, that "if you won't give us one of the Italian colonies, we should be quite content to have the Belgian Congo," which was a major source of uranium. See Herken, *op.cit.*, p. 50.

42. Herken, *op.cit.*, p. 53.

43. Yergin, *op.cit.*, p. 137; Larson, *op.cit.*, pp. 223–4.

44. Quoted in Alan Bullock, *Ernest Bevin. Foreign Secretary, 1945–1951*, New York: W.W. Norton, 1983, p. 137.

45. DBPO, series I, Vol. II, p. 496. This comment was contained in Halifax's quarterly report of December 4, 1945.

46. DBPO series I, Vol. II, p. 492: Roberts to Bevin, October 5, 1945.

47. Harriman and Abel, *op.cit.*, pp. 514–15, 519.

48. DBPO, series I, Vol. II, p. 568: Roberts to Bevin, October 26, 1945.

49. Molotov, "Doklad," p. 2.

50. Margaret Gowing, *Independence and Deterrence. Britain and Atomic Energy 1945–1952, Vol. 1, Policy-Making*, London: Macmillan, 1974, pp. 73–7; Richard Hewlett and Oscar Anderson, *The New World: A History of the United States Atomic Energy Commission, Vol. 1, 1939–1946*, Berkeley: University of California Press, 1990, pp. 455–69.

51. Gowing, *op.cit.*, p. 83.

52. Quoted by Scott Parrish, "A Diplomat Reports," *Cold War International History Project Bulletin*, Spring 1992, p. 21.

53. Hewlett and Anderson, *op.cit.*, pp. 469–72; Herken, *op.cit.*, pp. 66–8.

54. James F. Byrnes, *Speaking Frankly*, New York: Harper and Brothers, 1947, p. 111.

55. *Ibid.*, p. 122; James B. Conant, *My Several Lives*, New York: Harper and Row, 1970, p. 481.

56. Communiqué in FRUS 1945, ii, pp. 822–4.

57. DBPO series I, Vol. II, p. 855: record of meeting of the three foreign secretaries on December 24.

58. James B. Conant, *Moscow Diary*, December 24, 1945, Conant Papers, Harvard University.

59. *Ibid.* See also Conant, *My Several Lives*, p. 482.

60. Charles E. Bohlen, *Witness to History, 1929–1969*, New York: W.W. Norton, 1973, p. 249.

61. Zhukov reports that Stalin often found Molotov's stubbornness infuriating. In a conversation with the writer Konstanin Simonov, in *Marshal Zhukov: Polkovodets i chelovek*, Vol. 2, Moscow: Novosti, 1988, p. 201.

62. N.V. Novikov, *Vospominaniia diplomata: Zapiski 1938–1947*, Moscow: Politizdat, 1989, p. 306. A Soviet historian who worked in the Foreign Ministry at the time has called the London meeting "the first radical attempt at [atomic] pressure on the USSR." V.G. Trukhanovskii and N.K. Kapitonova, *Sovetsko–angliiskie otnosheniia 1945–1978*, Moscow: Mezhdunarodnye otnosheniia, 1979, p. 33. Trukhanovskii was in the Foreign Ministry at the time. The authors do not elaborate on their comment, except to imply that Britain and the United States wanted to end the wartime collaboration. On Soviet anxiety about atomic diplomacy see also A. Iu. Borisov, *SSSR i SShA. Soiuzniki v gody voiny 1941–1945*, Moscow: Mezhdunarodnye otnosheniia, 1983, pp. 259–60.

63. Novikov, *op.cit.*, p. 306.

64. Harry S. Truman, *Memoirs, Vol. 1. 1945: Year of Decisions*, New York: Signet Books, 1965, p. 604.

65. *Ibid.*, pp. 604–6. Whether Truman ever communicated the contents of the letter to Byrnes is not clear, but the letter does reflect his attitude at the time. See Robert J. Donovan, *Conflict and Crisis. The Presidency of Harry S. Truman*, New York: W.W. Norton, 1977, pp. 160–61.

66. Gaddis, *op.cit.*, pp. 282–90; Larson, *op.cit.*, pp. 247–9.

67. George F. Kennan, *Memoirs, 1925–1950*, Boston: Little, Brown, 1967, p. 295. The background to the telegram is described on pp. 290–95, and the text is given on pp. 547–59.

68. Novikov, *op.cit.*, pp. 314–15.

69. Larson, *op.cit.*, pp. 225–6. Bruce Robellet Kuniholm, *The Origins of the Cold War in the Near East*, Princeton: Princeton University Press, 1980, pp. 303–50.

70. McGeorge Bundy, *Danger and Survival*, New York: Random House, 1988, pp. 232–3.

71. US House of Representatives, Committee on International Relations, *Science, Technology, and American Diplomacy*, Vol. 1, Washington, DC: US Government Printing Office, 1977, p. 63. The formulation of US policy and the course of the negotiations are treated extensively in Hewlett and Anderson, *op.cit.*, pp. 531–619.

72. *A Report on the International Control of Atomic Energy*, New York: Doubleday, 1946.

73. On the writing of the report see Dean Acheson, *Present at the Creation*, New York: W.W. Norton, 1969, pp. 151–6; David E. Lilienthal, *The Journals of David E. Lilienthal, Vol. 2, The Atomic Energy Years, 1945–1950*, New York: Harper and Row, 1964, pp. 16–34.

74. *A Report on the International Control of Atomic Energy*, p. 34.

75. Hewlett and Anderson, *op.cit.*, pp. 577–8.

76. A.A. Gromyko, *Pamiatnoe*, 2nd edn, Book I, Moscow: Politizdat, 1990, pp. 346–7. Hewlett and Anderson, *op.cit.*, p. 583.

77. *A Report*, pp. 20–21.

78. See pp. 181, 185, 190, 196.

79. US Department of State, *Documents on Disarmament, 1945–1959, Vol. 1, 1945–1956*,

Washington, DC: US Government Printing Office, 1960, pp. 7–16.

80. Gromyko, *op.cit.*, p. 351.

81. Hewlett and Anderson, *op.cit.*, pp. 580–82; Thomas B. Cochran *et al.*, *Nuclear Weapons Databook, Vol. 2: US Nuclear Warhead Production*, Cambridge, Mass.: Ballinger, 1987, p. 151; Bertrand Goldschmidt, *The Atomic Complex*, La Grange Park, Illinois: American Nuclear Society, 1982, pp. 76–7.

82. Hewlett and Anderson, *op.cit.*, pp. 581–2.

83. *Ibid.*, pp. 606–7.

84. The text of this letter is in *Vestnik Ministerstva Inostrannykh Del SSSR*, July 15, 1991, pp. 39–40. The letter was also sent to three other officials at the Foreign Ministry: Vyshinskii, Dekanozov, and Malik.

85. *Ibid.*, p. 40.

86. *Ibid.*

87. V.M. Molotov, "Sovetskii soiuz i mezhdunarodnoe sotrudnichestvo," *Pravda*, October 31, 1946, p. 2.

88. *Sto sorok besed*, p. 85.

89. *Ibid.*, p. 84.

90. *Ibid.*

91. Hewlett and Anderson, *op.cit.*, pp. 607–18.

92. Bertrand Goldschmidt, "A Forerunner of the Non-Proliferation Treaty? The Soviet 1947 Proposals," unpublished paper, prepared for the Niels Bohr Centennial, 1985, pp. 14–15. Vladimir Batyuk, "The Baruch Plan and Russia," paper presented to the Cold War History Conference, Moscow, 1993.

93. Goldschmidt, *loc.cit.*, p. 9.

94. *Ibid.*, pp. 10–12; Batyuk, *loc.cit.*, p. 10.

95. As Goldschmidt points out, the Soviet proposal was in some respects similar in spirit to the Nuclear Non-Proliferation Treaty, which was signed in 1968. *Loc.cit.*, p. 10.

96. The Federation of American Scientists sent letters to Soviet scientists in 1946, asking them to respond to a series of questions about the utilization of atomic energy. The Foreign Policy Department of the Party Central Committee recommended that the Presidium of the Academy of Sciences arrange a meeting of the scientists who had received such letters to agree on the response to be made. The "answers should correspond to the position taken by Soviet representatives at the United Nations," M.A. Suslov to A.A. Kuznetsov, December 3, 1946. RTsKhIDNI f. 17, op. 128, t.1., d. 75. Kuznetsov was a secretary of the Central Committee, and Suslov worked in the Central Committee apparatus.

97. See the description of Skobel'tsyn by Frederick Osborn, "Negotiating on Atomic Energy, 1946–1947," in Raymond Dennett and Joseph E. Johnson (eds), *Negotiating with the Russians*, Boston: World Peace Foundation, 1951, pp. 224–5.

98. See, for example, Igor' Tamm, "Vnutriatomnaia energiia," *Pravda*, April 11, 1946; and Ia.I. Frenkel', *Osvbozhdenie vnutriatomnoi energii*, Moscow-Leningrad: izd. AN SSSR, 1946.

99. Gromyko, *op.cit.*, p. 276.

100. Wohlforth, *op.cit.*, pp. 98–9.

101. Paolo Spriano, *Stalin and the European Communists*, London: Verso, 1985, pp. 192–204; and Fernando Claudin, *The Communist Movement from Comintern to Cominform*, Harmondsworth: Penguin Books, 1975, pp. 307–70.

102. For comments on Litvinov's ideas and role see Alexander Dallin, "Allied Leadership in the Second World War," *Survey*, Winter–Spring 1975, pp. 15–16; and Vojtech Mastny, "The Cassandra in the Foreign Commissariat," *Foreign Affairs*, January 1976, pp. 366–76.

103. In a report he sent to Molotov from Washington in June 1943 Litvinov urged the Soviet Union to maintain much closer contact with Roosevelt who was, Litvinov thought, clearly willing to work with the Soviet Union. "Politika SShA v 1943 godu: Vzgliad Sovetskogo posla iz Vashingtona," *Vestnik Ministerstva Inostrannykh Del SSSR*, April 15, 1990, pp. 54–63.

104. Edgar Snow, *Journey to the Beginning*, New York: Random House, 1958, p. 315.

105. Richard C. Hottelet, "Soviet Union Can't be Trusted or Appeased, Diplomat Litvinov Warned Western World," *Washington Post*, January 21, 1952, p. 4.

106. Alexander Werth, *Russia at War, 1941–1945*, London: Pan Books, 1964, p. 839.

107. *Sto sorok besed*, pp. 96–7.

108. Z. Sheinis, *Maksim Maksimovich Litvinov: Revoliutsioner, diplomat, chelovek*, Moscow: Politizdat, 1989, pp. 422, 431.

109. Quoted in Robert Conquest, *Stalin: Breaker of Nations*, New York: Viking, 1991, p. 271.

110. E.S. Varga, *Izmeneniia v ekonomike kapitalizma v itoge vtoroi mirovoi voiny*, Moscow: Gospolitizdat, 1946.

111. *Sto sorok besed*, p. 78.

112. Larson, *op.cit.*, pp. 203–7. Control of the Straits had been a goal of Tsarist foreign policy.

113. Truman, *op.cit.*, p. 606.

114. Kuniholm, *op.cit.*, pp. 359–82.

115. *Sto sorok besed*, p. 103.

116. *Ibid.*

117. See Jonathan Haslam, "Soviet War Aims,"

paper presented at a conference on "The Rise and Fall of the Grand Alliance," University of East Anglia, September 1993.

118. Novikov's memorandum is entitled "US Foreign Policy in the Postwar Period," and a translation is published in *International Affairs*, 1990, no. 12, pp. 123–9.

119. Novikov, *op.cit.*, p. 353.

120. Novikov, *loc.cit.*, p. 123.

121. *Ibid.*, p. 124.

122. *Ibid.*, p. 128.

123. See, for example, I.I. Ermashev, *"Atomnaia diplomatiia" i mezhdunarodnoe sotrudnichestvo*, Moscow: Pravda, 1947; this is the text of a public lecture given in Moscow in December 1946.

124. "Otvety na voprosy zadannye moskovskim korrespondentom 'Sandei Taims', g-nom A. Vert poluchennye 17-go sentiabria 1946 g.," in McNeal, *op.cit.*, pp. 53, 54.

125. *Ibid.*, p. 56.

9. The Atomic Industry

1. CIA, *National Intelligence Survey, USSR, Section 73, Atomic Energy*, January 1951, p. 73–7.

2. CIA, Joint Atomic Energy Committee, *Status of the Soviet Atomic Energy Program, 4 July 1950*, CIA/SCI–2/50, p. 7. HSTL, PSF, National Security Council.

3. A.P. Aleksandrov, "Kak delali bombu," *Izvestiia*, July 28, 1988, p. 3.

4. G.D. Smit, *Atomnaia energiia dlia voennykh tselei*, Moscow: Transzheldorizdat, 1946. In the United States 1,000 copies of the report were made ready for release on August 12. Additions and deletions were made before an edition was prepared for wider distribution. The Soviet edition contains passages cut from the original version.

5. R. Kuznetsova, "Poka atomnaia bomba ne vzorvalas'," *Krasnaia Zvezda*, June 1, 1993, p. 2. The article consists of reminiscences by E. Slavskii, one of Vannikov's deputies, and later Minister of Medium Machine-Building. V.N. Novikov, "Shefstvo Berii," in *Beriia: konets kar'ery*, Moscow: Politizdat, 1991, p. 237. See also Sergei Leskov, "Lavrentii Beriia sumel by dobit'sia ekonomicheskogo protsvetaniia strany," *Izvestiia*, January 29, 1993, p. 10.

6. Jonathan E. Helmreich, *Gathering Rare Ores. The Diplomacy of Uranium Acquisition, 1943–1954*, Princeton: Princeton University Press, 1986, p. 48; on the origins of the trust see Margaret Gowing, *Britain and Atomic Energy, 1939–1945*, London: Macmillan, 1964, pp. 297–303.

7. Quoted by Helmreich, *op.cit.*, p. 48.

8. *Ibid.*, pp. 33–6, 56, 59.

9. FRUS 1945, ii, pp. 84–5.

10. Helmreich, *op.cit.*, pp. 60–68.

11. FRUS 1945, ii, p. 85.

12. Maclean became joint secretary of the Combined Policy Committee in February 1947, but did work connected with the bomb before this. Robert Cecil, *A Divided Life*, London: The Bodley Head, 1988, p. 70; Helmreich, *op.cit.*, p. 49. Merkulov's memorandum of February 28, 1945 to Beria contained information about uranium deposits around the world. "U istokov sovetskogo atomnogo proekta: Rol' razvedki," *Voprosy istorii estestvoznaniia i tekhniki*, 1992, no. 3, p. 122.

13. See pp. 101–2.

14. F.I. Vol'fson, N.S. Zontov, and G.R. Shushaniia, *Petr Iakovlevich Antropov*, Moscow: Nauka, 1985, p. 31.

15. Kuznetsova, *loc.cit.*

16. Vol'fson *et al.*, *op.cit.*, p. 30; and P.Ia. Antropov, "Shirokii nauchnyi diapazon," in *Dmitrii Ivanovich Shcherbakov, Zhizn' i deiatel'nost' 1893–1966*, Moscow: Nauka, 1969, p. 86.

17. Vol'fson *et al.*, *op.cit.*, p. 86. During the war he had been deputy to one of the members of the State Defense Committee, perhaps to Beria.

18. D.B. Shimkin, "Uranium Deposits in the USSR," *Science*, January 21, 1949, p. 59; F.I. Vol'fson, "Osnovnye cherty metallogenii zapadnogo Tian-Shania," *Izvestiia Akademii Nauk SSSR. Seriia geologicheskaia*, 1940, no. 3, p. 80 and map at p. 83.

19. Vol'fson *et al.*, *op.cit.*, p. 31; Antropov, *loc.cit.*, p. 86. Vernadskii refers to Tabashar in his diary (see p. 69), but I have used the more common Taboshary here.

20. Vol'fson *et al.*, *op.cit.*, pp. 31–2. This did not happen at once, however. The first uranium ore was apparently obtained in the summer of 1946, but only in limited quantity. Kuznetsova, *loc.cit.*

21. Vol'fson *et al.*, *op.cit.*, p. 33. The information about Combine No. 6's being subordinated to the First Chief Directorate comes from the CIA, *National Intelligence Survey*, p. 73–10.

22. Quoted by Vol'fson *et al.*, *op.cit.*, p. 33.

23. *Ibid.*, pp. 33–4. The mineralogist was Academician S.S. Smirnov.

24. *Ibid.*, pp. 34–5.

25. CIA, *National Intelligence Survey*, p. 73–11.

26. On mining in the Urals see Alexander Solzhenitsyn, *The Gulag Archipelago*, Vol. 2, London: Collins/Fontana, 1976, p. 575; on

the search for uranium in rivers and lakes see *Sovetskaia Atomnaia Nauka i Tekhnika*, Moscow: Atomizdat, 1967, p. 237.

27. CIA, *National Intelligence Survey*, p. 73–15.

28. I. Golovin and R. Kuznetsova, "Dostizheniia est'," *Pravda*, January 12, 1988, p. 3.

29. CIA, *National Intelligence Survey*, p. 15.

30. V. Gubarev, *V dvukh shagakh ot epitsentra*, Moscow: Sovetskaia Rossiia, 1979, pp. 58–9.

31. *Ibid.*, p. 60. In the 1950s an absorption process was adopted for producing uranium concentrates.

32. Jiri Kasparek, "Soviet Russia and Czechoslovakia's Uranium," *The Russian Review*, 1952, no. 2, p. 103. According to Konstantin Sorokin, a new agreement with Czechoslovakia was signed on November 23, 1945. See his "Das Manhattan-Projekt des Ostens," in Siegfried Fischer and Otfried Nassauer (eds), *Satansfaust: Das Nukleare Erbe der Sowjetunion*, Berlin: Aufbau Verlag, 1992, p. 42.

33. CIA, *National Intelligence Survey*, pp. 73–13, 73–14.

34. *Ibid.*, pp. 73–12, 73–13; Nikolai Grishin, "The Saxony Uranium Mining Operation ('Vismut')," in Robert Slusser (ed.), *Soviet Economic Policy in Postwar Germany*, New York: Research Program on the USSR, 1953, pp. 127–39. For extensive discussion of the uranium mining, see Norman Naimark, "The Soviet Occupation of Germany, 1945–1949," manuscript, 1993.

35. CIA, *National Intelligence Survey*, pp. 73–14, 73–15.

36. Deng Liqun, "On the Eve of and after the Peaceful Liberation of Xinjiang: One Page of Sino-Soviet Relations," *Jindai Shi Yanjiu* [Modern History Studies], 1989, no. 5, p. 149. I am grateful to Xue Litai for this reference.

37. Central Intelligence Agency, Joint Atomic Energy Intelligence Committee, *Status of the Soviet Atomic Energy Program*, July 4, 1950, CIA/SCI–2/50, p. 1. HSTL, PSF.

38. *Ibid.* A similar pattern emerges from private estimates: according to Shimkin, Eastern Europe supplied the Soviet Union with 10 metric tonnes of oxide in 1945, and with 150 metric tonnes in 1950 (Shimkin, *loc.cit.*, p. 147). Another source suggests that in 1946 Germany sent 135 tons of uranium ore (presumably concentrates) to the Soviet Union, 580 tons in 1947, and 900–920 tons in 1948.(Grishin, *loc.cit.*, p. 139.)

39. One scientist, who was working in 1952 on methods for extracting uranium from rock that contained very little of that mineral, has written that "the problem of obtaining the necessary quantity of uranium was at that time very acute for our country." V.M. Kolikov, "Na kafedre fiziki izotopov," in O.I. Sumbaev (ed.), *Akademik B.P. Konstantinov*, Leningrad: Nauka, 1985, p. 74.

40. CIA, *National Intelligence Survey*, p. 73–2.

41. "Delo Beriia," *Izvestiia TsK KPSS*, 1991, no. 2, p. 169.

42. Rosbaud to Goudsmit, September 16, 1945, Goudsmit Papers, Niels Bohr Library, American Institute of Physics, New York, Box 1, folder 25.

43. Nikolaus Riehl, "10 Jahre in goldenen Käfig. Erlebnisse beim Aufbau der sowjetischen Uran-Industrie," unpublished manuscript, p. 37. My thanks to Ulrich Albrecht for making this available to me.

44. *Ibid.*, pp. 12–14.

45. V.V. Goncharov, *Pervye (osnovnye) etapy resheniia atomnoi problemy v SSSR*, Moscow: Kurchatov Institute of Atomic Energy, 1990, p. 6.

46. Andreas Heinemann-Grüder, *Die Sowjetische Atombombe*, Berlin: Arbeitspapiere der Berghof-Stiftung für Konfliktforschung, 1990, p. 43.

47. Riehl, *loc.cit.*, pp. 15–22.

48. *Ibid.*, p. 22.

49. *Ibid.*, pp. 33–4.

50. *Ibid.*, p. 22; the date for the first delivery of uranium metal to Kurchatov's laboratory is confirmed in I.F. Zhezherun, *Stroitel'stvo i pusk pervogo v Sovetskom Soiuze atomnogo reaktora*, Moscow: Atomizdat, 1978, p. 79.

51. Riehl, *loc.cit.*, p. 23; Henry DeWolf Smyth, *Atomic Energy for Military Purposes*, Princeton: Princeton University Press, 1948, p. 93.

52. Riehl, *loc.cit.*, p. 24.

53. One of those involved in the process summarizes it thus: "chemical concentrate of uranium – obtaining pure compounds of uranium – obtaining uranium dioxide – preparation of a mixture of uranium dioxide and pure calcium – reduction smelting in an atmosphere of argon or helium – washing of the uranium powder in a weak acid solution – washing with water or spirit – drying of the powder – fusion of the powder into ingots." N. Galkin, "Znakom'tes' – uran," *Tekhnika – molodezhi*, 1975, no. 9, p. 15.

54. Riehl, *loc.cit.*, p. 27; Smyth, *op.cit.*, p. 93.

55. Riehl, *loc.cit.*, pp. 26–7.

56. Zhezherun, *op.cit.*, p. 106. By 1950, according to Riehl, the Elektrostal' plant was producing almost one metric ton of uranium metal a day; and, he writes, it was not the only such plant. *Loc.cit.*, p. 28.

57. Zhezherun, *op.cit.*, p. 66. There are, besides Zhezherun's detailed study, a number of accounts of the building of the reactor. A report written by Kurchatov and Panasiuk in 1947, "Stroitel'stvo i pusk pervogo v Sovetskom Soiuze uran-grafitovogo kotla s samorazvivaiushcheisia tsepnoi reaktsiei," has been declassified and published in I.V. Kurchatov, *Izbrannye trudy v trekh tomakh. Tom 3: Iadernaia energiia*, Moscow: Nauka, 1984, pp. 73–94. See also I.S. Panasiuk, "Pervyi sovetskii atomnyi reaktor," in *Sovetskaia atomnaia nauka i tekhnika*, Moscow: Atomizdat, 1967, pp. 19–44.

58. Goncharov, *op.cit.*, pp. 12–13; Zhezherun, *op.cit.*, p. 66.

59. I.S. Panasiuk, "Eto bylo v 1938–1946 godakh," in M.K. Romanovskii (ed.), *Vospominaniia ob akademike I.V. Kurchatove*, Moscow: Nauka, 1983, p. 26.

60. *Ibid.*, pp. 76–7; Zhezherun, *op.cit.*, pp. 79–85.

61. Zhezherun, *op.cit.*, pp. 84–5; Panasiuk, "Eto bylo," p. 23; Riehl, *loc.cit.*, p. 35; Kurchatov and Panasiuk, *loc.cit.*, pp. 82–3.

62. Riehl, *loc.cit.*; Zhezherun, *op.cit.*

63. Goncharov, *op.cit.*, p. 7.

64. Kurchatov and Panasiuk, *loc.cit.*, p. 83.

65. Zhezherun, *op.cit.*, pp. 98–103.

66. *Ibid.*, pp. 103–6; Kurchatov and Panasiuk, *loc.cit.*, pp. 83–4.

67. Zhezherun, *op.cit.*, pp. 106–10.

68. *Ibid.*, pp. 110–15; Kurchatov and Panasiuk, *loc.cit.*, pp. 85–7.

69. *Ibid.*, p. 87.

70. Zhezherun, *op.cit.*, p. 115.

71. Panasiuk, "Eto bylo," p. 26.

72. M.G. Pervukhin, "Vydaiushchiisia uchenyi i talantlivyi organizator," in Romanovskii, *op.cit.*, p. 10.

73. I.N. Golovin and Iu.N. Smirnov, *Eto nachinalos' v zamoskvorech'e*, Moscow: Kurchatov Institute of Atomic Energy, 1989, p. 9.

74. Richard G. Hewlett and Oscar E. Anderson, *The New World: A History of the United States Atomic Energy Commission, Vol. 1, 1939–1946*, Berkeley: University of California Press, 1990, p. 112, Zhezherun, *op.cit.*, p. 113.

75. Smyth, *op.cit.*, pp. 239–45.

76. *Ibid.*, p. 245.

77. Arnold Kramish, *Atomic Energy in the Soviet Union*, Stanford: Stanford University Press,

1959, p. 112; Zhezherun, *op.cit.*, pp. 117–19; Iu.V. Sivintsev, *I.V. Kurchatov i iadernaia energetika*, Moscow: Atomizdat, 1980, p. 40.

78. Zhezherun, *op.cit.*, pp. 116–19.

79. On April 11, 1945 he wrote a memorandum on intelligence received from the United States about reactor design. In this he wrote that "a uranium-graphite boiler with water cooling is the simplest technical form for realizing a boiler." "U istokov sovetskogo atomnogo proekta: rol' razvedki," *Voprosy istorii estestvoznaniia i tekhniki*, 1992, no. 3, p. 125.

80. V.I. Merkin, "Reshaiushchii eksperiment Kurchatova," in Aleksandrov (ed.), *Vospominaniia ob Igore Vasil'eviche Kurchatove*, Moscow: Nauka, 1988, p. 269.

81. Smyth, *op.cit.*, p. 108. During the fission of uranium-235 many of the neutrons emitted are captured by uranium-238 to form uranium-239, which has a half-life of 23 minutes and decays to form neptunium. Neptunium has a half-life of 2.3 days and decays in turn to form plutonium. It is this decay chain that makes it possible to use a nuclear pile to produce plutonium.

82. V. Gubarev, "Konstruktor reaktorov," *Pravda*, November 12, 1984, pp. 3, 6. N.A. Dollezhal', "Posle 1946 goda," in Aleksandrov, *op.cit.*, p. 233. N.A. Dollezhal', *U istokov rukotvornogo mira*, Moscow: Znanie, 1989, pp. 131–45.

83. Dollezhal', *op.cit.*, p. 147.

84. Dollezhal', *loc.cit.*, p. 233.

85. Goncharov, *op.cit.*, pp. 19–23.

86. Zhezherun, *op.cit.*, pp. 116–32.

87. V.K. Losev, "Ot palatok do promyshlennogo reaktora," in Aleksandrov (ed.), *op.cit.*, p. 263.

88. *Statement of Klaus Fuchs' to Michael Perrin*, in a letter of March 2, 1950 from J. Edgar Hoover to Admiral Souers. HSTL, PSF, pp. 6–7.

89. Goncharov, *op.cit.*, pp. 22–3.

90. Iu.N. Elfimov, *Marshal industrii. Biograficheskii ocherk o A.P. Zaveniagine*, Cheliabinsk: Iuzhno-ural'skoe izd., 1982, p. 177.

91. *Ibid.*, p. 129.

92. *The Memoirs of Herbert Hoover, Years of Adventure, 1874–1920*, New York: Macmillan, 1951, pp. 103–6, quotations from p. 106. Hoover noted, however, that when the Bolsheviks took over, "the very furies of ignorance were in the saddle." *Ibid.*

93. When US intelligence discovered that this was one of the main sites for the Soviet atomic industry, it went to Hoover's files to

learn something about the region.

94. Elfimov, *op.cit.*, p. 177.

95. Solzhenitsyn, *op.cit.*, pp. 78–9, 91.

96. US government intelligence document quoted in Zhores Medvedev, *Nuclear Disaster in the Urals*, New York: W.W. Norton, 1979, p. 197.

97. Gubarev, *loc.cit.*, p. 6; Elfimov, *op.cit.*, p. 182.

98. Losev, *loc.cit.*, p. 264.

99. I.N. Golovin, *I.V. Kurchatov*, 3rd edn, Moscow: Atomizdat, 1978, pp. 85–6; Dollezhal', *op.cit.*, p. 151.

100. O. Kviatkovskii, "Proshchanie s sablei," *Trud*, May 17, 1989, p. 3. *Bol'shaia Sovetskaia entsiklopediia*, 3rd edn, Vol. 23, Moscow: Sovetskaia entsiklopediia, 1976, p. 543.

101. V. Chalmaev, *Malyshev*, Moscow: Molodaia gvardiia, 1978, p. 167.

102. Elfimov, *op.cit.*, pp. 179–80, 185–6. Elfimov does not mention Slavskii or Muzrukov by name, but it is quite clear who they are from the biographies he gives. "Uranovyi proekt: iz vospominanii E. Slavskogo," *Pravitel'stvennyi vestnik*, April 1989, no. 7, p. 10.

103. Merkin, *loc.cit.*, p. 39.

104. D.S. Pereverzev, "Riadom s Kurchatovym," in Aleksandrov, *op.cit.*, pp. 385–6. Pereverzev was one of Kurchatov's bodyguards, who became devoted to Kurchatov and his memory.

105. Strict measures had been taken to prevent contamination, but boron, which could poison the pile, had been discovered in the graphite at one point. It turned out that the linoleum on the floor of the pile building contained boron; the linoleum was quickly removed. Golovin, *op.cit.*, p. 86.

106. Merkin, *loc.cit.*, p. 279.

107. Thomas B. Cochran and Robert Standish Norris, *Russian/Soviet Nuclear Warhead Production*, NWD 93–1, New York: Natural Resources Defense Council, September 8, 1993, p. 49.

108. Merkin, *loc.cit.*, p. 280.

109. Golovin, *op.cit.*, p. 87.

110. Merkin, *loc.cit.*, p. 281.

111. *Ibid.*

112. Interview with Golovin, October 21, 1990.

113. Goncharov, *op.cit.*, pp. 26–7. On the operation of the first production reactor see B.G. Dubovskii, "Takim ia pomniu I.V. Kurchatova," in Aleksandrov, *op.cit.*, p. 371. The reactor was decommissioned in 1987; Bill Keller, "Soviet City, Home of the A-Bomb, Is Haunted by Its Past and Future," *New York Times*, July 10, 1989.

114. L.V. Komlev, G.S. Sinitsyna, and M.P. Koval'skaia, "V.G. Khlopin i uranovaia problema," in *Akademik V.G. Khlopin, Ocherki, vospominaniia sovremennikov*, Leningrad: Nauka, 1987, p. 51.

115. Z.V. Ershova, "Moi vstrechi s akademikom V.G. Khlopinym," in *Akademik V.G. Khlopin*, p. 117; and M.L. Iashchenko-Kovalevskaia, "Vospominaniia," *ibid.*, p. 158.

116. Smyth, *op.cit.*, pp. 137, 139.

117. *Ibid.*, p. 139.

118. Iashchenko-Kovalevskaia, *loc.cit.*, pp. 158–9.

119. V.M. Vdovenko *et al.*, "Radiokhimiia," in *Sovetskaia Atomnaia Nauka i Tekhnika*, p. 262.

120. Ershova, *loc.cit.*, p. 117; Komlev *et al.*, *loc.cit.*, p. 52.

121. Boris Kurchatov, "Nekhozhenymi putiami," *Tekhnika – molodezhi*, 1975, no. 12, pp. 16–18. Boris Kurchatov gives April as the date, but the chronology in Aleksandrov, *op.cit.*, p. 462, gives May and June–August.

122. Vdovenko *et al.*, *loc.cit.*, p. 262.

123. Fuchs, Statement to Perrin, *loc.cit.*, p. 7.

124. Frank L. Parker, *Search of the Russian Scientific Literature for Descriptions of the Medical Consequences of the Kyshtym "Accident"*, Technical Report. Nashville: Environmental and Water Resources Engineering, Vanderbilt University, March 1983, p. 18.

125. In 1958 the Soviet Union recommended to China that it use a precipitation process. See John Wilson Lewis and Xue Litai, "Chinese Strategic Weapons and the Plutonium Option," *Critical Technologies Newsletter*, April/May 1988, p. 10.

126. Cochran and Norris, *op.cit.*, p. 52.

127. Diane M. Soran and Danny B. Stillman, *An Analysis of the Alleged Kyshtym Disaster*, LA-9217-MS, Los Alamos National Laboratory, January 1982, pp. 11–12.

128. Pervukhin, "Vydaiushchiisia," in Aleksandrov, *op.cit.*, p. 184; Komlev *et al.*, *loc.cit.*, p. 52.

129. See, for example, Elfimov, *op.cit.*, p. 186.

130. L.P. Sokhina, Ia.I. Kolotinskii, and G.V. Khalturin, *Dokumental'naia povest' o rabote khimiko-metallurgicheskogo plutonievogo tsekha v period ego stanovleniia (1949–1950 gg.)*, Cheliabinsk-65: Iuzhno-uralskoe izd., 1991, pp. 7–10.

131. *Ibid.*, p. 19.

132. *Ibid.*, p. 36.

133. *Ibid.*, p. 40.

134. *Ibid.*, p. 53.

135. *Ibid.*, p. 63. See also V. Gubarev, "Korolek

plutoniia," *Pravda*, January 2, 1979, p. 6; and Bochvar's obituary in *Pravda*, September 21, 1984, p. 3. Z. Ershova, M. Pozharskaia, and V. Fomin, "Milligrammy – eto nemalo," *Tekhnika – molodezhi*, 1976, no. 2, p. 49.

136. Cochran and Norris, *op.cit.*, pp. 49–51.

137. Leonid Iakimenko, "Kak byl poluchen pervyi eshelon tiazheloi vody," *Tekhnika – molodezhi*, 1976, no. 3, pp. 22–3; CIA, *National Intelligence Survey*, p. 73–18.

138. Iakimenko, *loc.cit.*, and CIA, *National Intelligence Survey*, and Vasilii Vladimirskii, "Rozhdenie reaktora, rozhdenie instituta," *Tekhnika-molodezhi*, 1975, no. 8, pp. 12–13.

139. No data have been published about the Cheliabinsk-40 heavy-water reactor.

140. Smyth, *op.cit.*, Chapters 9, 10, 11.

141. Aleksandrov, *loc.cit.*, p. 20.

142. Golovin, "Rossiiskii nauchnyi tsentr-Kurchatovskii institut," unpublished manuscript, 1992, pp. 12–13.

143. *Ibid.*

144. *Ibid.*, pp. 14, 19; Gerold Guensberg, "Defector Reveals How German Scientists Helped Break US Atom Bomb Monopoly," unpublished manuscript, n.d., p. 12; Cochran and Norris, *op.cit.*, pp. 116–17.

145. Golovin, *loc.cit.*, p. 19; Cochran and Norris, *op.cit.*, pp. 116–17.

146. Golovin, *loc.cit.*, p. 15.

147. CIA, *German Scientists at Sukhumi, USSR*, OSI/SR-2/49, October 31, 1949, p. 3; Manfred von Ardenne, *Ein glückliches Leben für Technik und Forschung*, 4th edn, Berlin: Verlag der Nation, 1976, pp. 161–2; Heinz Barwich, *Das Rote Atom*, Munich and Berne: Scherz Verlag, 1967, p. 31ff.

148. Max Steenbeck, *Impulse und Wirkungen*, Berlin: Verlag der Nation, 1977, p. 189.

149. Iurii Aleksandrovich Krutkov is an exception. He had become a corresponding member of the Academy in 1933, but had been arrested in the late 1930s. He worked in Tupolev's *sharaga* (prison design bureau) and went to Sukhumi when he was released from the *sharaga* at the end of the war. See Barwich, *op.cit.*, p. 72, and G.A. Ozerov, *Tupolevskaia sharaga*, 2nd edn, Frankfurt: Possev, 1973, pp. 40–41.

150. Steenbeck, *op.cit.*, pp. 188–9.

151. Barwich, *op.cit.*, p. 62; *Sergei L'vovich Sobolev*, Novosibirsk: Nauka Sibirskogo otdeleniia, 1969, p. 10.

152. Steenbeck, *op.cit.*, pp. 231–9.

153. Von Ardenne, *op.cit.*, pp. 185–6; CIA *The Problem of Uranium Isotope Separation by means of Ultracentrifuge*, Report No. DB-0-3, 633, 414, October 8.1957, p. 9.

154. *The Problem of Uranium Isotope Separation*, p. 26; Barwich, *op.cit.*, p. 103ff.

155. Golovin, *loc.cit.*, p. 18.

156. Pervukhin, *loc.cit.*, p. 12; Gerold Guensberg, "*The Soviet Centrifuge Program for Uranium Enrichment*," unpublished manuscript, November 1980, p. 6, gives the date as October 1948; Barwich, *op.cit.*, p. 106.

157. Golovin, *op.cit.*, p. 20.

158. *The Problem of Uranium Isotope Separation*, p. 26; Barwich, *op.cit.*, p. 103ff. Barwich writes that the Germans went to Verkhne-Nevinsk in October 1948, but the later date, which is given in *The Problem . . .* seems more plausible, since it fits in better with the general chronology of Soviet developments.

159. Barwich, *op.cit.*, pp. 106–7; *The Problem of Uranium Isotope Separation*, p. 10. This episode is confirmed by A.M. Petros'iants, "Chelovek slova i dela," in *Vospominaniia ob akademike Isaake Konstantinoviche Kikoine*, Moscow: Nauka, 1991, pp. 54–6.

160. Barwich, *op.cit.*, pp. 106–12.

161. Petros'iants, *loc.cit.*, p. 55.

162. Barwich, *op.cit.*, pp. 107–27. Confirmed by Petros'iants.

163. Petros'iants, *loc.cit.*, p. 56.

164. Golovin, *loc.cit.*, p. 24.

165. Steenbeck, *op.cit.*, pp. 273–9; *The Problem of Uranium Isotope Separation*, pp. 26–8.

166. *The Problem of Uranium Isotope Separation*, p. 32.

167. Work continued on electromagnetic separation, and also on development of the centrifuge. The first industrial centrifuge plant began operation in 1959 at Sverdlovsk-44.

168. *The Problem of Uranium Isotope Separation*, p. 32.

169. Golovin, *op.cit.*, p. 24.

170. Golovin, *loc.cit.*, p. 11.

171. Solzhenitsyn, *op.cit.*, Vol. 2, p. 393. See also Andrei Sakharov, *Vospominaniia*, New York: izd. im. Chekhova, 1990, p. 155.

172. Scientists and engineers were brought from prisons and camps to work on the project. The only *sharashka* (prison research institute) that can be identified with certainty is the institute for radiobiology and radiogenetics at Sungul, about 30 kilometers north of Kyshtym. The key figure there was N.V. Timofeev-Resovskii, who had worked in Germany from 1926 to 1945, where he had established a world reputation in radiation genetics and biophysics. Some of his German associates joined him at Sungul, and Nikolaus Riehl, who had been a friend of his in Berlin, became scientific director of the institute in 1950. The institute developed methods for measuring ra-

diation levels, and studied the effects of radioactive isotopes on living organisms. It seems to have been protected against Lysenkoism by the MVD, to which it was subordinate, and especially by Zaveniagin. See Riehl, *loc.cit.*, pp. 49–56; Daniil Granin, "Zubr," *Novyi Mir*, 1987, no. 2, pp. 40–43. See also Raisa Berg, *Sukhovei*, New York: Chalidze Publications, 1983, p. 224.

173. Grishin, *loc.cit.*, pp. 131–3.

174. "Dienstverpflichtungen zum Uranbergbau reissen nicht ab" (1948), Hoover Institution Archive, Sander Papers, Box 1, folder 9; "Arbeitsverhältnisse in Erzbergbau Aue," Sander Papers, Box 2, folder 5, p. 8. My thanks to Norman Naimark for making this material available to me.

175. CIA, *National Intelligence Survey*, pp. 73–7.

176. "Uranbergbau macht die Menschen zur Ruine," Hoover Institution Archive, Sander Papers, Box 1, folder 9, pp. 2–3.

177. "Uranbergbau." Patricia Kahn, "A Grisly Archive of Key Cancer Data," *Science*, January 22, 1993, pp. 448–51. For an extensive discussion see Naimark, *op.cit.*

178. Golovin, *op.cit.*, p. 11.

179. B.V. Nikipelov, A.F. Lyzlov, and N.A. Koshurnikova, "Opyt pervogo predpriatiia atomnoi promyshlennosti," *Priroda*, 1990, no. 2, pp. 30–38. After World War II the US Atomic Energy Commission set a dose limit of 36.5 rem per year for occupational exposure; the international standard today is 2 rem a year. (Rem stands for "roentgen equivalent man".) See Len Ackland, "Radiation Risks Revisited," *Technology Review*, February/March 1993, pp. 59, 61. An official report prepared in 1991 noted that at Cheliabinsk-40 "over 10,000 staff have been exposed to professional external and internal radiation in excessive doses." Between 1948 and 1968, 40 people suffered from acute radiation disease, of whom 8 died; 1,500 people were diagnosed as having "chronic radiation disease with dosages in multiple excess of the top level of toleration." The records show an increase in the death rate from malignant formations for those exposed to 25 rem a year and a total dose of 100 rem or more. *Proceedings of the Commission on Studying the Ecological Situation in Cheliabinsk Oblast*, Vol. 2, Moscow, 1991, p. 23. The commission was established by a decree of President Gorbachev on January 3, 1991.

180. Sokhina, *et al.*, *op.cit.*, p. 2.

181. *Ibid.*, *passim*.

182. Nikipelov *et al.*, *loc.cit.*, p. 32.

183. *Ibid.*, p. 31.

184. *Ibid.*, p. 32.

185. Cochran and Norris, *op.cit.*, pp. 65–8. This accident resulted in an increased incidence of leukemia among the exposed population. Mira Kossenko, Marina Degteva, and Nelly Petrushova, "Estimate of the Risk of Leukemia to Residents Exposed to Radiation as a Result of a Nuclear Accident in the Southern Urals," *PSR Quarterly*, December 1992, pp. 187–97. For extensive discussion see *Proceedings of the Commission*.

186. On September 29, 1957 a storage tank for radioactive waste at the chemical separation plant at Cheliabinsk-40 exploded, releasing 20 million curies of radioactive substances, of which 2 million entered the atmosphere and were spread over the countryside to the north-west. B.V. Nikipelov and E.G. Drozhko, "Vzryv na Iuzhnom Urale," *Priroda*, 1990, no. 5, p. 48. This issue contains several papers devoted to the accident.

187. The legacy of this approach can be seen in the nuclear accidents at Cheliabinsk-40 in 1957 and at Chernobyl in 1986.

10. The Atomic Bomb

1. Interview with Iu.B. Khariton, July 16, 1992; Khariton in V.S. Gubarev, *Arzamas-16*, Moscow: Izdat, 1992, pp. 21–2.

2. Interview with Khariton, July 16, 1992.

3. James H. Billington, *The Icon and the Axe*, New York: Vintage Books, 1970, pp. 200–3; *Sviatii Prepodobnyi Serafim*, Odessa: izd. Sv. Andreevskago Skita, 1903.

4. Virginia Cowles, *The Last Tsar*, New York: G.P. Putnam's Sons, 1977, p. 90.

5. Khariton in Gubarev, *op.cit.*, p. 22; Iu.B. Khariton and Iu.N. Smirnov, "O nekotorykh mifakh i legendakh vokrug sovetskikh atomnogo i vodorodnogo proektov," in *Materialy iubileinoi sessii uchenogo soveta tsentra, 12 ianvaria 1993 g.*, Moscow: Kurchatovskii institut, 1993, p. 46.

6. For a very clear description of the plutonium bomb see Margaret Gowing, *Independence and Deterrence. Vol. 2, Policy Execution*, London: Macmillan, 1974, p. 454ff.

7. Iurii Trutnev, in Gubarev, *op.cit.*, p. 51. Khariton in "Radi iadernogo pariteta," *Dos'e Literaturnoi Gazety*, January 1990, p. 18.

8. Interview with Khariton, July 16, 1992. The explosives institute was NII-6 (*Nauchno-issledovatel'skii institut-6*: Research Institute No. 6.)

9. P.T. Astashenkov, *Plamia i vzryv*, 2nd edn,

Moscow: Politizdat, 1978, p. 65; Iu. A. Khramov, *Fiziki, Biograficheskii spravochnik*, 2nd edn, Moscow: Nauka, 1983, p. 306.

10. Central Intelligence Agency, *Soviet Flame and Combustion Research and Its Relation to Jet Propulsion (including Rocket Propulsion)*, OSI/SR–6/49, June 1940, p. 15. J.G. Crowther, *Soviet Science*, London: Kegan Paul, 1936, pp. 179–85 describes the work of Khariton (here spelled Chariton) on explosives.

11. See the introductory essay in Ia.B. Zel'dovich, *Izbrannye trudy: Khimicheskaia fizika i gidrodinamika,* Moscow: Nauka, 1984, pp. 5–52.

12. On these three men see Andrei Sakharov, *Memoirs*, New York: Alfred A. Knopf, 1990, pp. 108–9.

13. V.A. Tsukerman and Z.M. Azarkh, "Liudi i vzryvy," *Zvezda*, 1990, no. 10, p. 144. On their wartime work see pp. 138–9, and on the invitation to join the atomic project, pp. 143–4. Nos 9 and 11 of the journal contain other installments of the memoirs of Tsukerman and Azarkh.

14. I.N. Golovin, "Rossiiskii nauchnyi tsentr – Kurchatovskii institut," unpublished manuscript, 1992, p. 18.

15. I.N. Golovin, *Kul'minatsiia*, Moscow: Kurchatov Institute of Atomic Energy, 1989, p. 3; A.P. Aleksandrov (ed.), *Vospominaniia ob Igore Vasil'eviche Kurchatove*, Moscow: Nauka, 1988, p. 469.

16. Documentary film on Khariton, *Nauchnyi Rukovoditel'*, 1993.

17. M. Rebrov, "Iadernyi sled," *Krasnaia Zvezda*, October 17, 1992, p. 5. He also apparently made a one-tenth scale model of the uranium-235 bomb.

18. V. Sergiichuk, "Vmeste s Kurchatovym," *Pravda Ukrainy*, October 26, 1984, p. 4.

19. He worked with Komel'kov. His contribution was to create a redundant system.

20. Interview with Khariton, July 16, 1992. Tsukerman and Azarkh, *loc.cit.*, pp. 148–9.

21. Sakharov, *op.cit.*, p. 108.

22. Golovin, *op.cit.*, p. 5.

23. Khariton and Smirnov, *loc.cit.*, p. 49.

24. Interview with I.N. Golovin, October 21, 1990.

25. Khariton and Smirnov, *loc.cit.*, p. 49. Interview with Khariton, July 16, 1992.

26. Al'tshuler "Tak my delali bombu," *Literaturnaia Gazeta*, June 6, 1990, p. 13. This is an interview with Al'tshuler. The narrow-gauge railway was soon converted to a normal line.

27. *Ibid.*

28. "Delo Beriia," *Izvestiia TsK KPSS*, 1991, no. 2, p. 168.

29. Sakharov, *op.cit.*, p. 108.

30. On secrecy and security see Sakharov, *op.cit.*, pp. 112, 115, 119; Al'tshuler, *loc.cit.*; Khariton and Smirnov, *loc.cit.*, pp. 36–7.

31. Sakharov, *op.cit.*, p. 115; Al'tshuler, *loc.cit.*

32. Khariton in Gubarev, *op.cit.*, p. 14.

33. Interview with Khariton, July 16, 1992.

34. Aleksandrov, "Gody s Kurchatovym," *Nauka i zhizn'*, 1983, no. 2, p. 23.

35. Iurii Abyzov, *Russkoe pechathoe slovo v Latvii, 1917–1944 gg., Part IV*, Stanford: Stanford Slavic Studies, 1991, pp. 260–61.

36. *Ibid.*

37. V.S. Emel'ianov, *S chego nachinalos'*, Moscow: Sovetskaia Rossiia, 1979, p. 233.

38. I.N. Golovin and Iu.N. Smirnov, *Eto nachinalos' v zamoskvorech'e*, Moscow: Kurchatov Institute of Atomic Energy, 1989, p. 9.

39. Al'tshuler, *loc.cit.*

40. V.B. Adamsky, "Becoming a Citizen," in *Andrei Sakharov: Facets of a Life*, Gif-Sur-Yvette: Editions Frontières, 1991, p. 27. I have translated this from the Russian text ("Stanovlenie grazhdanina") which Dr Adamskii kindly made available to me.

41. Sakharov, "Ia pytalsia byt' na urovne svoei sud'by," *Molodezh Estonii*, October 11, 1988, p. 2.

42. Khariton, in Gubarev, *op.cit.*, p. 14.

43. Tsukerman and Azarkh, *loc.cit.*, p. 151.

44. N.A. Dollezhal', *U istokov rukotvornogo mira*, Moscow: Znanie, 1989, p. 137.

45. *Ibid.*, pp. 137–9.

46. Max Steenbeck *Impulse and Wirkungen*, Berlin: Verlag der Nation, 1977, pp. 174–5; M.G. Meshcheriakov, "Akademik V.G. Khlopin: Voskhozhdenie na posledniuiu vershinu," unpublished paper, 1992, p. 28.

47. Al'tshuler, *loc. cit.* In an interview Sakharov said that although he knew something of Stalin's crimes in the late 1940s he was not aware of their full extent. Interview with A. Sakharov, June 15, 1987.

48. Sakharov, *op.cit.*, p. 97.

49. Konstantin Simonov, *Glazami cheloveka moego pokoleniia*, Moscow: izd. Pravda, 1990, p. 106.

50. Sakharov, *op.cit.*, p. 41.

51. Werner G. Hahn, *Postwar Soviet Politics*, Ithaca: Cornell University Press, 1982, pp. 58–9; 67–93.

52. *Ibid.*, p. 126.

53. N.G. Klueva and G.I. Roskin had developed an anti-cancer preparaton known as KR. At their request the manuscript of their monograph on the treatment of malignant tumors, which was published in Moscow, was taken to the United States in 1946 by

V.V. Parin, academician secretary of the Academy of Medical Sciences, and given by him to an American publisher. Stalin regarded this as betrayal of a state secret. Parin was sent to prison for twenty-five years, while Klueva and Roskin had to appear before a "court of honor," and were roundly condemned in the press. *Ibid.*, p. 127.

54. David Joravsky, *The Lysenko Affair*, Cambridge, Mass.: Harvard University Press, 1970, pp. 133–7; Zhores Medvedev, *The Rise and Fall of T.D. Lysenko*, New York: Columbia University Press, 1969, pp. 114–17; and V. Soifer, "Gor'kii plod," *Ogonek*, 1988, nos 1 and 2.

55. Soifer, *loc.cit.*, no. 2, p. 5.

56. Joravsky, *op.cit.*, pp. 137–9; Medvedev, *op.cit.*, pp. 117–23; Soifer, *loc.cit.*, no. 2, pp. 5–7.

57. *O polozhenii v biologicheskoi nauke. Stenograficheskii otchet sessii vsesoiuznoi akademii sel'skokhoziaistvennykh nauk imeni V.I. Lenina 31 iiulia-7 avgusta 1948 g.*, Moscow: Sel'khozizdat, 1948, p. 512.

58. Joravsky, *op.cit.*, p. 141; Medvedev, *op.cit.*, pp. 123–36; Soifer, *loc.cit.*, no. 2, pp. 7, 31.

59. Alexander Vucinich, *Empire of Knowledge, The Academy of Sciences of the USSR, 1917–1970*, Berkeley: University of California Press, 1984, pp. 220–28.

60. M.A. Markov, "O prirode fizicheskogo znaniia," *Voprosy filosofii*, 1947, no. 2, pp. 140–76; the controversy is discussed in detail in Loren R. Graham, *Science and Philosophy in the Soviet Union*, New York: Alfred A. Knopf, 1972, pp. 74–81. See also Vucinich, *op.cit.*, pp. 209–12.

61. A.A. Maksimov, "Ob odnom filosofskom kentavre," *Literaturnaia Gazeta*, April 10, 1948, p. 3; Hahn, *op.cit.*, pp. 79–82.

62. Graham, *op.cit.*, p. 79. It was the interpretation that was banned, not quantum mechanics as such.

63. A.S. Sonin, "Soveshchanie, kotoroe ne sostoialos'," *Priroda*, 1990, no. 3, p. 99. This is the first of three articles in successive issues of the journal by Sonin on the preparations for this conference.

64. *Ibid.*, p. 98.

65. *Ibid.*, p. 99.

66. On this see especially G.E. Gorelik, "Fizika universitetskaia i akademicheskaia," *Voprosy istorii estestvoznaniia i tekhniki*, 1991, no. 2, pp. 31–46.

67. P.L. Kapitsa, *Pis'ma o nauke*, Moscow: Moskovskii rabochii, 1989, pp. 216–17.

68. Ivanenko, who had been one of the first members of the nuclear seminar at Ioffe's institute, was vehement in asserting the priority of Soviet science. In 1948, for example, he complained in the Party's leading theoretical journal *Bol'shevik* that the Smyth Report had contrived "to set forth the important results of a large number of Soviet works, without so much as saying a word about Soviet science and its role in the physical discoveries of our time! Smyth tries to instill into his readers the idea that, in essence, only scholars from the Anglo-Saxon countries were capable of discovering all the modern conceptions about the structure of the atom and of the atomic nucleus, and about nuclear reactions" (D.D. Ivanenko, "K itogam diskussii po knige B.M. Kedrova 'Engel's i estestvoznanie'," *Bol'shevik*, 1948, no. 8, p. 69.) The bitterness of Ivanenko's criticism sprang from his belief that he had not received due recognition for formulting the neutron–proton model of the nucleus in 1932. The normal concern that scientists have about priority had become morbid and obsessive in Ivanenko's case.

69. Gorelik, *loc.cit.*, p. 37; Sonin, *loc.cit.*, *Priroda*, 1990, no. 4, p. 91. In February 1948 Professor A.A. Sokolov of Moscow University wrote to Zhdanov to complain that he and Ivanenko were not able to take part in the work of NIIF-2 (Skobel'tsyn's nuclear physics institute at Moscow University), and to accuse Landsberg, Landau, and Tamm of kowtowing to foreign physics. RTsKhIDNI, f. 17, op. 125. ed. khr. 618, pp. 110–11.

70. Sonin, *loc.cit.* (*Priroda*, 1990, nos 3, 4, and 5) summarizes the discussions.

71. *Ibid.*: no. 5, pp. 98–9.

72. *Ibid.*, p. 99.

73. Letter from I. Zorich, *Priroda*, 1990, no. 9, p. 106. I have been told the same story by other people, who heard it from Artsimovich.

74. Al'tshuler, *loc.cit.*; Sakharov, *op.cit.*, pp. 135–6; Khariton in Gubarev, *op.cit.*, p. 12.

75. Ia.B. Zel'dovich, "Fizika i Kurchatov," in Aleksandrov, *op.cit.*, p. 85. Zel'dovich notes that Kurchatov may have said "close down our shop (*zakryt' nashu lavochku*)."

76. *Filosofskie voprosy sovremennoi fiziki*, Moscow: izd. Akademii Nauk SSSR, 1952, p. 4. For criticism of Mandel'shtam, Landau, Frenkel', and Ioffe see, for example, pp. 22–5, 64–5, 297, 406.

77. The Russian word is *izdelie*, which some writers translate as "device" in this context. But "device" often implies something that is not a finished bomb, which is not the

meaning of the Russian word. *Izdelie* is closer to "gadget," the term used for the American bomb. *Izdelie* is used to refer to various weapons, e.g. missiles. It is used to avoid referring by name to the weapon. I have given *izdelie* its standard translation.

78. Iu.B. Khariton, "Nachalo," and M.A. Sadovskii, "S N.N. Semenovym v Kazani," in A.E. Shilov (ed.), *Vospominaniia ob Akademike Nikolae Nikolaeviche Semenove*, Moscow: Nauka, 1993, pp. 39, 131–5.

79. N.A. Vlasov, "Desiat' let riadom s Kurchatovym," in M.K. Romanovskii (ed.), *Vospominaniia ob akademike I.V. Kurchatove*, Moscow: Nauka, 1983, pp. 50–51.

80. V.S. Komel'kov, "Tvorets i pobeditel'," in Aleksandrov, *op.cit.*, p. 315.

81. The height of the tower is given by A.I. Burnazian in "O radiatsionnoi bezopasnosti," in Aleksandrov, *op.cit.*, p. 308; the workshop is mentioned by Pervukhin in "Vydaiushchiisia uchenyi i talantlivyi organizator," in Romanovskii, *op.cit.*, p. 13.

82. Fuchs was asked about the blast calculations for the Hiroshima and Nagasaki bombs; he was also asked about the Bikini test, and gave the formula for radiation intensity as a function of distance. He was asked no questions, and gave no information, about the Eniwetok (now spelled Enewetak) test. Fuchs's statement to Michael Perrin, in a letter from J. Edgar Hoover to Admiral Souers, March 2, 1950. HSTL, PSF, p. 6.

83. The most detailed description of the test is given by Golovin, *op.cit.* See also N.A. Vlasov, "Vblizi Kurchatova," in Aleksandrov, *op.cit.*, pp. 292–3; Komel'kov, *loc.cit.*, p. 315.

84. The Russian name for the Radiation Protection Service was *sluzhba radiatsionnoi bezopasnosti*.

85. Burnazian, *loc.cit.*, pp. 307–8. Burnazian was in overall charge of the Sungul Institute; see Zhores Medvedev, *Nuclear Disaster in the Urals*, New York: W.W. Norton, 1979, p. 29.

86. Golovin, *op.cit.*, p. 9.

87. Pervukhin, *loc.cit.*, p. 13.

88. Golovin, *op.cit.*, p. 11.

89. Pervukhin, *loc.cit.*, p. 13.

90. Golovin, *op.cit.*, pp. 13–14.

91. Pervukhin, *loc.cit.*, p. 13.

92. Barwich, *Das Rote Atom*, Murich and Berne: Scherz Verlag, 1977, p. 116.

93. Interview with Khariton, July 16, 1992.

94. Golovin, *op.cit.*, pp. 10–14.

95. See Chapter 3, p. 143.

96. Astashenkov, *op.cit.*, p. 79.

97. Golovin, *op.cit.*, pp. 14–16.

98. *Ibid.*, pp. 8–9, 18–19.

99. Communication from Iu.B. Khariton, July 1993.

100. Golovin, *op.cit.*, p. 20; Khariton, communication, *loc.cit.*

101. D.S. Pereverzev, "Riadom s Kurchatovym," in Aleksandrov, *op.cit.*, p. 386.

102. Astashenkov, *op.cit.*, p. 81.

103. V. Gubarev, "Fizika – eto moia zhizn'," *Pravda*, February 20, 1984, p. 8.

104. Komel'kov, *loc.cit.*, pp. 317–18.

105. Burnazian, *loc.cit.*, p. 309.

106. *Ibid.*, pp. 309–10.

107. *Ibid.*, p. 310.

108. *Ibid.*

109. M.G. Pervukhin, "Pervye gody atomnogo proekta," *Khimiia i zhizn'*, 1985, no. 5, p. 67. The US estimate of the yield of the explosion was also 20 kilotons, on the assumption that the bomb was like the bomb dropped on Nagasaki and tested at Alamogordo.

110. Burnazian, *loc.cit.*, p. 310; Komel'kov, *loc.cit.*, p. 318; Vlasov, "Vblizi Kurchatova," p. 293.

111. Khariton and Smirnov, *loc.cit.*, pp. 50–51.

112. *Ibid.* Khrushchev withdrew this latter privilege.

113. The list of awards was not published at the time or subsequently. I have pieced together this list from various works of reference.

114. Khariton and Smirnov, *loc.cit.*, pp. 39–40.

115. CIA Joint Atomic Energy Intelligence Committee, *Status of the Soviet Atomic Energy Program*, National Scientific Intelligence Estimate, NSIE–1 (CIA/SI 13–52), January 8, 1953, p. 11. HSTL, PSF.

116. Chuck Hansen, *U.S. Nuclear Weapons*, New York: Orion Books, 1988, p. 32.

117. Khariton and Smirnov, *loc.cit.*, p. 40.

118. *Ibid.*, p. 52.

119. Komel'kov, *loc.cit.*, p. 321.

120. A.R. Striganov, "I.V. Kurchatov – Kommunist," in Aleksandrov *op.cit.*, p. 396.

121. R.H. Hillenkoeter, Memorandum for the President, "Estimate of the Status of the Russian Atomic Energy Project," July 6, 1948. HSTL, PSF.

122. CIA, Nuclear Energy Branch, *Status of the USSR Atomic Energy Project*, OSI/SR–10/49, July 1, 1949, p. 1. HSTL, PSF.

123. Nadezhda Kozhevnikova, "Baloven' zhestokoi epokhi," *Sovetskaia kul'tura*, April 14, 1990, p. 15.

124. Fuchs's statement to Michael Perrin, *loc.cit.*,

p. 6.

125. *Ibid.*, p. 7.
126. "Foocase – Espionage (R) Interviews in England with Fuchs," Hugh H. Clegg and Robert J. Lamphere to Director, FBI, June 4, 1950, p. 29. HSTL, PSF.
127. Hans Bethe mentioned 18 months as a good figure, interview April 20, 1979; Rudolf Peierls was told by Artsimovich that he thought espionage saved the Soviet Union a year, interview with Peierls October 7, 1980. The JCAE of the US Congress concluded in April 1951 that atomic espionage had advanced the Soviet project "by 18 months as a minimum." US Congress, JCAE, *Soviet Atomic Espionage*, Washington DC: US Government Printing Office, April 1951, p. 5.
128. Gowing, *op.cit.*, p. 456.
129. *Ibid.*, p. 458.

11. War and the Atomic Bomb

1. G.K. Zhukov, "Korotko o Staline," *Pravda*, January 20, 1989, p. 3.
2. *Ibid.*
3. *Ibid.*
4. N.S. Khrushchev, *Khrushchev Remembers, Vol. 2: The Last Testament*, Harmondsworth: Penguin, 1977, p. 77.
5. "Otvet t-shchu Razinu," in Robert H. McNeal (ed.), *I.V. Stalin, Works, Vol. 3, 1945–1953*, Stanford: Hoover Institution Press, 1967, pp. 29–34.
6. "Prikaz narodnogo komissara oborony 23 fevralia 1942 goda No. 55," in Robert H. McNeal (ed.), *I.V. Stalin, Works, Vol. 2, 1941–1945*, Stanford: Hoover Institution Press, 1967, p. 39.
7. "Otvety na voprosy zadannye korrespondentom 'Sandei Taims', g-nom A. Vert poluchennye 17-go sentiabria 1946 g.," in McNeal, *op.cit.*, Vol. 3, p. 56.
8. "The Hiroshima and Nagasaki Tragedy in Documents," *International Affairs*, 1990, no. 8, p. 125.
9. *Ibid.*
10. *Ibid.*, p. 126.
11. *Ibid.*
12. *Ibid.*, pp. 125, 129.
13. "P.L. Kapitsa: Pis'mo Molotovu," *Vestnik Ministerstva Inostrannykh Del SSSR*, 1990, no. 10, p. 61.
14. "Kratkii obzor svedenii ob ispytanii atomnoi bomby v atolle Bikini," AVP f. 06, op. 8, p. 8, d. 113, p. 40.
15. V.L. Malkov, "Intelligence and Counter-intelligence in the Cold War Period," paper presented at the conference on "The His-

tory of the Cold War," Moscow, January 1993, pp. 25–6.
16. V.S. Gubarev, *Arzamas-16*, Moscow: Izdat, 1992, pp. 18–19.
17. JIC 329 of 3 November 1945 in the CCS 092 USSR (3–27–45) files, Record Group 218, National Archives.
18. David Alan Rosenberg, "American Atomic Strategy and the Hydrogen Bomb Decision," *Journal of American History*, June 1979, Vol. 66, p. 64.
19. *Ibid.*, pp. 66–7.
20. David Alan Rosenberg, "U.S. Nuclear Stockpile, 1945 to 1950," *Bulletin of the Atomic Scientists*, May 1982, pp. 25–30; "Nuclear Notebook: US Weapons Secrets Revealed," *Bulletin of the Atomic Scientists*, March 1993, p. 48.
21. For a discussion of this see Avi Shlaim, *The United States and the Berlin Blockade, 1948–1949*, Berkeley: University of California Press, 1983, pp. 234–40.
22. FRUS, 1948, i, p. 625.
23. NSC-30, "United States Policy on Atomic Warfare," *ibid.*, p. 628.
24. Quoted by Rosenberg, "American Atomic Strategy," p. 68.
25. *Ibid.*, pp. 68–9.
26. JCS 1953/1, May 12 1949, *Report by the Ad Hoc Committee to the Joint Chiefs of Staff on "Evaluation of Effect on Soviet War Effort Resulting from the Strategic Air Offensive,"* National Archives, Record Group 218 CCS 373 (10–23–48), sec. 1, bulky package 1, p. 6.
27. *Ibid.*, pp. 7–8.
28. *Ibid.*, p. 8.
29. FRUS 1949, i, pp. 481–2.
30. David Alan Rosenberg, "The Origins of Overkill," *International Security*, 1983, no. 4, pp. 16–17.
31. *Ibid.*, pp. 22–3.
32. "Nuclear Notebook."
33. Rosenberg, "Origins of Overkill," p. 15.
34. *Ibid.*, pp. 19, 29.
35. Walter S. Poole, *The History of the Joint Chiefs of Staff, Vol. 4, 1950–1952*, Wilmington: Michael Glazier, 1980, p. 168. The B-36 was slow and clumsy and required a 10,000-foot runway with 40 inches of subsurface construction. Alfred Goldberg (ed.), *History of the Strategic Arms Competition, 1945–1972, Part I*, Washington, DC: Office of the Secretary of Defense, Historical Office, March 1981, p. 27.
36. Poole, *op.cit.*, pp. 168–9.
37. *Ibid.*, pp. 169–70.
38. The United States and Britain had aircraft carriers, landing craft, and troop carriers,

while the Soviet Navy had none of these, and had far fewer cruisers, destroyers, and submarines. A similar picture emerges when strategic aircraft are compared.

39. Joint Intelligence Committee (Service Members), *Strategic Vulnerability of the USSR to a Limited Air Attack*, JIC 329, November 3, 1945, National Archives, Record Group 319, ABC 336 Russia (22 August 43), sec. 1–A, p. 2.

40. *Ibid.*, p. 3.

41. M.A. Garelov, "Otkuda ugroza," *Voenno-istoricheskii zhurnal*, 1989, no. 2, pp. 24–5.

42. *Ibid.*

43. The same source gives the naval balance for 1947: the US and the UK had 167 aircraft carriers of all classes, and 7,700 deck aircraft while the Soviet Union had neither; the US and UK had 405 submarines, the Soviet Union 173 (2.3:1); ships of the line and large cruisers 36:4 (9:1); cruisers 135:10 (13.5:1); destroyers and escorts: 1,059:57 (18.6:1). The Soviet Union had no landing craft, while in the 1947 the US had 1,114, as well as 628 troop carriers. *Ibid.*, p. 24.

44. On the restructuring of the ground forces see John Erickson, "The Evolution of the Soviet Ground Forces, 1941–1985," in John Erickson, Lynn Hansen, and William Schneider, *Soviet Ground Forces: An Operational Assessment*, Boulder: Westview Press, 1986, pp. 20–26. An effort was made to keep the best officers in the armed forces, and only 2.5 per cent of those with higher military education were demobilized. See S.A. Tiushkevich *et al.*, *Sovetskie vooruzhennye sily*, Moscow: Voenizdat, 1978, p. 374.

45. Garelov, *loc.cit.*, p. 24.

46. *Ibid.*, p. 25.

47. *Ibid.*

48. Matthew Evangelista, "Stalin's Postwar Army Reappraised," *International Security*, Winter 1982–1983, p. 114.

49. Garelov, *loc.cit.*, pp. 27–31.

50. David Glantz, "Soviet Military Strategy after CFE: Historical Models and Future Prospects," *Journal of Soviet Military Studies*, June 1990, pp. 268–9. US intelligence knew of the formations and units listed in the GSFG's operational plan; but it also identified another eight cadre divisions which are not mentioned in the plan (*ibid.*).

51. Evangelista, *loc.cit.*, pp. 118–19.

52. *Ibid.*, p. 119. In the drive to Berlin in the spring of 1945 the Red Army enjoyed superiority in the following ratios: 5.5:1 in manpower; 7.8:1 in artillery; 5.7:1 in tanks;

17.6:1 in aircraft. *Ibid.*, p. 120.

53. "Otvet t-shchu Razinu," p. 33. A careful distinction was drawn in Soviet military theory between the counterattack (*kontrataka*), which was tactical, the counterblow (*kontrudar*), which was operational, and the counteroffensive (*kontrnastuplenie*), which was strategic. (See, for example, Lieut.-Gen. P. Iarchevskii, "Kontrataki, kontrudary, kontrnastupleniia," *Voennaia Mysl'*, 1947, no. 3, pp. 18–27.)

54. Maj.-Gen. N. Talenskii, "Strategicheskoe kontrnastuplenie," *Voennaia Mysl'*, 1946, no. 6, pp. 3–16.

55. Quoted *ibid.*, p. 4.

56. *50 let vooruzhennykh sil SSSR*, Moscow: Voenizdat, 1968, p. 495.

57. Col. L. Vnotchenko, "Nekotorye voprosy teorii nastupatel'nykh i oboronitel'nykh operatsii (1945–1953 gg.)," *Voenno-istoricheskii zhurnal*, 1970, no. 8, pp. 34–5.

58. Maj.-Gen. M. Cherednichenko, "Razvitie teorii strategicheskoi nastupatel'noi operatsii v 1945–1953 gg.," *Voenno-istoricheskii zhurnal*, 1976, no. 8, pp. 38–45; see also his "Ob osobennostiakh razvitiia voennogo iskusstva v poslevoennyi period," *Voenno-istoricheskii zhurnal*, 1970, no. 6, pp. 19–30. See also M.M. Kir'ian (ed.), *Voenno-tekhnicheskii progress i vooruzhennye sily SSSR*, Moscow: Voenizdat, 1982, pp. 239–55.

59. V.S. Shumikhin, *Sovetskaia voennaia aviatsiia, 1917–1941*, Moscow: Nauka, 1986, p. 246. In Soviet usage the term "Air Forces" (*Voenno-vozdushnye sily*) is used rather than "Air Force," but I have used Air Force here as the generic term.

60. Shumikhin, *op.cit.*, pp. 245–9; M.N. Kozhevnikov, *Komandovanie i shtab VVS Sovetskoi Armii v Velikoi Otechestvennoi voine 1941–1945*, 2nd edn, Moscow: Nauka, 1985, pp. 30–32.

61. Shumikhin, *op.cit.*, p. 249.

62. A.D. Tsykin, *Ot "Il'i Muromtsa" do Raketonostsa*, Moscow: Voenizdat, 1975, p. 61.

63. Martin Gilbert, *Winston S. Churchill. Vol. 7: Road to Victory, 1941–1945*, Boston: Houghton Mifflin, 1986, p. 468.

64. General of the Air Force H.H. Arnold, *Global Mission*, New York: Harper, 1949, p. 469.

65. Robert Huhn Jones, *The Roads to Russia*; Norman: University of Oklahoma Press, 1969, p. 176; John R. Deane, *The Strange Alliance*, New York: Viking Press, 1947, pp. 229–30.

66. Jean Alexander, *Russian Aircraft since 1940*, London: Putnam, 1975, p. 357.

67. On the date of the first raid see Arnold, *op.cit.*, p. 480.

68. Alexander, *op.cit.*, p. 358.

69. Tupolev's design bureau was instructed to develop a four-engined bomber with a range of 3,000 kilometers, a speed of 600 km/h at 6,000 meters, and a bomb load of 5 metric tons; this was known as Project 64. See V.B. Shavrov, *Istoriia konstruktsii samoletov v SSSR 1938–1950 gg.*, Moscow: Mashinostroenie, 1978, pp. 354–5. In 1945 Miasishchev worked on the design of a bomber with four German JUMO-004 jet engines, with a range of 3,000 kilometers with one metric ton of bombs, and a speed of 800 km/h at 8,000 meters. See V.A. Fedotov, "Nauchno-konstruktorskaia deiatel'nost' V.M. Miasishcheva," in *Issledovaniia po istorii i teorii razvitiia aviatsionnoi i raketno-kosmicheskoi nauki i tekhniki*, Vol. 4, Moscow: Nauka, 1985, p. 47. See also Shavrov, *op.cit.*, p. 180. L.L. Kerber, *Tu – chelovek i samolet*, Moscow: Sovetskaia Rossiia, 1973, p. 172, refers to Il'iushin working on a similar design.

70. Shavrov, *op.cit.*, p. 355; Kerber, *op.cit.*, p. 173.

71. Shavrov, *op.cit.*, p. 354.

72. The Iak-15 was designed by the Iakovlev design bureau, which replaced the piston engine in the Iak-3 with the German JUMO-004 jet engine. The MiG-9 was designed by the Mikoyan bureau around the German BMW-003 engine. A.S. Iakovlev, *Sovetskie samolety*, 3rd edn, Moscow: Nauka, 1979, pp. 139–41; Heinz J. Nowarra and G.R. Duval, *Russian Civil and Military Aircraft, 1884–1969*, London: Fountain Press, 1971, pp. 152–3.

73. A. Iakovlev, *Tsel' zhizni*, 4th edn, Moscow: Politizdat, 1974, p. 431.

74. Kenneth R. Whiting, *Soviet Air Power*, Boulder: Westview Press, 1986, p. 127 gives a figure of 15,000 produced by 1953. Bill Gunston, *Aircraft of the Soviet Union*, London: Osprey, 1983, p. 175, writes that 5,000 were produced.

75. Shavrov, *op.cit.*, pp. 341–2.

76. Iakovlev, *Sovetskie samolety*, pp. 142, 153.

77. Col. B.G. Zabelok, "Razvitie taktiki i operativnogo iskusstva Voisk PVO strany," *Vestnik protivovozdushnoi oborony*, 1968, no. 2, p. 24.

78. *Voiska protivovozdushnoi oborony strany. Istoricheskii ocherk* (hereafter *Voiska*), Moscow: Voenizdat, 1968, pp. 346–7. A 130mm gun was developed to fire at targets between 12,000 and 16,000 meters, and passed its state trials in 1951. The Council of Ministers decided not to put it into production, however, but to recommend transition to surface-to-air missiles (SAMs) instead. This decision was later reversed, and the 130mm gun was deployed along with SAMs in the mid-1950s. Steven J. Zaloga, *Soviet Air Defence Missiles*, Coulsden: Jane's Information Group, 1989, pp. 31, 34. M.M. Lobanov, *Razvitie sovetskoi radiolokatsionnoi tekhniki*, Moscow: Voenizdat, 1982, p. 164.

79. Zaloga, *op.cit.*, pp. 10, 30. Interview with A.A. Basistov, December 5, 1992.

80. Lobanov, *op.cit.*, p. 158.

81. Lobanov, *op.cit.*, pp. 171–2.

82. *Ibid.*, pp. 172–4. An American evaluation of its performance in the Korean War concluded that it could detect a medium bomber like the B-47 at a range of 100km and an altitude of 3,300m, or at a range of 185km and an altitude of 10,000m *Zaloga, op.cit.*, p. 328.

83. Lobanov, *op.cit.*, pp. 174–6; Zaloga, *op.cit.*, 329–31.

84. Lobanov, *op.cit.*, pp. 178–80.

85. *Ordena Lenina Moskovskii Okrug PVO*, Moscow: Voenizdat, 1981, p. 185.

86. Zaloga, *op.cit.*, p. 340.

87. *Voiska*, p. 349.

88. *Ibid.*, p. 351.

89. *Ibid.*, pp. 349–50; *50 let*, p. 488.

90. *Voiska*, p. 349.

91. Col. N. Iakimanskii and Maj. V. Gorbunov, "Nekotorye voprosy razvitiia teorii operativnogo iskusstva i taktiki Voisk PVO strany v poslevoennyi period," *Voenno-istoricheskii zhurnal*, 1973, no. 3, p. 39.

92. *Voiska*, p. 356.

93. G.I. Pokrovskii, *Predposylki primeneniia energii atomnogo iadra v aviabombakh*, Moscow: Voenno-vozdushnaia inzhenernaia akademiia imeni prof. N.E. Zhukovskogo, 1946, p. 20. These conclusions are similar to those drawn by the JCS from the 1946 Bikini tests. They concluded that because of the scarcity of fissionable material the bomb would be used as a strategic weapon against urban industrial targets and not – except in extraordinary circumstances – against naval vessels or troop concentrations. See Rosenberg, "American Atomic Strategy," p. 67.

94. Pokrovskii, *op.cit.* There is no reason to assume that Pokrovskii was privy to secret information. He assumed, wrongly, that as little as one kilogram of plutonium or ura-

nium-235 would be needed for each bomb.

95. *Ibid.* and G.I. Pokrovskii, "Atomnaia energiia i perspektivy ee ispol'zovaniia," *Bloknot agitatora*, 1946, no. 15, p. 48.

96. The initial setbacks of the war could not be studied in a critical or objective way. See Matthew Gallagher, *The Soviet History of World War II: Myths, Memories and Realities*, New York: Frederick A. Praeger, 1963, pp. 37–78.

97. Interview with Col.-Gen. A.A. Danilevich, October 24, 1990.

98. Interview with Maj.-Gen. V.V. Larionov, November 13, 1990. An Instruction (*Instruktsiia*) is a document that contains instructions about the use of weapons or equipment.

99. Interview with Danilevich, October 24, 1990.

100. See the comments by Vladimir Larionov in his memoirs, *Bez voiny*, Kiev: Politizdat Ukrainy, 1982, pp. 71–187.

101. The US Strategic Bombing Survey was carried out at the end of World War II to assess the effects of the strategic bombing campaigns against Germany and Japan.

102. See, for example, V. Chalikov, "O roli strategicheskoi aviatsii," *Voennaia Mysl'*, 1946, no. 9; I. Krasnov, "O roli strategicheskikh bombardirovok v porazhenii Germanii," *Voennaia Mysl'*, 1947, no. 7; Colonel N. Chistov, "O zarubezhnykh vzgliadakh na rol' aviatsii v voine," *Voennaia Mysl'*, 1947, no. 9.

103. Col. M. Tolchenov, "Amerikanskaia pechat' o kharaktere budushchei voiny," *Voennaia Mysl'*, 1949, no. 6, p. 77.

104. Col. P. Fedorov, "O deistviiakh strategicheskoi aviatsii SShA vo vtoroi mirovoi voine," *Voennaia Mysl'*, 1949, no. 10, p. 66.

105. Maj.-Gen. of Tank Forces V. Khlopov, "O kharaktere voennoi doktriny amerikanskogo imperializma," *Voennaia Mysl'*, 1950, no. 6, pp. 67–78.

106. *Ibid.*, pp. 74–5.

107. *Ibid.*, p. 76.

108. Poole, *op.cit.*, pp. 161–2.

109. *Ibid.* See also Kenneth W. Condit, *The History of the Joint Chiefs of Staff: The Joint Chiefs of Staff and National Policy, Vol. 2: 1947–1949*, Washington, DC: Historical Division, Joint Secretariat, Joint Chiefs of Staff (declassified March 1978), pp. 294–302.

110. The "Offtackle" plan called for "attacks on 104 urban targets with 220 atomic bombs, plus a re-attack reserve of 72 weapons." Rosenberg, "Origins of Overkill," p. 16. Rosenberg in "American Atomic Strategy,"

p. 70, quotes a US admiral who wrote in an internal memorandum in January 1949 that "some authorities estimate that the damage done by strategic bombing of Germany was equivalent to 500 Atomic Bombs. But Germany did not surrender until her armies were defeated."

111. Interview with G.N. Flerov, November 17, 1990.

112. Soviet intelligence knew from Klaus Fuchs that the American stockpile was very small in the immediate aftermath of Hiroshima. (See p. 153.) Donald Maclean may have been able to provide some relevant information about United States raw materials requirements and production plans when he was secretary to the Combined Policy Committee in 1947 and 1948. See p. 174. By the 1950s samples of krypton-85 were being analyzed in order to assess the level of plutonium production in the United States (interview with G.N. Flerov, November 17, 1990).

113. Transcript of the Khrushchev memoirs, Columbia University, p. 384.

114. Litvinov, in his interview with Richard Hottelet in June 1946, commented that "if one side feels that its immense area and manpower, resources and dispersed industry safeguard it to a large extent, it will not be loath to use the bomb." Richard C. Hottelet, "Russians Did Not Realize Power of A-Bomb or Fear Atomic War, Litvinov Warned in '46," *Washington Post*, January 22, 1952, p. 11B.

115. John Erickson, *The Road to Stalingrad. Stalin's War with Germany*, Vol. 1, New York: Harper and Row, 1975, p. 223.

116. Goldberg, *op.cit.*, p. 257.

117. Glantz, *loc.cit.*, p. 269. Soviet sources confirm that the Soviet Union began to increase the size of its forces in 1949. See *50 let*, p. 480.

118. Thomas W. Wolfe, *Soviet Power and Europe, 1945–1970*, Baltimore: Johns Hopkins University Press, 1970, pp. 39–40. A memorandum from Admiral Hillenkoeter, director of Central Intelligence, to the White House on May 25, 1950 states that "new evidence clearly indicates that, since the summer of 1949, Soviet Armed Forces personnel strength has been increasing, as has been Soviet capabilities for aggressive military action" (HSTL). A CIA report in October 1951 noted that "for some time the USSR has been systematically strengthening its own and Satellite forces in Eastern Europe to maintain its relative advantage over growing Western strength." Special Esti-

mate: *The Strength and Capabilities of Soviet Bloc Forces to Conduct Military Operations against NATO*, SE-16, published October 12, 1951, p. 14. HSTL, PSF Intelligence File, Folder: SE Special Estimate Reports No. 10–18, Box 258.

119. Rokossovskii took his orders from Moscow, though he was a member of the Politburo of the Polish Party. A. Ross Johnson, Robert W. Dean, and Alexander Alexiev, *East European Military Establishments: The Warsaw Pact Northern Tier*, New York: Crane Russak, 1980, p. 20.

120. *Ibid.*, pp. 19–20.

121. CIA: Memorandum, "Status of Para-Military Forces in Soviet Zone Germany," July 7, 1950, pp. 1–2. HSTL, PSF. CIA Intelligence Memorandum No. 322, August 21, 1950: "Increased Capabilities of Paramilitary Forces in Soviet Zone Germany," pp. 1–3. HSTL, PSF.

122. Condoleezza Rice, *The Soviet Union and the Czechoslovak Army, 1948–1983*, Princeton: Princeton University Press, 1984, pp. 76–9.

123. Johnson *et al.*, *op.cit.*, p. 114.

124. Zoltan D. Barany, "Soviet Control of the Hungarian Military Under Stalin," *Journal of Strategic Studies*, June 1991, pp. 156–7.

125. *Handbook on the Satellite Armies*, Department of the Army Pamphlet No. 30–50–2, Washington, DC: Department of the Army, 1960, p. 3.

126. N.S. Khrushchev, "Preniia po dokladu tovarishcha N.S. Khrushcheva," *Pravda*, January 15, 1960.

127. Some sources put the origins of the naval build-up in 1946, but this appears to be wrong. See Goldberg, *op.cit.*, p. 268.

128. See Joint Intelligence Committee, *Implications of Soviet Armaments Programs and Increasing Military Capabilities*, JIC 436/2, January 16, 1956, p. 6. National Archives, Record Group 218, CCS 334 JIC (12–28–53), sec. 1. Robert Waring Herrick, *Soviet Naval Strategy*, Annapolis: US Naval Institute, 1968, pp. 63–4.

129. V. Chalmaev, *Malyshev*, Moscow: Molodaia gvardiia, 1978, pp. 320, 344.

130. Kir'ian, *op.cit.*, pp. 251–2.

131. Khrushchev, *op.cit.*, p. 49.

132. Vladimir Karpov, *Polkovodets*, Moscow: Sovetskii pisatel', 1988, p. 633.

133. *Ibid.*, pp. 634–5.

134. Pietro Nenni, *Tempo di Guerra Fredda. Diari 1943–1956*, Milan: SugarCo Edizioni, 1981, p. 537.

135. *Sto sorok besed s Molotovym: iz dnevnika F. Chueva*, Moscow: Terra, 1991, p. 100.

136. Interview with Col.-Gen. A.A. Danilevich, October 24, 1990.

137. *Ibid.* I have been told both that this was a film of the first Soviet tests, and that it was a film of the bombing of Hiroshima and Nagasaki; perhaps it was both.

138. Karpov, *op.cit.*, pp. 635–6; *Sovetskaia voennaia entsiklopediia*, Vol. 6, Moscow: Voenizdat, 1978, p. 313.

139. *Sovetskaia voennaia entsiklopediia*, Vol. 3, Moscow: Voenizdat, 1977, p. 92.

140. Garelov, *loc.cit.*, p. 24. The Joint Intelligence Committee of the JCS estimated in November 1948 that on August 1 the Long-Range Air Force consisted of 1,000 multi-engined bombers such as the Il-4, 600 Li-2 transports, and 200 Tu-4s. JIC 435/12, November 30, 1948, *Soviet Intentions and Capabilities, 1949, 1956/57*, p. 22. National Security Archive, Washington, DC.

141. Elements of the Long-Range Air Force would take part in the operation to establish air superiority in the initial phase of strategic offensive operations. Maj.-Gen. M. Cherednichenko, "Razvitie teorii strategicheskoi nastupatel'noi operatsii v 1945–1953 gg.," *Voenno-istoricheckii zhurnal*, 1976, no. 8, p. 42.

142. Shavrov, *op.cit.*, p. 358; *Andrei Nikolaevich Tupolev: grani derznovennogo tvorchestva*, Moscow: Nauka, 1988, p. 239.

143. Shavrov, *op.cit.*, pp. 350–58.

144. Kerber, *op.cit.*, p. 186. Stalin signed the document authorizing production. *Ibid.* The Tu-4 was the only aircraft to be distinguished in this way. A.N. Ponomarev, "Tvoria nevidannyi polet," *Znamia*, January 1980, p. 175.

145. US Intelligence estimated that there were 1,150 Tu-4s in the Soviet Air Force in mid-1955, and that production had ceased in 1953. See *Special Staff Study for the President, NSC Action No. 1328: Vol. III, Reproduction of Charts Used in Presentation of May 26, 1955*, Charts on Aircraft Production and Bloc Air Strength. Washington, DC: National Security Archive. Some writers estimate total production to have been as low as 400. See Gunston, *op.cit.*, 1983, p. 324. Alexander, *op.cit.*, p. 359 writes that 1,200 were built, of which 400 were delivered to the Chinese Air Force. On the modification of the Tu-4 to carry atomic bombs see Iu.B. Khariton and Iu.N. Smirnov, "O nekotorykh mifakh i legendakh vokrug sovetskikh atomnogo i vodorodnogo proektov," *Materialy iubileinoi sessii uchenogo soveta tsentra, 12 ianvaria 1993 g.*, Moscow: Kurchatovskii institut, 1993, p. 38.

146. Kerber, *op.cit.*, p. 216.
147. This judgment was soon borne out when US Air Force B-29s proved vulnerable to the MiG-15 in the Korean War and had to be switched from strategic missions to tactical support of ground operations. Kenneth R. Whiting, *Soviet Air Power*, Boulder, Colo.: Westview Press, 1986, p. 39.
148. Kerber, *op.cit.*, p. 216.
149. *Ibid.*, pp. 218–19. The engine was developed by A.A. Mikulin's design bureau.
150. *Ibid.*, p. 219.
151. A.S. Iakovlev, *Sovetskie samolety*, Moscow: Nauka, 1979, p. 143. For the range of Western estimates see Neta Crawford, *World Weapons Database Vol. 2: Soviet Military Aircraft*, Brookline Mass.: Institute for Defense and Disarmament Studies, 1987, pp. 106–20.
152. For the date of the test see *Andrei Nikolaevich Tupolev*, p. 240. It performed much better than the Iliushin bureau's competitive design, the Il-46, a scaled-up version of the Il-28 frontal bomber. *Ilyuschin und seine Flugzeuge*, Berlin: Transpress, 1976, pp. 67–8. It was called "Badger" by NATO.
153. CIA, *Appendices to NIE-64 (Part I): Soviet Bloc Capabilities through mid-1953*, December 24, 1952, National Archives: NNMM reference collection – CIA box, p. 13. At the end of 1952 there were 570 Tu-4s in western USSR, 300 in south-western USSR, and 100 in the Far East. *Ibid.*, p. 21. These forces could be redeployed relatively easily; "at least 30 airfields in the USSR and the Satellites are currently suitable for sustained medium bomber [i.e. Tu-4] operations, and about 75 others for limited medium bomber operations." *Ibid.*, p. 14.
154. *50 let*, p. 496; Kir'ian *op.cit.*, pp. 250–51.
155. S.A. Krasovskii, *et al.*, *Aviatsiia i kosmonavtika SSSR*, Moscow: Voenizdat, 1968, p. 347.
156. Cherednichenko, "Ob osobennostiakh," p. 22.
157. *Ibid.*
158. *Voiska*, p. 356.
159. CIA: Special National Intelligence Estimate, *Soviet Capabilities for Attack on the US through 1957*, SNIE 11-2–54, published February 24, 1954, pp. 5–6. HSTL, PSF.
160. Steven J. Zaloga, *Target: America*, Novato, Calif.: Presidio Press, 1992, pp. 48–9.
161. Shavrov, *op.cit.*, pp. 361–2, writes that the first test took place early in 1950, and implies that development of the plane started at the beginning of 1948.
162. Ponomarev, *Sovetskie aviatsionnye konstruktory*, 3rd edn, Moscow: Voenizdat,

1990, p. 45. Ponomarev, "Tvoria nevidannyi polet," p. 176. *Andrei Nikolaevich Tupolev*, p. 240.
163. D. Gai, *Nebesnoe pritiazhenie*, Moscow: Moskovskii rabochii, 1984, pp. 119; see also *Andrei Nikolaevich Tupolev*, p. 176, and G.A. Ozerov, *Tupolevskaia sharaga*, 2nd edn, Frankfurt: Possev, 1973, p. 52.
164. Gai, *op.cit.*, p. 119; *Andrei Nikolaevich Tupolev*, p. 240.
165. Alexander, *op.cit.*, p. 387. The Tu-95 is powered by the NK-12 engine which was designed with the help of Dr Ferdinand Brandner. See Alexander Boyd, *The Soviet Air Force since 1918*, New York: Stein and Day, 1977, pp. 222–3, and Ferdinand Brandner, *Ein Leben zwischen Fronten*, Munich: Verlag Welsermuehl, 1973, pp. 199–205.
166. Shavrov, *op.cit.*, pp. 176–80; Fedotov, *loc.cit.*, p. 47.
167. Fedotov, *loc.cit.*, p. 47; Gai, *op.cit.*, pp. 116–19.
168. Ozerov, *op.cit.*, p. 52.
169. Gai, *op.cit.*, pp. 138, 142.
170. Ozerov, *op.cit.*, p. 52; Alexander, *op.cit.*, pp. 289–90; see also Crawford, *op.cit.*, pp. 193–5.
171. Ponomarev, *op.cit.*, p. 234; Gai, *op.cit.*, pp. 158, 162.
172. US intelligence estimated that the Soviet Union had twenty 103Ms in operational units in mid-1955. See Special Staff Study for the President, NSC Action No. 1328, Vol. 3: *Reproduction of Charts Used in Presentation of May 26, 1955, Chart of Estimated Bloc Air Strength*, Washington, DC: National Security Archive.
173. CIA, *Scientific Research Institute and Experimental Factory 88 for Guided Missile Development, Moskva/Kaliningrad*, OSI–C–RA/60–2, March 4, 1960, p. 33. NII-88 was subordinate to the Seventh Chief Directorate of the Ministry of Armament.
174. *Ibid.*, p. 4.
175. G.S. Vetrov in A. Iu. Ishlinskii (ed.), *Akademik S.P. Korolev: uchenyi, inzhener, chelovek*, Moscow: Nauka, 1986, p. 300.
176. CIA, *Scientific Research Institute*, p. 5.
177. Vetrov, *loc.cit.*, p. 299.
178. P.N. Kuleshov, "Reaktivnaia artilleriia i ee budushchee," *Za oboronu*, no. 1–2, January 1947, p. 24. See also Col. N. Nikiforov, "Reaktivnaia artilleriia," *Za oboronu*, September 1946, no. 17–18, pp. 11–12; Engineer-Maj. A. Ivanov, "Letaiushchaia bomba Fau-2," *Za oboronu*, April 1946, no. 7–8, pp. 21–2.
179. V.S. Emel'ianov, *S chego nachinalos'*,

Moscow: Sovetskaia Rossiia, 1979, p. 219. Emel'ianov writes that Korolev approached him about this at the beginning of 1946. This seems too early but, whatever the exact date, the conversation indicates the pressure that Korolev was under at the time to achieve much greater ranges than the V-2.

180. Vetrov, *loc.cit.*, p. 299.

181. *Ibid.*

182. *Ibid.*; see also G. Vetrov, "Na puti k pervoi kosmicheskoi," *Nauka i zhizn'*, 1980, no. 2, pp. 12–13.

183. G.A. Tokaty, "Soviet Rocket Technology," in Eugene M. Emme (ed.), *The History of Rocket Technology*, Detroit: Wayne State University Press, 1964, p. 281. Tokaty defected from the Soviet Union in the late 1940s, and wrote extensively about his experiences there. Later Soviet publications confirm that there were meetings in the Kremlin in April 1947. See, for example, A.P. Romanov and V.S. Gubarev, *Konstruktory*, Moscow: Politizdat, 1989, p. 62.

184. I.M. Iapunskii, "Obosnovanie M.K. Tikhonravovym idei mnogostupenchatoi rakety raketnoi sistemy," *Iz istorii aviatsii i kosmonavtiki*, no. 36, Moscow: Akademiia nauk SSSR, 1979, p. 186. Soviet skeptics were not the only ones. See Vannevar Bush, *Modern Arms and Free Men*, New York: Simon and Schuster, 1949, pp. 85–7.

185. M.V. Keldysh, *Izbrannye trudy: Raketnaia tekhnika i kosmonavtika*, Moscow: Nauka, 1988, pp. 8–9; M.V. Keldysh (ed.), *Tvorcheskoe nasledie akademika Sergeia Pavlovicha Koroleva*, Moscow: Nauka, 1980, p. 328.

186. M.V. Keldysh, "O silovoi ustanovke stratosfernogo sverkhskorostnogo samoleta," in Keldysh, *Izbrannye trudy* p. 34. According to Tokaty, this project was discussed at the April 1947 meeting in the Kremlin.

187. CIA, *Scientific Research Institute*, p. 6; V. Tolubko, *Nedelin*, Moscow: Molodaia Gvardiia, 1979, p. 177.

188. Tolubko, *op.cit.*, pp. 174–9.

189. Keldysh *Tvorcheskoe nasledie*, p. 396; B.V. Raushenbakh (ed.), *Iz istorii sovetskoi kosmonavtiki*, Moscow: Nauka, 1983, p. 226.

190. Vetrov, in Ishlinskii (ed.), *op.cit.*, *loc.cit.*, p. 300.

191. Keldysh *Tvorcheskoe nasledie*, p. 544; Vetrov, in *Nauka i zhizn'*, pp. 13–14. I.K. Bazhinov and G.Iu. Maksimov, "Ob issledovaniiakh vozmozhnostei sozdaniia v SSSR pervykh moshchnykh sostavnykh raket i iskusstvennykh sputnikov zemli," in

Issledovaniia po istorii i teorii razvitiia aviatsionnoi i raketno-kosmicheskoi nauki i tekhniki, Vol. 7, Moscow: Nauka, 1989, p. 14.

192. O.G. Ivanovskii, *Naperekor zemnomu pritiazhen'iu*, Moscow: Politizdat, 1988, p. 148, makes it clear that the first rocket to carry a nuclear warhead was the R-5. Interview with Col.-Gen. Iu.P. Zabegailov, October 22, 1990.

193. Romanov and Gubarev, *op.cit.*, p. 65; see also Tolubko, *op.cit.*, pp. 175–6. Both of these sources imply that the meeting was held in 1947, or possibly in early 1948.

194. N.N. Flerov, "Delenie urana pod deistviem kosmicheskikh luchei na bol'shikh vysotakh," unpublished manuscript, p. 1. Interview with G.N. Flerov, November 12, 1990.

195. V.I. Prishchepa, "Iz istorii sozdaniia pervykh kosmicheskikh raketnykh dvigatelei (1947–1957)," in *Issledovaniia po istorii i teorii razvitiia aviatsionnoi i raketno-kosmicheskoi nauki i tekhniki*, Moscow: Nauka, 1981, p. 125.

196. *Ibid.*, p. 124.

197. Korolev makes this point in his draft design for the R-3 missile, in Keldysh *Tvorcheskoe nasledie*, p. 292.

198. The first volume of the draft design for the R-3 has been published *ibid.*, pp. 291–318, under the title "Printsipy i metody proektirovaniia raket bol'shoi dal'nosti."

199. Prishchepa, *loc.cit.*, p. 129.

200. I.K. Bazhinov and G.Iu. Maksimov, *loc.cit.*, p. 17; Keldysh, *Tvorcheskoe nasledie*, p. 293.

201. CIA, *Scientific Research Institute*, pp. 6–9; see also CIA, *The R-14 Project, a Design of a Long Range Missile at Gorodomyla Island*, Information Report No. CS-G-14851, August 26, 1953, pp. 1–35.

202. Keldysh, *Tvorceskoe nasledie*, p. 292.

203. Vetrov, in Ishlinskii (ed.), *op.cit.*, p. 302; Keldysh, *Izbrannye trudy*, p. 139.

204. Vetrov, in Ishlinskii, *op.cit.*, pp. 302–3; *Iz istorii sovetskoi kosmonavtiki*, Moscow: Nauka, 1983, pp. 232–4.

205. Vetrov, in Ishlinskii (ed.), *op.cit.*, p. 302; Keldysh, *Izbrannye trudy*, pp. 142–4.

206. Iapunskii, *loc.cit.*, p. 186.

207. Bazhinov and Maksimov, *loc.cit.*, pp. 15–17.

208. Iapunskii, *loc.cit.*, p. 186.

209. Tikhonravov was already thinking about the possibility of using such a rocket to put an artificial satellite into earth orbit, but he said nothing about this, knowing that such a suggestion would seem outrageous and ruin his case.

210. Iapunskii, *loc.cit.*, p. 186.

211. *Ibid.*, p. 319.
212. Bazhinov and Maksimov, *loc.cit.*, p. 20; Andrei Tarasov, "Ot lopaty do 'Burana'," *Pravda*, May 1, 1989, p. 4. In January 1952 Korolev presented a report on research into long-range cruise missile design, and concluded that a range of 8,000 kilometers could be attained by a missile with a ballistic first stage and a cruise second stage. See "Tezisy doklada po rezul'tatam issledovanii perspektiv razvitiia krylatykh raket dal'nego deistviia," in Keldysh, *Tvorcheskoe nasledie*, pp. 328–41, p. 334.
213. "Otvet tovarishcha I.V. Stalina korrespondentu 'Pravdy' naschet atomnogo oruzhiia," *Pravda*, October 6, 1951.
214. Poole, *op.cit.*, p. 167.
215. On the design philosophies of Tupolev and Miasishchev see Ozerov, *op.cit.*, pp. 52, 57 ff.

12. The War of Nerves

1. Harry S. Truman, *Memoirs, Vol. 2: Years of Trial and Hope, 1946–1952*, New York: Signet Books, 1965, pp. 127–9; Melvyn P. Leffler, *A Preponderance of Power*, Stanford: Stanford University Press, 1992, pp. 143–6.
2. N.V. Novikov, *Vospominaniia diplomata*, Moscow: Politizdat, 1989, p. 379.
3. FRUS 1947, ii, pp. 343–4.
4. George Kennan, *Memoirs, 1925–1950*, New York: Pantheon Books, 1967, pp. 325–6.
5. *Ibid.*, pp. 340–2; Leffler, *op.cit.*, pp. 157–64.
6. Novikov to Molotov, June 9, 1947; document reproduced in Galina Takhnenko, "Anatomy of a Political Decision: Notes on the Marshall Plan," *International Affairs*, July 1992, p. 116.
7. Molotov's instructions are reproduced *ibid.*, pp. 121–2.
8. V.M. Molotov, *Problems of Foreign Policy: Speeches and Statements April 1945–November 1948*, Moscow: Foreign Languages Publishing House, 1949, pp. 459–64.
9. Molotov drew this conclusion not only from British and French attitudes at the meeting, but also from intelligence about conversations between the British and the French and US Assistant Secretary of State William Clayton. See Mikhail Narinskii, "The Soviet Union and the Marshall Plan," Paper given at a conference on "New Evidence on Cold War History," Moscow, January 1993.
10. Molotov, *op.cit.*, p. 466.
11. Michael J. Hogan, *The Marshall Plan*, Cambridge: Cambridge University Press, 1987, p. 52.
12. *Sto sorok besed s Molotovym: iz dnevnika F. Chueva*, Moscow: Terra, 1991, pp. 88–9.
13. See Takhnenko, *loc.cit.*, pp. 122–5.
14. This memorandum has not been published, but Novikov provides a brief account, *op.cit.*, pp. 391, 394–5.
15. *Ibid.*, p. 396.
16. Dmitrii Volkogonov, *Triumf i tragediia*, Book II, 2nd edn, Moscow: Novosti, 1990, p. 487.
17. On the founding meeting of the Cominform see Jonathan Haslam, "The Soviet Union and the Foundation of the Cominform 1947," unpublished paper; Paolo Spriano, *Stalin and the European Communists*, London: Verso, 1985, pp. 292–306; Fernando Claudin, *The Communist Movement from Comintern to Cominform*, Harmondsworth: Penguin, 1975, pp. 455–79; Lilly Marcou, *Le Kominform*, Paris: Presses de la Fondation Nationale des Sciences Politiques, 1977, pp. 39–72.
18. *Informatsionnoe soveshchanie predstavitelei nekotorykh kompartii*, Moscow: Gospolitizdat, 1948, pp. 22–3.
19. *Ibid.*, p. 22.
20. *Ibid.*, p. 38.
21. *Ibid.*, p. 47.
22. On Stalin's approval see Volkogonov, *op.cit.*, p. 489.
23. Spriano writes that "no decision in the international Communist movement was ever more pragmatic and 'state-motivated' than the foundation of the Cominform in 1947. And never was the real motive more carefully buried in a flood of doctrinal argumentation and principled pronouncements." *Op.cit.*, p. 292.
24. Haslam, *loc.cit.*, pp. 30–3.
25. Spriano, *op.cit.*, p. 298.
26. On the postwar coalitions and the effect of the Cominform meeting see Charles Gati, *Hungary and the Soviet Bloc*, Durham, NC: Duke University Press, 1986, pp. 73–99, 108–23.
27. The Soviet ambassador in Belgrade complained in his dispatches to Moscow that the Yugoslavs put too much stress on the role of the Partisan movement in liberating the country. "Konflikt, kotorogo ne dolzhno bylo byt'," *Vestnik Ministerstva Inostrannykh Del SSSR*, 1990, no. 6, p. 54.
28. Iu.S. Girenko, *Stalin-Tito*, Moscow: Politizdat, 1991, pp. 336–7.
29. Milovan Djilas, *Conversations with Stalin*, Harmondsworth: Penguin, 1963, pp. 136,

141; Edvard Kardelj, *Reminiscences*, London: Blond and Briggs, 1982, p. 108.

30. N.S. Khrushchev, *Khrushchev Remembers: The Glasnost Tapes*, Boston: Little, Brown, 1990, pp. 102–3.

31. Pietro Nenni, *Tempo di Guerra Fredda: Diari 1943–1956*, Milan: SugarCo Edizioni, 1981, p. 400.

32. V. Chalmaev, *Malyshev*, Moscow: Molodaia gvardiia, 1978, p. 311. Malyshev's special responsibility for military technology and production was not announced at the time, but it has become clear since then.

33. In the autumn of 1947 Moscow set up a Committee of Information, headed by Molotov, to coordinate and evaluate foreign intelligence. This was a response to the creation of the CIA earlier in the year. Christopher Andrew and Oleg Gordievsky, *KGB: The Inside Story*, New York: Harper Collins, 1990, p. 381.

34. Molotov, *op.cit.*, p. 488.

35. See the memorandum of November 13, 1947 by Edmund A. Gullion, Special Assistant to Under-Secretary of State Lovett, FRUS 1947, i, p. 861.

36. "Zarubezhnye otkliki na doklad V.M. Molotova o tridtsatiletii Velikoi Oktiabrskoi sotsialistecheskoi revoliutsii," *Biulleten' Biuro informatsii TsK VKP(b): Voprosy vneshnei politiki*, no. 22(69), November 15, 1947, p. 2. RTsKhIDNI, f. 17, op. 128, t. 1, d. 265.

37. Alan Bullock, *Ernest Bevin: Foreign Secretary*, London: Heinemann, 1983, p. 489.

38. *Ibid.*, pp. 531, 547, 566–7; Kennan, *op.cit.*, p. 419; Avi Shlaim, *The United States and the Berlin Blockade, 1948–1949*, Berkeley: University of California Press, 1983, pp. 33–4, 149–50.

39. Hannes Adomeit, *Soviet Risk-Taking and Crisis Behavior*, London: Allen and Unwin, 1982, p. 81.

40. *Ibid.*

41. Shlaim, *op.cit.*, pp. 151–62; Adomeit, *op.cit.*, pp. 89–93. Frank Roberts, "Stalin, Khrushchev and the Berlin Crises," *International Affairs*, November 1991, p. 121.

42. Kennan, *op.cit.*, p. 420.

43. Djilas, *op.cit.*, p. 119.

44. Khrushchev, *op.cit.*, p. 165.

45. Haslam, *loc.cit.*, p. 27.

46. N.S. Khrushchev, *Khrushchev Remembers, Vol. 2: The Last Testament*, Harmondsworth: Penguin, 1977, p. 235.

47. One account says that Molotov was the mastermind of the blockade. Arkady Vaksberg, *Stalin's Prosecutor*, New York: Grove Weidenfeld, 1991, p. 280.

48. Alexander L. George and Richard Smoke, *Deterrence in American Foreign Policy: Theory and Practice*, New York: Columbia University Press, 1974, p. 118.

49. Andrei Gromyko, *Memoirs*, New York: Doubleday, 1989, pp. 391–2. This was in response to a question from Henry Kissinger, who asked why Stalin was prepared to risk war for the sake of an insignificant advantage. Gromyko added that Stalin was determined to avoid a general war, but that he would have resisted a Western attempt to relieve Berlin. See *ibid.*, p. ix.

50. Reports from Donald Maclean, who was at the British embassy in Washington until August 1948, may have made him feel more secure in his management of the crisis. Maclean would have known that there was no Western contingency plan to deal with the blockade, and also that the Western Allies were anxious to avoid war. Robert Cecil, *A Divided Life*, London: The Bodley Head, 1988, p. 87.

51. Shlaim, *op.cit.*, p. 288.

52. Djilas, *op.cit.*, p. 119.

53. Shlaim, *op.cit.*, pp. 235–40; Simon Duke, *US Defence Bases in the United Kingdom*, London: Macmillan, 1987, pp. 29–36.

54. Margaret Gowing, *Independence and Deterrence: Britain and Atomic Energy, 1945–1952, Vol. 1: Policy Making*, London: Macmillan, 1974, p. 311.

55. Shlaim, *op.cit.*, p. 239.

56. Adomeit, *op.cit.*, p. 137.

57. It is perhaps unimportant whether Stalin knew that the B-29s could not carry atomic bombs. They could, after all, be replaced by nuclear-capable aircraft, and even if he believed that they were nuclear-capable, he would apparently still have doubted the American willingness to go to war.

58. Shlaim, *op.cit.*, pp. 313–14; FRUS 1948, ii, pp. 999–1006; part of the Soviet record of these talks was published in *Moskovskie Novosti*, May 22, 1988, pp. 8–9.

59. Shlaim, *op.cit.*, p. 314; FRUS 1948, ii, p. 1005.

60. Shlaim *op.cit.*, pp. 330–1; Adomeit, *op.cit.*, pp. 101–2.

61. Shlaim, *op.cit.*, p. 380.

62. *Sto sorok besed*, p. 86; see also p. 15.

63. Duke, *op.cit.*, pp. 29–36.

64. See pp. 236, 237.

65. Soviet commentaries argue that the United States used the crisis as a pretext to deploy the B-29s to Britain; they do not present that transfer as a move in the crisis itself.

See, for example, S.I. Viskov and V.D. Kul'bakin, *Soiuzniki i "Germanskii Vopros" 1945–1949 gg.*, Moscow: Nauka, 1990, pp. 279–89.

66. I.V. Kovalev, "Istoriia bez 'belykh piaten': perelomnye gody v sovetsko-kitaiskikh otnosheniiakh (1948–1950)," interview with S.N. Goncharov, unpublished manuscript, 1990, pp. 14–15. I am grateful to Dr Goncharov for letting me see this document. Kovalev played an important role in the Soviet war effort in World War II, organizing the railways. In May 1948 Stalin sent him to China as his personal representative, and he held that position until January 1950.

67. Kovalev, *loc.cit.*, p. 16.

68. *Ibid.*

69. Shi Zhe, "I Accompanied Chairman Mao," *Far Eastern Affairs*, no. 2, 1989, p. 127. Shi Zhe was a member of Liu Shaoqi's delegation.

70. "Shortly after the fourth talk between Stalin and Liu Shaoqi, the Soviet side showed a documentary film on the test explosion of their atomic bomb." Shi Zhe, "On the Eve of the Birth of the New China," in *Mianhuai Liu Shaoqi*, Beijing, 1988, p. 224. See also Zhu Yuanshi, "Liu Shaoqi's Secret Visit to the Soviet Union in 1949," *Dang de Wenxian*, 1991, no. 3, p. 77. I am grateful to Xue Litai and John Lewis for these references. Liu returned to Beijing on August 14.

71. Sergei N. Goncharov, John W. Lewis, and Xue Litai, *Uncertain Partners: Stalin, Mao, and the Korean War*, Stanford: Stanford University Press, 1993, p. 71. Stalin turned down Liu's request to visit atomic installations.

72. See pp. 230, 238–40.

73. Stalin's remarks to Liu Shaoqi echoed his response to Churchill's "Iron Curtain" speech, which had been repeated in *Bol'shevik*, the Party's leading theoretical journal, in April 1949: "not a single great power at the present time, even if its government strives to, could raise a large army for a struggle against another great power, since at the present time no one can fight without his people, and the peoples do not want to fight." "Peredovaia: Bor'ba narodnykh mass za mir, protiv podzhigatelei novoi voiny," *Bol'shevik*, April 1949, no. 8, p. 3.

74. On the origins of the peace movement see Marshall Shulman, *Stalin's Foreign Policy Reappraised*, Cambridge, Mass.: Harvard University Press, 1963, pp. 80–103. See also

Lawrence S. Wittner, *One World or None*, Stanford: Stanford University Press, 1993, Chapters 10–13.

75. Claudin, *op.cit.*, pp. 576–82, gives a very skeptical account of the movement.

76. Kovalev, *op.cit.*

77. *Ibid.*, p. 17.

78. *Ibid.*

79. I.V. Stalin, "Vystuplenie na prieme v Kremle v chest' komanduiushchikh voiskami Krasnoi Armii," in Robert H. McNeal (ed.), *I.V. Stalin Works*, Vol. 2, 1941–1945, Stanford: Hoover Institution Press, 1967, pp. 203–4.

80. Khrushchev, *Khrushchev Remembers: The Glasnost Tapes*, p. 101.

81. Richard G. Hewlett and Francis Duncan, *Atomic Shield: A History of the United States Atomic Energy Commission, Vol. 2, 1947–1952*, Berkeley: University of California Press repr., 1990, p. 362.

82. *New York Times*, September 25, 1949.

83. Interview with I.N. Golovin, October 19, 1992.

84. Djilas, *op.cit.*, p. 119.

85. It was not foolish to think the test would not be detected. The United States had only just set up a system for detecting a Soviet test. In the spring of 1949 the US Air Force had deployed an interim monitoring system which used radiological methods. The US Navy had a small ground-based monitoring system. Britain was flying filter-equipped aircraft on detection missions. See C. Ziegler, "Waiting for Joe-1– Decisions Leading to the Detection of Russia's First Atomic Bomb Test," *Social Studies of Science*, 1988, no. 2, pp. 197–228.

86. A.P. Aleksandrov, "Gody s Kurchatovym," *Nauka i zhizn'*, 1983, no. 2, p. 20.

87. David Alan Rosenberg, "American Atomic Strategy and the Hydrogen Bomb Decision," *Journal of American History*, June 1979, pp. 78–9.

88. Marc Trachtenberg, "A 'Wasting Asset': American Strategy and the Shifting Nuclear Balance, 1949–1954," in his *History and Strategy*, Princeton: Princeton University Press, 1991, pp. 103–7.

89. G.M. Malenkov, *32-aia godovshchina Velikoi Oktiabr'skoi sotsialisticheskoi revoliutsii*, Moscow: Politizdat, 1949, p. 22. M. Suslov, "Zashchita mira i bor'ba s podzhigateliami voiny," *Bol'shevik*, December 1949, no. 23, p. 10.

90. FRUS 1950, i, p. 236.

91. NSC 68 has been much written about. See, for example, the collection of essays in Ernest R. May (ed.), *American Cold*

War Strategy: Interpreting NSC 68, Boston: Bedford Books of St Martin's Press, 1993.

92. FRUS 1950, i, pp. 259–60.
93. *Ibid.*, pp. 287–8.
94. See the comments on NSC 68 by the Bureau of the Budget and the Council of Economic Advisors, *ibid.*, pp. 298–311.
95. "Krakh diplomatii atomnogo shantazha," *Bol'shevik*, October 1949, no. 17, p. 49.
96. Malenkov, *op.cit.*, p. 21.
97. *Ibid.*, p. 18.
98. *Ibid.*, pp. 21–2. This last comment was greeted with stormy, prolonged applause.
99. *Ibid.*, p. 22.
100. *Ibid.*, p. 32.
101. Suslov, *loc.cit.*, pp. 18–20.
102. *Ibid.*, p. 22.
103. *Ibid.*, p. 21.
104. *Ibid.*, p. 26.
105. See the discussion in William Curti Wohlforth, *The Elusive Balance*, Ithaca: Cornell University Press, 1993, pp. 45–54.
106. It seems likely that these reflected genuine differences of approach, in view of the policies later adopted by Beria and Malenkov.
107. But Malenkov's approach did remain an important undercurrent in Soviet thinking about foreign policy in the last years of Stalin's life.
108. See pp. 240–41.
109. Khrushchev, *Khrushchev Remembers: The Glasnost Tapes*, pp. 100–1.
110. Iurii Smirnov, Interview with Iurii Khariton, *Izvestiia*, December 8, 1992, p. 3. This quotation is taken not from Khariton, but from Smirnov's commentary; no source is given.
111. Stalin, *O nedostatkakh partiinoi raboty i merakh likvidatsii trotskistskikh i inykh dvurushnikov*, Moscow: Politizdat, 1938, pp. 17–18.
112. Jiri Pelikan (ed.), *The Czechoslovak Political Trials, 1950–1954*, Stanford: Stanford University Press, 1971, p. 43.

13. Dangerous Relations

1. N.V. Novikov, who attended Marshall's meeting with Stalin in April 1947, found not the "collected leader of the Party and the country, unoppressed by age," whom he had met on the eve of the war. Stalin was now "an old, very old, tired man, who was apparently bearing the heavy burden of very great responsibility with great effort." N.V. Novikov, *Vospominaniia diplomata*, Moscow: Politizdat, 1989, p. 383. See also A.I. Rybin, "Riadom s I.V. Stalinym," *Sotsiologicheskie issledovaniia*, 1988, no. 3, p.
91.
2. N.S. Khrushchev, *Khrushchev Remembers*, Vol. 1, Harmondsworth: Penguin, 1977, p. 329.
3. *Sto sorok besed s V.M. Molotovym: Iz dnevnika F. Chueva*, Moscow: Terra, 1991, p. 324; see also p. 474.
4. Khrushchev, *op.cit.*, p. 328.
5. Arkady Vaksberg, *Stalin's Prosecutor*, New York: Grove Weidenfeld, 1991, p. 289.
6. Notably Marshall Shulman, in his *Stalin's Foreign Policy Reappraised*, Cambridge, Mass.: Harvard University Press, 1963.
7. Robert Tucker, *The Soviet Political Mind*, 2nd edn, New York: W.W. Norton, 1971, pp. 87–102. William Taubman argues that Soviet foreign policy became more rigid after 1949, with occasional and forceful probing for advantage. See his *Stalin's American Policy*, New York: W.W. Norton, 1982.
8. Edvard Kardelj, *Reminiscences*, London: Blond and Briggs, 1982, p. 108. An almost identical account is given by Milovan Djilas, *Conversations with Stalin*, Harmondsworth: Penguin Books, 1963, p. 141.
9. Shi Zhe, "I Accompanied Chairman Mao," *Far Eastern Affairs*, 1989, no. 2, p. 126.
10. I.V. Kovalev, "Istoriia bez 'belykh piaten:' perelomnye gody v sovetsko-kitaiskikh otnosheniiakh (1948–1950)," interview with S.N. Goncharov, unpublished manuscript, 1990, p. 28.
11. Stuart Schramm, *Mao Tse-tung*, Harmondsworth: Penguin, 1966, p. 150ff.
12. Kovalev, *loc.cit.*, p. 46.
13. *Ibid.*, pp. 11–12. Crossing the Yangtze did give rise to an incident that seemed to the Soviet Union to threaten to provoke Western intervention. In late April 1949, when two Royal Navy ships were damaged by PLA artillery fire on the Yangtze, Conservatives in the House of Commons called for war against Red China. Soviet troops on the Liaodun peninsula, and the Soviet Navy in Port Arthur and other Pacific bases, were brought up to full combat readiness. But the incident passed without further consequence. *Ibid.*, pp. 13–14.
14. Malenkov expressed a similar thought in his speech on November 6: "The victory of Chinese democracy opens a new chapter in the history, not only of the Chinese people but of all the peoples of Asia oppressed by the imperialists. The national liberation struggle of the peoples of Asia, the Pacific, and the entire colonial world has reached a new and considerably higher level." *32-aia godovshchina Velikoi Oktiabr'*

skoi sotsialisticheskoi revoliutsii, Moscow: Politizdat, 1949, p. 27.

15. Kovalev, *loc.cit.*, p. 29.

16. Schramm, *op.cit.*, p. 254.

17. The Joint Intelligence Committee argued in a report to the JCS in February 1950 that, as the Soviet atomic capability grew, "the attitude of the Kremlin will become more truculent, thus increasing the risk of war." (Report of the JIC to the JCS on *Implications of Soviet Possession of Atomic Weapons*, JIC 502, February 9, 1950, National Archives, Record Group 218, CCS 471.6.USSR (11–8–49), sec.1, p. 2.)

18. Kovalev, *loc.cit.*, pp. 31–3.

19. For a discussion of this aspect of Soviet policy, see Adam B. Ulam, *Expansion and Coexistence*, 2nd edn, New York: Praeger, 1974, pp. 514–16.

20. See in particular his "leaning to one side" speech of June 30, 1949, "On the People's Democratic Dictatorship," in *Selected Works of Mao Tse-tung*, Vol. 4, Beijing: Foreign Languages Press, 1967. He said that "the Communist Party of the Soviet Union is our best teacher and we must learn from it." p. 423.

21. This is a major argument of Sergei N. Goncharov, John W. Lewis, and Xue Litai, *Uncertain Partners: Stalin, Mao, and the Korean War*, Stanford: Stanford University Press, 1993.

22. The visit is discussed by Goncharov, Lewis, and Xue, *ibid.*, pp. 76–129.

23. For accounts of the visit see Shi Zhe, *loc.cit.*; Kovalev, *loc.cit.*; N. Fedorenko, "The Stalin–Mao Summit in Moscow," *Far Eastern Affairs*, 1989, no. 2, pp. 134–48; Wu Xiuquan, *Eight Years in the Ministry of Foreign Affairs*, Beijing: New World Press, 1985, pp. 5–23; Dmitrii Volkogonov, *Triumf i tragediia*, Book II, 2nd edn, Moscow: Novosti, 1990, pp. 496–500.

24. Wu Xiuquan, *op.cit.*, p. 13.

25. M. Suslov, "Zashchita mira i bor'ba s podzhigateliami voiny," *Bol'shevik*, December 1949, no. 23, p. 18.

26. Quoted by George Kennan, *Memoirs, 1950–1963*, New York: Pantheon Books, 1972, pp. 41–2.

27. Jonathan Haslam, "The Boundaries of Rational Calculation in Soviet policy towards Japan," in Michael Fry (ed.), *History, the White House and the Kremlin: Statesmen as Historians*, London: Pinter, 1991, p. 45.

28. See the discussion in Melvyn P. Leffler, *A Preponderance of Power*, Stanford: Stanford University Press, 1992, pp. 366–7. Bruce Cumings, in his *The Origins of the Korean War*, Princeton: Princeton University Press, Vol. 1, *1981*, Vol. 2, *1990*, rightly stresses the Korean origins of the Korean War. But the Soviet role is a matter of some moment too, not least for an understanding of Stalin's policy.

29. "O Koreiskoi voine 1950–1953 gg. i peregovorakh o peremirii," August 9, 1966. TsKhSD f. 5, op. 58, d. 266, p. 122. This is a brief history of the war prepared for Brezhnev and Kosygin on the basis of the Soviet Foreign Ministry archive.

30. Hao Yufan and Zhai Zhihai, "China's Decision to Enter the Korean War: History Revisited," *China Quarterly*, March 1990, p. 100.

31. "O Koreiskoi voine," p. 122.

32. *Ibid.*

33. N.S. Khrushchev, "Koreiskaia voina," *Ogonek*, 1991, no. 1, pp. 27–8. This is an expanded version of the section on the Korean War in Vol. 1 of the English-language edition of Khrushchev's memoirs.

34. Khrushchev, *loc.cit.*, p. 28. See also "O Koreiskoi voine," p. 122; Hao and Zhai, *loc.cit.*, p. 109.

35. "O Koreiskoi voine," p. 124.

36. Khrushchev, *loc.cit.*, p. 28; Hao and Zhai, *loc.cit.*, p. 100.

37. *Sto sorok*, p. 104. Molotov said that "the Koreans themselves thrust [the war] on us. Stalin said that we could not sidestep the national question of a unified Korea." Khrushchev gives a similar account of Stalin's reasons for supporting Kim; *loc.cit.*, p. 28.

38. See p. 124.

39. See Goncharov *et al.*, *op.cit.*

40. "O Koreiskoi voine," p. 123.

41. Yu Song-chol, *Hanquk Ilbo*, November 9, 1990. I have used the translation that appeared in FBIS–EAS–90–249, December 27, 1990. This translation includes several of Yu's articles, published on successive days. The reference here is to p. 27. Yu is a former head of the Operations Directorate of the North Korean General Staff.

42. Yu Song-chol, *loc.cit.*, p. 28.

43. Harry S. Truman, *Memoirs, Vol. 2: Years of Trial and Hope*, New York: Signet Books, 1965, pp. 385–6, 391.

44. A.A. Gromyko, *Pamiatnoe*, 2nd edn, Vol. 1, Moscow: Politizdat, 1990, pp. 249–50.

45. Rosemary Foot, *The Wrong War: American Policy and the Dimensions of the Korean Conflict, 1950–1953*, Ithaca: Cornell University Press, 1985, pp. 61–78.

46. Kim Il Sung and Pak Hon Yong to Stalin, September 29, 1950. This document is be-

ing transfened from the Russian Presidential Archive to TsKhSD. It does not yet have a file number. It is due to be published in the journal *Istochnik*, and in English in the *Journal of American-East Asian Relations* in February 1994. I am grateful to Kathryn Weathersby for making it available to me.

47. Hao and Zhai, *loc.cit.*, p. 104.
48. Khrushchev, *loc.cit.*, p. 28. Khrushchev does not give the date of his suggestion, but this seems to be the right period.
49. *Ibid.* Khrushchev's picture of Stalin's attitude is substantially confirmed by Chinese historians. Hao and Zhai, *loc.cit.*, p. 109. For a useful survey of Chinese writings see Chen Jian, *The Sino–Soviet Alliance and China's Entry into the Korean War*, Cold War International History Project, Washington, DC: Woodrow Wilson International Center for Scholars, 1992.
50. Hao and Zhai, *loc.cit.*, pp. 105–6. The quotation is taken from a later speech by Zhou Enlai in which he explained Mao's thinking to the Chinese People's Volunteers.
51. *Ibid.*, pp. 104–11.
52. The text of this telegram may be found in *Jianguo Yilai Mao Zedong Wengao, Vol. 1 (September 1949–December 1950)*, Beijing, 1987, pp. 539–41. I am grateful to Ifan Go for translating Mao's telegrams for me.
53. Hao and Zhai, *loc.cit.*, p. 110. According to Chen Jian, Stalin had agreed to provide this aid after the Inchon landing. *Op.cit.*, p. 26.
54. *Jianguo Yilai Mao Zedong Wengao*, pp. 543–4.
55. Chen, *op.cit.*, p. 29.
56. Hao and Zhai, *loc.cit.*, p. 111. Khrushchev refers to Zhou's meeting with Stalin, at which he was not present. He says that Stalin reported on it when he returned to Moscow from the Crimea, where it took place. According to Khrushchev's account, the issue discussed was whether or not China should enter the war. No mention is made of the question of Soviet air support. Khrushchev, *loc.cit.*, p. 28.
57. Chen, *op.cit.*, p. 29.
58. *Jianguo Yilai Mao Zedong Wengao*, pp. 552–3.
59. *Ibid.*, p. 556.
60. Gao Gang, "Doklad na konferentsii predstavitelei dobrovol'skoi armii, narodnoi armii i TsK Koreiskoi Trudovoi Partii," (February 1951), RTsKhIDNI f. 17, op. 137, ed. khr. 947, p. 7.
61. *Ibid.*, pp. 13–14.
62. "The Situation and Our Policy after the Victory in the War of Resistance against Japan," in *Selected Works of Mao Tse-tung*, Vol. 4, Peking: Foreign Languages Press, 1967, p. 21.

63. "Talk with the American Correspondent Anna Louise Strong," *ibid.*, p. 100. In the same interview Mao explained that he did not think an American attack on the Soviet Union was imminent. "The United States and the Soviet Union are separated by a vast zone," he said, "which includes many capitalist, colonial and semi-colonial countries in Europe, Asia, and Africa. Before the US reactionaries have subjugated these countries, an attack on the Soviet Union is out of the question." *Ibid.*, p. 99.
64. See Mark A. Ryan, *Chinese Attitudes toward Nuclear Weapons: China and the United States during the Korean War*, Armonk, New York: M.E. Sharpe, 1989, pp. 27–32. See also Goncharov, *et al.*, pp. 164–7.
65. Hao and Zhai, *loc.cit.*, p. 107.
66. Chen, *op.cit.*, p. 32.
67. Peng Dehuai, *Memoirs of a Chinese Marshal*, Beijing: Foreign Languages Press, 1984, pp. 474–7; Dean Acheson, *Present at the Creation*, New York: W.W. Norton, 1969, pp. 463–6.
68. Acheson, *op.cit.*, p. 475.
69. Hao and Zhai, *loc.cit*, p. 111; G. Lobov, "V nebe Severnoi Korei," *Aviatsiia i kosmonovtika*, 1990, no. 10, p. 34. Lobov was one of the Soviet Air Force commanders in Korea. The Soviet units were organized into the 64 Fighter Air Corps, which grew to 26,000 men by 1952, and was equipped mainly with MiG-15 fighter aircraft. An air force division consisted of several regiments, with perhaps 150 aircraft in all.
70. Lobov, *loc.cit.*, p. 34; Hao and Zhai, *loc.cit.*, p. 111.
71. Acheson, *op.cit.*, pp. 469–72.
72. Leffler, *op.cit.*, p. 400.
73. For a good account of how this impression was formed, see Robert J. Donovan, *Tumultuous Years: The Presidency of Harry S. Truman, 1949–1953*, New York: W.W. Norton, 1982, pp. 307–10.
74. Alan Bullock, *Ernest Bevin: Foreign Secretary, 1945–1951*, London: Heinemann, 1983, pp. 820–2.
75. Military planners in the Joint Staff, however, were discussing how the bomb might be used. Roger Dingman, "Atomic Diplomacy During the Korean War," *International Security*, Winter 1988–9, pp. 65–9. Attlee nevertheless sought assurances that Britain would be consulted, in line with the 1943 Quebec Agreement, before any decision to use the atomic bomb. He had to be content, however, with the hope expressed in the final communiqué that "world conditions"

would never call for the use of the atomic bomb, and with an assurance that he would be informed if the situation changed. Churchill was incensed to discover that the Quebec Agreement had thus been set aside, and wrote to Truman, asking him to agree that atomic weapons should not be used from British bases without prior British consent. The British Chiefs of Staff were also alarmed. Margaret Gowing, *Independence and Deterrence: Britain and Atomic Energy, 1945–1952, Vol. 1: Policy Making*, London: Macmillan, 1974, pp. 312–16. See also Simon Duke, *US Defence Bases in the United Kingdom*, London: Macmillan, 1987, pp. 64–72.

76. Robin Edmonds, *Setting the Mould*, New York: W.W. Norton, 1986, pp. 222–4; Rosemary J. Foot, "Anglo-American Relations in the Korean Crisis: The British Effort to Avert an Expanded War, December 1950–January 1951," *Diplomatic History*, Winter 1986, pp. 43–57; Bullock, *op.cit.*, pp. 823–4; Acheson, *op.cit.*, pp. 478–85.

77. Foot, *loc.cit.*, pp. 46–7, 50–1.

78. Leffler, *op.cit.*, pp. 400–1.

79. Donovan, *op.cit.*, p. 348.

80. Acheson, *op.cit.*, p. 516.

81. Peng Dehuai, *op.cit.*, pp. 479–80. "Win a quick victory if you can," Mao told him. "If you can't, win a slow one."

82. Gromyko to Vyshinskii, December 7, 1950. See note 46 above.

83. Wu Xiuquan, *op.cit.*, p. 75.

84. On December 13, 21, and 24 Mao sent Peng Dehuai cables urging him to cross the 38th parallel. See Hong Xuezhi, *KangMei YuanChao Zhangzheng Huiyi*, Beijing, 1990, p. 98; and Du Ping, *Zai Zhiynanjun Zongbu*, Beijing, 1989, p. 147. After the seizure of Seoul on January 4, 1951 Kim pressed Peng to engage in hot pursuit of UN forces. Peng was reluctant to do so, and Stalin supported him. My thanks to Xue Litai for these references and this information.

85. Robert Cecil, *A Divided Life*, London: The Bodley Head, 1988, pp. 105–15.

86. *Ibid.*, pp. 118. A cabinet paper reporting on Attlee's visit was among the documents found in Maclean's safe after his flight. *Ibid.*, p. 123. See also Christopher Andrew and Oleg Gordievskii, *KGB: The Inside Story*, Harper Collins, 1990, p. 395.

87. Acheson, *op.cit.*, p. 483; Bullock, *op.cit.*, p. 828.

88. Acheson, *op.cit.*, p. 487.

89. Bullock, *op.cit.*, p. 827.

90. Giorgio Bocca, *Palmiro Togliatti*, Rome: Editori Laterza, 1973, pp. 543–53. See also "Wollte Stalin Togliatti Kaltstellen?," *Osteuropa*, 1970, no. 10, pp. A703–A717.

91. See Lilly Marcou, *Le Kominform*, Paris: Presses de la Fondation Nationale des Sciences Politiques, 1977, pp. 113–19; Helmut Koenig, "Der Konflikt zwischen Stalin und Togliatti," *Osteuropa*, 1970, no. 10, pp. 699–706.

92. In his memoirs Eisenhower recalled that "in early 1951 the Indochina affair had come emphatically to my attention when I was Allied commander of the NATO troops with headquarters in Paris. The NATO defense needed greater French participation, but this was largely denied because of France's losses and costs in the Indochina war." Dwight D. Eisenhower, *The White House Years: Mandate for Change*, New York: Doubleday, 1963, p. 336.

93. Teresa Toranska, *Them: Stalin's Polish Puppets*, New York: Harper and Row, 1987, p. 46. Ochab does not give the date of this meeting, but from the context it is clear that he is referring to the meeting of January 1951. Ochab was First Deputy Minister of Defense and Chief Political Commissar in 1949–50, and Secretary of the Party Central Committee from 1950 to 1956. *Ibid.*, p. 34. Another account of this meeting is given by Karel Kaplan, on the basis of an interview with Alexej Čepička, who attended the meeting as Czechoslovak Minister of Defense. According to this account Stalin spoke of the need to prepare well for the military occupation of Western Europe within three or four years, before the United States had built up its forces to the point where it could transport reinforcements quickly to Europe and "bring its atomic superiority fully into play." Karel Kaplan, *Dans les Archives du Comité Central*, Paris: Albin Michel, 1978, pp. 162–6. No confirmation has been found, however, of this account of Stalin's speech.

94. *Ibid.*, p. 166.

95. Toranska, *op.cit.*, p. 46.

96. Eugene Zaleski, *Stalinist Planning for Economic Growth, 1933–1952*, Chapel Hill: University of North Carolina Press, 1980, p. 396. Jiri Pelikan, *The Czechoslovak Political Trials, 1950–1954*, Stanford: Stanford University Press, 1971, p. 100, confirms that in Czechoslovakia, and presumably in the other countries too, the February 1951 increases in industrial production meant increases in arms production.

97. Since he suspected many East European leaders of being Western spies, he may have thought that one of them would report

the military build-up to Washington or London. When Rudolf Slánský, who attended the Moscow meeting, was arrested in November 1951, "Stalin was triumphant.... He said he had sensed Slansky's real nature all along." (N.S. Khrushchev, *Khrushchev Remembers: The Glasnost Tapes*, Boston: Little, Brown, 1990, p. 133.) And if one of the leaders did not report it, then some lower-level official, who knew that a military build-up was now under way in Eastern Europe, might do so. Many officials would have known of the plans to expand arms production. These plans were approved at Central Committee plenary sessions in each of the three countries. The same point applies to Kaplan's version: if Stalin was intending to attack Western Europe, it made no sense to tell East European leaders whom he did not trust; if he was not intending to attack, it made sense to tell them only if he wanted that word passed to the West.

98. Strong voices were raised in the United States in favor of an isolationist policy. Herbert Hoover, for example, gave a speech calling for the preservation of the Western hemisphere above all else, on December 20. This was reprinted in full in *Pravda* on December 23, 1950.

99. Leffler, *op.cit.*, p. 377 points out that Soviet moderation in September 1950 had "inspired US risk-taking."

100. Parliamentary Report, *The Times*, February 13, 1951, p. 7.

101. Shulman, *op.cit.*, p. 169.

102. Stalin to Mao, August 28, 1951. See note 46 above.

103. Stalin to Mao, November 19, 1951. See note 46 above.

104. Pietro Nenni, *Tempo di Guerra Fredda. Diari 1943–1956*, Milan: SugarCo Edizioni, 1981, p. 537.

105. Yakov Rapoport, *The Doctors' Plot of 1953*, Cambridge, Mass.: Harvard University Press, 1991, p. 218.

106. N.G. Kuznetsov, "Krutye povoroty," *Pravda*, July 29, 1988, p. 3.

107. For an account of that discussion and its relevance for understanding this work see L.A. Openkin, "I.V. Stalin: Poslednyi prognoz budushchego," *Voprosy istorii KPSS*, 1991, no. 7, pp. 113–28.

108. For a good discussion of Varga's views see William Curti Wohlforth, *The Elusive Balance*, Ithaca: Cornell University Press, 1993, pp. 77–87.

109. *Ibid.*, p. 84.

110. *Ibid.*, p. 81.

111. J. Stalin, *Economic Problems of Socialism in the USSR*, Moscow: Foreign Languages Publishing House, 1952, p. 14.

112. *Ibid.*

113. *Ibid.*, p. 15.

114. Wohlforth, *op.cit.*, p. 85.

115. Nenni, *op.cit.*, p. 537.

116. Stalin, *op.cit.*, pp. 15–16.

117. Shulman, *op.cit.*, p. 244. Shulman juxtaposes these two kinds of war, and does not discuss how they are interrelated.

118. Though parts had appeared from February 1952 on.

119. Volkogonov, *op.cit.*, pp. 603–4.

120. Konstantin Simonov, *Glazami cheloveka moego pokoleniia*, Moscow: izd. "Pravda," 1990, p. 236.

121. *Ibid.*, p. 238. For Molotov's brief account of this see *Sto sorok*, pp. 465, 468–72. Stalin accused Molotov and Mikoian of being "rightists," though he did not use that term, but called them "Rykovtsy." (Aleksei Rykov was a member of the "Right Opposition," who had been in the Politburo from 1922 to 1930. He was tried with Bukharin and shot in 1938.) Molotov said that he could not understand the reasons for Stalin's attack on him.

122. Vaksberg, *op.cit.*, p. 305.

123. N.S. Khrushchev, "Secret Speech to the 20th Party Congress," in *Khrushchev Remembers*, Vol. 1, p. 625.

124. Robert Conquest, *Stalin: Breaker of Nations*, New York: Viking, 1991, pp. 309–10; Volkogonov, *op.cit.*, p. 584. On Voroshilov see Roy Medvedev, *All Stalin's Men*, Oxford: Basil Blackwell, 1983, p. 20.

125. Tucker's argument on this point seems to me to be borne out by later evidence. See Tucker, *op.cit.*

126. In the spring of 1952 Stalin ordered that 100 new tactical bomber divisions be created. The Air Force could not see the sense in so many bombers, but could not question Stalin's decision. It was this that led Ostroumov and his colleagues to conclude that Stalin was actively preparing for war. N.N. Ostroumov, "Armada, kotoraia ne vzletela," *Voenno-istoricheskii zhurnal*, 1992, no. 10, p. 40.

14. The Hydrogen Bomb

1. Andrei Sakharov, "It's an Absolute Necessity to Speak the Truth," *Moscow News*, November 15–22, 1987, no. 45, p. 14.

2. Andrei Sakharov, *Memoirs*, New York: Alfred A. Knopf, 1990, p. 164.

3. I.M. Khalatnikov, interviewed by G.E.

Gorelik, March 17, 1993.

4. *Ibid.* See also Iu.I. Krivonosov, "Landau i Sakharov v razrabotkakh KGB," *Voprosy istorii estestvoznaniia i tekhniki*, 1993, no. 3, pp. 123–31.

5. Herbert York, *The Advisors. Oppenheimer, Teller and the Superbomb*, San Francisco: W.H. Freeman, 1976, pp. 21–3; Peter Galison and Barton Bernstein, "In Any Light: Scientists and the Decision to Build the Superbomb, 1942–1954", *Historical Studies in the Physical Sciences*, 1989, Vol. 19, no. 2, pp. 270–1.

6. York, *op.cit.*, p. 22; Galison and Bernstein, *loc.cit.*, p. 271.

7. York, *op.cit.*, pp. 23–4. J. Carson Mark writes that "the general belief of those working on the problem at that time . . . was that some such design could be made to detonate, although it was fully understood that much study would yet be required to establish this fact and determine the most favorable pattern." See his *A Short Account of Los Alamos Theoretical Work on Thermonuclear Weapons, 1946–1950*, Los Alamos: Los Alamos Scientific Laboratory, LA-5647-MS, July 1974, p. 1.

8. Published in *Soviet Physics Uspekhi*, May 1991, pp. 445–6. The only date on the report is 1946.

9. Ia.I. Frenkel', "Atomnaia energiia i ee osvobozhdenie," *Priroda*, 1946, no. 5; reprinted in his *Na zare novoi fiziki*, Leningrad: Nauka, 1970. The quotation is taken from p. 367. It is not clear why Kurchatov did not draw Frenkel' into the project. Frenkel' may have been considered politically unreliable; or Kurchatov may have regarded him as too interested in qualitative concepts rather than in careful calculation. In 1946 a book was published in Vienna which discussed the possibility of using a fission bomb to initiate deuterium–deuterium reactions. Hans Thirring, *Die Geschichte der Atombombe*, Vienna: "Neues Oesterreich" Zeitungs- und Verlagsgesellschaft, 1946, pp. 130–4. The chapter dealing with the hydrogen bomb is reproduced in US Congress, Joint Committee on Atomic Energy, *The Hydrogen Bomb and International Control: Technical and Background Information*, Washington, DC: US Government Printing Office, July 1950, pp. 23–5.

10. "U istokov sovetskogo atomnogo proekta: rol' razvedki," *Voprosy istorii estestvoznaniia i tekhniki*, 1992, no. 3, p. 130.

11. Iu.A. Romanov, "Otets sovetskoi vodorodnoi bomby," *Priroda*, 1990, no. 8,
p. 20.

12. According to his confession to Perrin, "during 1947 Fuchs was asked on one occasion by the Russian agent for any information he could give about 'the tritium bomb'." Fuchs told Perrin that "he was very surprised to have the question put in these particular terms and it suggested to him (as had the earlier request for information about the electro-magnetic isotope separation process) that the Russians were getting information from other sources." *Statement of Klaus Fuchs to Michael Perrin*, January 30, 1950, p. 6, in a letter from J. Edgar Hoover to Admiral Souers, March 2, 1950, HSTL, PSF. This inference is not necessarily warranted, if one assumes that Soviet scientists had by this time given some thought to the conditions under which a thermonuclear explosion might be initiated. A transcript of Perrin's questioning of Fuchs records the following exchange: "They asked me what I knew about the tritium bomb, the super. I was very surprised because I hadn't told them anything about it. [Perrin] Let me get this clear. *They* asked *you* what you knew? [Fuchs] Yes . . . I hadn't told them anything about it. I was surprised." Norman Moss, *Klaus Fuchs*, New York: St Martin's Press, 1987, p. 144. Unknown to Perrin, the room where he took Fuchs's confession was bugged. A typist sat in the next room taking a (rather garbled) transcript of the conversation.

13. Moss (*ibid.*) implies that Fuchs gave information about the Super to Harry Gold while he was still at Los Alamos. But Fuchs's confessions to Perrin and to the FBI make it clear that Fuchs supplied this information only after he returned to Britain in the summer of 1946.

14. *Statement of Klaus Fuchs to Michael Perrin*, p. 6.

15. "Foocase – Espionage (R) Interviews in England with Fuchs," Hugh H. Clegg and Robert J. Lamphere to Director, FBI, June 4, 1950, p. 30. HSTL, PSF.

16. Sakharov, *Memoirs*, p. 94; interview with Iu.B. Khariton, July 16, 1992.

17. Sakharov, *Memoirs*, p. 101. The Russian edition makes it clear that Tamm was being asked to assess a particular design. Andrei Sakharov, *Vospominaniia*, New York: izd. im. Chekhova, 1990, pp. 139–40.

18. "Ot redkollegii," in E.L. Feinberg (ed.), *Vospominaniia o I.E. Tamme*, 2nd edn, Moscow: Nauka, 1986, p. 3.

19. V.L. Ginzburg and E.L. Feinberg, "Igor' Evgen'evich Tamm," in Feinberg, *op.cit.*,

p. 5; L.I. Vernskii, "V kabinete i vne ego," *ibid.*, pp. 83–4.

20. V.I. Ginzburg, interviewed by G.E. Gorelik and I.V. Dorman, March 28, 1992.

21. Sakharov, *Memoirs*, pp. 96–8.

22. *Ibid.*, pp. 94–6.

23. *Ibid.* Interview with A. Sakharov, June 15, 1987.

24. Sakharov, *Memoirs*, p. 93.

25. On Tamm's attitude see E.L. Feinberg, "Epokha i lichnost'," in Feinberg, *op.cit.*, p. 233. Sakharov, *op.cit.*, pp. 96–8.

26. "Stepen' svobody," *Ogonek* no. 31, 1989, p. 28.

27. Interview with Sakharov, "Ia pytalsia byt' na urovne svoei sud'by," *Molodezh Estonii*, October 11, 1988, p. 2.

28. Sakharov, *Memoirs*, p. 102. The September date comes from Igor' Golovin, "Rossiiskii Nauchnyi Tsentr – Kurchatovskii Institut," unpublished paper, 1992, p. 22. This fits in with the evidence on dates in G.E. Gorelik, "S chego nachinalas' sovetskaia vodorodnaia bomba?," *Voprosy istorii estestvoznaniia i tekhniki*, 1993, no. 1, p. 94. The terms "First Idea, Second Idea" etc. were invented by Sakharov for his memoirs.

29. Iu.A. Romanov, "Otets sovetskoi vodorodnoi bomby," *Priroda*, 1990, no. 8, p. 21; V.I. Ritus, "Esli ne ia, to kto?", *Priroda*, 1990, no. 8., pp. 11–13. This process was referred to by Sakharov's colleagues as "sakharizatsiia," which could be translated as "sweetening." *Sakhar* is the Russian for sugar.

30. Chuck Hansen, *US Nuclear Weapons: The Secret History*, New York: Orion Books, 1988, p. 45.

31. Sakharov, *Memoirs*, p. 102.

32. *Ibid.*, p. 103.

33. Romanov, "Otets sovetskoi vodorodnoi bomby," p. 21; Ritus, *loc.cit.*, p. 13.

34. V.S. Komel'kov writes that the transition to thermonuclear weapons was the logical next step, once the fission bomb had been tested. In his "Tvorets i pobeditel'," in A.P. Aleksandrov (ed.), *Vospominaniia ob Igore Vasil'eviche Kurchatove*, Moscow: Nauka, 1988, p. 321.

35. I.N. Golovin, *Kul'minatsiia*, Moscow: Institut atomnoi energii im. I.V. Kurchatova, IAE-4932/3, 1989, p. 21.

36. York, *op.cit.*, pp. 22–6; Galison and Bernstein, *loc.cit.*, pp. 273–83.

37. Galison and Bernstein, *loc.cit.*, pp. 281–2.

38. York, *op.cit.*, pp. 22–8; Mark, *op.cit.*, pp. 9–10. It was to the superbomb that Teller was referring when he wrote early in 1947 that "It has been repeatedly stated that future

bombs may easily surpass those used in the last war by a factor of a thousand. I share this belief." Edward Teller, "How Dangerous Are Atomic Weapons?," *Bulletin of the Atomic Scientists*, February 1947, p. 36.

39. Quoted in Galison and Bernstein, *loc.cit.*, p. 272.

40. *Ibid.*, pp. 281–2.

41. York, *op.cit.*, p. 76.

42. *Ibid.*, pp. 26–7.

43. Galison and Bernstein, *loc.cit.*, p. 283.

44. Lewis L. Strauss, *Men and Decisions*, New York: Doubleday, 1962, p. 217.

45. Galison and Bernstein, *loc.cit.*, pp. 284–8.

46. *Ibid.*, p. 288.

47. The other members who were present at the October meeting were Lee DuBridge, Cyril Smith, Hartley Rowe, and Oliver Buckley; Glenn Seaborg, who was absent, did seem to support the Super.

48. York, *op.cit.*, p. 156; the GAC's report is reproduced in York's book as an appendix. See also Galison and Bernstein, *loc.cit.*, pp. 288–95.

49. York, *op.cit.*, p. 155.

50. *Ibid.*, pp. 156–7.

51. *Ibid.*, pp. 157–8.

52. Galison and Bernstein, *loc.cit.*, p. 298.

53. FRUS 1949, i, pp. 588–95.

54. *Ibid.*, p. 595.

55. *Ibid.*, p. 587.

56. R. Gordon Arneson, "The H-bomb decision," *Foreign Service Journal*, May 1969, p. 29.

57. FRUS 1950, i, p. 513.

58. Galison and Bernstein, *loc.cit.*, pp. 305–6.

59. Robert Chadwell Williams, *Klaus Fuchs, Atom Spy*, Cambridge, Mass.: Harvard University Press, 1987, p. 119. MI5 had already begun survelliance of Fuchs in August. See Moss, *op.cit.*, p. 130, and Robert J. Lamphere and Tom Shachtman, *The FBI–KGB War*, New York: Berkley Books, 1987, pp. 80–7.

60. Galison and Bernstein, *loc.cit.*, pp. 310–12.

61. *Ibid.*, pp. 311–12. Sumner Pike, one of the AEC commissioners, remarked at a meeting of the commission on March 10 that this decision was a matter of "telling us to do what we are doing anyway, that is going after production as well as going after the test." JCAE Document cxxxviii, JCAE Executive Session, Classified, Box 5, National Archives. On the same day Molotov gave a speech in which he said: "All kinds of blackmailers from that camp yesterday tried to frighten us with the atomic bomb. Today they are trying to frighten [us] with the so-called 'hydrogen bomb,' which does not yet

exist in fact. They ought not brag in this way; while they were engaged in blackmail with their monopoly on the atomic bomb, Soviet people, as is known, did not lose any time in mastering the secret of the production of atomic energy and atomic weapons – let the blackmailers put that in their pipe and smoke it." "Rech' tov. V.M. Molotova," *Pravda*, March 11, 1950, p. 3.

62. York, *op.cit.*, p. 154.
63. Richard G. Hewlett and Francis Duncan, *A History of the United States Atomic Energy Commission. Vol. 2: 1947–1952: Atomic Shield*, Berkeley: University of California Press, 1990, pp. 439–41; Galison and Bernstein, *loc.cit.*, pp. 315–20; Daniel Hirsch and William G. Mathews, "The H-Bomb: Who Really Gave Away the Secret?," *Bulletin of the Atomic Scientists*, January–February 1990, pp. 24–6. Tritium must be produced in reactors or in accelerators; a reactor that can produce 1 kg of tritium can with the same neutrons produce on the order of 70 kg of plutonium.
64. Hewlett and Duncan, *op.cit.*, pp. 537–9.
65. By decreasing the volume of the deuterium it made sure that the energy lost to radiation decreased and the energy available for heating the nuclei increased. Hansen, *op.cit.*, pp. 49–50.
66. Lars-Erik de Geer, "The Radioactive Signature of the Hydrogen Bomb," *Science and Global Security*, 1991, vol. 2, pp. 351–63; Galison and Bernstein, *loc.cit.*, pp. 322–3; Hansen, *op.cit.*, pp. 49–50.
67. Galison and Bernstein, *loc.cit.*, pp. 322–4. Oppenheimer later said that the design being considered in 1949 "was a tortured thing that you could well argue did not make a great deal of technical sense. It was therefore possible to argue also that you did not want it even if you could have it. The program in 1951 was technically so sweet that you could not argue about that." US AEC, *In the Matter of J. Robert Oppenheimer*, Cambridge, Mass.: MIT Press, 1971, p. 251.
68. York, *op.cit.*, pp. 82–3; Hansen, *op.cit.*, pp. 56–60.
69. York, *op.cit.*, pp. 85–7; Hansen, *op.cit.*, pp. 61–8; Neil O. Hines, *Proving Ground*, Seattle: University of Washington Press, 1962, pp. 165–95.
70. Sakharov, *Memoirs*, pp. 117–18; V.L. Ginzburg, interviewed by G.E. Gorelik and I. Dorman, March 28, 1992.
71. Interview with Sakharov, June 15, 1987.
72. Sakharov, *Memoirs*, pp. 125, 156; interview with Iu.B. Khariton, July 16, 1992.
73. Golovin, *loc.cit.*, pp. 22–3.

74. N.A. Vlasov, "Desiat' let riadom s Kurchatovym," in M.K. Romanovskii (ed.), *Vospominaniia ob akademike I.V. Kurchatove*, Moscow: Nauka, 1983, p. 54.
75. *Ibid.*
76. Letter from S.L. Sobolev to the Central Committee science department proposing B.V. Kurchatov for candidate membership in the Academy of Sciences in the October 1953 elections. TsKhSD f. 5, op. 17, d. 409, p. 226. Boris was not elected.
77. A.P. Aleksandrov, "Kak delali bombu," *Izvestiia*, July 22, 1988, p. 3. The reference to Zhdanov is evidently to Iurii Zhdanov, who headed the section for science and higher educational institutions in the Central Committee apparatus in 1950–52.
78. *Ibid.*
79. Golovin, *loc.cit.*, pp. 22–3.
80. See O.I. Sumbaev (ed.), *Akademik B.P. Konstantinov*, Leningrad: Nauka, 1985, p. 289; and the memoir by A.I. Zaidel', "B.P. Konstantinov v moei pamiati," *ibid.*, pp. 45–6.
81. Sakharov, *Memoirs*, p. 159.
82. Golovin, *loc.cit.*, pp. 22–3. Once Konstantinov's plant was ready, that was used for isotope separation. The lithium-6 was used in two ways. It was combined with deuterium to produce lithium deuteride for the bomb. When bombarded by neutrons in the course of the explosion lithium produces tritium. Lithium-6.was also irradiated in a reactor to produce tritium for thermonuclear weapons.
83. V.S. Komel'kov, "Tvorets i pobeditel'," in Aleksandrov *op.cit.*, pp. 322–3; B. Korniakov, "Bez svintsovykh trusov," *Argumenty i fakty*, June 1991, no. 21. p. 4.
84. This was evidently Samuel Glasstone's *The Effects of Nuclear Weapons*, Washington, DC: US Government Printing Office, 1950.
85. Sakharov, *Memoirs*, pp. 171–3; Komel'kov, *loc.cit.*, pp. 322–3.
86. Golovin, *Memoirs*, p. 22.
87. Sakharov, *Memoirs*, pp. 160–61.
88. "Delo Beriia," *Izvestiia TsK KPSS*, 1991, no. 1, p. 145; Sakharov, *Memoirs*, p. 169.
89. "Rech' predsedatelia Soveta Ministrov SSSR tovarishcha G.M. Malenkova," *Izvestiia*, August 9 1953, p. 3.
90. Sakharov, *Memoirs*, p. 173.
91. Komel'kov, *loc.cit.*, p. 323.
92. *Ibid.*, p. 323; Sakharov, *Memoirs*, p. 174, gives a similar account.
93. Sakharov, *Memoirs*, pp. 174–5.
94. Komel'kov, *loc.cit.*, pp. 323–4; Sakharov, *Memoirs*, pp. 174–5; I.N. Golovin, *I.V. Kurchatov*, 3rd edn, Moscow: Atomizdat,

1978, p. 95.

95. Vlasov, *loc.cit.*, p. 42.

96. "Pravitel'stvennoe soobshchenie ob ispytanii vodorodnoi bomby v Sovetskom Soiuze," *Pravda* and *Izvestiia*, August 20, 1953, p. 2.

97. Interview with Khariton, July 16, 1992.

98. Komel'kov, *loc.cit.*, p. 322; Iu.B. Khariton and Iu N. Smirnov, "O nekotorykh mifakh i legendakh vokrug atomnogo i vodorodnogo proektov," in *Materialy iubileinoi sessii uchenogo soveta tsentra 12 ianvaria 1993g*, Moscow: Rossiiskii nauchnyi tsentr "Kurchatovskii Institut," 1993, p. 53. The photograph of the first Soviet bombs (see plate 43) shows that the bomb casing of the "Layer Cake" has about the same diameter as the first atomic bomb, even though it is much longer and has bigger stabilizers.

99. Interview with Hans Bethe, May 28, 1982.

100. Khariton and Smirnov, *loc.cit.*, p. 53; Iu. Zamiatnin, interview ed. by G.E. Gorelik, March 18, 1993.

101. Sakharov, *Memoirs*, p. 182; Khariton and Smirnov, *loc.cit.*, p. 53.

102. Interview with Bethe, May 28, 1982.

103. Richard G. Hewlett and Jack M. Holl, *Atoms for Peace and War, 1953–1961*, Berkeley: University of California Press, 1989, pp. 57–9. In 1962 Lewis Strauss, who was chairman of the AEC in August 1953, wrote that "we were able to test our first hydrogen bomb in November 1952. The Russians tested their first weapon involving a thermonuclear reaction the following August. The President's decision was not only sound but in the very nick of time." Strauss, *op.cit.*, p. 240.

104. In an interview on March 12, 1988 Khariton referred to it as a boosted bomb (*usilennaia bomba*). In a later publication he argued that it was the first thermonuclear bomb. Khariton and Smirnov, *loc.cit.*, p. 54.

105. See Chapter 11 of Sakharov, *Memoirs*.

106. "Delo Beriia," *Izvestiia TsK KPSS*, 1991, no. 2, p. 166.

107. A.A. Sokolov to M. Suslov, TsKhSD, f. 5, op. 17, d. 410, p. 247.

108. TsKhSD, f. 5, op. 17, d. 410, p. 266. The deputy head of the Central Committee's Department for Science and Culture wrote to Suslov in the same terms on October 20, 1953. *Ibid.*, p. 280.

109. "A Basis for Estimating Maximum Soviet Capabilities for Atomic Warfare," Memorandum for Mr Robert LeBaron, chairman of the Military Liaison Committee to the Atomic Energy Commission, February 16,

1950, pp. 2–3. HSTL, PSF.

110. LeBaron to Secretary of Defense, February 20, 1950. HSTL, PSF.

111. Central Intelligence Agency, Joint Atomic Energy Intelligence Committee, *Status of the Soviet Atomic Energy Program*, July 4, 1950, CIA/SCI-2/50, p. 4. HSTL, PSF. The Joint Committee was composed of representatives from the Departments of State, Army, Navy, and Air Force, and from the Atomic Energy Commission and the Central Intelligence Agency.

112. *Ibid.*, p. 5.

113. CIA, Joint Atomic Energy Intelligence Committee, *Status of the Soviet Atomic Energy Program*, December 27, 1950, p. 7. HSTL, PSF.

114. CIA, *Status of the Soviet Atomic Energy Program*, CIA/SI 113–51, July 28, 1951, p. 12. HSTL, PSF. This report stated that there was no specific evidence that the Soviet program "is or is not being directed toward the production of thermonuclear weapons."

115. CIA, *Status of the Soviet Atomic Energy Program*, National Scientific Intelligence Estimate, NSIE-1, January 8, 1953, pp. 7, 11. HSTL, PSF.

116. CIA, National Intelligence Estimate, NIE-65, FRUS 1952–4, viii, p. 1189.

117. Hans Bethe, "Memorandum on the History of the Thermonuclear Program," May 23, 1952. CD471.6, Office of the Secretary of Defense Records, RG 330, National Archives.

118. Edward Teller, "Comments on Bethe's History of Thermonuclear Program," August 14, 1952. Records of JCAE, Record Group 128, National Archives.

119. "Foocase – Espionage (R) Interviews in England with Fuchs," p. 28.

120. FRUS 1952–4, ii, Part 2, p. 998.

121. Interview with Bethe, May 28, 1982. De Geer, *loc.cit.*, Hirsch and Mathews, *loc.cit.*, p. 24. A fuller version of their paper was also published: *Fuchs and Fallout: New Insights into the History of the H-Bomb*, Los Angeles: Committee to Bridge the Gap, 1990.

122. Gurevich *et al.*, *loc.cit.*, p. 446.

123. Hirsch and Mathews, *loc.cit.*

124. Interview with Khariton, July 16, 1992.

125. Sakharov, *Memoirs*, p. 158.

126. Iu. Khariton, "Iadernoe oruzhie SSSR: prishlo iz Ameriki ili sozdano samostoiatel'no?," *Izvestiia*, December 8, 1992, p. 3. This revises the analysis I put forward in my "Soviet Thermonuclear Development," *International Security*, Winter 1979–80, pp. 192–7.

127. Sakharov, *Memoirs*, pp. 180–1.

128. *Ibid.*, p. 182.
129. Romanov, *loc.cit.*, p. 23.
130. Adamskii quoted by Iu.N. Smirnov, "Rytsar' nauki," *Priroda*, 1992, no. 2, p. 91.
131. Interview with Khariton, July 16, 1992.
132. Khariton, *loc.cit.*
133. Iu.A. Romanov, interviewed by G.E. Gorelik, November 11, 1992.
134. Sakharov, *Memoirs*, pp. 182–3.
135. *Ibid.*, p. 183. Malyshev was replaced as minister by Zaveniagin on February 28, 1955.
136. The decree, entitled "O mekhanizatsii ucheta i vychislitel'nykh rabot i razvitii proizvodstva schetnykh, schetno-analiticheskikh i matematicheskikh mashin," may be found in *Resheniia partii i pravitel'stva po khoziastvennym voprosam 1917–1967gg, vol. 3, 1941–1952 gody*, Moscow: Politizdat, 1968, p. 564. On the early development of computers see L.G. Khomenko, "Istoriia sozdaniia v AN USSR pervykh otechestvennykh EVM," *Ocherki istorii estestvoznaniia i tekhniki*, no. 36, 1989, pp. 74–6.
137. George Rudins, "Soviet Computers: A Historical Survey," *Soviet Cybernetics Review*, January 1970, p. 7; *Ocherki razvitiia tekhniki v SSSR. Mashinostroenie, avtomaticheskoe upravlenie mashinami i sistemami mashin. Radiotekhnika, elektronika i elektrosviaz'*, Moscow: Nauka, 1970, pp. 402–3. Khomenko, *loc.cit.*, pp. 76–80. BESM stands for *Bystrodeistvuiushchaia elektronnaia schetnaia mashina*: High-speed Electronic Calculating Machine.
138. Sakharov, *Memoirs*, p. 156.
139. "Intelligence Information for Use in the AFSWF Weapons Oriented Course (Advanced)," National Archives, Modern Military Branch, Record Group 218, Records of the US Joint Chiefs of Staff, 1954–6, CCS 334 JIC (12–28–55), sec. 3.
140. Sakharov, *Memoirs*, p. 188.
141. This description is taken from Sakharov, *Memoirs*, p. 190, and I.N. Golovin, "Kurchatov – Uchenyi, gosudarstvennyi deiatel', chelovek," in *Materialy iubileinoi sessii . . .* , *loc.cit.*, p. 14.
142. The distance is given in an interview with Khariton in V.S. Gubarev, *Arzamas-16*, Moscow: Izdat, 1992, p. 23.
143. Sakharov, *Memoirs*, p. 191.
144. Interview with Khariton, July 16, 1992. An American intelligence document prepared in February 1956 gives the same estimate for the yield. It states that "it was a two-stage thermonuclear weapon or device with a yield of about 1,600 kt. Both U-235 and U-233 were employed. It was exploded several

thousand feet in the air over the Semipalatinsk test site and was carried in an aircraft." "Intelligence Information." Khariton referred to this bomb in conversation as a "binary" bomb (*binarnaia bomba*). Interview with Khariton, March 12 1988.
145. Sakharov, *Memoirs*, p. 193.
146. "Rech' N.S. Khrushcheva," *Pravda*, November 28, 1955, p. 1.
147. Sakharov, *Memoirs*, p. 195.
148. Sakharov, *Memoirs*, p. 192. "Radi iadernogo pariteta," *Dos'e*, January 1990, p. 17. This is an interview with Khariton about Sakharov, but it contains excerpts from an unpublished interview that Sakharov had given to a correspondent of *Literaturnaia Gazeta* in January 1987.
149. "We will be happy if these bombs are never exploded over towns and villages," Khrushchev said. "Rech' N.S. Khrushcheva," *Pravda*, November 28, 1955, p. 1.
150. Sakharov, *Vospominaniia*, p. 258.
151. "Radi iadernogo pariteta." On Nedelin see V. Tolubko, *Nedelin*, Moscow: Molodaia gvardiia, 1979, p. 216. Nedelin was killed in 1960 when a Soviet missile blew up on the launch pad.
152. According to Khariton, the military in this period did not take the initiative in proposing the development of particular types of nuclear weapon. Interview with Khariton, July 16, 1992.
153. Sakharov, *Memoirs*, p. 193.
154. Sakharov, "Ia pytalsia."
155. Sakharov, *Memoirs*, pp. 197–233.
156. "So the test of November 22, 1955 became a turning-point in the life of Igor Vasil'evich. He took charge of no more tests at the test sites, and the chief thing for him now was the struggle for peace and the peaceful utilization of intra-atomic energy." Golovin, "Kurchatov – uchenyi, gosudarstvennyi deiatel'," in *Materialy iubileinoi sessii . . .* , p. 15.
157. Sakharov, *Memoirs*, p. 190.
158. Interview with Khariton, July 16, 1992.
159. Aleksandrov gives the date as 1953 in A.P. Aleksandrov, "Gody s Kurchatovym," *Nauka i zhizn'*, 1983, no. 2, p. 24. When I mentioned this to Sakharov, he asked, "Are you sure he wasn't referring to the 1955 test?" See also Golovin, "Kurchatov – uchenyi, gosudarstvennyi deiatel'," p. 15. Golovin ascribes this exchange to the period after the 1955 test.
160. York, *op.cit.*, pp. 96–103.
161. Barton J. Bernstein, "Crossing the Rubicon: A Missed Opportunity to Stop

the H-Bomb?" *International Security*, Fall 1989, pp. 132–60; McGeorge Bundy, *Danger and Survival*, New York: Vintage Books, 1990, pp. 214–19.

162. Sakharov, *Memoirs*, p. 99.

163. Interview with Khariton, March 12, 1988.

164. Landau's objection to working on nuclear weapons had more to do with his attitude to the regime than to nuclear weapons as such.

15. After Stalin

1. Zhukov's rehabilitation had begun even before Stalin's death. He was a delegate to the Nineteenth Party Congress and made a candidate member of the Central Committee. He returned to Sverdlovsk after the congress, but at the end of February 1953 he was summoned to Moscow. *Politbiuro, Orgbiuro, Sekretariat TsK RKP(b)-VKP(b)-KPSS: Spravochnik*, Moscow: Politizdat, 1990, p. 106; N.G. Pavlenko, "Razmyshleniia o sud'be polkovodtsa," in *Marshal Zhukov: polkovodets i chelovek*, vol. 2, Moscow: izd. APN, 1988, p. 138.

2. For a discussion of these changes see *XX s"ezd KPSS i ego istoricheskie real'nosti*, Moscow: Politizdat, 1991, pp. 10–12.

3. L.A. Openkin, "Na istoricheskom pereput'e," *Voprosy istorii KPSS*, 1990, no. 1, pp. 109–10.

4. *XX s"ezd.*, p. 29.

5. Deborah Welch Larson, "Crisis Prevention and the Austrian State Treaty," *International Organization*, Winter 1987, pp. 27–60.

6. N.S. Khrushchev, *Khrushchev Remembers*, Vol. 1, Penguin: Harmondsworth, 1977, pp. 345–66. The fullest account of Beria's arrest is given in three articles in *Krasnaia Zvezda*, March 18, 19, 20, 1988, under the title "Zadanie osobogo svoistva." These articles are based on an interview with Major-General I. Zub, one of those who arrested Beria.

7. "Delo Beriia," *Izvestiia TsK KPSS*, 1991, no. 2, p. 203.

8. *Izvestiia TsK KPSS*, 1991, no. 1, p. 145.

9. *Izvestiia TsK KPSS*, 1991, no. 2, p. 166.

10. M.G. Meshcheriakov, "Akademik V.G. Khlopin: Voskhozhdenie na posledniuiu vershinu," unpublished paper, 1992, p. 29.

11. *Izvestiia TsK KPSS*, 1991, no. 1, p. 145.

12. Malenkov, "Rech' predsedatelia Soveta Ministrov SSSR tovarishcha G.M. Malenkova," *Izvestiia*, August 9, 1953, p. 3.

13. For interesting discussions of Malenkov during this period see Openkin, *loc.cit.* and Elena Zubkova, "Malenkov, Khrushchev, i 'ottepel'," *Kommunist*, 1990, no. 14, pp. 86–94.

14. *XX s"ezd*, pp. 19–20; Iu.V. Aksiutin and O.V. Volobuev, *XX s"ezd KPSS: novatsii i dogmy*, Moscow: Politizdat, 1991, p. 55. The position of General Secretary had been abolished at the Nineteenth Congress, and it was only now that the new position of First Secretary was created.

15. Andrei Malenkov, *O moem otse Georgii Malenkove*, Moscow: Tekhnoekos, 1992, p. 115.

16. Aksiutin and Volobuev, *op.cit.*, pp. 59–60.

17. *Ibid.*, p. 62.

18. The "Secret Speech" is printed as an appendix to *Khrushchev Remembers*, pp. 580–643.

19. Central Intelligence Agency, *Appendices to NIE-64 (Part I): Soviet Bloc Capabilities, through mid-1963*, December 1952, p. 4. National Archives, NNMM Reference Collection – CIA box.

20. Vladimir Gubarev, "Muzei iadernogo oruzhiia," *Rossiskaia Gazeta*, October 20, 1992, p. 4.

21. G.G. Kudriavtsev, "Arkhipelag vozmezdiia," *Voenno-istoricheskii zhurnal*, 1993, no. 3, pp. 20–21.

22. Andrei Sakharov, *Memoirs*, New York: Alfred A. Knopf, 1990, p. 184; interview with Iu.B. Khariton, July 16, 1992. Arzamas-16 was later called the All-Union Research Institute of Experimental Physics, and Cheliabinsk-70 the All-Union Research Institute of Technical Physics.

23. Five graphite-moderated reactors and a chemical separation plant were built at Tomsk-7; the first reactor went critical in 1955. Three reactors and a separation plant were built at Krasnoiarsk-26, under ground. Thomas B. Cochran and Robert Standish Norris, *Russian/Soviet Nuclear Warhead Production*, NWD 93-1, Washington, DC: Natural Resources Defense Council, September 8, 1993, pp. 86–8, 96–101.

24. It made its first public appearance in the 1954 May Day flypast. About 2,000 are reported to have been produced by 1960. Neta Crawford, *Soviet Military Aircraft, Vol. 2 of World Weapon Database*, ed. Randall Forsberg, Brookline: Institute for Defense and Disarmament Studies, 1987, p. 114.

25. In May 1955 US intelligence estimated that there were 20 Miasishchev bombers in service; it did not know how many Tu-95s were in service. "Chart on Estimated Bloc Air Strength in Operational Units," in *Proposed Policy of the United States on the Question of Disarmament: Vol. 3: Reproduction of Charts Used in Presentation of May 26, 1955*, Washington, DC: National Security Ar-

chive. It was assumed that 500 Miasishchev bombers would be in service by mid-1960, *ibid.* In fact by 1960 there were only 35 in service, and about 110 Tu-95s. Crawford, *op.cit.*, p. 48.

26. N.S. Khrushchev, *Khrushchev Remembers, Vol. 2: The Last Testament*, Harmondsworth: Penguin Books, 1977, p. 72.

27. D. Gai, *Nebesnoe pritiazhenie*, Moscow: Moskovskii rabochii, 1984, p. 145.

28. A.N. Ponomarev, "Tvoria nevidannyi polet," *Znamia*, January 1980, p. 181.

29. Khrushchev, *Khrushchev Remembers*, p. 71.

30. Sakharov, *op.cit.*, pp. 180–81. Korolev used Tikhonravov's "packet" concept for the R-7: four identical rockets around a central booster. All engines were ignited at the same time, and the four first-stage rockets fell away when they had burned out. The engines – the four RD-107s and the RD-108 – were designed by Glushko's bureau. The first flight test took place in May 1957, and the first series production model was flight-tested in February 1959. It was this rocket that launched the first sputnik into earth orbit in October 1957. The R-7 was not satisfactory as a military missile, however, and only a handful were deployed. It was vulnerable to attack because it had to be launched from above ground, and because it took a long time to launch.

31. Khrushchev, *Khrushchev Remembers*, pp. 77–8.

32. *Iz istorii sovetskoi kosmonavtiki*, Moscow: Nauka, 1983, pp. 232–5. In May 1954 Korolev first submitted to the government a proposal for an artificial earth satellite. *Ibid.*, p. 233.

33. By Soviet terminology a missile with a range of more than 1,000 kilometers was considered a "strategic" missile.

34. Flight tests of the R-11 began in 1953. The ground forces version entered service in 1957, and was designed to provide nuclear firepower in support of ground forces operations; it was defined as an "operational-tactical missile." In 1959 the R-11 entered service with the Navy, for nuclear strikes against large industrial and administrative-political centers, and against military bases in coastal regions. *Iz istorii*, pp. 232–5; Mikhail Turetsky, *The Introduction of Missile Systems into the Soviet Navy (1945–1962)*, Falls Church: Delphic Associates, March 1983, p. 71.

35. On Iangel' see Khrushchev, *Khrushchev Remembers*, pp. 82–3; see also V. Gubarev, *Konstruktor. Neskol'ko stranits iz zhizni Mikhaila Ku'micha Iangelia*, Moscow:

Politizdat, 1977, pp. 71–74; V.S. Budnik, "O zhizni i deiatel'nosti Mikhaila Kuz'micha Iangelia," in *Pionery osvoeniia kosmosa i sovremennost'*, Moscow: Nauka, 1988, pp. 25–6. Among Iangel's first designs was the R-12 medium-range ballistic missile (known in the West as the SS-4). This was a modification of the R-5, with a range of 1,800–2,000 kilometers. It was flight-tested in 1957 and entered service in 1959. Iangel' also worked on an ICBM, known in the West as the SS-7, which blew up in 1960, killing Marshal Nedelin.

36. Steven J. Zaloga, *Soviet Air Defense Missiles*, Coulsden: Jane's Information Group, 1989, pp. 10, 32. This system was designed to repulse an air attack equivalent to three times that of the Anglo-American raid on Dresden in February, 1945. O.V. Golubev *et al.*, *Proshloe i nastoiashchee rossiiskikh sistem protivoraketnoi oborony (vzgliad iznutri)*, Moscow: Research Center, Committee of Scientists for Global Security, 1993, pp. 4–5.

37. This history is taken from a biographical sketch of G.V. Kisun'ko, head of the group that studied the problem, in "Den'gi na oboronu," *Sovetskaia Rossiia*, August 5, 1990, p. 4. Some thought had already been given to ABM defense from 1948 on by the Defense Ministry and the ballistic missile designers. See Golubev *et al.*, *op.cit.*, p. 5. Kapitsa worked on the problem of anti-ballistic missile defense at his *dacha* in the late 1940s and early 1950s. See his letters to Malenkov and Stalin on this subject in 1950. P.L. Kapitsa, *Pis'ma o nauke*, Moscow: Moskovskii rabochii, 1989, pp. 286–91, 294–5.

38. Matthew Evangelista provides useful case studies of the development of tactical nuclear weapons in both the United States and Soviet Union in *Innovation and the Arms Race*, Ithaca: Cornell University Press, 1988. On the US case see pp. 86–154. See also Robert A. Wampler, *NATO Strategic Planning and Nuclear Weapons 1950–1957*, Nuclear History Program Occasional Paper 6, College Park: Center for International Security Studies at Maryland, 1990, pp. 4–11.

39. Evangelista, *op.cit.*, pp. 169–95.

40. *Krasnoznamennyi prikarpatskii*, 2nd edn, Moscow: Voenizdat, 1982, p. 118. According to a US Army intelligence report, the exercise took place in October. US Department of the Army, General Staff, G-2, "Soviet Training for Atomic Warfare," March 7, 1955, p. 14. Army War College Library.

41. *Krasnoznamennyi prikarpatskii*, p. 118.

42. *Ibid.*, pp. 118–19.

43. It was apparently Ministry of Defense Order No. 00215, November 9, 1953 that initiated this training. This is summarized in US Department, "Soviet Training for Atomic Warfare," p. 3. Soviet sources are not as precise, but indicate that a decree to this effect was issued by the ministry at about this time. See, for example, V.G. Kulikov (ed.), *Akademiia General'nogo Shtaba*, Moscow: Voenizdat, 1976, p. 129.

44. Maj.-Gen. V.I. Makarevskii, in Tufts University–Moscow State University, *The Global Classroom – Part 2: At the Crossroads: Nuclear Weapons Strategies*, Television broadcast, April 9, 1988.

45. See, for example, *Krasnoznamennyi Severokavkazskii*, Rostov na Donu: Rostovskoe knizhnoe izdatel'stvo, 1971, p. 399; *Istoriia ordena Lenina Leningradskogo voennogo okruga*, Moscow: Voenizdat, 1974, p. 587.

46. Interview with Lt.-Gen. Iu.P. Zabegailov October 22, 1990.

47. See, for example, V. Khlopov, "O nekotorykh sovremennykh voennykh teoriiakh SShA," *Voennaia Mysl'*, 1954, no. 1; "Deistviia atomnogo oruzhiia," (excerpts from "The Effects of Atomic Weapons," published in the United States in 1950), *Voennaia Mysl'*, 1954, no. 3.

48. This account of the exercise is based on Lt.-Gen. (ret.) N. Ostroumov, "V zone iadernogo udara," *Aviatsiia i kosmonavtika*, 1990, no. 9; an interview with General Ostroumov, October 24, 1990; and on Vladimir Karpov, *Polkovodets*, Moscow: Sovetskii pisatel', 1985, pp. 524–6; V. Zmitrenko, "Vzryv, o kotorom mozhno teper' rasskazat'," *Krasnaia Zvezda*, September 29, 1989, p. 2; D. Efremov, "Ucheniia pod atomnym gribom," *Izvestiia*, October 14, 1989, p. 6; G. Sapunova, "Zharkii sentiabr' 1954-go," *Trud*, January 6, 1990, p. 3; B.P. Ivanov, "Atomnyi vzryv u poselka Totskoe," *Voenno-istoricheskii zhurnal*, 1991, no. 12, pp. 79–86; A. Khorev, "Chernoe pepelishche," *Krasnaia Zvezda*, June 9, 1992, p. 6; I. Osin, "Taina Totskikh uchenii," *Rossiiskaia gazeta*, June 12, 1992, p. 5; V. Bentsianov, "Nashi dushi iadernyi grib ne otravil," *Krasnaia Zvezda*, September 24, 1992, p. 2; V. Vedernikov, V. Moiseev, "V epitsentre iadernogo vzryva," *Rossiiskie vesti*, January 19, 1993, p. 1.

49. On the American exercises see Evangelista, *op.cit.*, pp. 131–3, 150–2. See also Howard L. Rosenberg, *Atomic Soldiers*, Boston: Beacon Press, 1980. The United States conducted exercises involving troops at the Nevada test site between 1951 and 1957.

Thomas B. Cochran *et al.*, *Nuclear Weapons Databook Vol. 2: US Nuclear Warhead Production*, Cambridge, Mass.: Ballinger, 1987, pp. 152–6. The press release for one of these exercises, in 1955, stated that its purpose was to teach "soldiers to view nuclear weapons in their proper perspective . . . that powerful though these weapons are, they can be controlled and harnessed . . . and that despite the weapons' destructiveness there are defenses against them on the atomic battlefield." *Ibid.*, p. 154. On the number of Soviet troops see Vedernikov and Moiseev, *loc.cit.*

50. Ivanov, *loc.cit.*, p. 79. Zhukov came to the test site periodically. On one occasion he watched a tank attack which was supposed to be passing through a contaminated zone. The tanks were moving slowly, so Zhukov stopped them and called all the tank commanders together. He asked whether any of them had taken part in the Berlin campaign, which Zhukov had commanded. When some of the men said they had, he asked them to mount a proper tank attack, which they did. Interview with Ostroumov, October 24, 1990.

51. Ostroumov, *loc.cit.*, p. 36.

52. One report refers to the two sides as North and South, another to East and West. See Osin, *loc.cit.*, and Vedernikov and Moiseev, *loc.cit.*

53. Efremov, *loc.cit.*

54. Karpov, *op.cit.*, p. 526.

55. Interview with Maj.-Gen. (ret.) V.V. Larionov, November 13, 1990.

56. Interviews with Col.-Gen. Iu.P. Zabegailov, October 22, 1990, and Ostroumov, October 24, 1990.

57. Sapunova, *loc.cit.*; Vedernikov and Moiseev, *loc.cit.*

58. Karpov, *op.cit.*, p. 526.

59. Interview with Col.-Gen. A.A. Danilevich, October 24, 1990.

60. New stress was placed on flexibility and mobility. John Erickson writes that "nuclear weapons employed on the battlefield now transformed maneuver into a process of exploiting to the fullest the nuclear strike in order to make the deepest possible penetration into enemy defenses, or conversely, to 'counter-maneuver' by moving Soviet troops out of range of an impending nuclear strike," in "The Evolution of the Soviet Ground Forces, 1941–1985," in John Erickson, Lynn Hansen, and William Schneider, *Soviet Ground Forces: An Operational Assessment*, Boulder, Colo.: Westview Press, 1986, p. 26.

61. I.N. Golovin, "Kurchatov – uchenyi, gosudarstvennyi deiatel', chelovek," in *Materialy Iubileinoi sessii uchenogo soveta tsentra 12 ianvaria 1993.g.*, Moscow: Rossiiskii nauchnyi tsentr "Kurchatovskii Institut," 1993, p. 13. The first nuclear weapons were assigned to the Air Force. The first nuclear-armed missile was the R-5. A combat version of the R-5 was tested with its ground equipment during 1955, and in February 1956 the R-5 was flight-tested with a nuclear warhead. *Iz istorii sovetskoi kosmonavtiki*, pp. 234–5.

62. Vladimir Gubarev, "Muzei iadernogo oruzhiia," *Rossiiskaia Gazeta*, October 20, 1992, p. 4.

63. Vladislav Zubok, "SSSR-SShA: put' k peregovoram po razoruzheniiu v iadernyi vek (1953–1955 gg.)," paper given at a conference on US–Soviet relations between 1950 and 1955, Ohio University, October 1988, p. 7.

64. Interview with I.N. Golovin, October 19, 1992.

65. Andrei Sakharov, *Memoirs*, New York: Alfred A. Knopf, 1990, p. 193. It seems that at one meeting they threatened to shoot each other.

66. N. Talenskii, "K voprosu o kharaktere zakonov voennoi nauki," *Voennaia Mysl'*, 1953, no. 9, pp. 20–30.

67. Although "military science" is the normal translation, "science of war" might be better; in any event the term means the systematic study of, or systematic knowledge about, war.

68. "K itogam diskussii o kharaktere zakonov voennoi nauki," *Voennaia Mysl'*, 1955, no. 4, pp. 16–22.

69. H.S. Dinerstein, *War and the Soviet Union*, New York: Praeger, 1959, and Raymond L. Garthoff, *Soviet Strategy in the Nuclear Age*, New York: Praeger, 1958 provide analyses of this discussion, and of other military writings of 1953–5.

70. "O nekotorykh voprosakh sovetskoi voennoi nauki," *Voennaia Mysl'*, 1955, no. 3, p. 3.

71. N. Bulganin, "O burzhuaznoi voennoi nauke (Otvet na vopros)," *Voennaia Mysl'*, 1955, no. 6, p. 3.

72. "Sovetskaia armiia – detishche sovetskogo naroda," *Voennaia Mysl'*, 1955, no. 2, p. 12. Zhukov pressed for intensive study of nuclear warfare when he became minister in February 1955. N.G. Pavlenko, "Razmyshleniia o sud'be polkovodtsa," in *Marshal Zhukov: polkovodets i chelovek*, Vol. 2, Moscow: Novosti, 1988, p. 138.

73. "US Weapons Secrets Revealed," *Bulletin of the Atomic Scientists*, March 1993, p. 48.

74. On the New Look see, for example, John Lewis Gaddis, *Strategies of Containment*, New York: Oxford University Press, 1982, pp. 127–97; David Alan Rosenberg, "The Origins of Overkill," *International Security*, Spring 1983, pp. 27–38.

75. David Alan Rosenberg, "A Smoking Radiating Ruin at the End of Two Hours," *International Security*, Winter 1981–2, pp. 3–38.

76. *Ibid.*, p. 25. This is a quotation from detailed notes made on the briefing by one of the officers who attended.

77. *Ibid.*, pp. 31–2. These figures are not in the SAC briefing, but in a briefing presented to the Joint Chiefs of Staff in a February 1955 by the Defense Department's Weapons Systems Evaluation Group. That briefing is also attached to Rosenberg's article.

78. *Ibid.*, p. 33.

79. *Ibid.*, pp. 30–31, 34.

80. *Ibid.*, p. 33.

81. On this issue see McGeorge Bundy, *Danger and Survival*, New York: Vintage Books, 1990, pp. 246–60; Marc Trachtenberg, "A Wasting Asset: American Strategy and the Shifting Nuclear Balance, 1949–1954," in his *History and Strategy*, Princeton: Princeton University Press, 1991, pp. 100–52. The Soviet Union was aware of a preventive war current in American thinking. An intelligence report prepared in December 1955 by the Committee of Information attached to the Foreign Ministry states that although the advocates of preventive war did not occupy key positions in the Eisenhower administration, their activities have "nevertheless to a significant degree increased the threat of war." "Ob izmeneniiakh v rasstanovke i sootnoshenii sil v burzhuaznykh krugakh osnovnykh kapitalisticheskikh stran po voprosam voiny i mira." TsKhSD, f. 5, op. 28, d. 285, p. 79.

82. P. Rotmistrov, "O roli vnezapnosti v sovremennoi voine," *Voennaia Mysl'*, 1955, no. 2. On not publishing his article see the editorial, "O nekotorykh voprosakh Sovetskoi voennoi nauki," *Voennaia Mysl'*, 1955, no. 3, p. 5.

83. Rotmistrov, *loc.cit.*, p. 20.

84. *Ibid.*

85. "O nekotorykh voprosakh," p. 5.

86. Matthew P. Gallagher, *The Soviet History of World War II*, New York: Frederick A. Praeger, 1963, pp. 153–75.

87. Dmitrii Volkogonov, *Triumf i tragediia*, Book 2, 2nd edn, Moscow: Novosti, 1990,

p. 136. See also Alexander Dallin, "Stalin and the German Invasion," *Soviet Union/ Union Soviétique*, 1991, nos 1–3, pp. 19–37.

88. "K voprosu o kharaktere sovremennoi voiny," *Voennaia Mysl'*, 1955, no. 8, pp. 3–17.

89. *Ibid.*, p. 10.

90. *Ibid.*

91. *Ibid.*, p. 13.

92. Khrushchev, *Vol. 2, The Last Testament*, p. 49.

93. *Ibid.*, pp. 49–58; Kuznetsov writes about his poor relations with Khrushchev and Zhukov in "Nashi otnosheniia s Zhukovym stali poistine dramaticheskimi . . . ," *Voenno-istoricheskii zhurnal*, 1992, no. 1, pp. 74–82. See also Robert Waring Herrick, *Soviet Naval Strategy*, Annapolis: US Naval Institute, 1968, pp. 67–72.

94. Michael McGwire, "Naval Power and Soviet Oceans Policy," in US Congress, Committee on Commerce, *Soviet Oceans Development*, Washington, DC: US Government Printing Office, 1976, pp. 81–2.

95. Khrushchev gave the 1955 figure in a speech to the Supreme Soviet in 1960. *Pravda*, January 15, 1960. Thomas W. Wolfe, *Soviet Power and Europe, 1945–1970*, Baltimore: Johns Hopkins University Press, 1970, pp. 164–6.

96. "Rech' tovarishcha G.M. Malenkova," *Pravda*, March 10, 1953, p. 1.

97. For example, "peaceful coexistence . . . is fully possible given the mutual desire to cooperate, readiness to perform obligations which have been assumed, observance of the principle of equality and non-interference in the internal affairs of states." "Otvet tovarishchu Stalina," *Pravda*, April 1, 1952.

98. Barton J. Bernstein, "The Struggle Over the Korean Armistice: Prisoners of Repatriation?" in Bruce Cumings (ed.), *Child of Conflict: The Korean–American Relationship, 1943–1953*, Seattle: University of Washington Press, 1983, pp. 261–307, esp. 296–307; see also Rosemary J. Foot, "Nuclear Coercion and the Ending of the Korean Conflict," *International Security*, Winter 1988–89, p. 96.

99. "O Koreiskoi voine 1950–1953 gg. i peregovorakh o peremirii," August 9, 1966. TsKhSD f. 5, op. 58, d. 266, p. 129. See Chapter 13, note 29 for a brief description of this document.

100. *Ibid.*, p. 130.

101. "Postanovlenie Soveta Ministrov SSSR," March 19, 1953, p. 1. This document is being transferred from the Russian Presidential Archive to TsKhSD. It does not yet have a file number. It is due to be published in the journal *Istochnik*, and in English in the *Journal of American-East Asian Relations* in February 1994. I am grateful to Kathryn Weathersby for making it available to me.

102. FRUS 1952–4, xv, pp. 788–9.

103. Foot, *loc.cit.*, p. 97; FRUS 1952–4, xv, p. 824.

104. "Zaiavlenie Ministra Inostrannykh Del SSSR V.M. Molotova po koreiskomu voprosu," *Izvestiia*, April 2, 1953.

105. FRUS 1952–4, xv, pp. 825–33.

106. *Ibid.*, xv, p. 1068.

107. *Ibid.*, pp. 1082–6.

108. Foot, *loc.cit.*, p. 99.

109. FRUS 1952–4, xv, p. 1110.

110. "Postanovlenie," p. 9.

111. FRUS 1952–4, xv, p. 1133.

112. Bundy, *op.cit.*, p. 239.

113. In his memoirs Eisenhower refers to earlier steps "to let the Communist authorities understand that, in the absence of satisfactory progress, we intended to move decisively without inhibition in our use of weapons." (Dwight D. Eisenhower, *The White House Years: Mandate for Change*, New York: Doubleday, 1963, p. 181.) He is not specific about these steps, so it is difficult to relate them to the shift in Soviet policy.

114. Foot, *loc.cit.*, p. 104.

115. Malenkov, "Rech'."

116. "Obrashchenie Tsentral'nogo Komiteta KPSS," *Izvestiia*, February 11, 1954, p. 1.

117. "Rech' tovarishcha N.S. Khrushcheva," *Pravda*, March 7, 1954, p. 1.

118. *Sto sorok besed s Molotovym: iz dnevnika F. Chueva*, Moscow: Terra, 1991, p. 496. Molotov had used the term in his March 10, 1950 speech, but in a special way: "We are wholly for the Leninist-Stalinist principles of peaceful coexistence of the two systems and for their peaceful competition. But we are well acquainted with the truth that while imperialism exists there exists also the danger of a new aggression, and that wars are inevitable in the presence of imperialism and its predatory plans." "Rech' tov. V.M. Molotova," *Pravda*, March 11, 1950, p. 3. In other words, peaceful coexistence might be desirable, but it was not possible.

119. *Sto sorok besed*, p. 496.

120. *Ibid.*, p. 497.

121. *Ibid.*

122. N.S. Khrushchev, *Khrushchev Remembers: The Glasnost Tapes*, Boston: Little, Brown, 1990, p. 148.

123. "Rech' tovarishcha G.M. Malenkova," *Izvestiia*, March 13, 1954, p. 2.

124. Herbert Dinerstein, *War and the Soviet*

Union, New York: Frederick A. Praeger, 1959, p. 74.

125. Peter G. Boyle (ed.), *The Churchill–Eisenhower Correspondence, 1953–1955*, Chapel Hill: University of North Carolina Press, 1990, pp. 123–4.

126. Malyshev to Khrushchev, April 1, 1954, enclosing a copy of the article entitled "Opasnosti atomnoi voiny i predlozhenie prezidenta Eizenkhauera." TsKhSD f. 5, op. 30, d. 16, pp. 38–44. I am grateful to Vladislav Zubok for drawing this document to my attention.

127. *Ibid.*, p. 39.

128. *Ibid.*, p. 40.

129. *Ibid.*, pp. 40–41.

130. *Ibid.*, p. 38.

131. *Izvestiia*, April 27, 1954, p. 7.

132. Quoted by Aksiutin and Volobuev, *op.cit.*, p. 60.

133. Quoted by Andrei Malenkov, *op.cit.*, p. 115. These are quotations from the minutes of the January 1955 plenum. The full stenographic report has not yet been made public.

134. Quoted by Openkin, *loc.cit.*, p. 116.

135. Quoted by Aksiutin and Volobuev, *op.cit.*, p. 61.

136. "Sud'by mira i tsivilizatsii reshaiut narody," *Kommunist*, March 1955, no. 4, esp. pp. 17, 18.

137. Mohammed Heikal, *Sphinx and Commissar: The Rise and Fall of Soviet Influence in the Arab World*, London: Collins, 1978, p. 129.

138. A.A. Roshchin, "Gody obnovleniia, nadezhd i razocharivanii (1953–1959 gg.)," *Novaia i noveishaia istoriia*, 1988, no. 5, p. 132.

139. *Ibid.*, p. 132.

140. For the July 1955 plenum see Aksiutin and Volobuev, *op.cit.*, pp. 63–4.

141. These elements were all present in the Soviet proposal to the UN General Assembly on September 24, 1953. The proposal was rejected by the Western powers. The proposal can be found in *Documents on Disarmament 1945–1959: Vol. 1 1945–1956*, Washington, DC: US Department of State, 1960, pp. 390–1. The fullest Soviet account of Soviet disarmament policy in this period is V.M. Khaitsman, *SSSR i problema razoruzheniia 1945–1959*, Moscow: Nauka, 1970; see p. 165 for this proposal. A helpful essay is Roshchin, *loc.cit.* Roshchin worked in the Foreign Ministry at the time, and was involved in the formulation of disarmament policy. The Soviet proposal of June 11, 1954 contained only minor modifications to the earlier Soviet position. *Documents on*

Disarmament, pp. 425–6.

142. *Documents on Disarmament*, pp. 456–67; Khaitsman, *op.cit.*, pp. 237–47.

143. Roshchin, *loc.cit.*, p. 131.

144. On this whole episode see Matthew Evangelista, "Cooperation Theory and Disarmament Negotiations in the 1950s," *World Politics*, July 1990, pp. 502–28; and V.M. Zubok, "Nebo nad 'sverkhderzhavami'," *SShA*, 1990, no. 7, pp. 47–55.

145. Roshchin, *loc.cit.*, p. 131.

146. Komitet informatsii pri MID SSSR, *O vozmozhnykh pozitsiiakh zapadnykh derzhav po osnovnym mezhdunarodnym voprosam na predstoiashchem soveshchanii glav pravitel'stv chetyrekh derzhav*, Gromyko to Suslov, July 7, 1955. TsKhSD f. 5, op. 28, d. 283, p. 84.

147. On the conference see Anthony Eden, *Full Circle*, London: Cassell, 1960, pp. 295–311; Eisenhower, *op.cit.*, pp. 503–31; FRUS 1955–7, v, pp. 361–535.

148. *50 let bor'by SSSR za razoruzhenie. Sbornik dokumentov*, Moscow: Nauka, 1967, p. 302.

149. Evangelista, *loc.cit.*, p. 522; Bundy, *op.cit.*, pp. 295–305.

150. FRUS 1955–7, v, p. 376. The prevailing winds in fact go from west to east.

151. *Ibid.*, p. 413.

152. Quoted by Bundy, *op.cit.*, p. 302.

153. Eden, *op.cit.*, pp. 368–9.

154. *Ibid.*, p. 306.

155. *Khrushchev Remembers: Vol. 1*, p. 427.

156. "Ob izmeneniiakh," p. 75. This assessment was prepared by the Committee of Information attached to the Foreign Ministry as part of the preparations for the Twentieth Party Congress.

157. "Rech' N.S. Khrushcheva," *Pravda*, November 28, 1955, p. 1. On the Committee of Information see Vladislav M. Zubok, "Soviet Intelligence and the Cold War: The 'Small' Committee of Information, 1952–53," Working Paper No. 4, Cold War International History Project, Washington, DC: Woodrow Wilson International Center for Scholars, December 1992, pp. 3–8.

158. *XX s"ezd KPSS*, vol. 1, Moscow: Politizdat, 1956, p. 36.

159. *Ibid.*, pp. 321, 455–6.

160. *Ibid.*, pp. 37–8.

161. The way in which Khrushchev put the issue in 1956 confirms that Stalin had been referring not only to war between capitalist countries but to the possibility of world war.

162. *Ibid.*, pp. 310, 320. On Malenkov see *ibid.*, p. 432.

16. The Atom and Peace

1. N.A. Dollezhal', *U istokov rukotvornogo mira*, Moscow: Znanie, 1989, p. 153.
2. *Ibid.*, pp. 153–4.
3. I.D. Morokhov (ed.), *Atomnoi energetike XX let*, Moscow: Atomizdat, 1974, p. 18; Dollezhal', *op.cit.*, p. 155.
4. D.I. Blokhintsev, "Pervaia atomnaia," *Voprosy istorii*, 1974, no. 6, pp. 110–12.
5. Dollezhal', *op.cit.*, p. 154.
6. Leipunskii's proposal is published in A.I. Leipunskii, *Izbrannye trudy. Vospominaniia*, Kiev: Naukova dumka, 1990, pp. 62–9.
7. *Ibid.*
8. *Sovetskaia atomnaia nauka i tekhnika*, Moscow: Atomizdat, 1967, p. 85. Fast-breeder reactors proved much more difficult to build than Leipunskii or anyone else, in the Soviet Union or outside, anticipated in 1950. The first Soviet experimental commercial breeder did not start up until 1973, the year after Leipunskii's death.
9. Dollezhal', *op.cit.*, pp. 155–6.
10. D.I. Blokhintsev, *Rozhdenie mirnogo atoma*, Moscow: Atomizdat, 1977, p. 41. The laboratory at Obninsk (later known as the Energy Physics Institute) had been set up at the end of the war with a group of physicists brought from Germany. Leipunskii became director in 1946. In the early years the laboratory worked on high-energy physics as well as reactor design. By 1950, however, the work on accelerators was concentrated at Dubna, to the north of Moscow, while Obninsk focused on reactor design and development. Blokhintsev took over from Leipunskii in 1950, and in the following year became scientific director of the power reactor project.
11. V.S. Komel'kov, "Tvorets i pobeditel'," in A.P. Aleksandrov (ed.), *Vospominaniia ob Igore Vasil'eviche Kurchatove*, Moscow: Nauka, 1988, p. 326.
12. "V sovete ministrov SSSR," *Pravda*, July 1, 1954, p. 1.
13. Blokhintsev, *op.cit.*, pp. 45–50; Dollezhal', *op.cit.*, pp. 166–7.
14. Dollezhal', *op.cit.*, p. 177.
15. *Ibid.*
16. Dollezhal', *op.cit.*, pp. 178–80; on the location of the reactor see Thomas B. Cochran and Robert Standish Norris, *Russian/Soviet Nuclear Warhead Production*, NWD 93–1, Washington, DC: Natural Resources Defense Council, 1993, p. 86. The first reactor at Tomsk-7, which was designed purely for plutonium production, went critical in 1955.
17. For a good discussion of the speech and its background see McGeorge Bundy, *Danger and Survival*, New York: Random House, 1988, pp. 285–93.
18. US Congress, Senate Committee on Foreign Relations, *Atoms for Peace Manual*, Washington, DC: US Government Printing Office, 1955, p. 3.
19. *Ibid.*, p. 5.
20. *Ibid.*, pp. 5–6.
21. *Documents on Disarmament 1945–1959: Vol. 1*, Washington, DC: Department of State, 1960, pp. 401–7.
22. *Ibid.*, p. 405.
23. FRUS 1952–4, ii, p. 1355.
24. The Soviet note is in *Atoms for Peace Manual*, pp. 269–74; the quotations are taken from p. 271.
25. "Opasnosti atomnoi voiny i predlozhenie prezidenta Eizenkhauera," TsKhSD f. 5, op. 30, d. 126, pp. 38–44. The analysis given in this article of the consequences of nuclear war was discussed on pp. 337–9.
26. *Ibid.*, pp. 42–4. The quotations are from p. 42.
27. Memorandum of the conversation, in FRUS 1952–4, ii, p. 1415.
28. *Ibid.*, p. 1416.
29. Richard G. Hewlett and Jack M. Holl, *Atoms for Peace and War 1953–1961*, Berkeley: University of California Press, 1989, pp. 228–9.
30. The Soviet *aide-mémoire* is given in FRUS 1952–4, Vol. ii, pp. 1567–9.
31. John Rigden, *Rabi: Scientist and Citizen*, New York: Basic Books, 1987, p. 240.
32. FRUS 1952–4, ii, pp. 1578–80.
33. "Soobshchenie TASS," *Izvestiia*, January 15, 1955; "Soviet Offers U.N. Atom Power Data," *New York Times*, January 15, 1955, p. 1.
34. "V sovete ministrov SSSR," *Izvestiia*, January 18, 1955, p. 1.
35. *Sovetskaia atomnaia nauka i tekhnika*, p. 375.
36. A.N. Lavrishchev at a press conference in Geneva, August 20, 1955. William L. Laurence, "Secrecy is Eased as Atomic Parley in Geneva Closes," *New York Times*, August 21, 1955, p. 1. The United States was concluding similar agreements with other countries at the time.
37. Iu.A. Khramov, *Fiziki: Biograficheskii spravochnik*, 2nd edn, Moscow: Nauka, 1983, pp. 51, 248.
38. FRUS, 1955–7, xx, p. 83.
39. Hewlett and Holl, *op.cit.*, pp. 370–1.
40. Kurchatov had chaired a commission in 1954 that pointed to a serious lag in Soviet nuclear physics, and blamed this in part on

unjustified secrecy and lack of contact with foreign scientists. On July 9, 1954 the Academy of Sciences adopted a resolution on the basis of this report. TsKhSD f. 5, op. 17, d. 458, pp. 48–52 for this resolution; pp. 53–77 for the report itself.

41. I.I. Novikov, "Ob organizatsii rabot," in Aleksandrov, *op.cit.*, p. 347. It was only at the last minute that the decision was taken to send a large delegation.

42. Blokhintsev, *op.cit.*, p. 93.

43. For a brief review of the topics discussed see Bertrand Goldschmidt, *The Atomic Complex*, La Grange Park: American Nuclear Society, 1982, pp. 257–60.

44. Blokhintsev, *op.cit.*, p. 92.

45. On the Presidium decree see the memorandum by A.M. Rumiantsev, head of the Central Committee Science and Culture department. TsKhSD f. 7, op. 17, d. 507, p. 270. On the late invitations to foreign scientists see Laura Fermi, *Atoms for the World: United States Participation in the Conference on the Peaceful Uses of Atomic Energy*, Chicago: University of Chicago Press, 1957, p. 39.

46. See the report on the foreign participants in the conference by S.T. Korneev, head of the Foreign Department of the Academy. TsKhSD f. 7, op. 17, d. 507, pp. 275, 283; Fermi, *op.cit.*, p. 39.

47. Fermi, *op.cit.*, p. 128.

48. Blokhintsev, *op.cit.*, pp. 93–4; Fermi, *op.cit.*, pp. 156–7.

49. Blokhintsev, *op.cit.*, p. 94.

50. V.I. Veksler was well known for having discovered, at the same time as Edwin McMillan at Berkeley and independently of him, the principle of the synchrocyclotron (or *avtofazirovka*) which made it possible to build much more powerful accelerators.

51. "An Assessment of the Geneva Conference by Sir John Cockcroft and Harwell Staff," September/October 1955, p. 13. PRO AB6.1627.

52. FRUS, 1955–7, xx, p. 212.

53. I.N. Golovin, *I.V. Kurchatov*, 3rd edn, Moscow: Atomizdat, 1978, p. 105.

54. I.V. Kurchatov, *Izbrannye trudy: Tom 3, Iadernaia energiia*, Moscow: Nauka, 1984, p. 168. He also pointed out that foreign industry was producing instruments of a higher quality than Soviet industry, and called for improvement in this respect.

55. Rudolf Peierls, *Bird of Passage*, Princeton: Princeton University Press, 1985, p. 266.

56. The quotations from Veksler and Rabi are both taken from Rigden, *op.cit.*, p. 245.

57. "Report on the International Conference on Peaceful Uses of Atomic Energy," August 31, 1955, p. 8. PRO AB16.1675. Goldschmidt describes the conference as "a remarkable success," *op.cit.*, p. 258.

58. Hewlett and Holl, *op.cit.*, pp. 312–16. The minutes of the discussions are in "Talks on Diversion of Fissile Material, Geneva, 22–9 August 1955," PRO AB6.1592.

59. The Pugwash movement had its origins in the "Russell-Einstein manifesto" of July 1955. This manifesto, signed by Bertrand Russell and Albert Einstein, as well as some other eminent scientists (but no Soviet scientists), called on scientists to come together "to appraise the perils that have arisen as a result of the development of weapons of mass destruction." Joseph Rotblat, *Pugwash – The First Ten Years*, New York: Humanities Press, 1967, pp. 12, 77–9.

60. On the early years of CERN see Victor Weisskopf, *The Joy of Insight*, New York: Basic Books, 1991, pp. 209–19.

61. *Sovetskaia atomnaia nauka i tekhnika*, pp. 377–8. V.S. Emel'ianov, *S chego nachinalos'*, Moscow: Sovetskaia Rossiia, 1979, pp. 216–18.

62. D.I. Blokhintsev, "Talantlivyi uchitel' organizatsii nauki," in Aleksandrov, *op.cit.*, pp. 420–21. "Otkrytie soveshchaniia po voprosu ob organizatsii Vostochnogo instituta iadernykh issledovanii," *Pravda*, March 21, 1956, p. 1. The original members were Albania, Bulgaria, Hungary, the GDR, China, North Korea, Mongolia, Poland, Romania, the Soviet Union, and Czechoslovakia.

63 Interview with Lt.-Gen. N.N. Ostroumov October 24, 1990. Ostroumov was the officer who was told to speak to the Commander-in-Chief of the Chinese Air Force.

64. John Wilson Lewis and Xue Litai, *China Builds the Bomb*, Stanford: Stanford University Press, 1988, pp. 38–9.

65. *Ibid.*, pp. 11–34.

66. *Ibid.*, p. 41.

67. *Ibid.*

68. *Ibid.*, p. 105.

69. *Ibid.*, p. 41.

70. M.Iu. Prozumenshchikov and I.N. Shevchuk, "Soviet–Chinese Relations," paper presented at a conference on "New Evidence on Cold War History," Moscow, 1993, p. 7.

71. N.S. Khrushchev, *Khrushchev Remembers: Vol. 2, The Last Testament*, Harmondsworth: Penguin, 1977, p. 93.

72. In his political history of nuclear energy, Bertrand Goldschmidt refers to the years from 1954 to 1964 as the period of euphoria. Goldschmidt, *op.cit.*, p. 253.

73. N. Bulganin, "*O zadachakh po dal'neishemu pod"emu promyshlennosti, tekhnicheskomu progressu i uluchshenii organizatsii proizvodstva. Doklad na plenume tsentral'nogo komiteta KPSS, 4 iiulia 1955 goda*, Moscow: Politizdat, 1955, pp. 9–10.

74. "'Nel'zia peredelyvat' zakony prirody' (P.L. Kapitsa I.V. Stalinu)," *Izvestiia TsK KPSS*, 1991, no. 2, p. 108. Kapitsa forgets here his own attitude to fission in 1939 and 1940.

75. Whether Stalin ever saw this letter is not clear. He did not reply to Kapitsa.

76. Fedor Burlatskii, "Posle Stalina," *Novyi Mir*, no. 10, 1988, p. 157.

77. See the note in P.L. Kapitsa, *Pis'ma o nauke*, Moscow: Moskovskii rabochii, 1989, p. 312.

78. V.S. Lel'chuk, *Nauchno-tekhnicheskaia revoliutsiia i promyshlennoe razvitie SSSR*, Moscow: Nauka, 1987, p. 92; *Ekonomicheskaia zhizn' SSSR: kniga vtoraia 1951–1965*, Moscow: izd. "Sovetskaia entsiklopediia," 1967, p. 487.

79. The following discussion is based on Kapitsa's letter of December 15, 1955, in Kapitsa, *op.cit.*, pp. 314–19. The Russian term *nauchnaia obshchestvennost'* carries the meaning of scientific public or scientific public opinion as well as scientific community.

80. *Ibid.*, p. 316.

81. D.V. Lebedev in "'Kruglyi stol.' Stranitsy istorii sovetskoi genetiki v literature poslednykh let," *Voprosy istorii estestvoznaniia i tekhniki*, 1987, no. 4, pp. 123–4.

82. Excerpts from the biologists' letter have been published. "Genetika – nasha bol'," *Pravda*, January 13, 1989, p. 4. On the same page is an article by Raisa Kuznetsova on the activities of Kurchatov and Tamm in defense of genetics.

83. Lebedev, *loc.cit.*, p. 124.

84. David Joravsky, *The Lysenko Affair*, Chicago: University of Chicago Press, 1970, pp. 157–62.

85. Kapitsa, *op.cit.*, pp. 317–18.

86. Nuclear scientists, notably S.L. Sobolev, took part in the rehabilitation of cybernetics, which had been condemned by militant philosophers as a bourgeois pseudoscience. Under the rubric of cybernetics – the science of control in machine and animal – Soviet scientists were able to offer some protection to theories in physiology and genetics that had been condemned. See David Holloway, "Scientific Truth and Political Authority in the Soviet Union," *Government and Opposition*, Summer 1970, pp. 345–67, and David Holloway, "Innovation in Science – the Case of Cybernetics in the Soviet Union," *Science Studies*, 1974, no. 4, pp. 299–337.

87. Andrei Sakharov, *Memoirs*, New York: Alfred A. Knopf, 1990, pp. 139–47; see also Marina Kuriachaia, "Upravliaemyi termoiad: Kto pervyi?" *Nezavisimaia gazeta*, June 1, 1993, p. 1.

88. I.N. Golovin, "U istokov sotrudnichestva," *Vestnik Akademii Nauk SSSR*, April 1986, pp. 115–16; I.N. Golovin and V.D. Shafranov, "U istokov termoiada," *Priroda*, 1990, no. 8, p. 28. See Golovin's report of a conversation with Kurchatov on December 31, 1950 in which Kurchatov showed his excitement about this project, *idem, Kurchatov*, pp. 96–101.

89. Manfred von Ardenne, *Ein Glückliches Leben für Technik und Forschung*, 4th edn, Berlin: Verlag der Nation, 1976, pp. 183–4. Jorge Sabato, a leading physicist in the Argentinian nuclear program, told me that at one of the Geneva conferences on the peaceful uses of atomic energy, A.P. Vinogradov stopped him and said, "So you're from Argentina. I have to thank you for helping me to get more resources for my research."

90. "Iz zapisok I.N. Golovina," *Priroda*, 1990, no. 8, p. 29. When General Meshik, who was responsible for security, said to Beria that Leontovich was a free thinker, Beria replied "You will watch him, he can't do any harm."

91. Joan Lisa Bromberg, *Fusion: Science, Politics, and the Invention of a New Energy Source*, Cambridge, Mass.: MIT Press, 1982, pp. 17–18, 32–3.

92. Vladimir Kogan, interviewed by G.E. Gorelik, June 23, 1993.

93. Bromberg, *op.cit.*, has some discussion of varying attitudes to classification and declassification in the United States. See pp. 30–31, 72–5, 89–90.

94. Kurchatov, "Rech' na XX s"ezde KPSS, 20 fevralia 1956 g.," in his *Izbrannye trudy: tom 3*, p. 171; Golovin, "U istokov sotrudnichestva," pp. 118–19; Komel'kov, *loc.cit.*, pp. 326–7.

95. Khrushchev, *op.cit.*, p. 93.

96. "Visit to the United Kingdom of Mr

Bulganin and Mr. Khrushchev, April 1956: Notes and Records prepared by the Interpreters," p. 4. PRO PREM 11 1626.

97. Sakharov, *op.cit.*, p. 147.

98. Golovin, *loc.cit.*, p. 119.

99. John Cockcroft, "Controlled Thermonuclear Fusion," in S.K. Runcorn (ed.), *Physics in the Sixties*, New York: Wiley, 1964, p. 32.

100. *Ibid.* According to Soviet sources, Cockcroft told Kurchatov that he had to go to Australia because his daughter was ill. Golovin, *loc.cit.*, p. 115.

101. I.V. Kurchatov "Nekotorye voprosy razvitiia atomnoi energetiki v SSSR," in Kurchatov, *op.cit.*, pp. 172–81.

102. I.V. Kurchatov "O vozmozhnosti sozdaniia termoiadernykh reaktsii v gazovom razriade," in Kurchatov, *op.cit.*, pp. 182–95.

103. "Notes on Lecture by Academician I.V. Kurchatov at Harwell, April 25, 1956 (prepared by Dr. Dunworth)," p. 1. PRO AB 16 1683 Russia.

104. PRO PREM 11 1611.

105. Telegram No 2301, from Foreign Office to Washington, April 27, 1956. PRO AB16 1683 Russia.

106. Notes on the meeting quoted in Bromberg, *op.cit.*, p. 72.

107. J.G. Beckerley, quoted in *Nucleonics*, June 1956, p. 43.

108. Bromberg, *op.cit.*, pp. 89–93.

109. Cockcroft, *loc.cit.*, p. 31.

110. "Visit to the United Kingdom . . . Notes and Records prepared by the Interpreters," *loc.cit.*, pp. 18–20.

111. S.E. Frish, *Skvoz' prizmu vremeni*, Moscow: Politizdat, 1992, pp. 364–6.

112. Letter to Khrushchev May 25, 1955. TsKhSD f. 7, op. 17, d. 507, pp. 257–9.

Conclusion

1. Quoted in Andrei Sakharov, *Memoirs*, New York: Alfred A. Knopf, 1990, pp. 399–400.

2. A.D. Sakharov, *Razmyshleniia o progresse, mirnom sosushchestvovanii i intellektual'noi svobode*, Frankfurt-am-Main: Possev-Verlag, 1970, p. 3.

Biographical Notes

Aleksandrov, Anatolii Petrovich (1903–94), physicist. Born in Ukraine. After graduating from Kiev University in 1930, he went to work at the Leningrad Physicotechnical Institute. From 1946 to 1955 he was director of the Institute of Physical Problems, and became director of the Kurchatov Institute of Atomic Energy in 1960. Joined the CPSU in 1962. Elected to the Academy of Sciences in 1953. President of the Academy from 1975 to 1986. Three times Hero of Socialist Labor (1954, 1960, 1973).

Alikhanov, Abram Isaakovich (1904–70), physicist. Born in Kars, then a part of the Russian empire (now Turkey). After graduating from the Leningrad Polytechnical Institute in 1928 he worked at the Leningrad Physicotechnical Institute. In 1945 he organized Laboratory No. 3, later named the Institute of Theoretical and Experimental Physics, and served as its director until 1968. Directed the creation of the first Soviet heavy-water reactor, and in 1954 was decorated a Hero of Socialist Labor. Elected to the Academy of Sciences in 1943.

Artsimovich, Lev Andreevich (1909–73), physicist. Born in Moscow, and graduated in 1928 from the University of Belorussia in Minsk. From 1930 to 1944 he worked at the Leningrad Physicotechnical Institute, where he headed the high-voltage laboratory. From 1944 he worked at the Kurchatov Institute for Atomic Energy. Elected to the Academy of Sciences in 1953; Hero of Socialist Labor (1969).

Beria, Lavrentii Pavlovich (1899–1953), party and state figure. Born in Merkheuli, Georgia. Joined the Bolsheviks in 1917. In 1921 Beria joined the Cheka, the predecessor of the NKVD. He served in the secret police through the 1920s, making a name for himself in various purges. In 1931 he was appointed First Secretary of the Georgian Communist Party. In 1938 he became deputy people's commissar for internal affairs, and in 1941 deputy chairman of the Council of Ministers. Chaired the Special Committee on the Atomic Bomb from 1945 to 1953. After Stalin's death in 1953, Beria was tried and executed for crimes against the state.

Bulganin, Nikolai Aleksandrovich (1895–1975), state and party figure. Born in Nizhnii Novgorod, Bulganin joined the Bolsheviks in 1917. In 1918–22 he worked in the All-Russian Cheka and in 1922–7 in the Supreme Council of the National Economy. From 1931 to 1937 he was chairman of the Moscow Soviet, and was a member of the Party Central Committee from 1934 to 1961. From 1947 to 1949 he was minister of the armed forces, and from 1953 to 1955 minister of defense. From 1955 to 1958 he was Premier, and from 1948 to 1958 he was in the Politburo. He held the title of Marshal of the Soviet Union from 1947 to 1958.

Dollezhal', Nikolai Antonovich (1899–), engineer. Born in Omel'nik, Ukraine, Dollezhal' graduated from the Moscow Higher Technical School in 1923. From 1942 to 1953 directed the All-Union Design, Planning, and Scientific Research Institute of Chemical-Mechanical Engineering in Moscow. Dollezhal' was the chief designer of the first Soviet plutonium production reactors. Elected to the Academy of Sciences (1962); Hero of Socialist Labor (1949).

Flerov, Georgii Nikolaevich (1913–90), experimental physicist. Born in Rostov-on-Don, Flerov graduated from the Leningrad Polytechnical Institute in 1938 and began work at Kurchatov's laboratory in the Leningrad Physicotechnical Institute. In 1940, together with Petrzhak, he discovered spontaneous fission. In 1955 he joined the CPSU, and in 1960 was named director of the laboratory of nuclear reactions at the Joint Institute of Nuclear Research at Dubna. Elected to the Academy of Sciences in 1968; Hero of Socialist Labor (1949).

Frenkel', Iakov Il'ich (1894–1952), theoretical physicist. Born in Rostov-on-Don, Frenkel' graduated from Petrograd University in 1916. From 1921 Frenkel' worked at the Leningrad Physicotechnical Institute, where he headed the theoretical department. Frenkel' was elected a corresponding member of the Academy of Sciences in 1929.

Ioffe, Abram Fedorovich (1880–1960), physicist. Born in Romny, Ukraine. After graduating from the St Petersburg Technological Institute in 1902, he worked in the laboratory of Wilhelm Roentgen, the discoverer of X-rays, in Munich. In 1906 Ioffe returned to work at the Polytechnical Institute in St Petersburg. Director of the Leningrad Physicotechnical Institute from 1923 to 1950. Elected to the Academy of Sciences in 1920. He joined the CPSU in 1942; Hero of Socialist Labor in 1955.

Kapitsa, Peter Leonidovich (1894–1984), physicist. Born in Kronshtadt, Kapitsa graduated from the Petrograd Polytechnical University in 1918. In 1921 Kapitsa went to the Cavendish Laboratory in Cambridge, where he worked for 13 years. In 1934 he was forced to stay in Russia; he set up the Institute of Physical Problems in Moscow. A member of the Academy of Sciences of the USSR (1939). Kapitsa won the Nobel Prize for Physics in 1978; Hero of Socialist Labor (1945).

Khariton, Iulii Borisovich (1904–), physicist. Born in St Petersburg, and educated at the Polytechnical Institute. Spent 1926–8 in Cambridge, where he received his Ph.D. When he returned to Leningrad, he took charge of a new laboratory to study explosives at the Institute of Chemical Physics. From 1939 to 1941, together with Zel'dovich, he did important research on nuclear chain reactions. Scientific director of Arzamas-16 from 1946 to 1992. Khariton joined the CPSU in 1956. A member of the Academy of Sciences (1953); three times Hero of Socialist Labor (1949, 1951, 1954).

Khlopin, Vitalii Grigor'evich (1890–1950), radiochemist. Born in Perm, graduated from Leningrad University in 1912. In 1915 began work at the Academy of Sciences' Radiological Laboratory, and in 1921 devised a process for extracting radium from uranium ore. In the following year Khlopin helped Vernadskii establish the Radium Institute in St Petersburg, and in 1939 became director of the Institute. Chairman of the Uranium Commission, 1940. He took charge of divising a method for the chemical separation of plutonium. Hero of Socialist Labor in 1949; elected to the Academy of Sciences in 1939.

Kikoin, Isaak Konstantinovich (1908–84), experimental physicist. Born in the town of Malye Zhagory, Kikoin graduated from the Leningrad Polytechnical Institute in 1930. From 1927 to 1936 he worked at the Leningrad Physicotechnical Institute. He joined Kurchatov's laboratory in 1943. After World War II he took charge of the gaseous diffusion and centrifuge methods of separating the isotopes of uranium. In 1947 he joined the CPSU. A member of the Academy of Sciences (1953); twice a Hero of Socialist Labor (1951, 1978).

Kurchatov, Igor Vasil'evich (1903–60), physicist. Born in Simskii Zavod in the southern Urals. Graduated from Crimean University in 1923, and two years later joined Ioffe's institute in Leningrad. In 1943 Kurchatov was appointed scientific director of the nuclear project; he held that position until his death in 1960. He joined the CPSU in 1948. Elected to the Academy of Sciences in 1943; three times Hero of Socialist Labor (1949, 1951, 1954).

Landau, Lev Davidovich (1908–68), theoretical physicist. Born in Baku, Landau graduated from Leningrad University in 1927. For the next five years, he did research at the Leningrad Physicotechnical Institute, and in 1932 moved to the Physicotechnical Institute in Khar'kov. In 1937 he went to Moscow to head the theoretical group of the Institute of Physical Problems. Imprisoned for a year, 1938–9. A member of the Academy of Sciences (1946); Hero of Socialist Labor (1954); Nobel Prize for Physics (1962).

Leipunskii, Aleksandr Il'ich (1903–72), physicist. Born in the village of Dragli, Poland, and graduated from the Leningrad Polytechnic Institute in 1926. He began work at the Leningrad Physicotechnical Institute, but in 1929 transferred to the Physicotechnical Institute in Khar'kov, serving as its director from 1932–7. He took charge of the development of breeder reactors after the war. Leipunskii was a member of the Ukrainian Academy of Sciences (1934), a Hero of Socialist Labor (1963), and member of the CPSU.

Malenkov, Georgii Maksimilianovich (1902–88), state and party figure. Born in Orenburg, Russia. Joined the Communist Party in 1920, then served in the Red Army in the Civil War. A leading member of the Moscow party committee in the 1930s, he was appointed secretary of the Central Committee in 1939. A member of the State Defense Committee (1941–5), he occupied key Party and government positions after the war. Chairman of the Council of Ministers, 1953–5. Removed from the Politburo (Presidium) in 1957.

Malyshev, Viacheslav Aleksandrovich (1902–57), state figure. Born in Ust'-Sysol'sk, graduated from the Velikie Luki Railroad Technicum in 1924 and joined the Communist Party two years later. People's Commissar of the Tank Industry during the war. Deputy Chairman of the Council of Ministers from 1947 to 1956. Minister of Medium Machinebuilding from 1953 to 1955. Hero of Socialist Labor (1944).

Molotov, Viacheslav Mikhailovich (1890–1986), state and party figure. Born in the village of Kukarka, joined the Bolsheviks in 1906. He studied at the St Petersburg Polytechnic Institute. Among his many titles and duties were Chairman of the Council of People's Commissars from 1930–41, and Peoples's Commissar (later Minister) of Foreign Affairs from 1939 to 1949 and from 1953 to 1956. From 1921 to 1957 he was a member of the Politburo.

Pervukhin, Mikhail Georgievich (1904–78), state and party figure. Born in the town of Iuriuzan', he joined the Communist Party in 1919. He studied electrical engineering and worked at various power stations. Became People's Commissar of the Electric Power Industry in 1939, and Deputy Chairman of the Council of People's Commissars in 1940. People's Commissar of the Chemical Industry during and after the war. Member of the Politburo from 1952 to 1957. Minister of Medium Machinebuilding, 1957–8. Hero of Socialist Labor in 1949.

Sakharov, Andrei Dmitrievich (1921–89), physicist. Born in Moscow, graduated from Moscow State University in 1942. In 1945 he began work at the Physics Institute of the Academy of Sciences. Recruited into the H-bomb program in 1948, Sakharov spent 1950–68 at Arzamas-16. An active campaigner for human rights in the 1970s, he was exiled to Gorky in 1980. He and his wife Elena Bonner were allowed to return to Moscow in 1987. Winner of the Nobel Peace Prize in 1975; elected to the Academy of Sciences in 1953; three times Hero of Socialist Labor (1953, 1956, 1962).

Semenov, Nikolai Nikolaevich (1896–1986), physicist and chemist. Born in Saratov, graduated from Petrograd University. From 1920 to 1931 he worked at the Leningrad Physicotechnical Institute, and in 1931 became director of the new Leningrad Institute of Chemical Physics. Received the Nobel Prize for Chemistry in 1956 for work on chain reactions done in the 1920s and 1930s. Elected to the Academy of Sciences in 1932. Member of the CPSU from 1947.

Skobel'tsyn, Dmitrii Vladimirovich (1892–1992), physicist. Born in St Petersburg, graduated from the University of Petrograd in 1915. From 1925 worked at the Leningrad Physicotechnical Institute. Joined the Physics Institute of the Academy of Sciences in 1937; director of this institute from 1951 to 1972. Elected to the Academy of Sciences in 1946; Hero of Socialist Labor (1969).

Tamm, Igor Evgen'evich (1895–1971), physicist. Born in Vladivostok, Russia. After graduating from Moscow University in 1918, Tamm taught physics at several higher educational institutions. In 1934 he began work at the Physics Institute of the Academy of Sciences. Member of the Academy of Sciences (1953). Hero of Socialist Labor (1953); in 1958 he received the Nobel Prize for Physics.

Vannikov, Boris L'vovich (1897–1962), party and state figure. Born in Baku, Azerbaijan, he joined the CPSU in 1919 and fought in the Civil War in the Caucasus. After a technical education he worked in industry; in 1937 he was appointed deputy people's commissar of the defense industry, and in 1939 people's commissar. People's commissar of munitions during the war; head of the First Chief Administration of the Council of Ministers from 1945 to 1953. Three times Hero of Socialist Labor (1942, 1949, 1954).

Vavilov, Sergei Ivanovich (1891–1951), physicist. Born in Moscow, he graduated from Moscow University in 1914. He became director of the Physics Institute of the Academy of Sciences in 1932. Elected to the Academy of Sciences in 1932, Vavilov became its president in 1945.

Vernadskii, Vladimir Ivanovich (1863–1945) mineralogist and geochemist. Born in St Petersburg, Vernadskii was appointed professor of mineralogy at Moscow University in 1890. He began the study of Russian radioactive minerals in 1911. Established the Radium Institute in Petrograd in 1922. Instrumental in setting up the Uranium Commission in 1940. Elected to the Academy of Sciences in 1912.

Zaveniagin, Avraamii Pavlovich (1901–56), state and party figure. Born in Uzlovaia. Member of the Communist Party since 1917. He directed the Magnitogorsk Metallurgical Combine from 1933 to 1937, then became First Deputy People's Commissar of Heavy Industry. From 1941–50, Zaveniagin served as the Deputy People's Commissar of Internal Affairs. Deputy to Vannikov at the First Chief Administration (1945–53); Minister of Medium Machinebuilding, 1955–6. Twice Hero of Socialist Labor (1949 and 1954).

Zel'dovich, Iakov Borisovich (1914–87) physicist. Born in Minsk, Belorussia, he began work at the Institute for Chemical Physics in 1931. In 1939–41 he did important research with Khariton on nuclear chain reactions. First head of the theoretical department at Arzamas-16. Elected to the Academy of Sciences in 1958; three times Hero of Socialist Labor (1949, 1953, 1956).

Zhukov, Georgii Konstantinovich (1896–1974), Marshal of the Soviet Union. Born in village of Strelkovka, Zhukov joined the Red Army in 1918. A key figure in the Soviet High Command in World War II, he was appointed deputy supreme commander in chief by Stalin in 1942. First Deputy Minister of Defense in 1953–5, and minister from 1955 to 1957. Four times Hero of the Soviet Union (1939, 1944, 1945, 1956).

Index